CW01262389

The War with God
THEOMACHY IN ROMAN IMPERIAL POETRY

Pramit Chaudhuri

OXFORD
UNIVERSITY PRESS

OXFORD
UNIVERSITY PRESS

Oxford University Press is a department of the
University of Oxford. It furthers the University's objective
of excellence in research, scholarship, and education
by publishing worldwide.

Oxford   New York
Auckland   Cape Town   Dar es Salaam   Hong Kong   Karachi
Kuala Lumpur   Madrid   Melbourne   Mexico City   Nairobi
New Delhi   Shanghai   Taipei   Toronto

With offices in
Argentina   Austria   Brazil   Chile   Czech Republic   France   Greece
Guatemala   Hungary   Italy   Japan   Poland   Portugal   Singapore
South Korea   Switzerland   Thailand   Turkey   Ukraine   Vietnam

Oxford is a registered trade mark of Oxford University Press
in the UK and certain other countries.

Published in the United States of America by
Oxford University Press
198 Madison Avenue, New York, NY 10016

© Oxford University Press 2014

All rights reserved. No part of this publication may be reproduced,
stored in a retrieval system, or transmitted, in any form or by any means,
without the prior permission in writing of Oxford University Press,
or as expressly permitted by law, by license, or under terms agreed with
the appropriate reproduction rights organization. Inquiries concerning
reproduction outside the scope of the above should be sent to the
Rights Department, Oxford University Press, at the address above.

You must not circulate this work in any other form
and you must impose this same condition on any acquirer.

Library of Congress Cataloging-in-Publication Data is available.
ISBN 978-0-19-999338-3

1 3 5 7 9 8 6 4 2
Printed in the United States of America
on acid-free paper

For Ayelet
and
for my parents

CONTENTS

Preface   ix
Texts and Abbreviations   xiii
Chronology of Poets and Emperors   xv

Introduction   1

1. Theomachy in Greek Epic and Tragedy   15
2. The Origins of Roman Theomachy: Lucretius and Vergil   56
3. Theomachy as Test in Ovid's *Metamorphoses*   82
4. Deification and Theomachy in Seneca's *Hercules Furens*   116
5. Theomachy in Historical Epic: Disenchantment and Remystification in Lucan's *Bellum Civile*   156
6. Paradigms of Theomachy in Flavian Epic: Homer, Intertextuality, and the Struggle for Identity   195
7. The War of the Worlds: Hannibal as Theomach in Silius Italicus' *Punica*   231
8. Theomachy and the Limits of Epic: Capaneus in Statius' *Thebaid*   256
9. The Politics of Theomachy   298

Epilogue   322

Bibliography   329
Index of Passages   357
General Index   375

PREFACE

The war with god ('theomachy') forms one of the foundational themes of mythology and literature, including the Christian story of Lucifer's rebellion, Ravana's domination of the Devas in the classical Hindu tradition, and the Greco-Roman myth of the battle between huge, serpent-legged Giants and the Olympian gods ('Gigantomachy').[1] The result of these conflicts is almost always the same: the gods, multiple or single, eventually emerge victorious and the cosmic order is maintained. Within Greco-Roman mythology, the early history of the universe witnesses some exceptions to this pattern: Cronus' usurpation of Uranus and Zeus' subsequent usurpation of Cronus demonstrate the possibility of successfully overturning the divine order in a way thoroughly alien to the monotheist conception of an omnipotent and eternal God. In practical terms, however, antagonism towards Zeus and his fellow Olympians appears as futile and disastrous as Satan's towards God.

Mortals, too, fight their own wars against the Olympian gods, but after the defeat of the supernatural and immortal Titans and Giants, human antagonism to the divine appears especially hopeless. Greek and Roman literature is filled with accounts of such human-divine clashes. Sometimes these battles are martial, like Capaneus' challenge to Jupiter and his consequent death by the god's thunderbolt (discussed in Chapter 8); at other times they are more figurative, as when Niobe's children are killed because she had boasted that her fertility was greater than that of the goddess Latona (Chapter 3). What brings these diverse conflicts together is a common threat to divine authority—a presumption on the part of the mortal 'theomach' to greater power than he or she actually possesses and a concomitant dismissal of the power of the gods. Those characters, and their representation in classical literature, are the broad subject of this book.

At first glance, the act of fighting against the gods appears paradigmatically impious and absurdly foolish: in opposing the divine, one rejects correct moral authority and misunderstands the order of power in the world. Thus, literary accounts of such conflicts have often been interpreted in a didactic vein, with the punishment of the rebels seen as a warning against arrogance and transgression and as an exhortation to religious piety. If the lesson against overreaching

---

[1] The relative status of Ravana and the Devas is made more complex by Ravana's godlike qualities and his invulnerability to all beings except humans. He is eventually killed by Rama, a human avatar of the god Vishnu. Hercules is a similarly ambiguous figure, both divine and human, who comes to the aid of the Olympians against the Giants yet in other myths attacks various gods (see Chapter 4).

seems simple, nevertheless the act of fighting against the gods provides a theme to which poets and playwrights have thought fit to return time and again. It is a story told by Homer and the Athenian tragedians, by Seneca and Statius, by Dante and Marlowe, by Milton and Shelley. Contemporary culture, too, has seized on the theme across multiple media—from the novelist Philip Pullman's Miltonic trilogy, *His Dark Materials*, to the blockbuster film *Clash of the Titans* and its sequel, to the video game series *God of War*. The common fascination with theomachy across time and place can be explained in part by specific cultural attitudes, but more compellingly by the sublime grandeur of such clashes: awesomely powerful individuals scaling mountains and city walls, holding back rivers in flood, scorning the gods, and standing at the centre of scenes crackling with divine lightning. Even as a scene of human failure, theomachy nevertheless seizes the reader's attention and proclaims its own importance.

A better understanding of these clashes can be achieved by shifting our focus from their inevitable and swift conclusion to their broader significance. These conflicts represent moments of critical tension when many of society's norms—not only religious, but also philosophical, political, and aesthetic norms—become the subject of negotiation. Theomachy thus illustrates crucial distinctions not just between piety and impiety but also between different kinds of belief, between political rivals or dynasties or even competing systems of government, and between contrasting visions of a genre or of art itself. The idea that opposition to god might signify more complex relationships is suggested, for instance, by Blake's notorious identification of Milton as being 'of the Devil's party without knowing it'. This book, however, moves beyond the question of whether an author was of one party or another, whether knowingly or not; rather, the fight with god itself, and all that it stands for, is the particular object of study.

There have been times when the enormous scope of theomachy suggested by the previous paragraphs was to be the scope of this book. The only remaining evidence of this, besides the epilogue, are the epigraphs at the beginning of each chapter, which attempt to give some flavour of the literary and conceptual reach of theomachy, sometimes in contexts that might initially seem very far removed from classical literature. There have also been times when I considered writing a much shorter book focused on Seneca and Statius, which would have corresponded much more closely to the original Yale dissertation on which this book is distantly based. The encouragement of others caused me to take a middle road, which has led to a fairly full (though by no means exhaustive) account of theomachy in classical, principally Roman imperial, poetry. By adopting this compromise I hope to have offered to my fellow classicists a reasonably substantial new reading of the epic and (to a lesser extent) tragic traditions, and to non-classicists a sense of how one might understand theomachy and what that understanding owes in particular to the literature of early imperial Rome. Since I deal with a tradition that is in important respects fairly unified, there is necessarily some repetition across chapters. I have kept the overlap, since I'm aware that the majority of readers will consult individual chapters rather than ploughing through the whole book. To those brave souls who do dare to read the book from cover to cover, I beg their indulgence. A book of this nature necessarily skims the surface of any number of important debates. In full acknowledgment of my scholarly debts, I have therefore erred on the side of citing too generously, with a correspondingly lengthy bibliography.

This book only arrived at its present form thanks to the help of numerous individuals and institutions. Susanna Morton Braund and David Quint supervised the original dissertation and have continued to offer invaluable advice; both typified the best qualities of Yale's joint Ph.D. program in Classics and Comparative Literature. Many people provided feedback on portions of the dissertation or influenced the resulting book in other ways. I am especially grateful to Alison Keith, who commented on several chapters of the manuscript with characteristic insight and generosity. My (then future) colleagues at Dartmouth College made shrewd observations on an early draft of Chapter 8; I thank them for their continuing collegiality. For advice, conversation, and many a comment I am also grateful to: Egbert Bakker, Alessandro Barchiesi, Victor Bers, Christopher Bond, Todd Curtis, Lesley Dean-Jones, Joseph Dexter, Denis Feeney, Kirk Freudenburg, Randall Ganiban, Philip Hardie, Christina Kraus, Giuseppe Mazzotta, William Metcalf, Carlos Noreña, Timothy Perry, Shilpa Raval, Claude Rawson, Haun Saussy, Celia Schultz, Christopher Star, Jelle Stoop, Stephen White, and Christopher Wood. I owe a more general debt to family, friends, and former teachers in the UK, India, and the US; thanks in particular to my great-uncle and great-aunt, Dr J. L. Majumder and Mrs E. Majumder.

I benefited enormously from a manuscript review seminar in 2012 sponsored by the Leslie Humanities Center at Dartmouth, for which I thank the centre's director, Colleen Glenney Boggs, as well as Jonathan Crewe, Adrian Randolph, and Isabel Weatherdon. An even greater debt of gratitude is owed to Jim Tatum, who generously read not only the manuscript (twice!) but also the dissertation (as well as giving me the idea for the book's title), and to Margaret Graver, whose rigour is second to none and whose support has been invaluable. Joseph Farrell and Stephen Hinds kindly agreed to participate in the seminar and gave me confidence that the book shouldn't shy away from the Augustan material because of any anxiety of influence. Stephen would also later turn out to have been one of the two anonymous referees for Oxford University Press, whose suggestions are responsible for many substantial improvements.

Several conference organisers and volume editors invited me to contribute material that ended up in the book in some form or other (any overlap with other publications is cited in the relevant place in the text): thanks in particular to Ralph Anderson, Emma Buckley, Helen Lovatt, Gesine Manuwald, and Carole Newlands. I'm also grateful to members of the Flavian Epic Network, who were present at many panels, and to audiences at Boston University, Dartmouth College, the University of Texas at Austin, Yale University, and several meetings of the American Philological Association.

The book couldn't have been written without considerable material support. The libraries at Yale, Dartmouth, and the University of Texas, and the enormous help provided by their staff, made it possible for me to quickly access a wide range of scholarship. Financial support came from the Beinecke Rare Book and Manuscript Library, the Charlotte Newcombe Foundation, and the Office of the Associate Dean for the Arts and Humanities at Dartmouth. A Dartmouth Junior Faculty Fellowship and sabbatical provided a crucial period of research leave in 2011–12. Since the writing of the book was largely complete by early 2013 (and much of it by mid-2012), I haven't been able to take close account of works appearing in 2013 or later. The one exception is Henry Day's book on Lucan, which the author generously shared with me ahead of publication.

The team at OUP USA has been encouraging, patient, attentive, and flexible—in short, an author's dream. Thanks in particular to my editor, Stefan Vranka, who was supportive of the project from the beginning and gave shrewd and substantive advice throughout the process of writing and publication. Thanks, too, to Stefan's colleagues Sarah Pirovitz, Natalie Johnson, and my incisive copyeditor, Ben Sadock. My research assistant, Michael Konieczny, hasn't just saved me from the proverbial countless embarrassments—he has improved the book on just about every page. Christine Hoskin provided invaluable help on the indices. Unfortunately, all this advice and oversight does not absolve me from the inevitable errors and stubborn judgements that remain; for those I claim sole responsibility.

The gratitude most difficult to express is also the deepest. For my parents I lack the words to do justice to their self-sacrifice, sense of tradition, and open-mindedness. Their generosity is all the greater for their knowing the cost. Finally, in the preface to my dissertation I thanked my wife, Ayelet Haimson Lushkov, for reading and improving every word, for inspiring its best ideas and ensuring its best presentation; I said that she puts everything into perspective and that I only wished I could do for her what she does for me. All of that remains true and truer still for everything that she's put into this (much longer) book. But I should really thank her for the most important thing of all—for being who she is.

P. N. C.

December 2013
Hanover, New Hampshire

TEXTS AND ABBREVIATIONS

Quotations of Latin are taken from the following main texts: Smith 1982 for Lucretius' *De Rerum Natura*, Mynors 1969 for Vergil's *Aeneid*, Tarrant 2004 for Ovid's *Metamorphoses*, Fitch 1987 for Seneca's *Hercules Furens*, Duff 1928 (based on Housman 1926) for Lucan's *Bellum Civile*, Delz 1987 for Silius Italicus' *Punica*, and D. E. Hill 1983 for Statius' *Thebaid*. For all other quotations I follow the texts used by the databases of the Thesaurus Linguae Graecae (TLG) and the Packard Humanities Institute (PHI). I have regularised Latin 'v' to 'u' in all quotations for the sake of consistency; titles of works and their abbreviations, however, retain the more common spelling with 'v' where applicable. Unless otherwise noted all translations are my own, though I have benefitted from consulting a variety of published translations.

Except when quoting others, I have used Latinised spellings of Greek names throughout in order to avoid inconsistency from chapter to chapter; so, 'Cronus' and 'Polynices', not 'Kronos' and 'Polyneikes'. The one exception is 'Herakles' / 'Hercules' to distinguish the hero of Euripides' play and Greek mythology on the one hand from Ovid's and Seneca's Roman hero on the other.

Abbreviations of ancient authors and works follow the conventions of the *OCD*; of journals, *L'Année philologique*. Exceptions and other abbreviations are as follows:

AJP	*American Journal of Philology*
ANRW	Vogt, J., H. Temporini, and W. Haase (eds.). 1972–. *Aufstieg und Niedergang der römischen Welt*. Berlin: de Gruyter.
BMC	Mattingly, H., and R. A. G. Carson (eds.). 1923–62. *Coins of the Roman Empire in the British Museum*. 6 vols. London: Trustees of the British Museum.
CA	*Classical Antiquity*
CIL	1862–. *Corpus Inscriptionum Latinarum*. Berlin: de Gruyter.
CP	*Classical Philology*
HSCP	*Harvard Studies in Classical Philology*
Keil	Keil, H. 1855–80. *Grammatici Latini*. 7 vols. + suppl. Leipzig: B. G. Teubner.
LIMC	1981–2009. *Lexicon Iconographicum Mythologiae Classicae*. 8 vols. + suppl. Zürich: Artemis Verlag.
Longin.	Longinus, *De Sublimitate*

LSJ	Lidell, H. G., R. Scott, and H. S. Jones. 1996. *A Greek-English Lexicon*. 9th edition, rev. Oxford: Oxford University Press.
Man.	Manilius, *Astronomica*
OCD	Hornblower, S., A. Spawforth, and E. Eidinow (eds.). 2012. *The Oxford Classical Dictionary*. 4th edition. Oxford: Oxford University Press.
OED	Simpson, J., and W. Weiner (eds.). 1989. *Oxford English Dictionary*. 2nd edition. 20 vols. Oxford: Oxford University Press.
OLD	Glare, P. G. W. (ed.). 1968–82. *Oxford Latin Dictionary*. Oxford: Oxford University Press.
PCPS	*Proceedings of the Cambridge Philological Society*
Rapt.	Claudian, *De Raptu Proserpinae*
RE	von Pauly, A. F., G. Wissowa, W. Kroll, K. Witte, K. Mittelhaus, and K. Ziegler (eds.). 1893–1980. *Paulys Real-Encyclopädie der classischen Altertumswissenschaft*. 83 vols. + indices. Stuttgart: J. B. Metzler.
TAPA	*Transactions of the American Philological Association*

CHRONOLOGY OF POETS AND EMPERORS

The following timelines on p. xvi provide a rough guide to the chronology of the Roman poets and of the emperors under whom they lived. Only those figures who feature prominently in this book are included here. Lucretius and Caesar appear in brackets since they predate the advent of the principate. For poets I have provided approximate birth and death dates; for emperors, both the year of birth and the span of their reign (beginning with the Battle of Actium for Augustus). All dates generally follow those supplied by the *OCD*.

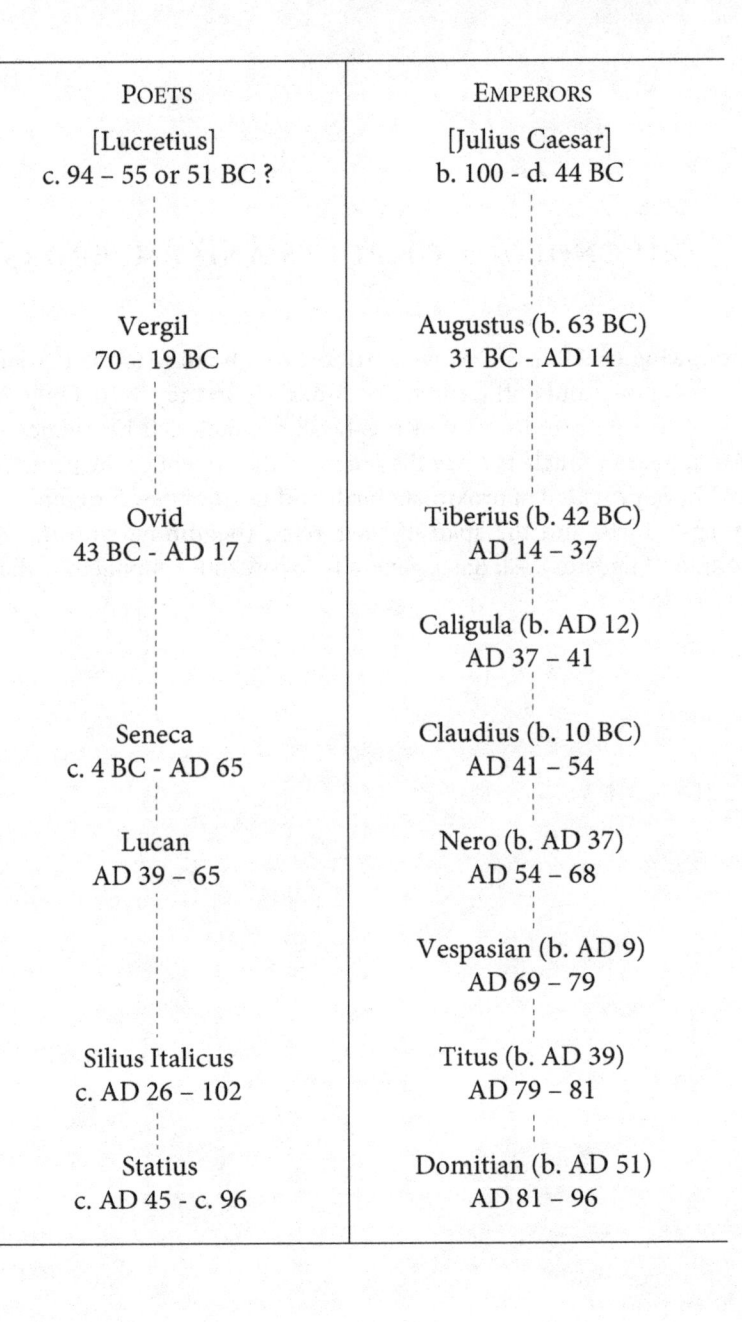

POETS	EMPERORS
[Lucretius] c. 94 – 55 or 51 BC ?	[Julius Caesar] b. 100 - d. 44 BC
Vergil 70 – 19 BC	Augustus (b. 63 BC) 31 BC - AD 14
Ovid 43 BC - AD 17	Tiberius (b. 42 BC) AD 14 – 37
	Caligula (b. AD 12) AD 37 – 41
Seneca c. 4 BC - AD 65	Claudius (b. 10 BC) AD 41 – 54
Lucan AD 39 – 65	Nero (b. AD 37) AD 54 – 68
	Vespasian (b. AD 9) AD 69 – 79
Silius Italicus c. AD 26 – 102	Titus (b. AD 39) AD 79 – 81
Statius c. AD 45 - c. 96	Domitian (b. AD 51) AD 81 – 96

Introduction

> High in the midst exalted as a god,
> The apostate in his sun-bright chariot sat
> Idol of majesty divine, enclosed
> With flaming cherubim, and golden shields.
>
> —JOHN MILTON

> I am thy child, as thou wert Saturn's child;
> Mightier than thee; and we must dwell together
> Henceforth in darkness. Lift thy lightnings not.
> The tyranny of heaven none may retain,
> Or reassume, or hold, succeeding thee.
>
> —PERCY BYSSHE SHELLEY

> My books are about killing God.
>
> —PHILIP PULLMAN

In the tenth book of Statius' epic poem, the *Thebaid*, the mortal hero Capaneus challenges the god Jupiter to battle. Statius declares the need for an appropriately lofty register to sing of this feat, freighting the divine confrontation with his own attempt at poetic originality (*Theb.* 10.827–31):

> hactenus arma, tubae, ferrumque et uulnera: sed nunc
> comminus astrigeros Capaneus tollendus in axes.
> non mihi iam solito uatum de more canendum;
> maior ab Aoniis poscenda amentia lucis:
> mecum omnes audete deae!

> Thus far of arms and trumpets, of swords and wounds: but now Capaneus must be raised to close battle against the star-laden vault.

> I must no longer sing in the customary manner of bards;
> a greater madness must be sought from the Aonian groves:
> dare with me all you goddesses!

Recent criticism has focused on the alignment between the ambitions of the hero and Statius himself to read Capaneus as a figure for the poetics of the *Thebaid*.[1] In particular, the attempt to fight Jupiter has been viewed as a metaphor for Statius' ambivalent relationship to Vergil, whose canonical status he both acknowledges and yet seeks to rival.[2] The theoretical basis for this kind of reading will be known to many from the work of Harold Bloom, who famously argued for a psychoanalytic model of literary tradition in which poets figured within their works their own struggles to surpass their predecessors and to innovate against the weight of tradition.[3] So pervasive and naturalised has Bloom's theory become, indeed, that few Statian critics feel the need to cite it, though one may detect a wry hint in Matthew Leigh's description of metapoetic readings as the 'dreariest of contemporary approaches to verse'.[4] The overfamiliarity of the metapoetic model, then, would seem to work against the thrill of Capaneus', and Statius', gambit.

To restore some sense of excitement to the episode one might move beyond the Bloomian concern with the canon, here represented by Vergil's *Aeneid*, to contemplate what lies at issue in the fight with the god: were Capaneus to defeat Jupiter, it would undermine the fundamental paradigm of power and source of authority in the epic tradition. For Statius the stakes are clear: if Capaneus succeeds, epic must give way to some new genre where human actors can defy all constraints.[5] At the same time, what could be more typical of epic than the martial hero striving to test his merit in battle and to earn immortal glory? Capaneus thus becomes doubly freighted with the burdens of generic identity and literary originality, the traditional hero taken to an innovative extreme. For epic to survive—to avoid becoming speculative philosophy

---

[1] Delarue 2000: 83–5, Lovatt 2001: 111–20, Leigh 2006.

[2] Leigh 2006: 235 suggests that *hactenus arma* (*Theb.* 10.827) refers not just to the content of the *Thebaid* until now but also to the earlier epic tradition. This is suggested by the presence of the Vergilian *incipit* (*arma*, *Aen.* 1.1) and by Statius' subsequently stated wish to depart from the customary ways of bards. Besides the list of arms, swords, etc., the one missing item from the typical content of epic is the *uirum* ('man' or 'hero') of Vergil's *arma uirumque*—has the genre lost its human centre or should we see Capaneus himself as a replacement for the traditional hero in the new breed of post-Vergilian epic?

[3] Bloom's theory is best represented by Bloom 1997 and 2003.

[4] Leigh 2006: 238; the article reveals a fascinating early modern prehistory to the metapoetic reading of Capaneus. Hardie 1993: 116–19 observes the applicability of Bloom's theory to all post-Vergilian Latin epic.

[5] McNelis 2007: 142 sees *hactenus arma* implying the imminent destruction of epic boundaries. Cf. Barchiesi 2001: 343–8 on the trumpet as a symbol for epic.

or science fiction—one of its most potent symbols must die, and so Capaneus does after being struck by Jupiter's thunderbolt.[6]

Leigh's anti-Vergilian reading of Capaneus points to a larger feature of the study of Silver Latin literature, namely, the strong hold exerted by Vergil on critical responses to imperial poetry.[7] Now, it would be a perverse critic indeed who failed to take account of the post-Augustan engagement with the *Aeneid*, but the sense of a Bloomian anxiety of influence threatens to circumscribe the significance of other texts with which the later works are in dialogue, to turn us, in short, into weaker readers. More problematically, the loudness of the dialogue with Vergil drowns out the wider intertextual conversation incorporating, among others, Lucretius, Ovid, Seneca, Lucan, and the Flavian epicists. At the same time, the focus on Vergil also leads to a downplaying of the culture and politics of Roman society in favour of largely literary interactions. The obvious limitations of such an approach are only amplified in the case of Neronian and Flavian authors whose literary models and whose historical context are available to us in much greater detail than for the Augustan poets and their predecessors. Indeed, looking beyond Vergil opens up perhaps the most exciting area of criticism of Silver Latin literature to date—the synthetic analysis that interprets the work in light of a multiplicity of intertextual relationships and simultaneously situates the poem within a literary network and within various cultural contexts.[8]

---

[6] Stanley Cavell draws a distinction between tragedy—the realm of human limitation—and speculative philosophy and science fiction, and then in turn between speculative philosophy and science fiction themselves. See Cavell 1999: 456–8. For the imposition of human limitation on fantasy see Bloom 1982: 200–23, esp. 212–13.

[7] I use the traditional term 'Silver Latin', without prejudice, as a convenient shorthand for post-Augustan Latin literature. In the case of Statius, the privileging of Vergil as an interpretive guide famously goes back to Dante's *Purgatorio*, but can be seen in recent criticism too (e.g., Ganiban 2007). For once we need not be coy about placing responsibility squarely on the shoulders of a particular individual. It is Statius himself who authorised such Vergilocentric scholarship just two lines before the end of his poem: *nec tu diuinam Aeneida tempta, / sed longe sequere et uestigia semper adora* ('do not test the divine *Aeneid*, but follow from afar and always worship its tracks', *Theb.* 12.816–17). Whether or not his poem obeys this injunction—and the evidence of *Silvae* 4.7 certainly suggests a more complicated relationship (cf. Leigh 2006: 223–5)—scholars have scrupulously followed the direction given by the author and have analysed the *Thebaid* with one eye on the *Aeneid*. The same tendency extends to scholarship on Silver Latin epic in general: see, e.g., Hardie 1993; cf. the title of Cowan (forthcoming), *After Virgil: The Poetry, Politics and Perversion of Roman Epic*. On the privileging of Vergil in studies of Senecan tragedy, note Staley 2010: 8: 'Seneca's tragedies are now regularly seen as epilogues to the *Aeneid*'. Cf. Putnam 1995: 246–85. Trinacty (forthcoming) broadens the Augustan intertextual base underlying the plays. On the distortions in our understanding of the republican epic tradition as a result of the dominance of the *Aeneid* see Elliott 2013.

[8] For Flavian epic, at least, the literary context is presently better served than the political: Lovatt 2005 is a fine example of an intertextual study; see also the essays in Manuwald and Voigt 2013; French scholarship in particular has taken the lead in this area, esp. Ripoll 1998 and Delarue 2000. The formative guide to the function of intertextuality in Latin poetry remains Hinds 1998. On the theoretical issues underlying discussions of intertextuality see Edmunds 2001. For a current reflection on practices and prospects see the essays in Baraz and van den Berg 2013. On Flavian epic and politics see Chapter 9.

The recent explosion of books and articles on Silver Latin epic and tragedy has given us a much fuller picture of the workings of individual authors and period style.[9] Yet with the exception of Denis Feeney's seminal study of the representation of the gods in classical epic, there has been no large-scale attempt to set the poetry in the contexts of both the Augustan and Greek traditions in addition to its Neronian and Flavian contexts.[10] Though much indebted to Feeney's work, this book differs in a number of ways, primarily in its focus on how the pressures placed by the mortal antagonist (or 'theomach') on the representation of the gods affect conceptions of specifically human capacities and limitations. Moreover, the treatment of a single theme allows for the inclusion not only of Senecan (and Attic) tragedy, which fell outside the remit of Feeney's study, but also of other texts and contexts from panegyric to philosophy, from lyric to historiography. This wide range of comparanda often shares important conceptual elements even where no direct allusion or even generic similarity is in play. And yet the ideas of warring against the gods, ascent to the heavens, and overcoming the obstacles of nature—even located in contexts as different as mythological epic, the imperial court, or Stoic philosophy—can inform each other in crucial and enlightening ways. At times, then, the relationship between texts described in this book can be thought of as very broadly intertextual, or better yet interdiscursive.[11] That is, the poetic texts derive significance not only from specific references or verbal overlap but also from what larger discourses—such as philosophy or imperial ideology—have to say about impiety or contending against the gods.[12] The war with god ('theomachy'), as this book will argue, fuels an interpretive process that exceeds the control of a single author or the parameters of a single text; and this book in turn is an exploration of the interpretive processes theomachy engenders and authorises in Latin literature, specifically the epic and tragic poetry of the first century AD.

Despite the ancient preoccupation with theomachy, however, no systematic study of the theme exists, no attempt has been made to explain its particular importance in imperial Rome, and no interpretation of Latin poetry has acknowledged its manifold symbolic functions. By contrast, the related theme of the Gigantomachy, to which the poets typically compare acts of human theomachy, has received considerable scholarly attention in the wake

---

[9] Besides the several books on the *Thebaid* cited in the notes thus far, I list here only the most recent English language monographs on the other authors of epic and tragedy: Staley 2010 (Seneca), Day 2013 (Lucan), Stover 2012 (Valerius Flaccus), Augoustakis 2010b (Silius, mostly).

[10] Feeney 1991.

[11] For a concise and up-to-date account of interdiscursivity see Riggsby 2006: 4–5; for a brief definition applied to the study of the *Aeneid* see Barchiesi 2002: 89–90. The category of interdiscursivity has gained currency in the field of critical discourse analysis, but its origins go back to the work of Michel Foucault; see Fairclough 2003: 19–39, esp. 37–9.

[12] These higher order connections will be a feature of Chapters 4, 5, and 9 in particular.

of Philip Hardie's groundbreaking study of the cosmic imagery of the *Aeneid*.[13] Gigantomachy's figuring of civil war, competition, and excess made it an apt image for the cultural and power struggles of the first century AD. The combination of the elevation of the emperor, the legacy of Hellenistic philosophies, and the sense of a rapidly changing society and culture placed extraordinary pressures on the traditional representation of gods in epic and tragedy, and hence made opposition to those gods of far greater intellectual interest to the poets of the time.

Critics have not adequately brought out, however, the important distinction between Gigantomachy and human-divine theomachy in fulfilling that poetic interest. In this respect the humanity of the theomach is fundamental. No matter how monstrous or Giant-like, and in Hercules' case even semi-divine, the theomach speaks the language of humanity and is thus capable both of offering a richer context for his radical aspirations and of inviting the audience to adopt an alternative view on the theological status quo. While writers may use the Gigantomachy to allegorise such intellectual ambitions—as the Epicurean poet Lucretius does in representing philosophical materialism, for example—the Giants do not give voice to those allegories, and their feats remain far distant in time and scale from the activities of humankind. Gigantomachic motifs are therefore inextricably entwined with, yet also distinct from, narratives of humans challenging gods. This book shows how the characterisation of the human theomach and the representation of human-divine theomachy enables a richer exploration of the nature, operation, and symbolism of divine power.

The book falls into roughly three parts, of which the first covers theomachy in Greek poetry and, especially, the development of theomachy in Augustan epic. These three chapters, on Homer and Attic tragedy, Lucretius and Vergil, and Ovid, introduce some of the main patterns and contexts that will be developed in the peculiar circumstances of later imperial Latin poetry. The remaining chapters can be divided dynastically, with chapters on Seneca and Lucan representing Neronian literature and Silius and Statius the Flavians. It's no accident that the latter take up a larger proportion of chapters than either their Augustan or Neronian counterparts, since Statius' Capaneus is, in many ways, a highpoint of the theme in ancient literary history. As many of the chapter epigraphs suggest, however, and as the book's epilogue will flesh out in a little more detail, theomachy has considerable staying power and has accordingly survived well into modernity. The snapshots of the Miltonic tradition at the head of this introduction, for example, represent but one aspect of classical theomachy's rich legacy.

Given the focus of the book on early imperial Rome and the genres of epic and tragedy, some related texts and figures lie beyond its scope. Even within epic, the voyage myths—the *Odyssey* and the Argonautic tradition—receive very

---

[13] Hardie 1986. On the role of Gigantomachy in Flavian epic see now Fucecchi 2013. On the place of the myth in Greek culture see the classic account of Vian 1952.

selective discussion since they engage theomachy far more infrequently and indirectly than their more martial counterparts.[14] Attic comedy does treat the subject of theomachy, especially in Aristophanes' *Birds*, but represents at most a minor influence on Roman theomachy. More germane in theme, if not influence, is the Aeschylean or pseudo-Aeschylean tragedy *Prometheus Bound*. Prometheus' Titanic nature, however, distinguishes him from the mortal antagonists of the divine in whom this book is interested. His possession of secret and powerful knowledge, in particular, means that his conflict with Zeus is conducted on different terms from the thoroughly imbalanced contest we see in the case of the human theomachies.[15] Finally, although I occasionally touch on the imitation of gods as a form of theomachy, the examples of Salmoneus, Haemus, and other imitators do not involve the mortal directly opposing or threatening to confront a god. Our main texts, moreover, do not provide detailed accounts or characterisation of these imitators, nor any direct speech indicating their motivation or objective. They thus remain a secondary thread in the story of theomachy.

The Terminology of Theomachy

Theomachy is a deceptively simple concept: literally, it is a war in which gods participate. Even so straightforward a definition, however, leaves many questions unanswered, and the symbolic potential of the war against god is already evident in the application of the relevant ancient terminology. I use the word 'theomach', from the Greek *theomachos* (LSJ s.v. θεομάχος), principally to designate a mortal who fights a god; 'theomachy', from *theomachia* (LSJ s.v. θεομαχία), to designate the fight itself, whether literal or figurative; and finally the adjective 'theomachic', which has no Greek equivalent, to describe the attitude or actions of the theomach. Modern scholars have largely followed Plato in reserving the word 'theomachy' for battles among the gods themselves, canonically the one narrated in *Iliad* 21 or the Gigantomachy.[16] Other ancient sources, however, use the constellation of Greek words to refer to mortals' battles against the gods, such as those of Homer's Diomedes or Patroclus.[17]

---

[14] Ovid's *Metamorphoses*, which is neither a martial nor a voyage epic, draws its theomachic interest principally from the genre of tragedy.

[15] By contrast, for example, it's the mortal aspect of the semi-divine Hercules that emerges especially clearly from Seneca's treatment of the hero's theomachy.

[16] Pl. *Resp*. 378d, Scymn. 637. On the intradivine theomachy in the *Iliad* see Chapter 1.

[17] The ancient commentators on the *Iliad* used the word θεομαχία and its cognates to refer both to battles amongst the gods and to conflicts between gods and humans. The bT Scholia ad *Il*. 20.4 and 21.470, for instance, refer to the battle of the gods in *Iliad* 21 as a theomachy. The b Scholia refer to Diomedes' *aristeia* in Book 5 as a theomachy (ad *Il*. 5.511: ἡ Διομήδους θεομαχία). The AT Scholia ad *Il*. 16.710 indicate that Patroclus' confrontation with Apollo in Book 16 was also thought of as a theomachy. The ancient commentary on Sophocles' *Ajax* (see pp. 000) uses the verb figuratively to describe Ajax's behaviour and attitude towards Athena.

Of all the Greek words related to this concept, the verb (LSJ s.v. θεομαχέω) is the most commonly found, and it is often used figuratively to describe heroes' arrogance towards the gods or opposition to what it is fated or natural.[18]

Outside modern scholarship, the English word 'theomachy' has its own long pedigree and has been used to mean 'opposition to the will of god'.[19] This meaning derives from late antique use of the Greek words by Christian authors, whose tracts frequently cast their theological opponents as theomachs, a rhetorical move to which English writers of the 16th and 17th centuries were particularly alive in the face of religious conflicts in Europe and the coming Enlightenment.[20] Lying behind all of these later Christian developments, however, was the classical Greek sense that opposition to the gods signified a wide range of challenges to intellectual and social norms, a sense that the Roman poets develop in powerful and influential ways.[21]

There is no direct Latin equivalent for the Greek word *theomachos*, but the phrase *contemptor deorum* ('despiser of the gods') and its variants convey all the impious and intransigent characteristics one could hope for. This is the term, for instance, that Vergil deploys to describe the tyrannical Mezentius and that Statius uses for the quintessentially theomachic Capaneus. Among their company we can also count numerous figures in Ovid's *Metamorphoses*— Pentheus, Pirithous, Erysichthon, and the Cyclops Polyphemus—all of whom, in one way or another, mount a serious challenge to the divine. When Romans talk about waging 'war' (*bellum*) against the gods, they too use the concept with different degrees of literalness. So, when Statius' Dis, god of the underworld, bids the Fury Tisiphone to 'seek one to carry the war to the gods' (*quaere deis qui bella ferat, Theb.* 8.76), he looks ahead to Capaneus' ascent into the sky and challenge to Jupiter—a literal transference of the war from the depths of hell to the divine heavens. Cicero and Livy, on the other hand, had already used the image of waging war against the gods to describe metaphorically (but only just) the impiety of Rome's foreign and domestic enemies—the Gauls and the Aequi; Verres, the tyrannical governor of Sicily; Flaminius, the consul who notoriously ignored the signs of the gods' disfavour.[22] What is implicit in all of

---

[18] See pp. 40–42, esp. n. 53.

[19] *OED* s.v. 'theomachy' 1a. The *OED* also records the rare 'theomachist', in place of which I use 'theomach', which I hope will sound more euphonic to modern ears.

[20] A search of the TLG database reveals that the vast majority of appearances of the verb in particular come from late antique Christian texts.

[21] For the broader semantics of the verb θεομαχέω and the contexts in which it can be applied see the discussions of the *Ajax* and *Bacchae* in Chapter 1.

[22] Cic. *Font.* 30 (Gauls), Livy 3.2.5 (Aequi), Cic. *Verr.* 2.4.72 (Verres), Livy 21.63.6 (Flaminius, on whom see Chapter 6). The Samnite leader Pontius attributes his nation's past defeats to fighting against the gods (Livy 9.1.11). The Romans could also deploy the concept of theomachy as metaphorically as the Greeks. In the context of a discussion about aging, for example, Cicero allegorises the Gigantomachy as a foolish and hopeless struggle against a natural process: *quid est enim aliud Gigantum modo bellare cum dis nisi naturae repugnare?* ('for what else is it to war with the gods, in the manner of the Giants, if not to fight against nature?', Cic. *Sen.* 5).

these scenes, and what is common to all usages of the word 'theomachy' and its various attendants, is the shared assumption that fighting the gods entails also a violent attack against the standing order, represented and embodied by the gods themselves. In contrast to the linguistic usage, however, what literary theomachy offers the reader is the opportunity to assess the moral value of the theomach himself, and thereby also to pass judgement on the world as we know it. In other words, a theomach is a sign with multiple, and shifting, referents: he can be a serious and principled opponent, or a rough and ignorant brute.[23] The semantics of theomachy, therefore, reside only partially in the word itself, and we must rely on context, literary as well as cultural, to define it fully.

Reading Theomachy in the Early Empire

In an influential article from 1984, Arnaldo Momigliano suggested that the transition from Caesar to Augustus saw poetry replace antiquarian studies and philosophy as the primary genre in which to think about religion:

> The men who represented the new [Augustan] age were neither scholars like Varro nor philosophers like Cicero: they were poets—Horace, Virgil, Propertius, Ovid, Manilius. It was a poet, Ovid, who undertook and did not quite complete the task of collecting the stories attached to the various festivals of the Roman calendar.[24]

Momigliano's example of Ovid's *Fasti* clearly illustrates the role of poetry in continuing the antiquarian and cultural study formerly associated with Varro; no less clear is the philosophical inheritance of the Augustan poets, especially from Lucretius.[25] Latin poetry could do more, however, than reveal the origins of Roman religion and engage in metaphysical debate—it could also bring philosophy and politics together in order to scrutinise contemporary pressures on religion and religious discourse.[26]

---

[23] I use the pronoun 'he' since the vast majority of theomachs are male, though Niobe is an important exception. It's a blind spot not only of ancient authors but, less excusably, of modern authors too that the powerful concept of fighting the gods has been largely restricted in this way. Observe, in this context, that Philip Pullman's *His Dark Materials* trilogy, inspired by Milton's *Paradise Lost*, features a young female protagonist—Lyra—but an older male theomach—Lyra's father, Lord Asriel.

[24] Momigliano 1984: 210–11.

[25] Cf. Feeney 1998: 46, with further references at n. 113. For an account of philosophy's continuing theological role in the early empire see Attridge 1978. On the reception of Lucretius in the Augustan poets, especially Vergil, see Mellinghoff-Bourgerie 1990, Hardie 2009b, and the essays in Armstrong et al. 2004.

[26] For literature's special cultural work in interacting with, but not replicating, various religious discourses see Feeney 1998: 141–2, 2004a: 4–8. Cf. Beard 1987, esp. 10 and 15 n. 32, and Woolf 2012: 200–5. On religion in Flavian epic see now the essays in Augoustakis 2013.

Precedent for this kind of integrative approach can be found in work on Cicero's *De Divinatione*. According to Brian Krostenko's reading of the text, the dialogue shows how philosophical traditions could combine with political realities—specifically, Caesar's use of 'religious symbolism to represent, and to justify, his own political supremacy'—to effect a change in religious beliefs, or at least to articulate new religious anxieties.[27] Indeed, politics, philosophy, religion, and literature always interrelate in various ways despite artificial attempts to separate them, such as the *theologia tripartita* of Scaevola and Varro, which divided the study of religion into three theologies: of the poets (*genus mythicon*), philosophers (*genus naturale*), and the state (*genus ciuile*).[28] Such categories are only a schematic representation of an idealised reality, and do not precisely reflect practices on the ground, whether of worshippers, sceptics, emperors, or poets. The effect of Hellenistic philosophy in particular on the poets' intellectual experimentation is well known, especially via the formative influence of Lucretius' *De Rerum Natura*, discussed in Chapter 2. The clearest example of such influence appears in Chapter 8, on Statius' *Thebaid*, where the impious figure of Capaneus uses Epicurean slogans in order to argue against the efficacy of divination. My concern, however, will be less to specify precise philosophical sources for the poetry—in most cases we lack evidence of a tight connection to a particular text or school of philosophy, and in any case the poets may have drawn eclectically from their reading—but rather to frame the poetic themes within a larger debate about the ways in which religious belief is grounded.[29]

Many of the episodes discussed in this book concern the role of the theomach in testing and shaping belief in, and beliefs about, the divine. When Ovid's Lycaon, discussed in Chapter 3, encounters a guest who gives signs of being a divinity, he disregards those signs in favour of tests intended to prove whether or not the figure is a god. Lycaon frames these tests, which turn out to be emphatically physical in nature, as clear and persuasive to any observer in response to the uncertainty of inferring divinity from signs. The episode thus enacts a conflict between the different ways in which one comes to have knowledge of the gods. While a lack of belief in a particular claim to divinity is importantly different from an outright denial of the very existence of gods, the connection between Lycaon's scepticism and a more extreme, euhemerist point of view is

---

[27] Krostenko 2000: 385; cf. Linderski 1982, Momigliano 1984, and Santangelo 2013: 10–36, and passim on the historical context. See also Gildenhard 2011: 246–384 on the relationship between theology and politics in Cicero's speeches. On the challenges faced by Cicero in reconciling Hellenistic philosophy and Roman religion see Beard 1986, Schofield 1986a, Brunt 1989.

[28] On the *theologia tripartita* see Lieberg 1973, Rüpke 2005. On the interrelation of philosophical theology and traditional cult see, e.g., Algra 2009 (on Stoicism). For a general account of Hellenistic philosophical theology see Mansfeld 1999; for more specialised studies see Essler 2011 and the relevant essays in Frede and Laks 2002 and Fish and Sanders 2011.

[29] For judicious warnings about overprivileging context over text in the interpretation of literature see Feeney 2004a: 18–20.

suggested by the episode itself and elaborated in several other myths in the *Metamorphoses*.[30] Comparison with Ovid's Niobe, for instance, highlights not only the epistemic interest common to both episodes but also the different kinds of objection raised against religious belief. Moreover, the subsequent Latin epic tradition shows religious belief subjected to repeated scrutiny along similar lines. Statius' Capaneus, for example, draws on the words of Lycaon as part of a comprehensive assault on the gods, an assault that conjoins epic theomachy with philosophically tinged scepticism and even atheism.[31] What emerges from these and other challenges is an emphasis not on disbelief per se but rather on the ways in which different beliefs contend in resolving various claims to divinity and the question of the existence of the gods.

In articulating various points of view pertaining to belief, epic could draw, as we have seen, on the tradition of religious and philosophical thought exemplified by Cicero and Lucretius. The comparatively greater liberties afforded to writers of fiction, however, enable the imperial poets to create a world in which the presence of the gods is tantalisingly close, at times visible, even tangible—strikingly unlike the real world in which the gods, at least fully animated gods, are well beyond reach.[32] In this mythical setting, with humans and gods so frequently intertwined, friction is to be expected. It's one thing to know distant gods through indirect communication, as the Romans did in their rituals, but quite another to face gods, or beings that may or may not be gods, up close. Under the pressing conditions created in the epic and tragic laboratories, knowing the divine becomes a more fraught concern, prompting a range of responses that include aggressively testing the gods. If the characters engaged in this activity are considered abrasive and impious, at least part of the explanation lies in the social norms and rival claims to authority threatened by their provocative challenge. Yet their desire for knowledge, and for security in that knowledge, can also be seen as an extension of what the Romans, whether in philosophy or religion, had already been doing for some time.

One of the many strands of contemporary theology was the empirical basis of Roman religion. Clifford Ando has argued that empirical analysis of the procedures and results of past rituals in order to ensure their future efficacy represented a fundamental component of Roman religion.[33] Empiricism of this sort, closely bound with divinatory practices and ritual protocols, contrasts with the position held, explicitly or implicitly, by many of the epic characters discussed

---

[30] Throughout this book I use the word 'scepticism' with its everyday meaning rather than as a technical term, i.e., to signify doubt or suspicion in general terms and not, unless otherwise indicated, to designate a particular philosophical school, such as Academic or Pyrrhonian scepticism.

[31] On atheism in classical antiquity see Bremmer 2007.

[32] On the interactions between different genres of belief see Feeney 1993: 242.

[33] See Ando 2008: xvi–xvii. Liebeschuetz 1979: 17 had already emphasised the empiricism of divinatory practices. For an ancient empiricist defence of divination see Quintus' arguments in *De Div.* 1 and the discussion in Schofield 1986a: 51–2, 62.

in this book. These antagonists of the gods subscribe to a much stronger empiricism, not only believing that knowledge is derived from experience and observation but also scrutinising, and often rejecting, otherworldy explanations for phenomena. Indeed, their suspicion of the supernatural leads them to question the very premises foundational to Roman religion. Rather than testing methods of communication with the divine, as the Romans so often did, they apply their empiricist approach to the prior question of whether it's possible to know the divine at all, and by extension whether the gods even exist. This contrast in epistemology, often expressed more simply in moral terms as a contrast between piety and impiety, proves fertile for the poets' thinking about religious belief: the episodes force rival premises, methods, and explanations into violent and spectacular conjunction. By placing these conflicts at the heart of their works, the epic poets expanded the cultural conversation to include the testing of the divine in the Romans' attempts to make sense of the epistemological, theological, and political concerns pertaining to belief.[34]

The most important reason for Roman literature's concentration on these issues, I suggest, was their topicality. The ever closer identification of divine and political power led to the introduction of new gods—beginning with Julius Caesar's deification—and generated a vigorous discourse on the relationship between the familiar Olympian gods and their new imperial partners. The origin and development of the emperor's elevated status, especially the imperial cult, provided an appropriate stimulus for thinking about the criteria and gradations of godhead and their implications for changing conceptions of the divine.[35] The attempt to establish the emperor as a figure near to, if not partaking of, divinity prompted a literary response in various genres, but especially epic, where the power of the gods played a key role in determining the nature of the world and the course of events.[36]

It's against this cultural context, for example, that Lucan's decision to abandon the conventional divine apparatus of epic in the *Bellum Civile*, the subject of Chapter 5, must be understood. Lucan's choice may be illuminated by a highly rhetorical passage in Book 7 (445–8), in which the narrator claims that in the

---

[34] Cf. Ando 2010a. A development of part of Ando 2008, it shares with my own argument a concern with multiple theological discourses (though treated from a historical rather than literary perspective).

[35] Although Roman generals had received divine honours as early as the mid-republic, the divine status and singular authority of the emperors differed by an order of magnitude. The bibliography on the imperial cult is extensive; the main accounts include: Weinstock 1971; Price 1984; Beard, North, and Price 1998: 1.140–9, 206–10; M. Clauss 1999; and Gradel 2002. Peppard 2011: 31–49 provides a convenient summary of the scholarship. On conceptual issues see R. Gordon 2001, Lipka 2009: 29–30 and 50, Iossif and Lorber 2011, Levene 2012; cf. esp. Versnel 2011: 439–92 on Greek attitudes to divine rulers. The loss of most Hellenistic epic is felt especially keenly in this area, since the relationship between those poems and the divinised rulers under whom they were composed would have provided important comparanda for the Roman material.

[36] See Feeney 2007: 133–5. For a fine account of the role of the imperial cult and the *theologia tripartita* in Ovid's exile poetry see McGowan 2009: 93–120.

face of the gods' allowing an evil such as the battle of Pharsalus to occur, traditional religious belief cannot be sustained: *mentimur regnare Iouem* ('we lie that Jupiter reigns', Luc. 7.447).[37] Further evidence of change in belief lies only a few lines later in the same speech (Luc. 7.455–9), when the narrator identifies one of the consequences of Pharsalus as the institution of imperial cult: *bella pares superis facient ciuilia diuos* ('civil wars will make deceased emperors equal to the gods', Luc. 7.457). The substitution of belief with disbelief (*mentimur*) goes some way to explaining why the epic could not maintain a traditional divine apparatus, which either would have looked quite hollow in light of the narrator's pronouncements or would have entirely undermined them. The coupling of disbelief with imperial cult further suggests a correlation between the conditions required for a change in belief and the conditions leading to a new state religion. It's important to note that Lucan is not engaging any individual component of religious belief here, such as an acceptance of the efficacy of one ritual or another, but rather the most extreme case possible—the question of the very power and identity of the gods—i.e., the kind of belief without which the edifice of Roman religion, imperial or otherwise, falls to dust.[38]

The conjunction of various streams of influence in imperial poetry meant that political theology and philosophical theology could be made to reflect on each other in novel and highly sophisticated ways: circumstances encouraged poets to consider how practical conceptions of power might affect one's metaphysical views, and how epistemological concerns might affect one's view of imperial ideology. The effects of such literary cross-fertilisation will be seen throughout this book, for the various episodes' theological concerns not only find expression through the idiom and conventions of epic and tragedy but also shape the evolution of theomachy over the course of the first century AD. Chapter 4, for instance, shows how Seneca triangulates his Hercules' attempted theomachy with other kinds of ascent to the heavens, political and philosophical, thereby widening the frame through which the hero's celestial aspirations are to be viewed.

The rise of the theomach during the early empire also marks a distinction between the poetry of the Augustan age and that of the mid to late years of the first century. Vergil and Ovid subject their gods to scrutiny, to be sure: they draw on some of the same philosophical thinking that will animate the later works, and they show a sensitivity to the conditions created by the evolving relationship between the emperor and the gods. But the Augustan poets' view of history was crucially different from that of the Neronian and Flavian authors. The later poets saw the system of the principate develop over time, the repeated

---

[37] On the whole passage see Chapter 5.
[38] By contrast, it's possible to countenance the dismissal of divination, for instance, without harm to religion and the belief in a divine being; this is, at least, the claim made at *De Div.* 2.148 (see Schofield 1986a: 57–60).

struggles for the throne, and even the ends and beginnings of entire dynasties (discussed in Chapter 9). That experience left its mark on their works: just as the conventions of imperial power were formed, tested, and broken by the emperor and his opponents, so too the conventions of genre—the power of the gods and the limits of heroism in epic and tragedy—became subject to similar experimentation.

The convergence of these various literary and cultural factors produced tragic heroes who sought an epic dominance of the world and the stage—such as Seneca's Atreus and Medea, for instance—and epic heroes whose careers closely followed a tragic plot, such as Silius' Hannibal (the focus of Chapter 7). The representation of heroism was thus defined less by generic conventions and more by an individual will to power that brought the hero into conflict with the gods, who still remained the clearest symbol of authority in the Roman world. It was characteristic of poetry from Seneca onwards to dramatise the coexistence of radically different attitudes to the gods in far more emphatic terms than even Ovid had depicted in the *Metamorphoses*—not the selective impiety of a Lycaon, Pentheus, Arachne, or Niobe, none of whom explicitly threatens the entire divine order, but rather the comprehensive claim of a maddened Hercules, Caesar, or Capaneus to revolutionise the world with which the audience was familiar.

Here, another concept is useful, which I term 'the theomachic sublime'. Sublimity has recently come back into vogue as an object of study, and the theomach, as Matthew Leigh has sketched out, makes for a particularly fine example of the phenomenon.[39] The frequent association of the sublime with storms, heights, and events of great magnitude sits comfortably with the *Sturm und Drang* of the theomachic moment, which regularly features thunderbolts, ascents, and moments of cosmic importance. In this sense, theomachy represents the apogee of a poem and its poetics.

Stephen Halliwell has recently contrasted two classic conceptions of the sublime, those of Kant and Longinus.[40] Whereas Kant identifies the sublime with a combination of elevation and frustration, and an awareness of the ultimate limits of thought, Longinus sees the sublime as a means of godlike transcendence.

---

[39] Leigh 2006. As recently as 2009, Philip Hardie could write that the 'sublime has been a rather understudied category in modern histories of Latin literature' (Hardie 2009b: 7). Thanks to Hardie's own work as well as that of a number of other critics, however, the scholarly landscape now looks very different. The philosophical turn in the scholarship further means that we can now profitably press beyond the surface of aesthetic features to consider the cognitive and symbolic role of the sublime in the representation of theomachy. On the sublime in Latin literature see also Conte 1994: 1–34, Schrijvers 2006, Porter 2007, Day 2013, Hardie 2013 , Young 2013. On the history and various theories of the sublime see, e.g., Shaw 2006, Axelsson 2007, Porter 2010, and the essays in Costelloe 2012. Here again my subject intersects with the work of Harold Bloom, who has had a long-standing interest in the Longinan and Lucretian concepts of the sublime, though largely focused on his specific concern with authorial influence (see most recently Bloom 2011).

[40] Halliwell 2012: 342.

The theomachic sublime, and by extension theomachy itself, contains elements of both conceptions contrasted by Halliwell.[41] On the one hand, it draws attention to paradoxes that cannot be resolved and powerful rival explanatory systems, but on the other hand it also suggests the capacity of either system to account for all that goes on in the world—whether natural or supernatural—and to reveal a higher truth to the limited human mind. The theomachies of imperial epic and tragedy, therefore, are far less dogmatic and prescriptive than a strictly moralising or philosophical reading would allow. Instead of the committed assertion of a particular world view, as in philosophy, the sublime experience associated with theomachy leaves genuinely open questions about the nature of the poetic fiction, its representational power, and its relationship to reality.

At the broadest level, then, the main argument of the book is that theomachy symbolises various conflicts of authority: the poets' attempts to outdo their literary predecessors, the contentions of rival philosophical views, and the violent assertions of power that characterise both autocratic authority and its opposition. By drawing on evidence from literature, politics, religion, and philosophy, this study reveals the various influences that shaped the intellectual and cultural significance of theomachy—from Stoic and Epicurean debates about the gods to the divinisation of the emperor, from poetic competition with Vergil and Homer to tyranny and revolution under the Julio-Claudian and Flavian dynasties. In particular, the Latin poets use the figure of the theomach to explore the implications of the threat he poses to the fictional world he inhabits and the Roman world represented through that fiction.[42] The theomach does not, however, provide an allegory for a single point of view to be weighed against an equally monolithic opposing view represented by the gods. Rather, the theomach allows the poet to put in play certain provocative and polysemous claims—Hercules' assertion of the limitlessness of his civilising power, for example, or Capaneus' various Epicurean and even atheistic challenges to conventional epic theology. In viewing these perspectives not as part of a binary opposition to be resolved in favour of one or the other verdict, but rather as part of an extended meditation on the problems posed by the relationship between gods and mortals, this book describes the role of the theomach in scrutinising the premises, limits, and possibilities of epic and tragedy, along with several of their most important contexts.

---

[41] And not only Halliwell's pairing of Kant and Longinus. One might equally well conjoin the demythologising Lucretian sublime described by Porter 2007 and Hardie 2009b with the theistic or spiritualistic sublime described by Chignell and Halteman 2012: 188–96. Theomachy stages a contest between these two forms of the sublime, leading to the corroboration, unsettling, or transformation of the reader's theological view.

[42] Cf. Lovatt 2001: 114.

1

Theomachy in Greek Epic and Tragedy

> And they said, Go to, let us build us a city and a tower, whose top *may reach* unto heaven; and let us make us a name, lest we be scattered abroad upon the face of the whole earth.
>
> —GENESIS 11:4
>
> This fable is for men who fight the gods.
>
> —AESOP
>
> This is what he kept saying to himself,
> 'How on earth can I get directly to Zeus?'
> Then he'd have little ladders made,
> and so he'd clamber up to heaven,
> until he fell off and smashed his head.
>
> —ARISTOPHANES

From the beginning of the classical literary tradition, the idea of theomachy provided a conceptual space for thinking about human capacities in relation to the ultimate paradigm of power—divinity. Coming into conflict with a god allowed for the clearest articulation of mortal limits, the nature and scope of divine power, and the fixity or fluidity of the boundary separating human beings from gods. Critics have treated these subjects before, though not usually as part of a specific and diachronic focus on human-divine antagonism, and certainly not with the Roman legacy in mind.[1] This chapter, therefore, has two primary goals. The first is to introduce the common and important features of Greek representations of theomachy in the *Iliad* and in Attic tragedy, our two main

---

[1] For a survey of theomachic scenes and allusions in Greek literature see Hogan and Schenker 2002, Yasumura 2011.

sources for theomachic scenes and imagery, in the first and second halves of the chapter, respectively. The second goal is to provide an initial sense of Roman theomachy's debts to, and distinctiveness from, its Greek models. The subsequent chapters will show how a number of different contexts, including Greek literature, combine to shape the form of Roman theomachy; in this chapter, I focus on a few key differences between the two traditions, the most important of which is the more direct and threatening antagonism between hero and god in the Roman examples. The presentation of the Greek material in this chapter responds to this second objective, with the result that the readings are shaped by the Roman reception of, and reaction to, Greek ideas. Readers of this book familiar with the basic contours of Greek theomachy and with the scholarship that I draw on may still wish to read the chapter both to get a broad sense of the major distinctions and to see how a Roman perspective might provide a different view of literary history.

Theomachy in the *Iliad*

The importance of theomachy to the *Iliad* is clear from the sequence of three heroic *aristeiai*—of Diomedes, Patroclus, and Achilles—that largely structure the ebbs and flows of battle over the course of the poem, and each of which culminates in physical conflict between the hero and one or more gods. The majority of my discussion of the *Iliad*, therefore, focuses on individual readings of these three episodes in chronological order. Each one sheds a slightly different light on the ways in which human-divine conflicts can be framed. Diomedes, for instance, illustrates the care and delicacy required in legitimising an attack on the gods; Patroclus reveals, by contrast, how a more direct antagonism with the gods threatens to break not only ethical norms but also the course of fate; while Homer uses Achilles, as the figure most like a god, to reflect on the distinction between mortals and immortals, and the ways in which boundaries can be pushed but ultimately still hold.[2]

Scenes of theomachy, moreover, are so heavily invested in concepts fundamental to epic—heroism and the gods—that they provide an especially suitable context for metapoetic thinking. The idea of competition at the highest level—which is what theomachy is—has a natural resonance with current theories of oral composition and its reflection in Homeric poetry, especially

---

[2] I use 'Homer' as shorthand to refer to the poetic tradition that created the *Iliad*. Although our text of the poem may only be a late, canonised form of one variant within a wider tradition, and although its form reflects the characteristics of oral composition, I take the text to be interpretable using many of the standard categories of criticism—narrative structure, characterisation, etc. For the sophistication attainable in oral composition see now Bakker 2013.

the *Iliad*'s frequent, yet often oblique, handling of myths relating to other generations of heroes, such as those involving Herakles or Thebes. But it's not competition alone that links theomachy to the rivalry of epic narratives—those other myths are often figured within the *Iliad* in theomachic terms, such as Dione's account of Herakles' assaults on gods, or the impiety of the Seven against Thebes. For that reason, my discussion of the *Iliad* attempts to triangulate the ideas of theomachy, generational conflict, and metapoetics. Finally, throughout the readings of the individual theomachies and related themes, the issues prominent in the *Iliad* are compared and contrasted with their Roman treatment.

DIOMEDES: DIVINE IMPULSION AND THE LEGITIMACY OF THEOMACHY

Early in Book 5, Homer prepares for the elevation of Diomedes through his *aristeia* by describing the hero in elemental terms (*Il.* 5.85–92):[3]

> Τυδεΐδην δ' οὐκ ἂν γνοίης ποτέροισι μετείη
> ἠὲ μετὰ Τρώεσσιν ὁμιλέοι ἦ μετ' Ἀχαιοῖς.
> θῦνε γὰρ ἂμ πεδίον ποταμῷ πλήθοντι ἐοικὼς
> χειμάρρῳ, ὅς τ' ὦκα ῥέων ἐκέδασσε γεφύρας·
> τὸν δ' οὔτ' ἄρ τε γέφυραι ἐεργμέναι ἰσχανόωσιν,
> οὔτ' ἄρα ἕρκεα ἴσχει ἀλωάων ἐριθηλέων
> ἐλθόντ' ἐξαπίνης ὅτ' ἐπιβρίσῃ Διὸς ὄμβρος·
> πολλὰ δ' ὑπ' αὐτοῦ ἔργα κατήριπε κάλ' αἰζηῶν

> You would not know which of the sides Diomedes was on,
> whether he was with the Trojans or the Achaeans.
> For he rushed over the plain like a river swollen
> by a winter storm, which flowing swiftly breaks up the dams.
> Neither the closed-in dams hold it back,
> nor do the walls of flourishing orchards stop
> its sudden onset when the thunderstorm of Zeus falls heavily,
> and the many fine works of strong men fall down before it.

The ostensible meaning of the introduction to the simile is straightforward— that Diomedes' swift movement all over the plain makes it impossible to identify him with one side or the other. The confusion, however, serves another purpose: it separates Diomedes from all the other combatants, whose movement and identities are easy to discern. The hero is then further distinguished from his peers through the river simile, which magnifies Diomedes' heroism. And yet the simile also subtly undercuts the mortal hero's awesome display of

---

[3] On Diomedes' *aristeia* in particular, and the topos of the *aristeia* in general, see Fenik 1968: 9–77, Krischer 1971: 13–90.

power, for behind the force of the river lies 'Zeus' storm'. The simultaneous elevation of a human while deftly reasserting divine control is characteristic of the *Iliad*'s treatment of martial heroism, especially in scenes of theomachy in which mortal and divine power are in explicit tension.

The viewing of the hero in elemental terms is an important technique for the Roman poets too. The theomach, in particular, takes on qualities of the natural world: Lucan's Caesar appears as an embodiment of lightning, while both Silius' Scipio and Statius' Capaneus will be compared to rivers. In these cases, however, the comparisons differ from the river simile describing Diomedes in one important respect: mention of the gods' power is typically absent or kept separate from the heroes' achievements. That distinction is already highly suggestive of a broader contrast between the Greek and Roman poets in their outlook on theomachy: the Roman heroes possess greater autonomy and unaided strength than their Greek counterparts.

The divinely sanctioned nature of most Iliadic theomachy is made explicit soon after the river simile. The goddess Athena herself licenses Diomedes to strike Aphrodite but expressly forbids him from attacking any of the other gods (*Il.* 5.129–32):

> τὼ νῦν αἴ κε θεὸς πειρώμενος ἐνθάδ' ἵκηται
> μή τι σύ γ' ἀθανάτοισι θεοῖς ἀντικρὺ μάχεσθαι
> τοῖς ἄλλοις· ἀτὰρ εἴ κε Διὸς θυγάτηρ Ἀφροδίτη
> ἔλθῃσ' ἐς πόλεμον, τήν γ' οὐτάμεν ὀξέϊ χαλκῷ.

> Now if a god comes here to test you,
> do not fight against the other immortal
> gods, but if the daughter of Zeus, Aphrodite,
> comes into the battle, strike her, indeed, with the sharp bronze.

Diomedes is thus able to do what no Roman theomach can: he wounds a god (*Il.* 5.330–7):

> ὃ δὲ Κύπριν ἐπῴχετο νηλέϊ χαλκῷ
> γιγνώσκων ὅ τ' ἄναλκις ἔην θεός, οὐδὲ θεάων
> τάων αἵ τ' ἀνδρῶν πόλεμον κάτα κοιρανέουσιν,
> οὔτ' ἄρ' Ἀθηναίη οὔτε πτολίπορθος Ἐνυώ.
> ἀλλ' ὅτε δή ῥ' ἐκίχανε πολὺν καθ' ὅμιλον ὀπάζων,
> ἔνθ' ἐπορεξάμενος μεγαθύμου Τυδέος υἱὸς
> ἄκρην οὔτασε χεῖρα μετάλμενος ὀξέϊ δουρὶ
> ἀβληχρήν.

> But Diomedes was pursuing Aphrodite with the pitiless bronze,
> recognising that she was a gentle goddess, not one of those
> who command the combat of men,
> neither Athena nor Enyo, sacker of cities.

> So when he reached her, chasing her through the thick crowd,
> the son of great-hearted Tydeus lunged forward
> and rushing with his sharp spear struck the top of her feeble hand.

Note how carefully Diomedes' action is made to appear legitimate. We already know that Athena has said that attacking Aphrodite, specifically, is permissible, but Homer here explains that among goddesses Aphrodite represents an acceptable target since she has no business being involved in battle. Moreover, in mentioning the obvious difference between Aphrodite and Athena, Homer reminds the audience of the divine authority behind Diomedes' action. Thus, however exceptional Diomedes' feat, the poem is emphatic in qualifying precisely how this theomachy might be considered reasonable and legitimate.[4]

After Diomedes wounds Aphrodite, the goddess claims the hero 'would even fight Zeus' (ὅς νῦν γε καὶ ἂν Διὶ πατρὶ μάχοιτο, *Il.* 5.362).[5] By the time she has fled to Olympus a few lines later, her already exaggerated concern appears to have grown in scale: οὐ γὰρ ἔτι Τρώων καὶ Ἀχαιῶν φύλοπις αἰνή, / ἀλλ' ἤδη Δαναοί γε καὶ ἀθανάτοισι μάχονται ('this is no longer a destructive war of Trojans and Achaeans, but now the Danaans are fighting even against the immortals', *Il.* 5.379–80).[6] The goddess's conception of an entire race of theomachic heroes may be hyperbolic, but some of the key moments in the poem will suggest that her anxiety is not altogether unjustified: Patroclus will attempt to scale the walls of Troy against Apollo in Book 16, and Achilles will provoke, and contend with, Scamander in Book 21. Nor are the Danaans alone in their theomachic urges. In response to Aphrodite's complaint, the goddess Dione tells her that other gods, too, have been attacked by mortals, such as the Aloidae's imprisonment of Ares or Herakles' assaults on Hera and Hades (*Il.* 5.382–404). Despite such outrages, Dione affirms the categorical difference between humans and gods (*Il.* 5.405–9):

> σοὶ δ' ἐπὶ τοῦτον ἀνῆκε θεὰ γλαυκῶπις Ἀθήνη·
> νήπιος, οὐδὲ τὸ οἶδε κατὰ φρένα Τυδέος υἱός
> ὅττι μάλ' οὐ δηναιὸς ὃς ἀθανάτοισι μάχηται,
> οὐδέ τί μιν παῖδες ποτὶ γούνασι παππάζουσιν
> ἐλθόντ' ἐκ πολέμοιο καὶ αἰνῆς δηϊοτῆτος.

> But in your case, the goddess bright-eyed Athena put him up to this.
> The son of Tydeus is a fool and does not know in his mind

---

[4] Turkeltaub 2010, esp. 143–4, argues that Diomedes' actions strain the neat distinction between piety and impiety, suggesting that particular conceptions of martial heroism entail impious behaviour. This is true (cf. below on Diomedes' attack on Aeneas, which Turkeltaub discusses), but it's important to recognise the efforts Homer goes to in order to make the theomachy appear legitimate. The contrast with Patroclus is telling, and even more so the contrast with the Roman theomachies. Similar to Turkeltaub is Barker and Christensen 2011: 31–2.

[5] Apollo echoes this concern at *Il.* 5.457.

[6] Cf. Juno's comparable claim at *Aen.* 1.46–8.

> that whoever fights the gods has a very short life,
> nor do his children by his knees call him father
> when he comes home from war and dire battle.

Despite the lesson that all theomachic heroes must ultimately die as a result of their transgression, it's important to observe a distinction between Diomedes' divinely assisted theomachy and the attacks of the heroes of old, such as Herakles, which appear to have been self-motivated, unaided, and grievous.[7] Dione thus puts Aphrodite's hysteria in perspective—not only will the hero inevitably be punished, but the wounding of Aphrodite, instigated by Athena and largely superficial, is in important ways less egregious than the transgressions of the past. Dione's speech thus also works against the elevation of Diomedes through his *aristeia*: measured against the *longue durée* of theomachy even Diomedes' feats fall short of earlier examples.

In citing Athena's involvement as mitigating Diomedes' theomachy, Dione continues the theme of qualifying and thereby, at least to some extent, legitimising the hero's actions. This situation of a god (Athena) putting a favourite (Diomedes) up against another god (Aphrodite) has no similar counterpart in Latin epic. In the *Punica*, for instance, Juno, who goes to extreme lengths to support Hannibal against the Romans, eventually restrains him from theomachy against Jupiter. Even an apparent counterexample reveals a clear difference from the Athena-Diomedes relationship. In the *Thebaid*, Dis wishes to send a mortal to fight against Jupiter as revenge for what he perceives to be an invasion of his domain. That mortal turns out to be Capaneus. And yet, despite the plausible argument that Dis inspires Capaneus to launch his theomachy, there is no question of legitimacy here. The impious Capaneus represents an entirely appropriate candidate to wage war on the gods, one who might do so with or without a divine impetus. The difference from the carefully parsed cooperation of Athena and Diomedes is stark, all the more so given that Capaneus despises all gods, whereas Diomedes makes no impious claims and obeys Athena's instructions to the letter. In fact, his obedience is highlighted when, towards the end of his *aristeia*, Athena chides him for weakness and cowardice in not fighting Ares, to which Diomedes responds by quoting back to the goddess her warning to attack Aphrodite alone (*Il.* 5.817–21).[8]

---

[7] According to the scholia, Dione's warning about the short life of the theomach encourages the audience to be pious: εἰς εὐσέβειαν δὲ ἡμᾶς διὰ τούτων παρακαλεῖ (bT Schol. ad 5.407). For a similarly didactic comment in the scholia to Sophocles' *Ajax* see Scholia ad *Aj.* 118 and my discussion further below. On the discrepancies between Dione's catalogue and Diomedes' *aristeia* see Sammons 2010: 24–38.

[8] For the Romans, in particular the Augustans, the episode of Aphrodite's wounding takes on greater significance because the goddess was at the time attempting to save Aeneas, founder of Rome and ancestor of the Julio-Claudian emperors. Thus, in both Vergil and Ovid, Venus refers back to Diomedes' wounding of her as a continuing anxiety when faced with potential harm to her descendants Aeneas and Julius Caesar (see Chapters 2 and 3). Precisely because Venus is so closely associated with Roman fortunes, however, her anxiety for herself and her nation is always unfounded: Venus may suffer the loss of Caesar, but no mortal ever comes close to harming her or destroying Rome.

PATROCLUS: OVERREACHING AND THE WALL

Homer further defines the limits of theomachy through the similarities and crucial differences between the theomachies of Diomedes and Patroclus. The excessiveness of Patroclus consists in the absence of a divine ally, as Athena was to Diomedes, and in the repetition of a theomachic pattern in direct contradiction of Apollo's warning. That pattern first appears halfway through Diomedes' *aristeia* (*Il.* 5.432–42):

> Αἰνείᾳ δ' ἐπόρουσε βοὴν ἀγαθὸς Διομήδης,
> γιγνώσκων ὅ οἱ αὐτὸς ὑπείρεχε χεῖρας Ἀπόλλων·
> ἀλλ' ὅ γ' ἄρ' οὐδὲ θεὸν μέγαν ἅζετο, ἵετο δ' αἰεὶ
> Αἰνείαν κτεῖναι καὶ ἀπὸ κλυτὰ τεύχεα δῦσαι.
> τρὶς μὲν ἔπειτ' ἐπόρουσε κατακτάμεναι μενεαίνων,
> τρὶς δέ οἱ ἐστυφέλιξε φαεινὴν ἀσπίδ' Ἀπόλλων·
> ἀλλ' ὅτε δὴ τὸ τέταρτον ἐπέσσυτο δαίμονι ἶσος,
> δεινὰ δ' ὁμοκλήσας προσέφη ἑκάεργος Ἀπόλλων·
> φράζεο Τυδεΐδη καὶ χάζεο, μηδὲ θεοῖσιν
> ἶσ' ἔθελε φρονέειν, ἐπεὶ οὔ ποτε φῦλον ὁμοῖον
> ἀθανάτων τε θεῶν χαμαὶ ἐρχομένων τ' ἀνθρώπων.

> Great-voiced Diomedes rushed at Aeneas,
> knowing that Apollo himself was holding his hands over him;
> but he dreaded not even the great god, and he ever desired
> to slay Aeneas and strip him of his famed armour.
> Then three times he fell on him desiring to kill him,
> and three times Apollo thrust back his bright shield;
> but when for a fourth time he rushed on like a god,
> Apollo the far-worker gave out a terrible cry and addressed him,
> 'Think, son of Tydeus, and give way! And do not aspire
> to equal the gods, since the race of immortal gods
> has never been like that of men who walk on the ground'.

The specific pattern of the attack—three attempts, a fourth time 'like a god', followed by a terrible cry—appears on only four occasions in the *Iliad*, once in reference to Diomedes here, twice performed by Patroclus, and once by Achilles.[9] Each occasion, as we shall see, is either explicitly theomachic or linked to theomachy. Apollo's response is quite clear: the repeated attack, even if directed against Aeneas rather than Apollo himself, implies an inflated sense of power and transgresses the boundary between mortal and divine. Whereas Diomedes obediently retreats after Apollo's warning, however,

---

[9] The phrase δαίμονι ἶσος ('like a god') appears on nine occasions in the poem (*Il.* 5.438, 459, 884; 16.705, 786; 20.447, 493; 21.18, 227), almost invariably in theomachic contexts. See Nagy 1979: 143–4.

Patroclus and Achilles will notably be more persistent and directly confrontational in their encounters with a god.

In Book 16, after Patroclus has killed Zeus' son Sarpedon, he ignores Achilles' earlier warning to repel the Trojans only from the plain (*Il.* 16.87–96) and instead pursues them up to the walls of the city, where he repeats Diomedes' earlier pattern of assault (*Il.* 16.698–709):

ἔνθά κεν ὑψίπυλον Τροίην ἕλον υἷες Ἀχαιῶν
Πατρόκλου ὑπὸ χερσί, περὶ πρὸ γὰρ ἔγχεϊ θῦεν,
εἰ μὴ Ἀπόλλων Φοῖβος ἐϋδμήτου ἐπὶ πύργου
ἔστη τῷ ὀλοὰ φρονέων, Τρώεσσι δ' ἀρήγων.
τρὶς μὲν ἐπ' ἀγκῶνος βῆ τείχεος ὑψηλοῖο
Πάτροκλος, τρὶς δ' αὐτὸν ἀπεστυφέλιξεν Ἀπόλλων
χείρεσσ' ἀθανάτῃσι φαεινὴν ἀσπίδα νύσσων.
ἀλλ' ὅτε δὴ τὸ τέταρτον ἐπέσσυτο δαίμονι ἶσος,
δεινὰ δ' ὁμοκλήσας ἔπεα πτερόεντα προσηύδα·
χάζεο διογενὲς Πατρόκλεες· οὔ νύ τοι αἶσα
σῷ ὑπὸ δουρὶ πόλιν πέρθαι Τρώων ἀγερώχων,
οὐδ' ὑπ' Ἀχιλλῆος, ὅς περ σέο πολλὸν ἀμείνων.

Then the sons of the Achaeans would have taken high-gated Troy
by the hands of Patroclus, for around and in front he raged with the spear,
if Phoebus Apollo had not stood on the well-built tower
thinking deadly thoughts against him, and aiding the Trojans.
Three times Patroclus went up on the corner of the high wall,
but three times Apollo thrust him back
pushing the bright shield with his immortal hands.
But when for the fourth time he rushed on like a god,
Apollo gave out a terrible cry and spoke winged words,
'Give way, god-born Patroclus. It is not fated now
that the city of the valiant Trojans be destroyed by your spear,
not even by that of Achilles, who is far better even than you.'

Here again we see the three formulaic elements: (1) τρὶς μέν...τρὶς δέ (three times); (2) ἀλλ' ὅτε δὴ τὸ τέταρτον ἐπέσσυτο δαίμονι ἶσος (a fourth attempt 'like a god'); (3) δεινὰ δ' ὁμοκλήσας (a great cry). There is a difference in the context, however. Although Diomedes had overreached inasmuch as he disregards Apollo's protection of Aeneas, it's important to distinguish Patroclus' direct confrontation with the god: he attempts to scale the wall against Apollo alone.[10]

---

[10] Moreover, as the scholia note, Diomedes' theomachy has the support of Athena, while Patroclus acts entirely on his own authority. The scholia are concerned with whether Diomedes and Patroclus retreat a short (τυτθὸν) or long (πολλὸν) distance from the god after their repeated assaults. Zenodotus preferred a short distance in both cases, while Aristarchus had Diomedes retreat a short distance and Patroclus retreat further. The scholia justify Aristarchus' reading on the grounds that Diomedes is

Patroclus' folly is greater still, since of the three theomachic heroes, Patroclus is also the only one to repeat the formulaic pattern of assaults (*Il.* 16.784–9):

τρὶς μὲν ἔπειτ' ἐπόρουσε θοῷ ἀτάλαντος Ἄρηϊ
σμερδαλέα ἰάχων, τρὶς δ' ἐννέα φῶτας ἔπεφνεν.
ἀλλ' ὅτε δὴ τὸ τέταρτον ἐπέσσυτο δαίμονι ἶσος,
ἔνθ' ἄρα τοι Πάτροκλε φάνη βιότοιο τελευτή·
ἤντετο γάρ τοι Φοῖβος ἐνὶ κρατερῇ ὑσμίνῃ
δεινός.

Then three times he leapt on them, the equal of swift Ares,
with a terrible shout, and three times he slew nine men.
But when for the fourth time he rushed on like a god,
then for you, Patroclus, did the end of life appear;
for Phoebus met you in the mighty conflict,
and he was terrible.

In the location where one might expect Apollo's shouted warning, the poet instead signals Patroclus' imminent death, a narratorial intervention made all the more striking by the apostrophe to the doomed hero. Patroclus is the only one of the three theomachs to perform the formulaic set piece twice, which he does in the space of a hundred lines, with the consequence that he is the only one of the three to die within the narrative of the poem.[11] Homer thus signals Patroclus' overreaching not just through explicit warnings in the narrative— from Achilles at the start of the book and from Apollo at *Il.* 16.707–9—but even at the level of lexical and formulaic repetition and difference.[12]

It's important to note also the ramifications of Patroclus' attack, namely, that contrary to fate the Greeks might have taken Troy, a feat which the audience knows would have short-circuited both Achilles' glory and the canonical mythology surrounding the city's fall. The passage thus closely identifies Patroclus' act of theomachy with the violation of fate, a counterfactual narrative which is finally aborted by Patroclus' death.[13]

---

hotheaded and has Athena's help (θερμὸς καὶ ἔχων Ἀθηνᾶν), while Patroclus is gentle and lacks divine aid (πρᾶος ὢν καὶ ὑπ' οὐδενὸς θεοῦ βοηθούμενος). See the AT Scholia ad *Il.* 16.710 and the bT Scholia ad *Il.* 5.443. Whatever the correct reading, the scholiasts' recourse to Patroclus' character to support Aristarchus' choice seems flimsy evidence indeed, especially in an episode when the hero seems anything but gentle. Cf. Muellner 1996: 15 n. 22.

[11] On the relationship between Patroclus' *aristeia* and death, including the idea of his possession by Ares, see Collins 1998: 15–45.

[12] Contrast Diomedes' obedience to Athena's orders (*Il.* 5.818). After his *aristeia*, Diomedes' return to human norms emerges especially clearly in his conversation with Glaucus, wherein he declares his refusal to fight the gods (*Il.* 6.128–9, 141) and relates the story of Lycurgus' theomachy and punishment (*Il.* 6.130–40). On the Lycurgus story, and the subject of mortals and immortals in general, see Lyons 1997: 69–102.

[13] While the poem often gives voice to hypothetical or counterfactual scenarios, such as Patroclus' sack of Troy, it ultimately cuts those possibilities off through divine intervention. Cf. *Il.* 2.155–6: ἔνθά κεν

Theomachy and the potential transgression of fate are systematically linked in the *Iliad*. Diomedes, for instance, at one point threatens to realise a similar counterfactual—to prematurely drive the Trojans back into their city—and so must be stopped by Zeus himself (*Il.* 8.130–4):

> ἔνθά κε λοιγὸς ἔην καὶ ἀμήχανα ἔργα γένοντο,
> καί νύ κε σήκασθεν κατὰ Ἴλιον ἠΰτε ἄρνες,
> εἰ μὴ ἄρ' ὀξὺ νόησε πατὴρ ἀνδρῶν τε θεῶν τε·
> βροντήσας δ' ἄρα δεινὸν ἀφῆκ' ἀργῆτα κεραυνόν,
> κὰδ δὲ πρόσθ' ἵππων Διομήδεος ἧκε χαμᾶζε.

> Now there would have been ruin and hard trouble for them,
> and they would have been penned like sheep in Troy,
> if the father of men and gods had not soon noticed.
> Thundering he released a terrible, shining thunderbolt
> and hurled it to the ground before the horses of Diomedes.

The prudent Nestor, whom Diomedes has just rescued, advises him to flee, spelling out the clear implication of the thunderbolt: ἀνὴρ δέ κεν οὔ τι Διὸς νόον εἰρύσσαιτο / οὐδὲ μάλ' ἴφθιμος, ἐπεὶ ἦ πολὺ φέρτερός ἐστι ('but no man can violate the will of Zeus, not even one very mighty, since he is far stronger', *Il.* 8.143–4).[14] As Daniel Turkeltaub has shrewdly observed, the thunderbolt alludes to the death of Capaneus, the father of Diomedes' charioteer, Sthenelus, and one of the Seven who failed to sack Thebes because of their impious folly (on which more below).[15] Zeus thus acts to prevent the realisation of the counterfactual and to suggest the impiety and inevitable doom in going against the warning. Taunted by Hector, Diomedes considers returning to the fray only to receive a clear divine response three times, and each time Zeus thunders (*Il.* 8.169–71):

> τρὶς μὲν μερμήριξε κατὰ φρένα καὶ κατὰ θυμόν,
> τρὶς δ' ἄρ' ἀπ' Ἰδαίων ὀρέων κτύπε μητίετα Ζεὺς
> σῆμα τιθεὶς Τρώεσσι μάχης ἑτεραλκέα νίκην.

> Three times he debated in his mind and heart,
> while three times from Mount Ida Zeus the counsellor thundered,
> giving a sign to the Trojans that victory in the battle inclined to them.

Ἀργείοισιν ὑπέρμορα νόστος ἐτύχθη / εἰ μὴ Ἀθηναίην Ἥρη πρὸς μῦθον ἔειπεν ('then beyond fate would the Argives have had their return, if Hera had not spoken a word to Athena'). When Zeus considers saving his son Sarpedon from his fate, Hera quickly sets him straight (*Il.* 16.433–58). See Morrison 1992 and 1997, Nesselrath 1992: 5–27, Louden 1993. Critics have generally underplayed the relation between theomachy and the contravention of fate, focusing instead on the ways that the counterfactuals might reflect the *Iliad*'s relationship to other heroic narratives.

[14] For the interweaving of thoughts of human and divine theomachy in this episode cf. *Il.* 8.210–11, where Poseidon dissuades Hera from opposing Zeus and echoes Nestor in asserting Zeus' superiority.

[15] Turkeltaub 2010: 142–3.

The narrative then moves away from any direct confrontation between Diomedes and Hector, despite the latter's repeated threats. Had Diomedes decided to turn back for a fourth time, the allusion to Capaneus gives the audience a clear sense of what would have happened. When Patroclus again attempts a fourth attack, he finds out that the gods' warnings are not hollow.

In provoking the audience's reflection on the relationship between theomachy and fate, Diomedes and Patroclus pave the way for Achilles, who fights the river god Scamander. When Achilles initially returns to battle, he gives Zeus reason to fear for the course of fate: δείδω μὴ καὶ τεῖχος ὑπέρμορον ἐξαλαπάξῃ ('I fear that even beyond fate he may destroy the wall', *Il.* 20.30). After Achilles fights the river and routs the Trojans, Apollo, too, shares Zeus' fear: μέμβλετο γάρ οἱ τεῖχος ἐϋδμήτοιο πόληος / μὴ Δαναοὶ πέρσειαν ὑπὲρ μόρον ἤματι κείνῳ ('for he was concerned for the wall of the well-built city, that the Danaans beyond fate might destroy it on that day', *Il.* 21.516–17). Apollo then deceives Achilles into pursuing him, thereby allowing the Trojans to flee into the city and preventing the Greeks from winning the war there and then. All three heroes who contend against the gods, therefore—Diomedes, Patroclus, and Achilles—threaten to contravene fate and raise the possibility of a future fashioned by human might alone; the gods must then intervene to place an upper limit on what can be achieved in the heroic *aristeia*. The act of theomachy thus reveals a delicate balance between the glimpse of an opportunity to revolutionise the epic world—by fundamentally changing the plot, for instance—and the inevitable prevention of change by the gods.

Two main features of Patroclus' theomachy play an important role in the Roman examples while also illustrating key differences. First, the connection between attacking a god and climbing a wall recurs in Hannibal's assault on the Capitol, which Silius repeatedly identifies with the walls of Rome, and in Capaneus' ascent of the walls of Thebes. Both heroes find their attempts ultimately blocked not by Apollo but by Jupiter, a scaling up of the divine opponent from the *Iliad* in accordance with the greater magnitude of the theomachies themselves. Lucretius, too, will represent his philosophical hero, Epicurus, ascending to the sky in a form of theomachy against superstition, as a result of which the walls of the world will fall away—an image for the unlimited view of the universe granted by philosophical knowledge. The interplay of philosophical and theomachic ascent represents a signal departure from the Homeric tradition, one that has a particular hold on the Roman imagination and will be seen in a variety of forms, including the inversion of the upward trajectory in Seneca's *Hercules Furens*.

Patroclus' vying against fate also carries over into the Roman tradition. It's important to observe, however, that for Patroclus the objective of his assault is to attack the city rather than the gods per se: he dies not because he persists in fighting Apollo but because he does not withdraw as Apollo warns him to do. That disobedience is at best a figurative fighting with the god after the more literal exploits on the wall a hundred lines earlier. In Roman theomachy, however, the idea of contravening fate or effecting the impossible involves a more direct opposition of hero and god. So, Hannibal wishes not only to defeat Rome, in defiance of history, but also to topple Jupiter from the Capitol. And Capaneus wishes not only to expose the gods as a fiction, in defiance of the poem's divine apparatus, but also, contradictorily, to defeat Jupiter in combat.

ACHILLES: MORTALITY AND DIVINISATION

In their relentlessness and antagonism with Apollo, both Diomedes and Patroclus foreshadow Achilles fighting Hector in Book 20 (*Il.* 20.441–9):

αὐτὰρ Ἀχιλλεὺς
ἐμμεμαὼς ἐπόρουσε κατακτάμεναι μενεαίνων,
σμερδαλέα ἰάχων· τὸν δ' ἐξήρπαξεν Ἀπόλλων
ῥεῖα μάλ' ὥς τε θεός, ἐκάλυψε δ' ἄρ' ἠέρι πολλῇ.
τρὶς μὲν ἔπειτ' ἐπόρουσε ποδάρκης δῖος Ἀχιλλεὺς
ἔγχεϊ χαλκείῳ, τρὶς δ' ἠέρα τύψε βαθεῖαν.
ἀλλ' ὅτε δὴ τὸ τέταρτον ἐπέσσυτο δαίμονι ἶσος,
δεινὰ δ' ὁμοκλήσας ἔπεα πτερόεντα προσηύδα·
ἐξ αὖ νῦν ἔφυγες θάνατον κύον.

But Achilles
leapt upon him furiously desiring to kill him,
with an awful shout; but Apollo snatched Hector up
so easily, as a god, and hid him in thick mist.
Then three times did swift-footed, shining Achilles fall on him
with his bronze spear, and three times he struck the deep mist.
But when for the fourth time he rushed on like a god,
then with a terrible cry he spoke winged words,
'Now again, you dog, you have escaped death'.

In this passage the same pattern and diction used of the other heroes' confrontations with Apollo—'three times…the fourth time he rushed on like a god'—concludes not with the god's terrible cry but with that of Achilles. Indeed, the formula used of Apollo at *Il.* 16.706 (δεινὰ δ' ὁμοκλήσας ἔπεα πτερόεντα προσηύδα) and in the first half of *Il.* 5.439 (δεινὰ δ' ὁμοκλήσας) is identical to the formula used of Achilles at *Il.* 20.448 (δεινὰ δ' ὁμοκλήσας); only context distinguishes between god and hero. That Achilles can usurp the god's role is indicative of the hero's almost superhuman stature, but it is also an augmentation of a theomachic pattern that began with Diomedes and continued through Patroclus.[16] Achilles' threat lies in his ability to make real the theomachic epithet 'like a god', even if only against mortal enemies.

Achilles appears most elevated above other mortals in his battle with the river god Scamander in Book 21, an episode I treat in detail in Chapter 6. Angered that Achilles has choked his riverbed with corpses and defiantly refuses to fight on the plain, Scamander turns his elemental force against the hero. Achilles' struggle against the raging and divine waters sets him apart from all of the other heroes and their conventional combat. Nevertheless, even Achilles' extraordinary powers are undercut when, faced with drowning, he depends for his survival on the intervention of Hera and Hephaestus. In Chapter 6, I compare three examples of the so-called *mache parapotamios*, or river battle, a topos used by both Silius and Statius. Set against their Homeric source, both Flavian scenes illustrate a development in the conception of heroism not only from Greek to Latin epic but also from Vergilian to Flavian epic. The latter half of the *Aeneid*, though it doesn't use the topos, takes up the question of who can assume Achilles' mantle as the paradigm of epic heroism. Vergil not only shows Aeneas to be that successor, he also suggests that Aeneas' piety makes him ultimately superior. The Flavian authors, however, take a different approach. They emulate the defining scene of Achilles' exceptionalism, but their theomachic heroes outdo him not so much in piety, but rather in the outlandishness of their physical feats. Even before any Olympian god intervenes, these mortal heroes, Silius' Scipio and Statius' Hippomedon, resist the river by virtue of their own might far more impressively than Achilles.

The *Iliad*'s turn from Achilles' *aristeia* to a battle among the gods—the other type of theomachy—further emphasises the gulf between mortal and immortal.[17] Zeus had authorised the intervention and combat of the gods at *Il.* 20.20–30 out of a concern that Achilles might sack Troy before its time, and the hero's subsequent *aristeia* certainly suggests his capacity to wreak massive destruction. Achilles' struggle with Scamander is itself embroiled in the divine theomachy, since Hephaestus' conflict with the river makes up one of the pairings of divine contestants drawn up following Zeus' speech (*Il.* 20.67–74). After Achilles routs the Trojans towards the city, the rest of the gods finally come to blows, but Zeus' laughter at the sight of the gods fighting (ἐγέλασσε, *Il.* 21.389) undermines any possible gravity. Among the gods, with nothing at stake, theomachy is but a parody.

---

[16] On the ritual antagonism of Achilles and Apollo see Nagy 1979: 142–50 (cf. 289–97), Muellner 1996: 10–18. The only other appearances of the 'three times...fourth time' formula in the *Iliad* occur during Achilles' lengthy *aristeia*, where it is applied to his opponents and thereby casts the hero in the structural position of Apollo—first, when Asteropaeus fails to dislodge Achilles' spear at the fourth attempt (*Il.* 21.177), and second, when Hector fails to outrun Achilles on their fourth circuit (*Il.* 22.208).

[17] On the gap between human and divine see J. Griffin 1980: esp. 152–8.

The subsequent encounter of Athena and Ares makes the parodic character of the divine theomachy readily apparent. The gods use a similar language of taunting as the heroes, and when Athena strikes Ares to the ground, the war god's fall is described in the same manner as the deaths of so many of the human combatants—his limbs loosened, his hair soiled with dust, his armour clanging about him (*Il.* 21.406–8). The crucial difference, of course, is that Ares' fall is just that, a fall, a piece of farce, and not a fatality, and it is precisely in that contrast that its poignancy lies.[18] Ares' discomfiture at the hands of Athena repeats a similar incident in Book 5, when she had helped Diomedes to wound the war god, (*Il.* 5.846–63). Ares refers to this episode in his opening challenge to Athena (*Il.* 21.396–8):

ἦ οὐ μέμνῃ ὅτε Τυδεΐδην Διομήδε᾽ ἀνῆκας
οὐτάμεναι, αὐτὴ δὲ πανόψιον ἔγχος ἑλοῦσα
ἰθὺς ἐμεῦ ὦσας, διὰ δὲ χρόα καλὸν ἔδαψας;

Do you not remember when you incited Diomedes, son of Tydeus,
to wound me, and you in open view took the spear
and drove it straight at me, and tore through my fair flesh?

Divine theomachy and human-divine theomachy are thus intertwined on two levels: first, by the larger structural connection between Achilles' *aristeia* and the intervention of the gods, and second, by Ares' explicit recollection of Diomedes' assault as he attempts to avenge himself on Athena. The interweaving of two kinds of theomachy, however, only draws attention to the triviality of the one and the gravity of the other.

If there is one brief moment in the *Iliad* where Achilles is assimilated to the gods in a more substantial—and disturbing—fashion, it is a simile from late in Book 21 (*Il.* 21.522–5):

ὡς δ᾽ ὅτε καπνὸς ἰὼν εἰς οὐρανὸν εὐρὺν ἵκηται
ἄστεος αἰθομένοιο, θεῶν δέ ἑ μῆνις ἀνῆκε,
πᾶσι δ᾽ ἔθηκε πόνον, πολλοῖσι δὲ κήδε᾽ ἐφῆκεν,
ὣς Ἀχιλεὺς Τρώεσσι πόνον καὶ κήδε᾽ ἔθηκεν.

And as, when smoke going to broad heaven rises
from a burning city, the anger of the gods spurs it on,
and it makes toil for many, and unleashes miseries,
so did Achilles cause toil and miseries for the Trojans.

As the first word of the poem, μῆνις in part referred to the resentment of the hero against another man, Agamemnon, but here it suggests the terrifying quality that makes a human most like a god. Here in the simile, Achilles, formatively linked to μῆνις, fulfils through his own wrath the anger of the gods that causes

---

[18] On his fall alluding to mortality see Purves 2006, esp. 201–3, with further references.

human sorrow.[19] Divine motivation and human action thus overlap in one and the same act of destruction. And yet the simile also points to its own fictive function—a poetic comparison that temporarily unifies aspects of the epic universe, human and divine, that typically remain far apart. Thus, Achilles is also mere smoke, an effect of fire rather than fire itself, driven on by something far more potent. The question of whether Achilles fulfils divine anger, merely resembles it, or in some sense even becomes it makes all the difference in the world, but it remains a question that the simile alone cannot answer. And read together with the rest of Achilles' *aristeia*, the simile appears to suggest that only in wreaking destruction can man ever become like god. This is the crucial double aspect of theomachy—on the one hand a moment of maximisation when the epic hero comes closest to god, but on the other hand the clearest demonstration of the fundamentally unbridgeable divide between the two.

We have noted a number of ways in which the Roman poets make theomachy a tenser and grander moment than in its Homeric incarnations, but it remains fundamentally true that however much the theomach may be elevated, the act itself is bound to fail and the hero doomed. Nevertheless, one exception is highly revealing. Lucan's Caesar substitutes for, and even displaces, the gods in a way that no other hero can. This becomes possible because the *Bellum Civile* lacks the traditional divine apparatus of epic, thus creating a vacuum which Caesar fills. As a forerunner of the deified emperors, Caesar illustrates an important problem posed for conventional epic theology by the novel status attainable by Rome's rulers. The effect of the imperial cult isn't limited to Lucan's godless poem, however, for across imperial epic the possibility of divinisation blurs the boundary that Homer is so concerned to preserve. Hence, Roman theomachies are coloured by the contemporary awareness that humans do in fact become gods and that the gods may be no more than humans in disguise.

FATHERS AND SONS: GENERATIONAL COMPETITION AND METAPOETICS

Human decline represents one of the well-known topoi of the *Iliad* and of Greek mythology. Whether Hesiod's account of the ages of man in the *Works and Days* or Nestor's self-aggrandising recollection of the feats of earlier generations, archaic epic emphasises the typical, even if not universal, degradation of human capacities over time.[20] Nowhere does this notion appear more

---

[19] On μῆνις as the anger of a god see Watkins 1977, Slatkin 1991: 85–105, Muellner 1996; Cairns 2003 offers a corrective to this view. At the beginning of Diomedes' *aristeia*, Aeneas tells Pandarus to shoot him with an arrow, but to be cautious in case he is an angry god (θεός... μηνίσας, *Il.* 5.177–8). It is conspicuously the theomachic hero who shows signs of divinity.

[20] Hes. *Op.* 109–201. For Nestor's boast see, e.g., *Il.* 1.266–72. On human decline in the *Iliad* see C. J. Mackie 2008: 34–40. On the epic's problematising of the topos, especially its suggestions that traditions about past heroes are unreliable and emulation of them unwise, see Turkeltaub 2010.

explicitly than in the *Iliad*'s repeated motif of a hero throwing a boulder that no two men of the audience's day might even lift.[21] Acts that typify the heroism of martial epic thus sit alongside an acknowledgement of the larger process of decline. These two contrasting visions of human capacities are brought into especially clear focus in the context of theomachy.

The contrast between heroes of the past and present, and their respective kinds of antagonism with the gods, appears within the narrative of the divine theomachy in Book 21. Poseidon recounts the story of his and Apollo's service to the ungrateful Laomedon, former king of Troy (*Il.* 21.450–7):

> ἀλλ' ὅτε δὴ μισθοῖο τέλος πολυγηθέες ὧραι
> ἐξέφερον, τότε νῶϊ βιήσατο μισθὸν ἅπαντα
> Λαομέδων ἔκπαγλος, ἀπειλήσας δ' ἀπέπεμπε.
> σὺν μὲν ὅ γ' ἠπείλησε πόδας καὶ χεῖρας ὕπερθε
> δήσειν, καὶ περάαν νήσων ἔπι τηλεδαπάων·
> στεῦτο δ' ὅ γ' ἀμφοτέρων ἀπολεψέμεν οὔατα χαλκῷ.
> νῶϊ δὲ ἄψορροι κίομεν κεκοτηότι θυμῷ
> μισθοῦ χωόμενοι, τὸν ὑποστὰς οὐκ ἐτέλεσσε.

> But when at length the glad seasons were bringing the end of our hire,
> then terrible Laomedon wronged us of all our wages,
> and he sent us away with threats.
> He threatened to bind together our feet and our hands above
> and sell us to far-lying islands.
> And he indicated he would cut off the ears of us both with the bronze.
> So we two went back with anger in our heart
> furious about our wages, which he promised but did not fulfil.

Like the early theomachs mentioned by Dione, such as Herakles and the Aloidae, and differently from Diomedes, Laomedon can credibly threaten to harm the gods. Even if the ultimate distinction drawn by Dione holds—namely, that gods are immortal and that humans will pay for acts of theomachy—the stories of Herakles and Laomedon suggest at least some diachronic shift in the position of humans relative to the gods.[22] This notion of the widening gap between god and mortal finds confirmation in an encounter between Achilles and Apollo at the beginning of Book 22. Apollo points out to Achilles the futility of hoping to close that gap (*Il.* 22.8–9, 13):

> τίπτέ με Πηλέος υἱὲ ποσὶν ταχέεσσι διώκεις
> αὐτὸς θνητὸς ἐὼν θεὸν ἄμβροτον;

---

[21] E.g., *Il.* 5.302–4.

[22] Even the early heroes were still ultimately in the gods' power. Athena, for instance, claims that Herakles would not have been able to return from Hades without her help (*Il.* 8.369). See C. J. Mackie 1999: 490.

> ...
>
> οὐ μέν με κτενέεις, ἐπεὶ οὔ τοι μόρσιμός εἰμι.
>
> Why, son of Peleus, do you pursue me with swift feet,
> yourself a mortal while I am an immortal god?
> ...
> You will not kill me, since I am not subject to fate.

In the face of this simple yet fundamental distinction, Achilles expresses his frustration in almost comically helpless terms: ἦ σ᾽ ἂν τισαίμην, εἴ μοι δύναμίς γε παρείη ('truly, I would take revenge on you, if I had the power', *Il.* 22.20). Laomedon's threats to cut off the gods' ears and to sell them into slavery are credible enough that they leave without their fee; Achilles, by contrast, can only fantasise about a vengeance that Apollo pre-emptively dismisses.

By contrast with Achilles, who reluctantly acknowledges his own impotence, the Roman theomachs, whether in the *mache parapotamios* or in the challenges to Jupiter, rarely concede. After Jupiter's thunderbolts fail to dissuade Hannibal, Juno has to reveal to him the gods themselves and practically drag him away (*abstrahit*, *Pun.* 12.728). Even after this revelation, in the last book of the *Punica*, Hannibal regrets not having dragged Jupiter from his throne on the Capitol. Rather than a sense of human decline, the Roman poets give the impression that their theomachic subjects are more powerful than ever, competing with the likes of Hercules, the Giants, and Titans. It is in these primal terms that Lucan figures the participants in Rome's civil war, Silius conceives of Hannibal's crossing of the Alps, or Statius imagines Capaneus' scaling of Thebes.

Some sense of how else Achilles' confrontation with Apollo might have been treated emerges from a comparison with the *Posthomerica* of Quintus of Smyrna. Written almost a thousand years later, anywhere from the second to fourth century AD, the *Posthomerica* shows a far more aggressive and confident Achilles.[23] After the slaughter at the river, treated in only a couple of lines, Quintus uses a series of counterfactuals to imagine Achilles killing all the Trojans, tearing down the gates, and leading the Greeks to raze the city (Quint. Smyrn. 3.26–9). The expansion on the Homeric trope, especially the physicality of the destruction of the gates, is already suggestive of a very different aesthetic from the *Iliad*. Like Homer, however, Quintus has Apollo appear to prevent a premature end to Troy, but, rather than deceiving Achilles into pursuing him, the god confronts the hero directly. Warned by Apollo to stop his slaughter, Achilles responds in striking fashion (Quint. Smyrn. 3.45–52):

> τοὔνεκ᾽ ἄρ᾽ οὐκ ἀλέγιζε θεοῦ, μέγα δ᾽ ἴαχεν ἄντην·
> Φοῖβε, τί ἦ με θεοῖσι καὶ οὐ μεμαῶτα μάχεσθαι

---

[23] On the much debated date of the *Posthomerica* see the summary at Maciver 2012: 3–5.

> ὀτρύνεις Τρώεσσιν ὑπερφιάλοισιν ἀμύνων;
> ἤδη γὰρ καὶ πρόσθε μ' ἀποστρέψας ὀρυμαγδοῦ
> ἤπαφες, ὁππότε πρῶτον ὑπεξεσάωσας ὀλέθρου
> Ἕκτορα τῷ μέγα Τρῶες ἀνὰ πτόλιν εὐχετόωντο.
> ἀλλ' ἀναχάζεο τῆλε καὶ ἐς μακάρων ἕδος ἄλλων
> ἔρχεο, μή σε βάλοιμι καὶ ἀθάνατόν περ ἐόντα.

> So he did not heed the god, but shouted loudly to his face,
> 'Phoebus, why do you urge me, even against my will,
> to fight against the gods, in defence of the arrogant Trojans?
> For already before you diverted and cheated me out of the battle,
> when first you saved Hector from destruction,
> of whom the Trojans boast loudly in their city.
> But draw back far away and go to the seat of the other gods,
> lest I strike you even though you are immortal'.

Whereas the Homeric Achilles wishes he had the power to take revenge on Apollo, Quintus' hero bids the god retreat to Olympus and even leaves open the possibility that, despite the god's immortality, nevertheless he might harm him.

Katherine King has rightly compared this Achilles, whose size is often compared to that of Giants and Titans, to the theomachic figure of Capaneus.[24] King doesn't claim that Capaneus, either Aeschylus' or Statius' version, is a source for Quintus, but she shows how the resemblance marks a significant departure from the Homeric Achilles. There has been some debate about the extent to which Quintus was influenced by Roman epic, if at all, a subject on which more work remains to be done, especially on the possible influence of post-Augustan writers.[25] We can nevertheless add this much to King's suggestion: in making Achilles more abrasively theomachic, Quintus follows, knowingly or not, a tradition defined by Latin epic of the early empire, which includes the many theomachs besides Capaneus, such as Caesar and Hannibal. As far as the tradition of theomachy is concerned, our extant evidence points to Neronian and Flavian literature in particular as the laboratory in which the most powerful developments occur. Thanks to Lucan, Silius, and Statius, the legacy of Homer's theomachic heroes had already, and forever, been transformed, and the *Posthomerica* may well reveal traces of that transformation.

---

[24] King 1987: 133–7. Cf. Carvounis 2007: 251–2 on the death of the Giant-like Ajax in *Posthomerica* 14.
[25] On the influence of Roman epic on the *Posthomerica* see U. Gärtner 2005, James 2007. Cf. Maciver 2012: 195: 'Also fruitful would be consideration of the similarities in style and intertextual behaviour between the *Posthomerica* and Latin hexameter works such as those by Claudian, or even the works by earlier poets like Statius'.

The *Iliad*'s contrast between the capacities of earlier heroes and the current generation does not pass without a response within the poem itself. In Book 4, Agamemnon attempts to rouse Diomedes to battle by comparing him to his father, Tydeus, and suggesting that the son lacks his father's courage.[26] Diomedes remains silent, but Sthenelus is quick to respond (*Il.* 4.401–10):

> ὣς φάτο, τὸν δ' οὔ τι προσέφη κρατερὸς Διομήδης
> αἰδεσθεὶς βασιλῆος ἐνιπὴν αἰδοίοιο·
> τὸν δ' υἱὸς Καπανῆος ἀμείψατο κυδαλίμοιο·
> Ἀτρεΐδη μὴ ψεύδε' ἐπιστάμενος σάφα εἰπεῖν·
> ἡμεῖς τοι πατέρων μέγ' ἀμείνονες εὐχόμεθ' εἶναι·
> ἡμεῖς καὶ Θήβης ἕδος εἵλομεν ἑπταπύλοιο
> παυρότερον λαὸν ἀγαγόνθ' ὑπὸ τεῖχος ἄρειον,
> πειθόμενοι τεράεσσι θεῶν καὶ Ζηνὸς ἀρωγῇ·
> κεῖνοι δὲ σφετέρῃσιν ἀτασθαλίῃσιν ὄλοντο·
> τῶ μή μοι πατέρας ποθ' ὁμοίῃ ἔνθεο τιμῇ.

> So he spoke, but mighty Diomedes did not address him at all
> since he respected the reproach of the honoured king;
> but the son of glorious Capaneus replied,
> 'Son of Atreus, don't speak lies, seeing as you have clear knowledge;
> we boast that we are far better than our fathers;
> and we captured the seat of seven-gated Thebes
> leading a smaller force under a stronger wall,
> trusting the omens of the gods and the aid of Zeus;
> but they perished by their folly;
> do not, then, hold our fathers in like honour with us.'

This is the strongest assertion of generational competition in the poem, and it comes from the son of Capaneus, who had defied Zeus himself. Sthenelus justifies the superiority of the Epigoni to their fathers, the original Seven, because of the greater difficulty of the task and the pious manner in which they perform it.[27] Despite the distinction he draws, however, Sthenelus' pride and competitiveness suggest that he, at least, isn't so different from his father after all, especially when his proud speech is contrasted with Diomedes' respectful submission to Agamemnon's authority (*Il.* 4.402; cf. 4.411–18).[28] The link between

---

[26] On this passage see Nagy 1979: 161–3, Turkeltaub 2010: 137–41, Barker and Christensen 2011.

[27] For the impiety of the Seven cf., e.g., Aesch. *Sept.* 427–31 and see below. Statius will write of Capaneus outstripping the deeds of his ancestors (*Theb.* 3.601–2), though that type of generational competition may owe as much to Roman aristocratic or dynastic notions as it does to the connection between theomachy and the overcoming of one's father.

[28] Barker and Christensen 2011: 26 with n. 1 note that Sthenelus' πειθόμενοι τεράεσσι θεῶν (*Il.* 4.408) is applied in modified form to Bellerophon at *Il.* 6.183. Bellerophon famously engages in a kind of theomachy when attempting to ride Pegasus to Olympus (alluded to obliquely at *Il.* 6.200). Underlying Sthenelus' claim to piety, then, is a trace of precisely the folly that he abjures.

generational competition and theomachy is further strengthened in Book 5 when Athena uses another negative comparison with Tydeus to rouse Diomedes to attack Ares (*Il.* 5.800–13). Thus, to match, or even beat, one's father is closely associated with fighting the gods, especially when the fathers have the impious pedigree of the Seven against Thebes.[29]

That theomachy and the supplanting of the father may be related notions fits with the pattern of divine usurpations in Greek mythology, such as Cronus' castration of Uranus and Zeus' defeat of Cronus. Moreover, Laura Slatkin has shown that the potential for theomachy lies at the heart of the plot of the *Iliad*.[30] Slatkin argues that the story of Thetis' power over Zeus (*Il.* 1.396–406) alludes indirectly to the better-known myth of Thetis' son being destined to be greater than the father, and Zeus' consequent yielding of Thetis to the mortal Peleus.[31] In the account in the *Iliad*, Thetis saves Zeus from a coup by other Olympian gods by unbinding him and summoning the hundred-handed Briareus, also known as Aegaeon, as a bodyguard. But the poet gives us the additional information that Briareus 'was greater in strength than his father' (ὃ γὰρ αὖτε βίην οὗ πατρὸς ἀμείνων, *Il.* 1.404). This apparently superfluous comment recalls the warning that Thetis' son too would be greater than the father.[32] Slatkin's observation can be pressed further. When Peleus, rather than Zeus, fathered Thetis' child, a potentially cataclysmic contest between Achilles and Zeus was avoided, but its energies were diverted to other instances in the poem. Its presence is felt not only in the power of Thetis or the elevation of Achilles but also in the chain of theomachies that reflect repeatedly, variously, and obsessively on the possibility of humans usurping the gods. Each element in the sequence builds up to the *aristeia* of Achilles, the hero who might have overthrown Zeus.[33]

The formula closely associated with theomachy in the *Iliad*—'three times … fourth time'—appears only once in the *Odyssey*, but tellingly in the context of father-son tension. This 'deliberate repetition of a significant formulaic utterance'—a technique which Egbert Bakker has termed 'interformularity'—points to larger connections between the contexts in which the formulae appear, contexts that mutually inform the interpretation of each passage.[34] Such an interformulary reading is invited when Telemachus attempts to string his father's bow (*Od.* 21.125–9):

---

[29] Cf. Turkeltaub 2010: 140–5.
[30] Slatkin 1991.
[31] See, e.g., Pind. *Isthm.* 8.26–47, Aesch. *PV* 755–68, and Slatkin 1991: 66–70.
[32] Slatkin 1991: 76–7 n. 26 expresses due caution about interpreting the *Iliad* against a mythology reconstructed from later sources. See also Nagy 1979: 346–7.
[33] The opening lines of Statius' unfinished *Achilleid*, quoted as an epigraph to Chapter 6, suggest that he, too, was alive to this way of interpreting the *Iliad*. Statius thus places theomachy front and centre of what he goes on to present as a putatively supra-Iliadic work (*Achil.* 1.3–7). Seneca's *Hercules Furens* will also develop the connection between theomachy and patricide, on which see Chapter 4.
[34] Bakker 2013: 10. I thank Egbert Bakker for bringing the diction of the *Odyssey* passage to my attention; cf. his own discussion at Bakker 2013: 100.

τρὶς μέν μιν πελέμιξεν ἐρύσσεσθαι μενεαίνων,
τρὶς δὲ μεθῆκε βίης, ἐπιελπόμενος τό γε θυμῷ,
νευρὴν ἐντανύειν διοϊστεύσειν τε σιδήρου.
καί νύ κε δὴ ἐτάνυσσε βίῃ τὸ τέταρτον ἀνέλκων,
ἀλλ' Ὀδυσεὺς ἀνένευε καὶ ἔσχεθεν ἱεμενόν περ.

Three times he made it tremble, eager to draw it,
and three times he relaxed his strength, though in his heart he hoped
to string the bow and shoot through the iron.
And now he would have strung it with his might, drawing it for the fourth time,
but Odysseus nodded and checked him in his eagerness.

The poet draws on the diction of theomachic assault, but he alters the pattern first by explicitly stating that Telemachus would have been successful and second through the intervention not of a god but of Telemachus' father (though Odysseus' nod recalls the divine aspect of Zeus).[35] Just as theomachy concludes in the assertion of divine superiority, so Odysseus here imposes his own authority on his son and on the plot: in neither case is authority to be replaced, even if the *Odyssey* passage suggests at least the potential for the son to supplant the father.[36] It's tempting to see in the passage a metapoetic reflection on the heroic trajectories of Telemachus and Odysseus and the implications for the epic. On this view, Telemachus' tension with his father reflects the poet's awareness that the son, after some growing pains, has attained maturity and may now be able to wrest the role of epic protagonist from an Odysseus who has passed his prime. The possibility is acknowledged but delicately suppressed through the simple action of Odysseus' divine nod, a nod that is no less than the poet's own gesture determining the course of the epic.[37]

Tension between father and son can facilitate other kinds of metapoetic reflection too. Since the formative work of Gregory Nagy and Richard Martin, in particular, Homeric scholars have found in the most agonistic moments of the poems a reflection of larger contests among epic and even non-epic traditions.[38] In a recent article, Elton Barker and Joel Christensen have argued that the *Iliad* makes selective and calculated use of the name and

---

[35] Cf. Achilles' usurping of Apollo's role at *Il.* 20.448. Though not in relation to this passage, Rutherford 1986: 159 sees Odysseus as like a god and identified with Athena; J. S. Clay 1983, rather counterintuitively, sees a tension between the hero and Athena.

[36] Stanford 1954: 60 sees Homer 'suggesting a latent father-son antagonism', on which see also Olson 1995: 176. Given that the prize for winning the archery challenge is Penelope's hand in marriage, her son's near success begs for a Freudian interpretation. Odysseus' potential vulnerability to his son is represented elsewhere in mythology by his ultimate death at the hands of Telegonus, his son by Circe. On fathers and sons and the dynamics of competition in the *Iliad* and *Odyssey* see Wöhrle 1999.

[37] Much has been written on the metapoetics of the *Odyssey*, but see most recently Bakker 2013.

[38] Nagy 1979, Martin 1989.

mythology of Thebes to distinguish itself from the epic tradition represented by the Cyclic *Thebaid*.[39] Focusing on the representation of Tydeus, a character shared with the *Thebaid*, they show how the *Iliad* evaluates and circumscribes Tydeus in order to promote its own, supposedly different, model of heroism. On this view, the generational tension between the Seven and the Epigoni (featuring in the speeches made before and during Diomedes' theomachy) reflects a larger tension between two rival epic traditions. In defining the limits of heroism, theomachy—whether allusive, as in the Odyssean example, or contextual, as in the Iliadic example—provides a stimulus to reflect on how else heroism might be conceived or the plot might be worked out, considerations that are likely to have been shaped by other poetic traditions.

The metapoetic reading of generational conflict has a similar pedigree in the study of Roman epic, too, and a special relevance to theomachy. Two factors in particular distinguish the Roman situation from the Greek one. First, the canonical status of Vergil and the diachronic relationship between his successors running from Ovid through Lucan down to the Flavians makes Harold Bloom's Oedipal model of literary filiation especially applicable. On this view, best represented by Philip Hardie, the Roman epic tradition defines itself by drawing on, reacting to, and tendentiously rereading Vergil's master text.[40] Theomachy in particular has emerged as a powerful metaphor for the Oedipal struggle against the father, where that father is a poetic rather than theological divinity. Capaneus, for instance, has been read as a figure for Statius' competition with Vergil, and beyond epic, Seneca's Hercules has been read as figuring a broader contest between Silver and Golden Latin.[41] The second factor that makes metapoetic interpretation operate differently in the Roman case is the availability of comparanda. Because we lack any substantial quantity of early Greek epic, it's difficult to ascertain precisely what the stakes were for the form of the genre (whether or not epic was conceived as a genre at the time), but in the case of the Roman examples, at least, there are fairly radical differences between the different kinds of epic: compendious, like the *Metamorphoses*, historical without gods, like the *Bellum Civile*, historical with gods, like the *Punica*, or mythological but subjecting the gods to sustained ethical and theological scrutiny, like the *Thebaid*. The availability of evidence thus allows us to draw far more detailed conclusions about the generic commitments signified by acts of theomachy.

---

[39] Barker and Christensen 2011: 35: 'the *Iliad* uses Theban material in a divisive way to achieve its ends and define itself against its competition and their shared tradition'.
[40] Hardie 1993.
[41] E.g., Leigh 2006 on Capaneus; C. A. J. Littlewood 2004: 107–27 on Hercules, esp. 120.

THE TOWER OF BABEL: MONUMENTALITY AND FAME

In Book 7, the Achaeans are said to build a great wall without offering the appropriate sacrifices to the gods, which causes Poseidon to worry that such a purely human feat will eclipse the fame of the Trojan wall built by himself and Apollo (*Il.* 7.446–53). Zeus reminds Poseidon that it's within his power to destroy the wall while reassuring him—echoing Poseidon's diction—that the god's fame, and not that of the Achaean wall, will spread as far as the dawn (σὸν δ' ἤτοι κλέος ἔσται ὅσον τ' ἐπικίδναται ἠώς, *Il.* 7.458). For a brief instant, however, the heroes of the war begin to make up some ground on, and even outstrip, their earlier counterparts, Herakles and Laomedon. The latter were able to threaten the gods in a way that Achilles cannot, but the Achaean wall can threaten to surpass the works of gods. The wall poses a more genuine threat than any of the heroes' literal theomachies, since Poseidon implies that while the wall stands it is indeed greater than his and Apollo's construction. Even if Zeus reasserts the extent of Poseidon's fame through an implicit contrast between the destruction of the wall and the immortality of the god, nevertheless in one respect—fame—mortals have the power to create something that exceeds the capacities of the gods.

In Book 12, the poem looks ahead to the destruction of the Achaean wall. The passage adopts an unusual temporal perspective: on the one hand it glances forward to the end of the war and the destruction of the wall by Poseidon and Apollo, achieved by a massive confluence of flood waters (*Il.* 12.13–33); on the other hand, the poet uses a past tense, as if looking back with a later audience on the matter of Troy: ὅθι πολλὰ βοάγρια καὶ τρυφάλειαι / κάππεσον ἐν κονίῃσι καὶ ἡμιθέων γένος ἀνδρῶν ('where many oxhide shields and helmets fell in the dust, and the race of semi-divine men', *Il.* 12.22–3).[42] The diachronic perspective emerges especially starkly through the word ἡμιθέων ('demigods', *Il.* 12.23). As Nagy has observed, this is the one instance of the word ἡμίθεος in Homer.[43] From the point of view of the audience, then, the heroes occupy a higher, more divine status than they do in the course of

---

[42] Scodel 1982 points out the connections between the twin aspects of building and flooding and Near Eastern and Biblical stories on similar themes; in all cases human impiety leads to divinely authorised obliteration. Cf. Nagler 1974: 147–56 on the Near Eastern background of Achilles' contest with Scamander. Inconsistencies in the poem's accounts of the wall have made it the object of much scholarly debate. Although in Book 12 it is said to remain until the end of the war, in Book 15 Apollo is described as destroying it as easily as a child scatters sand (*Il.* 15.361–6). One could reconcile the passages by arguing that Apollo damages only a part of the wall, but the tone of the two accounts is also at odds: in one version the wall is obliterated with a vast flood; in the other the god simply knocks it over. See, further, M. L. West 1969, T.W. Boyd 1995, Porter 2011.

[43] Nagy 1979: 159–61. The word ἡμίθεοι also occurs in Hesiod's *Works and Days*, where it appears in the account of the five ages and refers to the race of heroes who lived between the bronze and iron ages (*Op.* 160). Both in the retrospective character of the Iliadic passage and in the Hesiodic separation of ages, we see a clear break between the heroes of the Trojan war and the time of the audience.

the action of the poem. The Achaean wall thus combines the themes of the superiority of earlier generations and theomachic activity, but it does so with the novel twist of emphasising for once the superiority of the heroes of the *Iliad*.

Heroic decline in the *Iliad*, as we have seen, has two main phases: between Herakles or Laomedon and the heroes of the poem's own time, and between those heroes and the present of the audience, who lack the strength of their Iliadic ancestors. But where Achilles offers a glimmer that a human might, under other circumstances, have been born a god—and the supreme god at that—such possibilities are altogether absent for the audience of the *Iliad*. In this context it's salutary to consider the effect of the poem repeatedly floating the idea of antagonism with gods, and strongly associating such theomachic acts with the heritage of prior generations. The implications of this dual concern with theomachy and human history are bound up with Homeric epic's transmission of the past. The act of theomachy, whether literal in the case of Achilles' battle with Scamander or figurative, as in the case of the impiety of the Achaean wall, provokes the gods to threaten obliteration, that is, to eliminate the prospect of human immortality through fame and memory. Scamander claims he will bury Achilles under sand until his body cannot be found (*Il.* 21.316–23); Poseidon, too, will cover the shore with sand and leave no trace of the wall (*Il.* 12.27–33).[44] The idea of challenging the gods carries with it the epic poet's aspiration to defy the gods' authority over human fame, and epic itself thus begins to acquire a theomachic quality.[45] In other words, what physical might is for Herakles and construction is for the Achaeans—the means of wresting control from the gods—for the audience is represented by epic poetry. Admittedly, a poem that memorialises theomachy may be more heavily invested in defining and maintaining the conventional ethical norms of human behaviour than in defying divine authority.[46] This is, at least, the conservative pose of a narrator who calls on the divine Muse for aid and tells the story of the bard Thamyris, who boasted that he would defeat the Muses in contest, for which he was struck blind and lost the power of song (*Il.* 2.594–600).[47] Nevertheless, for all the decorum of that pose, the *Iliad* celebrates also the attempt to test those norms.[48]

---

[44] See Nagy 1979: 160.

[45] On the metapoetics of Iliadic heroism see Nagy 1979: 279–316, Martin 1989: 146–205, Ford 1992: 147–57. All three critics share a conception of the *Iliad* as essentially in competition with other epic traditions; for a different view see Scodel 2004.

[46] Buchan 2004: 107–32 reveals the tendencies within heroic ideology, especially as represented in the figure of Achilles, to exceed those norms and to annihilate the community founded upon them. On the construction of social and political norms in the *Iliad* see Yamagata 1994, Hammer 2002.

[47] On Thamyris, especially as a negative reflection of Homer, see Stanley 1993: 24, Scodel 2004: 6–7, Sammons 2010: 180.

[48] Homeric poetry faced another, completely different, charge of theomachic content from those who saw its portrayal of the gods as dangerously misleading (most famously Pl. *Resp.* 378d5–7). Feeney 1991: 5–56 relates how critics invoked and honed the concepts of poetic license and philosophical allegory in order to defend Homer from such charges. Heraclitus, a Homeric commentator of the first century AD, had sufficient confidence in his allegorical reading to venture the following counterfactual

The ideas of building or technology and fame have even stronger theomachic associations in Roman epic. Lucan's Caesar leads the desecration of a numinous grove in order to obtain wood for the construction of siege engines, and Silius' Scipio reverses Scamander's threat to obliterate Achilles when he threatens to re-channel and rename the Trebia. Latin poetry often expresses ambivalence about the enormous power of Roman technology, which could subject the natural world to human control in ways Homer could never have imagined. If theomachy reflected on the limits of human power, it's no wonder that the marvels of Roman engineering might have had an impact on the representation of the topos. Latin literature articulates a similar ambivalence about fame. On the one hand, poetic fame is the medium that raises to the stars both the heroes of epic, from Aeneas to Scipio Africanus, and the imperial subjects of panegyric, from Augustus to Domitian. But fame is also *fama*, the unpredictable and lightning-swift embodiment of rumour, which Vergil portrays as a sister of the Giants, and the most powerful of all opponents of the gods. The doubling of fame as a metonymy of both epic itself and its distorted other is one important instance of a more pervasive mirroring in a genre shaped by the Roman civil wars and compelled to play conflicting roles as panegyric and as critic of Roman culture. From this cauldron emerges a radically new approach to the theology of epic, one that draws on contemporary politics and philosophy to depict a world where humans can become divine, and the divine can altogether cease to exist. Theomachy is both the most potent symbol of this conflict and the richest medium through which to express it.

Theomachy in Greek Tragedy: Didacticism and Politics

That theomachy was a major theme in Greek tragedy is clear not only from surviving plays, such as Euripides' *Bacchae*, which dramatises Pentheus' struggle with Dionysus, but also from the subject matter of lost works. The Aeschylean Lycurgus trilogy or Sophocles' *Thamyris*, for instance, would have depicted conflicts with Dionysus and the Muses, respectively.[49] For the

---

claim: πάντα γὰρ ἠσέβησεν, εἰ μηδὲν ἠλληγόρησεν, ἱερόσυλοι δὲ μῦθοι καὶ θεομάχου γέμοντες ἀπονοίας δι' ἀμφοτέρων τῶν σωματίων μεμήνασιν ('if he [i.e., Homer] meant nothing allegorically, he was altogether impious, and sacrilegious stories full of blasphemous folly run riot through both epics', *Alleg. Hom.* 1.1–2). The word translated as 'blasphemous' is in Greek literally 'theomachic'. It is striking that the commentator's counterfactual image of the theomachic Homer assimilates the poet to his overreaching Diomedes, Patroclus, and Achilles.

[49] Other tragedies on theomachic themes include: Aeschylus' *Ixion*, *Niobe*, *Pentheus*, and *Xantriai* (about either Pentheus or the daughters of Minyas—possibly a satyr play); Sophocles' *Niobe*, *Ajax Locrus*, and *Salmoneus* (a satyr play); Euripides' *Bellerophon* (on which see Riedweg 1990); and several subjects dramatised by more than one playwright, such as Phaethon and Sisyphus. See further Kiso 1984, who argues for the importance of theomachy to Sophoclean tragedy on the basis of the titles of lost plays.

purposes of this study, the gravity of the loss is superseded only by the sorry state of the transmission of Hellenistic epic or early Roman tragedy. Nevertheless, enough Attic drama remains to allow a provisional sketch of the significance of the theomachic motif and to provide some context for later developments at Rome. The discussion in this part of the chapter is brief, since the antagonism to the divine represented in the extant tragedies has already received considerable scholarly attention. Moreover, it differs in kind from the martial theomachy with which Silver Latin authors were preoccupied, and on which this book focuses. That is not to say, however, that the two types of theomachy are unrelated, as the subsequent chapters will show: the legacy of tragedy will be felt especially strongly in Ovid's *Metamorphoses* (Chapter 3) and, naturally, Seneca's *Hercules Furens* (Chapter 4).

Both epic and tragedy have in common their use of theomachy to contemplate the ethical norms of human behaviour, especially the distinctions between piety and impiety, and the limits to which humans can test the gods.[50] But the example of the *Thamyris*, which must have dramatised the story of the singer's contest with the Muses, illustrates one of the main differences between the two genres' handling of theomachy: unlike epic, with its martial preoccupations, tragedy could devote its full attention to a broader range of theomachic acts, such as Niobe's boasting of her superiority to the goddess Leto, or Hippolytus' rejection of the worship of Aphrodite. In addition, as Jon Mikalson has pointed out, the divine patronage that can legitimise theomachy in the *Iliad*, such as Athena's support of Diomedes, has little place in tragedy:[51]

> In their various ways Ajax challenged Athena, Hippolytus Aphrodite, Pentheus Dionysus, and Neoptolemus Apollo. These kings and princes we may class as *theomachoi*, "god-fighters." Euripides evidently coined the verb θεομαχεῖν late in his career specifically to designate such behaviour (*Ba.* 45, 325, 1255, *IA* 1408), but the notion of a man fighting a god is as old as Homer. Homeric *theomachoi*, however, have their own divine champions who urge them into physical battle against another deity *and* ultimately protect them. The tragic *theomachoi* act on their own initiative and "fight," alone and in vain, against their divine opponents.

Although he elides certain nuances in Homeric epic highlighted in my earlier discussion, Mikalson rightly emphasises tragedy's isolation of the theomach. But what really distinguishes tragedy's treatment of the theme is the genre's inherently attentive and dialogic mode—its detailed representation of a small number of events through the competing perspectives of multiple agents—which gives theomachy emphases or inflections which the epic tradition had not brought out or fully explored.

---

[50] Cf. Halliwell 1990.
[51] Mikalson 1991: 159.

One of the features of tragic theomachy is the concentrated, at times even intimate, antagonism between hero and god. Aeschylus' *Seven Against Thebes*, for instance, characterises the Argive heroes as relentlessly impious and casts their downfall as punishment from the gods, while the *Bacchae* focuses especially closely on Dionysus' increasing manipulation of the hostile Pentheus. By incurring the wrath of god—either indirectly, through the Argives' impious boasts, or directly, through Pentheus' rejection of Dionysus—the heroes' theomachic behaviour appears thoroughly foolish and self-destructive. In that regard, the *Iliad* had already made the futility of theomachy explicit through, for example, the exchange between Achilles and Apollo in Book 22, when Achilles admits his impotence in the face of the god's immortality. In tragedy, however, the doomed fate of the protagonist that patterns the vast majority of plays makes the confrontation with the divine far more heavily laden with a sense of inevitable failure—so much so that the verb θεομαχεῖν could operate almost metaphorically, conveying futility with or without strong reference to the gods.[52] Thus, Euripides uses the verb in the *Bacchae* of Pentheus' opposition to Dionysus, a clear instance of human-divine antagonism, but he also uses it in the *Iphigenia at Aulis* with only the barest connection to theomachy as traditionally conceived. Towards the end of the *Iphigenia at Aulis*, Achilles commends Iphigenia for 'ceasing to fight the gods' (τὸ θεομαχεῖν γὰρ ἀπολιποῦσ', *IA* 1408), that is, for yielding to the gods' demand for her sacrifice in order to allow the Greek ships to sail to Troy. Iphigenia's initial reluctance to die can only be described as theomachy in the most figurative terms, especially when compared, for instance, to Pentheus' aggression against Dionysus. Indeed, the context of the verb casts Iphigenia's previous opposition to Calchas' prophecy (that is, to the will of the gods) as a refusal to yield to necessity, since the majority of the Greeks wish to sacrifice her for the greater cause: τὸ θεομαχεῖν γὰρ ἀπολιποῦσ', ὅ σου κρατεῖ, / ἐξελογίσω τὰ χρηστὰ τἀναγκαῖά τε ('for, ceasing to fight the gods, which are stronger than you, you have considered what is best and necessary', *IA* 1408–9).[53] Even though Iphigenia represents a chiefly metaphorical instance of theomachy, then, the use of the verb

---

[52] For a full account of the word as used in Greek tragedy and certain other contexts see Kamerbeek 1948.

[53] The semantic stretch of θεομαχεῖν from fighting the gods to resisting the inevitable is intuitive enough (cf. theomachy's relation to fate in the *Iliad*, discussed above). This more metaphorical usage can be seen in a number of later texts. In Xenophon's *Oeconomicus*, a farmer is said to be able to find out the quality of his soil and cultivate accordingly; to do otherwise is to fight the gods (*Oec.* 16.3). In the pseudo-Hippocratic letter to Damagetes, Hippocrates imagines telling Democritus that the world has two emotions, joy and grief, and to reject one is to fight the gods (*Ep.* 14.22). In Menander's *Eunuch*, Parmeno's advice to Thais not to resist love is expressed as an instruction not to fight the gods (fr. 162 K-T). Epictetus says that to desire impossible things and to obsess about another's welfare beyond one's control is to fight against god (*Diss.* 3.24.24; cf. 4.1.101: 'Why, then, do I fight against god? Why do I will what does not depend on the will?').

emphasises important aspects of how such acts were viewed—overbold and utterly ineffective.

The complex of impiety, futility, and destruction characteristic of typical theomachs, further accentuated by a frequent association with madness, has largely governed the critical response. Mikalson, for instance, observes the fixed pattern of such myths: 'The punishments vary, each suited to the character of the sinner, but the *theomachoi* always lose, and the power of the gods is always reasserted'.[54] Ruth Padel cites various accusations of madness against Hippolytus, Ajax, and Pentheus to conclude that '[m]adness both is, and is a punishment for, human transgression of divine law. It both incarnates, and punishes, offence to gods'.[55] Such approaches, while they may provide a good account of how some or even many members of the audience understood theomachy, neutralise the significance of the concept. If, by analogy, one were to focus entirely on the futility, madness, or transgression of theomachic acts in the *Iliad*, one might undervalue the heroic elevation of Achilles, the achievement of the Achaean wall, or the poem's implicit or explicit critique of the divine perspective. Similarly, what emerges from the treatment of theomachy and theomachic characteristics in tragedy is the conceptual power and variety of the theme, partly inherited from associations already activated by the *Iliad*, and partly emergent from new ways of looking at the implications of the relationship between human and god.[56] In the *Bacchae*, for example, Pentheus may err egregiously in rejecting the god, but the play allows the members of the audience a sustained hearing of his point of view and, therefore, a chance to evaluate for themselves the merits of rival outlooks. Even if Euripides' intent were ideologically conservative—an attempt to school the audience in the folly of Pentheus' extremism—the play's dialogic form nevertheless provides the audience with the opportunity to challenge the moral and political claims of the triumphant god at the close, not least in Cadmus' famous declaration that

---

[54] Mikalson 1991: 159, cf. 133–64.

[55] Padel 1995: 204, cf. 201–4.

[56] To explain the historical and cultural basis for the symbolic operation of theomachy in Greek literature is beyond the scope of this book, which attempts such explanations only for Roman epic and tragedy. But any parallel attempt for Greek literature would have to take into account developments in political and philosophical thought ranging from the Athenians' scrutiny of their own governmental system to their perceptions of other *poleis*, from the theology underlying civic religion to the manifold experimentations of the Sophists. The Sisyphus fragment (*TrGF* 43 fr. 19 Snell), attributed usually to Critias but occasionally to Euripides, offers a glimpse of just how radical the philosophical voice of tragedy could be (whether or not the passage is to be read as parody). Kahn 1997 links that voice to a philosophical tradition running from contemporary sophistry back through to Milesian cosmology. With the benefit of the limited yet significant evidence provided by the fragment, it's hardly surprising that tragic treatments of theomachy also engage philosophical concerns. On the Sisyphus fragment see also Sutton 1981. On atheism in classical Greece see Burkert 1985: 311–17, Bremmer 2007: 12–19. For another example of a cultural context for literary theomachy we might turn to the contemporary significance of ἀσέβεια ('impiety') within Athenian law; see, e.g., Versnel 1990: 123–31, Cohen 1991: 203–17. Much of the necessary contextualisation of tragic (and comic) theomachy will be accomplished by Tim Whitmarsh's forthcoming book.

'gods should not be like mortals in anger' (ὀργὰς πρέπει θεοὺς οὐχ ὁμοιοῦσθαι βροτοῖς, *Bacch.* 1348). Hard won though the lesson may be, it is only through Pentheus' intransigence that the play leads to the querying of Dionysus' conception of justice.

This part of the chapter, therefore, examines three plays especially concerned with theomachy and sampled from the three major authors of Attic tragedy: Aeschylus' *Seven Against Thebes* (*Septem*), Sophocles' *Ajax*, and Euripides' *Bacchae*. I argue that tragedy foregrounds certain important themes in the theomachic tradition, such as martial heroism and the analogy between divine and political authority, and prompts certain questions germane to the critical analysis of theomachy, chiefly, the effect of generic inflections and the problematic and negative character of tragic exemplarity. As in the previous discussion of the *Iliad*, each section will also contain a brief sketch of the key similarities and differences pertaining to the Roman texts that will be the subject of the remaining chapters.

AESCHYLUS' *SEVEN AGAINST THEBES*: IMPIETY AND INDEPENDENCE I

In the *Iliad*, heroes are often aided by gods, whether Athena's support during Diomedes' *aristeia*, or the repeated rescue of Aeneas by Apollo or Poseidon. Such divine assistance, typically reserved for the greatest heroes, functions as a sign of excellence, and yet the element of divine aid also confers a sense of artificiality on a character's merits. Aeneas, for instance, complains that he would stand a much better chance against Achilles if the latter did not have the help of some god or other (*Il.* 20.97–102).[57] Despite the potentially negative implications of benefitting from divine favour, however, not one of the heroes in the *Iliad* claims independence from the gods or rejects their help. To do so would be folly, as suggested by the contrast Sthenelus draws between the failure of the impious Seven against Thebes and the success of their sons who trusted in divine omens and the aid of Zeus (*Il.* 4.405–10).[58] In fact, there is only one

---

[57] There is, of course, some irony in Aeneas being the one to make this point given his own frequent dependence on divine aid.

[58] The even stronger case of mortals who challenge or fight the gods at their own behest is carefully distanced from the world of the heroes of the Trojan war. Dione's examples of Herakles and the Aloidae may technically be mortal, but their status is certainly ambiguous (*Il.* 5.385–404). In the case of the Aloidae, Dione elides the fact that their prodigious size renders them more akin to Giants (*Od.* 11.305–20), with whom they are often confused in the literary tradition. As the *Odyssey* passage further indicates, while their human father is Aloeus, they are born from the union of their mother with the god Poseidon, thereby distancing them even further from humanity. Herakles' status is similarly ambiguous given his descent from Zeus and eventual apotheosis. The *Iliad* provides four examples of theomachs who are less removed from other mortals, but none is especially closely related to the present time of the Trojan war: Thamyris' story is mentioned briefly in the catalogue of ships (*Il.* 2.594–600), Glaucus relates the tale of Lycurgus (*Il.* 6.130–40), and Achilles tells the story of Niobe (*Il.* 24.602–17);

direct assertion of human independence from the gods by a Homeric hero—the defiance of Locrian Ajax reported at *Od.* 4.499–511.[59] According to the story, Poseidon saves Ajax from the sea after wrecking his ship, but the hero attributes his survival to his own strength despite the gods: φῆ ῥ' ἀέκητι θεῶν φυγέειν μέγα λαῖτμα θαλάσσης ('he said that against the will of the gods he escaped the great abyss of the sea', *Od.* 4.504). Angered by this boast, Poseidon then drowns Ajax. The mythological tradition depicts Ajax as almost paradigmatically impious, as other accounts tell of his rape of Cassandra, who had taken shelter in the temple of Athena; indeed, in many versions it is Athena who destroys the hero.[60] Ajax's provocation of the gods, therefore, should be seen as a Homeric articulation—whether original or modified—of a more systematic mythological characterisation.

A human's explicit claim of independence from, or disregard for, the gods—a *hapax* in Homeric poetry—finds much more extensive expression in tragedy. Some inspiration for this theme may have derived from non-Homeric parts of the mythological tradition, such as the lost Cyclic *Thebaid* with its impious heroes. Aeschylus' tragic version of the myth, at least, addresses precisely the dismissal of divine power. In the play, a messenger reports that Hippomedon's shield carries an image of Typhon (*Sept.* 491–4), the monstrous threat to Olympus, while Eteoclus' bears an inscription defying Ares (*Sept.* 468–9). Parthenopaeus is even said to disdain the gods explicitly (*Sept.* 529–32):

> ὄμνυσι δ' αἰχμὴν ἣν ἔχει, μᾶλλον θεοῦ
> σέβειν πεποιθὼς ὀμμάτων θ' ὑπέρτερον,
> ἦ μὴν λαπάξειν ἄστυ Καδμείων βίᾳ
> Διός.

> He swears by the spear that he holds, daring to revere it
> more than god and above his own eyes,
> that in truth he will sack the city of the Cadmeans in spite of
> Zeus.

The logic of heroic self-assertion, familiar from the boasts of Homeric warriors, is here taken to a new and extreme conclusion—not just the hero's confidence in his own strength but the superiority of that strength to the will of the gods and the elevation of his spear in place of the gods' rightful worship.

Laomedon's manhandling of Apollo and Poseidon is marked as the stuff of the past. On the association between Thamyris and Capaneus in Statius' *Thebaid* see *Theb.* 4.182–6 with Parkes 2012: 133–5.

[59] The Phaeacians may violate Poseidon's sovereignty over the sea (*Od.* 13.128–83), but at no point are they said to provoke the god deliberately. There are, in addition, two examples of superhuman antagonism with the gods in the *Odyssey*, both of which the scholia associate with the term 'theomachy': the Cyclops Polyphemus (Schol. ad *Od.* 1.70) and the sons of Aloeus (Schol. ad *Od.* 11.317).

[60] Cf., e.g., Eur. *Tro.* 69–86, Apollod. *Epit.* 5.24–6.6, Verg. *Aen.* 1.39–45, 2.403–15.

And yet even Parthenopaeus' arrogance is not the most thoroughgoing expression of impiety in the play; that belongs to Capaneus.[61] Eteocles, the king of Thebes, emphasises the directness of Capaneus' challenge (*Sept.* 440–3):

Καπανεὺς δ' ἀπειλεῖ, δρᾶν παρεσκευασμένος,
θεοὺς ἀτίζων, κἀπογυμνάζων στόμα
χαρᾷ ματαίᾳ θνητὸς ὢν εἰς οὐρανὸν
πέμπει γεγωνὰ Ζηνὶ κυμαίνοντ' ἔπη.

And Capaneus threatens, ready to act,
dishonouring the gods, and, exercising his tongue
with foolish joy, though a mortal,
he sends loud and swollen boasts to Zeus in heaven.

The language of 442–3 reinforces a sense of Capaneus' superhuman aspirations, as the line ending θνητὸς ὢν εἰς οὐρανὸν ('though a mortal to heaven') suggests the action of the Giants or the Aloidae attempting to scale Olympus.[62] Although the full meaning of the sentence is clarified by 443, Eteocles' γεγωνὰ nevertheless hints at the sound of the word for Giant, γίγας.[63] The allusion gains support from the preceding speech of the messenger, which indeed describes Capaneus as a Giant (*Sept.* 424–31):

γίγας ὅδ' ἄλλος, τοῦ πάρος λελεγμένου
μείζων, ὁ κόμπος δ' οὐ κατ' ἄνθρωπον φρονεῖ,
πύργοις δ' ἀπειλεῖ δείν' ἃ μὴ κραίνοι τύχη·
θεοῦ τε γὰρ θέλοντος ἐκπέρσειν πόλιν
καὶ μὴ θέλοντός φησιν, οὐδὲ τὴν Διὸς
Ἔριν πέδοι σκήψασαν ἐμποδὼν σχεθεῖν.
τὰς δ' ἀστραπάς τε καὶ κεραυνίους βολὰς
μεσημβρινοῖσι θάλπεσιν προσήκασεν.

This one is another Giant, greater than the one described before,
but his boast intends something more than human,
and he makes terrible threats against our towers, which, I hope,
    chance will not fulfil;
for he says he will utterly destroy the city whether god is willing
or unwilling, and that not even conflict with Zeus,

---

[61] For the connection between impiety and boasting, especially in the *Septem*, see Canter 1937: 133–4 with 133 n. 5. Cf. Capaneus' punishment by Zeus at Soph. *Ant.* 127–40. For Capaneus' similar assertions of his own might in the *Thebaid* see Chapter 8.

[62] Cf. Bellerophon's attempt to fly to Olympus, which in Euripides' (fragmentary) play on the subject goes hand in hand with the hero's casting doubt on the gods' existence (see Riedweg 1990). On Bellerophon see also Chapter 4.

[63] On the responsions that structure the entire scene see Zeitlin 1982; cf. Vernant and Vidal-Naquet 1988: 273–300.

>though it fall before him in the plain, will stand in his way,
>and the lightning and thunderbolts
>he compared to midday heat.

The phrase οὐ κατ' ἄνθρωπον φρονεῖ (lit. 'thinks not in accordance with mankind'), coupled with Capaneus' explicit provocation of Zeus, further supports an association with the Giants. Thus, through verbal conceit and mythological analogy, the play raises human impiety and claims of independence to a cosmic level, as if mortals can recapitulate the primordial struggles for authority that tested and ultimately secured the power of the Olympian gods.[64]

The apparently simple didacticism of the *Septem*, however—the impression that the defeat of the fearsome Argives represents a straightforward triumph of piety over impiety—is complicated by at least two factors, one internal to the play, the other external. The course of the plot will see Eteocles, defender of Thebes and excoriator of the Argives' hubris, succumb to a similar arrogance, even if not outright theomachy, when he makes the fateful decision to fight his brother, Polynices, despite the protests of the chorus about the impiety of fratricide (οὐ θεμιστοῦ, 'not according to divine law' or 'sacrilegious', *Sept.* 694).[65] With the death of the king, what emerges from the play as a whole is the threat of impiety to the city both from without and from within. Moreover, if, as Froma Zeitlin has argued, tragedy used Thebes as a foil for Athens, the audience is likely to have seen the impious self-assertion described throughout the play as a danger to the welfare and democratic values of their own city.[66] Thus, theomachy, as the extension of reckless self-elevation and its ultimate symbol, begins to acquire a political valence that myths of this type, such as the Gigantomachy, had always left available for exploitation through the image of struggle between ruler and aspiring rebel, order and disorder.[67]

As we shall see in Chapter 8, many of Aeschylus' ideas are worked out more fully by Statius given the expanded scope afforded by the twelve books

---

[64] Critics have noted that in the *Phoenissae* Euripides plays on the shield ecphrasis of Aeschylus' *Septem* to link Capaneus and Prometheus. Euripides describes Tydeus as a kind of Prometheus figure: δεξιᾶι δὲ λαμπάδα / Τιτὰν Προμηθεὺς ἔφερεν ὡς πρήσων πόλιν ('[like] the Titan Prometheus [he] carries a torch in his right hand in order to burn the town', *Phoen*. 1121–2). The image clearly alludes to the shield of Capaneus in the *Septem*: ἔχει δὲ σῆμα γυμνὸν ἄνδρα πυρφόρον, / φλέγει δὲ λαμπὰς διὰ χερῶν ὡπλισμένη, / χρυσοῖς δὲ φωνεῖ γράμμασιν 'πρήσω πόλιν' ('he has as a symbol a naked man bearing fire, and the torch, his weapon, blazes in his hands, and it says in golden letters, "I shall burn the city"', *Sept.* 432–4). Thus, through the torch of Tydeus, Euripides reads Prometheus not just as the traditional bearer of fire but also as a kind of Capaneus. Aeschylus had already built a Promethean connection into his Capaneus through the word πυρφόρον, which alludes to one of his own (lost) plays, the *Prometheus Purphoros*. For discussion of the *Phoenissae* passage and the question of its authenticity see Mastronarde 1978, esp. 122–4.

[65] Cf. Creon (at the end) and the Seven (at the beginning) of Sophocles' *Antigone*.

[66] Zeitlin 1986.

[67] Cf. the representation of the Gigantomachy on the Parthenon, built some years after the production of the *Septem* in 467 BC.

of the *Thebaid*. At numerous points during the epic, for instance, Capaneus asserts his independence from the gods and resembles a Giant; what will set Statius' hero apart from his Aeschylean predecessor is a philosophical streak inherited from Lucretius, which will give his impiety greater intellectual significance than the mere blasphemy on show in the *Septem*. Furthermore, while Aeschylus' combination of impiety both within and outside the city plays a part in the *Thebaid* too, as one might expect, the political reading of theomachy in Chapter 9 shows that this ambivalent view of impiety is also inflected by its Roman imperial context, in which the emperor's divine aspirations figure him as both defender of and threat to the political and divine order. That double aspect of impiety is also a feature of the *Punica*, in which the figures of Hannibal (Chapter 7) and Flaminius (Chapter 6) not only share Capaneus' Giant-like qualities but also exemplify the twin threat of impiety to Rome both from her external enemy and from her own wrongheaded leaders.

SOPHOCLES' *AJAX*: IMPIETY AND INDEPENDENCE II

Sophocles' *Ajax* continues and deepens the political colouring of theomachic heroism through its protagonist's combined struggle against the authority of the gods and the leaders of the Greek army.[68] The opening scene of the play touches on both these conflicts, as the goddess Athena shows to Odysseus, hidden from Ajax's view, the madness inflicted by her on the once great warrior: we hear Ajax triumph over a captured and slaughtered herd of animals as he mistakenly perceives them to be his enemies—Agamemnon, Menelaus, and Odysseus himself. The deluded Ajax, in what will prove to be a particularly potent irony, sees Athena as a 'comrade in arms' (σύμμαχον, *Aj.* 117).[69] In a gnomic warning to Odysseus, however, the goddess makes clear that Ajax's madness is a punishment for arrogance towards the gods: ὑπέρκοπον / μηδέν ποτ' εἴπῃς αὐτὸς ἐς θεοὺς ἔπος... τοὺς δὲ σώφρονας / θεοὶ φιλοῦσι καὶ στυγοῦσι τοὺς κακούς ('never say an overweening word to the gods... the gods love those who think moderately and hate the wicked', *Aj.* 127–8, 132–3).

---

[68] On the dating of the *Ajax*, usually assigned to the 440s, see Finglass 2011: 1–11. This Ajax, son of Telamon and sometimes referred to as 'Greater' Ajax, differs from the Ajax from Locris mentioned above, who is the son of Oileus and sometimes known as 'Lesser' Ajax; as the following analysis will show, however, the two heroes share certain impious qualities.

[69] Margaret Graver has suggested to me that Ajax's arrogance is expressed by the very word σύμμαχον, since Ajax speaks of Athena as if she were on his level (pers. comm.). Ajax's imperious tone is important here (σοὶ δ' ἐφίεμαι, 'I bid you', *Aj.* 116) to distinguish the usage of σύμμαχος from more deferential examples, e.g., Aesch. *Sept.* 266, *Cho.* 2. Versnel 2011: 93–4 with n. 260 cites examples of Greeks invoking gods as *summachoi* in battle, but these prayers too are deferential, and in most cases the gods in question seem to be divinised heroes, like the Aeacides or Tyndarides, and not the first-rank Olympian gods.

A scholion on the first scene draws a more explicit connection between theomachy and madness as part of a larger, didactic point (Schol. ad *Aj.* 118):[70]

παιδευτικὸς ὁ λόγος καὶ ἀποτρεπτικὸς ἁμαρτημάτων· καὶ διὰ τοῦτο ἐπίτηδες καὶ τῷ Ὀδυσσεῖ καὶ τῷ θεατῇ ὑπέδειξε τὸν Αἴαντα δηλῶν ὡς ὁ πρότερον φρόνιμος καὶ πρακτικὸς νῦν ἐξέστη διὰ τὸ θεομαχῆσαι. καὶ τοῦτο δὲ Ὁμήρου παίδευμα, ὅτι, ἐφ' οἷς αὐχοῦσί τινες, τούτων στεροῦνται παρὰ τῶν θεῶν, ὡς καὶ Θάμυρις τῆς μουσικῆς καὶ Νιόβη τῶν τέκνων.

The account is instructive and deters transgressions; for this reason it purposefully shows Ajax both to Odysseus and to the spectator, making clear how one who was previously thoughtful and practical has now lost his senses because he fought with the gods. And this is also Homer's lesson, that some people boast of things of which they are then deprived by the gods, as both Thamyris of his music and Niobe of her children.

The scholiast seems to confuse madness as a result of theomachy and as a cause, but the general thrust of the comment is clear enough: arrogant behaviour towards the gods—a species of theomachy (θεομαχῆσαι)—is regularly punished, in Ajax's case by madness. That punishment, in turn, acts as a deterrent both for the internal audience of the play, here Odysseus, and for the Athenian spectators. Indeed, a contemporary audience, familiar with the mythological tradition, might have required little to no supplementary information about the nature of Ajax's impiety, which neither Athena nor the scholion specify. If, however, there were any doubt about the reasons for Athena's anger, the poet provides an explanation in a messenger speech much later in the play, through the reported words of the seer Calchas (*Aj.* 758–79):

> τὰ γὰρ περισσὰ κἀνόνητα σώματα
> πίπτειν βαρείαις πρὸς θεῶν δυσπραξίαις
> ἔφασχ' ὁ μάντις, ὅστις ἀνθρώπου φύσιν
> βλαστὼν ἔπειτα μὴ κατ' ἄνθρωπον φρονῇ.
> κεῖνος δ' ἀπ' οἴκων εὐθὺς ἐξορμώμενος
> ἄνους καλῶς λέγοντος ηὑρέθη πατρός.
> ὁ μὲν γὰρ αὐτὸν ἐννέπει· τέκνον, δόρει
> βούλου κρατεῖν μέν, σὺν θεῷ δ' ἀεὶ κρατεῖν.
> ὁ δ' ὑψικόμπως κἀφρόνως ἠμείψατο·
> πάτερ, θεοῖς μὲν κἂν ὁ μηδὲν ὢν ὁμοῦ
> κράτος κατακτήσαιτ'· ἐγὼ δὲ καὶ δίχα
> κείνων πέποιθα τοῦτ' ἐπισπάσειν κλέος.

---

[70] On theomachy and madness see Padel 1995. On the 'sanctimonious tone' of the scholion see Kamerbeek 1953: 43. For a similarly didactic comment cf. p. 20 n. 7 above. On the underappreciated merits of the scholia see Easterling 2006. Feeney 1993, however, rightly cautions against interpretive approaches excessively hidebound by the views of ancient critics.

τοσόνδ' ἐκόμπει μῦθον. εἶτα δεύτερον
δίας Ἀθάνας, ἡνίκ' ὀτρύνουσά νιν
ηὐδᾶτ' ἐπ' ἐχθροῖς χεῖρα φοινίαν τρέπειν,
τότ' ἀντιφωνεῖ δεινὸν ἄρρητόν τ' ἔπος:
ἄνασσα, τοῖς ἄλλοισιν Ἀργείων πέλας
ἵστω, καθ' ἡμᾶς δ' οὔποτ' ἐκρήξει μάχη.
τοιοῖσδέ τοι λόγοισιν ἀστεργῆ θεᾶς
ἐκτήσατ' ὀργήν, οὐ κατ' ἄνθρωπον φρονῶν.
ἀλλ' εἴπερ ἔστι τῇδε θἠμέρᾳ, τάχ' ἂν
γενοίμεθ' αὐτοῦ σὺν θεῷ σωτήριοι.

'Individuals grown excessive and useless
fall on grave difficulties sent from the gods',
said the seer, 'especially when someone born of human nature
then does not think appropriately for humans.
And Ajax, on his setting out from home,
was found foolish though his father spoke well.
For Telamon told him, "My son, desire to prevail with the spear,
but always to prevail with the help of god".
The other replied boastfully and foolishly,
"Father, with the help of the gods even a worthless man
might win victory; but I, even without them,
am confident in obtaining that glory".
So much he boasted. Then once again
in answer to divine Athena, when she was encouraging him
to turn a deadly hand against the enemy,
he spoke back with terrible and abominable words,
"My lady, stand beside the other Argives;
the battle line will never break where I am".
With such words did he win the unkind anger of the goddess,
for not thinking in a way appropriate to humans.
But if he survives this day, perhaps
with god's help we may save him'.

In the *Iliad*, Aeneas' complaint about the divine aid given to Achilles, however hypocritical, gently undermines the heroism of those who receive the support of the gods; Ajax turns that querying of heroism into a bald declaration: gods can elevate anyone, so the only true measure of merit is in achieving glory without them.[71] The claim of independence from the gods links the hero to his

---

[71] G. Zanker 1992 (also 1994: 64–71) argues that in the *Ajax* Sophocles scrutinises Homeric values and their inherent tensions. In this case, Sophocles suggests that in rejecting Athena's aid Ajax turns from a theomach in the style of the Iliadic Diomedes to a theomach of a more extreme sort, even if he does not actually fight a god.

Homeric namesake, Locrian Ajax, but the language of Calchas' account also identifies him with the more explicitly theomachic tradition represented by Aeschylus' Argives, in particular the repeated charge that Ajax does not think as men should (μὴ κατ' ἄνθρωπον φρονῇ, *Aj.* 761; οὐ κατ' ἄνθρωπον φρονῶν, *Aj.* 777; ὁ κόμπος δ' οὐ κατ' ἄνθρωπον φρονεῖ, *Sept.* 425).[72] Lest the audience believe Ajax's offence to Athena to be a recent aberration, Calchas claims that impious self-assertion is a consistent characteristic of the hero from the moment of his departure from Salamis through his fighting in the Trojan War. Now, after hearing of Ajax's persistent and arrogant dismissal of divine aid, in particular Athena's, we can feel the full irony of the maddened hero asking the goddess in the opening scene to stand by him as his ally (*Aj.* 117).[73] And in a further irony, the seer ends his speech by making the deliverance of Ajax contingent upon divine aid (σὺν θεῷ, *Aj.* 779), the very aid that Ajax so pointedly rejects (δίχα / κείνων, *Aj.* 768–9). At this point in the play, then, the scholiast on the very first scene appears to have been on the right interpretive track.

The impious claims attributed to Ajax need to be interpreted, however, in light of the play's interest in the theme of individual heroism versus hierarchical order.[74] The hero's boasts to his father and to Athena promote the value of individual heroism, the ability of one man to make a difference entirely through his own capacities. An alternative value system, however, is associated with Odysseus, whose frequent debts to Athena are pointedly mentioned by the goddess, and who operates skilfully within the command hierarchy of the Greeks. When such pragmatic values are in the ascendancy, and when the claims of the individual are overridden by the authority of the political order, the quality that once made Ajax an exceptional hero—his individualism—becomes a threat to the highly structured world of the Greek army, and by extension to Greek society.[75] After the suicide of Ajax just over halfway through the play, that political conflict is played out through the arguments about the hero's burial—forbidden by the Atreidae—and the different judgements about the legacy of Ajax's heroism. Menelaus, for instance, complains about Ajax's refusal to listen to the commands of his superiors (*Aj.* 1069–72), while Teucer disputes the very idea of Ajax's subordination, claiming that he came to the Trojan war independently of any fealty to Menelaus (*Aj.* 1099–1114). The ideological difference between the values of Ajax and his opponents, however, fails to mask an underlying similarity: at their extreme, both views are susceptible to impiety. In Ajax's case, that impiety consists in his boasts to Telamon and

---

[72] For translations see above. Knox 1961: 8–9 argues that Ajax acts like a god.

[73] Tyler 1974: 26–7 argues that Calchas' reported speech contains an accurate indication of Athena's motives and objectives in the play.

[74] On this theme see Knox 1961: 20–28.

[75] The play explicitly signals the relevance of its concerns to the city: Menelaus, for example, twice refers to the implications of Ajax's behaviour for the πόλις (*Aj.* 1073, 1082). On the contemporary significance of the 'Ajax dilemma' see Woodruff 2011.

Athena; in the case of the Atreidae, it consists in their denial of burial to the hero, as Odysseus points out near the close of the play: τοὺς θεῶν νόμους / φθείροις ἄν ('you would be destroying the laws of the gods', *Aj.* 1343–4).

The analogy between political and divine authority, and by extension between rebellion and theomachy, emerges especially clearly from a passage in the *Trugrede*, or 'deception speech', in which Ajax apparently resolves not to commit suicide, only to do so in the next scene. At one point, the hero quite unexpectedly speaks of bending to circumstances and the authority of others (*Aj.* 666–8):[76]

> τοιγὰρ τὸ λοιπὸν εἰσόμεσθα μὲν θεοῖς
> εἴκειν, μαθησόμεσθα δ' Ἀτρείδας σέβειν.
> ἄρχοντές εἰσιν, ὥσθ' ὑπεικτέον· τί μήν;
>
> For the rest we shall know how to yield to gods,
> and we shall understand how to revere the sons of Atreus.
> They are rulers, so they must be obeyed; well, why not?

Ajax describes both the gods and the Atreidae as authorities to be obeyed, and whether one reads the speech as deliberately ironic on his part or merely ambiguous, it makes little difference to the fundamental correspondence between divine and human rulers. Ajax himself, then, demonstrates the analogy between his disregard for Athena and the Greek leaders, in other words the analogy between theomachy and resistance to political hierarchy.[77]

Evidence in favour of an ironic reading of the speech can be found, according to a scholion, in the passage's diction (Schol. ad *Aj.* 666):

> ἐπιφθόνως ἔφρασεν, ἐν εἰρωνείᾳ ἀντιστρέψας τὴν τάξιν. ἔδει γὰρ εἰπεῖν θεοὺς μὲν σέβειν, εἴκειν δὲ Ἀτρείδαις. τοὐναντίον δὲ εἴρηκεν ὡς τῶν Ἀτρειδῶν νῦν δὴ θεομαχούντων.
>
> He speaks invidiously, out of irony switching the order. For one should say 'to revere the gods', and 'to yield to the Atreidae'. He says the opposite, as though the Atreidae are in that case fighting the gods.

The scholiast reads the unexpected reversal of verbs as casting the sons of Atreus as usurpers of the rightful place of the gods.[78] That the scholiast

---

[76] On the long-standing controversy of how one should read this speech and the intentions of the hero see Stevens 1986, Crane 1990, Hesk 2003: 74–103, all with further bibliography.

[77] Crane 1990: 94–101, esp. 96–9, argues that in the deception speech Ajax subtly displaces divine influence by focusing instead on the power of time. This reading suggests an attitude to the gods that is both related to and yet more sophisticated than the hero's earlier dismissals.

[78] See Kamerbeek 1953: 139, but note the qualifications at Finglass 2011: 334. Knox 1961: 16 with n. 85 compares σέβειν here to instances in the *Antigone*, where Creon also uses the verb to describe an attitude to political authority. Tim Perry has pointed out to me that the interchangeability of the verbs also

recognised the possibility of this ironic reading underscores the yet more essential point that the Atreidae, too, can be figured as theomachs (θεομαχούντων), whose impiety, although different from Ajax's excessive self-belief, is at the same time no less problematic. Thus, while Ajax's error in dismissing the divine may not be in doubt, the play forces its audience to consider whether the expunging of such individualistic figures genuinely serves the collective welfare, and whether Ajax's attention-grabbing form of impiety merely obscures the different, but equally dangerous, impiety of the Atreidae, who would abuse arguments from raison d'état to denigrate the contributions of the individual and who would ignore divine law to satisfy their personal grievances. Viewed through the lens of the *Ajax*, then, theomachy represents various kinds of threats to the welfare of the community, threats that may be less ostentatious than in Aeschylus' *Septem*, but are more well-defined and more suggestive of familiar conflicts within political discourse.[79]

The *Ajax* examines a particularly explicit combination of the madness and arrogance from which many tragic protagonists suffer, but within Roman tragedy Seneca hugely increases the intensity of these characteristics through the crazed theomachy of his Hercules. The main source for Seneca's play is Euripides' *Herakles*, or perhaps some Roman intermediary, but the *Ajax* better illustrates the tension between a mortal's excessive confidence in his own abilities and the greater power of the gods. Senecan tragedy differs from its Greek counterparts, however, in the framing of events on a cosmic scale and, especially in his *Thyestes* and *Medea*, in suggesting that some extraordinary figures may be justified in their sense of superiority. The political theme of the *Ajax* is also relevant to Roman theomachy. Seneca's Lycus is a type of theomach too, though on a much smaller scale than the maddened Hercules. As tyrant of Thebes, Lycus voices a pragmatic and cynical attitude both to politics and to certain aspects of mythology concerning the gods. It is to be expected that the balancing of individual and collective, which preoccupies the *Ajax* and many other Greek tragedies, would feature more heavily in the context of democratic Athens. Political debate in Senecan drama, on the other hand, centres almost exclusively on the rival claims of individuals—a reflection of the autocratic system under which the tragedies were composed.

EURIPIDES' *BACCHAE*: THE STRUGGLE FOR AUTHORITY

In the *Bacchae*, Euripides combines the political valence of theomachy with a direct representation of the theme when he depicts Pentheus, the king of

---

strengthens the analogy between divine and political authority and implicitly, therefore, between theomachy and rebellion (pers. comm.).

[79] On tensions between individualism and democracy in Athens, for instance, see Dynneson 2008: 100–1, 141–2.

Thebes, engaged in an active struggle against Dionysus and Bacchic cult. Pentheus denies the divinity of the new god and rejects his rites as a threat to the order of the city. More than the *Septem* and the *Ajax*, then, which depict heroic boasts of independence from the gods, Euripides' *Bacchae* distils theomachy into its purest form—the personal confrontation of mortal and god.[80] Indeed, this kind of conflict comes closest to its martial counterpart in epic, as Pentheus attempts to bind and even to fight the disguised Dionysus. Besides the immediate fact that Pentheus exhausts his energies trying to fight a mere apparition, his failure, as the god explains, is the inevitable consequence of his enterprise (*Bacch*. 635–6): πρὸς θεὸν γὰρ ὢν ἀνὴρ / ἐς μάχην ἐλθεῖν ἐτόλμησ' ('for, though a man, he dared to come to battle with a god').

In the earlier discussion of the *Iphigenia at Aulis*, we saw how Euripides employed the word θεομαχεῖν to signify futile struggle. That play, though not especially concerned with theomachy in any substantial way, was produced in the same trilogy as the *Bacchae*, a play which is, by contrast, thoroughly immersed in theomachy proper and uses forms of the verb θεομαχεῖν three times. Euripides' coinage (or perhaps early adoption) of the word encapsulates his developing interest in the semantic and intellectual reach of theomachy, a theme that had always engaged the playwright, as attested, for example, by the *Hippolytus* and the satyr play *Cyclops*, but which is investigated in new depth in the *Bacchae*. Where that theme might have subsequently led we will never know, since the trilogy containing the *Iphigenia at Aulis* and *Bacchae* represents the last work of Euripides, produced after his death in 405 BC.

In the *Bacchae*, the verb θεομαχεῖν has its full connotation of antagonism, referring quite specifically to Pentheus' opposition to Dionysus, as the god makes clear in the prologue: ὃς θεομαχεῖ τὰ κατ' ἐμὲ καὶ σπονδῶν ἄπο / ὠθεῖ μ', ἐν εὐχαῖς τ' οὐδαμοῦ μνείαν ἔχει ('[Pentheus] who fights against my divinity and rejects me from libations, and makes no mention of me at all in his prayers', *Bacch*. 45–6). Tiresias and later the maddened Agave, both of whom accede to the god's authority, characterise Pentheus as an agent of theomachy: κοὐ θεομαχήσω σῶν λόγων πεισθεὶς ὕπο ('and I will not fight the god persuaded by your words', *Bacch*. 325), ἀλλὰ θεομαχεῖν μόνον / οἷός τ' ἐκεῖνος ('but that one is only able to fight against the god', *Bacch*. 1255–6). Pentheus even orders an attack on the god's followers, to which the disguised Dionysus responds by saying that 'you should not take up arms against a god' (οὔ φημι χρῆναί σ' ὅπλ' ἐπαίρεσθαι θεῷ, *Bacch*. 789). Thus the *Bacchae*, certainly more than any other extant tragedy, blends the literal and metaphorical interpretations of theomachy: Pentheus' fight against god is futile on all levels.

It's shortly after this crazed assault that Pentheus entirely succumbs to his own moral weakness and the manipulation of Dionysus: determined to satisfy

---

[80] For the resemblance of Pentheus and Capaneus see Segal 1997: 128–31.

his salacious curiosity about the activities of the god's female followers, Pentheus abandons his scruples to dress up like a bacchant and is led by the god to his death at the hands of the women. In its futility, then, Pentheus' theomachy may be no different from any of the other examples we have seen of mortals trying to overcome an unbridgeable divide; what distinguishes it from the antagonism of other tragic and epic heroes, however, is its comprehensiveness: Pentheus denies the divinity of Dionysus, rejects his rites as a threat to the city, and punishes his worshippers. This all-out war against the new religion not only explains the subsequent severity of the god's revenge, it also redefines the political character of theomachy—from a symbol of arrogance or independence the fight with god has been transformed into a clash of irreconcilable world views encompassing theology and morality in addition to politics.[81] For Euripides, theomachy is not merely the expression of intransigence that leads to disaster, it is rather a reflection of a particular view of religion, society, and politics.[82] Pentheus sees himself as the defender of morality against eastern dissolution despite claims to the contrary that the Bacchic rites are in fact chaste. In the end, his crucial weakness will be his voyeuristic desire to see the bacchants for himself, a desire so strong that he is even willing to abandon his supposedly masculine values and dress like a woman. As misguided as Pentheus may be, his theomachy goes hand in hand with normative assertions about what religion should look like, how citizens should behave, and how leaders should rule.[83] Other tragedies had similar concerns, of course, but of extant works, the *Bacchae* most closely and explicitly ties these issues to the act or notion, even the vocabulary, of 'fighting against god'.

Among Roman texts, the *Bacchae* had a particular influence on Ovid's *Metamorphoses*. Although Ovid retells the story of Pentheus' fall in quite different form from Euripides, they both share an interest in common themes, especially the notion of a political and social struggle and the relation between sight and epistemology. Although we lack the same tragic sources for many of Ovid's other, related episodes, such as those of Lycaon and Niobe, it's clear that Ovid shows a sustained concern with the identification and criteria of divinity. Euripides' influential treatment of theomachy as a political and theological test of a new god has a clear resonance for the early imperial age, as it accustoms itself to the idea of its rulers as semi-divine or divine figures.

---

[81] For a reading of the *Bacchae* as representing a confrontation between two contrasting Athenian views of the importation of new gods see Versnel 1990: 156–205.

[82] I make no claims for Euripides' personal beliefs. Lefkowitz 1989 argues that the plays offer no evidence of Euripidean impiety or atheism.

[83] Having listed Dionysus' powers at some length, Tiresias warns Pentheus not to have too much confidence in his merely human authority: μὴ τὸ κράτος αὔχει δύναμιν ἀνθρώποις ἔχειν ('don't boast that power has force for men', *Bacch.* 310). Tiresias goes on to suggest a correlation between overconfidence in power and sickness of mind (*Bacch.* 311–12), a standard charge against theomachic figures like the Titans or Sophocles' Ajax.

The expansion of the semantics of theomachy to various other contexts—political and intellectual, for instance—is one of the most important contributions of Attic tragedy to the development of the theme. Theomachy isn't simply a literal or figurative assertion of superiority, but rather part of a world view. That view is invariably flawed, as one would expect in tragedy, but each individual play inflects the theomachic conception of the world in its own way, from emphatic claims of human independence to rejections of alternative visions of society.[84] Theomachy may ultimately reduce in each case to a kind of Achillean self-assertion, but it's precisely in the many layers of opposition to god—arrogant, irrational, reactionary, etc.—that we have a sense of theomachy's literary significance, its cultural importance, and its manifold variations across texts and periods.

---

[84] Cf. Euripides' *Hippolytus*, where Hippolytus' adherence to Artemis and consequent rejection of Aphrodite plays out a larger-scale opposition of chastity and love—Hippolytus' wilful rejection of the goddess of love is a challenge to love itself. Cf. p. 41 n. 53 above on the use of the word 'theomachy' in Menander's *Eunuch*.

2

The Origins of Roman Theomachy

LUCRETIUS AND VERGIL

> Thunderbolt and lightning—very very frightening me—
> Gallileo . . .
>
> —QUEEN

> They say miracles are past, and we have our philosophical persons to make modern and familiar things supernatural and causeless. Hence is it that we make trifles of terrors, ensconcing ourselves into seeming knowledge when we should submit ourselves to an unknown fear.
>
> —WILLIAM SHAKESPEARE

> IMP. CAESAR DIVI F. AVGVSTVS
>
> —CIL 6.702

Although we know the Roman epic tradition to have begun with an act of translation, we have little concrete idea of how its progenitors, Livius Andronicus, Naevius, and Ennius, viewed their genre, much less their reception of the Greek theomachic model.[1] The earliest Roman epic to come down to us intact is instead a highly unusual poem, Lucretius' didactic *De Rerum Natura*, and it is followed shortly by what many consider the genre's zenith, Vergil's *Aeneid*.[2] Both these texts are, of course, not only thoroughly Hellenised in their outlook but also Hellenistic in their aesthetic, and they stand as monuments to the Roman mediation of Greek influences as well as to the formation of a distinct Roman perspective.

These two very different poems have an important place in the development of the representation of theomachy. Lucretius' presentation of his

---

[1] On early Roman epic see Goldberg 1995, Feeney 1991: 99–128.
[2] On the relationship between Latin didactic and epic see Farrell 1991.

philosophical hero, Epicurus, as a kind of theomach brings into the poetic tradition a highly counterintuitive strain of thought, so that theomachy is no longer conceived as simply the direct antagonism between human and god, as it is in Homer and Attic tragedy. Instead, Lucretius uses theomachy as a metaphor for reconceiving the nature of the world and the relationship between gods and humankind. Lucretius influenced later poets, including Vergil, in a number of ways, but the effect of Epicurean theology in particular is striking. With its gods indifferent to human affairs, Epicureanism poses real problems within an epic context, where from Homer onwards gods typically take a direct, and often emotionally invested, role in the action. The first half of this chapter, therefore, outlines Lucretius' use of theomachy and examines Vergil's response in Book 4 of the *Aeneid*, which contains many of the epic's clearest echoes of Lucretius and Epicureanism.

The *Aeneid* presents problems of a slightly different kind when it comes to theomachy, not least because the poem superficially appears remarkably uninterested in this key epic topos. Neither Aeneas nor any of his opponents come close to imitating the more fantastical feats of Diomedes or Achilles, who could wound gods and fight rivers. That the *Aeneid* is an oddity in this regard emerges clearly not only from the return to, and prevalence of, the theme in subsequent epics, as we shall see in later chapters, but also from Vergil's own repeated flirting with, but ultimate avoidance of, theomachy within the *Aeneid* itself. Vergil briefly refers to Diomedes' wounding of Aphrodite, for instance, but he does so through a speech of Diomedes' filled with regret for the consequences of his overreaching, almost as if to verify the warnings of Homer's Dione about the inevitable disaster that must befall the human theomach. Moreover, the character who comes closest to fulfilling the role of theomach within the *Aeneid*, the impious Mezentius, is ultimately too old to pose a serious threat to Aeneas, let alone the gods—we are forced to settle for a theomach manqué.

These off-centre images of theomachy appear all the more striking when one takes into consideration the pervasive presence of Gigantomachic symbolism throughout the *Aeneid*. A sharp contrast appears between the grandeur of conflicts at the cosmic and metaphorical levels—the Battle of Actium cast as a Gigantomachic contest between Roman and Egyptian gods, for instance, or Aeneas compared to the hundred-handed Giant Aegaeon—and the absence of any such conflict from the plane of the human action.[3] That separation is purposefully engineered, I suggest, precisely because of the poem's investment in the value of piety, which is itself a mark of the wider influence of the Augustan context.

The combined pressure to make Aeneas both more pious than his epic predecessors and at the same time more powerful than the other heroes within the poem ensures that theomachy can only have an indirect and carefully hedged presence in the *Aeneid*. Gigantomachy, on the other hand, doesn't pose

---

[3] On Actium see *Aen.* 8.691–706 with Hardie 1986: 98–104. On the Aegaeon simile see pp. 78–80.

quite the same problems, since, with the important exception of the Aegaeon simile, it largely provides a framework within which to understand the cosmological imagery of the poem. This framework, as Hardie has shown in detail, serves the panegyrical aspect of the epic very well. As a combined response to the philosophical and political symbolism of Gigantomachy, drawing on Lucretius and Hellenistic Pergamum, respectively, the myth often functions in the *Aeneid* to emphasise religious conservatism and the preservation or restoration of order—both crucial concepts within Augustan ideology.[4] At other times, however, as in the Aegaeon simile, Vergil uses Gigantomachy to provoke reflection on the philosophical and panegyrical agenda underlying the typical usage of the imagery.[5] Theomachy, on the other hand, is rare and oblique, but its scarcity makes it stand out all the more against the background of the epic's pervasive piety.

The second half of the chapter, then, considers the question of why theomachy should be relatively absent from the *Aeneid*, as compared both to the *Iliad*, by which it is otherwise so influenced, and to later Roman epics, and what purpose its obliqueness serves. After looking at two examples of this phenomenon—what I have called the theomach manqué—I conclude the chapter by arguing that political considerations explain the subdued presence of theomachy in the epic. The need both to elevate Aeneas above his Greek predecessors and to emphasise the importance of piety in the context of Augustan ideology placed certain constraints on what the poem could do. What Vergil probably did not foresee, however, is that the Lucretian and Augustan strands—broadly speaking, philosophy and politics—would subsequently lead to a poetic tradition that utterly reversed the *Aeneid*'s take on theomachy. Far from keeping it at a safe distance, Roman imperial poetry would make theomachy fundamental to its nature.

The Revaluation of Theomachy in Lucretius' *De Rerum Natura*

Early in Book 1 of the *De Rerum Natura*, Lucretius describes Epicurus' attack on superstition, or *religio*, in figurative terms that recall Gigantomachy. Epicurus moves from looking up at *religio* in the sky (*tollere . . . oculos*, Lucr. 1.66-7) to standing above his enemy: *religio pedibus subiecta uicissim / obteritur* ('superstition was in turn cast underfoot and trampled', Lucr. 1.78-9).[6] Lucretius employs

---

[4] See Hardie 1986: 85-156, 209-13 on Gigantomachy in the *Aeneid*. On the role of religion in Augustan ideology, especially the simultaneous projection of conservatism alongside important innovations, see Galinsky 1996: 288-331 and Scheid 2005.

[5] Cf. O'Hara 1994: 217-24.

[6] Nonius quotes the phrase as *tendere oculos*, contrary to the manuscripts' consensus, but for our purposes the difference is immaterial, since I merely wish to show the direction of the philosopher's gaze and the subsequent elevation over *religio*.

strikingly violent and martial language to describe Epicurus' success: *obsistere*, 'to make a stand', 1.67; *effringere*, 'to break open', 1.70; *uictor*, 'victor', 1.75. This victory, however, consists in a mastery of scientific fact. In line with his overall goal of banishing fearful superstitions, Lucretius emphasises that supernatural phenomena such as *fulmina*, which in the minds of common folk confer truth on *religio*, present only a challenge and an incitement to Epicurus (Lucr. 1.68–71):[7]

> quem neque fama deum nec fulmina nec minitanti
> murmure compressit caelum, sed eo magis acrem
> inritat animi uirtutem, effringere ut arta
> naturae primus portarum claustra cupiret.

> whom neither stories of the gods nor thunderbolts
> nor heaven with its threatening roar held back, but all the more
> goaded the sharp courage of his mind to want to be
> the first to break the tight bolts of the gates of nature.

The combination of the violent ascent to heaven and the defiance of the thunderbolt shares a general resemblance with various accounts of the Gigantomachy and related enterprises, such as the Aloidae piling Ossa and Pelion on Olympus in order to reach the heavens.[8] The importance of that similarity, as Monica Gale has described, lies in the consequent moral revaluation of Gigantomachy:

> Lucretius reverses the traditional moral drawn from the myth throughout antiquity: rather than representing *hybris*, disorder and barbarity, the 'giants' have become heroic figures, challenging and overthrowing the tyranny of *religio*.[9]

---

[7] In the particular case of meteorological phenomena, ignorance and fear compel one to believe that they are instruments of divine will (Lucr. 5.1183–93). Lucretius concedes that our awe before the elements is a serious obstacle on the journey to *ataraxia*, and that these spectacular and destructive phenomena can drag an acolyte Epicurean back under the sway of *religio* (Lucr. 6.50–67; cf. 5.82–90). And so, after offering a scientific and demythologising account of lightning, he then questions with great rhetorical flourish whether any purpose whatsoever can be discerned in the activity of lightning (Lucr. 6.379–422). *Fulmina* destroy shrines, are wasted on the desert, and kill good and bad alike (Lucr. 2.1101–4 expanded in 6.379–422). The fact that such force doesn't appear to operate in divine interests, at least not in any obvious way, forms a strong part of Lucretius' argument against the divine causation of meteorological phenomena.

[8] On the Aloidae see *Od.* 11.305–20, and Chapter 1; cf. Typhon at Hes. *Theog.* 820–68.

[9] Gale 2000: 121. Cf. Gale 1994: 193:

> The Olympians are thus overthrown by the 'Giant' Epicurus as Uranus had been overthrown by Cronos, and Cronos by Zeus. It is significant that the defeats of Uranus and Cronos were often seen as punishments for their violence and cruelty, and the rule of Zeus equated with the establishment of justice. In Lucretius' eyes, the conventional gods are themselves tyrants, and the rebellion of the god/Giant Epicurus brings about the liberation of mankind.

See also Reiche 1971, Hardie 1986: 188, 209–13, D. Clay 1998: 184–6, Gigandet 1998: 327–33; Lucretius' Gigantomachic imagery is an odd omission from Innes 1979 on Gigantomachy and natural philosophy as literary themes.

Epicurus revises the Gigantomachy into a triumph not over the true gods but rather over tyrannical figments of the imagination—the superstitious beliefs held by the unenlightened majority. More successfully than any Giant, however, Epicurus raises all of us to the heavens: *nos exaequat uictoria caelo* (Lucr. 1.79). This is to be a Gigantomachy not of usurpation but of equality: the power of rational thought revealed by Epicurus enables each one of us to live a life of equanimity like the true gods themselves.[10]

In Book 5, Lucretius likens his own philosophical enterprise—specifically, the refutation of the belief in the immortality of the world—to Gigantomachy (Lucr. 5.113–21):

> multa tibi expediam doctis solacia dictis,
> religione refrenatus ne forte rearis
> terras et solem et caelum, mare sidera lunam,
> corpore diuino debere aeterna manere,
> proptereaque putes ritu par esse Gigantum
> pendere eos poenas inmani pro scelere omnis
> qui ratione sua disturbent moenia mundi
> praeclarumque uelint caeli restinguere solem
> immortalia mortali sermone notantes.

> I shall explain to you many consolations in learned words,
> so that by chance, bridled by superstition, you do not think
> that earth and sun and sky, sea, stars, and moon,
> are of divine body and must remain eternal
> and, therefore, you think it fair that, like the Giants,
> all those men are punished for their terrible crime—the ones
> who undermine the walls of the world by their own reasoning
> and wish to extinguish the bright sun in heaven,
> marking immortal things with mortal words.

When Lucretius infuses his philosophical iconoclasm with the violence of Gigantomachy through the images of 'undermining the walls of the world' and 'extinguishing the sun in heaven', he draws on a long-standing rhetorical motif within the philosophical tradition. The trope goes back at least as far as Plato's *Sophist*, in which the characters of Theaetetus and the Eleatic Stranger discuss the disagreement between materialists and idealists in terms of a Gigantomachy.[11] It's worth quoting the relevant passage at some length to illustrate the tradition inherited by Lucretius (Pl. *Soph.* 246a–c):

---

[10] For the claim that *ratio* can enable a life worthy of the gods, see Lucr. 3.319–22.
[11] On the literariness of the trope in the *Sophist* see Gigandet 1998: 329–30, Volk 2001: 103, Boys-Stones 2010: 36–9; on its philosophical significance see Brown 1998.

STRANGER: Moreover, there appears to be a kind of Gigantomachy going on amongst them on account of their dispute about being.
THEAETETUS: How so?
STRANGER: Some drag everything down to earth from heaven and the unseen, simply grasping rocks and oaks with their hands. For laying hold of all these things they confidently affirm this—that only things which can be handled or touched have being, because they define body and being as the same. And if anyone on the other side says that something without body has being, they utterly despise him and refuse to hear anything else.
THEAETETUS: Yes, you speak of terrible men: for I myself have often met with many of these.
STRANGER: For that reason those who dispute with them defend themselves very cautiously from above, from somewhere invisible, and vehemently contend that various mental and bodiless forms are real being; then with their arguments they break into small pieces the bodies of the other side and what the others call truth, instead calling it generation in motion rather than being. Between the two sides, Theaetetus, an immense battle over these things has always been waged.

The Giants, with their violent physicality and their attempt to overthrow Olympus, make for an apt mythical analogue for materialist philosophers, who seek to reduce heavenly things, such as the soul or the Forms, to entirely physical entities. The presentation of their position is laced with the moral judgement of the speakers, who attribute to the materialists an attitude of contempt (καταφρονοῦντες, *Soph.* 246b), and who see them as 'terrible men' (δεινοὺς ἄνδρας, 246b). By contrast, the nonmaterialists act cautiously (εὐλαβῶς, *Soph.* 246b) and occupy a strong position (ἄνωθεν ἐξ ἀοράτου, lit. 'from above, out of the invisible', 246b), which allows them to destroy their opponents' arguments (κατὰ σμικρὰ διαθραύοντες, 246c).[12] Thus, the impression of strength created by the comparison with the Giants quickly dissolves into weakness and failure. And yet, despite the decisiveness of the victory projected here, the conflict goes on. Indeed, the argument continues long after Plato not only in Lucretius' vision of the materialist Gigantomachy, in which he, unlike the Eleatic Stranger, sides with the Giants, but even in the *Thebaid*, as we shall see in Chapter 8.[13]

Lucretius claims that those who mistakenly hold a superstitious belief in the eternity of the world regard materialist philosophers like himself as impious, like the Giants. With its resolutely moral vocabulary (*ritu, poenas, scelere*), the

---

[12] Plato's κατὰ σμικρὰ plays on the atomism of the materialists, who get a taste of their own medicine. On the overvaluing of the material world and vulnerability to the invisible, see the discussion of Ovid's Niobe in Chapter 3.

[13] Volk 2001: 104–6 provides other examples of the trope, including the Lucretius passage.

passage implies that it is wrong to condemn materialist philosophers for supposed impiety, because that conception of impiety is founded upon a scientific error.[14] Lucretius thus reclaims the metaphor from Plato and gives it new value: Gigantomachy becomes a symbol of independence, rationalism, and resistance to the superstitions and prejudices of the ignorant. Lucretius practically reverses each and every point made in the *Sophist*: materialist philosophers are pious, not terrible; prudent, not reckless; deeply familiar with the realm of the invisible; and capable of breaking into small pieces not only others' arguments but also the very fabric of the world—for what could better describe their theory of atoms?

The combination of mythology and philosophy in the Gigantomachic metaphor has a further, aesthetic, effect—sublimity. The concept of the sublime—literally one of elevation, but traditionally also associated with transformative feelings of awe and revelation—has recently returned to the centre of scholarly discussions about the history of aesthetics and many of its major theorists, such as Kant and Burke.[15] Lucretius, in particular, has newly emerged as a key figure in the history of the sublime, who offers an important complement and contrast to Longinus' emphatically rhetorical, though in its own way also philosophical, treatment of the concept in the *Peri Hypsous*.[16] Lucretius' Gigantomachic metaphor offers an excellent example of the multiple aspects of the sublime: the image of the elevated philosopher flying in the face of the elements, as Epicurus does in Book 1, combined with the scientific revelation of the true nature of the world, replaces the sense of awe traditionally associated with religious experience with something new yet equally profound—the experience of the natural world both in all its vastness and in its minute, even invisible, detail.

For the subsequent history of theomachy these three aspects of Lucretius' Gigantomachic metaphor will be crucial—the revaluation of piety and impiety, the positing of a world made up of only material entities, and the sublimity of the poet's idiom and imagery. For epic, in particular, the Lucretian perspective proves especially fruitful as it allows poets to debate the moral robustness of the worlds they create—to ask how secure the theological

---

[14] Lucretius signals his reconception of impiety from the beginning of his work: *illud in his rebus uereor, ne forte rearis / impia te rationis inire elementa uiamque / indugredi sceleris. quod contra saepius illa / religio peperit scelerosa atque impia facta* ('In these matters I fear one thing, that you perhaps think you are embarking on the impious education of reason and entering on a path of crime. But in fact that very superstition has more often given birth to wicked and impious deeds', Lucr. 1.80-3). Lucretius supports this claim with the example of the sacrifice of Iphigenia to enable the Greek fleet to sail from Aulis.

[15] See pp. 13-14.

[16] See Conte 1994: 1-34, Porter 2007, Hardie 2009b (especially good on the reception of the Lucretian sublime in Latin literature), and Most 2012 on the relation of the Lucretian sublime to Longinus and its relevance to the modern art of Rothko, Newman, and others. On Longinus see, e.g., Halliwell 2012: 327-67, and Chapter 4.

framework that shapes our conceptions of right and wrong is—and to treat the very concept of fiction in a more sophisticated way. Later poets use the language and imagery provided by Lucretius to draw the reader's attention to the immaterial creations that sustain the illusory world of epic. The reader is thus invited to engage the fiction on an entirely new cognitive level, on which one is repeatedly driven to question the different implications of the world being like one thing or another. Theomachy provides a congenial, effective, and, above all, sublime idiom with which to shock and inspire the audience, bringing before their eyes an ostentatiously philosophical vision of the world, and in the process turning an epic topos into a moment of extraordinary intellectual power. In the history of theomachy, the full effect of Lucretius' legacy will only be felt in the works of later authors, most of all Statius. But the key figure who makes Lucretius of such importance to the epic system is Vergil, and so it is to the *Aeneid* that we now turn.

Epicureanism, Fiction, and Fama in *Aeneid* 4

Many Vergilian scholars have debated the significance of the concentration of Epicurean resonances in Book 4.[17] Vergil's ancient commentator Servius already noted several lines that allude to Epicurean ideas, such as the non-existence of the afterlife and the disinterest of the gods in human affairs. The characters who speak these lines, however—Anna, Dido, and Iarbas—behave in distinctively un-Epicurean ways: they offer sacrifices, act passionately, and appeal to the gods. The trio do not showcase Epicureanism, then, so much as misguidedly appropriate or ironically imitate its ideas. Were they more fully fledged Epicureans, indeed, one cannot help but think they would be far better off: Anna, one imagines, would warn Dido off the mental disturbances caused by romance, while Dido would react rather more phlegmatically to Aeneas' departure. The unfortunate casualty of this newfound equanimity, of course, would be the epic itself, left in tatters by the indifference of its erstwhile romantic martyrs. In order for Roman history to progress as it needs to, complete with Carthaginian enmity, it requires more impetus and conflict than an Epicurean outlook can generate. It is difficult to know, then, whether the characters' inconsistencies are designed to parody Epicureanism (i.e., because its adherents are hypocrites) or to defend it on the grounds that the characters themselves, at least, would benefit from following through on their rhetoric. In either case, however, the similarity across all three figures suggests that Vergil deliberately placed Epicurean slogans in the mouths of distinctively un-Epicurean characters. Whatever the reasons for this decision, its effect is to

---

[17] E.g., Adler 2003: 103–33, P. Gordon 1998, J. T. Dyson 1996.

prompt further questions about how and why Epicureanism is being deployed in this unexpected way.

The Epicurean allusions also form a striking contrast with the numerous passages in which the gods and the shades of the dead appear thoroughly invested in what happens on earth. At one level, then, the supernatural action of the poem simply explodes Epicurean claims. It is equally possible, however, to see the Epicurean allusions putting pressure on the audience's suspension of disbelief—do gods really come down in person to give orders to mortals? And if they do not, what does that mean for an interpretation of the poem? Through the further Epicurean voices of its North African characters, the whole Carthage episode proves a distraction not only from the mission of Rome's foundation but also from the theological premises grounding the plot of the poem and Roman history.[18]

Of particular relevance to these questions is Vergil's description of Fama, a personification of rumour and sibling of the Giants who incites Iarbas not only to anger but also to his Epicurean rhetoric. This network of relations, especially in conjunction with allusions to the *De Rerum Natura*, has recently received rich and detailed commentary from Philip Hardie.[19] Whereas Hardie's interests lie in the aesthetics of the sublime and in Fama herself, however, my concern is rather with the indirect way in which Vergil approaches the subject of theomachy, a topic further developed in the following sections. Finally, it should be noted that several issues raised here will play an especially important role in the discussions of later authors, in particular Ovid and Statius.

The Epicurean flavour of Book 4 is established early on.[20] In a speech designed to assuage Dido's anxiety about keeping faith with her dead husband, Anna rejects the hold exerted by the deceased: *id cinerem aut manis credis curare sepultos?* ('do you believe that ashes or buried shades are concerned with that?', *Aen.* 4.34). Servius long ago noted Anna's debt to Epicurean beliefs: *dicit autem secundum Epicureos, qui animam cum corpore dicunt perire* ('moreover, she says this following the Epicureans, who say that the soul dies with the body', Serv. ad loc.). Even more flavoured with Epicureanism is Dido's scepticism that the gods would trouble themselves to order Aeneas to leave Carthage (*Aen.* 4.376–80):[21]

---

[18] Hardie 2007b: 116.

[19] Vergil's Fama represents a leitmotif of Hardie's work, but the principal discussions are Hardie 2009b: 67–135 and 2012: 78–125.

[20] For the Epicurean associations of Carthage even in Book 1, especially in the curiously scientific song of the bard Iopas (*Aen.* 1.742–6), see P. Gordon 2012: 63–5, Mellinghoff-Bourgerie 1990: 27–8. On Iopas in general see Nelis 2001: 96–112.

[21] Cf. Serv. ad *Aen.* 4.379, who again points out the Epicurean background.

>   nunc augur Apollo,
> nunc Lyciae sortes, nunc et Ioue missus ab ipso
> interpres diuum fert horrida iussa per auras.
> scilicet is superis labor est, ea cura quietos
> sollicitat.
>
>   Now the augur Apollo,
> now the Lycian fates, now, sent by Jupiter himself,
> the messenger of the gods bears terrible orders through the air.
> Clearly this is a task for gods, this care disturbs
> their calm!

Both sisters' sarcastic challenges, however, merely parody Epicureanism proper, as Anna ends her speech by asking Dido to propitiate the gods with a sacrifice, while the impassioned Dido could not be further from the *ataraxia* prized by Epicureans.[22] Furthermore, the poem appears to offer a comprehensive rejoinder to any Epicurean doubts by showing Jupiter giving instructions to Mercury, and Mercury consequently accosting Aeneas. Book 6 will further depict an afterlife in which the spirits of dead, especially Anchises, very much concern themselves with what happens on earth. If the scepticism of Anna and Dido poses any threat to the integrity of the epic fiction, the effect is safely minimised when set against the frequency and importance of supernatural action throughout the poem. The sisters' Epicurean rhetoric sits at odds with an epic that not only includes Mercury and the spirit of Anchises but also begins with Juno's anger and ends with the indignation of Turnus' shade.

That same tension between Epicurean doubt and epic convention can be seen in the clearest allusion to Epicureanism in the poem, a speech by Iarbas addressing his father, Jupiter, also in Book 4. Hearing the rumour of Dido's affair with Aeneas, Iarbas complains that his proposal of marriage was rejected in favour of this effeminate foreigner, despite his many offerings to the god. The apparent inefficacy of sacrifice leads to far-reaching doubts (*Aen.* 4.208–10):

>   an te, genitor, cum fulmina torques
> nequiquam horremus, caecique in nubibus ignes
> terrificant animos et inania murmura miscent?
>
>   Or do we shudder in vain, father,
> when you hurl your thunderbolts, and are the fires in the clouds unseeing
> that terrify our minds and stir up empty rumblings?

---

[22] See Adler 2003: 115–16.

Servius again spells out the source of such rhetoric: TERRIFICANT ANIMOS ET RELIQUA *latenter secundum Epicureos locutus est* ('TERRIFY OUR MINDS ETC. He said this latently following Epicurus', Serv. ad *Aen*. 4.210). The rationalisation of lightning as a purely meteorological, and not theological, phenomenon was indeed a central concern in the *De Rerum Natura* (Lucr. 6.379–422), since even incipient Epicureans can fall back on superstitious beliefs in the face of terrible storms (Lucr. 6.50–67).[23] Iarbas is no pupil of the Garden, however, with his belief in his divine ancestry and lavish displays of religiosity. There is little reason, then, to see his rhetoric as anything more than a sign of frustration, a challenge intended to provoke Jupiter into responding and thereby validating the beliefs and rituals of his son. When Iarbas ends his speech on a similarly scathing note, he expects action, not silence: *nos munera templis / quippe tuis ferimus famamque fouemus inanem* ('we bring gifts to "your" temples, indeed, and foster your empty reputation', *Aen*. 4.217–18).[24] The response is instantaneous, dramatic, and utterly un-Epicurean (*Aen*. 4.219–21):[25]

> talibus orantem dictis arasque tenentem
> audiit Omnipotens, oculosque ad moenia torsit
> regia.
>
> As he was uttering these prayers and grasping the altars,
> the Almighty heard, and turned his gaze to the royal
> walls.

As with the Epicurean language of Anna and Dido, any suspicions raised by Iarbas' rhetoric are emphatically quashed both by the fact of his own religiosity and by the acute responsiveness of the gods.

Where Iarbas differs from Anna and Dido, however, is in the larger context of his speech, especially the appearance and effect of Fama described immediately beforehand. This monstrous personification of rumour, introduced at 4.173, spreads the story of Dido's affair and incites the jealousy of Iarbas: *incenditque animum dictis atque aggerat iras* ('she fires up his spirit with words and builds up his anger', *Aen*. 4.197). Beyond this more general effect, however, it's important to recognise the presence of *fama* within Iarbas' speech, in the closing line that speaks caustically of Jupiter's 'empty reputation' (*famam inanem*, *Aen*. 4.218). In drawing this direct, verbal

---

[23] See, esp., *ignorantia causarum conferre deorum / cogit ad imperium res et concedere regnum* ('ignorance of causes compels them to attribute things to the power of the gods and to concede their tyranny', Lucr. 6.54–5).

[24] The combination of *fama* here with *fulmina* and *murmura* above alludes to Lucretius' heroic image of Epicurus: *quem neque fama deum nec fulmina nec minitanti / murmure compressit caelum* ('whom neither stories of the gods nor thunderbolts nor heaven with its threatening roar held back', Lucr. 1.68–9). See Hardie 2012: 88–9.

[25] Hardie 1999: 99.

connection between Fama and Iarbas' sceptical rhetoric, Vergil raises important questions about the relationship between her and the gods. As Hardie has shown, Fama is, on the one hand, complicit with the will of Jupiter, even to the extent of foreshadowing and facilitating the subsequent actions of Jupiter and Mercury immediately following Iarbas' speech.[26] On the other hand, however, she represents misleading utterances of all kinds: *tam ficti prauique tenax quam nuntia ueri* ('clinging to falsehood and perversity as much as she announces the truth', *Aen.* 4.188). It is in that sense of a lie that Iarbas uses the word *fama* to provoke Jupiter—the god has been reduced to a mere rumour, fleeting and unreliable. The deployment of *fama* against the gods, however rhetorically intended by Iarbas, suits the personification very well. For as a sister of the Giants she shares their antagonism towards the Olympian gods (*Aen.* 4.178–80):[27]

> illam Terra parens ira inritata deorum
> extremam, ut perhibent, Coeo Enceladoque sororem
> progenuit.

> Mother Earth, incited to anger against the gods,
> bore her last, so they say, a sister to Coeus
> and Enceladus.

And yet Fama is also much more than a Giant. Indeed, the word *extremam*, which refers to extremity of degree as well of time and space, hints to that effect.[28] Whereas the Giants' purely physical threat to the gods was soundly defeated, Fama poses a more troubling conceptual threat—she inspires scepticism regarding their existence.

Fama has one further connection to Iarbas' speech that makes her kinship with the Giants of greater significance. As Hardie has identified, Vergil's description of Fama's movement (*mobilitate uiget uirisque adquirit eundo*, 'she thrives with motion and gains strength as she goes', *Aen.* 4.175) clearly alludes to Lucretius' account of the thunderbolt (Lucr. 6.340–2):[29]

> denique quod longo uenit impete, sumere debet
> mobilitatem etiam atque etiam, quae crescit eundo
> et ualidas auget uiris et roborat ictum

---

[26] Hardie 2012: 104–5.

[27] The immediately preceding description of her immense size and reach seems to precipitate the mention of the Giants: *mox sese attollit in auras / ingrediturque solo et caput inter nubila condit* ('soon she has raised herself into the air, and while she strides on the ground her head is hidden among the clouds', *Aen.* 4.176–7). See also Hardie 2009b: 88–93 and 2012: 99–100. On the ambiguity of *deorum* at 4.178 see Hardie 2009b: 72 n. 13.

[28] *OLD* s.v. *extremus* 4.

[29] Hardie 2009b: 71–2.

> Then, because it moves with sustained impetus, it must take up
> speed again and again, which increases as it goes
> and augments its powerful force and strengthens its impact.

These lines appear in the long section of the *De Rerum Natura* designed to offer a rational account of lightning, the same account that informs Iarbas' provocation of Jupiter at *Aen.* 4.208–10. What we have in the Lucretian-tinged description of Fama, then, is not only an ironic coupling of scientific rationalism (Lucretius' thunderbolt) with mythological personification (Fama's proverbial speed) but also a source for that same coupling in Iarbas, a resoundingly mythological son of Jupiter who nevertheless speaks like an Epicurean.[30] Fama thus spreads to the African king not only the rumour of Dido's affair but also something of her own paradoxically Lucretian nature. With his divine ancestry and superabundance of temples and sacrifices, Iarbas makes for an improbable theomach indeed. And, of course, he is no true theomach. Rather, he sounds like a belligerent version of Epicurus in part because he has been touched by Fama, a sister of the Giants who is herself described in Lucretian terms. Lucretius' materialist theomachy has thus come into this portion of the *Aeneid* in a highly counterintuitive way, transmitted by two very un-Epicurean figures in Fama and Iarbas.

Fama is a strikingly ambivalent entity—on the one hand lavishly mythologised, but on the other hand carrying on the work of Lucretius' demythologising Gigantomachy. But while the Giants represent powerful forces of disorder, their violence is simply directed outwards. In the case of Fama, by contrast, this tendency threatens to become self-destructive, even incoherent. For her capacity to cast doubt on the authority of Jupiter through the words of Iarbas not only affects the gods but can equally be turned on herself.[31] Her vivid personification easily collapses into pure and unsubstantial allegory—Fama becomes mere *fama*.[32] This doubleness is only to be expected, since the very nature of Fama makes her as likely to create one fiction as to undermine another. That sense of the uncontrollable and unknowable poses a real problem for a work such as the *Aeneid* that aspires to offer a particular, albeit nuanced, account of the world (*fama* as national tradition) and to avoid collapsing in a welter of competing, and ultimately undifferentiated, points of view (*fama* as mere rumour).[33] For while Fama is the means of establishing and consolidating a version of events through extension in space and time, by definition she

---

[30] Hardie 2012: 90. For further similarities between Fama and Iarbas see Hardie 2009b: 74–5.

[31] Hardie 2009b: 87.

[32] Note that when focalised through Jupiter's eyes, only three lines after Iarbas' pejorative use of the word, *fama* has its more positive meaning of 'fame': *oculosque ad moenia torsit / regia et oblitos famae melioris amantis* ('he turned his gaze to the royal city and the lovers forgetful of a better fame', *Aen.* 4.220–1). Jupiter thus restores Fama, for a time at least, to her purely abstract and non-threatening form even as the process she has fuelled continues unabated.

[33] Cf. Hardie 2009b: 85.

cannot grant any authority to a story or narrative, and she even threatens to undermine whatever authority might previously have belonged to such a narrative. In this way she figures the doubleness of all poetic fictions, which invite a suspension of disbelief while always remaining one step removed from the audience's material and, at one level, more credible world. Thus her presence in the text, whether she is conceived as complicit with or antagonistic to the gods, weakens the foundations upon which any confident reading of the poem's supernatural action, and indeed of the epic as a whole, can be based.

Once thought of as a product of Fama, as any utterance must be, fact becomes inextricably enmeshed with fiction, which has serious implications for epic, the poetry of fame and divine authority. Fama's stirring of Iarbas is bound up with this complex of myth-making and truth-destroying effects. Fama not only transmits a further, Lucretian voice—through her own similarity to the Lucretian *fulmen* and the effect on Iarbas' Epicurean outburst— she also threatens to recapitulate with greater success the Gigantomachy of her siblings, and of Epicurus too. For, rather than engaging in a head-on confrontation with the gods, as the Giants did, she instead contaminates the authority of the epic poet, the very authority that had previously relied upon, and in turn validated, the gods themselves. Vergil thus makes Iarbas' theomachic moment not only a product of Epicureanism but also—even earlier—an effect of Fama, a power that is at once fundamental to epic and yet deeply threatening to its working assumptions. As we shall see in subsequent chapters, the role of theomachy in scrutinising those assumptions represents an important part of Vergil's legacy to later poets.

The Theomach Manqué

The closest Vergil comes to putting a theomach amidst the action of the *Aeneid* is via the figure of Mezentius, twice describing the hero as a 'despiser of the gods' (*contemptor diuum*, *Aen.* 7.648; *contemptor deum*, *Aen.* 8.7).[34] Servius has this to say about the epithet: CONTEMPTORQUE DEUM MEZENTIUS *quis enim iustius quam sacrilegus contra pios et praepararet bellum et gereret?* ('MEZENTIUS DESPISER OF THE GODS For who could be more appropriate than a sacrilegious person to prepare and wage war against

---

[34] Vergil briefly mentions two other theomachs outside the main plot, who nevertheless appear in important locations in the poem. The description of Salmoneus in the underworld and his imitation of Jupiter (*Aen.* 6.585–94) marks the transition from the Giants to the proverbial sinners, Tityus, Ixion, and the rest. On Salmoneus see pp. 246–8, esp. n. 40. Near the beginning of the epic, Juno ends her speech by citing Pallas' destruction of Locrian Ajax. The image of Pallas using Jupiter's thunderbolt foreshadows Aeneas' Jupiter-like spear cast against Turnus at the end of the poem (cf. Hardie 1997c: 324 n. 27). *Serv. Dan.* ad 1.44 draws an intriguing connection between Vergil's representation of Ajax and a painting of Capaneus in a temple in Ardea (cf. Henderson 2000: 20–1). On Ajax see also Chapter 1.

the pious?' Serv. ad *Aen.* 8.7). The epithet will go hand in hand with the subsequent literary history of theomachy—applied to Ovid's Pentheus and Statius' Capaneus, for example—but in later uses it will almost invariably describe a more directly antagonistic relationship with the divine than that seen in the case of Mezentius. At most, Mezentius' opposition to Aeneas can be viewed as an indirect opposition to Jupiter, whose will is aligned with the interests of the Trojans.

A quick glance at the mythological figures with whom Mezentius is associated makes clear the difference between more and less explicitly theomachic characteristics. Homer's Polyphemus, for instance—savage and contemptuous of the gods—has long been viewed as an important source for the characterisation of Mezentius, but the Cyclops speaks far more confrontationally of Zeus than anything the Vergilian character says (*Od.* 9.273–8):[35]

> νήπιός εἰς, ὦ ξεῖν', ἢ τηλόθεν εἰλήλουθας,
> ὅς με θεοὺς κέλεαι ἢ δειδίμεν ἢ ἀλέασθαι.
> οὐ γὰρ Κύκλωπες Διὸς αἰγιόχου ἀλέγουσιν
> οὐδὲ θεῶν μακάρων, ἐπεὶ ἦ πολὺ φέρτεροί εἰμεν.
> οὐδ' ἂν ἐγὼ Διὸς ἔχθος ἀλευάμενος πεφιδοίμην
> οὔτε σεῦ οὔθ' ἑτάρων, εἰ μὴ θυμός με κελεύοι.

> You are a fool, stranger, or have come from afar,
> telling me to fear or avoid the gods.
> For the Cyclopes do not care for aegis-bearing Zeus
> nor the blessed gods, since we are far stronger.
> To avoid Zeus' enmity I would spare
> neither you nor your companions, unless my heart bid me.

Polyphemus' arrogance resembles that of many characters we shall come across in later chapters, but it has been much circumscribed in Mezentius, who never openly challenges the authority of Jupiter or claims superiority over the gods. The same scaling down is true of the simile comparing Mezentius to Orion (*Aen.* 10.762–8). Although the description of Orion's extraordinary size (*magnus*, *Aen.* 10.763; *supereminet*, *Aen.* 10.765) performs a typical function of similes, which is to cast Mezentius in hyperbolic terms, Vergil avoids any trace of the theomachic aspects of Orion's mythology, especially relating to Artemis.[36] Within the simile, however, one line alerts us to the ever-present,

---

[35] See Glenn 1971, and also Hardie 1986: 266–7, though I would slightly amend Hardie's claim on p. 266 that the 'impiety of Mezentius matches that of the Homeric Cyclops'. Jim Tatum reminds me that Polyphemus' impiety needs to be understood against the context of his descent and support from Poseidon (pers. comm.). The Cyclops has some limited justification for his attitude to Zeus, at least, given the tension between his divine father and uncle. Furthermore, Polyphemus' rhetoric sets up Odysseus as a theomach opposed to Poseidon.

[36] Some sources mention Orion competing with Artemis (Apollod. *Bibl.* 1.27), others his attempt to rape her (Aratus *Phaen.* 634–46). Cf. Sen. *HF* 12 and p. 120 with n. 9.

albeit distant, theomachic subtext: *ingrediturque solo et caput inter nubila condit* ('and while he strides on the ground his head is hidden among the clouds', Aen. 10.767). This line repeats word for word a line describing Fama (*Aen.* 4.177), which Hardie sees as a clear and deliberate connection not only between Orion and Fama but also including Mezentius and Polyphemus.[37] The pattern of association highlights the theomachic thread Vergil has sewn into his epic, yet at the same time the characterisation of Mezentius illustrates the deliberate limiting of theomachy in the poem's action and speech.

Mezentius' contempt for the gods corresponds to an improper and erroneous valuation of his own power: *dextra mihi deus et telum, quod missile libro, / nunc adsint!* ('now let my right hand, my god, and the weapon I poise to hurl, be favourable!' *Aen.* 10.773–4).[38] After the death of his son, Lausus, he makes his attitude to the gods more explicit still: *nec diuum parcimus ulli* ('nor do we show regard for any of the gods', *Aen.* 10.880).[39] But unlike Polyphemus or many of the later theomachs, Mezentius is willing to make certain concessions. Earlier in the scene, for example, he claims that his future lies in the hands of higher powers: *ast de me diuum pater atque hominum rex / uiderit* ('but about me the father of the gods and king of men will see', *Aen.* 10.743–4). And even his disregard for the gods needs to be placed in context: having seen Aeneas kill his son, his words express not so much impiety per se as the way in which grief can lead to an unbounded desire for vengeance.

Mezentius' limitations as a theomach are consistent with his declining physical powers. Despite his having the advantage of fighting on horseback against the unmounted Aeneas—Vergil describes the encounter as an 'unequal fight' (*pugna iniqua*, *Aen.* 10.889)—he is no match for his younger, stronger, and divinely armoured opponent.[40] Indeed, Vergil leaves us in little doubt that Mezentius is in the autumn of his career. The Etruscan hero tells his horse, Rhaebus, that they have lived long: *diu . . . uiximus* (*Aen.* 10.861–2); taken together with the description of his long beard and grey hair (*Aen.* 10.838, 844), and the fact that his son Lausus is of leadership and fighting age, the poet clearly conveys the impression of a warrior still strong, yet beyond his prime.[41]

---

[37] Hardie 2012: 99. Conte 2007: 163–6 emphasises Mezentius' monstrous and primeval associations as part of a larger argument for the moral complexity and capaciousness of the *Aeneid*. It's important to recognise, however, that it is far easier to be inclusive of, and humane towards, an opponent who poses little threat.

[38] Mezentius' divinisation of his spear arm alludes to a tradition that includes Aeschylus' Parthenopaeus (*Sept.* 529–30) and Apollonius' Idas (Ap. Rhod. 1.466–8), on which see S. J. Harrison 1991: 258, and that will continue with Silius' Flaminius and Statius' Capaneus.

[39] For the translation of *parcimus* as 'show regard for' see S. J. Harrison 1991: 278. See also Thome 1979: 155–6 and n. 402. Cf. Quint 2001: 57–8 for Mezentius replaying the role of the theomachic Patroclus.

[40] On the reception of this scene in the *Thebaid* see Chapter 8.

[41] The question of one's prime is a recurring feature of the second half the *Aeneid*. Evander regrets his old age and the consequent necessity for the young Pallas to fight (*Aen.* 8.560–71), and after his son's death he claims that if Pallas had been in his prime he would have defeated Turnus (*Aen.* 11.173–5). Whether this claim is true or merely the emotional words of a bereaved yet proud father, nevertheless

Not even the strongest theomach offers a seriously credible challenge to the gods, but Mezentius cannot offer one even to a mortal.

Mezentius' impiety lies not only in his lack of concern for the divine but also in his tyrannical rule, at least as reported by Evander: *quid memorem infandas caedes, quid facta tyranni / effera?* ('why should I recall the unspeakable slaughter, why the savage deeds of the tyrant?' *Aen.* 8.483–4).[42] The poet supports this negative judgement by contrasting Mezentius with his noble son Lausus, 'who deserves to be happier than under his father's rule and to have a father not at all like Mezentius' (*dignus patriis qui laetior esset / imperiis et cui pater haud Mezentius esset, Aen.* 7.653–4). The specific attack on Mezentius as a father suggests that the son's qualities have escaped paternal influence. The disjunction of father and son only highlights the tragedy of the latter's death when Lausus intervenes to save his father from Aeneas, thus wasting a good life for the sake of a bad one. But, as several critics have noted, the evidence of Book 10 paints a somewhat different picture of Mezentius—a brave warrior for whom death holds no fear, and whose speech provides some of the most reflective and moving moments of the poem.[43]

The most recent and vigorous defence of Mezentius comes from Leah Kronenberg, who emphasises the standard caveats about the negative assessment of the hero. Evander's account of Mezentius' cruelty, for instance, is never corroborated, and it is in any case subject to the natural prejudice arising from the lengthy war between the Arcadians and Latins (*Aen.* 8.55 and 8.472–4).[44] Kronenberg's principal goal, however, is to offer a radical allegorical reading of Mezentius as a kind of Epicurean, which contributes to an Epicurean reading of the whole poem. Her evidence is mainly drawn from Mezentius' attitude to death, his equanimity, and various intertexts with Lucretius and Philodemus.[45] She also explains Evander's allegation of Mezentius' method of torture (*Aen.* 8.485–8) as a philosophical allegory of materialism: Mezentius' binding of dead bodies to the living, as various passages from Aristotle and Cicero suggest, represents the Epicurean denial of the immateriality and immortality of the soul.[46] On Kronenberg's reading, then, Epicurean materialism has been rhetorically redefined as torture—the binding together of what should be

it raises the question of the timing of one's involvement in events. Apollo permits the young Ascanius one deadly intervention in the war before ordering him to cease because he is too young (*Aen.* 9.653–6). And, perhaps most importantly, the repeated stress on Turnus' youth (called *iuuenis* fourteen times, at *Aen.* 7.420, 435, 446, 456; 9.16, 806; 10.623, 686; 11.123, 530, 897; 12.19, 149, 598; *iuuentae* 7.473) assimilates him to the other doomed young warriors, Euryalus, Pallas, and Lausus, and suggests that he cannot hope to have parity with the seasoned combatant Aeneas. Behind Juno's use of *iuuenem* lies this pattern of fateful timing: *nunc iuuenem imparibus uideo concurrere fatis* ('now I see the young man meeting unequal fates', *Aen.* 12.149).

[42] For the traditional association of tyranny with impiety see, e.g., Pl. *Resp.* 568d7–8, 574d4–5, 575b7, and Chapter 9.
[43] See Thome 1979, Gotoff 1984.
[44] Cf. Kronenberg 2005: 408–10.
[45] Kronenberg 2005: 411–24.
[46] Kronenberg 2005: 408–10.

regarded as separate—and an ultimately philosophical difference has been distorted to serve Evander's own ends.

Kronenberg argues that an Epicurean reading of Mezentius destabilises conventional values of piety and impiety, just as we saw in the case of Lucretius. So, for instance, an Epicurean perspective not only undermines a simplistic notion of Mezentius' impiety, it also affects one's attitude to Aeneas' proverbial piety. Aeneas' rampage in Book 10, his offering of human sacrifice (*Aen.* 10.517–20), and the furious killing of Turnus at the end of the poem could hardly be further from Epicurean piety.[47] As Kronenberg acknowledges, however, even if her argument about Mezentius is true, the consequent reading of piety and impiety can claim no more authority than the alternatives that cast him as a savage and tyrannical figure.[48] In fact, the distinctly un-Epicurean world of the *Aeneid*, with its interventionist gods and largely fulfilled prophecies, militates against an Epicurean view.[49] Just as Mezentius opposes the fated and divinely appointed foreign leader of the Etruscans—Aeneas—and therefore indirectly opposes the gods themselves, so his Epicureanism seems to go against the poet's vision of the world to which he belongs. In this way, Mezentius continues the Epicurean associations and inconsistencies of the characters in Book 4, though far less openly and confrontationally.[50] If Mezentius puts in play a different way of looking at the poem, as Kronenberg suggests, he does so through the accumulation of such points of view rather than in isolation, and always with the possibility that those points of view are meant to be seen as in some way mistaken.

Mezentius raises the spectre of theomachy, but he is drained of much power: he doesn't go to the extremes that paradigmatic theomachs do, he is past his prime, and his philosophical attitude, such as it is, is relatively unthreatening. One critic, however, has offered a reading of Mezentius that suggests a new way of thinking about theomachy and its relation to philosophy. Before Kronenberg's expansive Epicurean reading of Mezentius, Antonio La Penna had already briefly suggested a similar idea, though he saw in the Etruscan's proud independence from the gods not Epicureanism in particular but rather an

---

[47] Kronenberg 2005: 425–8. On the allowances and limits of anger according to the Epicureans see Fowler 1997. Aeneas' distance from Epicureanism may also emerge from his seeing the 'strangely pale face' (*ora modis ... pallentia miris, Aen.* 10.822) of the dying Lausus. As Stover 2011: 356 and n. 26 notes, the phrase alludes to Vergil's own treatment of civil war at *G.* 1.477 as well as to Lucretius' ironic report of Ennius' account of phantoms in the underworld at Lucr. 1.123. What critics have not observed, however, is that Aeneas, while drawing on Lucretius' own ironic language, here views Lausus in a precisely anti-Epicurean way and in pointed opposition to Mezentius' Epicureanesque attitude to death. Vergil thus harnesses the tools of focalisation and intertextuality to figure a larger metaphysical conflict. On the Aeneas-Lausus scene in general see Putnam 1995: 135–40.

[48] See Kronenberg 2005: 408.

[49] Though see O'Hara 1990 on the problems pertaining to the prophecies in the poem.

[50] In that context, it's worth noting that the echo of Fama in the Orion simile may suggest the continuing, permeating effect of her Epicurean qualities.

attitude common to Epicureanism and Stoicism.[51] La Penna cites several passages, mostly from Seneca, that conceive of the *sapiens* as equal to or even surpassing the gods.[52] Whether or not La Penna is right to see these passages as a relevant context for understanding Mezentius, they do suggest one way in which the character might exceed, rather than fall short of, his theomachic predecessors, such as Polyphemus or Orion or the Giants. For however powerful and direct their opposition to the divine, the status quo is never really threatened. Mezentius may be far weaker, and far less confrontational, but read as a figure for philosophical autonomy he points to a completely different way of conceiving of theomachy—not as a physical or verbal contest against the gods but as a more effective means of equalling or bettering them. Mezentius' calm disregard for the gods may be more potent than any direct attack could ever be.[53]

Vergil's subduing of human-divine theomachy is most explicit in Book 11. When the Latins return from their embassy to Diomedes, the audience waits to hear whether the hero, one of the theomachs of the *Iliad*, will join the Italian war.[54] Finally, perhaps, Aeneas will meet an opponent worthy of him, one from whom he had to be saved in the *Iliad*, and by whom Aeneas wishes to have been killed in his despairing speech amidst the storm of Book 1 (*Aen.* 1.96–8):[55]

> o Danaum fortissime gentis
> Tydide! mene Iliacis occumbere campis
> non potuisse, tuaque animam hanc effundere dextra ...
>
> O bravest of the race of Greeks,
> son of Tydeus! Could I not have fallen on the plains
> of Ilion, and poured out this life at your hands ...

The audience knows perfectly well, of course, that Diomedes played no part in the Italian war, but Vergil uses the opportunity to banish any persistent Homeric memories of an Aeneas bested by Diomedes, from whom he had to be saved by the interventions first of his mother, Aphrodite, then of Apollo.[56] Vergil's awareness of Diomedes' superiority over Aeneas in the *Iliad* had emerged already at the end of Book 1, when in a memorable social faux pas Dido asks 'of what sort were the horses of Diomedes' (*quales Diomedis equi*, *Aen.* 1.752). These were, of course, once the prized horses of Aeneas before Diomedes

---

[51] La Penna 1999: 364–7.
[52] La Penna 1999: 365–6.
[53] This reading aligns Mezentius more closely with the kind of philosophical theomachy earlier attributed to Lucretius. By the time of Seneca's *Hercules Furens*, discussed in Chapter 4, there will be an even clearer case for the interplay of philosophical autonomy and theomachy.
[54] On Vergil's overall handling of Diomedes see Fletcher 2006, Nehrkorn 1971.
[55] Cf. Stahl 1981: 162–4, Lyne 1987: 132–5.
[56] For Aeneas' two near escapes from Diomedes see *Il.* 5.297–318, 431–53, and Chapter 1.

seized them, a fact of which Dido seems amusingly unaware despite her detailed knowledge of the Trojan War.[57]

Against this background, Vergil relates Diomedes' speech to the Latins as a palinode for his Homeric self. Full of disproportionately high praise for Aeneas, and following his heroic feats in battle in Book 10, the speech attempts to rehabilitate and consolidate the reputation of Aeneas in light of the *Iliad* (*Aen.* 11.282–7):

> stetimus tela aspera contra
> contulimusque manus: experto credite quantus
> in clipeum adsurgat, quo turbine torqueat hastam.
> si duo praeterea talis Idaea tulisset
> terra uiros, ultro Inachias uenisset ad urbes
> Dardanus, et uersis lugeret Graecia fatis.

> We have stood against his hard weapons
> and fought him hand-to-hand: trust that I know how large
> he looms over his shield, with what whirlwind force he hurls his spear.
> Had the land of Ida borne two such men besides,
> now the Dardanians would have reached Inachian cities,
> and Greece would be mourning their changed fates.

One could be forgiven for thinking that the intervening years have taken their toll on Diomedes' memory. The passage serves Vergil, however, rather better than it does the quoted speaker. The speech nods to Vergil's fashioning of all of Roman history as itself a kind of epic. For the Trojans would indeed conquer Greece with more men like Aeneas—once they became known as the Aeneadae, the Roman descendants of Aeneas. At the same time, Vergil elevates his own hero—and revises the Homeric narrative—through Diomedes' hard-earned wisdom, thus enabling the *Aeneid* and its protagonist to rise to the mark set by the *Iliad* and its Achilles. The last phase of the Italian war sees many of the warriors allude to, and recapitulate, the heroic identities of the *Iliad*, but despite their pretensions all will fall short of Achilles bar Aeneas himself.[58]

But Diomedes' palinode does more than magnify Aeneas and his descendants. After Aphrodite has been wounded by Diomedes, she flees to Olympus, where Dione reassures her of the inevitable disaster that befalls all theomachs, even those assisted by the gods. Diomedes, as we have seen, strains at human limits, but unlike Patroclus and Achilles shows more respect for the ultimate boundary between gods and mortals. Nevertheless, Vergil here presents

---

[57] Jim Tatum points out to me that Dido's question may be better understood not as a gauche misstep but rather as part of her characteristic repetition compulsion, which leads her to ask for stories she already knows (pers. comm.).

[58] Cf. Quint 1989: 35–43, 2001; Stahl 1981: 163.

Diomedes in a very different light. The hero regards his exile and the transformation of his companions into birds as punishment for his impious transgressions, especially his Iliadic theomachy, thus verifying what Dione had already predicted (*Aen.* 11.275–8):[59]

> haec adeo ex illo mihi iam speranda fuerunt
> tempore cum ferro caelestia corpora demens
> appetii et Veneris uiolaui uulnere dextram.
> ne uero, ne me ad talis impellite pugnas.
>
> I should really have expected all this from that very
> moment when, madly, I attacked divine bodies with my spear
> and injured Venus' hand with a wound.
> Do not, indeed, do not drive me to such battles.

No matter how integral to the fame of the hero, theomachy will have no place in this epic.[60] Indeed, Diomedes will go on to make piety a fundamental element of Aeneas' excellence, as if to further emphasise the contrast between Homeric and Vergilian heroism.[61] Piety will even elevate Aeneas above Hector: *ambo animis, ambo insignes praestantibus armis, / hic pietate prior* ('Both were outstanding in courage, both in excellence of arms, but this one in piety', *Aen.* 11.291–2). There could be no more profound recognition of the importance of Aeneas' piety than by the reformed *impius Tydides* (*Aen.* 2.163–4), the now remorseful theomach.

Thus, at the end of Book 10 and early in Book 11, Vergil offers his audience two versions of the theomach manqué—Mezentius, who cannot live up to his own billing as *contemptor deum*, and Diomedes, who has learned the folly of that course. In both cases, but especially in Diomedes' speech, Vergil suggests a further reason for the absence or failure of the theomach. When Diomedes says that he wishes to avoid 'such battles', he makes it sound as if a confrontation with Aeneas resembles his earlier encounter with Venus. Now, this could simply imply that the Trojans have divine support, as indeed they do, but his emphasis on Aeneas' power and excellence in particular suggests that to fight Aeneas is itself a kind of theomachy, and not merely because Venus may once again enter into battle. Jupiter confirms as much in Book 12 when he asks Juno what she hopes to achieve by her continued interference (*Aen.* 12.793–7):

---

[59] Cf. Stahl 1981: 173–4.
[60] In the divine council at the beginning of Book 10, Venus speaks sarcastically of being wounded by Diomedes again (*Aen.* 10.28–30). Although her tone is meant to convey outrage, it also highlights the implausibility of such an occurrence—this epic will not allow such things to happen.
[61] See Nehrkorn 1971: 575.

quae iam finis erit, coniunx? quid denique restat?
indigetem Aenean scis ipsa et scire fateris
deberi caelo fatisque ad sidera tolli.
quid struis? aut qua spe gelidis in nubibus haeres?
mortalin decuit uiolari uulnere diuum?

What now will be the end, wife? What at last remains?
You yourself know, and confess you know, that Aeneas as Indiges
is owed to heaven and is fated to be raised to the stars.
What are you devising? Or with what hope do you cling to the icy clouds?
Was it right that a god be injured by a mortal wound?

In echoing Diomedes' earlier phrase, *uiolaui uulnere*, Jupiter makes clear both that to fight Aeneas is to engage in Iliadic theomachy and that this would go a step too far for this epic, beyond even the extreme lengths to which Juno has so far been willing to go.[62] Moreover, in the subsequent duel with Turnus, we see a sign of Aeneas' elevated status in the comparison of his spear cast to a thunderbolt (*Aen.* 12.922–3), thereby aligning or identifying the hero with Jupiter.[63] Thus, Vergil changes the conditions of theomachy not only because the theomachs are no longer what they once were but also because in place of Olympian opponents we now find their proxy on earth.

Piety and Princeps

To say that Aeneas' alignment with Jupiter affects Vergil's handling of theomachy is to tell only half the story. For the elevation of Aeneas must be understood in the context of a larger religious, political, and cultural transformation at Rome whereby Augustus himself becomes more closely associated, and even identified, with the gods. The particular nature of Augustus' relationship to the divine has received a wealth of scholarly attention, but two basic sets of facts are sufficient for our purposes. First, even by the time of the composition of the *Aeneid*, Vergil would already have seen Augustus become progressively more affiliated with the gods, from the initial emphasis on divine parentage following Caesar's death through to the assimilation of his image to that of various deities in statuary and on coins, the incorporation of his name in prayers and hymns, and the fundamentally religious associations of his adopted cognomen, besides many other elements of a complex and evolving religious policy.[64] While none of these moves was in itself an unambiguous claim to

---

[62] For the deification of Aeneas see also *Aen.* 1.259–60. On Jupiter's allusion to Diomedes' speech see Fletcher 2006: 254, Nehrkorn 1971: 577–8.

[63] Hardie 1986: 147–50.

[64] Galinsky 1996: 312–22, Miller 2009: passim, esp. 15–53.

divinity proper, together they created a powerful aura. Second, whatever inhibitions Augustus may have felt about publicly claiming divinity, the poets were quite content to speak of him either as a god or in the gods' company. Vergil himself had already referred to the young Octavian as a *deus* in the first *Eclogue* (*Ecl.* 1.6), and Horace claims that Augustus will be considered a *praesens diuus* at *Carm.* 3.5.2.[65]

Augustus' close relationship with the gods, I suggest, put pressure on how epic, especially an explicitly Augustan epic, could deal with the figure of the theomach. In the *Iliad*, theomachy could elevate a hero, but in the contemporary climate, the figure who fights the gods can easily be read as in tension with the emperor, just as Diomedes and Mezentius are in tension with, and ultimately cede to, Aeneas. To the extent that Aeneas' opponents are described in heroic terms, their magnification is carefully circumscribed in a way that would no longer be possible if they could make a more compelling claim to inherit the mantle of Homer's fundamentally theomachic heroes. For Mezentius or Diomedes to enter the fray against the gods would be more than a mere fantastic distraction. Aeneas had already been depicted in the *Iliad* as inferior to his theomachic, Greek opponents—Vergil makes quite clear that this falling short will not happen again. With the additional alignment of Aeneas, Jupiter, and Augustus, such an elevation of an antagonist becomes almost inconceivable. Temporarily, at least, the principate had tempered one of the genre's defining excesses.

Another option closed off to Vergil was to cast Aeneas, rather than his opponents, in the theomachic mould. In effect, this would have been to identify the proto-Roman and proto-Augustan hero even more closely with Achilles to the extent of incorporating the Greek hero's theomachic qualities. But that route, too, becomes especially thorny given the importance of the concept of piety both to Aeneas' characterisation and as a fundamental Roman value cultivated and embodied by Augustus.[66] The moralising view of theomachy already seen in Dione's speech in *Iliad* 5, and more widely in Attic tragedy, intensifies due to the combined effect of Roman attitudes to piety and impiety and the emperor's identification with the Olympian gods. Moreover, it would have been all the more incoherent to depict *pius Aeneas* encountering a god in battle given that the Olympians are largely on his side with the pointed exception of Juno, whose opposition is purposefully indirect and conducted through intermediaries.

There is one moment in the epic, however, when Aeneas himself resembles a Giant or a theomach—the simile comparing him in his *aristeia* to Aegaeon fighting Jupiter (*Aen.* 10.565–70):

---

[65] Horace imposes a rather challenging condition, however, namely, the addition of the Britons and Persians to the Roman Empire.

[66] Cf. Galinsky 1996: 86–90 on the significance of piety on Augustus' *clipeus uirtutis*.

> Aegaeon qualis, centum cui bracchia dicunt
> centenasque manus, quinquaginta oribus ignem
> pectoribusque arsisse, Iouis cum fulmina contra
> tot paribus streperet clipeis, tot stringeret ensis:
> sic toto Aeneas desaeuit in aequore uictor
> ut semel intepuit mucro.
>
> Just as Aegaeon, who had a hundred arms, they say,
> and a hundred hands, and breathed fire from fifty mouths
> and chests, when against the thunderbolts of Jupiter
> he clashed with as many shields, and drew as many swords:
> so victorious Aeneas raged over the whole plain
> once his sword grew warm.

Tellingly, the passage forced at least one ancient reader into an interpretive knot (*Serv. Dan.* ad *Aen.* 10.567):

> IOVIS CUM FULMINA CONTRA quia dicitur flammam emisisse oribus suis contra Iouis fulmen. Homerus nihil dicit aliud, quam centum manus eum habuisse et auxilio eum Ioui adversus Neptunum, Iunonem et Mineruam fuisse. et forte aut suum ignem, aut Iouis, acceptum spirasse pro eo, ut sit 'contra' non aduersus Iouem, sed similiter, a pari, ut Terentius in Adelphis in capite comoediae 'ille ut item contra me habeat facio sedulo'.
>
> WHEN AGAINST JUPITER'S THUNDERBOLTS Because it is said that he emitted flame from his mouths against the thunderbolt of Jupiter. Homer says nothing other than that he had a hundred hands and helped Jupiter against Neptune, Juno, and Minerva. And whether he breathed his own fire or Jupiter's has accidentally been taken to be the same thing, so that *contra* means not 'against Jupiter', but 'similarly', 'equally', as at the beginning of Terence's *Adelphoe*, 'and I do everything I can to make sure that he likewise holds me dear'.

The commentator, whether Servius himself or someone else, describes a way of construing the Latin that must, on any reading, seem implausible and quite perverse. The point of the simile is not to make Aeneas seem like one of Jupiter's monstrous defenders, as related in Homer and Hesiod, but rather to show the extreme nature of his fury.[67] Critics have argued about the significance of the simile, whether it represents Aeneas' harnessing of crude violence for necessary ends, or draws attention to the moral ambiguities of civil war, or even undermines the panegyrical symbolism of Gigantomachy.[68] It's

---

[67] On the Homeric Aegaeon/Briareus see Chapter 1.
[68] See Hardie 1986: 154–6, O'Hara 1994: 218–21, Kronenberg 2005: 406, 425–6. On possible justifications for anger see Thornton 1976: 132–3, 205 n. 88; Braund and Gilbert 2003.

reasonable to think that even ancient readers might have differed in their responses. To prior interpretations I would add that the simile evokes the theomachic route open to, but not taken by, Vergil. Driven into a frenzy by the death of Pallas, Aeneas appears at his most Achillean, and concomitantly at his most theomachic: only a few lines before the simile, Aeneas even kills a priest of Apollo and Diana (*Aen.* 10.537–42).[69] What Vergil gives us, then, is a mere glimpse of what might have been the case under other circumstances, if the *Aeneid* and its protagonist hewed more closely to Homeric tradition.

There remains one final way in which Vergil accommodates theomachy into the poem, and it too is indirect. In fact, the reading emerges most explicitly in Ovid's *Metamorphoses*. Close to the end of the poem, when Venus bemoans the imminent assassination of her descendent Julius Caesar, she offers a litany of her and her family's sufferings, amongst which she lists Diomedes' wounding of her as well as Aeneas' toils (*Met.* 15.760–78).[70] Venus speaks of the anxiety of seeing her son having 'to fight with Turnus, or, if we speak the truth, with Juno rather' (*bellaque cum Turno gerere, aut, si uera fatemur, / cum Iunone magis, Met.* 15.773–4). Venus' rhetorical exaggeration here may allude to her similar hyperbole in *Iliad* 5, when she extrapolated from the example of Diomedes to an entire Greek army of theomachs.[71] Venus naturally views Diomedes' impious attack against her as completely different from Aeneas' innocent war with Juno. Indeed, she describes the latter in terms of theomachy precisely in order to highlight Aeneas' piety by contrast with Diomedes' overreaching. The distinction may seem clear enough: Diomedes directly confronts and humiliates a goddess with the assistance of another goddess, Athena, while Juno persecutes a hero who bears no ill will towards her.[72] In the act of waging war, as Venus puts it, Juno is the active agent, not Aeneas. But the expression *bella gerere* is more than just an exaggeration. Within it lies the implication that any kind of opposition to a god is a form of war, whether or not one intends to fight the god; all that matters is the divine perception of antagonism. So, irrespective of Venus' irony, Aeneas' pursuit of an aim contrary to Juno's will is sufficient to be described as a kind of theomachy. Unlike most theomachies, however, Aeneas gets the better of his divine opponent.[73] Despite Juno's hostility, he succeeds in perpetuating the Trojan race through the founding of Rome, which will one day destroy the goddess' favoured city of Carthage. But that success depends on Jupiter's will and his resolution with Juno. In that way, Aeneas' theomachy is legitimised in the same way that

---

[69] On the reception of this scene in the *Thebaid* see Chapter 8.
[70] See Chapter 3.
[71] *Il.* 5.379–80, on which see Chaper 1.
[72] In Silius' *Punica*, Juno will take a different view, framing the foundation of Rome as a spurning of her (*Pun.* 1.42).
[73] Randall Ganiban reminds me that Aeneas' fury at the close may equally be read as a sign of Juno's triumph (pers. comm.). Seneca's *Hercules Furens*, on which see Chapter 4, rereads the *Aeneid* along these lines.

Diomedes' had been, through the support and authority of a god, even against another of the gods. It is telling, however, that this more explicitly theomachic reading of the *Aeneid* is suggested not by Vergil himself but by Ovid, an author who, as we shall see in the next chapter, has no qualms about tackling the subject head-on.[74]

---

[74] On Ovid as a tendentious yet insightful rereader of the *Aeneid* see Papaioannou 2005.

3

Theomachy as Test in Ovid's *Metamorphoses*

> The other disciples therefore said unto him, We have seen the Lord. But he said unto them, Except I shall see in his hands the print of the nails, and put my finger into the print of the nails, and thrust my hand into his side, I will not believe.
>
> —JOHN 20:25

> Not the man who denies the gods worshipped by the multitude but he who affirms of the gods what the multitude believes about them is truly impious.
>
> —EPICURUS

> And I believe in the pie and the tartlet:
> the one is the mother and the other is the son;
> and the true Paternoster is the pork liver.
>
> —LUIGI PULCI

Scholars of Greek and Roman religion have only recently returned to belief as a concept worthy of further investigation after many years of regarding it as anachronistic and overly laden with Christianising assumptions.[1] In tandem with this renewed interest, I attempt to restore some measure of confidence in the validity and relevance of the concept of belief by examining its role in several episodes in Ovid's *Metamorphoses*, a work formative for later poets'

---

[1] Beard 1986: 34: 'It seems doubtful, for example, that "belief" and "disbelief"—with their suggestion of the personal commitment characteristic of modern world religions—are appropriate terms for the analysis of traditional Roman religion'. On Christianising preconceptions see, e.g., Price 1984: 10–15, Feeney 1998: 12–14, J. P. Davies 2004: 4–7, Ando 2008: x–xii, though to speak of Christianising assumptions homogenises the variety and complexity of Christian thought (see Feeney 1998: 12 n. 2, 15). For consideration of belief in Greek religion, see T. Harrison 2000 and (forthcoming), Versnel 2011: 539–59; for both Greek and Roman religion see the essays in R. Anderson (forthcoming). This chapter significantly expands on Chaudhuri (forthcoming b).

handling of theomachy.[2] What often distinguishes the Ovidian and post-Ovidian narratives of theomachy is their interest in testing the empirical criteria of divinity—the observable features or actions that signify divine power and justify belief. Though the origins of that interest lie in Lucretius and Vergil, as we saw in the previous chapter, the themes of testing and belief take centre stage from Ovid onwards.

Through a series of close readings of different types of theomachic challenge—from Lycaon's test of Jupiter's identity, through Pentheus' rejection of Bacchus, to Hercules' fight with the river god Achelous, among several other episodes—the chapter shows how the *Metamorphoses* engaged and commented on the topic of religious belief, especially through the voices of its sceptical and violent characters. I focus on these scenes not only because they chart a range of sceptical enquiry but also because of their detailed representation of debate between different points of view. Thus, the Lycaon episode emphasises more general issues of sign-inference, while the story of Niobe foregrounds materialism, and that of Hercules suggests alternative measures by which to identify and evaluate divine power. What emerges overall, I argue, is an emphasis not on disbelief per se but rather on the ways in which different beliefs contend in resolving various claims to divinity and the question of the existence of the gods.

Tellingly, the strong philosophical colouring of these particular myths represents a significant change from their Greek counterparts. One reason for this, as the previous chapter already began to suggest, is the stimulus of imperial religion. Contemporaries were sensitive to a transition taking place in the kind of status achievable by a human and the implications for conceptions of divine power. As we shall see in the coming chapters, views on this transition could vary from conservative to radical, from uncertain to antagonistic, and from irreverent to panegyrical—contrasts which would only grow over time as Romans had the opportunity to witness and adjust to evolving institutions. In this climate it became increasingly difficult to separate Olympus from the Palatine, and hence increasingly intuitive to subject the gods of epic to questions pertaining to the rulers of Rome. The languages of myth and philosophy provided an especially powerful resource with which to interpret the new world order.[3]

As a result of this context, and therefore perhaps more than any previous poet, Ovid makes theomachy central to a larger enquiry into the nature of the divine. That enquiry, begun in earnest in the *Metamorphoses* and continued in

---

[2] Studies of belief in epic have typically examined questions of fictionality and myth (e.g., Feeney 1991, Wheeler 1999: 162–93, Feldherr 2010); this chapter focuses specifically on the criteria of religious belief.

[3] On Ovid's use of Capaneus to represent his relationship with Augustus in the exile poetry see Chapter 9.

the poetic tradition over the course of the century, touches on the premises underlying not only religion and imperial ideology but also those artistic forms of expression—pre-eminently the epic genre—that attempt to represent the gods. For in attacking the divine the theomach forces the reader to engage art's capacities and limits head-on, in particular art's adequacy to give an account of the authorising force and ultimate object of artistic representation, an object that nevertheless always exceeds and eludes representation—the gods.

Guess Who's Coming to Dinner: Lycaon

At the beginning of the *Metamorphoses*' first tale of human transformation, Jupiter calls a council of the gods to report the crimes and punishment of the Arcadian king, Lycaon. Since, according to Jupiter, Lycaon's wickedness typifies all humans, the god declares his intent to wipe out the human race by flood and begin anew. The context of the council scene strongly assimilates Olympus to the Palatine (*Palatia caeli*, 'the Palatine of heaven', *Met*. 1.176) and Jupiter to Augustus (*nec tibi grata minus pietas, Auguste, tuorum est / quam fuit illa Ioui*, 'the devotion of your people is no less pleasing to you, Augustus, than theirs [the gods'] was to Jupiter', *Met*. 1.204-5). This poetic gambit emphatically politicises the subsequent story and draws a symbolic connection between divine and human power.[4] Unsurprisingly, then, this episode has often garnered scholarly attention as an example of Ovidian political allegory, usually focusing on the authoritarianism of Jupiter and his control of the narrative of Lycaon's supposed wrongdoing.[5] My concern here, however, is with a less obvious theme, that of the manner in which the different participants' beliefs are established.[6]

---

[4] The passage at *Met*. 1.171-6 also pictures the gods as members of the Roman Senate, on which see W. S. Anderson 1997: 168-70, Barchiesi 2008b. Due 1974: 71-2 and Barchiesi 2008b: 128-32 also discuss the ambiguity of *Caesareo* at *Met*. 1.201. Reference to conspiracy against Augustus, rather than or in addition to Julius Caesar, increases the sense of political urgency in the lead-up to Jupiter's account.

[5] E.g., Due 1974: 71-3, 103-7. For Rosati 2002b: 274 the narration by Jupiter thematises the problems of the authority of power and word; cf. O'Hara 2007: 116-18. For a legal reading of the episode as a case of *maiestas* see Balsley 2011. Habinek 2002: 51-2 reads Jupiter's response to Lycaon in terms of Roman imperial policy.

[6] Brief but insightful commentary at Feldherr 2002: 169-72, esp. 171-2: 'It might even be argued that Lycaon's outrage results less from his attempt to deprive the gods of the honour due them than from his scrupulous belief in the reality of appearances and his efforts to use those appearances to distinguish different orders of being'. Feldherr 2010: 39 touches on Lycaon's empiricism but focuses principally on the theme of sacrifice (131-49); cf. Barkan 1986: 26-7. Wheeler 1999: 172-81 discusses disbelief primarily in terms of political opposition. Klein 2009, esp. 197-8, discusses belief in the Perseus episode in the context of fictionality and metapoetry (note the link between credibility and testing at *Met*. 4.747-9). Cf. the different forms of evidence and argument employed by Pythagoras (e.g., *Met*. 15.356-61), on which see Beagon 2009.

Jupiter begins his report by informing the council that Lycaon has already been punished for his crimes (1.209–10). The subsequent recollection of events functions as a post-factum justification not only of the punishment of Lycaon but also of the sentence against humankind. In contrast to the extant Greek versions of the myth, Jupiter's language as he describes his undercover visit to the earth shows an abiding concern with issues of evidence and proof as central to both his and Lycaon's actions (*Met.* 1.211–15):[7]

> contigerat nostras infamia temporis aures;
> quam cupiens falsam summo delabor Olympo
> et deus humana lustro sub imagine terras.
> longa mora est quantum noxae sit ubique repertum
> enumerare; minor fuit ipsa infamia uero.

> The infamy of the age had reached my ears;
> hoping the rumour false I glided down from the top of Olympus
> and, a god in human form, wandered the earth.
> It would take a long time to enumerate how much crime I found
> everywhere; even the infamy was less than the truth.

Paraphrasing the sequence of thought here may help to clarify Ovid's focus on epistemological procedures: Jupiter hears a rumour of human wickedness, acknowledges the possibility that the information may be false, attempts to establish its truth or falsity through direct observation, and gathers evidence that demonstrates the initial report to have been overly conservative.[8] With due allowances for Jupiter's rhetorical craft—without any other testimony he is at liberty to misrepresent humanity as he pleases—the theme of verification through personal experience or autopsy is nevertheless emphatic. It's as if Jupiter wishes to convey due diligence in establishing the facts before destroying humankind. Although the god's genocidal intent has a long mythological pedigree—we know, for instance, of similar plans by Zeus in the early phases of the epic tradition—the importance given to the god's intellectual and investigative procedures is an unusual twist.[9]

Ovid's preoccupation with matters of knowledge and enquiry continues as Jupiter becomes the object of Lycaon's own fact-finding mission (*Met.* 1.220–3):[10]

---

[7] See Forbes Irving 1990: 90–5, 216–18.

[8] The word *imagine* (*Met.* 1.213) may suggest the appearance of (divine) statuary (cf. Lucr. 6.420, Cic. *Dom.* 112). On the relationship between image and deity in the ancient world and the cognitive processes involved in epiphanic experience see Platt 2011, esp. 50–76. But Ovid may also suggest a further sense of *imago*, namely, an ironic allusion to Epicurus' image of the divine seeping into our awareness, a conception which could seem to some to be tantamount to atheism (Cic. *Nat. D.* 2.76). Although the precise implications are unclear, the use of the word *imago* coheres with the entire episode's concern with perceiving divine qualities.

[9] On Zeus' destruction of humankind see the D Scholia ad *Iliad* 1.5 and Scodel 1982.

[10] For the common ground between Jupiter and Lycaon see Feldherr 2010: 133–4.

> signa dedi uenisse deum, uulgusque precari
> coeperat; inridet primo pia uota Lycaon,
> mox ait 'experiar deus hic discrimine aperto
> an sit mortalis, nec erit dubitabile uerum'.

> I gave signs that a god had come, and the people began
> to pray; Lycaon first mocked their pious prayers,
> then said, 'I shall test with clear distinction whether this one is god
> or mortal, nor will the truth be open to doubt'.

Jupiter's narration implies that the signs he gave ought to have been sufficient for Lycaon to recognise his divinity, as the *uulgus* did, and his rhetoric makes clear that he, at least, expects his audience to evaluate the beliefs and actions presented as two stark alternatives.[11] In speaking of *pia uota* and in showing the *uulgus* to have correctly identified him, Jupiter clearly indicates that the *uulgus* are morally and epistemologically on the right track.[12] By contrast, the impious Lycaon, who 'mocks' (*inridet*) pious prayers, takes a very different approach from the *uulgus*, one characterised by scepticism and empiricism. The vocabulary attributed to Lycaon shows a clear interest in testing and proof: *experiar* ('I shall test'), *aperto* ('clear'), *discrimine* ('distinction'), *dubitabile* ('doubtful'), and *uerum* ('truth').[13] The verb *experiar*, in particular, strongly suggests the acquisition of knowledge by empirical testing.[14] On the one hand, then, Jupiter's narrative guides the reader to validate the epistemological approach of the *uulgus*, but on the other hand Lycaon's language, whether or not Jupiter represents it accurately, emphasises the problems of credibility and proof that Jupiter's divine signs, and inference from them, leave open.

---

[11] Lee 1984: 97, citing *Aen.* 5.647, suggests that *signa* possibly refers to Jupiter's divine appearance. For *signa* implying a more indirect knowledge cf. Cicero's remark on the abilities of diviners, who, 'even if they do not discern causes themselves, nevertheless discern the signs and marks of causes' (*etsi causas ipsas non cernunt, signa tamen causarum et notas cernunt, Div.* 1.127).

[12] The attitude of the reader will depend in part on how one understands the word *uulgus*, on which see further my discussion of the Pierides episode below. The character of Marcus in Cicero's *De Divinatione* advocates for the authority of various religious practices and beliefs precisely out of respect for the *opinionem uulgi* (*Div.* 2.70), though there too one might wonder whether the connotations of *uulgus* do not colour how we should read Marcus' claim.

[13] *aperto* may even be an etymological play on *experiar*, if Ovid was aware of the notion, recorded by Priscian, that the words were etymologically connected (Keil 2.400.15).

[14] The verb *experiri* often has a strong sense of testing by experience or observation, e.g., Cic. *Cael.* 58 (testing poison), Livy 27.13.8 (proving courage in battle). On the legal sense of *experiri* as 'going to court' and its relevance for the Lycaon episode see Balsley 2011: 60–1. Dante will use the cognate Italian word *esperto* in the *Inferno* to describe both Odysseus' excessive thirst for knowledge of the world (*Inf.* 26.97–9; note that his curiosity about the vices and worth of humankind resembles that of the Ovidian Jupiter) and the Giant Ephialtes' desire to test his power against Jupiter (*Inf.* 31.91–2). The linking of intellectual presumption and theomachy has a basis in Christian history—that is, Satan's corruption of God's creation through the tree of knowledge—but Dante also follows a pattern of classical myth and diction.

Jupiter claims that Lycaon's test, such as it was, was to attempt to kill him in his sleep (*Met.* 1.224–6):

> nocte grauem somno necopina perdere morte
> me parat—haec illi placet experientia ueri!
> nec contentus eo est.

> He prepared to kill me at night in the depths of my sleep,
> unexpectedly—this test of the truth seemed good to him!
> But he was not satisfied with this.

Jupiter's language (*experientia, ueri*) sarcastically echoes the earlier quotation of Lycaon (*experiar, uerum*) in order to mock the scientific pretensions of his antagonist. The noun *experientia*, even more clearly than the earlier use of *experiar*, signifies knowledge attained by experience and observation. Thus Varro deploys the noun to describe one of the ways in which human beings learn agricultural techniques, and Lucretius uses it to describe the means by which we make progress in technology, arts, and civilisation.[15] The medical author Scribonius Largus, writing some fifty years after Ovid, explicitly ties *experientia* to the provision of proof (*Compositiones* ep. 1): *medicamenta usu experientiaque probata* ('medicines tested by use and experience').[16] It's that sense of trial, error, and advance—all subject to observation or other sensory experience—that underlies Ovid's use of *experiar* and *experientia* and emphasises the profound difference between the intellectual responses of the *uulgus* and Lycaon. What Jupiter's sarcasm sidesteps, however, is the logic of the test: for what more categorical distinction can there be between a god and an imposter than mortality itself?

It's unclear what is meant by Jupiter's claim that Lycaon 'was not satisfied' (*Met.* 1.226) with this test, but like any good empiricist Lycaon tries another method: only through experience, it seems, can Lycaon know whether his guest is really a god or an imposter. Lycaon's second test, Jupiter goes on to report, is to offer the visitor human flesh to eat, which, far from deceiving the god, incites him to assume his true form and bring retribution on the household (*Met.* 1.226–31).[17] Jupiter's anger and his transformation of Lycaon into a wolf cast the episode as a clear moral lesson. But—and this fact is generally neglected by commentators—Lycaon does, in an obvious sense, succeed. The test of Jupiter's identity verifies, in however dramatic and impious fashion, the

---

[15] *Rust.* 1.18.7–8, Lucr. 5.1448–53.

[16] On the relationship between medical and philosophical, especially Epicurean, empiricism see Giovacchini 2012.

[17] Lycaon's attempted trick has mythological precedents, such as the feast of Tantalus or Prometheus' ruse at Mecone, in both of which the distinction between human and god is maintained by the gods' ability to see through the mortal deception. For the link with Prometheus see Feldherr 2010: 131–4; for Tantalus see Forbes Irving 1990: 91–4; see also Barchiesi 2005: 178.

belief of the *uulgus* based on Jupiter's *signa*. In other words, Lycaon provokes Jupiter to appear as the reader knows the god, the fully fledged mythological deity of epic, and not as the *uulgus* knows the god, through the indirect evidence of signs. Whereas Jupiter's allegations of wrongdoing seek to alienate the divine audience from Lycaon, the god's deliberate emphasis of the themes of testing and observation brings Lycaon's perspective closer to that of the human audience. Further, Lycaon's motivation in the first place to test matters of uncertainty had already been validated by Jupiter's own impulse to verify rumour through direct observation of humankind. Ovid thus imbues Jupiter's account with a capacity for endorsing a broad empiricism even as the god tolerates only a circumscribed and unidirectional application of the method.

To gauge how a contemporary reader might have responded to the story we can return to the beginning of the episode and Ovid's series of analogies between Olympus and Rome. With those explicit comparisons in the background, it's difficult to set aside the political implications of Ovid's handling of the myth. When Lycaon interrogates the ambiguous status of the stranger—is he human, is he divine, and how can one know?—thought of recent changes in the politico-religious sphere regarding the status of the emperor cannot be far away. Other poets had already tangled with the question of Augustus' status, most explicitly Horace in *Odes* 1.12. But where Horace's poem gently raises the question of Augustus' ambiguous status within a highly panegyrical discourse, Lycaon's test of the stranger's claim to divinity, at least according to Jupiter's version of events, is characterised by antagonism, impiety, and violence.[18] If we are to see contemporary allegory in this episode—and Ovid's introduction makes it hard not to—then Lycaon's scrutiny of Jupiter's status suggests one, especially adversarial, response to Augustan religious innovations, of which the imperial cult is only the most glaring example.[19]

And yet the emperor alone does not explain the particular features of Ovid's Lycaon story, even if he forms the inescapable context for many readers' interpretations. The highly original elements of empiricism and sign-inference that Ovid brings to the myth point to religious and philosophical contexts that precede imperial innovations. Enquiring into the criteria of divinity embroils Ovid in questions fundamental to Hellenistic philosophy as well as to the hermeneutic practices of civic religion, such as augury and haruspicy: how to

---

[18] *Odes* 1.12 represents an enquiry into what Augustus is—man, god, or hero. But as a piece of panegyric it can simply duck the difficult question of how one attains such a status (though Horace's implication is that poets have a crucial role in elevating Augustus; see Feeney 1998: 111–14, and cf. Du Quesnay 1995 on *Odes* 4.5). For Ovidian scepticism about anthropomorphised gods see Feldherr 2010: 40. On Ovid's negotiation of the divine aspect of the emperor in his exile poetry see McGowan 2009: 63–120. Cf. Chapter 9 for Statius' response to this ode of Horace.

[19] On the tension between religious novelty and political resistance see the discussion of the *crimen maiestatis* in Bauman 1967 and 1974. For a broad survey of religious restoration and innovation under Augustus see Galinsky 1996: 288–331, Liebeschuetz 1979: 55–100.

interpret signs; what counts as a sign; what is the nature of the connection between sign, source, and result; what are the relative merits of speculative and empirical methods of enquiry; and, finally, what is the nature of the gods.[20] These kinds of question, amply discussed in texts such as Cicero's *De Natura Deorum* and *De Divinatione*, are here transplanted, mutatis mutandis, to the epic genre. The enquiries set in motion by Lycaon thus stimulate a range of questions—philosophical and political—about the very criteria of divinity, questions that will be developed over the course of the poem.

Seeing and Knowing: Semele and Pentheus

In the Theban cycle of *Metamorphoses* 3, Ovid explores the themes of sight and knowledge that Attic tragedy had linked so closely to the city of Thebes, especially through the figure of Oedipus. Indeed, by omitting any lengthy account of Oedipus, Ovid only draws attention to the influence of this absent presence on Book 3's various stories of misperception, familial trouble, and desire gone wrong. So much is well known.[21] And yet, as the previous reading of the Lycaon episode suggested, the themes of sight and knowledge are not the exclusive preserve of Thebes, despite the long shadow cast by Oedipus. Rather, Thebes offers an excellent opportunity to investigate further the ways in which one could come to see and know, and hence to believe in, a god. If Ovid inherits some of these epistemological concerns with vision from the broad mythology surrounding the city, however, the specific issue of divinity centres on one particular figure—Bacchus—and the questions generated by the advent of this new god. Once again, the notion of theomachy plays a significant role as Bacchus comes into conflict with his human cousin, Pentheus, whose relation to, and rejection of, the god Ovid conceives in emphatically perceptual terms. Moreover, Ovid had already made the link between theomachy and misperception not only through the formative example of Lycaon's failure to recognise Jupiter but also through the story of Bacchus' birth, as the competition between Semele and Juno over their respective claims to Jupiter hinges on the same issues of recognition and testing.

Ovid makes theomachy a feature of the Semele story not only as a prelude to Bacchus' later conflict with Pentheus but also, more explicitly, through Juno's own reaction to Semele's pregnancy (*Met.* 3.263–6):[22]

> ipsa petenda mihi est; ipsam, si maxima Iuno
> rite uocor, perdam, si me gemmantia dextra

---

[20] On sign-inference in ancient philosophy see Allen 2001, Giovacchini 2012: 106–15. Cf. the Lycaon-inspired empiricism of Capaneus discussed in Chapter 8.
[21] Gildenhard and Zissos 2000, Hardie 2002b: 165, Janan 2009: 156–67, Keith 2010.
[22] Cf. the opening of Seneca's *Hercules Furens* discussed in Chapter 4.

sceptra tenere decet, si sum regina Iouisque
et soror et coniunx—certe soror.

I must attack her; I must destroy her, if I am rightly called
almighty Juno, if it is fitting that I hold in my right hand
the jewelled sceptre, if I am queen and Jupiter's
sister and wife—at least sister.

Through the series of conditionals Juno claims that her very identity is at stake in this theomachic contest over Jupiter—by destroying her rival she confirms her own status in heaven.[23] That same notion of compromised identity recurs a few lines below, when Juno explains why this infidelity in particular is so serious (*Met.* 3.268–72):

concipit (id deerat!) manifestaque crimina pleno
fert utero et mater, quod uix mihi contigit, uno
de Ioue uult fieri: tanta est fiducia formae.
fallat eam faxo; nec sum Saturnia si non
ab Ioue mersa suo Stygias penetrabit in undas.

She has conceived (only that was lacking!) and bears the visible crime
in her full womb and wishes to become—what scarcely applies to me—
the mother of a child by Jupiter: so great is her confidence in her beauty.
I shall make it lead her astray; nor am I Saturnia, if she will not
be overwhelmed by her Jupiter and penetrate the Stygian waves.

What troubles Juno most is the pregnancy itself, which proves Jupiter's infidelity and raises Semele, as the mother of Jupiter's child, to the equivalent of Juno herself (despite the exaggeration in *uix*, since Juno in fact bears at least three children by Jupiter).[24] Triggered by the thought of this challenge, Juno once again declares her own identity to be contingent on Semele's death. The reasonableness of Juno's anxiety is less important here than the terms in which she couches that worry: identity and proof of identity. Besides the loaded word *manifesta* (*Met.* 3.268), which already signals the importance of visibility

---

[23] Jim Tatum reminds me that Ovid's allusion here to *Aen.* 1.46–9 is laced with wit: if Juno was insecure in the *Aeneid*, when she called herself 'Jupiter's sister and wife' (*Iouisque / et soror et coniunx*, *Aen.* 1.46–7), how much more insecure must she be now when forced to play the part of the—unusually chaste!—sister (pers. comm.). Further, the Vergilian Juno had complained that she had to do battle with one nation for so many years (*Aen.* 1.47–8); her Ovidian counterpart, on the other hand, complains about one woman now rendered effectively the equivalent of the entire Trojan race. Finally, Ovid develops the earlier Juno's concerns about worship and honour (*Aen.* 1.48–9) into a larger theme in the *Metamorphoses*, one bound up with questions of belief and involving many of Ovid's gods.

[24] In addition to Ares, Hebe, and Eileithuia, a variant tradition has Hephaestus born from both Hera and Zeus rather than Hera alone (Cic. *Nat. D.* 3.55). If the Eris said to be a sister of Ares at *Il.* 4.440–1 is to be considered more than figurative, then by implication she too would be a daughter of Zeus and Hera.

as a criterion of proof, some hint of the impending concern with appearance and reality also lies in the phrase *fiducia formae*. Although it primarily refers, as elsewhere in the poem, to confidence in one's beauty, it also suggests a trust in 'outward appearance' (*OLD* s.v. *forma* 13).[25] Semele's *fiducia formae* is thus doubly responsible for her downfall: Juno will take advantage not only of Semele's vanity but also of her inability to discern true divinity. To some extent, then, we have here a recapitulation of the Lycaon episode, or at least of several issues central to that episode, most prominently the link between theomachy and the testing of identity.[26]

These themes are taken up straightaway as Juno disguises herself as Semele's old nurse (*Met.* 3.275–8) in order to warn her that Jupiter may in fact be a human imposter (*Met.* 3.280–6):[27]

>   'opto
> Iuppiter ut sit' ait, 'metuo tamen omnia; multi
> nomine diuorum thalamos iniere pudicos.
> nec tamen esse Iouem satis est; det pignus amoris,
> si modo uerus is est, quantusque et qualis ab alta
> Iunone excipitur, tantus talisque rogato
> det tibi complexus suaque ante insignia sumat'.

>   'I wish
> that he is Jupiter', she says, 'but I fear all such things; many men
> have entered chaste bedrooms in the name of the gods.
> But it is not enough to say that he is Jupiter; let him give proof of his love,
> if it really is him, ask him to embrace you,
> as great and awesome as when received by high Juno,
> and to put on first his distinguishing tokens'.

The irony of Juno's warning about the difficulties of identifying a god is straightforward enough, but it raises genuinely thorny, if familiar, issues about how one can know a god. Although Juno's purpose is to have Semele unwittingly overwhelmed by Jupiter, her advice nonetheless suggests that there is no real test for divinity besides epiphany itself—the manifest and unambiguous appearance of the god. And indeed, this was the conclusion of the Lycaon episode too, when finally Jupiter's nature was proven by the revelation of his true form and the concomitant destruction of Lycaon's palace.

Semele arrives at a similar end through rather different means, of course, foolishly requesting a *pignus amoris* from Jupiter that results in her death. Despite

---

[25] For the standard meaning of the phrase cf. *Met.* 2.731, 4.687, 8.434, 14.32.

[26] In Semele's case, unlike that of Lycaon, the theomachy is seemingly initiated by the god rather than the human, though Juno sees things differently. We should remember, however, that since Jupiter narrates, and hence has total control over, the story of Lycaon, the question of who may have instigated the theomachic contest is hardly straightforward.

[27] On identity and disguise in the episode see von Glinski 2012: 75–7.

her innocence, however, the form of her demise reinforces the theomachic quality of the episode: Jupiter's lightning may here function as the least subtle of sexual symbols, but it is also the force hurled against those who would test the boundary between human and divine—against not only Lycaon, for example, but also Phaethon, who sought to imitate Apollo.[28] Juno thus engineers the form of Semele's death not only to confirm the difference between mortal and divinity but also, it seems, in order to corroborate the theomachic narrative with which she began. Ovid even describes the thunderbolt in such a way as to emphasise the curiously pseudo-theomachic role played by Semele (*Met.* 3.302–4):

> qua tamen usque potest, uires sibi demere temptat
> nec, quo centimanum deiecerat igne Typhoea,
> nunc armatur eo; nimium feritatis in illo est.

> And yet as far as he can he tries to lessen his own strength,
> nor does he arm himself now with that fire with which he had hurled down hundred-handed Typhoeus; there is too much savagery in that.

The entire episode is thus made to resemble, and yet fall short of, theomachy proper, especially in Jupiter's reluctant use of the thunderbolt. In some crucial respects, however, the episode preserves the characteristic threads of other theomachic episodes—the mechanisms of proving divine identity, the threat to divine authority, and possibly even the desire to elevate oneself to the level of a god.

Several of these concerns carry through into the final episode of Book 3, in which Pentheus, king of Thebes, refuses to recognise the divinity of Bacchus, attempts to prevent the worship of the god in the city, and eventually dies at the hands of the god's crazed followers, including Pentheus' own mother. Already in the *Bacchae* Euripides had made the themes of sight and knowledge important features of the story of Pentheus' theomachy. Critics have noted how the tragedy plays with multiple senses of the concept of recognition, slipping between mere identification of an individual and a deeper acknowledgement of that individual's nature and power.[29] In the *Metamorphoses*, Ovid places that tradition within a larger discourse about seeing and knowing the divine that had begun with Lycaon and continues right through to the end of the poem. Ovid emphasises the importance of that epiphanic discourse within the Pentheus episode by combining two separate myths about the recognition of Bacchus: inserted into the story of Pentheus is a parable, drawn from the *Homeric Hymn to Dionysus*, about the failure of the

---

[28] Semele and Phaethon are further connected by the requests they make of the gods. When testing Apollo's paternity, Phaethon also seeks a favour that the god subsequently regrets granting (*Met.* 1.747–2.102). The similarity suggests Semele's ambition to exceed mortal limits, as Juno had originally feared. Nonnus gives the deified Semele a proud and confrontational speech against Hera at *Dion.* 9.208–42

[29] See, e.g., J. Gregory 1985, Goldhill 1988, Segal 1997.

Tyrrhenian sailors to recognise the god.[30] Ovid's conjoining of the two Dionysiac myths—partly inherited from Pacuvius' lost tragedy *Pentheus*—thus develops a long-standing literary, especially tragic, preoccupation with the concept of recognition while offering a fuller account of the nature and variety of epiphanic experience.[31]

Pentheus' theomachic credentials were firmly established in the *Bacchae*, as we saw in Chapter 1, and they are no less clear in the *Metamorphoses*. Ovid designates the Theban king a 'despiser of the gods' (*contemptor superum Pentheus*, *Met*. 3.514), who alone scoffs at Tiresias' power of prophecy (*Met*. 3.513–16).[32] Tiresias predicts that Pentheus' refusal to honour Bacchus will result in a horrific demise at the hands of his mother and aunts. And yet for Pentheus the sudden corruption of the masculine values of Thebes renders the question of Bacchus' divinity moot. There will be no test of divinity here, in the manner of Lycaon or Semele, but rather an exposure of mere pretence: *ego actutum (modo uos absistite) cogam / adsumptumque patrem commentaque sacra fateri* ('I shall immediately (just you stand aside) compel him to confess his borrowed father and invented rites', *Met*. 3.557–8). As Tiresias warned, however, Pentheus' theomachy, and ultimately his death, will instead demonstrate the power, and hence the reality, of Bacchus' godhead.

Pentheus also listens to an admonitory tale from a prisoner, a follower of Bacchus named Acoetes. The captive, a former helmsman, recounts a story in which his fellow sailors come across a beautiful young boy, whom Acoetes himself identifies as a god: *specto cultum faciemque gradumque; / nil ibi quod credi posset mortale uidebam* ('I regarded his dress, appearance, and rank: I saw nothing there which could be thought mortal', *Met*. 3.609–10). Acoetes announces as much to his comrades and prays to the boy, but the rest of the sailors, sceptical of the claim, disavow his prayers. Despite the helmsman's protestations, the 'impious crew' (*impia turba*, *Met*. 3.629, *manus impia*, *Met*. 3.656) promises safe passage to the boy while in reality planning to sell him. When the deceit is eventually exposed mid-voyage, a series of miraculous and terrifying occurrences reveals the boy as Bacchus and culminates in the men's transformation into dolphins; Acoetes alone is spared and joins the Bacchic cult. Although Acoetes had initially expressed uncertainty about which god in particular the boy might be (*Met*. 3.611–12), he identifies the boy as Bacchus in the course of the narrative, presumably with the benefit of hindsight: *tum denique Bacchus / (Bacchus enim fuerat)* ('then finally Bacchus (for it was Bacchus)', *Met*. 3.629–30); *ait Liber* ('said Liber', *Met*. 3.636). Given Pentheus' rejection of Bacchus' godhead, the didactic quality of Acoetes' tale is clear enough: disaster awaits those who would doubt the god.

---

[30] The hymn, the seventh in most collections, is longest of the extant Homeric hymns to Dionysus.
[31] On Pacuvius as a source for Ovid see *Serv. Dan.* ad *Aen*. 4.469 and Otis 1970: 400–1.
[32] Ovid thus not only maintains the characterisation of Pentheus in the *Bacchae* but also links him to Lycaon, and before him Vergil's Mezentius (on whom see Chapter 2).

Furthermore, the sailors' inability to see Bacchus for who he is looks very much like Pentheus' own error, especially when Acoetes himself begins to resemble Bacchus.[33] While Pentheus' slaves prepare to torture Acoetes to death, the doors open of their own accord and the prisoner is mysteriously and spontaneously released from his chains (*Met.* 3.697–700). This supernatural escape recalls the Dionysus of Euripides' *Bacchae*, who similarly evades binding and incarceration.[34] If Acoetes is indeed Bacchus, how apt that he should swear by the god that his tale is true, adding that 'no god is closer than he' (*nec enim praesentior illo / est deus*, *Met.* 3.658–9).[35] Pentheus thus fails to recognise the god in two senses, religious and perceptual.

And yet one should be careful not to overemphasise the correspondence between Acoetes' story and the case of Pentheus.[36] For the inset narrative makes the act of identifying the god a relatively straightforward matter of morality: the pious Acoetes simply senses the boy's divinity from his appearance, while the impious crew possess no such belief. It's certainly possible to read Pentheus' ignorance in the same way as the crew's, as a product of his impiety. But thus far in the *Metamorphoses* the moralistic approach to identifying a god has been anything but straightforward. Indeed, in the programmatic episode of Lycaon, the conjoining of recognition and morality was the means by which Jupiter justified his plan to destroy humankind, but it was a distinctly rhetorical move, and one which effaced some significant problems raised by his own representation of events. A similar issue arises here, since Acoetes' account is complicated not only by the potential bias of the narrator, now a follower of the god, but also by the possibility that Acoetes may himself be Bacchus, an identification which would necessitate that at least some details of the narrative are false. In short, it certainly aligns with the god's interests for the audience to see a close correspondence between the impious sailors and Pentheus, and to accept Acoetes' straightforward recognition of the god, but for the reader primed by Ovid's sustained scrutiny of cases of epiphany and the very concept of recognition, Acoetes' tale oversimplifies an enormously complex set of cognitive processes and contextual factors.

One immediately striking difference between the two stories pertains to epiphany itself. For, while the inset tale, in accordance with its hymnic origins, describes the revelation of Bacchus, the framing story does not.[37] Even if Acoetes is the god, he does not reveal himself in his divine form. Unlike the *Bacchae*, which ends by bringing Dionysus onstage in his own persona, and not as the

---

[33] See Barchiesi and Rosati 2007: 229–30.

[34] Eur. *Bacch.* 616–41.

[35] See Eur. *Bacch.* 500, 502.

[36] See W. S. Anderson 1997: 399: the sailors 'serve as clear warning prototypes for Pentheus'; Feldherr 2010: 189: 'the narrative being told to Pentheus describes the situation in which he finds himself—disbelieving a god who appears before him'; Liveley 2011: 53–4 describes Acoetes' speech as 'clearly indicating where Ovid's sympathies lie'.

[37] On the importance of epiphany to the *Homeric Hymn to Dionysus* see Jaillard 2011.

Stranger of earlier scenes, Ovid's *Metamorphoses* provides no equivalent resolution: Book 3 simply concludes with Pentheus' death and the consequent acceptance of Bacchus by the Thebans.[38] For Philip Hardie, the interplay of the two narratives—rather than one or the other—constitutes a telling account of Bacchus' power:[39]

> Acoetes' narrative is witness to the power of Bacchus as supreme manipulator of his own absence and presence, able to withhold and reveal his identity at will, the power through which he avenges himself on a Pentheus unable to reveal his presence, though present, to his deluded mother and aunts, and unable to use the true story of Actaeon as a warning to them of what they are doing at that very moment.

On this reading, the god represents a mastery of form—of being and not being—unavailable to the human characters, but instead characteristic of the *Metamorphoses* itself, with its thoroughgoing problematisation of the boundary between fiction and reality. If the traditional object of epiphany is to see the god, Ovid's two alternative accounts of Bacchus provide a means by which to see the god in a deeper sense, that is, to know him as a being both fundamentally present and absent, and not simply as the anthropomorphised form inherited from a hymn or tragedy.[40] The poem's exploitation of the resources of fiction and reality thus creates a new kind of epiphany altogether.

And yet Ovid always leaves room to question such all-encompassing claims to power. For the story of Pentheus only achieves resolution when the king goes to see for himself the activities of the bacchants. Both Hardie (see above) and Andrew Feldherr view Pentheus' obsession with presence as a flaw, but I would emphasise that autopsy, as self-destructive as it is, remains the only way to prove the god's power and to bring the plot of the episode to a conclusion.[41] Ultimately, Bacchus is as dependent on presence as Pentheus, since the proof of the god's power comes from seeing the punishment of the king. Moreover, Ovid himself hints at the essential importance of autopsy as an authorising claim. At one point he compares Pentheus' anger to a raging river, 'such as I myself have seen' (*sic ego . . . uidi*, *Met.* 3.568–9). For Feldherr, this narratorial intrusion suggests 'that Pentheus is to be figured only by things that can really be seen'.[42] But Ovid's assertion of presence also validates the simile and reminds

---

[38] The closest we get to a proper epiphany of Bacchus is the appearance of the god's attributes in the episode of the Minyeides in the next book (*Met.* 4.389–98), on which see Keith 2010.

[39] Hardie 2002b: 168–9.

[40] Hymns and tragedies play on the idea of presence or absence, of course, but both genres place a premium on actual epiphany, whether indirectly, through a hymn's narrative of divine revelation, or directly, through tragedy's use of the deus ex machina. On further generic tensions underlying the Pentheus episode, especially between epic and tragedy, see Keith 2002.

[41] Feldherr 2010: 186, with n. 38.

[42] Feldherr 2010: 186; cf. McNamara 2010: 191–3.

the audience that acts of comparing, identifying, describing—the stuff of the *Metamorphoses*, indeed of all art—entail a claim to authority, of which autopsy is a powerful instance.

Furthermore, Ovid suggests that, in terms of seeing and knowing, the inset tale does not, in fact, map all that well onto the conclusion of the Pentheus story. Acoetes claims that he knew the young boy's divinity merely by looking at him (*specto*, *Met.* 3.609), and he becomes a worshipper of the god following an especially clear-cut case of epiphany. This is not, however, the experience of the Thebans: *talibus exemplis monitae noua sacra frequentant / turaque dant sanctasque colunt Ismenides aras* ('warned by such examples, the Theban women throng the new rites and give incense and worship the holy altars', *Met.* 3.732-3). Witness not to an epiphany but to the punishment of a transgressor, the Theban women believe in Bacchus in a very different way from Acoetes.[43] Whether that cognitive difference matters to the now-established god is, of course, a moot question. But for the reader, at least, the closing lines of the book suggest that Pentheus' theomachy, and his corresponding affirmation of autopsy, have achieved something after all. Pentheus succeeds in exploding Acoetes' bland morality fable by revealing the absence of any grounds for sure recognition and identification of divinity beyond the display of maximal power.

In challenging the moralisms that undergird Acoetes' world view, Pentheus hardly elevates his own moral status—indeed, Ovid makes no bones about Pentheus' tyrannical qualities. The effect of that challenge, however, is to put in question the relation between morality and power already at stake in the Lycaon and Semele episodes. If Bacchus need only demonstrate his supremacy in order to secure worship, then why does Acoetes emphasise matters of morality and justice in his story? The question becomes more pressing in light of Feldherr's politicised reading of the episode in which both Pentheus and Bacchus mediate aspects of imperial power, especially as projected through imperial spectacle.[44] Both figures' concern with optics—whether Pentheus' privileging of autopsy or Bacchus' mastery of illusion and invisibility—evokes the visual aspects of Augustan power, from monumental art and public spectacles to the urban sight lines created and disrupted by imperial building projects.[45] Pentheus' desire to make an example of Acoetes' death (*Met.* 3.579-80) and Bacchus' similar use of Pentheus both illustrate the importance of demonstrating power for all to see. But Acoetes' insistence on a capacity for seeing that is ethically, as well as perceptually, correct, together with the subsequent undermining of this position, points to a real struggle to appear not only powerful

---

[43] Pace W. S. Anderson 1997: 409: 'The populace agree with Acoetes'.

[44] My concerns here differ somewhat from those of Feldherr, whose interests lie, first, in the fluctuating referentiality of Pentheus and Bacchus vis-à-vis the emperor, and second, in the use of the contemporary experience of spectacle as a hermeneutic aid to reading the text. See Feldherr 2010: 180-98.

[45] See also Barchiesi 2008a and 2009 on the Phaethon episode.

but also in the right. Indeed, Pentheus had begun the entire episode with a lengthy diatribe against the Bacchic religion's new paradigms of behaviour, which threaten to undermine the masculine values the king proudly identifies with Thebes from its very foundation. The conclusion of the episode not only leaves the moral high ground vacant, it suggests that power is not properly established until the populace really do agree with Acoetes' moral conviction. The success with which gods are able to create that conviction, and the implications for imperial authority, will form part of Ovid's continued engagement with theomachy.

Art and Morality: The Pierides and Arachne

The central aim of this chapter is to show how Ovid's major episodes of theomachy thematise issues of belief in the gods and the criteria of divinity. One slight exception to this pattern is a pair of stories which focus on, and develop, a concern with the morality of the divine, which had also played a part in the episodes of Lycaon and Pentheus. This shift is no mere diversion for variety's sake, however, but rather part of Ovid's attempt to show the many levels on which theomachy functions and the many ways in which the reader must rely on such tests in order to acquire proper knowledge of the gods. The two episodes—the musical competition between the Pierides and the Muses in Book 5 and the weaving contest between Arachne and Pallas in Book 6—show the gods deeply invested in projecting and defending an august image of themselves against the deflating characterisations presented both by their human opponents and by the poem itself.

Ovid's account of the relationship between art and moral critique represents one of the well-worn topics of scholarship on the *Metamorphoses*.[46] Given the abundance of excellent work on the subject, therefore, this section restricts itself to making two brief points directly pertaining to theomachy: first, that the Pierides portray their iconoclastic art—and thus theomachy itself—as more intellectually challenging and rich in content than the conventional song of the Muses, and second, that Arachne's art provokes the goddess Pallas by exposing a distinction between power and moral authority. Theomachy thus tests the claims of theodicy, a test that has implications not only for the gods of the poem but also, Ovid will hint, for an imperial ideology closely aligned with the authority of the Olympians. The argument, then, is preoccupied not so much with the form of theomachic art as with the assertions it makes about the nature of the gods.

Like the tale of Lycaon, Ovid narrates the Pierides' singing contest with the Muses not in his own voice but through the report of one of the victorious

---

[46] See, e.g., Leach 1974, Johnson and Malamud 1988, Harries 1990, P. J. Johnson 2008.

Muses, who describes the event to Pallas (*sic orsa deae dea*, *Met.* 5.300). The juxtaposition of *deae dea* emphasises not only the casual intimacy between the two goddesses—we should expect no scrutiny from this interlocutor—but also the true divinity of the Muses: a challenge to them is as serious as a challenge to Pallas or the other gods and raises the same issues of power and authority. Indeed, lest we consider musical contest of less importance than theomachy proper, the Muse describes it as a 'battle' (*proelia*, *Met.* 5.307). As a result, it becomes impossible to disentangle any reliable representation of the contest from the potential bias of the narrator. The Muse's value judgements highlight the problem: *intumuit numero stolidarum turba sororum* ('the crowd of foolish sisters swelled with pride in their number', *Met.* 5.305). Moreover, the Muse gives remarkably short shrift to the Pierid singer—just over ten lines of summary—as compared to the three hundred lines recapitulating the song of the Muses' own representative, Calliope.[47] And yet, as with Lycaon, the content of the report can nevertheless point to underlying conflicts more substantial than mere insult to the gods.

The Muse-narrator reports that the Pierides framed the contest as one between learned and shallow poetry: *desinite indoctum uana dulcedine uulgus / fallere* ('cease to deceive the uneducated mob with your empty sweetness', *Met.* 5.308–9). The diction is suggestive of the vocabulary of literary aesthetics, especially the Hellenistic ideals of originality and refined learning that were so influential on Roman poetry. So, for instance, Horace's claim to 'hate the ignorant crowd and shun them' (*odi profanum uulgus et arceo*, *Carm.* 3.1.1) alludes to Callimachus' very similar claim to 'loathe common things' (σικχαίνω πάντα τὰ δημόσια, *Epigr.* 28.4).[48] The Pierides' language only strengthens the case for reading the episode as a commentary on the aesthetic values of the *Metamorphoses*, a case already compelling because of the episode's preoccupation with the relative merits of different kinds of song.[49] I want to approach the metapoetic implications in a slightly different way than usual, however—not in order to disagree with other critics, but rather to show how literary critical and theological concerns can overlap. Rather than tracing a connection to Horace and Callimachus, then, what happens if we read the Pierides' derogatory attitude to the *uulgus* as an intratextual reference to the Arcadian *uulgus* of the Lycaon episode (*Met.* 1.220), whose pious belief in the divinity of Jupiter contrasted with the scepticism of Lycaon? As we have already seen in the cases of Semele and

---

[47] See Rosati 2002b: 299–301.

[48] For the influence of Callimachus on Roman, especially Augustan, poetry, see Hunter 2006, Barchiesi 2011, and Acosta-Hughes and Stephens 2012: 204–69. J. J. Clauss 1989 sees the presence of Callimachean imagery throughout this whole section of the *Metamorphoses*, focusing in particular on the episode of the Lycian farmers in Book 6.

[49] For an extensive reading of Calliope's story of Persephone from a metapoetic angle see Hinds 1987b. Zissos 1999: 109–12 discusses the importance of Calliope's pandering to the crowd of nymphs, while 'the Pierides are depicted as losing because they are out of touch with the audience' (111).

Pentheus, and will continue to see in later episodes, Lycaon's behaviour and the issues raised by his conduct are formative for the characterisation of Ovidian theomachy. By alluding to the Arcadian *uulgus*, then, Ovid combines the Pierides' literary snobbery with a tradition of testing the claims of the gods.

The subject of the Pierid's song is the Typhonomachy, a myth closely associated or even identified with Gigantomachy. Indeed, according to the Muse, the Pierid 'ascribes undeserved honour to the Giants and belittles the deeds of the great gods' (*bella canit superum falsoque in honore Gigantas / ponit et extenuat magnorum facta deorum*, Met. 5.319-20). In particular, the Pierid describes the gods fleeing Typhoeus in fear and hiding themselves in the guise of animals (*Met.* 5.321-31). Thus, while the Pierides may not question a particular claim to divinity, as Lycaon and Pentheus do, they nevertheless threaten to radically revise fundamental notions about the power and dignity of the gods. For this reason Calliope spends the first few lines of her song reminding the audience of Typhoeus' eventual defeat and imprisonment under Etna (*Met.* 5.346-58). Her response is all the more effective for the casual way in which she neutralises the force of the Pierid's song, since Typhoeus represents little more than a piece of local colour used to introduce Sicily and the central story of the rape of Proserpina. In terms of rhetoric, then, as well as the well-known conclusion of the Typhonomachy, Calliope offers a devastatingly dismissive rejoinder to the Pierid, whose song is presented as not only tendentious but also trivial. Moreover, the Muses' eventual victory, coupled with the Pierides' transformation into magpies (*Met.* 5.662-78), makes the contest seem a thoroughly one-sided affair.

But before buying too readily into the way in which the Muse-narrator presents events, it's important to notice how both the summary of the Pierid song and the manner of Calliope's response prevent, and avoid, any close engagement with the song's content. The narrator gives the reader little more to go on than a moralising and distinctly slanted account. One salient detail, however, provides a possible explanation for why, beyond its diminution of divine authority, the Pierid's song might have been regarded as dangerous and why Calliope responds in the particular way that she does. That detail is the Pierid's revaluation of the Gigantomachy.

In disputing the conventional account of the Gigantomachy, the Pierid recalls Lucretius' similar revaluation in his defence of materialist philosophers in the *De Rerum Natura*, discussed in the previous chapter. In that same passage from Book 5, Lucretius claims that he will explain his materialism in 'learned words' (*doctis dictis*, Lucr. 5.113), thus framing his philosophical project in terms suggestive of Hellenistic aesthetics. There's reason to believe that the Pierides' own promotion of superior learning is also a matter of Hellenistic philosophy and not just Hellenistic aesthetics alone. Their notion that poetic 'sweetness' appeals to common tastes exemplifies Lucretius' own concern, expressed in *De Rerum Natura* 1, to make his difficult philosophy more palatable to the audience through the medium of poetry.[50] Without that sweetness, indeed, the philosophy turns off most people, whom Lucretius describes as the *uolgus* (Lucr. 1.945). Moreover, the context of the whole passage in *De Rerum Natura* 1 is suffused with explicit mentions not only of the Muses but also of the Hellenistic literary ideal of originality, both of which feature prominently in Ovid's episode.[51] If the Pierid made good on the claim to offer a more sophisticated song than the Muses, however, the Muse-narrator and Calliope give little opportunity to see it.[52] At the end of the contest the Muse-narrator will describe Calliope's song as 'learned' (*doctos cantus*, Met. 5.662), almost as a riposte to the Pierides' earlier claim, but the word perhaps elides the particular learning—of a philosophical kind—that the Pierides had meant, but of which we see barely a glimpse.

And yet the Lucretian flavour of the Pierid song may be traced in some of the features of Calliope's dismissive response. For she vividly connects the seismic and volcanic activities of Etna to the presence of Typhoeus, from the flames emitted from the Giant's mouth to his struggles that shake the earth. This emphatically mythological description stands in pointed contrast to Lucretius' natural scientific account of Etna (Lucr. 1.722–5, 6.680–702), and it participates in a tradition of demythologising and remythologising accounts by not only Lucretius but also Vergil (G. 1.471–3, Aen. 3.570–82), and, some years after the *Metamorphoses*, by the unknown author of the *Aetna*.[53] Indeed, Calliope's song as a whole could hardly be more anti-Epicurean, or more generally anti-rationalising, from Dis' immediate fear that Etna's eruptions might reveal the terrified shades, through the various machinations and consequent sufferings of the gods, to the mythical aetiologies for seasonal and agricultural changes. These features, I suggest, respond to an aspect of the Pierid's song that we are never allowed to see head-on. Although the Pierid's theriomorphic image of the gods may bear little resemblance to an Epicurean view, we must remember that it serves the interest of the Muse-narrator to depict the song as straightforwardly beyond the pale rather than as a troubling challenge to conventional theology.[54] Certain details, however, hint at the Muses' ignorance or suppression of the Pierid's meaning. In a similar way, Jupiter's tendentious account of Lycaon nevertheless left enough clues to reconstruct a more significant challenge to a conventional view of how one knows a god—a view

---

[50] Lucretius draws an analogy between the honey used to sweeten a cup of bitter medicine (*mellis dulci liquore*, Lucr. 1.938) and the sweet honey of the Muses (*musaeo dulci melle*, Lucr. 1.947). For his originality see esp. Lucr. 1.926–30.

[51] Six words relating to 'Muse' or 'Pierus' appear between Lucr. 1.925 and 947.

[52] Against the reading offered by Hinds 1987b: 128–32 I would only emphasise his own qualifications at 166–7 n. 40.

[53] See Glauthier 2011: 87–132. Cf. Hardie 1988, which argues for Ovid's remythologisation of Lucretius in the Narcissus episode.

[54] Rosati 2009 argues that the Pierid's theriomorphic song manipulates the relationship between Greek and Egyptian religion.

represented by the *uulgus*. It is worth recalling, then, that Lycaon's rationalistic and empiricist urge hinted at a scientific, perhaps even Epicurean, allegory. On such a reading of Lycaon, we can now see a philosophical, as well as theomachic, connection running from his own testing of the god to the learned song of the Pierides. Theomachy is not for the masses, but for an elite steeped in Hellenistic thought and values.

Ovid continues the theme of artistic competition in the subsequent episode of Arachne, which begins Book 6. In her weaving contest with the goddess Pallas, Arachne, like the Pierid singer, creates theriomorphic images of the gods. Unlike the song of the Typhonomachy, however, which represents the fleeing and terrified gods in a manner very different from that described elsewhere in the *Metamorphoses*, Arachne's images capture the gods in flagrante, as Ovid himself so often depicts them. In the cases of Europa and Danae, moreover, she even reproduces stories already treated in the poem. This correspondence, coupled with the artistic theme, has naturally led to a number of metapoetic readings of the episode. Like the treatment of the singing contest, however, I wish to shift attention from the different styles of art created by Pallas and Arachne—more ordered on the one hand and more fluid on the other—to the particular way in which Arachne's theomachic art responds to and provokes Pallas. For it's not merely Arachne's temerity that angers the goddess, nor even her success, but above all her effectiveness in undermining the image of the gods projected by Pallas.

Most acts of theomachy culminate in the revelation of a god's identity or true power, but this is almost the starting point of the Arachne episode. Her bold claim to weave better than Pallas summons the goddess in disguise, and her face-to-face challenge provokes the goddess to cast off her disguise and take up the contest. Whereas in the other cases of theomachy, then, the process of revelation or epiphany tells us something about the gods, that work is now displaced onto the art created by Pallas and Arachne.

Pallas' tapestry has a strongly didactic purpose. In the middle it depicts her own victory over Neptune in the contest to be the patron deity of Athens, while in the four corners appear smaller scenes showing the metamorphic punishments of mortals who sought to supplant or better the gods. She includes these last figures, in particular, 'so that her rival for praise might understand by these examples what prize to expect for her mad daring' (*ut tamen exemplis intellegat aemula laudis, / quod pretium speret pro tam furialibus ausis, Met.* 6.83–4). Pallas' triumph over Neptune only amplifies the warning: mortals lose contests with the gods; she wins them. But beyond the obvious admonitory lesson the tapestry also emphasises a particular image of the gods—as benefactors of humankind and patrons of cities, who dominate the centre of the world and relegate their opponents to the periphery. Moreover, while the corner scenes show mortals subject to metamorphosis at the hands of the gods, the central image depicts that same transformative power being used for positive ends: Pallas strikes the ground with her spear and causes an olive tree—her gift to Athens—to rise up miraculously from the earth. The gods themselves, however, are familiar and unchanging (*Met.* 6.72–4):

> bis sex caelestes medio Ioue sedibus altis
> augusta grauitate sedent. sua quemque deorum
> inscribit facies: Iouis est regalis imago.

> The twelve gods, with Jupiter in the middle, sit in their high thrones
> with august dignity. Each of the gods is marked out
> with their own appearance: the image of Jupiter is regal.

The deliberate emphasis on divine majesty and constancy—why else bother to mention that the gods possess their own appearance?—rejects the theriomorphic images of the gods in the *Metamorphoses*, in the song of the Pierid, and, as Ovid will go on to describe, in Arachne's tapestry. Before getting to Arachne, however, it's important to note the obvious pun in *augusta grauitate*. A contemporary audience is unlikely to have missed the allusion to the name of the emperor. The wordplay suggests a correlation between Pallas' conception of divine authority and that of Augustus—solemn, regal, well-ordered, and intolerant of any rival.[55] On this reading, Arachne's very different representation of the divine not only works against Pallas' image but also becomes a critique of an Augustan self-image.

The image of the gods as grave bearers of authority, invested in the foundation of cities, is precisely what Arachne undermines in her own tapestry. Not only are they shown occupied in the pursuit of love, but their metamorphosed forms graphically expose the gods' tendency to adopt other guises for less worthy purposes. Ovid highlights the opposition between the two visions of the gods by ironically applying the same language of divine appearance to Arachne's images: *omnibus his faciemque suam faciemque locorum / reddidit* ('to all of them she restored their own appearance and the appearance of the surroundings', *Met.* 6.121–2). The sense of a true, discernible identity—Pallas' *sua facies*—becomes hard to sustain when the same phrase is applied to the gods' theriomorphic forms, especially given the corrective *reddidit*. Ovid attributes Pallas' angry response to resentment at Arachne's success: *doluit successu flaua uirago / et rupit pictas, caelestia crimina, uestes* ('the golden war goddess was pained at her success and tore the cloth embroidered with heavenly crimes', *Met.* 6.130–1). But that success goes beyond formal or aesthetic excellence; rather, it bespeaks the acuity and rhetorical effectiveness of Arachne's alternative view of the gods.

In touching a divine nerve, Arachne shows how theomachy can offer a penetrating critique of an image of the gods—not just a literal image but also a rhetorical and ideological projection. Arachne's story thereby touches on the

---

[55] Cf. Fowler 2007: 7–10 on the Augustan ideology of comportment.

political sphere, as Ovid hints through the punning allusion to the emperor's name. It's impossible to know what Augustus' response might have been, but the episode makes clear that while punishing the theomach may demonstrate the gods' power, it does not undo the damage done to an authority predicated on a particular, moral conception of the gods or, indeed, of the emperor.[56]

After a series of explorations of the theme in the early books of the *Metamorphoses*, the Arachne episode suggests that the gods do, in fact, have a vested interest in projecting moral authority. One could infer as much from the Lycaon episode, too, but there Jupiter had delivered such a one-sided version of events that it becomes difficult to reject with any certainty—even if one doubts—the moral gap he describes between the pious and the impious. The episode of Pentheus pushed the issue of morality in a slightly different direction, as it posed a question about whether assertions of morality and piety have any real value or whether they are simply the ornamentation of divine power. Books 3–6 frequently return to, and develop, the idea that the gods, at least, genuinely believe their ethical characterisation to be of some significance, even if that characterisation is ultimately self-serving. What sets the Arachne episode apart from the others, however, is the difficulty of seeing her as just another Lycaon or Pentheus or even a Pierid. Her arrogance towards Pallas may recall these other examples, but she is neither a savage nor a tyrant, and her art equals, if not betters, that of the gods. She clearly resists, therefore, the easy moral judgements passed on the other cases, and she shows theomachy to be an effective instrument of moral critique turned against the arch-moralisers of the poem—the gods themselves. Like the Pierid song, then—but more explicitly and successfully—Arachne's tapestry points to the techniques by which the gods project and defend their claims to authority. Once again theomachy both reveals the gods and challenges conventional beliefs in the nature of divinity.

A Material Girl in a Material World: Niobe

The episode of Niobe immediately follows that of Arachne, a connection as thematically consistent as it is mythologically specious. Although Ovid wholly manufactures a link between the two women, there is no mistaking the genuine overlap in their competitive attitudes to the gods, and the complementary ways in which they put pressure on conventional beliefs about the divine. Fundamental to the myth of Niobe has always been the element of boasting: the Theban queen vaunts her fourteen children over the goddess Latona's mere two.[57] Ovid, perhaps uniquely, frames this claim to superiority in terms of

---

[56] Cf. pp. 298–9 on the representation of Arachne on the frieze of Domitian's Forum Transitorium.
[57] Sources differ over the exact number of children (see Forbes Irving 1990: 295), but the element of fecundity is common to all versions.

the very criteria for belief in divinity (*Met.* 6.170–2): *'quis furor auditos'* inquit */praeponere uisis / caelestes?'* ('What madness is this', she says, 'to prefer gods merely heard of to those actually seen?').[58] As in the story of Lycaon, Niobe requires observable evidence prior to the acknowledgement of a deity. Ovid thus harnesses a story usually regarded as a morality tale of human vulnerability and misplaced pride and redirects it to the question of why one should believe in a particular god, or even, as I shall suggest at the end of the section, in conventional conceptions of divinity.[59]

The objects of Niobe's ire in this passage are the Theban women, who, in contrast to Niobe's own scepticism, follow the prophetess Manto in accepting Latona's godhead and offering her worship (*Met.* 6.157–64). As in the Lycaon episode, here too the divine communication is indirect: Manto asserts that Latona speaks through her (*ore meo Latona iubet*, *Met.* 6.162), a claim supported by the narrator's description of the prophetess as inspired by god (*diuino concita motu*, *Met.* 6.158). But whereas the Arcadians worshipped Jupiter as a result of the god's signs of divinity (however unclear those signs may be to the reader), the Theban women's worship of Latona is couched as obedience (*paretur*, *Met.* 6.162) to a reported instruction from the god. This indirectness precisely represents the problem described by Niobe as one of 'gods merely heard of'—there are not even any *signa* to be seen. By contrast with the Theban women, the queen rejects Latona based on the supposed superiority of visible criteria of divinity over the invisible, the material over the immaterial.[60] She spells out the consequence of this way of thinking in two words, 'my godhead' (*numen meum*, *Met.* 6.172): according to the evidence she is about to present, Niobe herself, rather, can truly lay claim to being a god.

Niobe offers several arguments to support her own claim to divinity: kinship with elevated mortals and gods (*mihi Tantalus auctor, / cui licuit soli superorum tangere mensas; / ...Iuppiter alter auus*, 'Tantalus is my father, to whom alone it was allowed to touch the tables of the gods;...Jupiter is my other grandfather', *Met.* 6.172–6), the fear of her subjects (*me gentes metuunt Phrygiae*, 'the Phrygian peoples fear me', *Met.* 6.177), royalty (*me regia Cadmi / sub domina est*, 'Cadmus' palace is under my rule', *Met.* 6.177–8), wealth (*inmensae*

---

[58] Ivana Petrovic has suggested to me that *caelestes* may be a (typically Ovidian) witticism explaining that the gods are simply above Niobe's resolutely earthbound vision (pers. comm.). Pentheus, too, had used similar diction when attacking the worship of Bacchus (*quis furor*, *Met.* 3.531).

[59] As with Ovid's treatment of Lycaon, no other extant version of the Niobe myth offers his emphatically sceptical characterisation, even in cases where Niobe is described as a god (Soph. *Ant.* 834, *El.* 150). See Forbes Irving 1990: 17, 294–7.

[60] On the invisibility of Roman gods, as discussed in Christian sources, see Ando 2010b. Some strands of that later debate—'regarding the representation of the invisible; invisibility as an index of metaphysical valuation; the susceptibility of matter to sense-perception; and the limits imposed on human understanding by embodiment' (Ando 2010b: 69)—can also be seen in the Ovidian passages discussed here.

opes, 'immense wealth', *Met*. 6.181), beauty (*digna dea facies*, 'face worthy of a goddess', *Met*. 6.182), and above all her many children (*huc natas adice septem / et totidem iuvenes*, 'add to this seven daughters and as many sons', *Met*. 6.182–3).[61] Against this imposing list of assets she contrasts the status of the once vagrant Latona (*Met*. 6.186–91), and even casts doubt on her lineage, implying either its unimportance or its fictitiousness by referring to Latona's father as 'Coeus, whoever he is' (*nescioquoque Coeo*, *Met*. 6.185).[62] The queen then declares, imprudently, that her sheer quantity and quality of goods render her impervious to fortune (*Met*. 6.193–7). After one final disparagement of Latona's modest fertility as all but childlessness, she orders the people to cease their worship of the goddess (*Met*. 6.197–202).[63]

Latona's response, addressed to her children Apollo and Diana, echoes Niobe's concerns. The goddess asserts her pride in her children and her position in the pantheon, and demands the protection of her worship (*Met*. 6.206–9):

> en ego uestra parens, uobis animosa creatis,
> et nisi Iunoni nulli cessura dearum,
> an dea sim dubitor perque omnia saecula cultis
> arceor, o nati, nisi uos succurritis, aris.
>
> See, I, your mother, proud of your birth,
> and willing to yield to no goddess except Juno,
> am doubted as to my divinity, and am denied worship at the altars
> through all the ages, unless you, my children, come to my aid.

Ovid's epistemological focus in the episode emerges clearly from Latona's response. Rather than the typical anger of a deity at a mortal's rejection or contempt, Latona's anxiety responds precisely to the terms set by Niobe—the criteria that constitute divinity. Latona freely admits the significance of the challenge: she fears not only that Niobe's words have put her divinity in doubt but also that such doubt threatens her worship in perpetuity.

---

[61] For Niobe's speech as a parody of the hymnic genre see Barchiesi 1999: 124, W. S. Anderson 1972: 176–7. Platt 2011: 67 reads the Homeric Hymns, for instance, as narratives 'in which humans learn to read correctly the *sēmata* of divine presence and recognise the special qualities of divine bodies'. By contrast, Niobe's hymn to herself offers a completely different account of divinity—the *sēmata* of her own 'godhead' undermine Latona's divinity—and the epiphany that it elicits (the subject and implied purpose of most hymns) is oddly non-apparent—Latona herself does not appear and Apollo and Diana are invisible. On Ovid's use of hymn in general see Syed 2004.

[62] The intended rhetorical force of *nescioquoque Coeo* comes from the contrast Niobe sets up between her own lineage, including Jupiter, and a 'mere' Titan. But there may be a further, cultural layer of significance to the uncertainty signified by *nescioquoque*. Roman prayer language often adopted a catch-all form, of the *si(ue)* or *quisquis* type, in order to minimise the possibility of failed communication with the divine (see Hickson 1993: 33–5, 40–3). In Niobe's dismissive language may be heard a parody of the Romans' attempts in their prayers to manage uncertainty.

[63] Despite Niobe's injunction, however, the Theban women continue to worship Latona privately (*Met*. 6.203): *tacito uenerantur murmure numen* ('they worship her godhead with silent murmurs'), and this continued worship, in its way, already signifies a rejection of Niobe's materialist criteria.

That particular problem is resolved, at least at the level of plot, by the manner of Latona's vengeance against Niobe. Latona's wish for the queen to be made childless (*Met.* 6.212–13) is a matter of retaliation, but it also suggests the goddess's anxiety about Niobe's new criteria for divinity, a central element of which was her superior fecundity. At the same time, through the elimination of the main visible proof of the queen's claim to divinity, Latona strengthens the counterargument for privileging the unseen and the immaterial over more materialist grounds for belief. Accordingly, Apollo and Diana slay the children unseen, *tecti nubibus* ('hidden in clouds', *Met.* 6.217). When Apollo slays the sons at least his arrows are visible, but when Diana kills the daughters the poet gives us no indication of the forms of their deaths beyond the fact that their wounds are various. The girls simply appear to keel over dead, in one case agonised by 'an unseen wound' (*uulnere caeco, Met.* 6.293). The true gods' efficacy and invisibility are the ultimate disproof of Niobe's criteria of divinity and any belief that rests upon those criteria.[64] And yet once again, just as with Lycaon's provocation of Jupiter, the gods do become manifest, in a sense, following the challenge laid down by Niobe (*Met.* 6.313–5):

> tum uero cuncti manifestam numinis iram
> femina uirque timent cultuque inpensius omnes
> magna gemelliparae uenerantur numina diuae.

> Then all men and women truly fear the manifest
> anger of the divinity, and they all worship more urgently
> the great godhead of the twins' divine mother.

From an epistemological perspective, then, the sceptic's testing seems an especially powerful, albeit impious and hazardous, way of forcing the divine to reveal itself.

Just as cultural contexts enrich our understanding of Ovid's handling of the Lycaon myth, so too they illuminate his Niobe, though here the focus shifts slightly from identification of a god to the very criteria of divinity. Niobe's argument—that visible, material criteria define a god—are likely to have struck at least some contemporary readers as especially pertinent. In a world where the emperor's elevated status went hand in hand with lineage, power, and wealth, the force of Niobe's claims, especially at *Met.* 6.172–83, appears considerably more compelling. At one point in the poem Ovid even directly comments on the importance of Augustus' lineage for Caesar's, and ultimately Augustus' own, deification: *ne foret hic igitur mortali semine cretus, / ille deus*

---

[64] One might see invisible gods as the first step towards a rationalisation of supernatural influence. The invisibility of Diana's arrows makes it impossible to distinguish between divine intervention and disease, which were in any case traditionally associated (see, e.g., Apollo's anger and the plague of *Iliad* 1; cf. B. Holmes 2010: 49). On this view, however, Niobe's claim to divinity would be no less undermined—not because she is inferior to the gods, but because there are no such things as gods. I owe this point to David Quint.

faciendus erat ('therefore, so that this one [Augustus] would not be born of mortal seed, the other [Caesar] had to be made a god', *Met.* 15.760–1). The emperor, whose power is not only visible through diverse forms such as monuments and coinage but also explicitly tied to genealogy, thus validates Niobe's criteria of divinity and thereby facilitates reading against the grain of Ovid's story: if the road to becoming more than human is a matter of possessing and obtaining the right assets, then perhaps one should be less persuaded by—or at least less fixated on—the power of the invisible.[65] As in the Lycaon story, the imperial context thus creates a slippage from scepticism about a single claim to divinity to outright scepticism. For while Niobe's suspicion of 'gods merely heard of' may be directed at Latona alone—the queen readily acknowledges other gods, such as her own grandfather, Jupiter—once one gives importance to perceptible criteria of divinity, suspicion easily encompasses any god who cannot provide such proof of status.[66]

How to Be a God: Achelous and Hercules

If in the previous instances of theomachy Ovid used conflicts between humans and gods to meditate on the identity and criteria of divinity, he does so even more explicitly in the case of the fight between Hercules and the river god Achelous in Book 9, an episode related by Achelous himself. The battle against a river, as we saw in Achilles' struggle with Scamander in Chapter 1, offers a paradigmatic and canonical example of epic theomachy. What sets Ovid's episode apart, however, is not only the question of Hercules' ambiguous status—part human and part divine—but also the larger context of Achelous' narrative, which includes various stories concerning the power of the gods related towards the end

---

[65] The result of such a reading of the Niobe episode is to place Augustus in tension with the very gods, especially Apollo, with whom he took such pains to align himself (see, e.g., Miller 2009: index s.v. 'Augustus/Octavian'), and to suggest that despite his vaunted renewal of traditional religion he was in some ways its greatest threat. On Augustus' image as reviver of religion see the references at p. 88 n. 19. Feldherr 2010: 301 suggests another similarity between Niobe and Augustus: the latter lost many prospective heirs. Niobe featured prominently in Augustan art, in particular on the doors of the Temple of Palatine Apollo, in which capacity she served as a more conventional warning against hubris (see Galinsky 1996: 213–24). On the relationship between the depiction of Niobe on the temple doors and in Prop. 2.31 see Miller 2009: 200–4.

[66] Although Niobe acknowledges Jupiter's divinity, by doubting Latona she raises the spectre of a *sorites*-style argument against the existence of all gods. The original purpose of such arguments, such as those attributed to Carneades by Cicero (*Nat. D.* 3.43–52) and those of Sextus Empiricus (*Math.* 9.182–90), was not to promote atheism, but rather to attack certain theological principles (see Burnyeat 1982, who takes the Stoics to be the main target, and Meijer 2007: 193–206, who sees the argument as having a wider application). But the logical conclusion of such arguments, however rhetorically intended, was a denial of the divinity of the traditional gods. Ovid may flag Niobe as an especially appropriate conduit for such *sorites* arguments because of her own implicitly quantitative criteria of divinity: the more criteria one satisfies—proximity of relationship to gods, wealth, beauty, fecundity, etc.—and the more of each criterion that one possesses, the better one's claim to godhead.

of Book 8. The idea of divine power is made more complicated still by the context of Hercules' apotheosis, narrated shortly after the fight. For in light of the hero's eventual divinity, it becomes difficult to decide whether it is Hercules or Achelous who should be regarded as the theomach—the 'mortal' fighting the river god, as Achelous alleges, or the river god fighting a superior power.

Ovid puts the question of divine power into play immediately following Achelous' first story, which identifies several nearby islands as the bodies of transformed nymphs and of Achelous' own lover, Perimele. In contrast to the rest of the river god's audience, who believe the story, Pirithous, yet another example of a scorner of the gods, expresses scepticism about the entire category of metamorphic tales (*Met.* 8.611–16):

> factum mirabile cunctos
> mouerat; inridet credentes, utque deorum
> spretor erat mentisque ferox, Ixione natus:
> 'ficta refers nimiumque putas, Acheloe, potentes
> esse deos' dixit, 'si dant adimuntque figuras'.
> obstipuere omnes nec talia dicta probarunt...

> The wondrous deed had moved them
> all; but the son of Ixion mocked their credulity,
> since he was a despiser of the gods and possessed of an unbridled spirit,
> saying: 'You report fictions, Achelous, and think the gods
> too powerful if they give and take away forms'.
> All were shocked and did not approve such words.

Pirithous' mockery recalls the similar attitude of Lycaon to the credulity of the Arcadian *uulgus* (*inridet*, *Met.* 1.221). Beyond a common concern with true and false claims, however, Pirithous explicitly doubts the transformative power of the gods that has been on show for the preceding eight books of the poem. One of his companions, Lelex, attempts to banish his doubt by relating the story of Baucis and Philemon.[67] In particular, Lelex introduces and concludes the tale by emphasising the grounds for believing it—autopsy and reliable report. He has seen the place himself (*ipse locum uidi*, *Met.* 8.622), and has heard the story from trustworthy old men who have no reason to lie (*haec mihi non uani (neque erat, cur fallere uellent) / narrauere senes*, *Met.* 8.721–2). If Lelex is trying to make his point in terms that Pirithous or other sceptics might appreciate, however, he falls some way short of his goal. He has established the existence of a tradition, to be sure, but not its truth. That traditions could be

---

[67] On Pirithous and Lelex as representing different kinds of beliefs in fictions see Feeney 1991: 229–32, Wheeler 1999: 167–71, Gildenhard and Zissos 2004: 67–8, Fabre-Serris 2009, Feldherr 2010: 54–8; A. H. F. Griffin 1991: 66–7 attributes some of Ovid's characterisations to the influence of Nicander. My interest lies less in the metapoetics of belief in the gods, and more in the way that the didactic stories of Book 8 will lead to a very different treatment of belief in divine power in Book 9.

false is a piece of commonplace knowledge, as the genre of historiography in particular so frequently attests.[68] Lelex's lesson, however superficially tailored to Pirithous, seems rather to continue the morally didactic examples seen throughout the poem thus far.[69] He even recalls making an offering at the site with the following words: *cura deum di sunt, et qui coluere coluntur* ('those who care for the gods become gods, and those who have worshipped them are worshipped in turn', *Met.* 8.724).

Achelous follows Lelex with an equally transparent moral allegory, this time illustrating the perils of impiety rather than the rewards of piety. Although ostensibly told to satisfy Theseus' curiosity (*Met.* 8.725–7), the story of Erysichthon clearly responds to Pirithous. In describing Erysichthon as one 'who would scorn the power of the gods' (*qui numina diuum / sperneret*, *Met.* 8.739–40), Achelous alludes to Pirithous, who had earlier been characterised by the narrator as a *deorum spretor* (*Met.* 8.612–13). For his desecration of a grove of Ceres, Erysichthon is afflicted with insatiable hunger, leading eventually to him consuming his own body. The connection of impiety with immoderate desire offers a stark warning to Pirithous, who in the mythological tradition attempts to rape Persephone, for which he will remain eternally trapped in the underworld like his father, Ixion, an archetypal criminal. Lelex's and Achelous' morality tales, then, will prove ineffective, a typical sign of the theomach's intransigence.

It's important to observe, however, that the heavy-handedness of the two stories applies not only to their moral didacticism but also to the way in which they signal the existence of divine power. Baucis and Philemon witness miraculous goings-on before Mercury and Jupiter baldly announce that they are gods (*di sumus*, *Met.* 8.689) and explain that the rest of the impious neighbourhood will be punished for denying the two gods hospitality. The episode, especially the eventual drowning of the neighbours in a swamp, recalls in miniature the story of Lycaon while also taking up the end of the flood narrative in the episode of Deucalion and Pyrrha.[70] Two pious couples are thus contrasted with one impious sceptic. But Lelex has made the matter of identifying the gods—a real point of contention even in Jupiter's report about Lycaon—almost comically straightforward: Mercury and Jupiter don't just provide signs of their divinity; they declare it outright. Correspondingly, Achelous presents Erysichthon as knowingly disregarding unambiguous signs of divine power in Ceres' grove—her oak bleeds, and the nymph within it explicitly warns of Erysichthon's punishment. The two stories respond to Pirithous' scepticism

---

[68] See Marincola 1997, esp. 117–27.

[69] Green 2003 distinguishes between the moralistic agenda underlying Lelex's narration and the contrasting reading Ovid makes available to the reader of the *Metamorphoses*.

[70] The maximal contrast between the figure of the theomach and Deucalion and Pyrrha goes back to Pind. *Ol.* 9.29–46. Intriguingly, the theomach in question in the ode is Herakles, though Pindar distances himself from the story. Ovid, as we shall see, moves in the opposite direction, from Deucalion and Pyrrha to Hercules as theomach.

with sledgehammer subtlety, emphasising the presence of the divine at every turn. The problem with this rhetorical strategy in the context of the *Metamorphoses* as a whole is that the scenarios described by Lelex and Achelous do not possess the epistemological and metaphysical nuances that have made issues of divinity so thorny in the earlier episodes of the poem. Pirithous' scepticism about divinely caused transformations may be misguided, but it simply will not suffice to solve the harder cases, like those of Lycaon and Niobe, by adverting to easier ones, like those of Baucis and Philemon and Erysichthon. Indeed, in eliding the difference between hard and easy cases Lelex's and Achelous' protests sound a little too insistent and appear correspondingly unconvincing. That disparity, which we might reframe as a difference between an oversimplified theory about the divine and a more nuanced reality, is well illustrated by the very next story that begins Book 9, the contest between Achelous and Hercules.

Achelous ends Book 8 by offering perhaps the most convincing response to Pirithous—his own capacity to change shape (*Met.* 8.879–83). But Achelous' subsequent account of his losing struggle with Hercules diminishes the relative importance of metamorphosis as a power of the gods. Moreover, the river god even resembles Pirithous in expressing a sceptical attitude to what he regards as the fiction of Hercules' divine origins. The issue of the divinity of Hercules will in due course lead to the narration of his eventual apotheosis, but the prior story of the contest puts an unusual spin on the concept of theomachy precisely because, as Achelous says, Hercules 'was not yet a god' (*nondum erat ille deus*, *Met.* 9.17). Framed in this way, the river god affirms the traditional hierarchy of divine and human: *turpe deum mortali cedere* ('it is disgraceful for a god to cede to a mortal', *Met.* 9.16). Achelous then argues that the story of Jupiter's paternity is either false or proof of Alcmena's adultery: *elige, fictum / esse Iouem malis an te per dedecus ortum* ('choose whether you prefer that Jupiter is a fiction or that you are born through disgrace', *Met.* 9.25–6). The use of *fictum* looks back to Pirithous' own words to Achelous in the previous book (*ficta*, *Met.* 8.614). Further, although here *fictum* clearly refers to the claim of Jovian paternity, the Latin itself hints at an even more radical possibility—that Jupiter is a fiction and does not really exist. Achelous does not intend such an impiety, of course—he himself is a god—but the irony only amplifies the effect of recalling the scepticism originally voiced by Pirithous.

In the course of the theomachy itself, Achelous' powers of metamorphosis—which Pirithous had believed to be beyond the capacities of the gods—cannot compete with the sheer physical force of Hercules. If that does not sufficiently unsettle our conception of the divine, Hercules himself returns to the sceptical theme in the very next episode. Poisoned by his unwitting wife, he contrasts his suffering with the imagined welfare of his enemy Eurystheus; the perceived injustice leads Hercules to doubt the existence of the gods: *et sunt qui credere possint / esse deos?* ('and are there those who could believe that the gods exist?', *Met.* 9.203–4). And yet the danger of such radicalism is averted when Jupiter confirms his parentage and accepts the hero into heaven. In that light, the earlier discussions of divine power in Book 8 rather seem to miss the point: all the shape-shifting and the manipulation of external forms pale by comparison with the greatest metamorphosis of all—the making of a new god.

Hercules' divinisation has an especially crucial significance in that it represents a paradigm for a series of Roman apotheoses described towards the end of the poem, culminating in the deification of Caesar and Augustus.[71] If the new gods of the Roman world follow in Hercules' footsteps, the challenge presented by Pirithous and Achelous makes them appear both more and less divine: more so because of their extraordinary yet manifest power, like that of Hercules, and less so because metamorphosis—the process that turns them into gods—is the very thing that the poem, whether through the voice of Pirithous or others, so often calls into question.[72]

Rulers, Gods, and the Poet: The Romanisation of Theomachy

After a substantial gap, during which the poem shifts its attention from the gods to the age of heroes and early Roman history, Ovid briefly returns to the subject of theomachy towards the end of the *Metamorphoses*, beginning with the narrative of Caesar's assassination and running through to the poet's epilogue. Like the episode of Achelous and Hercules, the combination of Caesar's death and apotheosis puts an unusual spin on theomachy: thanks to Caesar's eventual divinisation, Ovid raises an entirely human act of murder into something of mythical proportions. At the same time, Ovid avoids the kind of detailed scrutiny of the criteria of divinity, which the earlier episodes of theomachy had so thoroughly examined. The absence of such scrutiny is made all the more pointed by a clear ring composition tying the end of the poem to its beginning: the narrative of Caesar's murder recalls the programmatic tale of Lycaon, in which the assassination was first mentioned.[73] Here in Book 15, however, there is no obvious sign of the poet's previous concerns with doubt and testing. The disappearance of the more confrontational aspects of theomachy will come as no surprise given the explicitly Augustan context. Indeed, since Ovid turns from the divinisation of Caesar to glance towards the similar future awaiting the emperor, this could hardly be the place to emphasise aggressive scepticism or resistance, no matter how distanced from the poet's own voice. And yet two important factors impinge on any reading

[71] See Feeney 1991: 205–24.
[72] For apotheosis as a category that encourages thinking about belief and disbelief see Feeney 1998: 110–11 and Hardie 2009a: 13.
[73] White 2002: 14.

of the poem's denouement. The first is the difficulty of ignoring the effect of all the previous episodes of theomachy in the poem, an effect made all the more present to the reader by the recollection of Lycaon through Caesar. The second factor is Ovid's own epilogue, which famously casts the poet as in tension with Jupiter. But alongside these reasons to see a continuing pressure placed on claims to divinity, the epilogue also suggests that Ovid takes a leaf from the emperor's book in deploying such claims to his own advantage.

The transition from the arrival of Asclepius to the narrative of Caesar emphasises a new concern with specifically Roman gods: *hic tamen accessit delubris aduena nostris; / Caesar in urbe sua deus est* ('yet this one approached our shrines a stranger; Caesar is a god in his own city', *Met.* 15.745–6). Unlike Asclepius, and earlier Bacchus and Hercules, whose status is owed to their power and divine father, Ovid draws attention to the unusual process by which one can now become a god: it was not so much Caesar's achievements that led to his deification 'as his descendant' (*quam sua progenies*, *Met.* 15.750). A few lines later, Ovid makes the reversed causality even more explicit: *ne foret hic igitur mortali semine cretus, / ille deus faciendus erat* ('therefore, so that this one [Augustus] would not be born of mortal seed, the other [Caesar] had to be made a god', *Met.* 15.760–1). Whatever the means of Caesar's deification, however, the fact of his becoming a god goes along with a renewed interest in theomachy. When Venus sees the impending murder of Caesar, she interprets it as yet another attack on her and her descendants, citing the examples of her wounding by Diomedes and Aeneas' persecution by Juno. In referring to one of the paradigmatic episodes of theomachy from the *Iliad*, however, and in casting Aeneas' struggles as a 'war . . . with Juno' (*bella...cum Iunone*, *Met.* 15.773–4), Venus not only seeks the sympathy of the other gods but also associates the killing of Caesar with acts of fighting the divine.[74] Theomachy has thus become Romanised, a double process that applies a mythical theme to historical reality and gives history the character of myth.

The blurring of mythical tradition and recent history was nowhere more evident than in the *Aeneid*, whose influence is felt throughout the *Metamorphoses* but especially in the last books. Venus' speech brings that Vergilian dialectic between myth and history right up to contemporary Rome. Not only does Venus interpret Caesar's murder according to mythical paradigms, she also acts as if this event is part of epic tradition rather than history (*Met.* 15.803–6):

> tum uero Cytherea manu percussit utraque
> pectus et Aeneaden molitur condere nube,
> qua prius infesto Paris est ereptus Atridae
> et Diomedeos Aeneas fugerat enses.

[74] Note the double valence of theomachy—both as a wilful impiety and as a divine persecution of a pious hero.

> But then Venus struck her breast with both
> hands and strove to hide Aenean Caesar in a cloud,
> as earlier Paris was snatched from hostile Menelaus,
> and Aeneas had fled the sword of Diomedes.

If the mere thought of Venus rescuing Caesar, as she rescues others in the *Iliad*, does not sufficiently play on the reader's suspension of disbelief, Ovid drives the point home with the single word *uero*. On the one hand it has its usual and straightforward function of an adversative, contrasting the viciousness of the assassins with the desperate action of Venus. But, on the other hand, its etymological meaning, 'in truth', puts the idea of Venus' epic intervention—indeed the whole mythico-historical construct implied by *Aeneaden*—under some pressure.[75] Ovid thereby provokes the reader to doubt not the story itself—which is clearly fantastical—but rather the underlying Augustan narrative about divine origins and associations that enabled such stories to exist. Fundamental to that narrative is the idea of divine genealogy, whether backwards through Aeneas and the maternity of Venus or forwards through the agency of Augustus: *ut deus accedat caelo templisque colatur / tu facies natusque suus* ('you and your son will ensure that he enters heaven a god and is worshipped in the temples', *Met.* 15.818–9). The introduction of new gods and the demonstration of divinity have been crucial themes of the poem, especially the first half, and Ovid returns to them here. Moreover, the killing of Caesar—the act that precedes and leads to his divinisation—recalls, in particular, the striking simile used in the Lycaon episode, which compared the gods' outrage at Lycaon's impiety to the anger of the Roman people towards Caesar's assassins (*Met.* 1.199–205). The interaction of myth and history is not, however, confined to explicit passages that blend, and alternate between, the two realms, as in the accounts of Lycaon and Caesar. Rather, these passages affirm the potential of myth always to impinge on historical reality. The theomachic resonances of the death of Caesar merely emphasise that any and all episodes of divine-human conflict in the poem have points of contact with contemporary Rome as well as the mythical tradition.

Ovid's decision to allude to, rather than spell out, the mutual implications of the various parts of his poem seems entirely judicious given the power of the *princeps*, of which Ovid famously fell foul. But an overly direct interrogation of imperial ideology was also rendered unnecessary, so thoroughly had the groundwork been laid in the earlier episodes. From Lycaon onwards, theomachy consistently tests claims about the identity of gods, the true criteria of divinity, and the ethical norms established by conventional piety. The ring

---

[75] Cf. Gladhill 2012, paragraph 24, on the allusion to *Aen.* 1.33 (*tantae molis erat Romanam condere gentem*) in Ovid's *Aeneaden molitur condere*: 'The hiding of the *Aeneis* in a cloud is an intertextual gesture to the underlying implications behind Vergil's *moles*, the establishment of a poetically authorized Augustan Rome'.

composition that links the first episode of metamorphosis to the last thereby reactivates the whole set of questions that Lycaon had initiated. For this reason Ovid can well afford to adopt a lighter touch in this final, semi-historical narrative about the gods than he had in the case of Pentheus, Niobe, and the other theomachs—Caesar's assassins, by contrast, are given little characterisation at all, let alone an epistemological remit. However, while the reader well versed in issues of sign-inference, autopsy, and ethical scrutiny may possess a battery of objections to the more grandiose claims of imperial ideology, the power of those claims remains very much real and unaffected by individuals' scepticism. It seems unlikely, then, that the main purpose of Ovid's less confrontational denouement was merely to reiterate earlier questions. Rather, Ovid accepts the remarkable ideological dexterity of Augustus, a man whom our sources record as a religious traditionalist as well as an innovator, one who cultivated the worship of the gods, imitated them, and even created them. It is not only because of an understandable caution, then, that Ovid responds to Augustus with a subtlety not evident in earlier episodes treating claims to divinity. That subtlety can also be put down to a new appreciation of the nature of divinity, one made richer and more nuanced by the variety of examinations undertaken in the early books of the poem.

Nowhere is that appreciation more evident than in Ovid's closing gambit, an epilogue through which the poet signals a deeply ambivalent relationship both to divinity and to the emperor. On the one hand, Ovid boasts that his work is invulnerable to 'Jupiter's anger' (*Iouis ira*, *Met.* 15.871), as well as fire, iron, and the passage of time. Besides this troping of permanence, one might reasonably wonder why Jupiter should be angry at the work in the first place, though the poem's representation of the god and the challenges to him offer a ready answer. A hint of imperial censorship, too, cannot be far away.[76] Read in the light of Ovid's subsequent exile, the wrath of Jupiter functions as a staple analogy and metaphor for Augustus' own attitude to the poet.[77] The *Metamorphoses*, Ovid seems to suggest, defies god and, by implication, the emperor.[78] And yet the terms in which Ovid frames his defiance—his poetic immortalisation—owe a good deal to the emperor. The poet's catasterism follows that of Caesar, which Augustus had affirmed, and it also resembles the emperor's own deification, at which Ovid had already glanced: *super alta*

[76] The threat of censorship increases the sense of the *Metamorphoses*' dangerousness, whether or not Ovid entertained the possibility seriously.

[77] Cf. Lowrie 2009: 376 n. 40, and see in general her discussion at 374–82. See also my treatment of Ovid's exile poetry in Chapter 9. Jim Tatum points out to me that the last words in the *Metamorphoses* used of Augustus and Ovid himself are, respectively, *absens* ('absent', *Met.* 15.870) and *uiuam* ('I will live', *Met.* 15.879) (pers. comm.). Might this diction—with each word placed emphatically at the final foot of the hexameter—hint at a reversal of fortunes between immortalised emperor and exiled poet (cf. *OLD* s.v. *absum* 1b)? On rereading the *Metamorphoses* from the perspective of Ovid's exile poetry see Hinds 1985.

[78] Pace Galinsky 1975: 254.

perennis / astra ferar ('I shall be borne above the high stars, eternal', *Met.* 15.875–6).[79] The topoi of poetic catasterism and flight flourish in the Augustan period, but nowhere is the link with the elevation of the emperor more visible than in this epilogue.[80] Moreover, Ovid figures his fame not only as analogous to imperial ascent but also as dependent on Roman power (*quaque patet domitis Romana potentia terris / ore legar populi*, 'wherever Roman power extends over conquered lands, I shall be read by the lips of the people', *Met.* 15.877–8). Scholars have pointed out before the complicity between Ovid and Augustus, the figurehead of Roman power, but I would like to draw attention to a striking consequence of the poet's double aspect as antagonist and analogue of the emperor.[81] At the close of the *Metamorphoses* Ovid himself has become subject to the scrutiny to which his poem has so consistently subjected claims to divine power or of divine identity. And yet the trace of theomachy glimpsed in Ovid's defiance of Jupiter's anger disappears with the assertion of the poet's own divinisation. Indeed, the consequences of the poet's canonical status will remain tantalisingly outside the scope of the work and without the author's explicit self-commentary. The twinning of those themes of theomachy and divinisation, however—more intimately connected than even in the earlier episodes of the *Metamorphoses*—represents a dynamic that will be fundamental to the subsequent poetic tradition.

---

[79] Note how the diction of Ovid's catasterism looks back to the previous two: *illa dies* (*Met.* 15.873) and *aeui* (874) point to *illa dies* and *aeuo* (both 868) in reference to Augustus; *spatium* (874), *alta* (875), and *astra* (876) point to *spatioso* (849), *altius* (848), and *astris* (846) in reference to Caesar. Observe also, however, that Caesar must be carried by Venus (*intulit*, 846, *tulit*, 847), whereas Ovid can rise through his own power (*ferar*, 876).

[80] E.g., Verg. *Ecl.* 5.51–2, 56–7; *G.* 3.8–9; Hor. *Carm.* 1.1.35–6, 2.20.1–5, 3.30.1–9. Wickkiser 1999: 135–6 notes the hyperbole of Ovid's *super astra*, where most deifications are placed among the stars or in the heavens.

[81] Wickkiser 1999: 136–9, Habinek 2002, esp. 51–9. For the instability of comparisons here see O'Hara 2007: 128–30. For the power and limitations of Ovid's textual apotheosis, as compared to Caesar's and Augustus' astral apotheoses, see Hardie 1997b: 189–95.

4

Deification and Theomachy in Seneca's *Hercules Furens*

> He is the culmination of man in the ancient world.
> —GUSTAVE FLAUBERT

> How ridiculous are mortals' boundaries!
> —SENECA

> For you are poets, and we too are poets treating the same things, rivalling you as artists and actors of the noblest drama.
> —PLATO

Hercules is by nature a figure defined by extremes, whether in terms of his proverbially great strength, insatiable appetites, or the extent of his travels. In one of the clearest signs of the hero's exceptionalism, the Olympians must rely on his aid to win their battle against the Giants. At the same time, the mythological and literary traditions also suggest a tension between Hercules and the gods, from the outright theomachy against Hades and Hera mentioned by Dione in *Iliad* 5 and against Achelous in *Metamorphoses* 8 through to more subtle associations related to his heroic acts and even his genealogy.[1] The idea of Hercules as a theomach, then, is at once both jarring and strangely apt. Jarring, because Hercules is a son of Jupiter and traditional ally of the gods, and a future deity himself; appropriate, because theomachy is the paradigmatic act of extremism, chafing against the limits of mortality just as Hercules himself fights Hades and strives to become a god.

---

[1] On Dione's speech at *Il.* 5.392–404 see Chapter 1; on Achelous Chapter 3. Hardie 1986: 110–18 detects some Gigantomachic notes in Hercules' overcoming of Cacus in *Aeneid* 8, though he views them as signs of the forces of order appropriating the elemental powers of disorder. On Hercules' inability to control his violence in the Salian hymn at *Aen.* 8.285–305, see Heiden 1987. Padilla 1998: 56 n. 150 notes that 'Tzetzes, *On Lycophron* 640, refers to a tradition of Herakles as the son of Briareus'.

Seneca's *Hercules Furens* (*HF*) makes more of the idea of Herculean theomachy than any other text we know of. The tragedy opens with Juno voicing her anxiety that Hercules will seize Jupiter's throne, and when later the hero is afflicted with madness he imagines himself waging war on the gods. Seneca thus doubly jolts his audience, first, by hinting at a theomachy greater than any before—this is one hero who poses a genuine threat to the gods; second, by making that theomachy a failure on an unprecedented scale—far from ascending to the stars, Hercules mistakenly kills his wife and children. The twinning of the themes of theomachy and deification was already fairly clear in the Hercules narrative of the *Metamorphoses*, where the hero fought Achelous in part to prove his claim to divinity, shortly before achieving his apotheosis. Seneca, however, makes the conjoining of those themes utterly fundamental to his play: Juno almost stakes her divinity on stopping Hercules from becoming a god, Hercules hallucinates that the gods bar him from heaven before imagining himself launching a theomachy, and numerous other passages in the work discuss either the criteria of divinity or acts of theomachy.

Scholarship on the play has primarily focused on the moral assessment of the hero, especially Hercules' responsibility for his frenzied actions. Questions of character and will are more difficult to parse in Seneca's tragedy than in Euripides' version of the myth, which would certainly have been one, and possibly even the main, source for the *HF*.[2] In the Greek play, Lyssa, the personification of madness, explicitly brings about Herakles' frenzy, at which the first half of the drama hints only obliquely.[3] In the Senecan version, by contrast, the onset of madness coincides with no visible, external interference, and the content of Hercules' hallucination not only corresponds to Juno's initial fears but also fits plausibly with the attitude he has already shown to Dis and Juno. As a result, while some critics put the extremity of his behaviour down to the malign influence of Juno, the majority—and currently orthodox—view sees an essential continuity in the behaviour of the hero in sanity and madness.[4]

The intense focus on questions of character and responsibility, however, has led to a fairly narrow treatment of the distinctively Senecan themes of deification and theomachy. Where critics have looked to contemporary politics, aesthetics, or philosophy for illuminating contexts, they have done so largely in

---

[2] Braden 1993 argues that differences from Euripides should be taken into consideration when interpreting the play, since Seneca would at the very least have been familiar with the Greek version. Tarrant 1978 and 1995 cautions against overprivileging Greek models without knowledge of now lost Roman intermediaries.

[3] On Euripides' *Herakles* see Papadopoulou 2005, esp. 1-2 on earlier critics' frequent charges that the play is, in Gilbert Murray's phrase, 'broken-backed' (Murray 1946: 112).

[4] Mitigating arguments emphasising Juno's role: Herington 1966: 456, Motto and Clark 1981 (cf. 1988: 261-6), Lawall 1983: 11, Zwierlein 1984: 12-21, Billerbeck and Guex 2002: 25-9. Arguments emphasising Hercules' negative characterisation: Henry and Walker 1965; Bishop 1966; W. S. H. Owen 1968: 302-8; Braden 1970: 23-5; 1993; Galinsky 1972: 168-70; Zintzen 1972; Shelton 1978; Fitch 1979; 1987; Segal 1983: 234-5; Papadopoulou 2004; E. R. Wilson 2004: 98-112; Riley 2008: 51-91.

isolation. This chapter, by contrast, draws on a variety of prose and poetic texts including Suetonius' biography of Caligula, the treatise *On the Sublime* attributed to Longinus, and Seneca's philosophical works, in order to illustrate various contemporary discourses that use the imagery of ascent to the heavens or the rhetoric of antagonism against the gods, and reads the *HF* against those contexts. I argue, in particular, that Seneca alludes to a number of alternative paths to godhead—political, poetic, and philosophical—some of which appear more viable than Herculean theomachy. Imperial deification, poetic immortality, and the elevation of the wise man all intersect with the themes and diction of the *HF*, and they were all the more likely to occur—either individually or collectively—to an author or reader steeped in the literature and experience of the mid-first century AD. The chapter thus begins with a close reading of Juno's prologue that establishes the basic twinning of the themes of deification and theomachy (those who know the play well may wish to skip this part), while the following three sections examine the political, poetic, and philosophical contexts in turn.

The mention of Seneca's philosophical writings in the previous paragraph will for some readers immediately raise a host of questions that are best dealt with at the outset. We need not belabour the long-standing debate about the relationship between the philosophy and the tragedies, nor the question of whether they even have the same author.[5] Critics have agreed that Senecan prose provides an important context for the poetry, but they differ on whether the drama should be seen as supporting, testing, or rejecting Stoicism.[6] I take the position that the tragedies, as works of poetry, necessarily have a wider range of reference, authorial intention, and readerly reception than a strictly Stoic interpretation—whether Stoic or anti-Stoic—can reflect. That is not to say that any interpretation, including my own, can do justice to all contexts or that no interpretation should follow Stoic lines of thought, since this would arbitrarily exclude an important and available context—indeed, my final section exploits precisely this resource. A reader with strong philosophical sympathies, for instance—whatever their philosophical leanings, and whether or not Seneca is the author of both the prose and the tragedies—is liable to read the themes of deification and theomachy in the *HF* from a perspective shaped

---

[5] The most recent overview of Stoic interpretation of the tragedies is Hine 2004, which contains numerous further references and lays out the various schools of thought (following Mayer 1994). See also C. A. J. Littlewood 2004: 15–57; the essays by Ker and Tarrant in Volk and Williams 2006; the essays by Schiesaro, Wray, and Busch in Bartsch and Wray 2009; Staley 2010; and Star 2012: 62–83. For the view that Seneca Philosophus and Tragicus are not the same individual see Ahl 2008: 14–16. Throughout this book I refer to Seneca the Younger as the author of both sets of works, though most of the readings could remain largely as they are even if the author of the tragedies were someone else.

[6] Staley 2010 offers the most recent and trenchant argument in favour of a Stoic interpretation of the tragedies. Schiesaro 2003, with whose metapoetic readings Staley frequently disagrees, sees greater tension between the tragedies and the philosophy. For a reading of the *HF*, in particular, against a Stoic context see Auvray 1989, though her concerns are quite different from mine.

by philosophical discourse. I use mostly Stoic texts to illustrate that discourse because the imagery and expression of Stoicism are closest to what we see in the *HF*, but I also cite Epicurean *comparanda*: a shared philosophical sensibility is much more relevant to my reading than any doctrinal differences. Accordingly, the interpretations offered should not be thought of as defining a single, dominant message, but rather as illustrating different contextual views of a single theme—views which will turn out to have certain key features in common. As the Stoic question nicely illustrates, I hope that the combination of contexts drawn on throughout the whole chapter, and indeed in the book, will loosen up the strictures placed on criticism and shortcut some of the narrower debates in which the field of Latin literary criticism occasionally becomes mired.[7]

Juno

Juno has the longest opening monologue of any character in the ten tragedies transmitted under Seneca's name. Her expansive speech introduces the themes of divinisation and the struggle for authority that dominate the play. Indeed, her very first words show a concern with divine status (*HF* 1–5):

> soror Tonantis—hoc enim solum mihi
> nomen relictum est—semper alienum Iouem
> ac templa summi uidua deserui aetheris
> locumque caelo pulsa paelicibus dedi.
> tellus colenda est; paelices caelum tenent.

> Sister of the Thunderer—for this name alone
> is left me—I, a widow, have deserted ever-unfaithful Jupiter
> and the regions of highest heaven,
> and driven from the sky I have yielded my place to concubines.
> I must court the earth; concubines hold the sky.

She proceeds to list various constellations in the sky, which represent the catasterism of Jupiter's lovers and illegitimate sons (*HF* 6–18). Thus, from the very opening of the play, divine status is related to cosmic dislocation and competition.[8] Superiority and inferiority are literalised in spatial terms, as Juno is forced to leave the heavens for earth and bridles at the loss of her rightful position. Juno's opposition of earth and heaven (*tellus…caelum, HF* 5), moreover, is suggestive of the myth of the Gigantomachy, in which the sons of

---

[7] Besides philosophically sectarian interpretations, compare political readings of texts as either pro-imperial or anti-imperial (on which see Chapter 9).
[8] The opening line alludes to Juno's speech in Ovid's Semele episode (*Met.* 3.266), which is similarly concerned with the way human overreaching is construed by the goddess (see Chapter 3).

the earth attempt to overthrow the gods of Olympus. Although the phrase *tellus colenda est* primarily refers to Juno's unwilling departure from heaven and occupation of earth (*OLD* s.v. *colo* 1 'to inhabit'), it also suggests the 'worship' of Earth as a deity (*OLD* s.v. *colo* 6). With this secondary meaning in mind, Juno becomes aligned no longer with Olympus but with the earth—the ultimate source of monstrous power, the mother of the Giants and of the beasts that plague humanity and Hercules. Already in the first five lines, then, we are introduced to the theme of cosmic disorder that will run through the whole of the play.

Within the list of constellations, Juno points specifically to Orion: *ferro minax hinc terret Orion deos* ('here menacing Orion terrifies the gods with his sword', *HF* 12), an image that introduces the idea of theomachy before even the first mention of Hercules.[9] She then cements the theme of human-divine rivalry and deification through her specific fear about Alcmene, whose current superiority would be strengthened by the apotheosis of her son, Hercules (*HF* 21–6, especially *astra promissa*, 'promised stars', *HF* 23). Juno appears especially anxious about the cosmic disorder Hercules generates from birth, whether in the form of the lengthened night of his conception (*in cuius ortus mundus impendit diem*, *HF* 24) or the consequently increasing number of constellations as mother and son both will become fixed in the heavens (*pariterque natus*, *HF* 23).[10] At the same time, her emphasis on Hercules' unique birth provides some justification for the promise of deification: he was marked from the beginning as exceptional, as well as disruptive of the normative cosmic order.

However likely the deification of mother and son may be, Juno refuses simply to concede without a fight (*HF* 27–9):

> non sic abibunt odia: uiuaces aget
> uiolentus iras animus, et saeuus dolor
> aeterna bella pace sublata geret.
>
> My hatred will not just go away: my violent mind
> will pursue living anger, and fierce pain
> will abolish peace and wage eternal wars.

Juno's anger, sense of grievance, and relentless aggression recall her portrayal in the *Aeneid*, where she displays unrelenting hatred towards the defeated Trojans,

---

[9] Orion is not born from one of Jupiter's affairs, hence Fitch 1987: 123: 'The inclusion of Orion in Juno's list is puzzling'. Fitch explains Orion's presence by his chasing of the Pleiades at the time of his catasterism. I would argue that Seneca's emphasis of Orion's theomachic aspect also recalls his attempted rape of Diana. Orion thus foreshadows the equally mighty and sexually aggressive Hercules. W. S. H. Owen 1969 argues for the variant reading of A (*fera coma hinc exterret*), thereby dropping any mention of Orion; both Fitch 1987 and Billerbeck 1999 follow E, however, as do I.

[10] On Seneca's use of cosmic imagery to destabilise straightforward ideas about Hercules' deification see W. S. H. Owen 1968: 302–8.

now turned usurpers first of her favoured Carthage and then of Italy: *necdum etiam causae irarum saeuique dolores / exciderant animo* ('and not even now had the causes of anger and savage pains fallen from her mind', *Aen.* 1.25–6); *Iuno aeternum seruans sub pectore uulnus* ('Juno, keeping an eternal wound beneath her breast', *Aen.* 1.36).[11] But whereas in the *Aeneid* Juno is foiled by a combination of the historical necessity of Rome's foundation and the panegyrical demands of Augustan ideology, the dark world of Senecan tragedy presents no such obstacles for the goddess. If Aeneas, in a sense, won his theomachy against Juno and in the process enabled Rome to exist, Seneca's allusion reminds us that Juno's anger remains relevant half a century after the *Aeneid* and that the object of her anger, while superficially Hercules, is at heart always Rome.

And yet, as soon as she declares her bellicose intent, she bemoans the inefficacy of her powers against a hero whose seeming invincibility threatens to defy the generic laws of tragedy (*HF* 30–42):

> quae bella? quidquid horridum tellus creat
> inimica, quidquid pontus aut aer tulit
> terribile dirum pestilens atrox ferum,
> fractum atque domitum est. superat et crescit malis
> iraque nostra fruitur; in laudes suas
> mea uertit odia; dum nimis saeua impero,
> patrem probaui, gloriae feci locum.
> qua Sol reducens quaque deponens diem
> binos propinqua tinguit Aethiopas face,
> indomita uirtus colitur et toto deus
> narratur orbe. monstra iam desunt mihi,
> minorque labor est Herculi iussa exequi
> quam mihi iubere; laetus imperia excipit.

> What wars? Whatever fearful thing the hostile earth begets,
> whatever sea or air has brought forth,
> terrible, dread, noxious, cruel, savage,
> has been broken and tamed. He overcomes and grows through ills
> and enjoys my anger; to his own praises
> he turns my hatred; by ordering such cruelties,
> I have proved his paternity, I have given scope to his glory.
> Where the Sun, leading back the day and laying it down,
> has touched both Ethiopian tribes with his close torch,
> his untamed valour is worshipped and in the whole world
> he is spoken of as a god. Now monsters fail me,
> and it is a lesser labour for Hercules to fulfil orders,
> than for me to give them; he receives my commands gladly.

---

[11] See Fitch 1987: 131.

The goddess's seeming impotence against a mortal raises the question of how she can possibly get the better of Hercules over the course of this tragedy. The earth, which she now inhabits and possibly even worships, has already been tamed by Hercules—indeed, Juno's opposition only magnifies his glory. Despite the typical dominance of gods on the tragic stage, Juno seems as unlikely to prevail here as in the *Aeneid*, reduced back to her epic role by the hero's transcendence of all obstacles.

Further, through her commands, Juno feels that she has provided Hercules with the opportunity to prove descent from Jupiter (*HF* 35–6).[12] Her anxiety seems belated, however. Through his valour, the hero has already earned the status of a god (*HF* 39–40), a kind of deification by word of mouth.[13] Moreover, Hercules has become a substitute for the Olympian gods, since the people can call on him with greater reliability than calling on the gods above. His effectiveness, unlike that of conventional prayer to the gods above, is wholly manifest—he destroys threats to civilisation and his spoils, such as the skin of the Nemean lion, advertise his victory.[14] Hercules' deification thus seems to be a fait accompli, a mere formal recognition of an already prevalent belief. It is precisely the constructedness of this belief, however—its dependence on what society chooses to believe and value—that creates an opportunity for Juno. The people have conferred de facto divine status upon Hercules because of his protection of them and his civilisation of the world—contingent facts that can be undone or at least severely undermined. As Juno herself has already made abundantly clear at the outset of her monologue, honour and status represent fundamental criteria of divinity, and even a dejected Juno can still muster powerful resources. Were Hercules to suffer a similar reverse, it's as yet unclear whether his merely constructed divinity could be sustained.

Of all his trials, Juno describes in greatest detail Hercules' most recent challenge—the abduction of Cerberus from the underworld. Her sense of futility, and consequent anxiety, increases as the hero not only satisfies her commands but also threatens to exceed them (*HF* 46–56):[15]

> nec satis terrae patent:
> effregit ecce limen inferni Iouis
> et opima uicti regis ad superos refert.

---

[12] Thus pre-empting the sceptical question raised by Achelous in Ovid's *Metamorphoses* (*Met.* 9.23–6), on which see Chapter 3 above. Cf. Ps.-Sen. *HO* 147–50.

[13] Fitch 1987: 133 states that *colitur* in line 39 need only mean that the people honour, rather than worship, Hercules. I would argue that *colitur* must at least suggest worship. In the context of treating the hero as a *deus*, the distinction between honour and worship is, at best, a fine one.

[14] From this perspective Hercules can appear to pose a rather more genuine threat to all the gods, not only Juno, since he makes the gods unnecessary. The portrayal of a benefactor of humankind as an antagonist of the gods recalls Prometheus, who is himself a kind of theomach.

[15] I here adopt the text of Billerbeck; Fitch 1987 follows Leo in moving 49 after 54 for the sake of continuity of thought. Since Juno's rhetoric reflects her anger and anxiety, however, improvements to her logic, and to the transmitted text, are unwarranted (see Billerbeck 1999: 210–12).

> parum est reuerti, foedus umbrarum perit:
> uidi ipsa, uidi nocte discussa inferum
> et Dite domito spolia iactantem patri
> fraterna. cur non uinctum et oppressum trahit
> ipsum catenis paria sortitum Ioui
> Ereboque capto potitur et retegit Styga?
> patefacta ab imis manibus retro uia est
> et sacra dirae mortis in aperto iacent.

> Even the earth does not extend far enough:
> See, he has broken the threshold of infernal Jupiter
> and brings back the spoils of the defeated king to the upper world.
> It is not enough to return, the covenant of the shades has been undone:
> I saw him myself, I saw him, having shattered the night of the underworld
> and having subdued Dis, vaunting to his father the spoils
> of his brother. Why did he not drag him defeated and burdened
> by chains—the very one who shares an equal lot with Jupiter—
> and become master of captured Erebus and lay bare the Stygian world?
> A path has been opened back from the deep shades,
> and the sanctities of dread death lie in the open.

Hercules' penetration of the underworld literalises the crossing of boundaries, both spatially and in terms of appropriate human action.[16] The passage brings out the violence with which Hercules destroys divisions between worlds and mixes darkness and light (*effregit limen, nocte discussa*). Juno refers to Dis as conquered (*uicti*) and subdued (*domito*), and even envisages his capture (*HF* 52-4). By describing Cerberus as the spoils of Jupiter's brother (*fraterna*, emphasised by enjambment), and by mentioning that Dis drew an equal lot to Jupiter (*paria sortitum*), Juno identifies the gods of upper and lower worlds and thereby suggests that it's a small step from threatening Dis to threatening Jupiter himself.[17] The rhetorical questions at *HF* 52-4 culminate in the image of Hercules as the new sovereign of the underworld, exposing what had previously remained hidden, and assuming a divine role equal to his father's.[18] Juno thus imagines deification by force—an act of theomachy—and a consequent revolution in the nature of the underworld, no longer a repository and prison safely removed from sight and interaction. Juno goes on to describe Hercules parading Cerberus through the cities of Argos (*HF* 57-9), an act she interprets in typically self-centred fashion as a triumph over her (*de me triumphat, HF* 58). While she fears the sight of Cerberus, Hercules shows himself less afraid than gods, whether the Sun (*HF* 60-1) or Juno herself (*HF* 61-3), and so his

---

[16] Boundaries: Fitch 1987: 134-5.
[17] See Fitch 1987: 136-7.
[18] Juno's claim is not unfounded—Hercules asserts as much after he returns from the underworld: *si placerent tertiae sortis loca, / regnare potui* ('if the regions of the third lot pleased me, I could have reigned', *HF* 609-10).

triumphal aspect becomes more than a celebration of success or a mockery of Juno—it marks his superiority over the gods.

At this point Juno dismisses these and earlier complaints as too light (*leuia sed nimium queror*, *HF* 63). She then explicitly voices the fear of theomachy to which all previous anxieties have been leading (*HF* 64–74):

> caelo timendum est, regna ne summa occupet
> qui uicit ima; sceptra praeripiet patri.
> nec in astra lenta ueniet ut Bacchus uia:
> iter ruina quaeret et uacuo uolet
> regnare mundo. robore experto tumet,
> et posse caelum uiribus uinci suis
> didicit ferendo; subdidit mundo caput
> nec flexit umeros molis immensae labor
> meliusque collo sedit Herculeo polus.
> immota ceruix sidera et caelum tulit
> et me prementem: quaerit ad superos uiam.

> It is heaven we must fear for, lest he seize the highest kingdoms,
> who conquered the lowest; he will snatch his father's sceptre.
> He will not come to the stars by a slow path, as did Bacchus:
> he will seek a way by ruin and wish
> to rule in an empty world. He swells with his tested might,
> and by carrying it has learnt that heaven can be conquered
> by his own strength; he set his head under the world
> and the labour of that immense weight did not bend his shoulders
> and the sky sat more firmly on Hercules' neck.
> His head unmoved bore stars and heaven
> and my pressure: he is seeking a path to the gods.

Juno casts the move from infernal to celestial conquest as a natural progression from one realm to the next. In the goddess's imagination, Hercules' deification by force contrasts with Bacchus' *lenta uia*. The distinction she draws between the two entrances into heaven implies an argument a fortiori: bad enough that Bacchus became a god, but at least he came without violence and without threatening the existing order; Hercules, on the other hand, will not only become a god, he will do so by asserting his superiority over all the other gods.[19] As Juno hates Bacchus and his subtle apotheosis, a fortiori she hates Hercules and his more violent aspect. Juno finds further evidence for Hercules' potential destabilisation of the cosmos, ironically enough, in his ability to support the world in Atlas' place (68–74), a feat that has provided empirical

---

[19] The phrase *lenta uia* is rich in irony: to Juno's divine eyes Bacchus' apotheosis may seem gentle, especially in contrast to her fears about Hercules, but to mortals Bacchus seems disproportionately threatening and destructive (see Chapters 1 and 3).

evidence of his might (*robore experto, didicit ferendo*), greater even than the strength of Atlas (*melius*).[20]

After this long, ever-increasing build-up of Hercules' power and ambition, Juno seems to have little recourse to stop the hero from accomplishing whatever he wills (*HF* 75–82), and instead she bids her anger advance, as if more intense emotion will enable her to achieve what she otherwise cannot (*perge, ira, perge, HF* 75).[21] Again she alludes to Hercules' alleged theomachic intent (*magna meditantem, HF* 75) as if it's a certainty; indeed, her own desire to confront him personally, and not to rely on instruments such as monsters and tyrants, threatens to make the theomachy a reality (*HF* 76–8). However, she then turns to other means, namely, the Titans and Typhoeus or Enceladus (*HF* 79–82):

> Titanas ausos rumpere imperium Iouis
> emitte, Siculi uerticis laxa specum,
> tellus Gigante Doris excusso tremens
> supposita monstri colla terrifici leuet.
>
> Send out the Titans who dared to burst the rule of Jupiter,
> open the hollow at the top of Sicily,
> let the Dorian earth, trembling when the Giant shakes,
> raise the buried neck of the terrible monster.

For fear that Hercules will launch a theomachy, she threatens, apparently without a trace of irony, to release the paradigmatic theomachs of mythology.[22]

Unfortunately for Juno, Hercules 'has already defeated' opponents of this sort when he came to the gods' aid during the Gigantomachy (*sed uicit ista, HF* 84). The act of conquering such potent theomachs sets Hercules up as a protector of order, but his supremacy also suggests that he has the potential to become the ultimate theomach himself, especially if one follows Juno's own logic: just as Hercules is assimilated to the monsters he has conquered, so too his victory over the Giants turns him, potentially, into one of them.[23] Accordingly, Juno hits upon the idea of turning Hercules against himself: *quaeris Alcidae parem? / nemo est nisi ipse; bella iam secum gerat* ('do you seek an equal for Alcides? There is no one except himself; now let him wage war with himself', *HF* 84–5); *i nunc, superbe, caelitum sedes pete, / humana temne* ('now go, proud one, seek the gods' abodes, despise what is human', *HF* 89–90). She now freely encourages the hero to pursue what she sees as his ultimate goal of deification because

---

[20] Fitch 1987: 141–2 argues convincingly for the readings of E, *experto* (68) and *melius* (72), over those of A, *expenso* and *medius*.

[21] For further discussion of this kind of self-address see below, p. 148 n. 88.

[22] See Fitch 1987: 144–5 for possible confusion of Typhoeus with Enceladus.

[23] Dauge 1981: 33–4 sees an ambivalence between Herculean and Titanic characteristics as fundamental to Roman identity.

the very habits and abilities that have brought him so much success in the past will now, in true tragic form, lead to his destruction.

Having complained from the beginning of her speech about disorder in the cosmos, Juno now threatens to bring that same disorder out from the underworld up to the surface in order to defeat Hercules: *iam Styga et manes feros / fugisse credis? hic tibi ostendam inferos* ('do you believe you have now escaped Styx and the fierce shades? Here will I show you hell', *HF* 90-1). By invoking hellish powers to act on earth, she exacerbates the acts of inversion and revelation she had earlier decried. She adds that she will call on Discord, a figure buried in darkness and trapped by a mountain (*HF* 92-4), a description that may represent an obscure mythology, but whose content, if not its vocabulary, immediately recalls the image of the Giant trapped beneath Etna at *HF* 79-82.[24] The similarity and proximity of the images yields a stark conclusion: abstract powers, like Discord, will now be made to do the work of Giants. What Juno goes on to describe is not, then, a list of monsters, but rather various personifications (*HF* 96-8): Crime (*Scelus*), Impiety (*Impietas*), Error (*Error*), and Frenzy (*Furor*)—the last of which she emphatically claims as the chosen agent of her resentment (*HF* 99). Unlike Euripides, Seneca offers no immediate and embodied cause such as Lyssa to do his explanatory work; Juno's ultimate recourse is to entities of the most abstract and internal kind—they may have personified form but, unlike Lyssa, they will not appear on stage.[25] This change is perfectly in tune with the interiority that characterises Seneca's philosophy: the greatest threats to the Stoic come from within.[26] It fits also with Juno's plan of turning Hercules against himself, using his own strength against him. We should be careful, however, not to over-allegorise the text. An animated and psychologically plausible goddess has been speaking for nearly a hundred lines; there seems little reason, at least at this point in the play, to minimise her presence and agency in favour of the psychological forces she describes.[27] Much of the power of this play springs from the conjunction of a traditionally vivid deity together with the invisible yet pervasive operation of forces of nature and of mind.

Inspired by madness (*HF* 109-12), Juno finally devises a way to manipulate Hercules' exceptionalism to his disadvantage: *hic prosit mihi / Ioue esse genitum*

---

[24] One could venture some lexical overlap in the two passages. If we follow the MSS, as does Fitch 1987, *specus* (*HF* 94) echoes the unproblematic *specum* (*HF* 80). However, *specus* renders it very difficult to construe an image of Discord's dwelling or prison, leading Bentley to conjecture *latus* (adopted by Fitch 2002). In addition, *oppositi* (*HF* 94) might pick up *supposita* (*HF* 82). Whether or not one is convinced by such lexical arguments, the basic image of the peril buried deep underground, and Juno's desire to release it, connects the two passages.

[25] Cf. the Nurse's even more radical demythologisation of *Amor* at Sen. *Phaed.* 195-203, with which compare the famous speculative question of Nisus at *Aen.* 9.184-5.

[26] See, e.g., *Ep.* 71.37.

[27] On allegorical interpretation of the gods in classical literature see Feeney 1991; on psychology in Senecan tragedy see Schiesaro 2003.

('now let it avail me that he is born of Jupiter', *HF* 117–18). Ultimately, Juno's perversion of Hercules' heroism has as its goal his exclusion from heaven: *scelere perfecto licet / admittat illas genitor in caelum manus* ('after the crime is completed, let his father admit those hands into heaven', *HF* 121–2). Thus, at the close of the prologue Juno's final thoughts remain fixed on the idea of Hercules becoming a god. If she had feared that the hero's violence would lead to theomachy and the overturning of the world order, she now sees that the same violence can be twisted to his detriment and to the maintenance of the status quo. It remains for the rest of the tragedy to play out this dialogue between divinity and monstrosity.

Deification and Tyranny

The idea of Hercules' conquest of the underworld, and possibly of heaven too, has an earthly counterpart: the tyrant Lycus has seized control of Thebes in Hercules' absence.[28] A lengthy agon takes up most of Act 2, in which Lycus attempts to secure his own legitimacy as ruler in part by attacking the claims made for Hercules' exceptionalism by Amphitryon and Megara, Hercules' father and wife.[29] A substantial portion of the debate centres on the question of Hercules' eligibility for divine status, thus continuing and further emphasising the main theme of Juno's prologue. Seneca's particular interest in these issues—Euripides, by contrast, spends far less time discussing Herakles' future deification—reflects the influence of contemporary discourse about imperial cult and apotheosis.[30] Various texts, such as Seneca's *Apocolocyntosis* and Suetonius' biography of Caligula, provide a context for reading the *HF* as an exploration of the issues raised by the divinisation of the emperor, whether after death or even in life. Against that background, Hercules' failed theomachy will appear to settle, temporarily at least, the question posed in the agon—he cannot forcibly attain to divinity, the desire for which is nothing but madness and a route to self-destruction.

Amphitryon and Megara open the scene by praying for Hercules' return from the underworld. In the course of his speech, Amphitryon proclaims

[28] On Lycus' correspondence to the paradigmatic tyrant of Seneca's *De Clementia* see Rose 1979–80: 136. On the parallelism of Hercules and Lycus, see Bishop 1966, Rose 1979–80: 137–9, Papadopoulou 2004. The fact that the same actor in Euripides' version played both parts emphasises the assimilation of hero and tyrant (see Ruck 1976). The question of the performance or non-performance of Senecan drama notwithstanding (on which see see Boyle 1997: 10–12 and the essays in T. Harrison 2000), Seneca too allows for the same actor to play both parts, though Kohn 2013: 93–5 argues for a different arrangement of parts.

[29] See Rosenmeyer 1989: 82.

[30] E. R. Wilson 2004: 102 also notes Seneca's greater interest in the theme of political tyranny, on which see further below.

Thebes' close connection to the gods, even hinting at his own hopes for Hercules (*HF* 265–7):

> haec quae caelites
> recepit et quae fecit et (fas sit loqui)
> fortasse faciet...

> This [land] which has received gods
> and which has already made gods and (may it be acceptable to say)
> perhaps will still make them...

When Lycus subsequently enters and describes his plan to marry Megara, his speech ends with a reference to Amphitryon as 'Alcides' true progenitor' (*uerus Alcidae sator*, *HF* 357). With this entirely unprompted detail, Lycus casts doubt on Hercules' paternity. In attempting to replace a king whose origins are not only noble but also supposedly divine, it is natural for Lycus, a parvenu (*HF* 337–41), to attack inflated claims about birth.[31] As we have already seen from Juno's speech, however, any reference to Hercules' birth has greater significance than the local characterisation of Lycus—it ties into the larger questions of the criteria for Hercules' deification and the scope of his power.

The subject of Hercules' paternity comes up again later in the scene, after Megara has emphatically rejected Lycus' proposal and the argument between them turns to the possibility of Hercules' return (*HF* 436–8):

LYC. tenebrae loquentem magna Tartareae premunt.
MEG. non est ad astra mollis e terris uia.
LYC. quo patre genitus caelitum sperat domos?

LYC. Tartarean darkness crushes the boaster.
MEG. There is no easy way from the earth to the stars.
LYC. Born from what father does he hope for the homes of the heavenly gods?

Read in light of Amphitryon's words earlier in the scene (*subitusque ad astra emerget*, 'suddenly he will emerge to the stars', *HF* 276), Megara's phrase *ad astra* would seem to refer to Hercules' return from the darkness of the underworld. Lycus, however, takes Megara's words as referring to Hercules' admission to the heavens.[32] Together with Lycus' previous insistence on Amphitryon

---

[31] Cf. the *nouus homo* Gaius Marius' similar contrast between degenerate aristocracy and his own energy and achievements at Sall. *Iug.* 85. Although at first Lycus' speech appears to contrast him with the noble Hercules (cf. Amphitryon at *HF* 268–70, where I follow Fitch in reading *ignarum*), the idea of old versus new blood takes on a different meaning in the context of Hercules' attempt to join the established Olympian gods. Juno, for example, sees Hercules as an arriviste who makes claims based on *uirtus* no differently from Lycus. As will be seen below, the emperors too could be regarded as men on the make trying to join an elite club.

[32] Cf. Henry and Walker 1965: 16–17.

being Hercules' true father, the implication of *HF* 438 is clear: Hercules is not divinely born and so cannot hope to ascend to the stars as a god.

Amphitryon pre-empts Megara in responding to this denial (*HF* 439–47):

> miseranda coniunx Herculis magni, sile;
> partes meae sunt reddere Alcidae patrem
> genusque uerum. post tot ingentis uiri
> memoranda facta postque pacatum manu
> quodcumque Titan ortus et labens uidet,
> post monstra tot perdomita, post Phlegram impio
> sparsam cruore postque defensos deos
> nondum liquet de patre? mentimur Iouem?
> Iunonis odio crede.

> Wretched wife of great Hercules, be silent;
> it is my part to return to Alcides his true father
> and birth. After so many noteworthy deeds by that great hero
> and after he pacified by his hand
> whatever the rising and setting Titan sees,
> after so many monsters have been subdued, after Phlegra
> spattered with impious blood and after he defended the gods
> is there still room for doubt about his father? Are we lying about Jupiter?
> Believe the hatred of Juno.

Amphitryon's logic agrees with Juno's inasmuch as Hercules' deeds are regarded as sufficient proof of his paternity. Again, the implication naturally follows that, as the true son of Jupiter, he is entitled to aspire to heaven. Lycus, however, takes issue with the very premise—fundamental to classical mythology—of cross-breeding between immortals and mortals: *quid uiolas Iouem? / mortale caelo non potest iungi genus* ('why do you offend Jupiter? Mortal kind cannot be joined with heaven', *HF* 447–8).[33] When Amphitryon responds that this is the origin of several gods (*HF* 449), Lycus changes the subject to Hercules' slavery (*HF* 450). Similarly, when faced with the example of Bacchus as evidence of the trials of divine birth (*HF* 457–8), Lycus again evades the point by simply asserting that to be wretched signifies mortality (*HF* 463). For Lycus, then, even if tradition suggests otherwise, gods are gods, men are men, and there is no traffic between them.

Lycus' sceptical attitude to deification appears thoroughly out of place not only given the standard mythology surrounding Hercules and other figures, like Bacchus, but also because of contemporary developments in politics and religion. In the historical tragedy *Octavia*, written in the style of Seneca not long after his death, the image of seeking a path to heaven has a clear political

---

[33] Lycus' use of the strong word *uiolas* (*OLD* s.v. *uiolo* 1) for a moment turns Amphitryon into a kind of theomach.

resonance.[34] At one point in the *Octavia*, the character of Seneca himself attempts to persuade Nero, using arguments drawn from the historical Seneca's *De Clementia*, that mercy is the route to deification: *petitur hac caelum uia* ('heaven is sought by this path', Ps.-Sen. *Oct.* 476).[35] Nero, however, offers a powerful rejoinder at *Oct.* 527–32, where he declares that arms, loyalty, and an heir—not mercy—are in fact the way to be worshipped as a god.[36] Similar political resonances can be heard in the *HF* too. The first choral ode, which contrasts Hercules' overreaching with the chorus's wish for a quieter and more secure life, had already brought certain aspects of Roman culture into the compass of the play. In comparing rustic innocence to urban ambition, for instance, the chorus alludes to the Roman custom of *salutatio* (*HF* 164–6) and the legal quarrels of the forum (*HF* 172–3; *fori*, *HF* 172). Most striking of all, however, is a passage towards the end of ode (*HF* 192–5):

> alium multis Gloria terris
> tradat et omnes
> Fama per urbes garrula laudet,
> caeloque parem tollat et astris;
> alius curru sublimis eat

> Let glory give another to many lands
> and let chattering rumour praise him
> through all the cities,
> and raise him equal to heaven and stars;
> let another ride high in a chariot.

With its mention of widespread fame and elevation to the stars, the passage recalls Juno's complaint about the geographical extent of Hercules' renown and his popular deification (*HF* 37–40). The image of the chariot, on the other hand, suggests the triumphal procession, which temporarily accorded the *triumphator* near-divine (though, importantly, not actually divine) status, and which under Augustus had become a strictly imperial prerogative.[37] The intratextual and contextual echoes thus combine to assimilate Hercules' status and aspirations to elements of Roman ambition: in both the mythological and political scenarios human achievement culminates in elevation to the stars.[38]

---

[34] On the authorship and date of the *Octavia* see Ferri 2003: 5–30.

[35] Cf. Marti 1952: 35–6.

[36] Boyle 2008: 194, 205.

[37] On the triumph see Beard 2007. On all the Roman touches in the choral passage see Fitch 1987: 162, 174–80. The chariot of line 195 alludes not just to the triumph but also to the story of Phaethon (Fitch provides a detailed comparison of the first half of the ode to the *parodos* of Euripides' *Phaethon*). The story of the boy who tried to play god (specifically his father, the Sun) has a general resonance with the *HF*, which is concerned with Hercules' qualification to be a god. On Phaethon see further below. The role of the ever-troubling Fama in raising one to the heavens already casts a Gigantomachic shadow over the passage (cf. Chapter 2).

[38] The following argument develops Fitch 1987: 18–20. Cf. Braden 1970: 23–5, Papadopoulou 2004: 277–9.

In an article on Seneca's *Thyestes*, Katharina Volk invokes the context of imperial deification:[39]

> The idea that human beings, especially powerful rulers, could become stars and/or gods was, of course, perfectly acceptable at the time of Seneca. Ever since Julius Caesar had been turned into a comet after his death, it had become expected for the Julio-Claudian emperors to be posthumously deified (though not all of them were) and to be treated already during their lifetime, if not as gods, then at least as future gods.[40]

Volk is absolutely right to note the close association of emperor and divinity, though how naturalised that association was in the mid-first century remains unclear. Emperors may have sought posthumous deification, but the decision whether or not to approve it lay with the senate. It's important to stress the political negotiation that would have gone into the process of deification by senatorial decree and, more importantly, the conceptual negotiation that would have taken place in reconciling pre-existing religious attitudes and beliefs with this relatively new practice within a new political system.[41] Neither Tiberius nor Caligula were deified, as Volk points out, and even if the *HF* was written after Claudius' deification, this was by no means a settled practice.[42]

Work by Duncan Fishwick, Simon Price, and Ittai Gradel, amongst others, has by now established how important imperial-divine relations were to the politics of the day, especially the negotiation of the status of the emperor both during his life and posthumously through the custom of imperial cult.[43] Seneca's attitude to Claudius' apotheosis in the *Apocolocyntosis*, for example, emphasises the importance of appropriate criteria for divinity, a concern equally evident in the *HF*, whether or not the two works are by the same author.[44] In the satire, the deified Augustus lays out the consequences of admitting Claudius into heaven with the other gods and deified humans: *quis credet? dum tales deos facitis, nemo uos deos esse credet* ('who will believe in him? While you make gods of such a kind, no one will believe that you are gods', *Apocol.* 11.4). Deification thus has implications not only for the individual in question, whose

---

[39] On deification in the *Thyestes* see below and Chapter 5.

[40] Volk 2006: 196.

[41] See Beard and Henderson 1998: 191, and esp. 198: 'Consecration, then, was for any emperor, and at any coronation, never automatic, but always, critically, in question. It must always have been the product of a complex process of (tacit, occluded, or open) negotiation about whether to, how to, and (especially) how not to, consecrate particular figures'.

[42] On the dating of the *HF* see Fitch 1987: 50–3.

[43] Fishwick 1987–2005, Price 1984, Gradel 2002. Price 1987 argues convincingly for deification as a site for the negotiation of authority between emperor and senate.

[44] On the authorship of the *Apocolocyntosis* see Eden 1984: 6–8. I take the standard, albeit uncertain, position that the satirist and tragedian are one and the same. Even if it had a different author, however, the *Apocolocyntosis* would still provide contextual support for my main argument that the *HF*'s concern with deification draws on contemporary issues.

eligibility for divinity must be established, but also for the existing gods and for worshippers—the credibility of the entire system lies at stake.[45] While Augustus seeks to prevent the divinisation of Claudius on grounds of unsuitability, Juno tries to bar Hercules for fear of two different consequences—first, that his apotheosis might further shame her, and second, that he might usurp Jupiter. Notwithstanding these differences in motivation, however, both Juno and the stakeholders of the early principate share a concern that adding a new god might have negative consequences for the present ones, and as a result some working out of the various claims must take place—by debate or by sheer force.

In Act 4 of the *HF*, as madness descends on Hercules, he imagines his ascent to heaven (*HF* 959–63):

> astra promittit pater.
> —quid, si negaret? non capit terra Herculem
> tandemque superis reddit. en ultro uocat
> omnis deorum coetus et laxat fores,
> una uetante.

> My father promises the stars.
> What if he should refuse? The earth cannot hold Hercules
> and at last gives him up to the gods. See, of its own accord
> the whole assembly of gods calls me and opens the doors,
> though one goddess forbids it.

The image of the assembly of gods admitting Hercules to heaven, however crazed, parallels the situation in the *Apocolocyntosis*, where the newly deceased emperor Claudius waits expectantly on the decision of the council of gods whether to welcome him into their company. For the forbidding Juno of the *HF* we can instead read an Augustus protective of his relatively new, and elite, club. The comparison between the two situations, however, emphasises a difference: unlike Claudius, Hercules might just be able to force his way into heaven and overturn the existing order. Whatever the process of deification for Hercules, the element of force causes it to differ markedly from the satirical example of Claudius. In the *HF*, Seneca is interested in the question of one's suitability for deification, but even more so in the wider implications of asserting one's power in such an extreme fashion. Apotheosis and its flip side, theomachy, become for Seneca a touchstone for the evaluation of Hercules, just as the senatorial award of deification is a touchstone for the evaluation of emperors. In depicting deification and theomachy as inextricably intertwined, the *HF* suggests greater pessimism about the nature of imperial autocracy and its excessive ambitions than does the *Apocolocyntosis*, where personal animosity

---

[45] Cole 2006 argues that we should see the satire as salvaging deification from becoming a total farce.

towards Claudius allowed Seneca to draw an especially sharp division between good and bad candidates for deification.

The phrase *non capit* in the passage above alludes to a speech by Apollo in the *Aeneid*, in which the god praises Iulus as the descendant and ancestor of gods (*dis genite et geniture deos*, *Aen.* 9.642) before declaring that Troy lacks the scope for Iulus' glorious future: *nec te Troia capit* ('nor does Troy contain you', *Aen.* 9.644). The reference to Iulus' divinised descendants, Caesar and, proleptically, Augustus, is clear enough from *geniture deos*, but the phrase *nec capit* and its Senecan intertext allude to another, non-Roman, divinised ruler, Alexander the Great. Plutarch records Philip of Macedon saying the following to his son on perceiving his extraordinary talent: ζήτει σεαυτῷ βασιλείαν ἴσην· Μακεδονία γάρ σ' οὐ χωρεῖ ('seek out a kingdom equal to yourself, for Macedonia cannot contain you', Plut. *Alex.* 6.8).[46] Alexander makes an especially good analogue for Hercules, since he claimed descent both from Hercules himself through his father, Philip, and from Zeus through his mother, Olympias, who was impregnated, according to legend, by Zeus Ammon in the form of a serpent.[47] Alexander's eventual deification, moreover, would set a precedent for Hellenistic monarchies and through them for Roman deification.[48] Unlike Alexander and Iulus, however, Hercules defies the limits not of a country or city, like Macedonia or Troy, but of the very earth itself. Furthermore, it's not a father or god who extols the hero but Hercules himself.[49] Finally, where Philip and Aeneas may have prepared their sons for success—in Alexander's case far greater success than his father had—Hercules will, if necessary, defy the gods, including Jupiter, in his ascent. That violent aspect is crucial in redefining the process of deification.

John Fitch has observed that Hercules' threats to enter heaven by force (*recipis et reseras polum? / an contumacis ianuam mundi traho?* 'Do you receive me and unbar the sky? Or do I pull down the door of stubborn heaven?', *HF* 963–4) find an analogue in Caligula's similar threats to Capitoline Jupiter, as reported in Suetonius' biography: ἤ μ' ἀνάειρ' ἤ ἐγὼ σέ ('raise me up or I'll raise you!', *Calig.* 22.4).[50]

---

[46] As Fitch 1987: 368 notes, the story was clearly known to Seneca's father, who attributes a very similar comment to Cestius Pius: *orbis illum suus non capit* ('his world does not contain him', Sen. Rh. *Suas.* 1.5).

[47] Plut. *Alex.* reports both Alexander's Herculean lineage (2.1) and the legend of the snake (3.1–4).

[48] For Alexander's deification and its legacy see Weinstock 1971: index s.v. 'Alexander'; Rawson 1975; Badian 1981, 1996; Spencer 2002.

[49] Statius alludes to the same idea in the *Achilleid*, when Chiron observes the destiny of the young Achilles to exceed his current surroundings: *nunc illum non Ossa capit, non Pelion ingens / Pharsaliaeue niues* ('now Ossa does not contain him, nor huge Pelion or the Thessalian snows', *Achil.* 1.151–2). The Gigantomachic associations of Ossa and Pelion, however, clearly mark Achilles as being in the mould of Hercules rather than Iulus, all the more so given the theomachic note sounded by the very opening lines of the poem (see epigraph to Chapter 6).

[50] Fitch 1987: 368. Caligula is quoting Ajax's words to Odysseus during their wrestling match in the funeral games for Patroclus (*Il.* 23.724); see Wardle 1994: 216. Since Caligula is talking to a statue of the god, the verb has the sense of 'remove' or 'uproot'.

Fitch gives no more than the bare reference, and one might think that the point of the comparison is Caligula's supposed madness. To some extent this must be true: the perception, biased or otherwise, of Caligula's madness and monstrosity provides a cultural context for interpreting Hercules' own descent into madness and monstrosity.[51] But we can press this cultural context further, especially by taking account of an alternative report of Caligula speaking the same words in Seneca's own *De Ira* (*Ira* 1.20.8–9):[52]

> ad pugnam uocauit Iouem et quidem sine missione, Homericum illum exclamans uersum: ἤ μ' ἀνάειρ' ἤ ἐγὼ σέ. quanta dementia fuit! putauit aut sibi noceri ne ab Ioue quidem posse aut se nocere etiam Ioui posse. non puto parum momenti hanc eius uocem ad incitandas coniuratorum mentes addidisse; ultimae enim patientiae uisum est eum ferre qui Iouem non ferret.

> He summoned Jupiter to battle, and even to the death, shouting this verse of Homer: 'raise me up or I'll raise you'. What madness! He thought that he couldn't be harmed even by Jupiter, or that he himself could harm even the god. I do not think that this exclamation of his was of little moment in exciting the minds of the conspirators; for it seemed the very limit of endurance to put up with a man who would not put up with Jupiter.

Caligula is here provoked to anger by lightning interrupting a pantomime, an illustration of the emperor's triviality and sense of disproportion. More important than the cause, however, is Seneca's conclusion—that for the conspirators the tipping point of Caligula's excess could plausibly be his bathetic theomachy. The attempt to fight the gods is thus not so much a revolution in itself, as the maddened Hercules sees it, but rather the moment when the tyrant ensures his own downfall.

Indeed, the political critique of Caligula, and subsequently of Nero and Domitian, focuses in large part on their relations with the gods—excessively imitative and even antagonistic.[53] In the Suetonian account, Caligula's threat to

---

[51] On the presentation of Caligula as a typical tyrant in Senecan prose see Tarrant 2006: 14–15; for allusions to Caligula in the *De Clementia* see Braund 2009: index s.v. 'Caligula'. On the historical relations between Seneca and Caligula see M. T. Griffin 1992: 51–7, 213–15. Suetonius and Dio provide most of our information about the emperor. Philo also paints a negative portrait, but this may partly be the product of his Jewish perspective on the notoriously anti-Jewish emperor. On Caligula's divinity see the equally hostile Josephus at *AJ* 19.4–6. On the possible influence of Claudian propaganda on our sources see Barrett 1990: 172–80. Barrett's biography also offers the fullest and least hostile modern account of Caligula's reign; see also Winterling 2011. On Caligula's cult and the standard methodological caveats see Simpson 1996.

[52] Cf. Dio 59.28.6.

[53] Further examples of antagonism between Caligula and Jupiter: *Calig.* 33.1, 57.3, 58.2–3. Suetonius labels Nero a *religionum contemptor* (*Ner.* 56.1). His biography shows many of the same tyrannical characteristics that we see in Caligula, and indeed Nero is even said to have admired his uncle Caligula

Jupiter appears in a lengthy passage describing the emperor's unprecedented attempts to secure worship as a god during his lifetime.[54] The context of the passage reveals the close connection between Caligula's divine aspirations and his particular understanding of the institution of the principate. In response to a discussion between foreign kings on their relative claims to nobility, Caligula, quoting Homer, declared that there should be 'one lord and king' (εἷς κοίρανος ἔστω, εἷς βασιλεύς, *Calig.* 22.1).[55] Suetonius alleges that the emperor was quite taken with this idea (*Calig.* 22.1-2):

> nec multum afuit quin statim diadema sumeret speciemque principatus in regni formam conuerteret. uerum admonitus et principum et regum se excessisse fastigium, diuinam ex eo maiestatem asserere sibi coepit.

> And he was not far from assuming at once a diadem and changing the appearance of the principate for the form of monarchy. But being advised that he exceeded the distinction of leaders and kings, he began to arrogate to himself a divine majesty.

Suetonius depicts Caligula as pursuing the logical extension of imperial autocracy—first by abandoning the charade of republicanism, and then by analogising the power of the *princeps* to the only valid comparandum—divinity. As exaggerated as Caligula's antagonism with Jupiter may be, the idea of theomachy captures the desire of the tyrant to pre-empt senatorial approval—the normal prerequisite of post-mortem deification—in favour of asserting sole power. Through Hercules' Caligulan madness, then, Seneca suggests that apotheosis strays all too easily into theomachy just as imperial ideology collapses all too easily into tyranny. The distinctions so clearly drawn between Augustus and Claudius in the *Apocolocyntosis* are seen in a quite different light from the perspective of the *HF*, which, like Suetonius' biography many years later, focuses on the inevitable implications of absolute—or seemingly absolute—power.

As the foregoing hopefully makes clear, a vital distinction between Seneca's view of imperial divinisation and that of Vergil or Ovid emerges as a result of the intervening years. Seneca could make systemic observations based on his experience of the patterns and nuances of different emperors' ideologies and legacies. Moreover, with his long and distinguished involvement in politics, he

---

(*Ner.* 30.1). Cf. Tac. *Ann.* 15.45 for Nero's committing of sacrilege. Jupiter signals his dissatisfaction with the whole dynasty of Julio-Claudians in the last year of Nero's reign, as related at the beginning of Suetonius' *Life of Galba*: *ac subinde tacta de caelo Caesarum aede capita omnibus simul statuis deciderunt, Augusti etiam sceptrum e manibus excussum est* ('and when immediately afterwards the temple of the Caesars was struck from heaven all the heads fell at once from the statues, even Augustus' sceptre was struck from his hands', *Galb.* 1.1). On Domitian see Chapter 9.

[54] For the historical validity of these claims see Barrett 1990: 140-53, Simpson 1996, Gradel 2002: 140-59.

[55] The quotation comes from Hom. *Il.* 2.204-5.

was an especially privileged—and interested—witness to those various negotiations and developments. The resulting insights, however tendentious, make his treatment of deification and theomachy quite different from anything we have seen in previous chapters: the political—and specifically imperial—aspect of theomachy comes into its own. As much as Hercules' characterisation may be coloured by Seneca's experience of particular individuals, the hero represents a larger and more systemic concern—the nature of autocracy.

Madness and the Sublime

Caligula represents merely one of the contexts relevant for interpreting the madness of theomachy, though it's perhaps the most directly political. As we have seen, the literary tradition makes fighting the gods emblematic of wrongheaded thinking, whether the literal madness of Sophocles' Ajax or the more metaphorical kind attributed to Euripides' and Ovid's Pentheus. What these examples lack, however, is the sense of elevation created in Hercules' mad fantasy. However unreal, Hercules opens up a view of the scale and significance of human possibility, one correlate of which is imperial deification. The association between madness and theomachic ascent is well represented by the myth of Bellerophon, in which the hero attempts to enter Olympus on the winged horse Pegasus, only for Zeus to send a gadfly to madden the horse and throw Bellerophon to earth.[56] The ambition and fall of Bellerophon, also famed as a tamer of beasts and destroyer of monsters, is a close mythical analogue for Hercules' own trajectory in the *HF*, and were we to have a more substantial portion of Euripides' *Bellerophon*, we might expect to see some overlap with the content of Seneca's play.[57] We have better luck, however, with another mythical figure whose story focuses on these same themes of madness, ascent, and fall—Phaethon.

The myth of Phaethon's failed attempt to drive the chariot of his father, the Sun, was also the subject of a play by Euripides, of which we have a few fragments, but it's the version in Ovid's *Metamorphoses* that has a direct connection to Hercules' imagined theomachy.[58] Ovid makes Phaethon's divine birth a matter of dispute with another son of a god, Epaphus, which motivates Phaethon to seek out his father and prove his paternity. Although not literally

---

[56] See, e.g., Pind. *Isthm.* 7.44–7. When Glaucus relates the story of Bellerophon to Diomedes in *Iliad* 6 he only glancingly alludes to Bellerophon's theomachic aspect (*Il.* 6.200). But the allusion offers a subtle warning to Diomedes, whose acts of theomachy took up much of the previous book (see Chapter 1).

[57] On Euripides' play, which was not the only treatment of the myth but was the one most likely to have influenced Seneca, see Riedweg 1990.

[58] C. A. J. Littlewood 2004: 107–27 discusses the wider relevance of (mostly Euripides') Phaethon to the *HF*.

mad, it's repeatedly suggested that Phaethon is out of his wits: Epaphus, for instance, calls him *demens* (*Met.* 1.753) for believing his mother's claim that his father is the Sun god. After Phaethon comes to the palace of the Sun and seeks proof of his paternity, the god grants him anything he desires, which turns out to be the opportunity to drive his father's chariot. Despite his father's plea that he wish for something wiser (*sapientius*, *Met.* 2.102), Phaethon 'burns' (*flagrat*, *Met.* 2.104) to drive the chariot, a verb suggestive of madness as well as desire.[59] Most crucially for the *HF*, in the course of his ride Phaethon sees, or imagines, the constellations coming alive (*Met.* 2.193–200):[60]

> sparsa quoque in uario passim miracula caelo
> uastarumque uidet trepidus simulacra ferarum.
> est locus, in geminos ubi bracchia concauat arcus
> Scorpius et cauda flexisque utrimque lacertis
> porrigit in spatium signorum membra duorum;
> hunc puer ut nigri madidum sudore ueneni
> uulnera curuata minitantem cuspide uidit,
> mentis inops gelida formidine lora remisit.

> Also, scattered everywhere in the heavens
> he sees with alarm the marvellous forms of huge beasts.
> There is a place where Scorpio bends his claws in twin arcs
> and, with his tail and his curving arms on both sides,
> spreads his body over the space of two star signs;
> when the boy saw this creature drenched in the sweat of black poison
> threatening to wound him with its curved sting,
> robbed of his wits by cold fear, he dropped the reins.

As Fitch has noted, the Ovidian passage is recalled towards the beginning of Hercules' madness (*HF* 944–52):[61]

> primus en noster labor
> caeli refulget parte non minima Leo
> iraque totus feruet et morsus parat.
> iam rapiet aliquod sidus: ingenti minax
> stat ore et ignes efflat et rutilat, iubam
> ceruice iactans; quidquid autumnus grauis
> hiemsque gelido frigida spatio refert
> uno impetu transiliet, et uerni petet
> frangetque Tauri colla.

---

[59] For *flagro* used to describe the effect of desire and madness cf. Cic. *Verr.* 2.4.75: *ita flagrare cupiditate atque amentia coepit*. For the madness of Phaethon cf. also Nonn. *Dion.* 38.190: μαίνετο δ' ἱπποσύνης μεθέπων πόθον ('he madly pursued his desire to drive the chariot').

[60] On allusion to Lucretius in this passage see p. 151 n. 98 below.

[61] Fitch 1987: 364–5.

> See, my first labour,
> the Lion, shines in no small part of heaven
> and all seething with rage prepares to bite.
> Now he will seize some star: threatening with his huge
> maw he stands and breathes fire and blazes red, shaking
> his mane on his golden neck; whatever stars sickly autumn
> and cold winter with its frozen tracts bring back
> he will leap over in one bound, and he will attack
> and break the neck of the spring Bull.

Even without any verbal overlap, the common conceit of the zodiacal signs appearing animate and dangerous to the disturbed mind connects both passages.[62] Phaethon's literal loss of control and the subsequent threat of fire engulfing the earth become internalised and personal for Hercules, whose mental loss of control will evoke a Gigantomachic act of destruction, while in reality it leads to the killing of his own family.

One option at this point would be to use the political themes critics have seen in Ovid's Phaethon episode—especially dynastic succession and the topography of the imperial city—in conjunction with my earlier discussion of deification to circle back to the historical context of the *HF*.[63] Rather than turning immediately to the play's external political meaning, however, I want to approach theomachy from a new direction by attending to the language and aesthetics of the episode, focusing especially on the ideas of passion, elevation, and revelation—key constituents of the concept of the sublime. The consequent readings of Seneca's imagery are primarily literary and philosophical, but by the end of the chapter we shall see how they operate in dialogue with the political reading offered above.

In the case of both Phaethon and Hercules, excessive ambition, however disastrous, proceeds from a spirit of admirable daring and allows the reader the opportunity of a glimpse of the world from an extraordinary perspective, a view typically unavailable to humankind.[64] The combined senses of height, scale, awe, and exceptionalism created by the visions of the two heroes are characteristic of the sublime, a concept associated with the aesthetic theory of Longinus, usually dated to the first century AD, but also with a philosophical tradition evident in Plato, Lucretius, and Seneca.[65] Critics have noted, moreover,

---

[62] Seneca was well acquainted with Ovid's treatment of Phaethon: he quotes extensively from it at *Prov.* 5.10–11.

[63] See Schmitzer 1990: 89–107, Barchiesi 2008a and 2009. Succession and Roman topography are both subjects close to Seneca's heart, especially in the *Thyestes*.

[64] Phaethon's epitaph commemorates his daring: *hic situs est Phaethon, currus auriga paterni, / quem si non tenuit, magnis tamen excidit ausis* ('here lies Phaethon, driver of his father's chariot, which even if he did not control, nevertheless he fell in a great undertaking, *Met.* 2.327–8). On the sublime view from above see Day 2013: 153–6.

[65] My use of the name 'Longinus' is merely a shorthand and should not be taken as a commitment to identifying the author with any particular individual. On the treatise, its author, and its date see

the particular applicability of the concept to Neronian and Flavian poetry with its ostentatiously grand depictions of the world and the superhuman actions of its outsized personalities.[66]

As the Greek title of Longinus' work, *Peri Hypsous*, implies, an important feature of the sublime is the notion of loftiness (LSJ s.v. ὕψος).[67] Several of Longinus' citations from the *Iliad* demonstrate that magnitude, too, goes together with height as a means of conveying the sublime—as in Homer's simile comparing the stride of Hera's horses to the distance seen by a man sitting on a hilltop (*Il.* 5.770–2 ap. Longin. 9.5), or the description of Poseidon's enormous stature (*Il.* 13.18–19, 27–9 ap. Longin. 9.8). Longinus' examples, moreover, although almost exclusively Greek, are suggestive of the Neronian and Flavian fascination with theomachy. At 8.2 he cites Homer's description in the *Odyssey* of the Aloidae piling Pelion on Ossa (*Od.* 11.315–17), a familiar Gigantomachic motif. Both size and theomachic intent, are, of course, especially relevant to Hercules' madness, where the two are often intertwined (as they are in the tradition more generally). Thus, after Hercules' disturbed vision of the constellations, his speech evokes immense extension in space, for example the swollen seas (*tumida cesserunt freta*, *HF* 955), but it's the dimension of height in particular that's so inherently connotative of his striving towards sublimity: *in alta mundi spatia sublimis ferar* ('let me be carried on high to the lofty spaces of the cosmos', *HF* 958). His theomachic declaration ten lines later is as explicit as they come, and it culminates with an image of violent and inexorable ascent (*HF* 965–73):

> dubitatur etiam? uincla Saturno exuam,
> contraque patris impii regnum impotens
> auum resoluam. bella Titanes parent,
> me duce furentes; saxa cum siluis feram
> rapiamque dextra plena Centauris iuga.
> iam monte gemino limitem ad superos agam;
> uideat sub Ossa Pelion Chiron suum,
> in caelum Olympus tertio positus gradu
> perueniet aut mittetur.
>
> Is there still doubt? I shall strip the bonds from Saturn,
> and against my impious father's unbridled tyranny
> I shall release my grandfather. Let the Titans prepare war,
> raging under my leadership; I shall carry rocks and forests

---

Russell 1964: xxii–xxx. On reading Seneca with Longinus see Staley 2010: 42–7, C. A. J. Littlewood 2004: 121–7, Schiesaro 2003: 127–30, Michel 1969. On the sublime in Senecan philosophy see Williams 2012. See Chapter 2 above for my discussion of the Lucretian sublime.

[66] See Schrijvers 2006, Day 2013, Hardie 2013.

[67] The Latin equivalent of ὕψος is *sublimitas*, which along with its cognate adjective *sublimis* can be seen to have the same range of literary critical usage (cf. Quint. 1.8.5). See Leigh 2006: 230 with n. 56.

>   and seize ridges full of Centaurs in my right hand.
>   Now with twin mountains I will drive a path to the gods;
>   let Chiron see his Pelion under Ossa,
>   and, placed third, Olympus will reach heaven
>   or be hurled there.

The image of Hercules piling one mountain on top of another to reach his goal is a marker of his excess and frenzy, but it's also a reminder of the hero's ability to shape the world to suit his own needs. Hercules' speech contains a further image which contributes to its sublimity—his vision of disruption on a massive scale, from the underworld all the way to the heavens. Longinus sees such disruptions as a function of the enormous scale of Homer's theomachy amongst the gods (Longin. 9.6, after quoting *Il.* 21.388 and 20.61–5):[68]

> ἐπιβλέπεις, ἑταῖρε, ὡς ἀναρρηγνυμένης μὲν ἐκ βάθρων γῆς, αὐτοῦ δὲ γυμνουμένου ταρτάρου, ἀνατροπὴν δὲ ὅλου καὶ διάστασιν τοῦ κόσμου λαμβάνοντος, πάνθ' ἅμα, οὐρανὸς ᾄδης, τὰ θνητὰ τὰ ἀθάνατα, ἅμα τῇ τότε συμπολεμεῖ καὶ συγκινδυνεύει μάχῃ;

> Do you see, my friend, how the earth is torn from its foundations, Tartarus itself is laid bare, the whole world is overturned and parted asunder, and all things together—heaven and hell, things mortal and things immortal—share in the conflict and the dangers of that battle?

For the poets of the Neronian and Flavian age, that sense of universal peril, and the idiom in which it is expressed, becomes not only a common feature of their works but also, unlike for Homer, the product of human-divine theomachy rather than a consequence of battles among the gods.[69]

Besides the imagery used by Hercules, the madness that motivates his speech also has a sublime quality (Longin. 8.4):

> θαρρῶν γὰρ ἀφορισαίμην ἂν ὡς οὐδὲν οὕτως ὡς τὸ γενναῖον πάθος, ἔνθα χρή, μεγαλήγορον, ὥσπερ ὑπὸ μανίας τινὸς καὶ πνεύματος ἐνθουσιαστικῶς ἐκπνέον καὶ οἱονεὶ φοιβάζον τοὺς λόγους.

> I would affirm with confidence that there is no tone so lofty as that of genuine passion, in its right place, when it bursts out in a mad gust of enthusiasm and as it were fills the speaker's words with frenzy.

---

[68] Longinus quotes from two different descriptions of the divine theomachy as if they are a single passage; on this and other conflations of Homer see Usher 2007. Translations of Longinus here and elsewhere follow those of Roberts 1907 with slight adaptations.

[69] The fine distinction between theomachy and Gigantomachy brings us back to a political reading of the play. If Fitch 1987: 369 is right to see Hercules' Gigantomachic language as an allusion to Hor. *Carm.* 3.4.42–58, it's clear that the challenge to Augustus symbolised by the Giants in Horace has become far more ambiguous in Seneca: Hercules represents a threat to the divine and, by implication, political order, while at the same time he figures the excesses of imperial power. For a full discussion of this kind of doubleness see Chapter 9.

Deification and Theomachy in Seneca's Hercules Furens

As so often in his treatise, Longinus is here thinking not of characters within a work, like Hercules, but rather of poets and orators themselves. It's tempting, therefore, to see Hercules' madness as reflecting a poetic frenzy felt by Seneca.[70] Longinus offers support for this view in a later passage that assimilates Euripides to the playwright's own Phaethon (Longin. 15.4):[71]

ἆρ᾽ οὐκ ἂν εἴποις, ὅτι ἡ ψυχὴ τοῦ γράφοντος συνεπιβαίνει τοῦ ἅρματος καὶ συγκινδυνεύουσα τοῖς ἵπποις συνεπτέρωται; οὐ γὰρ ἄν, εἰ μὴ τοῖς οὐρανίοις ἐκείνοις ἔργοις ἰσοδρομοῦσα ἐφέρετο, τοιαῦτ᾽ ἄν ποτε ἐφαντάσθη.

Would you not say that the soul of the writer mounts the chariot at the same moment and shares in the dangers and in the flight of the horses? For it could never have imagined such things had it not been borne equally swiftly on that heavenly labour.

Applied to the *HF*, such a metapoetic reading places Seneca in a particularly odd predicament vis-à-vis his hero, since, while all the signs of sublimity are present, the situation depicted is a hallucination.[72] Phaethon, by contrast, may eventually fall, but his journey while it lasts is spectacular. The sublimity of Seneca's language, on the other hand—clearly effective in its evocation of height and grandeur—contrasts sharply with his character's inability to get off the ground.[73]

Hercules' vision of reaching the stars, attaining to his father's throne, and doing so irrespective of the gods has a clear resemblance to the jubilant rhetoric of Atreus towards the end of the *Thyestes* (*Thy*. 885–8):

> aequalis astris gradior et cunctos super
> altum superbo uertice attingens polum.
> nunc decora regni teneo, nunc solium patris.
> dimitto superos: summa uotorum attigi.
>
> I stride equal with the stars and above all men
> touching the high heaven with my proud head.

---

[70] Cf. Leigh 2006: 233–4 on Statius.

[71] Cf. C. A. J. Littlewood 2004: 122–6.

[72] Cf. Staley 2010: 44 on Seneca's Atreus, quoting Sen. *Ira* 1.20.2: *omnes quos uecors animus supra cogitationes extollit humanas altum quiddam et sublime spirare se credunt; ceterum nil solidi subest, sed in ruinam prona sunt quae sine fundamentis creuere* ('all those whom a mad soul raises beyond human thoughts believe that they breathe forth something lofty and sublime; but there is no substance in it, and what they build without foundations is prone to collapse').

[73] Longinus asserts that the true sublime elevates the reader and causes him to exult as if he produced the sublime language himself (Longin. 7.2). Applied to the context of drama, rather than epic or oratory, Longinus' statement leaves unclear whether we identify more closely with the character or the author, and therefore whether we resent Hercules' fall or share Seneca's truly elevated perspective. Longinus' comparison of the effect of sublimity to a thunderbolt (δίκην σκηπτοῦ) at 1.4 puts the reader of the sublime in the novel position of a theomach who survives the thunderbolt and is improved by the experience.

Now I have the adornments of rule, now the throne of my father.
I release the gods: I have attained the summit of my prayers.

Atreus, the tyrant par excellence, isn't simply describing his elation through a metaphor of altitude ('high as a kite', 'over the moon', 'on cloud nine', etc.); rather, he identifies with, and even surpasses, the gods themselves, as a subsequent exclamation makes clear: *o me caelitum excelsissimum / regumque regem!* ('O, I am the highest of gods, king of kings!', *Thy.* 911–12).[74] As with Hercules' distortion of the sublime—not real but merely hallucinated loftiness—Atreus' elevation to the divine is of a peculiarly deviant kind, inspired as it is by the realisation of a grotesque revenge—to have his brother consume the flesh of his own dead sons. As the successful director of his own theatre of cruelty, however, Atreus represents perhaps the most self-reflexive of Senecan protagonists.[75] By comparison with Atreus' mastery of the plot of his own play, Hercules' misperception and vulnerability hardly make him out to be an author figure, however reflective of Senecan poetics he might otherwise be.[76]

In fact, it is precisely by separating metapoetry from the familiar conceit of authorial symbolism that we better appreciate the implications of Hercules' language. It's instructive here to compare two famous and self-evidently metapoetic passages from the Augustan poets that do reflect on their authors, and which both concern ideas of sublimity and deification similar to those we see in the *HF*. At the end of Horace's first ode, the poet looks to be canonised by his patron, Maecenas: *quodsi me lyricis uatibus inseres, / sublimi feriam sidera uertice* ('but if you place me among lyric bards, I shall strike the stars with my lofty head', *Carm.* 1.1.36).[77] Seneca may be alluding to this passage at *HF* 958–9—*sublimis* picking up Horace's *sublimi*, and perhaps an aural echo of Horace's *feriam* in Hercules' *ferar*. Ovid alludes to the Horatian passage (along with the similarly metapoetic *Carm.* 3.30) at the end of the *Metamorphoses*: *super alta perennis / astra ferar* ('I shall be borne above the high stars, eternal', *Met.* 15.875–6). Here, too, Seneca may pick up Ovid's *alta*, *astra*, and *ferar* at *HF* 958–9. Both Horace and Ovid express considerable confidence about their reaching the

---

[74] Tarrant 1985: 217, Volk 2006: 194–5.

[75] On Atreus as metapoetic figure see Schiesaro 2003. Atreus' dismissal of the gods immediately after he rejoices at holding the throne of his father joins together theomachy and filial succession in strongly Bloomian terms. Hercules, by contrast, fails in his all too literal attempt to succeed his father. The difference between the two figures suggests Bloom's characterization of strong and weak poets, respectively (see Bloom 1997). The question of paternity and status common to both plays also returns us to the Homeric concern with generational competition (see Chapter 1).

[76] Cf. Staley 2010: 46 and 147 n. 40, though more can be made of Littlewood's approach than Staley suggests.

[77] On the gigantism, rather than ascent, implied by the image see Hardie 2009b: 122–3, Farrell 2007: 189; cf. Nisbet and Hubbard 1970: 15. On the metapoetic implications of Atreus' allusion to this ode at *Thy.* 885–6 see Schiesaro 2003: 59.

stars, and it's precisely in comparison to that confidence—resoundingly justified by Seneca's time—that Hercules' own words ring so hollow: he speaks the well-known language of poetic elevation while firmly rooted to the ground. Furthermore, the Augustan poets are careful to make their immortality contingent on others, whether on Maecenas, the Muses, the poet's audience, or the continuation of Roman power.[78] Hercules, by contrast, envisages a violent ascent in a sequence of first person singular verbs, his only concession to collaboration the unleashing of the Titans to fight under his leadership.

Whether or not one sees direct allusion to the Augustan poets here, the existence of common interests and forms of expression among these texts is sufficient to illustrate two important distinctions: first, the poets succeed in reaching the stars, or at least seem likely to succeed, whereas Hercules does not; second, the poets depend on others for this success, whereas Hercules assumes a greater autonomy. Much like the context of political deification discussed earlier, Seneca's language presents us with multiple models of how to become divine, and the evidence of these canonical metapoetic texts reveals yet further ways, beyond the obvious fact of hallucination, in which Hercules has got the wrong idea.[79] Rather than mining such intertexts for their implications about Seneca's authorial self-conception, we can derive far clearer conclusions about how different contexts affect our view of deification and theomachy—two major, explicit, and inseparable themes of the play. By the time we come to our third and last context for deification—philosophy—we shall see that the notion of Hercules' error has been well established, while the play subtly hints at more viable and sensible alternatives.

The language in which Hercules imagines his own ascent to the sky finds its closest analogue at the end of Seneca's *Medea*, when Jason sees Medea aloft in her chariot and takes her triumph as proof that there are no gods: *per alta uade spatia sublime aetheris, / testare nullos esse, qua ueheris, deos* ('travel on high through the lofty spaces of the aether, and bear witness where you fly

---

[78] Note, e.g., *Romana potentia* and *ore populi* at *Met*. 15.877–8 (on the Ovidian passage in general see Chapter 3). Cf. Hor. *Carm*. 3.30.7–16. The second choral ode of the *HF* makes a similar point about the power of song being dependent on external authority. Dis may have been conquered by Orpheus' song (*uincimur*, *HF* 582), but he retains the authority to impose conditions on the victor (*lege tamen data*, *HF* 583). Hercules, by contrast, departs the underworld with a free gift, Theseus (*HF* 806), and could have ruled in Dis' place (*HF* 609–10). Hercules' eventual madness thus recalibrates the relationship between song and physical force.

[79] Contrast Hercules', and Caligula's, ambitions with Jupiter's prophecy about the deification of Aeneas, which highlights not only the god's own authority but also Venus' physical transportation of her son: *sublimemque feres ad sidera caeli / magnanimum Aenean* ('you will bear great-hearted Aeneas high up to the stars of heaven', *Aen*. 1.259–60). Venus' action here positively reinterprets the less glorious moment in the *Iliad* when she had to snatch her son away from Diomedes; Ovid alludes to the Vergilian passage, and its Homeric background, at *Met*. 15.803–6, 844–6 (see Chapters 2 and 3).

that there are no gods', *Med.* 1026–7). The linguistic coincidence with Hercules' speech is very close (*in alta mundi spatia sublimis ferar, / petatur aether, HF* 958–9) and highly suggestive.[80] As with Atreus, Medea's and Hercules' ability and propensity to go beyond human limits in terms of power or moral norms threatens, or even does away with, the gods: in Medea's case, Jason interprets her elevation and the seeming absence of divine retribution as proof that gods do not exist; in Hercules' case, the hero's desired ascent to heaven veers towards theomachy, a threat that Juno fears from the outset.[81] It's important to note, however, that as the one Senecan tragedy to include a divine actor, Juno, the *HF* accordingly avoids the sceptical rhetoric of the other plays. In the last section of this chapter I shall argue that the *HF* in its own way suggests a rejection of conventional divinity, but for now it's sufficient to note that the conceptual ambit of the superhuman in Senecan tragedy includes not merely the idea of a physical threat to the gods, as voiced by Juno, but also an intellectual threat to the gods which renders them absent, impotent, or non-existent.

The argument of this section has attempted to explain why Seneca takes an image in many ways emblematic of the sublime and turns it on its head—Hercules' ascent is frenzied, impious, and a mere delusion. The answer, I suggest, lies in distinguishing and evaluating alternative ways—both within and outside Senecan tragedy—of achieving what Hercules desires and yet spectacularly fails to realise. The guiding concepts of madness and sublimity highlight the gap between mortal and god, and in turn make the reader hyperconscious of the different ways that gap can be conceived—as the overreaching of a Phaethon or Hercules, as the poetic yearning for eternal fame, or as the creation of a theological vacuum.[82]

---

[80] Since the relative dating of the two plays cannot be established on the basis of current evidence, the direction of the allusion between the two plays, and any consequent interpretation, must for now remain a mystery. Fitch 1981 argues that the two plays should be grouped together in terms of date of composition, perhaps in the early 50s AD.

[81] At *Thy.* 1077–92 Thyestes prays to Jupiter to strike Atreus down with his thunderbolt, explicitly calling for the weapon used in the Gigantomachy, but the play ends without any divine intervention: Atreus, like Medea, represents the only source of power in his play (see Schiesaro 2003: 151–3). The *HF* is less stark and more open to possibility than the other two plays.

[82] The effect of madness also emphasises the gap between human and divine. In the prologue, Juno uses madness as inspiration to achieve her destructive ends, calling on the Furies to attack her (*HF* 110–11). By contrast, Hercules' 'sight' of Tisiphone (*HF* 982–6) seems to act as the trigger for the misrecognition and slaughter of his family. Hercules' killing of his wife Megara also has a theomachic aspect to it—the hero imagines that he has got hold of Juno and by her death is liberating Jupiter (*HF* 1018–19). Towards the end of his rampage Hercules sarcastically claims to have sacrificed Lycus' family for Juno, calling his offerings worthy of her (*te digna, HF* 1038). Note the ironic recollection of his earlier prayers 'worthy of himself' (*meque dignas, HF* 927). The switch from killing Juno (i.e., Megara) to provoking her is a symptom of his madness, but it's worth noting that his unknowing fulfilment of the goddess's desire does, in some sense, do her honour: the sacrifice of his own family is clear testament to Juno's power.

Virtus, Equanimity, and the Gods

In their fourth and final ode the chorus ponder, amongst other things, Hercules' state of mind (*HF* 1082-99), a subject upon which the final act will dwell. When Hercules awakes to learn that he has killed his wife and children, he declares his intent to commit suicide. Amphitryon and Theseus respond by undermining the various justifications for Hercules' suicide: they question his responsibility for his earlier actions, the effectiveness of suicide as a means to avoid shame, and the very nature of heroism. It may seem, then, that the play has shifted its concern away from deification and theomachy towards matters of moral judgement both private and public. Two main points, however, encourage a continued focus on the issues discussed so far: first, as we shall see, traces of the theomachic instinct surface even in the supposedly sane Hercules; second, the involvement of the gods, or lack thereof, necessarily comments on the capacities of humans to resolve their affairs and decide their own fates. The latter point invites reflection on various philosophical contexts that cast the wise man as equal to or surpassing the gods. Viewed in this way, the tragedy offers another alternative route to divinity, very different from the apotheosis and theomachy with which the earlier portions of the play were concerned. Whether Hercules is at all capable of pursuing such a path is of course a central question; in the end, I argue that he is not.

When Hercules recognises his own responsibility for the brutal deaths of his family, Amphitryon attempts to place the blame squarely on the shoulders of Juno: *crimen nouercae; casus hic culpa caret* ('the crime is your stepmother's; this misfortune is free from fault', *HF* 1201).[83] Hercules, however, after calling for terrible punishment against himself, considers suicide the only appropriate recourse: *inferis reddam Herculem* ('I shall return Hercules to the underworld', *HF* 1218).[84] In response to his son's repeated claims of guilt, Amphitryon suggests that the demands of Herculean heroism might be best satisfied by another course of action: *nunc Hercule opus est: perfer hanc molem mali* ('now there is need of a Hercules: endure this weight of evil', *HF* 1239). This alternative, then, produces a new choice for Hercules, not between vice and virtue as such but between life and death, between the unyielding determination of a Sophoclean Ajax and a more rehabilitative and patient heroism.

The play's concern with suicide isn't limited to Hercules but also includes the subsequent threat by Amphitryon to kill himself (*HF* 1302-13). Seneca's

---

[83] Cf. *hoc Iuno telum manibus immisit tuis* ('Juno sent this weapon into your hands', *HF* 1297). Amphitryon is claiming that Hercules blames himself for something he could not help. Railing against things one has no control over is, as noted earlier, a kind of 'theomachy'; indeed, that is how the Stoic Epictetus uses the word (*Diss*. 3.24.24 and 4.1.101). Cf. p. 41 n. 53.

[84] On the implications of Hercules' references to himself in the third person, which Seneca deploys far more than Euripides, see Fitch and McElduff 2002: 25. Hercules thus creates the impression of having separate personae, with the present 'I' looking objectively upon earlier versions of himself. The validity of this distancing move comes under scrutiny in the final act.

philosophical writings on suicide and the manner of his own death have made the subject of even greater interest and have enriched the critical treatment of the theme.[85] What remains to be observed, however, is the relation between suicide and the tragedy's dominant themes of deification and theomachy. That there is such a relationship is clear from evidence both external and internal to the play. According to a passage from another Senecan tragedy, the *Agamemnon*, suicide can place one in an ambivalent position vis-à-vis the gods (*Ag.* 604–9):

> solus seruitium perrumpet omne
>   contemptor leuium deorum,
>   qui uultus Acherontis atri,
>   qui Styga tristem non tristis uidet
>   audetque uitae ponere finem:
> par ille regi, par superis erit.

> He alone will break through every servitude,
> a despiser of the fickle gods,
> who looks not sadly at the face of black Acheron,
> nor the grim Styx,
> and who dares to put an end to his life:
> that man will be equal to a king, equal to the gods.

The phrase *contemptor deorum* has a rather different sense here from the superficial designation of impiety that was applied to Vergil's Mezentius and Ovid's Pentheus, though there too we saw how it could take on greater theological significance.[86] In this choral ode, however, Seneca puts the phrase to striking use not only by dissociating it from impiety but also by tying it to equality with the gods. The chorus's intent is hardly theomachic, but their words bear on how we might read the connection between theomachy and suicide in the *HF*. Characterised as scornful of the gods and conceived as a means of rising to the level of the divine, suicide provides a novel means of reconciling Hercules' various attitudes—more or less legitimate—to entering heaven. However, it rather seems as though Hercules will fall short once again, for at no point in the final act does Hercules appear to possess the kind of calm detachment described by the chorus of the *Agamemnon*.

True to his deeply embedded instincts, Hercules imagines the form of his death as directly confrontational with the gods: he envisages himself being struck by Jupiter's lightning and occupying the place of Prometheus (*HF* 1202–10). When he wonders whether he should cremate his 'body spattered

---

[85] E. R. Wilson 2004: 88–112 discusses the relevance of Senecan philosophy to Hercules' choice whether to live or die. On the general topic of suicide in Seneca see T. D. Hill 2004: 145–82, Ker 2009.

[86] See Tarrant 2006: 12 on the *Agamemnon*. On Mezentius see Chapter 2, on Pentheus Chapter 3. Cf. Narducci 2002: 388–95 on Lucan's Cato.

with impious blood' (*cruore corpus impio sparsum*, *HF* 1217), he unknowingly echoes Amphitryon's description of the site of the Gigantomachy: *Phlegram impio / sparsam cruore* ('Phlegra spattered with impious blood', *HF* 444–5). Thus, instead of a composed acceptance of death, Hercules' fancies assimilate him to Titans and Giants. At a more conscious level, Hercules threatens the kind of suicide that entails maximal collateral damage (*HF* 1287–94):

> tota cum domibus suis
> dominisque tecta, cum deis templa omnibus
> Thebana supra corpus excipiam meum
> atque urbe uersa condar, et, si fortibus
> leue pondus umeris moenia immissa incident
> septemque opertus non satis portis premar,
> onus omne media parte quod mundi sedet
> dirimitque superos, in meum uertam caput.

> The entire city with its homes
> and masters, the Theban temples with all the gods
> shall I receive over my body
> and I shall bury myself beneath the city overthrown, and
> if the toppled walls fall as but a light weight for my strong shoulders
> and I am not fully covered and crushed by the seven gates,
> then the whole weight that sits at the centre of the universe
> and separates the gods shall I turn upon my head.

The passage clearly shows that neither Hercules nor the play is finished with theomachy. The threat to destroy temples and their divine images represents one form of impiety, while the imagined collapse of the city walls and even the heavens recalls the terms so often used of Gigantomachy. We might usefully contrast Hercules' attitude with Seneca's ideal response to a natural disaster—in this case, dying in an earthquake—in the *Natural Questions* (*QNat.* 6.2.8–9).[87] While Seneca takes solace from the fact that his own death entails the shaking of the world (*orbe concusso*), it is not because of the concomitant collective disaster (*publicam cladem*), but rather because it is a solace (*solacium*) to see that the earth too is mortal (*terram quoque uidere mortalem*). This peculiarly pointed qualification, whether or not it's truly consoling, contrasts sharply with the attitude of Hercules, who, far from being a victim of a natural disaster, instead desires to effect one, thus becoming one with such elemental forces as reside in the

---

[87] See Williams 2012: 228–30, and 257: 'earthquakes... offer a powerfully suggestive metaphor here [in *QNat.* 6] for any significant disaster or affliction, public or private, physical or psychological, that destabilizes life'. Mazzoli 1968: 366 and 1970: 258 argues that the Vagellian quotation in the *QNat.* passage comes from a poem about Phaethon and conjectures that these words are spoken by the boy as he asks to drive his father's chariot. Cf. Duret 1988: 141–2. If correct, Hercules' vision of disaster may continue and further nuance the relationship with Phaethon seen earlier in the play. On Seneca's positive reinterpretation of the Phaethon myth in his prose see Tarrant 2006: 3.

depths of the earth from which he recently returned. Hercules' language thus strongly suggests a continuity in his overreaching—before, during, and after madness—and an attitude that parodies the proper response to catastrophe.

At this point, with the play poised to see another burst of theomachic energy, matters come to a sudden and swift resolution. Amphitryon falls back on his last resort, telling Hercules that he will have to commit suicide in the full knowledge that this will cause his grief-stricken father to do the same. Presented with this stark ultimatum Hercules relents and gives up what is most characteristic of him, the impulse of *uirtus*, in favour of obedience to his father: *succumbe, uirtus, perfer imperium patris* ('yield, my valour, endure my father's command', *HF* 1315).[88] In a play so concerned with paternal authority, that concession figures a more general subordination to the existing order, and a renouncing of his divine parentage. For now, at least, the threat of theomachy would seem to have abated, and Juno's initial fear quelled.

As in the final act of Euripides' play, Theseus invites Hercules to find redemption at Athens (*HF* 1341–4; cf. *Her.* 1313–39):

> nostra te tellus manet.
> illic solutam caede Gradiuus manum
> restituit armis; illa te, Alcide, uocat,
> facere innocentes terra quae superos solet.

> My land awaits you.
> There Gradivus returned his hand purified
> of slaughter to warfare; that land calls you, Alcides,
> which is accustomed to make gods innocent.

The example of Gradivus—Mars—is a Senecan addition.[89] While Athens can offer other examples of purification, such as Orestes, it's notable that Theseus cites the example of a god, a status which Hercules once sought but which has now been indelibly coloured by the disasters following from his lofty ambition. Theseus, however, recognises that it may nevertheless be appropriate to compare Hercules to the gods. Despite all that has happened over the course of the drama, the facts Juno laid out at the beginning of the play have not been disproven: Hercules is still the son of Jupiter, already hailed as a god on earth, and aware of the promise of deification.[90] If he behaves like the gods, and looks to their

---

[88] See E. R. Wilson 2004: 108 for discussion of the conflict between heroic instinct and paternal authority. In bidding his *uirtus* to give way, Hercules reverses his earlier, more typically heroic command that his valour rise (*exsurge, uirtus, HF* 1157). The idea of speaking to one's *uirtus* can be compared with other Senecan characters' frequent addresses to their 'spirit' or *animus* (e.g., perhaps most famously Medea at *Med.* 41, 895, 937, 976, 988). Cf. also Juno's address to her anger at *HF* 75. On self-address in Senecan tragedy see Star 2012: 62–83.

[89] For Mars Gradivus see, e.g., Livy 1.20.4.

[90] The final act of Euripides' play, by contrast, has Herakles emphatically reject Zeus as his father in favour of Amphitryon: πατέρα γὰρ ἀντὶ Ζηνὸς ἡγοῦμαι σ' ἐγώ ('for I regard you as my father instead of Zeus', *Her.* 1265).

example for rehabilitation, perhaps he is simply preparing for his new company.[91] Moreover, even though the end of the tragedy shows Hercules in great distress, his particular emotional response to his situation may seem less appropriate to a human than to a god. His anguish seems mostly predicated on shame and the loss of status, rather than regret, and in his futile desire to flee somewhere where he is not known (*HF* 1321–41)—even the underworld—he recalls the Juno of the prologue, shamed into finding refuge outside Olympus.

By the end of the tragedy it seems we are no closer to answering what exactly Hercules has or will become. If Hercules is still as much a son of Jupiter as before, if his future still holds deification, and if the choice to live is his greatest glory yet, then Juno has suffered a resounding defeat.[92] But the play is less concerned with the definition of Juno's success or failure than with the assessment of Hercules as a hero. For one thing, there is no deus or dea ex machina to impose their resolution of the drama and their interpretation of events. Instead, the absence of the gods, just as at the end of Statius' *Thebaid*, places front and centre the importance of human methods of negotiation and reconciliation.[93] In filling the vacuum created by the gods' absence, humanity achieves—intellectually, at least—a similar result to a successful theomachy, perhaps even a better result, since it dispenses with the gods without the need for recriminations, denials, or threats of combat. Ultimately, both the fable of Mars purified by the Areopagus and the similar prospect of Hercules looking to Athens for redemption demonstrate the subordination of gods and demigods to the most powerful human procedures and rituals. If the reader thinks that by going to Athens the assimilation to Mars brings Hercules closer to the gods, then the implications of the final act of the play have been seriously misunderstood: divinity—Hercules' constant aspiration—is not what it once was.

There is one way, however, for Hercules to have his cake and eat it—to achieve divinity without lapsing into the ambitious, violent, and even theomachic hero of old: Hercules could learn to become wise. The final act of the tragedy, with its frequent mentions of endurance of adversity, valour, and emotional restraint, repeatedly recalls the characteristics traditionally associated with philosophical wisdom.[94] That particular conception of wisdom, or *sapientia*, opens the door to a different way of becoming divine. In Letter 98, for

---

[91] See Papadopoulou 2004: 275.

[92] Lawall 1983: 22 sees in the play's resolution a Herculean victory: 'Once again, Juno has succeeded not in destroying Hercules but only in setting him up for a triumph greater than his preceding triumphs (cf. 33 and 312f.), because it is a triumph over himself, to which nothing else is equal (cf. 84f.)'. Cf. Motto and Clark 1981. E. R. Wilson 2004: 109–12 generally follows Fitch 1987 and Braden 1993 in her pessimistic reading of the close.

[93] See Chapter 8.

[94] Compare, e.g., Theseus' encouragement to Hercules (*surge et aduersa impetu / perfringe solito*, 'rise and break through adversity with your accustomed force', *HF* 1274–5) with Seneca's statement at Helv. 5.1 *nec secunda sapientem euehunt nec aduersa demittunt* ('neither do favourable events elate the wise man nor do adverse events cast him down'); cf. *Ben.* 6.35.1. Compare also Hercules' *uincatur mea / Fortuna dextra* ('let Fortune be conquered by my right hand', *HF* 1271–2) and Theseus' response

instance, which discusses not only endurance of misfortune but also the specific examples of losing one's children or wife, Seneca contrasts merely mortal goods with something greater: *nam illud uerum bonum non moritur, certum est sempiternumque, sapientia et uirtus; hoc unum contingit inmortale mortalibus.* ('for that true good does not die, but it is fixed and eternal, consisting of wisdom and virtue; this is the only immortal thing to touch mortals', *Ep.* 98.9). The ability to endure his misfortune is a true test of Hercules' equanimity, and thus of whether he might be able to attain the elevated status of the *sapiens*, or wise man. In another epistle, Letter 73, Seneca makes entirely explicit the kind of apotheosis that follows from equanimity and self-control (*Ep.* 73.14–16):

> sapiens tam aequo animo omnia apud alios uidet contemnitque quam Iuppiter et hoc se magis suspicit quod Iuppiter uti illis non potest, sapiens non uult. credamus itaque Sextio monstranti pulcherrimum iter et clamanti 'hac itur ad astra, hac secundum frugalitatem, hac secundum temperantiam, hac secundum fortitudinem'. non sunt dii fastidiosi, non inuidi: admittunt et ascendentibus manum porrigunt. miraris hominem ad deos ire? deus ad homines uenit, immo quod est propius, in homines uenit: nulla sine deo mens bona est.

> The wise man sees and scorns all things belonging to others as calmly as does Jupiter, and he esteems himself more because while Jupiter cannot make use of them, the wise man does not wish to do so. Let us therefore believe Sextius when he shows the path of greatest beauty and cries, 'This is the way to the stars, this is the way, by following frugality, self-restraint, and courage'. The gods are not disdainful or envious; they admit you and stretch out a hand as you climb. Do you marvel that man goes to the gods? God comes to men—no, what is closer, he comes into men: without god no mind is good.

Wisdom, Seneca unambiguously asserts, leads to divinity. It is then tempting to read Seneca's rhetorical question—*miraris hominem ad deos ire?*—as a response to other, less plausible kinds of apotheosis, mythical and imperial.[95] Armed with equanimity and moral self-sufficiency, the *sapiens* may achieve a more realistic goal than entering the heavens as a new god or breaching them

---

(*nunc magna tibi / uirtute agendum est*, 'now you must act with great valour', *HF* 1276–7) with *Ep.* 71.30: *sapiens quidem uincit uirtute fortunam* ('the wise man, indeed, conquers fortune with valour').

[95] In an article on the *Apocolocyntosis*, Green 2010: 275 n. 4 draws a sharp distinction between what he takes the phrase *ad deos ire* to mean—'the Stoic notion of a man's intrinsic connection with the divine'—and other idioms conveying apotheosis proper (e.g., *caelum ascendentem*, *Apocol.* 1.2). This distinction is blurred, however, by Seneca's thoroughly rhetorical language, in which he can conceive of the Stoic as making a way to the stars and as being equal to god, concepts very much in evidence in the passages quoted in this section. This rhetorical colouring is important for the interpretation of both the Letters and the *HF*: it facilitates the productive comparison of different concepts of going to the heavens and equalling the gods, whatever the underlying niceties might be.

as a theomach: rather than joining or replacing the gods, one can learn how to live like them.[96] Compared to the optimism of the letter, however, the final act of the play is studiously ambiguous and vague, which makes for a mysterious and powerful end to the drama. Whatever we, the audience, might think about alternative forms of divinisation, the characters are left to figure matters out for themselves, and it remains unclear whether Hercules could even follow the path suggested by Sextius, Seneca, and other philosophers.

The concept of the wise man as equal to the gods is common to Stoicism and other Hellenistic philosophies. As we saw in Chapter 2, for instance, Lucretius can depict Epicurus as a god rising up to the heavens.[97] Like Lucretius, Seneca too envisages philosophy raising one to level of the gods (*Ep.* 41.4):

> si hominem uideris interritum periculis, intactum cupiditatibus, inter aduersa felicem, in mediis tempestatibus placidum, ex superiore loco homines uidentem, ex aequo deos, non subibit te ueneratio eius?

> If you see a man unafraid of dangers, unaffected by desires, happy in adversity, peaceful in the midst of storms, beholding men from a higher place, equal with the gods, will veneration for him not come upon you?

Such philosophical ascents contrast sharply with Hercules' failed ascent in Act 4, where his febrile visions of the constellations coming alive represent the kind of dangerous falsehood that natural science, whether Epicurean or Stoic, seeks to explode.[98] The irony is all the more acute, of course, since Hercules is proverbially famous for subduing the natural world, a reputation to which the *HF* often adverts. By enduring *aduersa* (*HF* 1274), however, Hercules has the opportunity to make up for his grievous error in Act 4 and, like the man imagined by Seneca in Letter 41, achieve the ascent the hero has always desired.

---

[96] Cf. Lucr. 3.319–22 and my discussion of Epicurean theomachy in Chapter 2. For the distinction between equanimity and conventional divinity in the *HF*, one need look no further than Juno, a goddess characterised by her anxious and wrathful state of mind.

[97] The idea of a philosophical ascent to the gods is present in Plato too, notably in the *Phaedrus*, where the ascent is enabled by the (positive) madness of love. Even philosophers can suffer a great fall, however: cf. Lucr. 1.716–41, where Lucretius treats Empedocles' legendary fall into a volcano as symbolic of his scientific error. Just as Lucretius' sublime language raises up both Empedocles and the reader, only for the reader to be able to appreciate the extent of Empedocles' fall (Hardie 2009b: 89–90, 216–17), so too Hercules' theomachic sublime has the same effect of intensifying the reader's experience of Hercules' error, all the more so once the reader sees that philosophy offers a real and lasting elevation.

[98] The passage of Ovid's Phaethon episode to which Hercules' hallucination alludes may itself allude to Lucretius. Not only does Ovid's anagrammatic wordplay at *Met.* 2.193–4 (*passim miracula...simulacra*, the verbal rearrangement further signalled by *sparsa...in uario*) contain one of the key terms of the account of visual perception in *De Rerum Natura* 4 (*simulacra*), but the word *miracula* is also part of a play on words in that same book of Lucretius (*miracula* and *auricularum* at Lucr. 4.592–4, on which see Gale 1994: 135 n. 20). Seneca alludes to the Ovidian passage (though seemingly not the wordplay) in a discussion of stargazing at *Ep.* 90.43 (on which see Degl'Innocenti Pierini 2005).

In another letter to Lucilius, Seneca can speak of philosophy in even more explicitly deifying terms: 'sic itur ad astra'. hoc enim est quod mihi philosophia promittit, ut parem deo faciat; ad hoc inuitatus sum, ad hoc ueni: fidem praesta ('"Thus does one go to the stars". For this is what philosophy promises, to make one equal to a god; to this have I been summoned, to this have I come: keep your promise', Ep. 48.11).[99] Seneca here quotes Apollo speaking to Iulus at Aen. 9.641, a Vergilian passage to which, as we saw earlier, the HF also alludes.[100] The phrase ad astra, together with Seneca's claim of being invited to become like the gods, overlaps with the HF, especially Hercules' theomachic speech in which he speaks of his father's promise of the stars (astra promittit pater, 959) and the gods summoning him to heaven (uocat / omnis deorum coetus, HF 961–2). Thus, in addition to my earlier suggestions of ruler cult and the literary sublime as relevant contexts for understanding apotheosis and theomachy in the HF, one should add another context—the philosophical sublime.[101] That Seneca intends the latter as an alternative to imperial deification in particular seems clear from their conjoining in Ep. 48: he quotes Apollo's ideologically laden speech, which adverts to the apotheosis of Caesar, only to pivot to the quite different idea of philosophy's promise of divinity.[102] Beyond its rehabilitative implications, then, the model of the sapiens has a particular relevance for Hercules, since it offers the hero the possibility of divinity at the very moment when thought of literal apotheosis may be furthest away.

In Chapter 2, I discussed Antonio La Penna's argument that these philosophical claims about equality with, and independence from, the divine were important for a reading of Vergil's Mezentius.[103] The philosophical rhetoric to which La Penna refers is much more obviously relevant for a reading of Seneca's Hercules. Nowhere is this more evident than in the further claim that the sapiens not only equals but even surpasses god (Ep. 53.11–12):

> est aliquid quo sapiens antecedat deum: ille naturae beneficio non timet, suo sapiens. ecce res magna, habere inbecillitatem hominis, securitatem dei.

> There is something in which the wise man excels god: god does not fear thanks to the privilege of nature, the wise man thanks to himself. Behold a great thing, to have the weakness of man, the security of god.

---

[99] Cf. Ep. 92.30, where Seneca claims that a virtuous man 'equals the gods' (deos aequat), and Sil. Pun. 1.611.

[100] See p. 133 above.

[101] Indeed, sublimitas is one of the components of the summum bonum at Sen. DVB 9.4.

[102] Note the same allusion in the earlier passage quoted from Ep. 73, where the words itur ad astra appear in the mouth of Quintus Sextius, a philosopher of the mid to late first century BC. Whether the phrase should be taken as proverbial or as a deliberate allusion to the Aeneid on Sextius' part (in which case the quotation comes from relatively late in Sextius' life), for Seneca and Seneca's readers, at least, the phrase would have recalled the famous Vergilian passage and its ideological import.

[103] La Penna 1999: 364–8. See pp. 73–4.

Seneca is here more likely to be working out a rhetorical theme than to be saying in all seriousness that the wise person is better than god. But what may be merely rhetorical to Seneca Philosophus, as so often, takes on a quite different significance in Seneca Tragicus. My point is not that the wise man is literally a theomach, of course, but rather that theomachy can be understood metaphorically in much the same way that Lucretius reinterpreted the theme.[104] That metaphor, however rhetorical, provides an illuminating context for understanding the development of the themes of deification and theomachy in the *HF*: Hercules pursues an overly literal conception of how to become, or even exceed, the gods. From a philosophical point of view, then, one answer to the play's conundrum concerning apotheosis lies precisely in wisdom, which offers a different kind of divinisation in stark contrast both to the earlier aspirations of Hercules and to contemporary imperial practice.

Philosophy had often adopted Hercules as an allegorical figure, of course, most famously in Prodicus' allegory of the choice between vice and virtue.[105] Stoicism too, and indeed Seneca himself, had used Hercules as a philosophical exemplar.[106] Here, however, Seneca offers something subtler than allegory, though he can rely on the tradition created by Prodicus and others to make the reader more receptive to philosophical connotations.[107] Rather than deploying Hercules as an overt symbol, Seneca gives the hero a new and deliberately imprecise significance, one that inherits Euripides' theological interest but puts it to different use. In making a choice regarding suicide and the value of external goods, like his reputation, Hercules has the opportunity to think and act philosophically, and thereby to achieve a deification—or theomachy—very different from the earlier conceptions appearing in the play. Not for Seneca the Euripidean moment at which Herakles explicitly attacks the poets' conceptions of the gods (*Her.* 1340–6), but rather the question of how one might become a god, an enquiry inspired by philosophy and politics in equal measure.[108]

---

[104] Cf. Seneca's attribution of similar rhetoric to Epicurus: *intra quae quisquis desiderium suum clusit cum ipso Ioue de felicitate contendat, ut ait Epicurus* ('whoever limits his desire within these bounds can contend in happiness with Jupiter himself, as Epicurus says', *Ep.* 25.4). For other such sentiments in Stoic and Epicurean thought see La Penna 1999: 366–7. A strikingly similar idea—though voiced with real bitterness—appears in the mouth of Euripides' Amphitryon: ἀρετῇ σε νικῶ θνητὸς ὢν θεὸν μέγαν ('I conquer you in virtue, though I am a mortal and you a great god', *Her.* 342).

[105] Prodicus' allegory is related at Xen. *Mem.* 2.1.21–34.

[106] See, e.g., Cic. *Fin.* 3.66.1–8, Sen. *Ben.* 1.13.3, *Tranq.* 16.4, Tietze Larson 1991.

[107] Assuming Seneca Tragicus and Philosophus are one and the same, that an author might wish to explore a different facet, or even an entirely dissimilar representation, of a character should come as little surprise. The calm and respectful Odysseus of Sophocles' *Ajax*, for instance, bears little resemblance to the same character in the *Philoctetes*. Moreover, to read the Hercules of the *HF* as encompassing Seneca's understanding of the whole literary history and symbolism of the hero would be misguided, just as it would be to read the Aegaeon simile of *Aeneid* 10 as entirely definitive of Aeneas' character.

[108] On the strangely philosophical outburst from Euripides' Herakles, see Silk 1985, Mastronarde 1986, Lawrence 1998.

The thematic unity across the play, however—while it may reaffirm the importance of deification—doesn't help to determine whether or not Hercules in fact achieves any kind of deification, especially of the philosophical sort.[109] To my mind, the last act offers little grounds for seeing Hercules as even an incipient *sapiens*—neither is he self-sufficient, nor does he anywhere seem to be arriving at equanimity. In fact, his final request that Theseus return him to the underworld (*redde me infernis*, HF 1338) shows little progress from his earlier threat to commit suicide (*inferis reddam Herculem*, HF 1218). We can now see, however, that as a result of his persistent misunderstanding Hercules falls short of the prize he has sought for so long: the obsessive and literal-minded desire to become a god distracts from a suppler concept of divinity and a more realistic path of attainment. In alluding to philosophical contexts, the play's language thus indicates how we might read the final act—as a continued debate and negotiation of the nature of divinity, but on a completely different plane from what came before.

If the various contexts for deification and theomachy—political, poetic, and philosophical—all highlight Hercules' failure, there are nevertheless grounds for seeing a more complicated picture. In the poetic and philosophical realms, at least, the conception of the sublime shows either authors or wise men raised up to look down on the world, and in the context of the HF to look down on the frenzied Hercules in particular. But as Longinus states, it is only through the sublime that writers are elevated in the first place: τὸ δ' ὕψος ἐγγὺς αἴρει μεγαλοφροσύνης θεοῦ ('sublimity lifts them near to the great mind of god', Longin. 36.1). That sublimity—at least in literary terms—is best represented by Hercules' grandiose theomachic vision. However much Seneca might turn the sublime on its head by audaciously wedding it to an impious hallucination, it's nevertheless through Hercules' madness and failure that the audience experiences the sublime. It is only thanks to Hercules' theomachy, in other words, that the play succeeds as a work of art, and, more importantly from a didactic perspective, that the audience becomes hyperconscious of the different ways of ascending to the heavens. Hercules is no mere negative exemplum, then, but rather the enabling fiction of our own sublimity. That heuristic role represents a key part of Seneca's contribution to the poetics of theomachy.

Like his Augustan predecessors, Seneca reaffirms theomachy as a theme of substance and provokes the reader to interpret mythical acts in distinctly non-mythical terms. But as the intellectual and political climate of the first century AD focused writers' attention on the changed possibilities for one's relationship with the divine, so too the engagement with theomachy became ever

---

[109] Motto and Clark 1981: 116 speak of Hercules' 'super-godliness', but the essay misses the continuous twinning of the themes of deification and theomachy right through the play up to and including the possibilities of Hercules' suicide or purification. The idea that Hercules does achieve a philosophical divinisation is examined in the Pseudo-Senecan *Hercules Oetaeus*, on which see Galinsky 1972: 173–83, Tietze Larson 1991.

more direct. Seneca's profound and radical vision of deification and theomachy, expansively treated in the *Hercules Furens*, exploits the potential of a theme that would come to dominate a different genre in the second half of the century: epic. Whether or not they allude to Seneca's Hercules, Lucan's Caesar, Silius' Hannibal, and Statius' Capaneus will all engage a recognisably similar set of issues and will return to the same question of the place of the human relative to the cosmos and to god.[110]

---

[110] A study of the influence of Senecan tragedy on imperial Latin poetry, especially epic, is a desideratum (preliminary work on Statius, for instance, includes Venini 1971: 55–80, Frings 1992). The theological legacy of the *HF* also makes a distinctive contribution within the larger field of Seneca's influence on English Renaissance tragedy: Marlowe's Tamburlaine and Milton's Samson approach the question of divine power from different angles, for instance, but in doing so both heroes draw on the special status and ambitions of Seneca's Hercules. On Tamburlaine see, e.g., Braden 1985: 186–9, and the epilogue below. Cf. Chaudhuri (forthcoming a) on Senecan tragic theology in *Titus Andronicus*.

5

Theomachy in Historical Epic
DISENCHANTMENT AND REMYSTIFICATION IN LUCAN'S *BELLUM CIVILE*

> In truth, there is nothing, so miserable, hateful, cruel and irreligious as civil war, for it is an enemy against law, nature, and God, it pulls down the seats of justice, throws down the altars of religion, digs up the urns of their parents, disperses the dust and bones of their dead ancestors, spills the blood of their fathers, sons, brethren, friends and countrymen, and makes a total destruction and dissolution.
>
> —MARGARET CAVENDISH

> Such things the younger gods do,
> ruling all beyond justice.
>
> —AESCHYLUS

> As it is, the world ends because neither the all too human gods, with their armies and quarrels, nor the fiery thinker know how to save it.
>
> —A. S. BYATT

In Lucan's *Bellum Civile* (*BC*), the notorious absence of the gods removes the possibility of any conventional scene of theomachy. Rather counter-intuitively, however, that very absence makes the issue of theomachy more pressing within the poem, for the removal of the gods goes hand in hand with the proliferation of figures who exemplify different kinds of theomachy—Caesar, the narrator, Pompey, and even Cato.[1] Some of these are more explicit than others: Caesar,

---

[1] For a convenient list of the most important scholarship on the absence of Lucan's gods see Day 2013: 106 n. 4; Feeney 1991: 250–301 remains paramount. I often use 'Lucan' as an alternative to the less committal 'narrator' or 'poet', but the question of authorial identity is especially problematic in this poem given the changes in narratorial tone and the author's self-consciousness about the function of narrative. On this topic see, e.g., Masters 1992, Bartsch 1997, Leigh 1997, Henderson 2010, Ormand 2010.

for example, represents an especially ambiguous kind of theomach, since the poet repeatedly emphasises both the gods' favour towards him and his characteristic impiety and scepticism, attitudes typically associated with antagonists of the divine. Pompey and Cato, on the other hand, exemplify a tension with the gods that arises from the seeming opposition, impotence, or non-existence of the divine. The absence of the gods therefore provides a fascinating perspective on theomachy, as various figures take on the role of theomach and god, thereby expanding the range of application of the topos and further destabilising the moral and theological foundations of epic that had already been undermined by Lucretius and Ovid, among others.

More specifically, as this chapter argues, Lucan uses the imagery of theomachy to play two competing concepts—disenchantment and remystification—against each other. In the *BC*, that disenchantment is emphatically political as well as theological. Whereas in the previous chapters the relationship between imperial politics and theomachy—however potent—remained largely implicit, Lucan is the first Roman author to make that relationship savagely explicit. In Book 7 of the *BC*, the narrator notoriously declares the practice of imperial deification to be a form of vengeance upon the gods for having allowed the Battle of Pharsalus, and as a consequence the fall of the republic, to occur (Luc. 7.455–9). As we have seen in other works, reflection on the political reality and ideology of the principate frequently goes hand in hand with philosophical thinking. Accordingly, earlier in the same outburst the narrator claims—with a cavalier disregard for consistency—that there are no gods and that Jupiter does not reign (Luc. 7.445–7). The emotional intensity of the moment offers a ready explanation for how the speaker can in almost the same breath both reject the gods and take comfort from revenge against them. Yet one might also interpret this passage in another way, as a doubly radical voice that takes both traditional religion and its imperial evolution as targets of its ire. But before parsing this passage, to which we shall return later in the chapter, it's important to recognise that the notion of theomachy embedded here raises two immediate questions: who is fighting whom, and who, if anyone, counts as divine for the purposes of this poem—the Olympian gods, Caesar, the emperors, the republicans, or even the narrator himself?

Precisely because of passages like that in Book 7, the *BC* is regularly viewed as the product of a cynical mind in a disillusioned age.[2] By the time of the epic's composition under the emperor Nero, the monarchical system of the principate had been consolidated and naturalised, even if the Roman world could still be subject to considerable turmoil, as it would be in the civil wars following Nero's fall in AD 68, itself only three years after Lucan's own death. Nevertheless, the

---

[2] E.g., Tarrant 1997: 65.

contours of imperial power and the models of good and bad rulership were already fairly well established in the Julio-Claudian dynasty. However hysterical the tone of the narrator, then, the condition of Rome to which he was responding was hardly novel. Against this historical context, Lucan's minimisation of the divine presence looks not only like a firm nod to the genre of historiography but also like part of a larger sociocultural disenchantment that came with the experience of almost a century of imperial rule.[3] But in opposition to this disenchantment—a view of the *pax deorum* as forever destroyed, or even of the gods as distant or non-existent—was a powerful force of remystification: humans had become gods, and those gods were more palpable than ever before. It is that dialogue between rival theologies—a negative one critical of convention, and a positive one forming entirely new customs—that animates much of Lucan's poem and turns its representation of theomachy into a site where these issues can be imagined, explored, and in some way comprehended.

The chapter consists of three sections, each treating the different theomachic aspects of the main protagonists and the narrator. Part 1 examines the grove-cutting scene at Massilia in Book 3 to show how Lucan plays with the notion of disenchantment. Building on the work of Matthew Leigh, I read the symbolic rationalism of Caesar against the episode's key intertext of Ovid's Erysichthon. Erysichthon's punishment of insatiable hunger, a condition that metaphorically applies to Caesar, raises important questions about the relationship between divine power and human character that complicate Leigh's account. Part 2 then focuses on the account of the Battle of Pharsalus in Book 7 to show how Caesar shifts from a figure of disenchantment to one of remystification, effectively filling the void left by the absence of the gods. In the course of this movement, however, the narrator emerges as another rationalising theomach, driven to cast doubt on the gods by the breakdown of even minimal theological expectations. Part 3 shows how remystifications proliferate in the latter part of the poem, in particular through the simultaneously divine and theomachic aspects of Pompey and Cato. Departing from Henry Day's study of the Lucanian sublime, I argue that the narrator envisages a cycle of theogony and theomachy while the characters, much like Seneca's Hercules, fail to see the possibility of a true divinisation, one that might close the cyclical pattern. Like his uncle, I suggest, but more explicitly, Lucan figured competing notions of how one might be like, or struggle against, the gods. The key difference is that by putting multiple models of divinity and theomachy in his text, Lucan opens up to greater scrutiny characteristics that Seneca had treated far more allusively.

---

[3] On historiography and the *BC* see Feeney 1991: 250–73. On the effect of the system of the principate on Lucan's poem cf. Roche 2009: 1–3.

Massilia: Disenchantment and Desire

The theme of disenchantment emerges especially clearly in the episode of the Massilian grove in *BC* 3, in which Caesar leads his men in cutting down a sacred wood to supply timber for the siege.[4] When his soldiers fear to desecrate the ancient and numinous grove, Caesar himself is the first to take an axe to a tree (Luc. 3.436-9):[5]

> 'iam ne quis uestrum dubitet subuertere siluam,
> credite me fecisse nefas'. tum paruit omnis
> imperiis non sublato secura pauore
> turba, sed expensa superorum et Caesaris ira.

> 'Now so that none of you hesitates to overturn the wood,
> believe that I did the crime'. Then the whole crowd obeyed
> his commands, not without anxiety nor with fear put aside,
> but weighing out the anger of the gods against that of Caesar.

In the traditional reading of Lucan's epic the troops would seem to have chosen correctly, since the gods are conspicuous only by their absence. The Massilians, however, take a different view, of which the poet is pessimistically sceptical (Luc. 3.446-9):

> muris sed clausa iuuentus
> exultat; quis enim laesos inpune putaret
> esse deos? seruat multos fortuna nocentes,
> et tantum miseris irasci numina possunt.

> But the young men shut within the walls
> exult; for who would think that the gods are harmed
> with impunity? Yet fortune guards many guilty people,
> and the gods can be angry only with the wretched.

Whether because Caesar's anger is greater or more real than the gods' or because Caesar's fortune allows him to act with impunity, his cutting of the grove undermines any confidence in the justice, or even the existence, of the gods.

---

[4] In the *Thebaid*, the pyre of Opheltes requires its own grove-cutting. Although the scene (*Theb.* 6.84-117) alludes to the passage in Lucan, the instruction comes from one of the more pious figures in the poem, Amphiaraus (*Theb.* 6.84-5; see Newlands 2002: 292). Statius' description ends with a simile comparing the act to the sacking of a city, a similar conflation of the acts of deforestation and conquest to what we see in Lucan. Most scenes of tree-cutting (e.g., in Homer, Ennius, Vergil, and Statius) describe preparations for burial, whereas Caesar will be associated with the denial of burial (on which see below).

[5] For a metapoetic interpretation of the episode see Masters 1992: 25-9. On Caesar's tree-felling alluding to Aeneas see Thomas 1988. On the metapoetics of entering an ancient wood see Hinds 1998: 11-14.

The episode has received extensive discussion from Matthew Leigh, who has persuasively argued that Lucan creatively expands upon the historical Caesar's supposed disregard for superstition.[6] Lucan does this in part by drawing on various models of rationality and intellectual progress, from Lucretius' pioneering Epicurus to Octavian's clearing of the dark and supposedly pestilential woods of Avernus.[7] Furthermore, compared to his poetic and mythical models, such as Erysichthon and Lycurgus, Caesar pointedly fails to be punished for his supposedly sacrilegious act. Although the siege is ultimately unsuccessful, the subsequent naval battle later in the book leads to the Massilians' bloody defeat, and Caesar's impiety and rapaciousness go unpunished. For Leigh, this impunity is a powerful reflection of what Lucretius and Octavian, in their distinctive ways, had already shown—that a bold, even revolutionary, figure can dispel even the most persistent of superstitions. Moreover, in attributing this almost certainly fictional act to Caesar, Lucan not only alludes to Octavian's historical clearing of Avernus, but he also suggests the roots of Octavian's rationalism: 'Caesar stands on the cusp between an age of faith and an age of scepticism'.[8] Caesar is thus figured as a trailblazer, one who represents the scepticism that Octavian will inherit and apply, but that scepticism, I would add, will eventually be turned against Augustus and his successors.

What Chapter 3 showed—and where Leigh's reading of Massilia must be situated in a larger context—is that the scepticism of the post-Caesarian age could be explained less as a product of individual and conspicuously rationalistic acts and more as a response to quite the opposite tendency identified with Caesar and especially Augustus—a profound remystification achieved through the near identification of mortal and divinity. Thus, two of the prominent strands running through the previous chapters—scepticism and divinisation—are intertwined in one and the same figure: Lucan's Caesar, against whose anger even divine wrath is found wanting, is at once theomach and god.

Leigh sees Caesar's rationalism as itself a kind of theomachy manqué:

> The hero who reveals the absence or impotence of the gods is one who is frustrated in his fundamental desire to perform the truly grand and charismatic deed of matching himself against those gods.[9]

Whereas in the Augustan context, for example, Vergil's Mezentius and Diomedes were not up to the task of fighting Aeneas, let alone the gods, Lucan's

---

[6] Leigh 2010: 208.

[7] Leigh 2010: 209–10 (Epicurus), 219–28 (Octavian). See also Day 2013: 136–43, who expands on the Lucretian and Longinan features of the episode.

[8] Leigh 2010: 202. On the fictionality of Caesar's grove-cutting see Phillips 1968: 299, Hunink 1992: 168; on the historical events that may have influenced Lucan's scene see S. L. Dyson 1970. Frederiksen 1984: 334, quoted by Leigh 2010: 223, draws a more general connection between Caesar's and Octavian's sense for symbolic spectacle: 'Octavian had however learned from his adoptive father the uses in the quest for public attention of spectacular alterations of the physical environment'.

[9] Leigh 2010: 202.

Caesar, by contrast, finds himself in entirely the wrong kind of epic—a godless one—to prove his impressive theomachic credentials.[10] As Henry Day observes of Leigh's point, however, theomachy—traditionally a paradigm of failure and self-destruction—may represent a poor substitute for one able to secure for himself the even greater glory of attaining divine power.[11]

That sense of usurping and even surpassing a divine prerogative, as Day points out, is already evident in the grove-cutting episode.[12] Although the wood has long remained untouched by lightning (Luc. 3.408–10), a traditional instrument of divine power, it is nevertheless felled by Caesar, who famously embodies the thunderbolt, or *fulmen* (Luc. 1.151–7).[13] From this perspective, Caesar's destruction of the ancient grove represents less an act of rationalism than the trampling of older gods by newer ones. Human-divine theomachy is thus implicated with the other type of theomachy fought among gods or other supernatural powers. Before pursuing Day's insight about Caesar's re-mystification further, however—especially its force in Lucan's account of the Battle of Pharsalus in Book 7—it's important to parse Caesar's relationship to the gods in the scene at Massilia more carefully. One should not be too quick to accede to Caesar's self-elevation without questioning whether he really is as impervious to punishment as his behaviour implies and as the episode superficially suggests.

In fact, Leigh takes Caesar's impunity for cutting down the grove as more clear-cut than is strictly warranted, especially compared to the primary literary model of Ovid's Erysichthon. The difference from Ovid serves Leigh's argument about the move from mythology to history, or from republic to empire, very well: starting with the civil wars an impious figure like Erysichthon—i.e., Caesar—need no longer fear divine retribution. But it's important to recognise that in the *Metamorphoses*, as we saw in Chapter 3, the story of Erysichthon was deployed as a morality tale by the river Achelous to correct the scepticism of Pirithous regarding divine power. In other words, Erysichthon did not represent, for Ovid at least, a straightforward demonstration of the fact of divine retribution but rather merely one rhetorical move in a larger theological dialogue both in that passage of the *Metamorphoses* and across the poem as a whole. Furthermore, Lucan's Caesar doesn't offer a simple response to Ovid based on the presence or absence of the gods. For the distinction

---

[10] On Vergil's Mezentius and Diomedes as theomachs manqués see Chapter 2.

[11] Day 2013: 143: 'But, as the poem progresses, Caesar seems less concerned to "match" himself with the gods than to put himself in their place, asserting his position as their demonic surrogate'.

[12] Cf. Caesar's arrogance in the storm scene of Book 5 (esp. Luc. 5.579–80), on which see generally Matthews 2008, Day 2013: 143–56.

[13] Day 2013: 138–9. On the comparison of Caesar to lightning in *BC* 1 and its relation to Lucretius' explanation of the force of the thunderbolt (Lucr. 6.323–9) see Day 2013: 115–16 (cf. my discussion of the Lucretian passage at pp. 67–8). Cf. also Lucan's similar description of the (divinised) Alexander as a *fulmen* (Luc. 10.34).

emphasised by Leigh between Erysichthon's punishment and Caesar's seeming impunity tells only part of the story. Although critics have often noted Caesar's similarity to Erysichthon, it's worth revisiting the overlap between the two texts to show how the condition of the two characters is in one fundamental way very similar—they are both characterised by excessive desire—even if the theological contexts appear quite different.[14]

In brief, Ovid recounts how the Thessalian king Erysichthon cuts down an oak sacred to Ceres, for which he is cursed with never-ending hunger, and, as a result, he consumes his entire wealth and eventually devours his own body. Lucan's description of Caesar cutting the tree echoes Ovid's language in a number of places (I have emphasised those Latin words common to both sets of passages):[15]

>   primus raptam librare bipennem
> ausus et aeriam ferro proscindere quercum
> effatur merso uiolata in robora ferro...(Luc. 3.433–5)

>   He first dared to grab an axe
> and swing it, and to cut down the lofty oak with iron,
> and when the iron sank deep into the desecrated wood, he declared...

> ille etiam Cereale nemus uiolasse securi
> dicitur et lucos ferro temerasse uetustos.
> stabat in his ingens annoso robore quercus,
> una nemus...(Met. 8.741–4)

> He is even said to have desecrated Ceres' wood with an axe
> and to have outraged the ancient groves with iron.
> There stood among these a huge oak with years of strength,
> itself a forest...

Both Caesar and Erysichthon begin by ordering others to perform the act but, on seeing their hesitation, grab an axe in order to do the job themselves: *raptam bipennem* (Luc. 3.433); *rapta securi* (Met. 8.754). When one slave tries to stop Erysichthon from felling the tree, the king decapitates him with the axe. With this story in the literary background, we may be less surprised that Caesar's troops fear their general more than the gods: any reader of Ovid knows exactly what awaits an imprudent objector. On the other hand, the Massilians believe that the gods will punish Caesar, as, for instance, Ceres punishes Erysichthon. The Lucanian world is of course different from the Ovidian one, and if Caesar is eventually punished in 44 BC, that will prove too late for the Massilians. Moreover, the fact that Ovid's oak bleeds (Met. 8.762) and that the dying tree

---

[14] On the intertextuality see Phillips 1968: 298–9.
[15] Lucan may also pick up the vocabulary of the Ovidian passage at other points in the scene: *lucus numquam uiolatus* (Luc. 3.399), *uetustas* (Luc. 3.406).

nymph prophesies Erysichthon's punishment (*Met.* 8.771–3) makes more clear-cut the narrative of cause and effect, crime and retribution.

Punishment notwithstanding, Erysichthon and Caesar do share a similar condition of insatiable hunger—literal in Erysichthon's case, metaphorical in Caesar's. Both men have a need that exceeds all proportion and even the limits of what the world can provide:

> sed non in Caesare tantum
> nomen erat nec fama ducis, sed nescia uirtus
> stare loco, solusque pudor non uincere bello;
> acer et indomitus, quo spes quoque ira uocasset,
> ferre manum et numquam temerando parcere ferro,
> successus urguere suos, instare fauori
> numinis, inpellens, quidquid sibi summa petenti
> obstaret, gaudensque uiam fecisse ruina. (Luc. 1.143–50)

> But in Caesar there was not just
> a name nor the fame of a general, but a valour that knew not
> how to stand in one place, and his only shame was not to conquer in war;
> he was keen and unrestrained, wherever hope and anger called,
> to bring force and never lightly to spare the sword,
> to press his successes, to pursue the favour
> of god, driving on whatever blocked him as he sought the heights
> and rejoicing to have made a path by ruin.

nec mora, quod pontus, quod terra, quod educat aer
poscit et appositis queritur ieiunia mensis
inque epulis epulas quaerit; quodque urbibus esse
quodque satis poterat populo non sufficit uni. (*Met.* 8.830–3)

And there was no delay, but whatever sea, or earth, or air brings forth,
he demands, and though meals are served he complains of hunger
and amid feasts he seeks feasts; and what could be enough for cities
and for a nation is not enough for one.

There is no lexical allusion here, to be sure, but the common idea of relentless desire is clear enough. Moreover, Erysichthon's instant need for food (*nec mora*, *Met.* 8.830) characterises Caesar's impatience more generally: Massilia is only conquered with 'a delay' (*una mora*, Luc. 3.392), and much to his frustration (*inpatiens haesuri Martis*, 'impatient of the sluggish war', Luc. 3.453).[16] And as if to emphasise the conjunction of profanity and extremes of desire, immediately after the desecration of the grove Caesar turns to Spain, explicitly described as

---

[16] The grove itself, and the reluctance of his troops to cut it down, causes a further delay, and one may even notice a play on the words *mora* (Luc. 3.392) and *nemora* (Luc. 3.395). On the relationship between Caesar and *mora* see Masters 1992: 3–10 and passim.

the *extrema mundi* ('the furthest reaches of the world', Luc. 3.454). The central difference between the limitless desires of Erysichthon and Caesar, however, is that the punishment of the former is the latter's very condition of being. Caesar's hunger, as it were, does not lead to the same symbolic, and heavily moralised, end suffered by Erysichthon, in which Ceres translates the king's refusal to heed conventional limits (represented by his killing of the tree nymph) into a far more self-destructive form of limitlessness. But what need is there for divine intervention when the transgressor, like Caesar, already suffers the relevant punishment by his very nature? In effect, the punishment precedes Caesar's crime.

Perhaps more problematic for the gods, however, and for belief in the gods, is that once mortals embrace such a debased and excessive condition, as Caesar seems to, the whole notion of punishment and suffering—one incentive to piety—becomes hopelessly undermined. In other words, Ovid's Erysichthon and Lucan's Caesar do not simply offer contrasting paradigms of divine power, as Leigh argues, but rather the Ovidian intertext invites reflection on what Lucan's doing away with the gods really implies—whether Lucan allegorises divine power through Caesar's constant yearning, or whether Caesar truly eliminates the gods as an explanatory and moral force.

The significance of Ovid's Erysichthon touches not only Caesar but also the wider condition of the Roman people. So, when attempting to quell the mutiny in Book 5, Caesar accuses his troops of greed in terms that clearly recall Erysichthon, claiming that for them 'not even this world suffices' (*quibus hic non sufficit orbis*, Luc. 5.356; cf. *Met.* 8.832-3 above, especially *non sufficit uni*). Caesar thus attributes to his men the very appetite that he himself possesses (cf. Luc. 10.456), an irony made more pointed by the fact that the mutineers are at this point weary of conquest and bloodshed. Indeed, they had already accused him of insatiability: *quid satis est, si Roma parum est?* ('What is enough, if Rome is too little?', Luc. 5.274). But despite the soldiers' protestations, and despite the fact that the presence of Erysichthon is most visible in and around Caesar, Lucan makes perfectly clear from early in the poem that the perverse union of desire, especially avarice and hunger, and limitless expansion afflicts Roman society as a whole.[17] When the poet laments the excesses and eventual self-destruction that follow in the wake of empire (1.158-82), among the various topoi of luxury, violence, and moral degeneracy, he speaks of 'hunger [that] spurned earlier diets' (*mensasque priores / aspernata fames*, Luc. 1.163-4). At the climax of the passage, financial woe, which Lucan posits as a major cause of the war, is described in the metaphorical language of hunger and greed: *usura uorax* ('devouring usury', Luc. 1.181), *auidum fenus* ('greedy interest', Luc. 1.181).[18] As formative as this passage from *BC* 1 is, however, an even

---

[17] Cf. the endlessness of civil war discussed by Masters 1992: 216-59, Quint 1993: 147-57.
[18] Cf. *deuorat* (*Met* 8.827), *auidas* (829), and *uoracior* (839) used of Erysichthon. In this light, Lucan's description of the Romans as not the kind of people 'whom their own liberty could nourish' (*quem sua*

clearer sense of the importance of the theme of hunger emerges from Book 4, when Caesar grants clemency to the starved and thirsting army of Afranius. The description of the soldiers drinking deeply from the rivers—sated by water alone—prompts the poet to launch another tirade against the vices of greed and extravagance, including gluttony: *quaesitorum terra pelagoque ciborum / ambitiosa fames et lautae gloria mensae* ('ostentatious hunger for food sought over land and sea and the glory of a sumptuous feast', Luc. 4.375–6).[19] The outburst seems a little misplaced, as if the poet seeks any opportunity to wedge in a rather clichéd complaint about decadence, whether in reference to Caesar's age or Lucan's own. But the popularity of the theme of immoral luxury, familiar from the satirists from Horace to Juvenal, risks deadening what is clearly an important and interconnected idea in the *BC*: hunger, as a metaphor for excessive desire, is one of the defining characteristics not only of Caesar but also of the Roman people both during and after the civil war. Erysichthon is no longer the exception but rather the rule.

Finally, in Book 10, Lucan will return to the language of Ovid's Erysichthon more clearly than ever before. Describing the feast held by Cleopatra for Caesar, the poet says that 'they laid out a banquet on gold, whatever land, air, sea, or Nile yielded' (*infudere epulas auro, quod terra, quod aer, / quod pelagus Nilusque dedit*, Luc. 10.155–6). According to the narrator, the feast shows a level of luxury then unfamiliar to Rome (Luc. 10.108–10), even as corrupted by greed as the city appears in Book 1. Lucan here looks ahead to the topos of extravagance that becomes so closely associated with wealth under the empire. More intriguing than the clichéd castigation of contemporary mores, however, is the timing of the allusion to Erysichthon. For here in Egypt, at last, Caesar will for the first time appear vulnerable, uncertain, and protected by fortune alone when the Egyptians assault the palace (Luc. 10.439–85). To be sure, not long into the attack Caesar returns to his former, energetic self. But the signs of weakness and the possibility of his death follow on suggestively from Cleopatra's Erysichthon-like feast, at which Caesar might very well have been murdered, the poet claims, had the assassins not feared the ensuing chaos (Luc. 10.422–5). Near the close of the poem as we have it, then, Lucan suggests that Caesar and Rome are on the self-destructive course implied by the mythological paradigm of Erysichthon. Whether that hunger—that desire—proves the world to be more disenchanted or remystified, however, as the Massilia episode encourages us to enquire, is a question to which we shall return.

---

libertas... pasceret, Luc. 1.172) makes perfect sense: they preferred a diet of something more extravagant than mere freedom. Later in the same book, Curio speaks of Caesar's *liuor edax* (Luc. 1.288) in a speech that lures Caesar with thoughts of world domination (esp. Luc. 1.283–91). On the conjunction of material need and irreligion both in the Massilia episode and in Caesar's violation of the treasury in the temple of Saturn (also in *BC* 3) see Fantham 1996.

[19] Cf. *Met.* 8.830 above: *quod pontus, quod terra, quod educat aer*...

Pharsalus: Gods Old and New

THE ECLIPSE

Book 7 of the *BC* opens with a description of the sun's reluctance to shine upon on the battlefield of Pharsalus (Luc. 7.1–6):

segnior, Oceano quam lex aeterna uocabat,
luctificus Titan numquam magis aethera contra
egit equos cursumque polo rapiente retorsit,
defectusque pati uoluit raptaeque labores
lucis, et attraxit nubes, non pabula flammis,
sed ne Thessalico purus luceret in orbe.

More slowly than the summons of eternal law,
sorrowful Titan never drove his steeds from Ocean harder against
the heavens, and turned back his course with the sky dragging him on.
He wanted to endure an eclipse and the suffering of his stolen
light, and he drew clouds towards him, not to feed his flames
but lest he shed a pure light in the world of Thessaly.

The idea of the sun withholding its light from impious acts is a commonplace of classical literature, which Vergil (*G.* 1.466–8) and Ovid (*Met.* 15.785–6) had employed in their accounts of Caesar's murder, and which Seneca had made such a focal point of the *Thyestes*, in particular in the choral ode sung at the very moment when Thyestes unwittingly feasts on the flesh of his own sons (*Thy.* 789–884).[20] Ovid also describes Phoebus refusing to cast light on the world after the death of his son Phaethon, a myth itself variously connected with both the *Georgics* and the *Thyestes*, and which in Ovid's version bears some lexical overlap with the opening of *BC* 7 (*Met.* 2.381–93):[21]

---

[20] Cf. *Thy.* 120–1, 776–8, 784–8, 891–2. Among the portents in *BC* 1, Lucan compares an eclipse to the one in the Thyestean myth (Luc. 1.540–4). Statius' fraternal duel—a paradigm of civil war—will also cause an eclipse (*Theb.* 11.119–35). The importance of the end of *G.* 1 to the *BC* is clear from the epic's proem, on which see Putnam 1995: 223–6, Henderson 2010: 487–8, and Thompson and Bruère 2010: 109–16 (who also discuss the significance of the *Georgics* for Lucan's panegyric to Nero). Two other elements of the *Georgics* passage will be of particular relevance for Lucan's treatment of Pharsalus: Vergil's interest in the signs portending Caesar's death lie behind Lucan's similar interest in the ominous signs before the battle (on which see below), and Vergil's image of the farmer coming across the bones of the combatants is expanded at the end of *BC* 7 (furthermore, *grandia ossa* at *G.* 1.497, besides its Homeric resonance, may also suggest the Gigantomachy motif so important to Lucan). The allusions to the end of *G.* 1 at the opening and close of *BC* 7 (see below for similar ring composition in the *Thyestes*), coupled with the allusions in Lucan's proem, illustrate not only the importance of the Vergilian passage but also the skilful architectural design of the *BC*. Cf. Narducci 2002: 58–9.

[21] For the sun's refusal to shine cf. also *Met.* 2.329–31, 394–400. On the relevance of Phaethon to the eclipse in the *Georgics* see Gale 2000: 35–6. Immediately prior to the first mention of the eclipse in the *Thyestes*, Seneca describes a drought in terms suggestive of Phaethon's near incineration of the earth; see, e.g., Tarrant 1985: 104 on *Thy.* 108 alluding to *Met.* 2.255–6.

squalidus interea genitor Phaethontis et expers
ipse sui decoris, qualis cum <u>deficit</u> <u>orbem</u>
esse solet, <u>lucem</u>que odit seque ipse diemque
[datque animum in <u>luctus</u> et <u>luctibus</u> adicit iram]
officiumque negat mundo. 'satis' inquit 'ab aeui
sors mea principiis fuit inrequieta, pigetque
actorum sine fine mihi, sine honore <u>laborum</u>.
quilibet alter <u>agat</u> portantes lumina currus;
si nemo est omnesque dei non posse fatentur,
ipse <u>agat,</u> ut saltem, dum nostras temptat habenas,
orbatura patres aliquando fulmina ponat.
tum sciet ignipedum uires expertus <u>equorum,</u>
non meruisse necem qui non bene rexerit illos.'

Meanwhile, Phaethon's father was in mourning and without his
ornaments, as he is when he goes into eclipse,
and he hates the light and himself and the day
[and he casts his mind to grief and to grief adds anger]
and denies his charge to the world. 'It is enough', he says,
'my lot has since the dawn of time been unrequited, and
work without end wearies me, and labours without honour.
Let someone else drive the chariots that bear the light;
if there is none, and all the gods admit themselves unable,
let him do it, so that, while he tries out our reins, he puts
aside for once the lightning bolts that bereave fathers.
Then he will know, when he's tried the strength of my fire-footed steeds,
that he who did not guide them well did not deserve death'.

Although the shared vocabulary is to be expected in any description of an eclipse, Lucan's particular mention of the mournful aspect of the sun (*luctificus*) recalls Phoebus' sorrow in the *Metamorphoses* (*luctu*, *Met.* 2.329; cf. *luctus*, *Met.* 2.124), an allusion which nicely conveys Lucan's own emotional response to Pharsalus.[22] The contexts of the other poetic eclipses, too, have a bearing on this pivotal moment in the *BC*. Vergil and Ovid, for example, represent the sun as mourning Caesar's death, but Lucan's application of the same image to Pharsalus suggests both a displacement of the Augustan poets' sympathy for Caesar as well as a larger imagistic connection between Caesar's greatest crime, Pharsalus, and his moment of punishment, the assassination, which lies outside the scope of the poem.[23]

---

[22] Moreover, if the soundplay in *luctus et luctibus* (*Met.* 2.384) is genuinely Ovidian (Tarrant brackets the line as inauthentic), or at least pre-Lucanian, it may have contributed to Lucan's concentration of similar sounds in *lex*, *luctificus*, *lucis*, and *luceret*. Elsewhere in the *BC* passage, Lucan plausibly also draws on the diction of the *Thyestes* chorus, especially Seneca's *rapis*, *uocat*, *aetherio*, *cursu*, and *equos* scattered throughout *Thy.* 793–804.

[23] For the book's proleptic glances ahead at Caesar's death see Luc. 7.596, 781–3.

There is, however, a larger theme that connects all of these eclipses—divinisation. Both accounts of Julius Caesar's death occur in contexts that either allude to Octavian's deification (*G.* 1.498–501) or explicitly address the deification of both Julius Caesar and, proleptically, Augustus (*Met.* 15.832–70).[24] The story of Phaethon, moreover, concerns his attempt to prove his divine paternity and to act in a godlike way. Indeed, when in Book 1 Lucan envisages Nero's future deification, he does so in terms that allude to Phaethon (Luc. 1.47–52):

>   seu sceptra tenere,
> seu te flammigeros Phoebi conscendere currus,
> telluremque nihil mutato sole timentem
> igne uago lustrare iuuet, tibi numine ab omni
> cedetur, iurisque tui natura relinquet,
> quis deus esse uelis, ubi regnum ponere mundi.

>   Whether it pleases you to hold the sceptre,
> or to mount the flaming chariot of Phoebus,
> and to roam an earth that is unafraid of a changed sun
> and your wandering fire, every god
> will yield to you, and nature will leave up to you
> which god you wish to be, where in the world to place your kingdom.

The idea of driving Phoebus' chariot, combined with the detail that the earth would not fear the change of sun, not only evokes the myth of Phaethon but also suggests, by contrast, Nero's success at performing the task. It has been argued that the allusion to Phaethon's destructive folly implies criticism of Nero as an overreacher or source of catastrophe for the world, and that Lucan's attempts to place a positive spin on the myth merely provide the necessary cover for that criticism.[25] Whether or not such a subversive reading is correct, however, the allusion to Phaethon in the context of deification strengthens a similar association in Book 7.

The *Thyestes*, too, conjoins solar imagery and the theme of divinisation. The choral ode that reflects on the eclipse is immediately followed by Atreus' triumphant claim to have risen to the stars and to discharge the gods (*Thy.* 885–8).[26] Atreus then draws on the language of the sun's illumination to describe the moment of revelation to his brother, thus casting himself as the sun god: *etiam die nolente discutiam tibi / tenebras, miseriae sub quibus latitant tuae* ('even if the day is unwilling I shall scatter the darkness from you, under which your miseries are hiding', *Thy.* 896–7).[27] A few lines further, by realising that power

---

[24] On the deifications at the end of the *Metamorphoses* see Chapter 3.

[25] Hinds 1987a: 28–9, citing as supporting evidence another allusion to Phaethon (*Met.* 2.298ff.) at Luc. 1.74; see also Roche 2009: 8–9, 153. For the view against, see Dewar 1994.

[26] Cf. pp. 141–2 above.

[27] Volk 2006 argues that Atreus' assumption of the role of the sun god should be read as a critique of Nero, who also projected a close identification with the sun. Volk's historicist reading is attractive,

of illumination quite literally (*aperta multa tecta conlucent face*, 'the open hall gleams with many torches', *Thy.* 908), Atreus even manages, if only for a moment, actually to usurp the place of the absent sun.

These various scenes of eclipse from Vergil to Seneca are associated with a wide range of divinisations—more or less literal, and more or less explicitly theomachic. With this association in mind, what I wish to suggest—and what will become clear later in Book 7—is that the image of the eclipse at the opening of the book, though primarily meant to suggest the impiety of Pharsalus, also points to the battle's theological consequences—the creation of new gods. The status of these gods, however, and their relation to the Olympian gods remains at this point very much undecided. Rather, what matters is that the opening image suggests the imminence of an event with powerful, yet profoundly uncertain, implications for the world, an event that can be figured as ultimately restorative (according to a positive reading of the Augustan poets or the panegyric of Nero), unintentionally catastrophic (if read through Phaethon), or utterly diabolical (if read through Atreus).

THE SEMANTICS OF GIGANTOMACHY

One of the principal means by which Lucan ties the civil war to the idea of a change in the divine order is through the—by now very familiar—motif of Gigantomachy. Early in Book 7 the poet compares the preparations of Pompey's army before the battle to the activities of the gods before Phlegra (Luc. 7.144–50):

> si liceat superis hominum conferre labores,
> non aliter Phlegra rabidos tollente gigantas
> Martius incaluit Siculis incudibus ensis,
> et rubuit flammis iterum Neptunia cuspis,
> spiculaque extenso Paean Pythone recoxit,
> Pallas Gorgoneos diffudit in aegida crines,
> Pallenaea Ioui mutauit fulmina Cyclops.

> If one may compare the works of men to those of gods,
> not otherwise, when Phlegra raised the rabid Giants,
> did Mars' sword grow hot on the Sicilian anvils,
> and the tip of Neptune's trident grew red in the flames again,
> and Paean forged again the arrows with which Python was stretched out,
> Pallas scattered the Gorgon's locks over her aegis,
> the Cyclops changed the thunderbolts of Pallene for Jupiter.

even if the chronology is uncertain, but the connection between the displacement of the sun and criticism of the Caesars, and therefore of Nero too, is more decisive in *BC* 7. What *BC* 7 suggests, however, is that Lucan's reading of his uncle's *Thyestes*, whenever it was composed, would have shared common ground with Volk's interpretation. On the *Thyestes* and *BC* 7 see in general Ripoll 2009.

By comparing the Pompeians to the Olympian gods, Lucan implies that the Giants should be associated with the Caesarians.[28] Earlier in the poem, by contrast, the allegory had been deployed more ambivalently.[29] In Book 3, when the Massilians make their case for neutrality to Caesar, they represent their position as that of humankind vis-à-vis the Gigantomachy, all the while remaining ostensibly non-committal about the particular identities of the gods and Giants (Luc. 3.312–20):

> at, si funestas acies, si dira paratis
> proelia discordes, lacrimas ciuilibus armis
> secretumque damus. tractentur uolnera nulla
> sacra manu. si caelicolis furor arma dedisset,
> aut si terrigenae temptarent astra gigantes,
> non tamen auderet pietas humana uel armis
> uel uotis prodesse Ioui, sortisque deorum
> ignarum mortale genus per fulmina tantum
> sciret adhuc caelo solum regnare Tonantem.

> But if you prepare fatal armies and terrible battles
> in your discord, we shed tears for civil war
> and stand apart. Let no hand interfere with
> sacred wounds. If frenzy had armed the gods,
> or if the earth-born Giants were attacking the stars,
> yet human piety would not dare to aid Jupiter
> with arms or prayers, and ignorant of the fate of the gods
> the human race would know only through bolts of lightning
> that the Thunderer still reigned in the sky alone.

The allegory conveys a sense of deference to superiors: the Massilians simply wish to keep out of a conflict between higher powers. The passage allows for the Caesarians to be identified with the Giants or with Jupiter. On the one hand, the very idea of Gigantomachy frames the civil war as one between usurpers and the representatives of the status quo, and hence suggests that it is Caesar who represents the Giants against the old guard of the republic. For the Massilians, that impious association will be substantiated by Caesar's subsequent desecration of the grove, discussed in the previous section. On the other hand, in taking lightning (*fulmina*, Luc. 3.319) to be a sign of Jupiter's victory, the Massilians also allude to Caesar's close association with the *fulmen*, beginning with the formative simile used to describe him at *BC* 1.151–7 (*qualiter*

---

[28] See Day 2013: 173–5, and 172 n. 164 for further references on Lucan's reversal of the outcome of the Gigantomachy.

[29] Masters 1992: 39–40 discusses the application of Gigantomachic imagery to both Caesarians and Pompeians alike; cf. Feeney 1991: 297–9.

expressum uentis per nubila fulmen, 'as a thunderbolt forced through the clouds by winds', Luc. 1.151).[30]

In rejecting the Massilians' plea to remain neutral, Caesar implicitly denies the force of the allegory: whether or not civil war is like the Gigantomachy, one cannot abstain from what is a universal conflict. Indeed, Caesar even puts pressure on the larger allegorical practice that uses the gods to define ethical and political norms for mortals. That use of allegory only works if mortals accept the premise of divine exemplarity and superiority, but if mortals rise to the level of the gods, then they can determine norms for themselves while appropriating and reconstructing prior models of divine action.

The tendency to reshape the semantics of Gigantomachy is evident from near the very beginning of the poem in the panegyric to Nero (Luc. 1.33–8):

quod si non aliam uenturo fata Neroni
inuenere uiam magnoque aeterna parantur
regna deis caelumque suo seruire Tonanti
non nisi saeuorum potuit post bella gigantum,
iam nihil, o superi, querimur; scelera ipsa nefasque
hac mercede placent.

But if the fates found no other way for the advent of Nero
and the eternal kingdom was obtained by the gods at great cost
and heaven could not serve its Thunderer
except after the wars of the savage Giants,
then, O gods, we complain of nothing; those crimes and abominations
are pleasing at this price.

Here, as we might expect, the emperor is clearly aligned with Jupiter, though Lucan makes the novel move of casting Gigantomachy as a positive step inasmuch as it enables not only the gods' secure grasp on heaven and Jupiter's supremacy but also the rule of Nero. Several critics have understandably seen this claim as preposterous even within the hyperbolic context of imperial panegyric.[31] Leaving aside the intractable question of the passage's subversiveness, however, it's important to observe the contrast in the alignment of Jupiter and the Giants between the panegyric in Book 1 and Pharsalus in Book 7. Here Jupiter corresponds to what will become the imperial side, while in Book 7 the Olympians are analogous to the Pompeians.

There are two basic ways of approaching this change in meaning and tone, one more explanatory in its purpose, the other more interpretive. First, one

---

[30] On the simile see Day 2013: 107–16.
[31] For the ambiguity of the panegyric see Due 1962: 93–102; Thompson 1964; Jenkinson 1974; Ahl 1976: 47–9; Hinds 1987a: 26–9, 1998: 87–8; W. R. Johnson 1987: 118–23; Feeney 1991: 298–301; Leigh 1997: 23–6; N. Holmes 1999; O'Hara 2007: 131–42; Roche 2009: 7–10; Grimal 2010. For objections and qualifications see Dewar 1994; cf. Nelis 2011.

explanation for the shift derives from the long-standing claim, based on the evidence of the ancient biographical tradition, that Lucan's relationship with the emperor broke down sometime after the initial publication of the first three books, and that the poet's increasing hostility towards Nero and the principate began to show much more clearly in the later books.[32] On this view, the move from aligning the Olympian gods with the Julio-Claudians to aligning them with the Pompeians tracks Lucan's own growing disenchantment with the emperor and the imperial system. As tempting as this biographical explanation may be, however, we shall shortly see the serious problems it faces from the poet's turn against the gods later in Book 7.

The interpretive approach doesn't depend on biographical evidence, which may well be unreliable, but rather focuses on the context of each of the Gigantomachy passages: the first is spoken in a panegyric, the second by a supposedly neutral party, and the third by an increasingly partisan narrator. Instead of attributing these shifts to the biography of the poet and focusing on a linear change of tone over time, one can trace different voices within the same poem that evoke, support, and challenge each other. The point is not merely that Lucan's use of Gigantomachy is ambivalent, nor that different parties have reason to deploy the myth in different ways, though both those things are true. Rather, the accumulation of competing perspectives makes Gigantomachy an important reference point in a larger debate about the relationship between gods and mortals, a debate that cannot simply be reduced to a single-issue conflict about piety or impiety, republic or empire, conventional theology or scepticism, but which incorporates these and other points of religious, political, and philosophical contention.

THE POWER OF THE GODS

Immediately after the Gigantomachy analogy in Book 7, Lucan spends some considerable time describing the portents before the battle and their interpretation both by the participants and, to emphasise the global consequences, by those in far-flung parts distant from Thessaly (Luc. 7.151–206). Some portents are drawn from the historiographical record, while others are likely the invention of poetic hyperbole.[33] The narrator acknowledges an uncertainty about the status of these signs, whether they are real or the product of fear (Luc. 7.172–6):

> iam (dubium, monstrisne deum nimione pauori
> crediderint) multis concurrere uisus Olympo
> Pindus et abruptis mergi conuallibus Haemus,
> edere nocturnas belli Pharsalia uoces,
> ire per Ossaeam rapidus Boebeida sanguis.

---

[32] See Fantham 2011.
[33] On the portents before Pharsalus see Plut. *Caes.* 47 with the commentary of Pelling 2011: 373–6.

Already (it is uncertain whether men trust in portents of the gods
or their own excessive fear) Pindus seemed to many to collide with
Olympus, and Haemus to sink in sheer valleys,
Pharsalus to issue sounds of war at night,
and Lake Boebeis, near Ossa, to run with blood.

The image of clashing mountains and the mention of Olympus and Ossa further associate the impending battle with the Gigantomachy.[34] But in equivocating whether the vision is a true portent or simply a fearful imagining—especially through the diction of doubt and belief—the poet once again scrutinises the Gigantomachic allegory: the reader is left unsure whether Pharsalus should be seen as a second Gigantomachy on a par with the first, a lesser copy of the mythical original, or a realisation more palpable than any myth.

Despite the concentration of unnatural, or supernatural, occurrences, Lucan leaves unclear the ultimate source of power behind these signs, behind the outcome of the battle, and, by implication, even behind the larger operation of the universe. Besides human fear as a creator of portents, Fortune is first said to reveal the future through the signs (Luc. 7.151–2), but also Jupiter (Luc. 7.197) and Nature (Luc. 7.201–2). Even if these diverse causes can be reconciled, however, it's difficult to accommodate the narrator's further claim that Caesar prayed successfully to the Eumenides and the powers of the underworld (Luc. 7.168–71). The proliferation of powers—Olympian, Stoic, chthonic—leaves entirely uncertain which, if any, should be considered allegorical and how one might go about determining the true metaphysics of the world.

These implicit anxieties about divine power come to the surface of the text in an astonishing outburst from the narrator (Luc. 7.445–59):

> sunt nobis nulla profecto
> numina: cum caeco rapiantur saecula casu,
> mentimur regnare Iouem. spectabit ab alto
> aethere Thessalicas, teneat cum fulmina, caedes?
> scilicet ipse petet Pholoen, petet ignibus Oeten
> inmeritaeque nemus Rhodopes pinusque Mimantis,
> Cassius hoc potius feriet caput? astra Thyestae
> intulit et subitis damnauit noctibus Argos:
> tot similes fratrum gladios patrumque gerenti
> Thessaliae dabit ille diem? mortalia nulli
> sunt curata deo. cladis tamen huius habemus
> uindictam, quantam terris dare numina fas est:
> bella pares superis facient ciuilia diuos;

---

[34] Cf. also Luc. 7.475–84.

> fulminibus manes radiisque ornabit et astris
> inque deum templis iurabit Roma per umbras.

> Truly we have no
> gods: when the times are seized by blind chance,
> we lie that Jupiter reigns. Will he look on from high
> heaven, though he holds the thunderbolt, at the Thessalian slaughter?
> Will he really assail Pholoe, assail Oeta with his fires
> and the forest of innocent Rhodope and the pines of Mimas,
> and will Cassius rather strike this [Caesar's] head? He brought stars
>   to Thyestes
> and condemned Argos to sudden night:
> will he then give daylight to Thessalia,
> bearing so many like swords of brothers and fathers? Mortal affairs
> are no god's care. Yet from this disaster we have
> vengeance, as much as is right for gods to give the earth:
> civil wars will make deceased emperors equal to the gods;
> Rome will adorn the spirits of the dead with thunderbolts and haloes
>   and stars
> and in the temples of the gods she will swear by shades.

In the Massilians' allegory of the Gigantomachy in Book 3, they claimed that mortals would assume from seeing lightning in the sky that 'Jupiter still reigned' (*regnare Tonantem*, Luc. 3.320). Now the narrator, despite his earlier attribution of lightning to Jupiter (Luc. 7.197), uses the same phrase as the Massilians to reject belief not only in the rule of Jupiter but even in the gods tout court (Luc. 7.445–7).[35] That a profound sense of injustice can lead to scepticism is hardly original to Lucan. An epigram transmitted in the scholia to Persius, supposedly dating from around the 30s BC, conveys a remarkably similar sentiment: *marmoreo Licinus tumulo iacet, at Cato paruo, / Pompeius nullo: credimus esse deos?* ('Licinus lies in a marble tomb, but Cato in a small one, Pompey in none: do we believe that gods exist?' Schol. ad Pers. 2.36). What sets the passage in the *BC* apart, however, is the force and anger with which the poet speaks, reaching a pitch of such emotional intensity that all thoughts of consistency vanish.[36] With its elevation of chance and the assertion that the gods do not care for mortals, the passage at times has the flavour of Epicureanism.[37] But the poet goes further, interpreting the fact that Jupiter doesn't intervene directly as proof that the gods do not exist. As the passage reaches its rhetorical climax, the narrator even claims that this disaster achieves

---

[35] Lucan here also responds to Hor. *Carm.* 3.5.1–2; cf. Leigh 1997: 93 n. 33.

[36] On this passage see Feeney 1991: 281–3, 297–8; Bartsch 1997: 111; Leigh 1997: 93–9; Narducci 2002: 58–66. Sklenář 2003: 8–9 privileges the single, nihilistic aspect over the inconsistencies.

[37] For the possibility of a politicised Epicureanism see Momigliano 1941, Fowler 1989.

some measure of vengeance on the gods, as Pharsalus paves the way for humans to be raised up as their equals.[38] The sharp differences between the various positions smack of despair and frustration, to be sure, but they also represent a powerful battery of attacks on traditional epic theology, as if the narrator at last offers an explanation for the strange character of the poem thus far.[39] Finally, if mortals really do effect a form of revenge upon the gods, the poet thereby articulates what exactly a successful theomachy looks like in Roman society, that is, no less than a theological revolution that undoes the fundamental distinction between god and man—the imperial cult.

It's important to notice that in this rhetorically charged passage near the centre of Book 7, Lucan alludes back to the opening description of the sun's reluctance to shine. But whereas there I pinpointed a range of more or less implicit intertexts, here the poet explicitly refers to the myth of the Thyestean banquet. Moreover, just as I argued that the initial allusion to Seneca's treatment of the eclipse in his *Thyestes* brings to mind Atreus' self-divinisation, so here, I would suggest, the Senecan tension between Atreus and the gods, if the gods even exist, is reimagined as a tension between the Caesars and the equally dubious gods. The fact that imperial deification is mentioned so explicitly here also reinforces the original claim that Ovid's account of the eclipse in *Met.* 15 and the subsequent deification of Caesar and Augustus are alluded to as well. Thus, what was a mere hint on the poet's part at the opening of the book becomes fully apparent as we reach the crucial halfway point, as if to emphasise yet further the historical and religious consequences of the battle. If Ovid had been relatively light-handed in his treatment of the practice of deification, Lucan's repeated allusion to the Thyestean banquet highlights how much more obviously theomachic the relationship between the Caesars and the gods has become by the

---

[38] Note also that mention of the mountains of Rhodope and Mimas at line 450 suggests two episodes of overreaching: Rhodope and her husband, Haemus, are changed into mountains for comparing themselves to Zeus and Hera (cf. Ov. *Met.* 6.87–9), while Mimas is one of the Giants. We are primed, therefore, for the action that Jupiter ought to take against the similarly presumptuous Caesar and his successors.

[39] On the absence of the gods from Lucan's epic cf. Ahl 1976: 69; for an altogether different view of the gods as continuing to have a powerful, albeit impersonal, presence see Fantham 2003. On the narrator's inconsistencies regarding the gods throughout the poem see Bartsch 2012; cf. Chapter 8 for the significance of similar inconsistencies in the characterisation of Statius' Capaneus. Unlike the *BC*'s narrator, Caesar, and Pompey too, consistently believe in the favour of the gods. In the speech to his troops before the battle, Caesar claims that the gods are nearby and on his side (Luc. 7.297–8), and a little later on he even addresses them directly (Luc. 7.311). Pompey, too, invokes the gods in his speech immediately following Caesar's (Luc. 7.348–55). Moreover, after the battle, Caesar sees the bloodshed as proof of fortune and divine favour: *fortunam superosque suos in sanguine cernit* (Luc. 7.796). In their explicit statements about the gods, then, both Caesar and Pompey are far more conventional than the narrator in the range of supernatural entities they acknowledge and the nature of their relationship with the divine. This difference is no doubt partly attributable to the genre. The actors of historical epic, no matter how avant-garde Lucan's treatment, are, with the exception of the ostentatiously ahistorical Erichtho, unable to see their world through the wide-ranging perspective of a poet looking back at events and their metaphysical meaning.

time of Nero. Moreover, the change takes place not only over the course of the Julio-Claudian dynasty but even across the span of Lucan's poem. For whereas in the panegyric in Book 1 the poet could describe the gods merely yielding to Nero (*cedetur*, Luc. 1.51), in Book 7 that relationship has become altogether more antagonistic, reminiscent of the theomachs of mythology, and—with the representation of tyrannical emperors in mind—the theomachs of history.[40]

CAESAR THE GOD

In asserting that the emperors will be equal to, and in tension with, the gods, the narrator makes more piquant still the comparisons between human and divine common to epic. Soon afterwards, for instance, the poet describes Caesar's action on the battlefield in typically aggrandising terms (Luc. 7.567–71)

> quacumque uagatur,
> sanguineum ueluti quatiens Bellona flagellum,
> Bistonas aut Mauors agitans, si uerbere saeuo
> Palladia stimulet turbatos aegide currus,
> nox ingens scelerum est.

> And wherever he roams,
> just as Bellona shakes her bloody flail,
> or Mars drives on the Bistonians, when with the harsh scourge
> he lashes his steeds terrified by the aegis of Pallas,
> a great night of crimes falls.

The diction used of Bellona recalls her appearance in the scene of Actium depicted on the shield of Aeneas: (*cum sanguineo sequitur Bellona flagello*, 'Bellona follows with her bloody flail', *Aen.* 8.703).[41] Lucan thereby emphasises a double irony—that the goddess of Roman victory should be a figure for Caesar in a civil, not a foreign, war, and that despite Augustan propaganda Actium, too, was part of a civil war. Beyond the irony, however, the very nature of comparison between Caesar and the gods has become almost impossibly ambiguous. For his superhuman level of activity—inciting his troops, healing them, supplying arms, and directing the battle (Luc. 7.557–81)—undermines the force of the simile: it cannot have its intended aggrandising function if the subject—Caesar—already seems to be a more effective, and certainly more tangible, replacement for the gods.[42]

---

[40] Cf. Chapter 4 on deification and theomachy in Seneca's *Hercules Furens*, with particular reference to Caligula.

[41] Cf. Putnam 1995: 238–9, and 222–45 on the wider role of allusions to the *Aeneid* in casting Caesar as divine; also Esposito 2012: 113–15.

[42] Cf. Feeney 1991: 296. Caesar's activity here conveys the speed that he shows throughout the poem (see, e.g., Roche 2009: index s.v. 'Caesar, speed'). This quality, too, has a place in the theomachic tradition.

There are other supernatural entities whose status and influence further complicate our understanding of Caesar's relationship to the gods—the Furies. Earlier in the book the narrator poses a series of rhetorical questions implying that Caesar can call on the support of hell (Luc. 7.168–71):

> (at tu, quos scelerum superos, quas rite uocasti
> Eumenidas, Caesar? Stygii quae numina regni
> infernumque nefas et mersos nocte furores
> inpia tam saeue gesturus bella litasti?)

> But you, Caesar, what gods of crimes, what Furies
> did you rightly summon? Which gods of the Stygian realms
> and hellish abomination and madness steeped in night
> did you pray for, on the verge of waging impious wars so savagely?

In suggesting that Caesar can draw on the nether powers, Lucan aligns him with the witch Erichtho from Book 6 (also a theomachic figure), as well as Vergil's Juno, who summons Allecto in *Aeneid* 7 to incite the Latin war. Madness appears prominently in the first line of the passage describing Caesar's activity in the battle: *rabies populis stimulusque furorum* ('the frenzy of peoples and goad to their rage', Luc. 7.557). Lucan goes so far as to claim not that Caesar creates frenzy but that he is himself a *rabies*, thereby making him a personification of madness. Lucan further enhances the identification through allusions to the effect of Vergil's Allecto on Amata (*stimulis*, Aen. 7.405), the Latin mothers (*furores*, Aen. 7.406), and the dogs of Iulus (*rabiem*, Aen. 7.479). And yet, despite the attempt to turn Caesar into a kind of Fury in his own right, after the battle the general has terrifying visions of the dead that figure him as a tragic victim of madness, an object of the Furies rather than their substitute (Luc. 7.777–80):

> haud alios nondum Scythica purgatus in ara
> Eumenidum uidit uoltus Pelopeus Orestes,
> nec magis attonitos animi sensere tumultus,
> cum fureret, Pentheus, aut, cum desisset, Agaue.

> Not otherwise did Pelopian Orestes, not yet cleansed on the
> Scythian altars, see the face of the Furies,
> nor did they feel more wracking disturbance of the mind,
> either Pentheus, when he raged, or Agave, when she stopped.

For in *Iliad* 22 even the swift-footed Achilles bemoans his inability to catch and harm Apollo (see p. 30–1), but now, almost a thousand years later, the gods seem finally to have been caught. Roche 2009: 20 lists other similarities between Caesar and Achilles. On the political semantics of Caesar's velocity see Willis 2011: 36–55. On the characteristic of swiftness in the historical Caesar's own *Bellum Civile*, see Grillo 2012: 14–36.

The comparison to Orestes is especially suggestive, for the canonical version of the myth—Aeschylus' *Eumenides*—is as much concerned with the power of the Furies relative to the Olympian gods as it is concerned with Orestes himself.[43] The example of Orestes, who plays the familiar role of the human at the mercy of higher powers, throws the more complex case of Caesar into high relief, for here Caesar seems prey to the very same powers—the Furies—to which the narrator had earlier attributed his success. Moreover, the book has already flagged the issue of supernatural powers vying for control, from the leitmotif of the Gigantomachy to the tension between deified emperors and the gods. In Book 3, Caesar, as rationalist theomach, had brought harm to the ancient gods of the Massilian grove, seemingly with impunity. But now, as a newly remystified figure, he threatens to replace the gods of Olympus and of Rome. And yet, just when Caesar paves the way for his divinisation, Lucan reminds the reader of his mortality and of his subjection to the terrors of the mind. The description of Caesar's mental torment is partly, of course, mere wish fulfilment on the part of the narrator. But, as we shall see in the next section, it also offers a pointed contrast to the self-control of Pompey and Cato in the last phase of the poem. That distinction will be significant for Lucan's sketching of two alternative conceptions of divinity, one imperial, as seen in Book 7, the other more philosophical.

Before we get to that point, however, it's important to round off the discussion of Book 7's theological concerns by noticing how one very brief passage near the end returns to key themes from earlier in the book and from earlier in the poem, too. The passage briefly describes Caesar arranging a feast in view of the battlefield and the corpses (Luc. 7.792–4):

> epulisque paratur
> ille locus, uoltus ex quo faciesque iacentum
> agnoscat.
>
> That place
> is made ready for feasts, from which he might recognise
> the faces and expressions of the dead.

The passage primarily emphasises the barbarism of Caesar, but the mention of feasting next to human bodies hints at the various myths of cannibal feasts involving theomachic figures—Lycaon, Tantalus, and, most pertinently, Atreus.[44] Atreus, of course, is a leitmotif of the book, invoked subtly through the opening eclipse and explicitly by the narrator halfway through the book.

---

[43] On this passage see Esposito 2012: 106–12. Cf. the Aeschylean epigraph to the chapter, *Eum.* 162–3.

[44] Cf. also Ovid's account of Tereus in *Met.* 6, whose rape and silencing of Philomela assimilates him to a god, but whose unwitting consumption of his son's flesh ultimately exposes him as mortal. Seneca's Atreus famously cites the example of Tereus' feast (*Thy.* 272–8).

In all of these myths the feast marks the crucial moment when either the theomach is exposed, as in the case of Lycaon, or the gods fail to appear, as in Seneca's *Thyestes*. Atreus, moreover, takes the flight of the sun—indeed, the whole zodiacal system, according to the chorus—as the basis for yet further theomachic rhetoric (*Thy.* 893–5):

> utinam quidem tenere fugientes deos
> possem, et coactos trahere, ut ultricem dapem
> omnes uiderent!

> Would that I were able to hold back the fleeing
> gods, and drag them back unwilling, so that they might all see
> my vengeful feast!

It's precisely that need to turn one's dire achievements into a spectacle for the gods—however rhetorically, and whether they truly exist or not—that reappears in Lucan's psychologising of Caesar (Luc. 7.797–9):

> ac ne laeta furens scelerum spectacula perdat,
> inuidet igne rogi miseris caeloque nocenti
> ingerit Emathiam.

> And so that the madman might not lose the sight of his crimes,
> he begrudges the wretched the flames of the pyre and casts Emathia
> at the guilty heavens.

Thus, the *Thyestes* looms especially large for the reader of *BC* 7—one of several intertexts for the opening account of the eclipse, mentioned again in the narrator's purple passage in the middle of the book, and forming a ring composition through the final allusion to the feast. What the eclipse at the opening of the book had hinted at only suggestively—the disappearance of the gods and the elevation of man—by its end has become an explicit and dominant theme.

Perhaps the most revealing episode in this context, however, is not a myth as such, but rather Suetonius' report of a banquet held by Octavian, at which the young triumvir and his guests dressed up as the Olympian gods, with Octavian himself appearing as Apollo.[45] It is valuable not, perhaps, as a direct source for Lucan, but as an illustration of the network of images and associations important for *BC* 7. Of particular relevance to Lucan's reflection on feasting and the gods is an anonymous, but apparently well known, lampoon about the banquet quoted by Suetonius (*Aug.* 70):[46]

---

[45] Suet. *Aug.* 70.
[46] See Miller 2009: 30–9, esp. 37–8, for possible allusion to the historical Caesar through the phrase *auratos thronos*.

cum primum istorum conduxit mensa choragum,
   sexque deos uidit Mallia sexque deas,
impia dum Phoebi Caesar mendacia ludit,
   dum noua diuorum cenat adulteria:
omnia se a terris tunc numina declinarunt,
   fugit et auratos Iuppiter ipse thronos.

As soon as that table of scoundrels found a choragus,
   and Mallia saw six gods and six goddesses,
while Caesar, impiously, plays a false Phoebus,
   while he feasts on the new adulteries of the gods:
then all the deities took themselves away from the earth,
   and Jupiter himself fled his golden throne.

That human wickedness drives the gods from the earth is a notion familiar from the end of Catullus 64 (384–408) or Ovid's account of ages of humankind (*Met.* 1.149–50), and which ultimately derives from Greek myth. The anonymous composer of the lampoon, therefore, casts Octavian's and his guests' identification with the gods precisely as representative of that mythical wickedness and as the cause of the Olympians' departure. The collocation of three elements—the transgression of mortal limits, feasting, and the absence of the gods—situates the lampoon within the mythical tradition of impious feasts, and the particular element of Octavian's presumption illustrates the quality that Lucan will see in, or retroject on, Caesar. Even in the slight detail of the feast at Pharsalus, then, Lucan recapitulates some of the central themes of Book 7.

And not only of Book 7. For the image of Caesar feasting in such grotesque circumstances not only alludes back to the grim diet of the witch Erichtho in Book 6 (Luc. 6.538–53) but also picks up the poem's larger thematics of hunger as a symbol for excessive desire. Like his analogue, Erysichthon, in Book 3, and like the impious and greedy populace of Rome described in Book 1, Caesar's limitless desire is framed in terms of food. And yet, unlike the mythological examples of feasting and hunger, and as we saw earlier in the discussion of Massilia, Caesar's transgressive desire prompts no immediate punishment or response. No god appears, and no gods depart, because to all intents and purposes they were never in the world of the poem. Once again Caesar seems to defy mythological paradigms, not so much displacing the gods as simply filling the vacuum created by their absence, and exploiting that absence to do with impunity what no figure—historical or mythical—has done before.

Book 7 puts on display the extremes of disenchantment and remystification. The narrator's outburst halfway through condenses both positions, as, on the one hand, he abandons any conventional theology for atheist and Epicurean alternatives, yet, on the other hand, his disenchantment culminates in reinterpreting the imperial cult as a form of revenge upon the gods for allowing Pharsalus to occur. This discrepancy reflects a larger tension in the book and indeed in the poem as a whole, as the figure most closely identified with disenchantment—Caesar himself—becomes subject to remystification as he increasingly resembles a proto-emperor and effectively substitutes for the gods who have been so pointedly absent from the poem. There is at least one way, however, in which Caesar's scepticism and divinisation can be reconciled. In representing a rationalistic and progressive spirit, as he does at Massilia for instance, Caesar threatens gods who had been explicitly characterised as ancient. At Pharsalus, however, the narrator identifies Caesar with new, imperial gods in tension with the Olympians. That cycle of the rise of new powers threatening and even displacing the old is itself a traditional myth of progress, whether the Oresteian and Promethean accounts of Olympians riding roughshod over ancient powers or the Gigantomachic account of the strengthening of order by being tested by the forces of disorder. Whether Caesar should be identified more closely with the Giants, Furies, or Olympians, however, or whether he is an entity greater or lesser than these, Lucan leaves studiously vague. As a consequence, Pharsalus may be an end point of the republic, but it's only one of many moments in a larger theogonic-theomachic cycle that has far from run its course.

Versions of the Sublime: More Gods, More Theomachy

In the previous chapter, we saw how Seneca exploited aesthetic and philosophical conceptions of the sublime in order to suggest different interpretations of the divinisation and theomachy of Hercules. Where the *BC* differs from Senecan drama in this regard is in the opportunity afforded by epic to refract the sublime through different characters, as opposed to the concentration on the protagonist characteristic of tragedy. So, for instance, various elements of the sublime are seen in Caesar, Pompey, and Cato, as well as in the poet's accounts of various physical and meteorological phenomena from clashing mountains to torrid deserts, and from sea storms to ecpyrosis. Moreover, each of these diverse visions of the sublime has a powerful claim to authority that differs markedly from Hercules' hallucination and failed theomachy. Not only does Caesar manage to force his way into heaven, as we have seen, but the defeated Pompey, too, will achieve a form of apotheosis at the beginning of Book 9. At the same time, the narrator reflects on the ultimate superiority of nature over mortal affairs in sublime terms, whether through the storm that prevents Caesar from reaching Italy in Book 5 or through the decomposition of the dead after Pharsalus, a process which stands metonymically for the cataclysm that will destroy the universe.

The coexistence of these multiple idioms and domains of the sublime, each interacting with the others, has now received extensive and insightful discussion from Henry Day.⁴⁷ Two Lucanian symbols of the sublime, in particular, receive the majority of Day's attention—the Caesarian sublime, which in its simultaneous challenge to, and arrogation of, divine power strains at the limits of mortality, and the Pompeian sublime, which by articulating the rupture between republic and empire fashions the past into a constant reminder of what has been lost to the present.⁴⁸ Where these two sublime heroes intersect most explicitly, however, is in their claims to apotheosis. For Day, the process of Pompey's catasterism caps a highly counterintuitive trajectory of the sublime—from an unmarked and unknown grave, contrasted with the great and lofty tombs of the divinised Ptolemies and Pharaohs, Pompey achieves a truer apotheosis, one that predicates immortality on the memory and preservation of an ideal, vividly realised in Pompey's commingling with the minds of Brutus and Cato.⁴⁹

Day's concern with the tropes of verticality and magnitude that characterise the sublime leads to a rich analysis of the paradoxes that structure the passage from Pompey's burial to apotheosis: the low and humble reaches the heavens; the small and confined exceeds all bounds.⁵⁰ My interest, however, lies in the various notions of theomachy that suffuse this part of the text, especially the continuation of the idea of new gods replacing old that we see at Massilia and Pharsalus, and of ever new conceptions of divinity. What this last phase of the extant poem shows (and here we can ignore for the moment Lucan's intended scope) is the appearance of other, alternative figures of the divine to rival the Caesarian model, not only Pompey but also Cato.⁵¹

The first clear sign of Pompey's impending apotheosis comes in the narrator's complaint that other figures, unlike Pompey, have their divinity associated with a wide locale (Luc. 8.800–2):

> si tota est Herculis Oete
> et iuga tota uacant Bromio Nyseia, quare
> unus in Aegypto Magni lapis?

> If Hercules has all of Oeta
> and Bacchus all the peaks of Nysa, why
> is there only one rock in Egypt for Magnus?

The context of the passage is the inadequacy of Cordus' short and hasty funerary inscription—*hic situs est Magnus* ('here lies Magnus', Luc. 8.793)—to do justice to Pompey's numerous achievements; by comparison with the scope of a small, inscribed rock, Hercules and Bacchus have the whole mountains of Oeta and Nysa associated with their names. But through the comparison with

---

⁴⁷ Day 2013.
⁴⁸ Day 2013: 106–78 (Caesarian sublime), 179–233 (Pompeian sublime).
⁴⁹ Day 2013: 219–33.
⁵⁰ Day 2013: 219–29.
⁵¹ On the intended scope of the *BC* see Stover 2008, Tracy 2011.

these semi-divine, and later fully divine, figures, Lucan also glances ahead to Pompey's own celestial destiny. Moreover, these gods represent only the first set of comparanda in a series that will culminate, at the end of the book, with Jupiter himself.

The next divinities to appear also signify more than their immediate context suggests (Luc. 8.831–4):

> nos in templa tuam Romana accepimus Isim
> semideosque canes et sistra iubentia luctus
> et, quem tu plangens hominem testaris, Osirim:
> tu nostros, Aegypte, tenes in puluere manes.

> We accepted your Isis in Roman temples
> and half-dog gods and the rattles that demand wailing
> and Osiris, whom you, lamenting, testify is a mortal man:
> but you, Egypt, hold our shades in your dust.

The poet here emphasises the irony and injustice of Egyptian gods being accepted and worshipped in Rome while Pompey remains in Egypt, kept not in temples but in the dust. Besides Isis, the passage describes two gods whose iconography and mythology have an additional significance for Pompey—Anubis, the dog-headed god, and Osiris, whose association with the afterlife and immortality derives from the myth of his death at the hands of his jealous brother, Set (associated by classical authors with Typhon).[52] In particular, the words *semideos* and *hominem*, though primarily referring to Anubis' appearance and Osiris' mortality, respectively, draw attention once more to the porous boundary between human and divine already suggested by the examples of Hercules and Bacchus. In this passage the narrator's use of *semideos* and *hominem* carries an implicitly pejorative tone, since the Egyptian gods include those who are but half-divine and half-bestial, or who are in fact merely human. In Book 9, however, the Egyptian gods recur in a context that is not pejorative but outright theomachic. One of Pompey's sons, Gnaeus, threatens to take revenge on Egypt for the murder of his father, a threat that includes among its targets deified kings and gods (Luc. 9.153–61):

> non ego Pellaeas arces adytisque retectum
> corpus Alexandri pigra Mareotide mergam?
> non mihi pyramidum tumulis euolsus Amasis
> atque alii reges Nilo torrente natabunt?
> omnia dent poenas nudo tibi, Magne, sepulchra.

---

[52] For the identification of Set, the usurper, with the monstrous Typhon, brother of the Giants, see, e.g., Hdt. 3.5.3, Diod. Sic. 1.85.5. Caesar's Gigantic qualities and his refusal to tolerate a superior (Luc. 1.125) make his conflict with, and defeat of, Pompey resonate with the myth of Set/Typhon and Osiris. In Egyptian mythology that conflict continues through Osiris' son, Horus, just as Pompey's legacy is carried on by not only his own sons but also his figurative successors, Brutus and Cato.

> euoluam busto iam numen gentibus Isim
> et tectum lino spargam per uolgus Osirim,
> suppositisque deis uram caput.

> Shall I not plunge the citadels of Pella and the shrine that protects
> the body of Alexander in the sluggish Mareotis?
> Shall not Amasis, dragged from the tombs of the pyramids,
> and those other kings swim the swollen Nile?
> Let all their tombs pay the penalty, Magnus, for your lack of burial.
> I shall hurl Isis, god of the nations, from her grave,
> and I shall scatter Osiris, swathed in linen, among the crowd,
> and I shall burn [my father's] head with gods for kindling.

The objects of Gnaeus' threats escalate from the bodies of the divinised rulers Alexander and Amasis to the images of Isis and Osiris, though Gnaeus speaks as if he will burn the very gods themselves. His diction regarding Osiris in particular is striking—*spargam*—as if he will recapitulate the dismemberment of Osiris by Set in Egyptian mythology. Thus, Gnaeus knowingly takes on the Giant-like role of Set/Typhon and becomes yet another in the *BC*'s long list of theomachs. Gnaeus' anti-Egyptian theomachy represents an extreme form of the narrator's own imperialism, but it also develops an idea already seen in Vergil's account of Actium, where the Roman gods face 'monstrous deities of every kind' (*omnigenumque deum monstra*, *Aen.* 8.698).[53] But whereas Vergil devotes but a few lines to representing a cosmic theomachy of gods fighting gods, Lucan shows the radically transformed aesthetic of his age by putting in Gnaeus' mouth a detailed threat to launch a theomachy of man against gods.

However, as Gnaeus' mention of Alexander suggests, and as we have seen many times over, the character of theomachy is determined not only by aesthetics but also by politics. Thus, immediately following the poet's indignant response to the acceptance of Egyptian cult at Rome, he focuses his resentment once again on the imperial cult (Luc. 8.835–7):

> tu quoque, cum saeuo dederis iam templa tyranno,
> nondum Pompei cineres, o Roma, petisti;
> exul adhuc iacet umbra ducis.

> Nor did you, O Rome, yet demand the ashes of Pompey,
> though you already gave temples to the savage tyrant;
> the shade of your leader still languishes in exile.

The narrator apostrophises and accuses Rome just as—*tu quoque*—he had done to Egypt. Moreover, he amplifies the sense of injustice which pervades

---

[53] Lucan's imperialism is reflected, for instance, in his regret that the energy and sacrifice of civil war could not have been turned onto an external foe and truly global domination (Luc. 1.9–23).

this whole section by contrasting the temples devoted to Caesar—the 'tyrant' who inspires the imperial cult—with the continued separation of even Pompey's ashes from Rome.

Unlike Gnaeus, however, who would desecrate tombs and burn gods in revenge for his father's death, the poet envisages a different solution to the problem created by Caesar's and his successors' divinisation—the creation of yet another god (Luc. 8.843–50):

> satis o nimiumque beatus,
> si mihi contingat manes transferre reuolsos
> Ausoniam, si tale ducis uiolare sepulchrum.
> forsitan, aut sulco sterili cum poscere finem
> a superis aut Roma uolet feralibus Austris
> ignibus aut nimiis aut terrae tecta mouenti,
> consilio iussuque deum transibis in urbem,
> Magne, tuam, summusque feret tua busta sacerdos.

> O enough and too much blessed,
> if it fell to me to transfer the dug-up shades
> to Ausonia, to violate such a tomb of our leader.
> Perhaps, when Rome would demand from the gods
> an end to sterile fields or fierce winds,
> or excessive heat or earthquake,
> You will pass, Magnus, into the city by the counsel and command
> of the gods, and the high priest shall carry your urn.

Here the narrator imagines himself importing Pompey's remains to Rome to function as a kind of tutelary deity, similar to the transfer of Asclepius in 293 BC during a great plague, or of Magna Mater in 205/4 BC during the Second Punic War.[54] These divine arrivals were, however, a feature of republican history and religion, and so Lucan's vision of the importation of a Pompeian cult contrasts pointedly with the form of deification associated with, and following on from, Caesar.[55]

The creation and transfer of a new deity, and the implicit turn from the principate back to the republic, represent a threat not only to the new imperial gods but even to Jupiter himself. The poet imagines a traveller coming across Pompey's grave in Egypt and esteeming this site above that devoted to Jupiter

---

[54] On the relationship between such importations and the Roman rite of *euocatio* (the summoning of a deity from the enemy to the side of Rome) see Blomart 1997, Gustafsson 2000. The importation of Pompey's ashes may also allude to the famous episode of Agrippina's bringing back of Germanicus' ashes (Tac. *Ann.* 3.1).

[55] Ovid had suggestively juxtaposed, yet contrasted, the cults of Asclepius and Caesar in the final book of the Metamorphoses (esp. *Met.* 15.745–6). Lucan, as so often, makes a more radical division between republican and imperial practice.

on nearby Mount Casius (*non... manesque tuos placare iubebit / et Casio praeferre Ioui?* 'will [the grave] not compel him to placate your shade and to hold you above Casian Jupiter?', Luc. 8.855–8).[56] Here is yet another instance of the low—Pompey's sand-bound grave—surpassing the high—Jupiter's lofty shrine—to add to the many other counterintuitive reversals noted by Day. The theomachic note, however, is worth dwelling on, for Mount Casius is linked to Zeus' defeat of Typhon after the gods fled to Egypt (Apollod. *Bibl.* 1.41), and to the nearby area of the Serbonian marshes, 'which the Egyptians call the exhalations of Typhon [i.e., Set]' (ἃς Τυφῶνος μὲν ἐκπνοὰς Αἰγύπτιοι καλοῦσι, Plut. *Ant.* 3.6).[57] In this loaded geographical context, even the rhetorical elevation of Pompey can seem to turn him into another Typhon.

A sequence of sharp comparisons follows, which emphasises the opposition of Pompey to both Jupiter and the divinised Caesars (Luc. 8.858–64):

> nil ista nocebunt
> famae busta tuae: templis auroque sepultus
> uilior umbra fores. nunc est pro numine summo
> hoc tumulo Fortuna iacens: augustius aris
> uictoris Libyco pulsatur in aequore saxum.
> Tarpeis qui saepe deis sua tura negarunt,
> inclusum Tusco uenerantur caespite fulmen.

> No grave shall harm
> your fame: buried in temples and gold
> you would be a meaner shade. Now Fortune, lying in this tomb,
> stands for the highest god: more august than the altars
> of the victor is a rock beaten on the African shore.
> Those who often deny their incense to the Tarpeian gods
> worship the lightning bolt enclosed in the Etruscan turf.

The reference to burial in temples and gold recalls the imperial *templa* at Luc. 8.835 and once again promotes Pompey at the expense of the deified Caesars.[58] But the phrase *pro numine summo* also implies that Fortune, in her new Pompeian guise, is in tension with the god one would expect to be *summus*—Jupiter.[59] The next word—*augustius*—then takes the reader back to competition with divinised humans, here allusively pointing to Augustus.[60] Finally, the

---

[56] Day 2013: 230. For the similar privileging of the shade of Amphiaraus over Apollo see *Theb.* 8.335–8 and p. 288 n. 90 below.

[57] For Ovid's treatment of the myth of Typhon see Chapter 3. Zeus seems to have been associated with two mountains, both called Casius. Lucan clearly refers to the one near Pelusium and Pompey's tomb (cf. Plin. *HN* 5.68), but the other, located near the present-day Turkish/Syrian border, has similar mythological associations (on which see Lane Fox 2009: 243–58). Apollodorus says that Casius overhangs Syria, and so may be referring to this latter mountain, though the gods' flight to Egypt and the fact that ancient Syria also bordered Egypt suggest that he, too, meant the same mountain as Lucan.

[58] Cf. Luc. 9.10–11, Day 2013: 223.

[59] Day 2013: 230.

[60] Day 2013: 223.

alternation between references to Jupiter and the emperors concludes with the aphoristic analogy in which Etruscan ritual is elevated above the worship of the entire Tarpeian, i.e., Capitoline, pantheon—that is, above the gods who play such a limited role in the poem as well as their imperial successors.[61] Although the reference to Etruscan ritual may seem somewhat opaque to us, its basic implication is clear enough: just as some reject the luxury and novelty that characterise mainstream imperial religion in favour of a simpler and more old-fashioned form of worship, so too the cult of Pompey may also be preferred to those of other gods.[62]

Day has well discussed how all the unusual antitheses drawn thus far support the poet's claim that the absence of a tomb actually amplifies the memory and fame of Pompey: *proderit hoc olim, quod non mansura futuris / ardua marmoreo surrexit pondere moles* ('one day it will be a boon that no high monument of heavy marble has risen up to remain for posterity,' Luc. 8.865–6).[63] The emphasis placed on the lack of a tomb, the constant reference point of the last section of Book 8, recalls once again the epigram transmitted in the scholia to Persius: *marmoreo Licinus tumulo iacet, at Cato paruo, / Pompeius nullo: credimus esse deos?* ('Licinus lies in a marble tomb, but Cato in a small one, Pompey in none: do we believe that gods exist?', Schol. ad Pers. 2.36).[64] In the epigram, the absence of Pompey's tomb signifies a larger injustice that in turn leads to a querying of the gods' existence—for how could they let this happen? That sense of doubt, which the narrator had expressed so aggressively in Book 7, is reinterpreted once more in Book 8—the disbelief is now directed towards the very story of Pompey's burial, thus assimilating him to Jupiter (Luc. 8.869–72):

> ueniet felicior aetas,
> qua sit nulla fides saxum monstrantibus illud;
> atque erit Aegyptus populis fortasse nepotum
> tam mendax Magni tumulo quam Creta Tonantis.

> A happier age shall come,
> when no faith will hold with those who point to that rock;
> and perhaps for our descendants, Egypt, with her claim to Magnus' tomb, will be as false as the Crete of the Thunderer.

By analogy with the paradigmatically false claim that Crete holds Jupiter's burial, Pompey's lack of a tomb becomes a powerful sign not of the absence of

---

[61] As Day 2013: 231 points out, in this analogy it is Pompey who is associated with the *fulmen*, the symbol of sublime power that for most of the poem attaches to Caesar.

[62] On the rather mysterious reference to Etruscan ritual see Mayer 1981: 189, who summarises the explanations offered in the *Commenta Bernensia*. For the contrast between wealthy and humble worship here see *Comm. Bern.* ad Luc. 8.863 (Usener 1869: 286–7).

[63] Day 2013: 227–9.

[64] Cf. *Pompeio...tumulum* (Luc. 8.713), *iaceat nullo* (714), *tumulus* (816), *tumulo...iacens* (861), *tumulo* (872).

the gods but of the creation of a new god. Despite the poet's apparent optimism, however, a sense of uncertainty nevertheless persists, for the comparison between Egypt and Crete reinforces the simultaneously analogous and antagonistic relationship between Pompey and Jupiter that suffuses the last section of Book 8, a relationship that mirrors Caesar's own ambivalent position as both favourite and usurper of the gods.

Finally, the absent tomb should also be considered within the context of the epic tradition. Homer had canonically tied the lack of proper burial to fame, oblivion, and the limits of mortality when the river Scamander threatens to bury the overreaching Achilles in mud and silt and to deny him a tomb (*Il.* 21.318–23).[65] In the *BC*, by contrast, it's precisely that absence that guarantees Pompey's fame, and that makes him both like the gods and at the same time a potential threat to them. In moving away from the notion that the gods can determine mortal renown, and in rejecting the connection between monumentality and fame, Lucan follows the lead of Horace and Ovid in developing a strand of Homeric theomachy.[66] Whereas the Augustan poets, however, had staked their immortality on their art and on the continuity of Roman power and traditions, Lucan makes Pompey's immortality contingent on a political ideal at odds with the current ideology. In Pompey's deification Lucan invents a challenge both to the existing Olympian gods and to the imperial pantheon to come: the making of a god promises with it the preservation of a powerful memory.[67]

Lucan's Book 9 opens with a striking realisation of the apotheosis to which Book 8 has led—a vivid description of Pompey's ascent to the heavens (Luc. 9.1–4):[68]

> at non in Pharia manes iacuere fauilla,
> nec cinis exiguus tantam conpescuit umbram:
> prosiluit busto semustaque membra relinquens
> degeneremque rogum sequitur conuexa Tonantis.
>
> But the shade did not linger among the Pharian embers
> nor did so little ash hold such a great shade:
> it leapt from the pyre and, leaving behind its half-burned limbs
> and the unworthy bier, followed the dome of the Thunderer.

The passage opens with a strong adversative—'but not'—as if to correct a reader's misapprehension that Pompey's role simply ended with his death. But

---

[65] See pp. 203–4.

[66] Cf. pp. 142–3 on Horace, Ovid, and Seneca. Homer had already treated human memory as a form of defiance against the gods (see pp. 37–8), an idea developed by Silius (pp. 207–10).

[67] Cf. Day 2013: 225–31. On the role of memory in Lucan see Gowing 2005: 82–101.

[68] A sceptical reader might have inferred from the equivalence made between Jupiter and Pompey at the end of Book 8, for instance, that both god and man are dead and nothing more.

since the signs of Pompey's coming deification were fairly clear in Book 8, the adversative here isn't so much a correction as an emphatic affirmation of what the poem had already suggested. In the movement from Book 8 to Book 9, then, the narrator gestures at a world defined not by clear beginnings and endings but by ever-present possibilities: neither the formal ending of a poetry book nor even death itself is conclusive; rather, any denouement contains within it the seeds of a new narrative and of a new creation.

The narrator's voice at the opening of Book 9 represents Pompey's catasterism according to a Stoic model of the afterlife of the *sapiens*, in which souls ascend to the lunar sphere.[69] Now that Pompey has achieved a measure of elevation unattainable by Egyptian kings and emperors (*non illuc auro positi nec ture sepulti / perueniunt*, 'those encased in gold and buried with offerings of incense do not reach there', Luc. 9.10–11), the narrator's voice would seem to be more optimistic. Robert Sklenář, however, has pointed out that this model is not only a debatable one within Stoic philosophy but that, even if Lucan adopted it wholesale, the character of Pompey in the *BC* hardly conforms to the very criteria for catasterism specified by the poet—those 'harmless in life' (*innocuos uita*, Luc. 9.8).[70] It's worth recalling at this point that as early as Book 2 Cato, even though he eventually opts to fight on Pompey's side, had alleged that Pompey too, much like Caesar, promised himself world rule (Luc. 2.320–2). Moreover, even Pompey's insertion among the 'demigods' (*semidei*, Luc. 9.7), while on one reading entirely positive, on another reading recalls the description of Anubis as *semideos* in the previous book (Luc. 8.832)—whether we are to see Pompey as clearly distinct from the Egyptian god or unsettlingly similar remains impossible to resolve. Where the narrator's voice in this passage differs from Book 8 is in the normalisation of the relationship between Pompey and Jupiter. Occupying the lunar sphere below the celestial abode of the gods, Pompey's spatial location and explicitly semi-divine nature ease the theomachic tensions raised in the previous book: a clear hierarchy separates Pompey from the true gods. Indeed, far from reaching further up into the heavens, his spirit descends back to earth to join with the body and mind of Brutus and Cato (Luc. 9.17–18). And yet the idea of theomachy will not recede for long, for it's in Cato that we find our newest model of divinity and theomach.[71]

When Cato is presented with the opportunity to consult the oracle of Jupiter Ammon, he is inspired to respond by the god within him: *ille deo plenus tacita quem mente gerebat, / effudit dignas adytis e pectore uoces* ('he, filled with the god that he bore in his silent mind, poured out from his breast

---

[69] Schotes 1969: 74–5.
[70] Sklenář 2003: 126–7.
[71] Note, too, that in opposing the increasingly divine Caesar, Cato and Brutus are engaged in another theomachy of sorts. Cf. Chapter 3's discussion of the assassination of Caesar in the *Metamorphoses*.

a speech worthy of the shrine', Luc. 9.564–5). That god, of course, is Pompey, who had earlier settled 'in Cato's mind' (*mente Catonis*, Luc. 9.18). Inspired by a *deus*, Cato's speech is weighed against that of Jupiter's own oracle. Cato uses a series of rhetorical questions to cast doubt on the special status of the oracle, asserting instead the immanence of divine power throughout the world (Luc. 9.574–80):[72]

> nec uocibus ullis
> numen eget, dixitque semel nascentibus auctor
> quidquid scire licet. sterilesne elegit harenas
> ut caneret paucis, mersitque hoc puluere uerum,
> estque dei sedes nisi terra et pontus et aer
> et caelum et uirtus? superos quid quaerimus ultra?
> Iuppiter est quodcumque uides, quodcumque moueris.

> Nor does god
> need any voice, for the maker told us at birth
> whatever we were permitted to know. Did he choose these barren sands
> to prophesy to a few, and did he sink the truth in this dust,
> and is god's seat other than earth, sea, air,
> heaven, and valour? Why do we seek gods further?
> Jupiter is whatever you see, whatever you contemplate.

On the one hand, Cato's respect for the divine emerges clearly from the passage, but equally notable is the readiness with which he challenges cultic belief and practice. In assessing that challenge, however, context is paramount, especially the way in which the cult is characterised. Lucan had earlier taken care to distinguish Jupiter Ammon from the Roman Jupiter: *sed non aut fulmina uibrans / aut similis nostro* ('but neither brandishing thunderbolts nor similar to our own', Luc. 9.513–14). As with the distinctions drawn in Book 8 between Pompey and the Egyptian gods, similarly here, Lucan's distancing of Ammon makes it more permissible that Cato should be so dismissive of the traditional conception of a god. Moreover, the narrator fully endorses Cato's scepticism (Luc. 9.584–6):

> sic ille profatus
> seruataque fide templi discedit ab aris
> non exploratum populis Hammona relinquens.

> Thus Cato spoke,
> but he preserved the credibility of the temple and departed from its altars
> leaving Ammon, untested, to the peoples.

The poet clearly implies through the phrase *seruata fide* that it is only by Cato's departing that people's faith in the oracle is preserved—were he to have tested

---

[72] I follow Housman's punctuation here rather than Duff's.

it, the oracle would no longer win credence. Thus, the narrator esteems the combination of Pompey's divine inspiration and Cato's theology above at least one (safely foreign) manifestation of Jupiter himself. The contest is so one-sided, indeed, that Cato can afford to spare Jupiter's blushes—an act of clemency worthy of Caesar himself.

Cato and Caesar are in many ways, of course, antitypes of each other. This opposition is established from early in the poem when the narrator remarks that 'the victorious cause pleased the gods, but the defeated cause pleased Cato' (*uictrix causa deis placuit, sed uicta Catoni*, Luc. 1.128). Indeed, Cato's reluctant decision to support Pompey follows from his belief that Caesar represents the primary threat to the republic and to freedom. Cato's antithetical relationship to Caesar is well captured in the desert march of Book 9 through the repeated emphasis of his resistance to hunger and thirst.[73] Already in Book 2 the poet says of Cato that 'for him it was a feast to have conquered hunger' (*huic epulae, uicisse famem*, Luc. 2.384). When in the Libyan desert a soldier offers Cato a drink of water from his helmet, the general sharply rejects any implication that he might not be able to endure the heat and thirst before casting aside the helmet: *sic concitus ira / excussit galeam, suffecitque omnibus unda* ('thus roused by anger he knocked the helmet away, and the water sufficed for all', Luc. 9.509–10). The anger of Cato, coupled with the language of sufficiency, recalls Caesar's quelling of the mutiny in Book 5, when he claims that for his troops 'not even this world suffices' (*quibus hic non sufficit orbis*, Luc. 5.356), which as we saw above alludes to the appetite of Erysichthon. Lucan thus depicts Cato as the diametric opposite of the insatiable Caesar and Erysichthon, his capacity to overcome bodily needs highlighted again and again.[74]

Like Caesar, however, and like Pompey too, Cato becomes yet another candidate for deification. In an apostrophe to Rome, the narrator offers a panegyric to Cato that echoes the praise of Pompey and responds to the divinisations of Caesar and Nero (Luc. 9.601–4):

> ecce parens uerus patriae, dignissimus aris,
> Roma, tuis, per quem numquam iurare pudebit,
> et quem, si steteris umquam ceruice soluta,
> nunc, olim, factura deum es.

> Behold, the true father of his country, worthiest of your altars,
> Rome, in whose name it is never shameful to swear,
> and whom, if you ever stand up freed from your chains,
> now, one day, you will make into a god.

---

[73] Note also the energy Cato shows in helping his men endure the pain of death (Luc. 9.884–9), which recalls the energy shown by Caesar at Pharsalus (Luc. 7.557–81).

[74] Cf., e.g., Luc. 9.591–3, 617–18.

The concepts of worthiness and shame, coupled with the conditional clause looking ahead to Rome's liberation from the yoke of tyranny, openly contrast the putative apotheosis of Cato with the historical deifications of the emperors. The narrator's insistence on imagining these public cults devoted first to Pompey and now to Cato nevertheless sits oddly with the kind of Stoic deification he actually attributes to Pompey, one contingent not on the worship of the people nor on the political context but on virtue. Instead, he simply perpetuates the theogonic-theomachic cycle, with new gods created in order to displace the old. For the narrator, this pattern is therapeutic: by repeating the crucial act of human divinisation, but at the same altering the character and values of those divinised, the great error of the past will finally be rectified.[75] But the same pattern of displacement equally implies the endlessness of the process by which new gods are created to struggle with their predecessors. That theomachic quality was evident in Caesar, Pompey, and Cato, who undermines Jupiter Ammon, and whom the poet had from the beginning of the *BC* placed in opposition not only to Caesar but also to the gods (Luc. 1.128).

Furthermore, just as Pompey seems to ill deserve his Stoic apotheosis, so too even Cato, figurehead of Stoic wisdom, falls short of the ideals he is supposed to represent. So, for instance, Sklenář observes that Cato's subjection to anger (*concitus ira*, Luc. 9.509) is the opposite of the self-control one would expect from a true *sapiens*.[76] In this way, both the narrator and the characters—even those the narrator suggests, or one might naturally expect, to know better—gesture towards, yet ultimately parody, the proper, Stoic route to the heavens. As with so many other questions in the poem, it remains resolutely unclear whether this failure altogether undermines the plausibility of the Stoic ideal or leaves it intact as a goal that others, if not the characters of the *BC*, might attain. Ultimately in either case, as with Seneca's Hercules, it is to theomachy that these individuals are drawn, for there seems no other idiom and no other method available through which to take charge of their world.

Cato, Caesar, and the *Hercules Oetaeus*

In this chapter and the previous one we have seen how a theomachic reflex characterises the heroes of Senecan tragedy and Lucan's epic, and shadows both political and philosophical conceptions of apotheosis. Some confirmation of this habit can be found in a text that combines allusions to Seneca's Hercules and Lucan's three protagonists—the pseudo-Senecan *Hercules Oetaeus* (*HO*).

Composed probably during the Flavian period, the tragedy dramatises the events surrounding Hercules' death, cremation, and deification on Oeta.

---

[75] On the Freudian relationship between repetition and change and its application to the epic tradition see Quint 1993, esp. 131–57 on the *BC*.

[76] Sklenář 2003: 90.

As one might expect from this subject matter, both Ovid's account of Hercules' death and apotheosis and Seneca's treatment of Hercules' madness are frequent points of reference for the author of the *HO*. As Matthew Leigh has noted, however, the text twice alludes to Lucan's Cato, too.[77] Describing the moment Hercules lays himself on the pyre, Philoctetes exclaims, 'what triumphing victor ever stood so happy in his chariot?' (*quis sic triumphans laetus in curru stetit / uictor? HO* 1683–4). The lines pick up Lucan's praise of Cato in Book 9 (Luc. 9.598–600):

> hunc ego per Syrtes Libyaeque extrema triumphum
> ducere maluerim, quam ter Capitolia curru
> scandere Pompei.
>
> I would rather lead this triumph through the Syrtes
> and the ends of Libya, than thrice climb the Capitol
> in Pompey's chariot.

The privileging of Cato's march over the elevation of the triumph—a moment when man comes closest to god—will culminate, as we have seen, in the narrator's hope for Cato's own deification.[78] The juxtaposition of endurance with apotheosis makes for an apt analogue for Hercules, whose endurance of Nessus' poison and the flames of the pyre allegorises the Stoic quality required for true greatness and precedes his ascent to heaven. Philoctetes emphasises Hercules' calm state of mind even amidst pain, again alluding to Cato: *iacuit sui securus* ('free from cares of self he lay', *HO* 1693; cf. *securumque sui* 'without care for self', Luc. 2.241).

Leigh observes, however, that in other ways Hercules has more in common with Lucan's Caesar, as when he fells a sacred grove to build his funeral pyre (*HO* 1618–41), thus affirming 'the continuing titanic tendency in his character'.[79] For Leigh, Lucan's heroes represent contrasting paradigms: 'Yet, if the Hercules of the *Hercules Oetaeus* acquires the philosophical virtues of Lucan's Cato, he also retains some of the reckless self-assertion of Caesar'.[80] As we have seen over the course of this chapter, however, Lucan's ostensible contrasting of Caesar, Cato, and Pompey is accompanied by a frequently theomachic subtext that unites all three figures in a cycle of theogony and antagonism with gods variously conceived. Rather than portraying Hercules as a combination of paradigmatically positive and negative models, then, the allusions to the *BC* equally suggest the inextricability of one model from the other. Indeed, in the very last lines of the *HO*, when Hercules has finally achieved the apotheosis for which he has waited so long, and which eluded his counterpart in Seneca's

---

[77] Leigh 2010: 229 n. 95.
[78] Cf. also the image of the triumph at Sen. *HF* 195 and my discussion in Chapter 4.
[79] Leigh 2010: 229–32, esp. 232.
[80] Leigh 2010: 230.

tragedy, the chorus ends the play on a tantalising note as it asks the divinised hero to continue to protect them from monsters (*HO* 1994–6):

> tu fulminibus frange trisulcis:
> fortius ipso genitore tuo
> fulmina mitte.

> You, break them with forked thunderbolts:
> more mightily than your very sire
> hurl the thunder.

At the very moment when the audience might expect all theomachic anxieties—whether in this play or in the hero's prior mythology—to have been resolved once and for all, the chorus, with a breathtaking lack of awareness, wills the son to supersede the father.

The proliferation and overlapping of theomachic identities observed in Seneca and Lucan is an especially common feature of Flavian epic and, if the conventional dating of the *HO* is correct, of Flavian tragedy too. But, as the presence of the divinised Hercules on stage near the end of the *HO* suggests, there is a new means by which theomachy takes an even more central position in the literature: through the return of the gods that Lucan had excluded comes the renewed possibility of the physical confrontation between mortal and god.

6

Paradigms of Theomachy in Flavian Epic
HOMER, INTERTEXTUALITY, AND THE STRUGGLE FOR IDENTITY

Of great-hearted Achilles, the offspring feared by the Thunderer
and forbidden to succeed to his father's heaven,
tell me, goddess.

—STATIUS

The world of Flavian epic is, at one level, emphatically remystified. After Lucan notoriously omitted the traditional divine apparatus from his *Bellum Civile*, the Flavian poets return to a superficially Vergilian theology of highly active and interventionist deities. The two martial epics, in particular—Silius Italicus' *Punica* and Statius' *Thebaid*—put the presumptions of overreachers, such as Hannibal and Capaneus, in tension with a reinvigorated pantheon of Olympian gods. And yet in representing theomachy directly, the poems already reveal a crucial difference from their Vergilian model, which studiously avoided open conflict between the human and divine realms. One important stream of influence includes the theomachic confrontations in Ovid's *Metamorphoses* and the tragic tradition, which naturally flows closer to the surface of Statius' mythological, Theban theme than to Silius' historical subject matter. The single source, however, that provides the main impetus and formal pattern for both epicists' treatment of theomachy is Homer.[1] The debt of Flavian epic to the *Iliad* and *Odyssey* has been scrupulously documented by Herbert Juhnke, whose substantial and painstaking accumulation of parallels and allusions has long provided literary critics with an invaluable resource.[2] Recent developments in the study of intertextuality, however, enable a more nuanced understanding of literary influence, temporality, and the interaction of text and context.[3]

---

[1] For the status of Homer in Flavian epic see, e.g., Silius' praise of him at *Pun.* 13.781–91.
[2] Juhnke 1972.
[3] See p. 3 n. 8.

It's against such a background, then, that this chapter attempts to sketch the basic contours of Flavian theomachy, before the later chapters treat the individual poems in greater detail and with an eye to their larger thematic coherence. Focusing on two quite different case studies, I illustrate the main debts to, and departures from, the Homeric epics and the subsequent tradition. The first case study examines the *mache parapotamios*, the epic topos of the struggle between mortal and river god, of which we have no extant examples between the *Iliad* and the Flavian epics. The second case study takes a different approach by looking at the synchronic as well as diachronic intertexts for the topos of the agon between a seer and a theomach. Focusing on Silius' argument between Flaminius and Corvinus, and the subsequent account of the battle of Trasimene, I combine evidence from the Greek epic tradition, connections to a near-contemporary agon in Statius' *Thebaid*, and intratextuality within the *Punica* itself to show how a multilayered representation of theomachy can be interpreted.

A final word on chronology: the contemporaneity of Silius and Statius poses problems for ascertaining which author might have influenced the other. Both epics were composed over a number of years during the reign of Domitian, with Silius probably finishing (or failing to finish) after Statius.[4] My argument, however, concerns itself with similarities and differences across texts rather than questions of an author's originality or responsiveness to another text. Hence, while leaving open the possibility of direct allusion from one epicist to the other, the subsequent readings are largely unaffected by the chronological uncertainties.[5]

Once More unto the Breach: The *Mache Parapotamios*

The *mache parapotamios* represents perhaps the clearest example of human-divine theomachy to feature in the *Iliad*, the *Punica*, and the *Thebaid*.[6] Moreover, unlike the rather anomalous case of Diomedes' divinely assisted wounding of Aphrodite and Ares, the river battle topos distinguishes between the deeds of heroes performed with the help of the gods and those without. It thereby provides an especially revealing perspective on the true capacities of mortals to contend

---

[4] See Wistrand 1956; Bassett 1963; McDermott and Orentzel 1977; Ahl, Davis, and Pomeroy 1986: 2493; Laudizi 1989: 29–54. Wilson 2013 cautions against viewing the *Punica* as a strictly Flavian poem.

[5] For a refreshingly flexible handling of the relationship between the two epics, similar to my own, see Lovatt 2010. Regardless of chronology, any reader of both epics will have had their understanding of one influenced by the other. On the interpretability of various types of intertextuality, some clearly non-allusive, see Hinds 1998: 17–51.

[6] For a later version of the topos, see the battle between Dionysus and Hydaspes in Book 23 of Nonnus' *Dionysiaca*, on which see Schmiel 2003. Because of his divine origins, however, Dionysus can impose himself on the river in a way that the mortal theomachs cannot (cf. Hercules' defeat of Achelous discussed in Chapter 3).

with the divine. In this section, therefore, I survey the relevant episodes in the three epics, focusing on the different ways that the texts frame the relative power of gods and mortals. Homer, for instance, goes to great lengths to emphasise the divine or near-divine qualities of Achilles in his struggle against the river Scamander, but the episode nevertheless strongly reaffirms the categorical distinction between humans and gods. By contrast, the two Flavian epicists downplay the divine qualities of their theomachs while at the same time showing them in crucial ways to be more powerful than their Iliadic predecessor. In addition, Silius and Statius associate the increased power of their heroes with different aspects of the authors' Flavian context: Silius' Scipio, father of Africanus, harnesses the power of Roman engineering, while Hippomedon's theomachy exemplifies a metapoetic competitiveness typical of Flavian epic.

ILIAD 21: ACHILLES-SCAMANDER

Achilles fights the river god known as Scamander to mortals but as Xanthus to the gods in Book 21 of the *Iliad*. Towards the beginning of the hero's long *aristeia*, the poet describes the Trojans fleeing Achilles like locusts from a fire (*Il.* 21.12–16). The simile continues a pattern of fire imagery associated with Achilles in Book 20 and foreshadows the elemental conflict to come between hero and river, and then between the river and Hephaestus.[7] The simile also marks the place where Achilles leaps into the river after the Trojans 'like a god' (δαίμονι ἶσος, *Il.* 21.18). The rest of Achilles' *aristeia* functions, in consequence, almost as an extended analysis of the significance of the fire simile and the δαίμονι ἶσος formula. Some parts of the narrative elevate the hero to the level of the divine, while others show that his resemblance to fire and to god, suggested at the opening of the *aristeia*, falls crucially short of truly elemental and divine power.[8]

Achilles makes a provocative claim about the power of the river god in taunting the corpse of one of his opponents, Lycaon (*Il.* 21.130–2):[9]

οὐδ' ὑμῖν ποταμός περ ἐΰρροος ἀργυροδίνης
ἀρκέσει, ᾧ δὴ δηθὰ πολέας ἱερεύετε ταύρους,
ζωοὺς δ' ἐν δίνῃσι καθίετε μώνυχας ἵππους.

Not even the fair-flowing river with his silver eddies
will protect you, though you have long sacrificed many bulls to him,
and thrown single-hoofed horses, still living, into his eddies.

---

[7] Achilles is described in terms of a forest fire at *Il.* 20.490–4; Hector claims he would fight Achilles even if his hands were like fire at *Il.* 20.371–2. See Whitman 1958: 138–44, King 1987: 18–19, C. J. Mackie 1998 (with slight differences at C. J. Mackie 2008: 180–6).

[8] On the theomachic associations of the δαίμονι ἶσος formula see Chapter 1.

[9] On the Lycaon scene see E. T. Owen 1946: 208–10, Schein 1984: 147–9. On the systematic concern with burial, or lack thereof, over the course of Achilles' *aristeia* see Whitehorne 1983: 133–5.

Achilles' dismissal of the Trojans' worship of their local river deity as ineffective undermines the system of hoped-for reciprocity underlying many of the prayers within the poem.[10] Achilles here does more than simply challenge the efficacy of sacrifice, however; rather, he casts the river god as impotent in the face of his own onslaught. Predictably, Achilles' boastful speech elicits a response from the river Scamander, thus marking a shift whereby the hero now leapfrogs his human opponents and engages a higher, divine order of the world (*Il.* 21.136–8):

> ὣς ἄρ' ἔφη, ποταμὸς δὲ χολώσατο κηρόθι μᾶλλον,
> ὅρμηνεν δ' ἀνὰ θυμὸν ὅπως παύσειε πόνοιο
> δῖον Ἀχιλλῆα, Τρώεσσι δὲ λοιγὸν ἀλάλκοι.
>
> So he spoke, and the river grew more enraged at heart,
> and pondered in his heart how to stop the work
> of shining Achilles, and to keep the Trojans from ruin.

That the river should be angered at the deaths of his worshippers would need no explanation, but the comparative, μᾶλλον, is striking. In saying that the river grew 'more enraged' the poet implies that Achilles' provocation caps an ascending series of attacks, over and above the destruction he has caused, and that it is that provocation which finally incites Scamander to respond. Achilles' self-aggrandising claims, dismissive of religious practice and even of the god himself, therefore recalibrate the relationship between mortal and immortal, and they do so emphatically, with the mortal Achilles asserting his agency over the divine river.

Achilles further exacerbates the tension between himself and Scamander with a second boastful speech over the body of an opponent, Asteropaeus, the descendant of another river (*Il.* 21.184–99):

> κεῖσ' οὕτως· χαλεπόν τοι ἐρισθενέος Κρονίωνος
> παισὶν ἐριζέμεναι ποταμοῖό περ ἐκγεγαῶτι.
> φῆσθα σὺ μὲν ποταμοῦ γένος ἔμμεναι εὐρὺ ῥέοντος,
> αὐτὰρ ἐγὼ γενεὴν μεγάλου Διὸς εὔχομαι εἶναι.
> τίκτέ μ' ἀνὴρ πολλοῖσιν ἀνάσσων Μυρμιδόνεσσι
> Πηλεὺς Αἰακίδης· ὃ δ' ἄρ' Αἰακὸς ἐκ Διὸς ἦεν.
> τὼ κρείσσων μὲν Ζεὺς ποταμῶν ἁλιμυρηέντων,
> κρείσσων αὖτε Διὸς γενεὴ ποταμοῖο τέτυκται.
> καὶ γὰρ σοὶ ποταμός γε πάρα μέγας, εἰ δύναταί τι
> χραισμεῖν· ἀλλ' οὐκ ἔστι Διὶ Κρονίωνι μάχεσθαι,
> τῷ οὐδὲ κρείων Ἀχελώϊος ἰσοφαρίζει,

---

[10] Examples of such prayers abound in the *Iliad*: e.g., Agamemnon claims his past sacrifices to Zeus as grounds for the god's aid (*Il.* 8.238–44); before shooting at Menelaus, Pandarus vows a great sacrifice to Apollo, the archer god (*Il.* 4.119–21). On sacrifices and offerings in Greek religion see Burkert 1985: 54–73.

οὐδὲ βαθυρρείταο μέγα σθένος Ὠκεανοῖο,
ἐξ οὗ περ πάντες ποταμοὶ καὶ πᾶσα θάλασσα
καὶ πᾶσαι κρῆναι καὶ φρείατα μακρὰ νάουσιν·
ἀλλὰ καὶ ὃς δείδοικε Διὸς μεγάλοιο κεραυνὸν
δεινήν τε βροντήν, ὅτ' ἀπ' οὐρανόθεν σμαραγήσῃ.

Lie as you are! It is hard to struggle against the children
of the mighty son of Cronus, even for one born of a river.
You say that your birth is from the wide-flowing river,
but I boast descent from great Zeus.
The man who fathered me rules over the many Myrmidons,
Peleus, son of Aeacus; and Aeacus was born of Zeus.
So, as Zeus is greater than the rivers that murmur seaward,
so the line of Zeus is greater than the line of a river.
For beside you is a great river, if he can defend you
at all; but one cannot fight with Zeus son of Cronus.
With him not even mighty Achelous vies,
nor the great strength of deep-flowing Ocean,
from whom all rivers and every sea
and all springs and deep wells flow;
but even he fears the lightning of great Zeus,
and his dread thunder, when it crashes from heaven.

Many heroes advertise their ancestry in epic poetry, often in combination with the kind of competitive verbal play that we see here, with Achilles using his genealogy to trump the lineage of his opponent.[11] What stands out in this passage, however, is Achilles' further (and, in context, unnecessary) goading of Scamander for not being able to save Asteropaeus. Achilles' confidence derives from a belief in a fixed hierarchy, where his descent from Zeus trumps that of the descendants of any lesser deities. But in provoking Scamander, a god, Achilles comes close to inflating his own position in the hierarchy he has articulated: he may well surpass Asteropaeus, but he ought to be wary of suggesting that he can disregard the river itself. At the beginning of the book, Scamander, or Xanthus, had been introduced as a son of Zeus: 'eddying Xanthus, whom immortal Zeus fathered' (Ξάνθου δινήεντος, ὃν ἀθάνατος τέκετο Ζεύς, *Il.* 21.2). Achilles thus hazards the temper not only of a god but also of a fellow descendant of Zeus.[12]

---

[11] Achilles is responding to Asteropaeus' own genealogical boast at *Il.* 21.153–60. On this kind of trumping, or 'flyting', in Homer see Martin 1989: 66–77, Parks 1990, H. S. Mackie 1996: 43–83, Kyriakou 2001, Hesk 2006. On similar verbal play (called 'capping') by competitors in oral performance see Collins 2004. The tradition has modern analogues in calypso wars and the answer songs of contemporary rap, on which see Wald 2012 (I thank Ben Sadock for the reference).

[12] Achilles' concern with hierarchy in this passage contrasts slightly with the point he had earlier made to Lycaon, namely, that all men die, including better men than Lycaon, such as Patroclus or even Achilles himself (*Il.* 21.106–13). There, Achilles minimised the importance of hierarchy when weighed

In the face of Achilles' provocation and his continued slaughter of the Trojans along the river, Scamander directly addresses the hero and calls on him to desist (*Il.* 21.214–20):

ὦ Ἀχιλεῦ, περὶ μὲν κρατέεις, περὶ δ᾽ αἴσυλα ῥέζεις
ἀνδρῶν· αἰεὶ γάρ τοι ἀμύνουσιν θεοὶ αὐτοί.
εἴ τοι Τρῶας ἔδωκε Κρόνου παῖς πάντας ὀλέσσαι,
ἐξ ἐμέθεν γ᾽ ἐλάσας πεδίον κάτα μέρμερα ῥέζε·
πλήθει γὰρ δή μοι νεκύων ἐρατεινὰ ῥέεθρα,
οὐδέ τί πῃ δύναμαι προχέειν ῥόον εἰς ἅλα δῖαν
στεινόμενος νεκύεσσι, σὺ δὲ κτείνεις ἀϊδήλως.

Achilles, you are powerful beyond men, and do evil
beyond men; for the gods themselves ever protect you.
If the son of Cronus has granted you to destroy all the Trojans,
at least drive them from my stream and do your dire work on the plain.
See, my lovely streams are filled with corpses,
nor can I in any way pour my waters into the bright sea
being choked with the dead, while you slaughter like ruin.

Scamander concedes Achilles' elevation 'beyond men', but the emphatic enjambment of ἀνδρῶν followed by the attribution of his success to divine aid— 'for the gods always protect you'—reminds the hero of the contingency of that elevation and the fixity of the hierarchy against which he chafes. With that premise in view the river strikingly foregoes the opportunity to assert his divine authority, preferring to adopt a conciliatory tone in explaining why the hero should fight elsewhere. Achilles agrees to relocate the slaughter from the river to the plain—'it will be... as you order' (ἔσται ταῦτα... ὡς σὺ κελεύεις, *Il.* 21.223)—but within the space of ten lines he leaps back into the river. Critics have found no satisfactory explanation for why Achilles reverts back to fighting in the river, which has naturally led to debate about the composition of this episode and the suggestion that Achilles' return to the river is simply an inelegant prerequisite of the subsequently added theomachy.[13] In terms of the narrative alone, however, it looks very much as if Achilles flagrantly disregards Scamander's appeal and his own earlier agreement to abide by it, thus further provoking the river.

---

against the shared fate of mortals; here, Achilles focuses on the widely differing power of mortals consequent upon their birth. This shift from one speech to the next characterises Achilles' increasing confidence in parallel with his ever more superhuman feats.

[13] See Richardson 1993: 70. Only a brief passage separates Achilles' assent to Scamander and his leaping back into the river, in which time Achilles lunges at the Trojans 'like a god' (δαίμονι ἶσος, *Il.* 21.227), a pointed position for a formula closely associated with theomachy. In the same passage Scamander castigates Apollo for not assisting the Trojans (*Il.* 21.228–32). It is striking that the unanswered appeal to Apollo results in the immediate return to the river of Achilles, Apollo's mortal doublet and antagonist, and in the consequent theomachy between hero and river.

At this point the river bursts into flood to destroy Achilles. The description of the struggle with Scamander is lengthy and amplifies the heroism of Achilles, but it also emphasises the disparity between human and elemental god (*Il.* 21.240–2):[14]

δεινὸν δ' ἀμφ' Ἀχιλῆα κυκώμενον ἵστατο κῦμα,
ὤθει δ' ἐν σάκεϊ πίπτων ῥόος· οὐδὲ πόδεσσιν
εἶχε στηρίξασθαι.

The swirling wave rose terribly around Achilles,
and the river pushed him back as it fell on his shield; nor could
he find a sure foothold.

The passage represents a powerfully sublime moment as the seething and swollen flood surrounds the hero. That Achilles should even place his shield in the way of the water is an impressive feat, but Homer's language has the hero bested from the very outset, with the river thrusting him back as he loses his footing.[15] In the Flavian epics we shall see how the image of the hero holding his shield against the force of the river marks a key point of comparison, and subtle contrast, with Achilles. But in the *Iliad*, the power hierarchy is immediately apparent, and Achilles is left with little choice but to flee without ever having really begun a theomachy proper. As sublime as the imagery and diction is, with Scamander's 'surface blackening' (ἀκροκελαινιόων, *Il.* 21.249) and 'great roar' (μεγάλῳ ὀρυμαγδῷ, *Il.* 21.256), it builds expectations for a contest that never really gets off the ground.

In the context of this elemental turmoil, and given the enormous disparity between mortal and god, the poet describes the river's pursuit of Achilles through a highly unexpected simile (*Il.* 21.257–64):

ὡς δ' ὅτ' ἀνὴρ ὀχετηγὸς ἀπὸ κρήνης μελανύδρου
ἂμ φυτὰ καὶ κήπους ὕδατι ῥόον ἡγεμονεύῃ
χερσὶ μάκελλαν ἔχων, ἀμάρης ἐξ ἔχματα βάλλων·
τοῦ μέν τε προρέοντος ὑπὸ ψηφῖδες ἅπασαι
ὀχλεῦνται· τὸ δέ τ' ὦκα κατειβόμενον κελαρύζει
χώρῳ ἔνι προαλεῖ, φθάνει δέ τε καὶ τὸν ἄγοντα·
ὣς αἰεὶ Ἀχιλῆα κιχήσατο κῦμα ῥόοιο
καὶ λαιψηρὸν ἐόντα· θεοὶ δέ τε φέρτεροι ἀνδρῶν.

---

[14] Nagler 1974: 147–63 relates the river fight of Achilles and Scamander to Near Eastern flood and creation myths. Fenno 2005: 498–502 reads the battle as part of a systematic antagonism between salt and fresh water, where the Greeks are associated with the sea and the Trojans with rivers.

[15] Achilles here defends himself with the shield made by Hephaestus, on which is depicted the greatest river, Ocean. Even such magnificent objects and representations, however, pale in comparison with actual divine power: Achilles will be saved not by a product of Hephaestus but by Hephaestus himself.

> As when a man drawing a channel leads from a dark spring
> a stream of water amid his plants and orchards,
> with a pickaxe in his hands, removing obstacles from the ditch—
> and as it flows all the pebbles beneath
> are swept along; and flowing quickly it murmurs
> down a sloping place, and even overtakes the man leading it—
> so did the wave of the river ever catch Achilles
> even though he went swiftly; for the gods are mightier than men.

The simile suggests that the river catches the man unawares, at a point where he might have thought he had controlled the stream. That peripeteia represents in miniature the transition from Achilles' earlier provocations of the river to his current plight. As so often in Homer, however, the world of the simile is far removed from the world of war and supernatural conflict: Scamander is no gentle stream, and Achilles is no farmer. The narrative of an entirely animate river overwhelming the hero offers a pronounced contrast with the image of man's taming of the natural world through the civilisation of agriculture and irrigation. Thus the simile, rather than accommodating the world of epic to everyday experience, achieves the opposite effect—through dissonance it highlights the special nature of epic action and discourse. Furthermore, the concluding words of the passage—'for the gods are mightier than men'—offer a distinctively epic explanation for the river's catching of Achilles, very different from the topographical explanation in the simile. Indeed, the words powerfully reaffirm the point which Homer's description of the theomachy has already made self-evident: Achilles is no match for Scamander. The closing words also recall a speech of Hector in Book 20, in which he rouses the Trojans by pointing to the emptiness of Achilles' threatening rhetoric: καί κεν ἐγὼ ἐπέεσσι καὶ ἀθανάτοισι μαχοίμην, / ἔγχεϊ δ' ἀργαλέον, ἐπεὶ ἦ πολὺ φέρτεροί εἰσιν ('I too could fight even the immortals with words, but with the spear it would be hard, since they are far mightier', Il. 20.367–8). Hector thus shows an awareness of what Achilles, despite his exceptional abilities and bravado, will have to learn: though Achilles twice casts doubt on the power of Scamander, in the end he experiences the vastly superior strength of the god.

At the end of a bitter and desperate prayer for aid, Achilles describes his own predicament in terms of another simile (Il. 21.281–3):

> νῦν δέ με λευγαλέῳ θανάτῳ εἵμαρτο ἁλῶναι
> ἐρχθέντ' ἐν μεγάλῳ ποταμῷ ὡς παῖδα συφορβόν,
> ὅν ῥά τ' ἔναυλος ἀποέρσῃ χειμῶνι περῶντα.

> But now it has been fated that I be caught by a miserable death,
> enclosed in a great river like a swineherd boy
> whom a torrent sweeps away as he tries to cross it in winter.

The simile of the innocent rustic may reflect Achilles' self-conception amidst despair, but it's at the same time extraordinarily disingenuous for ignoring both his achievement in surviving the initial assault of Scamander and the fact of his repeated provocation of the river. It's also tellingly within the same sphere of human activity as the narrator's own simile, which cast him as a farmer irrigating his fields. The difference between farmer and swineherd, however, is pronounced, furthering the deterioration of Achilles' status and agency: the narrator's farmer attempts to control nature and is overtaken, but the swineherd, without the benefit of technological knowledge and faced with a greater challenge, is entirely at nature's mercy. Achilles, who started out vaunting his divine stock, is left considerably, and progressively, worse off than when he entered the river.

The divine aid that now comes to Achilles, initially in the support of Poseidon and Athena, promises finally to create a genuine contest, just as in Book 5 Diomedes had been able to wound even the gods with the help of Athena. Achilles at first appears to have some success (*Il.* 21.302–4), but this initial burst only spurs Scamander to draw on the support of another river, the Simois, ἵνα παύσομεν ἄγριον ἄνδρα, / ὃς δὴ νῦν κρατέει, μέμονεν δ' ὅ γε ἶσα θεοῖσι ('so that we might stop this brutal man, who now prevails, and who strives to equal the gods', *Il.* 21.314–15).[16] Scamander ends his speech by claiming that he will bury Achilles under sand until his body cannot be found (*Il.* 21.318–23):

> κὰδ δέ μιν αὐτὸν
> εἰλύσω ψαμάθοισιν ἅλις χέραδος περιχεύας
> μυρίον, οὐδέ οἱ ὀστέ' ἐπιστήσονται Ἀχαιοὶ
> ἀλλέξαι· τόσσην οἱ ἄσιν καθύπερθε καλύψω.
> αὐτοῦ οἱ καὶ σῆμα τετεύξεται, οὐδέ τί μιν χρεὼ
> ἔσται τυμβοχόης, ὅτε μιν θάπτωσιν Ἀχαιοί

> And him
> will I enwrap in sands and pour over him abundant silt
> beyond measure, nor shall the Achaeans know where to gather
> his bones; below so much mud will I cover him.
> Even here shall be his tomb, nor shall he have need
> of a heaped-up mound, when the Achaeans conduct his funeral.

Scamander's threat must be understood against the context of every Iliadic hero's desire for fame, or *kleos*. *Kleos* provides a means by which humans can achieve a form of immortality, and the *Iliad* reflects on the role of the tomb, in

---

[16] Scamander sees Achilles' animal ferocity (he describes him as ἄγριον) as a way of competing with the gods, thus aligning the bestial and the divine (cf. King 1987: 13–28). Those extremes are normally distinguished, rather than assimilated, in Greek literature (see Detienne 1981). Shay 1994, on the *Iliad* and the modern psychology of war, characterises the berserker as someone who feels superhuman and can also behave like an animal.

particular, in transmitting the fame of the hero.[17] Here, however, Scamander imagines the absence of any burial of, or monument to, Achilles—in other words, the obliteration of the hero's memory and claim to immortality. And it's a threat that looks to be realised when once again the flood appears about to overwhelm Achilles (*Il.* 21.324–7). What enables Achilles to survive is further divine assistance. Seeing his plight, Hera bids Hephaestus to burn the river until she signals that he stop. The subsequent narrative leaves Achilles behind to describe a full-dress theomachy between the gods, but one in which Hephaestus is as superior to Scamander as Scamander had been to Achilles. The river quickly concedes: "Ἥφαιστ', οὔ τις σοί γε θεῶν δύνατ' ἀντιφερίζειν, / οὐδ' ἂν ἐγὼ σοί γ' ὧδε πυρὶ φλεγέθοντι μαχοίμην ('Hephaestus, none of the gods can measure up to you, nor would I fight you, burning with fire like this', *Il.* 21.357–8). That we have come to an entirely different order of conflict from Achilles' embryonic theomachy is made especially clear by the emphasis placed on fire: Achilles had begun his *aristeia* compared to fire (*Il.* 21.12–16), but now we see the immense disparity between a mere simile and the true divine element.[18]

While Hera's favour may indicate and magnify Achilles' heroism, it's important to note that it also serves divine self-interest. Hephaestus follows to the letter Hera's instruction to repel Scamander, despite any protestations, until she tells him to relent. Scamander must eventually turn to Hera herself, promising not just to keep out of Achilles' way but even to refrain from protecting Troy from the fire of the Greeks. It's this all-important second concession that prompts Hera to call off her son's assault: "Ἥφαιστε σχέο τέκνον ἀγακλεές· οὐ γὰρ ἔοικεν / ἀθάνατον θεὸν ὧδε βροτῶν ἕνεκα στυφελίζειν ('Hephaestus, hold back, my glorious child; for it is not seemly to mistreat an immortal god so for the sake of mortals', *Il.* 21.379–80). This simple dismissal concludes Achilles' battle with the river god. At first, it may look as though Hera politely resolves the tension with Scamander by re-establishing the categorical and moral distinction between humans and gods: the river ultimately remains one of them. But Hera herself was the one to urge her son to burn Scamander in the first place, so her claim about the seemliness of divine infighting appears highly disingenuous. And yet, in a way, she speaks truthfully, and revealingly, when she says that such things should not be done for the sake of mortals. For Hephaestus' prolonged burning of Scamander, at Hera's instruction, continues

---

[17] A particularly striking example of the relationship between a tomb and a hero's fame is the scenario imagined by Hector in Book 7, in which he envisages passing sailors seeing the tomb of his opponent and remarking that Hector had killed him. 'Thus one day will somebody speak', Hector continues, 'and my fame shall never die' (ὥς ποτέ τις ἐρέει· τὸ δ' ἐμὸν κλέος οὔ ποτ' ὀλεῖται, *Il.* 7.91). It is a striking sign of Hector's self-regard that the tomb advertises not its occupant's fame but Hector's.

[18] C. J. Mackie 1998 rightly argues that Achilles' apparent invulnerability to Hephaestus' fire sets him apart from the other heroes of the poem and is, for a variety of reasons, suggestive of his immortality. My point is rather that, despite this elevation, the context of the river battle makes clear how ultimately limited Achilles in fact is.

until the river promises not to interfere with the sack of Troy. Achilles' epic, perhaps even hyper-epic, battle with the river is finally seen in proportion, merely one part of a divine power play much greater in significance and temporal scope. In this way, Homer's episode of the *mache parapotamios* not only shows Achilles to be inferior to the river god, but it also illustrates the relative smallness of human action within the gods' frame of reference.

PUNICA 4: SCIPIO-TREBIA

For all that Hannibal appears to be the main theomach of the *Punica*, the first, and indeed only, true theomachy in the poem is fought by a Roman, Publius Scipio, father of the future Africanus. Over the course of the two battles related in *Punica* 4, at the Ticinus and the Trebia, Silius reflects on many of the same issues arising from *Iliad* 21 pertaining to the boundaries of human and divine power, culminating with Scipio's confrontation with the Trebia and the consequent problem of what exactly Homeric theomachy might signify in the case of a historical character acting in a Roman epic context.[19] Perhaps surprisingly, Scipio—not even one of the protagonists of the poem—emerges as in some ways more powerful than Homer's Achilles; it is no longer divine birth that allows a hero to strain at the limits of mortality, but rather the distinctively Flavian character of Silius' epic and, as we shall see, of Statius' *Thebaid*, too.

Early in Scipio's *aristeia* at the battle of the Ticinus, Silius compares the consul to Boreas stirring up the Aegean Sea, causing shipwrecks and drenching the Cyclades (*Pun.* 4.243–7). The comparison with the divine, and characteristically violent, north wind has the local function of aggrandising Scipio, but through the focus on water imagery it also looks ahead to the hero's confrontation with the river in the following battle. Already we are primed to see Scipio as more than merely mortal, and indeed as harnessing the kind of power himself that will subsequently be used against him by the Trebia towards the end of the book.

Scipio's major human opponent is the huge Gaul Crixus, whom Silius, following epic and mythological tradition, characterises as a Giant. In describing Crixus as 'thundering around' (*circumtonat*, *Pun.* 4.253) an opponent, Silius evokes the sound and fury of a storm, an apt image for Gigantomachic struggle.[20] When a few lines later Scipio and Crixus are about to fight a duel, Silius makes the Gigantomachic imagery explicit through a simile comparing the Gaul to the Giant Mimas: *quantus Phlegraeis Telluris alumnus in aruis / mouit signa Mimas caelumque exterruit armis* ('as great as the son of Earth, Mimas, marched on the Phlegraean fields and terrified heaven with his arms',

---

[19] See Santini 1991: 63–113 on the importance of the topos for the *Punica* as a whole, and 80–91 on the Trebia scene in particular, as well as Juhnke 1972: 13–24 for the relationship to the Homeric scene.
[20] See, e.g., Stat. *Theb.* 3.595–6.

Pun. 4.275–6). When Scipio fells Crixus, 'the earth groans, struck by his vast armour' (*percussa gemit tellus ingentibus armis, Pun.* 4.294).[21] The modern convention of capitalisation that distinguishes *Telluris* in the simile at 275 from *tellus* at 294 oversimplifies a deliberate ambiguity: the earth groans not just because of the weight of Crixus' armour but also because his death recalls—perhaps even recapitulates—the death of her son. Scipio is thus elevated through a series of mythological associations, first through the Boreas simile, and second through his killing of Crixus-Mimas.[22]

The associative imagery used of Scipio at the Ticinus aligns the consul with the gods and prepares the reader for the truly elemental encounter later in the book. The next battle's location at the river Trebia affords Silius the opportunity to represent the topos of the *mache parapotamios* and thus to engage Homer's canonical version in *Iliad* 21.[23] When Silius describes Scipio's entrance into the battle, he deploys a loaded simile comparing him to a river which tears away part of a mountainside and sweeps away animals and woods (*Pun.* 4.520–4).[24] The full significance of the simile will not emerge for a little while longer, when the man compared to a river will actually fight a river. Here, just before introducing the heroics of Scipio and Hannibal, Silius declares that not even Homer's tongue could tell of the leaders' feats in battle: *non, mihi Maeoniae redeat si gloria linguae* ('not even if the glory of the Maeonian tongue were to return...', *Pun.* 4.525). It will soon become clear that this reference to Homer, immediately following the river simile used of Scipio, gestures towards Achilles' theomachy against Scamander in *Iliad* 21, which prepares the way for Silius' own experiment with the topos.

---

[21] Silius follows this line with a simile comparing the crash to the dropping of masonry blocks into the sea to lay foundations for the houses of wealthy Romans. The sublime and cataclysmic imagery of a mountain clashing with the angry sea (*diuisaque caerula pulsu / illisum accipiunt irata sub aequora montem, Pun.* 4.298–9) elevates the use of wealth and technology into a kind of theomachy in which the Romans dominate the realms of earth and water. Silius here alludes to a Vergilian simile (*Aen.* 9.710–16) describing the fall of the Giant-like Bitias from the thunderbolt-like javelin of Turnus in terms of masonry dropped into the sea. Vergil even highlights the Gigantomachic subtext by including in the simile reference to Jupiter's imprisonment of Typhoeus under the island of Ischia (on this episode see Hardie 1986: 144–5, 1994: 220–5). At the Trebia, too, Scipio will assert his dominance over water.

[22] Thus aligning the consul with Zeus or Ares, each of whom is said to have defeated Mimas. See Eur. *Ion* 212–15 (Zeus), Ap. Rhod. 3.1226–7 (Ares).

[23] For a detailed inventory of the episode's allusions to the *Iliad* and to other texts see Spaltenstein 1986: 318–22.

[24] For the theomachic implications of similes comparing men to rivers, see pp. 17–18 on Diomedes and p. 290 n. 98 on Capaneus. Silius will later compare the Carthaginian elephants driving through the Trebia to 'a cliff shorn and flung down from a mountain' (*proruta cautes / auulsi montis, Pun.* 4.600–1), which, by alluding back to the simile used of Scipio (*auulsum montis...latus, Pun.* 4.522), makes the idea of the *mache parapotamios* especially monstrous and novel. Note that the comparison of Scipio to the river that breaks the mountainside makes him appear even more powerful than the elephants, which are compared to the falling cliff. We can thus see how features of the *Punica* that in the past may have been taken to demonstrate a lack of invention of Silius' part—here a near repetition of a simile—in fact represent his originality in handling epic topoi.

Whereas Homer personalises Scamander from the outset, describing the river's reaction to Achilles even before the conflict over the choking of the river with corpses, Silius does so only gradually in the case of the Trebia. The first mention of the Trebia in the course of the battle is studiously vague: *tum Trebia infausto noua proelia gurgite fessis / incohat ac precibus Iunonis suscitat undas* ('then with his unlucky swell the Trebia begins new battles against the tired Romans, and rouses his waves at Juno's request', *Pun.* 4.573–4).[25] We never, in fact, see Juno make this request, and so we have only a minimal sense of the river's motivation for the attack. It is only after its initial assault that the Trebia, like Scamander, becomes filled with corpses and weaponry (*Pun.* 4.625–6). And whereas Scamander grows angry at Achilles' provocations and explicitly complains about the clogging of his riverbed, Silius pointedly delays anthropomorphising the Trebia until later in the scene. As a result of the Trebia's lack of anthropomorphisation, at least on a Homeric scale, Silius' descriptions of the surging river as angry (*ferox, Pun.* 4.639, *furit* 640) leave it very unclear whether these terms should be understood as metaphorical or real. If real, the river's anger seems perplexing and without cause unless one recalls Scamander's response in the *Iliad* and imputes it to the Trebia. Silius thus keeps the reader in mind of the Homeric intertext, which continuously informs Scipio's *aristeia* even as Silius' narrative departs from its model in important ways, such as the ambiguous nature of the Trebia.

From the very beginning of the *mache parapotamios*, Scipio's heroism appears greater than Achilles': while Scipio, too, enters the river and kills countless opponents, he does so despite being hampered by the wound he received at the Ticinus (*Pun.* 4.622–4). When the Trebia bursts into flood, moreover, Scipio responds not with fear, like Achilles (δείσας, *Il.* 21.248), but with more violent anger (*accensa...uiolentius ira, Pun.* 4.642)—Scipio thus becomes more Achillean than Homer's own paradigmatically wrathful hero. Most impressively, whereas Achilles cannot himself harm Scamander, Scipio can avail himself of the resources of Roman technology to make a credible threat to reduce and block the course of the Trebia (*Pun.* 4.643–8):

> 'magnas, o Trebia, et meritas mihi, perfide, poenas
> exsolues' inquit. 'lacerum per Gallica riuis
> dispergam rura atque amnis tibi nomina demam,
> quoque aperis te fonte, premam, nec tangere ripas
> illabique Pado dabitur. quaenam ista repente
> Sidonium, infelix, rabies te reddidit amnem?'

> 'O Trebia, you will pay great and deserved penalties
> to me', he said. 'I will tear you into streams and scatter you

---

[25] Livy 21.54.9 writes that overnight rains had swelled the Trebia before the battle, a fact which may have suggested to Silius the possibility of including the topos of the river battle.

across the Gallic fields, and I will deprive you of the name of river, and I will stop you at the spring where you rise, nor shall it be allowed you to touch the banks and flow into the Po. What sudden madness, wretch, has turned you into a Carthaginian river?'

Even if Silius has only partially personalised the river by this point, Scipio addresses the Trebia directly. Unlike Achilles, who has no legitimate complaint against Scamander, Scipio implies that the Trebia's location in the Italian peninsula ought to entail a loyalty to Rome.[26] Scipio rather occludes the fact, evident from the early books of the *Punica*, that northern Italy was not strictly Roman territory during this period, as attested by the alliance of many of its long-standing Gallic inhabitants with Hannibal. To a Flavian reader of the first century AD, however, by which time the Trebia had long been part of Roman territory, Scipio's view would have appeared entirely normal: this was land that would eventually, necessarily, be incorporated into the Roman Empire, and on that basis its rivers should assist Rome, not her enemies. Scipio's threat to control the river presents a striking contrast to the relative impotence of Homer's Achilles in the same situation. In particular, Scipio's language of hydroengineering resonates less with the Iliadic passages directly describing Achilles and rather with the simile of the famer irrigating his orchards (*Il.* 21.257–64). Homer's simile, however, only highlighted by contrast Scamander's vast superiority to Achilles, whereas Scipio not only raises the idea of human mastery over water to an entirely different order from Homer's farmer, but also speaks with an authority derived from the poem's Roman context. For the idea of dominating and reducing a river has a particular contemporary resonance for Silius' audience.[27] In the previous book of the *Punica*, Silius had praised Vespasian for his pacification of the Rhine (*Pun.* 3.599). And Domitian, too, bridged the Volturnus through the construction of the Via Domitiana, a feat represented by Statius in *Silvae* 4.3, in which the river praises the emperor for curbing its violent floods.[28] Thus, Scipio's threat to the Trebia not only draws on a familiar thematic connection between technological progress and theomachy—Caesar's felling of the Massilian grove in Lucan's *Bellum Civile*, for instance, or Xerxes' historical bridging of the Hellespont—it also articulates an especially Flavian claim to authority in theomachic terms.[29]

---

[26] On Roman ideology and morality in Silius' episode see Juhnke 1972: 22–3.

[27] Strabo 5.1.11 reports that M. Aemilius Scaurus ordered the draining and canalisation of the area around the Trebia for agricultural purposes. See Santini 1991: 85.

[28] Stat. *Silv.* 4.3.72–94, on which see Coleman 1988: 122–6 and Newlands 2002: 301–9.

[29] Cf. Hannibal's fording of the Rhone at 3.442–65 with Santini 1991: 91–4. On the manipulation of nature as theomachy see p. 206 n. 21 above, and the discussion of Caesar's grove-cutting in Chapter 5. Caligula is reported to have ridden across the Gulf of Baiae in similar fashion to Xerxes (Suet. *Calig.* 19, Joseph. *AJ* 19.5–6), on which see Wardle 2007. For other comparanda, including Caesar at Luc. 4.141–3, see Santini 1991: 84–5, as well as 97–113 for suggestive comments about the tension between nature and science. On the relationship between theomachy and Flavian ideology see Chapter 9.

Scipio's superiority to Achilles consists not only in the credibility of his threat but also in his greater success at resisting the river: *arduus aduersa mole incurrentibus undis / stat ductor clipeoque ruentem sustulit amnem* ('the general stood tall against the surge of oncoming waves, and withstood the rushing river with his shield, *Pun.* 4.651–2).[30] And although the Trebia rises in flood about him, undermines his footing, and rushes against his shield, Scipio—unlike Achilles—does not flee. It's at this point, in the face of the Scipio's threats and unyielding resistance, that Silius finally, and fully, anthropomorphises the Trebia (*Pun.* 4.659–66):

> tum madidos crines et glauca fronde reuinctum
> attollit cum uoce caput: 'poenasne superbas
> insuper et nomen Trebiae delere minaris,
> o regnis inimice meis? quot corpora porto
> dextra fusa tua! clipeis galeisque uirorum,
> quos mactas, artatus iter cursumque reliqui.
> caede, uides, stagna alta rubent retroque feruntur.
> adde modum dextrae aut campis incumbe propinquis.'

> Then the river raised his dripping locks and his head bound
> with blue-green weeds and said, 'Do you threaten to exact further arrogant
> penalties and to erase the name of the Trebia,
> O enemy of my realms? How many corpses do I carry,
> felled by your hand! I have left a course choked
> with the shields and helms of men whom you slew.
> You see my deep pools grow red with carnage and flow backwards.
> Put a limit to your might or else attack the nearby fields'.

Although systematic allusion to *Iliad* 21 has prepared the reader for the explicit intervention of the river, nevertheless the graphic description of the Trebia, including direct speech, represents a striking moment in the historical epic: Scipio's theomachy consists not merely of poetic hyperbole, nor the threat of reducing and rechannelling the river, but of a Homeric confrontation between a mortal and a vividly realised deity. By attributing to the Trebia the same complaint as Homer's Scamander, however—namely, that the hero's *aristeia* has resulted in the choking of the river—the Trebia's speech elides an important discrepancy: it had actually begun its assault on the Romans before Scipio's *aristeia* and in response to the request of Juno (*precibus Iunonis*, *Pun.* 4.574). Whereas Homer portrays Achilles' arrogance as an important and credible cause of Scamander's anger, Silius makes the Trebia appear far more disingenuous in its self-justification, thus legitimising Scipio's own attitude to the river.[31]

---

[30] Santini 1991: 86.
[31] See Juhnke 1972: 17, but cf. Santini 1991: 82–3 for similarities between Scipio and Hannibal that make the Roman hero appear more transgressive, and thus more like Achilles.

Besides Silius' Roman colouring of the theomachy, it's also important to note that the Trebia's fear of losing its name and identity reverses one aspect of the Iliadic encounter, where Scamander threatens to obliterate all trace of Achilles and to deny him a tomb (*Il.* 21.318–23). By the time of the Flavian era, the power dynamic between mortal and god has shifted to the extent that humans can now threaten to do to gods what once only gods could do to mortals.[32] Although the rest of the episode proceeds according to the Homeric pattern, with Scipio appealing to the gods to die on land (*Pun.* 4.670–5) and Vulcan burning the river into submission (*Pun.* 4.675–95), it is notable that the resolution is ultimately brought about not by a divine negotiation about the future of the war—as in the case of Hera and Scamander's agreement about the future sack of Troy—but through a promise not to carry out Scipio's earlier threat: *tum demum admissae uoces et uota precantis / orantique datum ripas seruare priores* ('then at last the voice and prayers of the petitioner were heard, and he was allowed, as he asked, to keep his former banks', *Pun.* 4.696–7). The Trebia, in other words, must appeal to the gods to prevent the realisation of a mortal's threat—a situation far different from that in *Iliad* 21, where Achilles was largely an irrelevance to the larger divine power play.

THEBAID 9: HIPPOMEDON-ISMENUS

In Book 9 of the *Thebaid*, Statius, too, reworks Achilles' struggle against Scamander in Hippomedon's theomachy against the river god Ismenus. Like Homer, Statius foregrounds the testing of the physical limits of the human body, but he also uses allusions to, and differences from, the Iliadic scene to distinguish his conception of epic heroism and to comment on the place of the *Thebaid* within the epic tradition. Like Silius, Statius makes Hippomedon's feats appear greater than those of Achilles; indeed, they are greater even than Scipio's. Statius is far more ostentatious than Silius, however, in reflecting on his episode's relationship to the *Iliad* and on the poetological function of rivers in the literary tradition.

Statius' metapoetic interest emerges from the opening of Hippomedon's *aristeia*, when the poet invokes the Muses (*Theb.* 9.315–18):

---

[32] Homer already shows awareness of the relationship between theomachy, memory, and human technology and construction through his treatment of the Achaean wall, on which see Chapter 1. Whereas for Homer, however, the destruction of the wall and, in particular, the *mache parapotamios* reassert divine authority, Silius shows how, in the Flavian era, even an episode figurative of divine supremacy can now point to the very real power of mortals over their world. The idea of obliterating or preserving the name of a god is also suggestive of the practice of *damnatio memoriae*, which was a real possibility in the case of Caligula and Nero, but which would only officially occur for the first time with Domitian (see Flower 2006). I am not suggesting that Silius alludes to debates over whether to condemn the memories of former emperors, but rather that the existence of those debates creates a context in which the relationship between theomachy and memory can take on a new significance different from that in Homer's time.

> nunc age, quis tumidis magnum expugnauerit undis
> Hippomedonta labor, cur ipse excitus in arma
> Ismenos, doctae nosse indulgete sorores:
> uestrum opus ire retro et senium depellere famae.

> Come now, learned sisters, grant me to know what toil
> overcame great Hippomedon in the swollen waves,
> why Ismenus himself was roused to arms:
> it is your task to go back and drive off the decay of old age from fame.

The myth of the Seven already requires Hippomedon to die, but the watery manner of his death is Statius' Homerically inspired invention.[33] The Muses are summoned as if to recount an ancient but once famous story, alluding to Homer's *mache parapotamios*. The subsequent narration, however, in combining an Iliadic episode involving a different character—Achilles—with a novel treatment of Hippomedon, represents a self-consciously hybrid creation.[34] Literary repetition thus opens the way for literary competition, in this case specifically with Homer, though one may suspect, if Statius and Silius composed their epics in book order, that here, relatively late in the *Thebaid*, Statius was also responding to the equivalent scene from relatively early in the *Punica*.[35]

The trigger for Hippomedon's theomachy and demise is his repetition of Achilles' actions. Just as Achilles kills Asteropaeus, a river-born youth (though not a descendant of Scamander), Hippomedon slays Crenaeus, Ismenus' own grandson. As so often, Statius emphasises the impious characterisation of the Argive heroes, here through the words of Crenaeus: *sacrum amnem, sacrum (et miser experiere!) deumque / altrices inrumpis aquas* ('this is a sacred stream, sacred—and miserably shall you die!—disrupting waters that have nourished gods', *Theb.* 9.342–3). Without responding, Hippomedon simply attacks his opponent (*nihil ille, sed ibat / comminus*, 'he said nothing, but met him in combat', *Theb.* 9.343–4). The detail of Hippomedon's silence contrasts with the later reports of Crenaeus' mother and Ismenus, who both allege the hero's boastful arrogance. First, Crenaeus' mother complains: *ecce furit iactatque tuo se in gurgite maior Hippomedon* ('see, Hippomedon rages and boasts himself the greater in your flood', *Theb.* 9.393–4); then Ismenus describes Hippomedon 'proudly rejoic[ing] in the spoils and blood of an innocent boy' (*tumidus spoliis et sanguine gaudes / insontis pueri*, *Theb.* 9.442–3).[36] For the mother and grandfather

---

[33] On Hippomedon's theomachy see Klinnert 1970: 88–99, 112–18; Vessey 1973: 294–8; Dewar 1991: 118–19; Lovatt 2005: 119–28; McNelis 2007: 135–7. Juhnke 1972: 24–44 gives a detailed account of the similarities and differences between the Homeric and Statian scenes.

[34] There may also be a further irony in Hippomedon's preceding Achilles in mythological time. Cf. Lovatt 2001: 120 n. 31.

[35] On the chronology of the composition of the *Punica* see p. 196 n. 4 above; on that of the *Thebaid* see Dewar 1991: xvii.

[36] The narrator offers no evidence of these actions in the text. See Lovatt 2005: 122–3.

of the slain youth to exaggerate Hippomedon's offence is perfectly comprehensible, but an additional reason for their allegation of the hero's audacity lies with the Homeric source for this episode. For Achilles, unlike Hippomedon, rages (*Il.* 21.33), vaunts (*Il.* 21.130–2, 184–99), and even triumphantly despoils the descendant of a river (*Il.* 21.182–3). In a witty acknowledgement of the power of tradition, Statius has the Homeric past resound so loudly that the characters of the *Thebaid* mistakenly impute distant echoes of Achilles to Hippomedon.

Ismenus stakes his vengeance on the difference between his own godhead and Hippomedon's mortality: *ni mortalis ego et tibi ductus ab aethere sanguis* ('unless I am a mortal and your blood comes from heaven', *Theb.* 9.445). Although Hippomedon's physical strength certainly elevates him above the average mortal, Ismenus' rhetoric is clearly ironic. The weighing of divinity and mortality becomes more pointed, however, when we recall that Achilles explained his superiority to Asteropaeus on the grounds of his own direct descent from Zeus (*Il.* 21.184–99). The Iliadic context thus emphasises by contrast Hippomedon's mortality. Moreover, god and mortal are separated not only in nature but also in the complete absence of any communication between them. Whereas Scamander and Achilles initially address each other to communicate their wishes (*Il.* 21.214–26), Ismenus only complains to Jupiter before attacking Hippomedon without any verbal preface. Furthermore, whereas Achilles can rely on divine aid to save him, Hippomedon's prayer (*Theb.* 9.506–10) only ensures that his death comes on dry land, rather than by drowning. Beyond the physical confrontation, then, there is little interaction between the human and divine realms, unlike the highly and explicitly intertwined worlds of gods and mortals in the *Iliad*.

Against this background, the narrator describes Hippomedon's purely human resistance to the river in manifestly heroic terms (*Theb.* 9.469–72):[37]

> stat pugna impar amnisque uirique,
> indignante deo; nec enim dat terga nec ullis
> frangitur ille minis, uenientesque obuius undas
> intrat et obiecta dispellit flumina parma.

> An unequal fight holds river and man alike,
> while the god grows indignant; for the man does not turn his back nor
> is he broken by any threats, but he meets the waves as they
> come, and thrusting his shield forward he repels the waters.

The word *impar* naturally suggests the god's advantage over the mortal, but the rest of the passage forces the reader to wonder whether it isn't in fact

---

[37] Hippomedon, like Achilles, technically fights two rivers. Just as Scamander calls on the aid of Simois, so Ismenus draws on Asopus. Since only one river is personified in the theomachies themselves, however, I refer to only one river in my analysis.

Hippomedon who fares better, especially since his pushing back of the waters with his shield pointedly surpasses Achilles' efforts, and even those of Silius' Scipio, who merely stands his ground against the Trebia.[38] Hippomedon's mistake, however, is to become yet more like Achilles. Instead of remaining silent, he taunts the river, accusing him of effeminacy (*Theb.* 9.476-80). Ismenus' second assault (*Theb.* 9.481-510) proves the god's superiority over the mortal, and Hippomedon can pray for no more than to die on land (as does Scipio; cf. *Pun.* 4.670-5). Statius thus makes his river theomachy into a purer combat between mortal and immortal without the complications of Achilles' divine assistance and the parallel battle between Scamander and Hephaestus, and without Silius' similar interventions.

As well as presenting an opportunity to compete with Homer, and perhaps Silius too, Statius' theomachy possesses in its very elemental nature a strain of metapoetic imagery.[39] Callimachus had long ago made the swollen river a symbol of grandiose epic poetics.[40] Statius draws on this tradition, even flagging the metapoetic imagery by placing 'swollen waves' (*tumidis undis*, *Theb.* 9.315) in the very first line of the invocation to the Muses.[41] Together with the grandiose connotation of the river in spate, Charles McNelis also notes that the image of the 'swollen river' appears near the beginning of Lucan's Bellum Civile in the account of Caesar's crossing of the Rubicon (*tumidum amnem*, Luc. 1.204).[42] Jamie Masters has argued of the Lucanian passage that Caesar's crossing involves the poet in a complex dynamic of reluctance and complicity, where Lucan at once both obstructs and narrates the progress of civil war, with the river—first swollen and obstructing Caesar, then reduced and compliant— standing as a kind of objective correlative for the poet's own ambivalence towards Caesar.[43] Statius' metapoetic gambit is somewhat different from Lucan's. The invocation to the Muses at the opening of Hippomedon's theomachy signals a purple passage through which the poet will compete with Homer. The grandiosity required for such a poetic contest is represented in the figure of the swollen river, but within the narrative itself the cause of the river's greater intensity is rather the sheer physical force and the provocation of Hippomedon. Thus, the theomachy as a whole—both Hippomedon's might and the river's

---

[38] Moreover, Hippomedon had killed Crenaeus despite the opposition of the river (*Theb.* 9.344-5).

[39] On the storm imagery in the episode see Lovatt 2005: 124-8; Hardie 2013: 129 spots links with the Vergilian, as well as Homeric, sublime. For other metapoetic features of this episode, focused on the ecphrasis of Crenaeus' shield, see Chinn 2010.

[40] Callim. *Hymn* 2 105-13.

[41] The Muses are specifically called 'learned' (*doctae*, 9.317), a characteristic closely associated with Hellenistic poetry and its Roman descendants (see Dewar 1991: 120). McNelis 2007: 135-7 reads the metapoetic thrust of Hippomedon's theomachy as part of a sustained dialogue between Callimachean and non-Callimachean poetics, the latter of which temporarily emerges victorious through the triumph of the river in flood. On the pervasive influence of Callimachean poetry on Roman literature see most recently Hunter 2006.

[42] McNelis 2007: 120-1.

[43] Masters 1992: 1-10.

response—becomes the means by which Statius outdoes his predecessors and achieves poetic fame.[44] It's important to emphasise, moreover, the starker opposition between mortal and immortal than in the equivalent Homeric scene. The effect of this is not only to magnify the heroism of Hippomedon but also to highlight the different implications of theomachy in the two epics: where Homer often undercuts the elevation granted Achilles' *aristeia* by drawing attention to divine support, Statius pushes to the brink the notion that a mortal on his own might just overcome the gods, a notion we shall examine in greater detail in Chapter 8.

Flaminius, the Agon, and Intertextual Characterisation

In *Punica* 5, just before the fateful battle of Trasimene, Silius narrates an agon between the consul Flaminius and a certain Valerius Corvinus over the notoriously ill omens observed as the Roman army marches to meet the Carthaginians.[45] Silius exploits the freedom provided by the epic genre to exaggerate the prodigies: whereas Livy, for instance, records that Flaminius fell from his horse and that one of the standards could not be pulled from the ground, Silius describes, among other unsettling occurrences, the earth bleeding at the removal of the standards (*Pun.* 5.66–9) and even spectacular signs sent by Jupiter himself (*Pun.* 5.70–4):[46]

> ac super haec diuum genitor terrasque fretumque
> concutiens tonitru Cyclopum rapta caminis
> fulmina Tyrrhenas Thrasymenni torsit in undas,
> ictusque aetheria per stagna patentia flamma
> fumauit lacus atque arserunt fluctibus ignes.

> Moreover, the father of the gods shook land and sea
> with thunder and from the furnaces of the Cyclopes he seized
> bolts of lightning and hurled them against the Tuscan waves
>   of Trasimene,
> and struck by heavenly flame throughout its suffering waters
> the lake smoked and fires burned on its tides.

The image of the god hurling thunderbolts provides more than a splash of epic colour—it makes the presence of the divine an explicit feature of the episode,

---

[44] McNelis 2007: 137, following Dewar 1991: 144, argues that the outdoing of Homer lies in Hippomedon's greater success against the river compared to Achilles.

[45] This section of the chapter is a slightly revised version of Chaudhuri 2013.

[46] On Silius' use of sources here see Lucarini 2004: 113–14, Pomeroy 2010: 30–1. Livy 22.3.11–12 reports the prodigies, on which see Levene 1993: 38–43. Silius' omen of the bull fleeing the altar (*Pun.* 5.63–5) hints at the similarly inauspicious attempt to sacrifice a calf when Flaminius entered office (Livy 21.63.13–14), as well as alluding to Verg. *Aen.* 2.223–4 (cf. Spaltenstein 1986: 340); Lovatt 2013a: 63 sees allusion to Luc. 7.151–84. Cf. Cic. *Div.* 1.77 = Coelius fr. 20P.

which therefore has a direct bearing on the substance of the argument between Flaminius and Corvinus on the validity of omens as an index of divine favour or disfavour.

The agon itself, unlike the prodigies, has no equivalent in the sources. Although Polybius and Livy report the consul's rashness, impiety, and the disagreement with his advisors over military strategy, the dispute isn't framed in terms of the interpretation of omens, and no individual is singled out.[47] Cicero, following Coelius Antipater, does record a disagreement between Flaminius and the *pullarius*, but the exchange extends only to a few words, which are much transformed and expanded in Silius' *agon* (Cic. *Div*. 1.77 = Coelius fr. 20P). Indeed, the figure of Corvinus, who appears neither in other sources nor anywhere else within the *Punica*, seems to be a fiction invented solely for the purpose of this agon.[48] Moreover, Silius draws particular attention to the scene through the emotional intensity of the narrator's voice immediately prior to Corvinus' introduction (*Pun*. 5.75–8):

> heu uani monitus frustraque morantia Parcas
> prodigia! heu fatis superi certare minores!
> atque hic, egregius linguae nomenque superbum,
> Coruinus...
>
> Alas for futile warnings and prodigies vainly delaying
> the Parcae! Alas for gods unable to contend with the fates!
> At this point, excelling in speech and of distinguished name,
> Corvinus...

The repeated mentions of fate—in both personified and abstract forms—succinctly emphasise the inevitability of the coming disaster despite Corvinus' intervention, but they also prepare the way for the subsequent argument to elaborate on the role of human beliefs and actions—specifically, those of Flaminius—in leading to such a dire outcome.

In adapting the historiographical character of Flaminius and inserting him into a fictitious agon, Silius naturally drew inspiration from the epic tradition. The argument between one character mindful of omens and another dismissive of supernatural knowledge exemplifies an epic topos with roots stretching back to Homer, and passing through Apollonius Rhodius to Silius' contemporary Statius.[49] In each of these instances, as with Flaminius and Corvinus, imprudent scepticism—or, in the more extreme cases, impious folly—contends with pious caution. As several critics have noted, however, Silius' scene has particularly strong resemblances, especially in Flaminius' speech, to Statius'

---

[47] Polyb. 3.80.3–82.8, Livy 22.3.4–14. Polybius mentions neither omens nor impiety.

[48] For the supposed genealogy of this Corvinus see below.

[49] I discuss these examples of the topos below. See also Neri 1986: 2016–17, Fantham 2006, Stover 2009, Lovatt 2013a: 60–5.

agon between the impious Capaneus and the seer Amphiaraus in *Thebaid* 3.[50] While history, and indeed epic, has generally not been kind to Flaminius, an intertextual kinship with the theomach Capaneus threatens to turn his rashness and neglect of ritual into a far greater impiety.[51] Is this simply another example of epic hyperbole, or is there something more to be said for reading one character against the other?

Flaminius provides an apt example of Silius' typological characterisation, whereby different characters are linked by common features across the *Punica* in order to offer a sustained examination of a particular type of heroism and its attendant strengths and weaknesses.[52] These links are not only intratextual but also intertextual as Silius accommodates within his range of characterisation allusions to key figures within the preceding epic and historiographical traditions. Because of the difficulty in establishing any relative chronology for the *Punica* and the *Thebaid*, however, critics have been reluctant to press the intertextuality between Flaminius and Capaneus.[53] By focusing on the similarities and differences between the two heroes across a range of shared features—valour, impiety, and Gigantomachic imagery—the following argument attempts to explain the implications of the intertextuality not only for a reading of Flaminius but also for his place within the heroic economy of the *Punica*. I use Capaneus as a foil here, not as a focus of the enquiry in his own right, partly for reasons of scope and partly because the relationship between the two characters is not symmetrical: given his relatively greater importance within the *Thebaid*, Capaneus informs a larger proportion of Flaminius' characterisation than vice versa.[54]

TOPOI AND INTERTEXTUALITY

The agon over omens is part of a long-standing epic topos, which has certain standard characteristics, such as a disregard for the divine, accusations of cowardice, and overconfidence in one's might. Not all instances of the topos are exactly alike, however, and two canonical examples are worth looking at in order to show how Silius' and Statius' versions have a particular affinity. The first example of the type occurs between Hector and Polydamas in *Iliad* 12 just

---

[50] Neri 1986: 2035–6, Ripoll 1998: 340–2, Nau 2005: 170–2. On Capaneus, see Chapter 8 below.

[51] On Flaminius' flaws see Ahl, Davis, and Pomeroy 1986: 2521; Ripoll 1998: 341–2.

[52] J. Griffin 1985: 183–97, discussing Vergil, offers a classic account of the benefits of reading characters typologically. See also Ariemma 2010, on the *Punica*, which focuses primarily on Varro and his connections to Flaminius and Minucius (cf. Marks 2005: 19–20 with footnotes, 23 n. 29; Tipping 2010a: 109–10). On exemplarity as a model through which to understand heroism in the *Punica* see Tipping 2010a: 7–13. On Livy's similar method of typological characterisation see Chapter 3 of Levene 2010, esp. 170–2 on Flaminius.

[53] On the chronology see p. 196 above.

[54] Moreover, other characters, such as Vergil's Mezentius and Ovid's Lycaon, have considerably greater bearing than Flaminius on Statius' Capaneus (see Chapter 8).

before the Trojans breach the Achaean wall, an action that will eventually lead to the return of Achilles to the fighting and to Hector's death.[55] When the Trojans are alarmed by an inauspicious bird omen, Polydamas warns Hector of the dire implications and recommends that they call off the attack on the ships, concluding that 'this is how a prophet would respond, who understood the portents clearly in his heart, and the people would listen' (ὧδέ χ' ὑποκρίναιτο θεοπρόπος, ὃς σάφα θυμῷ / εἰδείη τεράων καὶ οἱ πειθοίατο λαοί, *Il.* 12.228–9). Hector replies by setting up an opposition between his own confidence in the support of Zeus and the meaninglessness of bird omens (*Il.* 12.233–43):

> εἰ δ' ἐτεὸν δὴ τοῦτον ἀπὸ σπουδῆς ἀγορεύεις,
> ἐξ ἄρα δή τοι ἔπειτα θεοὶ φρένας ὤλεσαν αὐτοί,
> ὃς κέλεαι Ζηνὸς μὲν ἐριγδούποιο λαθέσθαι
> βουλέων, ἅς τέ μοι αὐτὸς ὑπέσχετο καὶ κατένευσε·
> τύνη δ' οἰωνοῖσι τανυπτερύγεσσι κελεύεις
> πείθεσθαι, τῶν οὔ τι μετατρέπομ' οὐδ' ἀλεγίζω
> εἴτ' ἐπὶ δεξί' ἴωσι πρὸς ἠῶ τ' ἠέλιόν τε,
> εἴτ' ἐπ' ἀριστερὰ τοί γε ποτὶ ζόφον ἠερόεντα.
> ἡμεῖς δὲ μεγάλοιο Διὸς πειθώμεθα βουλῇ,
> ὃς πᾶσι θνητοῖσι καὶ ἀθανάτοισιν ἀνάσσει.
> εἷς οἰωνὸς ἄριστος ἀμύνεσθαι περὶ πάτρης.

> If you really say this in seriousness,
> then the gods themselves have surely destroyed your wits,
> you who urge me to forget the counsels of thundering Zeus,
> which he himself promised to me and assented to,
> while you bid me obey the omens of long-winged birds,
> which I neither look to nor heed in the slightest
> whether they fly on the right to the dawn and sun
> or on the left to the cloudy west.
> Let us obey the will of great Zeus,
> who rules over all mortals and immortals.
> The single best omen is to defend one's homeland.

It's important to note that Hector's opposition to Polydamas is based not on outright impiety, as we shall see in some of the later examples, but rather on a misplaced privileging of his own relationship to the gods, an error of which Flaminius, too, will be guilty. Hector goes on to assert that Polydamas' true motive for advocating withdrawal is cowardice (*Il.* 12.244–50):

> τίπτε σὺ δείδοικας πόλεμον καὶ δηϊοτῆτα;
> εἴ περ γάρ τ' ἄλλοι γε περὶ κτεινώμεθα πάντες

---

[55] On this scene, and Hector and Polydamas more generally, see Taplin 1992: 157–60, Redfield 1994: 143–53, Schofield 1986b: 18–22.

νηυσὶν ἐπ' Ἀργείων, σοὶ δ' οὐ δέος ἔστ' ἀπολέσθαι·
οὐ γάρ τοι κραδίη μενεδήϊος οὐδὲ μαχήμων.
εἰ δὲ σὺ δηϊοτῆτος ἀφέξεαι, ἠέ τιν' ἄλλον
παρφάμενος ἐπέεσσιν ἀποτρέψεις πολέμοιο,
αὐτίκ' ἐμῷ ὑπὸ δουρὶ τυπεὶς ἀπὸ θυμὸν ὀλέσσεις.

Why are you afraid of war and battle?
If all the rest of us die about
the ships of the Greeks, you should not fear to die;
for your heart is neither staunch nor warlike.
But if you flee the battle or persuading anyone else
with words turn them from the war,
straightaway struck by my spear you will lose your life.

Hector's accusations and threats, which are also formative for the topos, do not prevent him from responding more positively to Polydamas' advice in the following book, namely, that the Trojans should regroup before deciding whether to launch another assault or withdraw to the city (*Il.* 13.723–53). The opportunity for a more considered strategy is lost, however, when, with the consent of Zeus, the Trojans advance even to the point of setting fire to the Achaean ships, a success which turns to disaster when the tide of battle turns and the Trojans are caught far from the city. Later in the epic, after Achilles has routed the Trojans, Hector worries that if he retreats to the city he will have to endure Polydamas' reproaches for not heeding his earlier warnings to be more cautious (*Il.* 22.99–103). It is striking, however, that even when Hector imagines such reproaches, he doesn't conceive his fault as a misplaced trust in Zeus, but rather overconfidence in his own prowess: Ἕκτωρ ἧφι βίηφι πιθήσας ὤλεσε λαόν ('Hector has destroyed the army, trusting in his own might', *Il.* 22.107). It is this overconfidence in one's own strength and in one's individual capacity to determine the course of events that will come to typify the figure of the sceptical or impious hero.

The element of impiety appears more emphatically in the agon between Idas and the seer Idmon in Apollonius' *Argonautica*.[56] As Jason sits brooding during a feast, Idas interprets his reticence as cowardice and boastfully explains why there should be nothing to fear (Ap. Rhod. 1.466–71):

ἴστω νῦν δόρυ θοῦρον, ὅτῳ περιώσιον ἄλλων
κῦδος ἐνὶ πτολέμοισιν ἀείρομαι, οὐδέ μ' ὀφέλλει
Ζεὺς τόσον ὁσσάτιόν περ ἐμὸν δόρυ, μή νύ τι πῆμα
λοίγιον ἔσσεσθαι μηδ' ἀκράαντον ἄεθλον
Ἴδεω γ' ἑσπομένοιο, καὶ εἰ θεὸς ἀντιόῳτο·
τοῖόν μ' Ἀρήνηθεν ἀοσσητῆρα κομίζεις.

---

[56] See J. J. Clauss 1993: 79–80 and, on the scene's reception in Statius' *Thebaid*, Stover 2009, esp. 440–5.

> Let my rushing spear be witness now, with which beyond all others
> I carry off glory in wars—nor does Zeus aid me
> so much as my spear—that no grief
> shall be deadly nor any challenge unfulfilled
> while Idas follows, even if a god should encounter us;
> such an aid am I whom you bring from Arene.

In claiming to depend on his spear more than Zeus and in promising to overcome even a god, Idas is situated within a tradition of impious heroes in Greek literature, including Capaneus and Parthenopaeus in Aeschylus' *Seven Against Thebes*.[57] The seer Idmon responds that Idas' boasts dishonour the gods and thereby threaten to bring disaster; to illustrate his point he invokes the myth of the gigantic sons of Aloeus (Ap. Rhod. 1.481–4):

> τοῖα φάτις καὶ τοὺς πρὶν ἐπιφλύειν μακάρεσσιν
> υἷας Ἀλωιάδας, οἷς οὐδ᾽ ὅσον ἰσοφαρίζεις
> ἠνορέην, ἔμπης δὲ θοοῖς ἐδάμησαν ὀιστοῖς
> ἄμφω Λητοΐδαο, καὶ ἴφθιμοί περ ἐόντες.

> Such boasts, the story goes, the sons of Aloeus poured out
> against the gods, whom you in no way equal
> in strength, but they were nevertheless both slain by the arrows
> of Leto's son, though they were mighty.

The sons of Aloeus, whose feats were often conflated or confused with the Gigantomachy, provide a well-known paradigm of human overreaching. In the *Iliad*, for instance, the goddess Dione cites another story of the Aloidae binding Ares as an example of mortal transgression, though she leaves implicit their later downfall at the hands of Apollo (*Il.* 5.383–91).[58] The dismissal of omens, and by extension of prophetic figures, implies a disregard for the basic sources of authority by which the will of the gods was known in the ancient world. It's a small step from there, passages like Apollonius' suggest, to an impious disregard for the gods themselves, analogous to mythological acts of theomachy. Idas finally rounds off the agon by casting doubt on the power of prophecy and threatening the seer (Ap. Rhod. 1.487–91):

> ἄγρει νυν τόδε σῇσι θεοπροπίῃσιν ἐνίσπες,
> εἰ καὶ ἐμοὶ τοιόνδε θεοὶ τελέουσιν ὄλεθρον
> οἷον Ἀλωιάδῃσι πατὴρ τεὸς ἐγγυάλιξε·
> φράζεο δ᾽ ὅππως χεῖρας ἐμὰς σόος ἐξαλέοιο,
> χρειὼ θεσπίζων μεταμώνιον εἴ κεν ἁλῴης.

---

[57] Cf. *Septem* 427–31 (Capaneus) and 529–32 (Parthenopaeus). Wißmann 2000: 453–4 argues that Apollonius' agon alludes to the confrontation of Tydeus and Amphiaraus in the *Septem*.
[58] See Chapter 1.

> Come now, tell me this in your prophecies,
> whether the gods will fulfil the same ruin for me too
> which your father promised to the Aloidae.
> But consider how you might escape from my hands unharmed
> if you are caught making a prophecy empty as the wind.

Where Hector had warned Polydamas neither to flee nor to dissuade the Trojans from battle on the basis of his interpretation of omens, Idas threatens Idmon not for actions consequent upon prophetic interpretation but for the act of interpretation itself. Apollonius' agon thus offers a starker and more fundamental opposition between attitudes to omens and prophecies, which accompanies an equally sharp contrast in attitudes to the gods themselves.

Silius and Statius draw on different aspects of this tradition in their own versions of the topos.[59] Both scenes describe ill omens pointing to military disaster, which in the *Thebaid* take the form of an elaborate augury and bird omen figuring the deaths of the Argive champions.[60] An agon then follows in which sceptical dismissals and exhortations to battle (by Flaminius and Capaneus, respectively) militate against the insistence on the validity of omens as signs of divine will (by Corvinus and Amphiaraus). To the extent that Corvinus also offers strategic advice to wait for the other consul (*Pun.* 5.96–100), he combines the historiographical record of disagreement between Flaminius and his aides with the warnings of Polydamas in *Iliad* 13. What sets the Statian agon apart from the other intertexts as a compelling comparandum for the Silian passage, however, is the combination of language and context. A few passages in particular, laid out in the table below, demonstrate clear overlap in detail and diction between Flaminius and Capaneus (I have emphasised those Latin words common to, or sharing a similar function in, both sets of passages).[61]

Flaminius' claims about the sword as its own augur, the superstition of omens, and the sufficiency of valour as a divine force all have close counterparts in Capaneus' language.[62] Capaneus also tells Amphiaraus not 'to postpone the day of battle with veins and the sighting of birds' (*uenisque aut alite uisa / bellorum proferre diem*, *Theb.* 3.665–6), an order which could just as easily be given by Flaminius to Corvinus. Moreover, Flaminius' indignation at the prospect of being forced to hold his position while Hannibal continues to

---

[59] See Juhnke 1972: 83–5, with a catalogue of Homeric parallels listed on p. 388; Neri 1986: 2016 n. 233, 2035. On the Statian agon in its own right, see Chapter 8.

[60] *Theb.* 3.460–551. Vessey 1973: 154, Fantham 2006: 155, and Stover 2009: 446 all suggest an intertextual connection between the Statian augury and the competing interpretations of a bird omen by Liger and Bogus at *Pun.* 4.101–42. On both scenes see Ripoll 2002: 936–60.

[61] For earlier references in the scholarship to these similarities cf. p. 216 n. 50 above.

[62] Cf. also *uanis auibus* (*Theb.* 3.652) and *classica* (*Theb.* 3.662) with the *Punica* passages above, and *inertia* (*Theb.* 3.660) with *inerti* (*Pun.* 5.121). Both Capaneus and Flaminius have a common source in Vergil's Mezentius (cf. *Aen.* 10.773, Ripoll 1998: 341–2), who in turn looks back to Apollonius' Idas (cf. S. J. Harrison 1991: 258).

Punica	
quippe monent superi. similes ne fingite uobis, / classica qui tremitis, diuos. sat magnus in hostem **augur** adest **ensis**, pulchrumque et milite dignum auspicium Latio, quod in armis **dextera** praestat. *Pun.* 5.117–20	Sure, the gods warn us! Don't imagine the gods similar to you, /who tremble at the clarion call. The sword is a great enough /augur against the enemy, and it is an omen both beautiful /and worthy of a Roman soldier that my right hand shows in arms.
deforme sub armis uana superstitio est; dea sola in pectore **Virtus** bellantum uiget. *Pun.* 5.125–7	For armed men /empty superstition is a disgrace; valour is the only goddess /that flourishes in the hearts of warriors.
nam dum nos **augur** et extis quaesitae fibrae uanusque **moratur** haruspex ... *Pun.* 5.162–3	For while the augur and the fibres /sought from the entrails and the empty soothsayer delay us ...
Thebaid	
uirtus mihi numen et **ensis**, / quem teneo! *Theb.* 3.615–16	Valour is my god and the sword that I hold!
tuus o furor **auguret** uni ista tibi, ut serues uacuos inglorius annos et tua non umquam Tyrrhenus tempora circum clangor eat. quid uota uirum meliora **moraris**? *Theb.* 3.648–51	Let that frenzy of yours augur those things for you /alone, that you may preserve your empty years without glory /and the Tyrrhenian clangour may never surround /your head. Why do you delay the better wishes of men?
illic **augur** ego *Theb.* 3.668	There [in battle] I shall be augur
sunt et mihi prouida **dextrae** / omina Cf. *Theb.* 10.485–6	Prescient too are the omens of my right hand

lay waste to Italy and while the Roman defeat at the Trebia haunts the consul's dreams (*Pun.* 5.121–9) corresponds to Capaneus' outrage at the thought of the ambush of Tydeus going unavenged (*Theb.* 3.653–5).[63] This overlap goes well beyond any similarities with the other examples of the topos: by contrast, in the *Iliad*, Hector does not declare his sword to be a substitute for prophecy, nor his valour to be a god, and in the *Argonautica*, where Idas does make similar claims, his argument with Idmon does not concern the interpretation of a set of omens, nor the decision whether to fight. The application to Flaminius of language used of Capaneus, a theomach who will challenge Jupiter to battle in Book 10 of the *Thebaid*, appears strikingly disproportional even accounting for poetic licence. Yet it's precisely the identification of the intertextuality—whether or not Silius was writing with Capaneus in mind—that invites an enquiry into the nature and extent of Flaminius' impiety.

---

[63] For the historiographical source of Flaminius' rhetoric see Livy 22.3.10, Cic. *Div.* 1.77 = Coelius fr. 20P.

A SPECTRUM OF IMPIETY

When Corvinus and the other Romans pray that Flaminius not 'struggle with the gods' (*caelicolis contendere*, *Pun.* 5.104), they mean that he should not defy the omens.[64] The act of disregarding omens before battle recalls other episodes in Roman history, such as Claudius Pulcher's drowning of the sacred chickens during the First Punic War, all of which are followed by Roman defeat.[65] This sceptical attitude to omens marks Flaminius as one who defies standard religious practice, and harmonises with the senatorial criticism recorded by Livy—angered by the new consul's decision to avoid his religious duties at Rome and enter office at Ariminum, they protest that 'Gaius Flaminius was waging war not only with the senate, but now even with the immortal gods' (*non cum senatu modo sed iam cum dis immortalibus C. Flaminium bellum gerere*, Livy 21.63.6). Flaminius' Capaneus-like rhetoric, however, retrospectively casts the shadow of a greater impiety over the significance of the words *caelicolis contendere*.[66]

Whether Silius directly alludes to Statius or the two heroes simply share a structural and lexical similarity within epic discourse, the phrase *caelicolis contendere* points to the type of literary role Flaminius is about to play and the likely consequences for the army. The Statian intertext suggests that Flaminius, far from comprehending the metaliterary hint not to act like a theomach, insists on over-assiduously playing the role of impious hero, who might literally fight the gods. And yet, unlike Capaneus, Flaminius' antagonism to the divine never rises above his dismissal of the omens. So, whereas Capaneus goes as far as to speak of the gods as a human fiction (*primus in orbe deos fecit timor! Theb.* 3.661), Flaminius readily acknowledges the gods.[67] Indeed, he even encourages one of his men to carry the *spolia opima* to the temple of Jupiter (*Pun.* 5.167–8)

---

[64] *Pun.* 5.103–4: *nunc superos de Flaminio, nunc deinde precari / Flaminium, ne caelicolis contendere perstet* ('they pray now that the gods do not fight over Flaminius, now that Flaminius does not persist in struggling against the gods'). Though the Romans do not know it, there is a sense in which Flaminius, far from opposing the gods, actually facilitates their will, for Juno herself is said to have chosen Flaminius to bring about this defeat (*Pun.* 4.709–10).

[65] On Claudius Pulcher see Cic. *Div.* 1.29 and 2.20 (both books of the *De Divinatione* discuss several examples of generals ignoring omens, including Flaminius; cf. *Nat. D.* 2.7–8), Livy, *Per.* 19, Suet. *Tib.* 2.2. Among the inauspicious signs described by Silius before the battle of Trasimene, the sacred chickens refuse to eat (*Pun.* 5.59–62); cf. Cic. *Div.* 1.77 = Coelius fr. 20P.

[66] Cf. Neri 1986: 2036. Silius subtly foreshadows the episode's theomachic theme in the aetiology of the lake's name: 'for you, Trasimene, could compete in beauty with the gods' (*nam forma certare deis, Thrasymenne, ualeres*, *Pun.* 5.16). Cf. *Pun.* 5.76: *heu fatis superi certare minores!* ('alas for gods unable to contend with the fates!').

[67] For the apparent inconsistency in Capaneus' attitude to the gods see Chapter 8. Flaminius' language can also hint at more radical beliefs: one may read as more than rhetorical, for instance, the claim that *Virtus* is the 'only goddess' (*dea sola*, *Pun.* 5.126) in the hearts of warriors (cf. Livy 22.5.2); and when Flaminius tells Corvinus not to 'imagine' the gods to be similar to him, the verb *fingite* (*Pun.* 5.117) raises the possibility that gods are simply fashioned to fit human conceptions. On the divinisation of *uirtus* in the republic see McDonnell 2006: 209–12. For Lovatt 2013a: 65, 'Flaminius' rhetoric of secular scorn for sacred authority is itself a cover for his true self-absorption'.

and another to perform the rites of Apollo on Mount Soracte (*Pun.* 5.179–81). Analogous sentiments are, unsurprisingly, never voiced by Capaneus.

The intertextuality here thus reveals a spectrum of impiety, at the one end of which lie familiar episodes of aristocratic arrogance and rashness, which manifests itself primarily in the rejection of ritual (as with the drowning of the sacred chickens), and at the other end of which lies all-out theomachy. Invoking that spectrum, I suggest, introduces into the *Punica* an important discourse on impiety and the human relationship with the divine. Silius ostentatiously reinserts the gods into his historical epic, a narrative choice not just the opposite of Lucan's but also, necessarily, much more emphatic than Livy's, whose divine apparatus, such as it is, responds to the generic demands of historiography rather than epic.[68] Silius' gods, rather, descend from the interventionist gods of Vergil—they have anthropomorphised form, they involve themselves in the action and the plot of the poem, and they have favourites with whom they directly interact, whether Juno's guardianship of Hannibal or Venus' enfeebling of the Carthaginians at Capua.[69] With such a strong divine presence in the poem, the fate of Rome, and thus the course of the epic, hangs in part on the direct connection between actions on earth and in heaven: Hannibal, repeatedly cast as impious, is a threat to Rome; Scipio, repeatedly cast as pious, is its saviour. That Flaminius' impiety goes hand in hand with his jeopardising of Roman fortunes is part of the historiographical tradition, to be sure, but Silius has clearly gone beyond the parameters of his source. Flaminius' intertextual similarity to Capaneus encourages us to read his language not as mere epic window dressing for a historical account, but rather, and more ambitiously, as a component or index of the heroic and theological economy of the *Punica*. Flaminius' characterisation, in fact, dovetails with the presentation of Hannibal and Scipio, the iconic heroes of the epic—a dualism highlighted by the Statian intertext.[70]

IRONY, REVERSAL, AND FORESHADOWING

The role of Flaminius as counterfoil or precursor to other characters in the *Punica*, especially in terms of his relationship to the divine, emerges from the ambivalence of his heroism. In particular, various aspects of his characterisation associate him with one side or the other in the mythical Gigantomachy, which suggests further overlap with Capaneus and has deeper implications for the construction of heroism in the *Punica*. As part of this larger system of

---

[68] For Livy's manipulation of religious material to fit the requirements of the genre see Levene 1993. For Silius' handling of the gods see Feeney 1991: 301–12.

[69] Juno, for instance, saves Hannibal's life at Zama at *Pun.* 17.567–80; Venus intervenes at Capua at *Pun.* 11.385–409.

[70] On Capaneus' ambivalence with respect to the gods and Giants see Chapter 8.

associations, Flaminius rhetorically casts the Gallic tribe of the Boii, whom he had defeated in an earlier campaign, as Giants (*Pun.* 5.110–13):

> quas ego tunc animas dextra, quae corpora fudi
> irata tellure sata et uix uulnere uitam
> reddentes uno! iacuere ingentia membra
> per campos magnisque premunt nunc ossibus arua.
>
> What lives I took with my right hand, what bodies I laid low,
> born from the angry earth and scarcely giving up their life
> at one blow! Their huge limbs lay throughout the plains
> and now they press the fields with their large bones.

Like the comparison between Crixus and Mimas in Book 4, Flaminius' allusion to the Giants primarily rests on the Gauls' proverbially imposing stature, though it may also hint at the myth of their descent from the Giant Keltos.[71] The association is clearly signalled, moreover, by *irata tellure sata*, which alludes to the myth of the Giants' origin from Earth.[72] Consequently, the rhetorical conceit also represents Flaminius himself as a Hercules- or Jupiter-like figure, and in any case as a hero who restores order against the destructive violence of the Giants.

Silius, however, goes on to undermine the stability of Flaminius' self-aggrandising rhetoric. When the consul readies himself for battle, Silius draws particular attention to the helmet Flaminius had won in the earlier battle against the Boii, in which he defeated their king, Gergenus (*Pun.* 5.130–9):[73]

> nec mora iam medio coetu signisque sub ipsis
> postrema aptabat nulli exorabilis arma.
> aere atque aequorei tergo flauente iuuenci
> cassis erat munita uiro, cui uertice surgens
> triplex crista iubas effudit crine Sueuo;
> Scylla super fracti contorquens pondera remi
> instabat saeuosque canum pandebat hiatus,
> nobile Gergeni spolium, quod rege superbus
> Boiorum caeso capiti illacerabile uictor
> aptarat pugnasque decus portabat in omnes.

---

[71] Spaltenstein 1986: 345. The association goes back to the Great Altar of Pergamum, which depicted the Gigantomachy in commemoration of the defeat of the Gauls (cf. Hardie 1986: 120–43).

[72] Cf. *Pun.* 4.275–6. For the Giants as children of Earth see, canonically, Hes. *Theog.* 183–6. Cf. Verg. *Aen.* 4.178–83, where Earth, angry with the gods (*ira inritata deorum*, *Aen.* 4.178), is said to have given birth to Fama, sister of the Giants Coeus and Enceladus. Further hints of the Gigantomachy may also be found in the multiple blows required to kill the Gauls (cf. the deaths of several Giants described in the account of the Gigantomachy at Apollod. *Bibl.* 1.34–8), and in the sound of *premunt ossibus*, which may allude to the Giants' piling of the mountains of Ossa and Pelion (cf., e.g., Sen. *Thy.* 812, *Aetna* 49).

[73] The reading *Gergeni* (following Delz) is problematic (cf. *Gargeni* in Duff's Loeb), but the name of the chief—whether or not that is what is designated by *Gergeni*—doesn't affect the particular argument made here.

> Now, without delay, amidst his company and by the
>   standards themselves,
> he put on his arms for the last time, open to no entreaty.
> The hero's helmet was strengthened with bronze
> and the tawny hide of a sea calf, and from its top rose
> a triple crest spreading a mane of Suevian hair;
> a Scylla brandishing a heavy broken oar
> stood above and opened the savage jaws of her dogs:
> the noble spoil of Gergenus, which—unbreakable—the proud
> victor had put on his head after slaying the king of the Boii,
> and he bore the trophy into all his battles.

The act of putting on an opponent's arms in epic has several inauspicious precedents, such as Hector's donning of the armour of Patroclus in the *Iliad* or Turnus' wearing of Pallas' sword belt in the *Aeneid*.[74] Silius, too, emphasises the direct line between Flaminius' death and his earlier triumph over Gergenus by the repetition of the verb *apto* before the battle of Trasimene (*postrema aptabat arma*, *Pun.* 5.131) and after the defeat of the Gallic king (*aptarat*, *Pun.* 5.139). Furthermore, just before Flaminius' death, Ducarius bids his fellow Gauls avenge the earlier defeat (*Pun.* 5.652–5):

> nec uos paeniteat, populares, fortibus umbris
> hoc mactare caput. nostros hic curribus egit
> insistens uictos alta ad Capitolia patres.
> ultrix hora uocat.
>
> Fear not, my countrymen, to sacrifice this life
> to the brave shades. This is the man who stood in his chariot
> and drove our defeated fathers to the high Capitol.
> The hour of vengeance calls.

By wearing the helmet, Flaminius comes to resemble his erstwhile opponents, and through his disastrous leadership he himself fulfils the vengeance desired by the Gauls. A further consequence of the assimilation of the consul with a Gaul, however, follows from Flaminius' own rhetoric: his presenting the earlier battle as a Gigantomachy is now turned on its head, as he resembles not only a

---

[74] The ecphrasis of Flaminius' helmet (*Pun.* 5.130–9) also hints at further intertextuality with Capaneus, this time with the catalogue in *Thebaid* 4, especially when the passage is taken together with the two lines immediately following (*loricam induitur; tortos huic nexilis hamos / ferro squama rudi permixtoque asperat auro*, *Pun.* 5.140–1). Compare the diction of the *Punica* passage with the similar words, cognates and sounds at *Theb.* 4.165–74: *uertice, iuuencis, terga, super, aenae* (with Silius' *aere*), *squalet* (with *squama*), *triplici, ramosa* (with *remi*), *aspera, fuluo* (with *flauente*), *auro, torpens* (with *contorquens*), *ferro, nexilis*. Many of these words represent standard vocabulary for the type scene, of course, and Spaltenstein 1986: 347–8 has pointed out other, Vergilian, source passages, but the density of overlap with Statius suggests that a more specific connection to Capaneus is present. On the Statian passage see Parkes 2012: 126–30.

Gaul but by extension also a Giant. At this point, the previous Statian intertexts acquire even greater potency, since the *Thebaid* describes Capaneus as the most Giant-like of epic heroes, who even bears a representation of a Giant on the crest of his helmet.[75] In using language in the agon that fits with the characterisation of a theomach, Flaminius thus pre-empts and strengthens his assimilation to a Giant, a resemblance that itself emerges from his own ambivalent allusions to Gigantomachy.

Flaminius' agon with Corvinus plays on and deepens his complex relations to both Gaul and Giant. Like Flaminius, Corvinus' role in this regard is encapsulated in the description of his helmet (*Pun.* 5.78–80):

> Coruinus, Phoebea sedet cui casside fulua
> ostentans ales proauitae insignia pugnae,
> plenus et ipse deum...
>
> Corvinus, on whose golden helmet sits the bird of Phoebus,
> showing the emblem of his ancestral battle,
> and he himself full of the god...

As his name and the mention of an ancestral battle indicate, Corvinus traces his descent from Marcus Valerius Corvus (or Corvinus; both names are attested).[76] Livy records Corvus' defeat of a Gaul in single combat with the mysterious aid of a raven that suddenly sat on the Roman's helmet and attacked his opponent during the duel (Livy 7.26.1–5). In identifying Corvinus in this way, Silius offers the reader two rival claimants to be the most pre-eminent opponent of the Gauls, either Corvinus through his familial legacy or Flaminius through his defeat of the Boii. In arguing against the genealogically loaded figure of Corvinus, however, Flaminius already sets himself in opposition to an anti-Gallic figure and thus hints at the multiple roles he will play as both Roman commander and Gaul.

The description of the raven as *Phoebea ales* follows the standard mythological association of the bird with Apollo.[77] In drawing attention to a divine element, Silius' periphrasis for *coruus* recalls that the raven in Valerius Corvus' duel was viewed as a portent indicating the will of the gods.[78] The mention of Phoebus also hints at Corvinus' prophetic status, especially when Silius states that his speech is inspired by the gods (*plenus et ipse deum*, 5.80).[79] This

---

[75] For Capaneus as Giant see, e.g., *Theb.* 10.849–52, 4.175–6 (the Giant on his helmet; on this and other Gigantic associations in the catalogue scene see S. J. Harrison 1992).

[76] See Volkmann, s.v. 'Valerius' (137), *RE* VII A, 2413–18, with Oakley 1997: 238–9, on Livy's Corvus.

[77] Cf. Spaltenstein 1986: 342.

[78] Livy 7.26.4: *quod primo ut augurium caelo missum laetus accepit tribunus, precatus deinde, si diuus, si diua esset qui sibi praepetem misisset, uolens propitius adesset* ('the tribune first received this happily as an omen sent from heaven, then he prayed that whoever sent the bird—whether god or goddess—be favourable and propitious').

[79] Cf. Spaltenstein 1986: 342: 'Sil. s'inspire aussi de la réputation prophétique du corbeau, qui justifie la prescience de Corvinus'.

seer-like characterisation, implied already by the structural role Corvinus occupies within the topos of the agon, and similar to that of Polydamas, Idmon and Amphiaraus, is further strengthened by Corvinus' explicit regard for the gods (*ne dedignare secundos / exspectare deos*, 'do not disdain to wait for the favour of the gods', *Pun.* 5.87–8). Although Corvinus plays the part of the pious counsellor well, Silius invites the reader to see a profound doubleness entailed in Flaminius' opposition. On the one hand, and on his own rhetoric, Flaminius appears as the Gaul-killing (and thus also Giant-killing) hero who has regard for Jupiter and Apollo; on the other hand, however, his hostility to Corvinus symbolically places him in opposition to Apollo, as a Gaul/Giant figure whose Capaneus-like speech pits him against Jupiter, and indeed all the gods.

Intriguingly, the oscillation between Giant and anti-Giant in Flaminius' characterisation corresponds to the grander, and more explicit, dialectic Statius uses for Capaneus: though much more consistently Giant-like than Flaminius, Capaneus too figures himself as a Giant-killer when he threatens a serpent sacred to Jupiter: *at non mea uulnera.../.../ effugies.../.../ non, si consertum super haec mihi membra Giganta / subueheres* ('you will not escape my wounds... not even if you carried a Giant upon those limbs to battle against me', *Theb.* 5.565–70).[80] In itself, the double association of an epic hero with Giant and anti-Giant is nothing new: as we saw in Chapter 2, Vergil famously compares Aeneas to Aegaeon, a simile that challenges the reader to reflect on the nature of the hero's piety. But what sets Flaminius and Capaneus apart from that kind of ambivalence is the explicit way in which their own rhetoric, not just the voice of the poet, plays with the theme of the Gigantomachy. Both Flaminius and Capaneus knowingly draw on the imagery of the Giants in order to magnify their own heroism, though they do so without the self-awareness to see the full implications for themselves.

Flaminius' oscillation between Giant and anti-Giant is all the more striking because it reflects a larger dualism fundamental to the heroism of the *Punica*— the tension between the Gigantism of Hannibal and the Jovian symbolism of Scipio.[81] The former, as we shall see in the next chapter, will come perilously close to theomachy when he attacks Rome in the face of Jupiter's lightning in Book 12. Indeed, even his patron goddess, Juno, accepts that the hero has overreached: *cede deis tandem et Titania desine bella* ('yield to the gods at last and cease your Titanic wars', *Pun.* 12.725). Scipio, on the other hand, claims descent from Jupiter, an old legend that Silius relates through the mouth of Scipio's mother, Pomponia, in the underworld (*Pun.* 13.615–47).[82] Moreover, the closing

---

[80] On the duality of Capaneus here and elsewhere see Lovatt 2005: 133–6. For the common conception of Giants as 'serpent-legged' cf., e.g., *anguipedum* (Ov. *Met.* 1.184); they are frequently represented as such in art (*LIMC* s.v. *Gigantes*).

[81] See Fucecchi 1990b, Marks 2005: 168–9, Tipping 2010a: 68.

[82] Cf. Livy 26.19.6–7. The bibliography on the Scipionic legend is extensive, but Walbank 1967 remains seminal.

lines of the epic not only reiterate and legitimise the story but also compare Scipio in his triumph to Hercules after the Gigantomachy (*Pun.* 17.649–54):[83]

> aut cum Phlegraeis confecta mole Gigantum
> incessit campis tangens Tirynthius astra.
> salue, inuicte parens, non concessure Quirino
> laudibus ac meritis, non concessure Camillo.
> nec uero, cum te memorat de stirpe deorum,
> prolem Tarpei, mentitur Roma, Tonantis.

> ... or like the Tirynthian, having destroyed the might of the Giants,
> triumphed over the Phlegraean plains, touching the stars.
> Hail, undefeated father, not yielding to Quirinus
> in glory or merit, nor yielding to Camillus.
> Nor in truth, when she recalls your divine origins,
> does Rome lie that you are the offspring of the Tarpeian Thunderer.

With this apparent polarisation of Hannibal and Scipio in mind, let us turn back to Flaminius. The defeat at Trasimene suggests two interpretations of Flaminius' own Gigantism: either it's his impiety—his Giant-like quality—that leads to the disaster, as Corvinus' warning implies, or he isn't quite Giant-like enough and is simply bested by someone who plays that role more convincingly, that is, Hannibal.[84] We see a similar pattern in the case of Capaneus when in *Thebaid* 9 he kills Hypseus, son of the theomachic river Asopus; Hypseus may inherit some of his father's theomachic boldness, but he is no match for the ultimate theomach of the poem.[85] The pattern of being outperformed by a superior instantiation of the type is equally applicable to the relationship between Flaminius and Scipio. Flaminius' description of his defeat of the Gauls as a kind of Gigantomachy suggests a certain Jovian pretension, which is only partially substantiated in Flaminius' individual feats during the battle itself when his assault is compared to a storm sent by Jupiter (*Pun.* 5.384–91). But if any character can make the case for channelling the authority of Jupiter, however rhetorically, it is Scipio, whose supposed descent from the god is given such emphasis by the poet. Beyond the obvious follies of Flaminius' military strategy, then, in epic terms his failure seems to consist in not living up to the

---

[83] Cf. Hardie 1997a: 159–60, esp. 159: 'a resumptive allusion to a hero and a myth central to the imagery of the whole poem'.

[84] Moreover, Hannibal both associates himself, and is associated with, the Gauls: see, e.g., *Pun.* 2.33–5 (cf. Tipping 2010a: 65 n. 38 for further references). There is some irony in Flaminius' warning to the fleeing Roman soldiers that they 'are giving Hannibal fire and sword against the Tarpeian shrine of the Thunderer' (*uos in Tarpeia Tonantis / tecta faces ferrumque datis*, *Pun.* 5.635–6) when Flaminius himself has shown qualities that align him with a theomach.

[85] Asopus' theomachy is related at *Theb.* 7.320–7, Hypseus offers a theomachic prayer at *Theb.* 7.730–5, and Capaneus kills Hypseus at *Theb.* 9.546–59. That Statius is pitting one theomach type against another in sequence in *Thebaid* 9 is made clear by Hypseus' own triumph over the body of Hippomedon (*Theb.* 9.540–6), who had fought the river god Ismenus (*Theb.* 9.446–539).

potential of his own symbolism, which must ultimately be realised by other characters.

Such a typological intra- and intertextual approach clarifies the effect of the overlap with Statius' Capaneus for a reading of Flaminius: first, by sharpening the connection between Flaminius and Hannibal, the resemblance to Capaneus emphasises Flaminius impious and destructive nature; second, the points of contrast with Capaneus assimilate Flaminius more closely to an anti-Giant figure, like Scipio, and hence the Statian intertext emphasises Flaminius' failure to follow through on his Jovian posturing. Separating these opposing implications so neatly, however, is perhaps too clinical a dissection of Silius' method of characterisation. Indeed, such apparently clear distinctions can be a more generally problematic consequence of intertextuality as a reading practice. The tendency to atomise characters by identifying particular local sources for individual elements obscures the more complex intertextual structures that exist in the poem. Seeing the dualism within Flaminius as representing two contrasting types of heroism in the *Punica* already emphasises the composite nature of literary characterisation and the possibility of separating some qualities from others. It's important to remember, however, that these qualities exist within the unified body of Flaminius, whose identity and attributes should not be differentiated, explained, and evaluated in exclusively atomising ways.

The importance of this point emerges more clearly in light of recent scholarship, which has taken a rather dark view of the significance of Scipio's triumph at the close of the poem. For these critics, Scipio too has an inherent dualism in his character, and instead of ushering in an era of Roman glory, his supremacy is seen as instrumental in Rome's decline and as the fulfilment of what Hannibal had failed to accomplish.[86] This dualism, on the ambivalent reading of the *Punica*, is not unique to Scipio but rather has an apt precedent in Flaminius, though the relationship between them doesn't become fully visible until read as part of a greater discourse on impiety and heroism. That discourse is deepened by the intertextual links between Flaminius and Capaneus, which—whether or not they involve direct allusion—go well beyond anything in Livy or the earlier instances of the agon topos in emphasising the scene's Gigantomachic imagery and Flaminius' unawareness of the significance of his own impieties. Flaminius thus represents a more intractable problem in the very nature of epic heroism, namely, the difficulty of controlling or even harnessing destructive characteristics like Gigantism or impiety. This line of

[86] See, e.g., Tipping 2010a: 185–92 (cf. Tipping 2007: 235–9, 2010b: 215–18), Jacobs 2010: 137–9. See, *contra*, Marks 2005 for a positive account of Scipio. Note also the final image of Scipio's speech in the debate of Book 16, in which he argues for an assault on Carthage; let Hannibal attack Rome, Scipio declares, 'if he doesn't hear before then the temples of his people crackling in Roman flames' (*si templa suorum / non ante audierit Rutulis crepitantia flammis, Pun.* 16.696–7). On the one hand this is just revenge for Hannibal's own attempts at theomachy, and it is of a similar type to the positive, nationalistic theomachy depicted on the Shield of Aeneas. At the same time, however, the image has the disconcerting effect of casting Scipio as Hannibal's theomachic double.

interpretation, then, takes intertextuality not just as a guide to an epic's composition and narrative structure but rather as a way of approaching the interface between the microscopic relations among texts and their macroscopic implications.

Putting Vergil into Perspective

Critics have devoted considerable attention to Flavian epic's debt to the *Aeneid*, the importance of which will feature more clearly in the following chapters.[87] As this chapter has shown, however, Silius and Statius also owe a good deal to Greek epic, as well as to each other's experiments with that tradition.[88] For as much as they were returning to a more Vergilian epic model after the radicalism of Lucan's *Bellum Civile*, the increasing fascination with theomachy made Homer's repeated examinations of the theme of particular relevance. When Vergil had the heroes of the second half of the *Aeneid* vie to claim the mantle of Achilles, for example, the theomachic element surfaced only obliquely, as in the Aegaeon simile applied to Aeneas. However, if we compare just the opening of Statius' *Achilleid* quoted in the epigraph to this chapter, we observe not only Statius' ambition of representing Achilles directly but also the immediate sense of a tension between the hero and Jupiter. The 'feared offspring' to which Statius refers alludes to the prophecy that Thetis' son would surpass his father, and although Achilles is not Jupiter's son, the potential theomachic symbolism surrounding him is nevertheless the theme that Statius chooses to place front and centre.[89] For all the *Achilleid*'s much discussed playfulness in the two books Statius composed, we have no idea how the poem might have continued once Achilles entered battle.[90] Given these opening lines, however, and the theomachic preoccupations of the *Thebaid* and of the contemporary *Punica*, it's difficult to believe that the same concerns would not have played an important part in the remainder of the *Achilleid* too. As the two case studies in this chapter have shown, theomachy and its topoi not only offered the metapoetic opportunity for poets to match their heroes, and their works, with their predecessors, they also provided an idiom through which to reflect on the physics and ethics of human and Roman power.

---

[87] For the scholarship's focus on the *Aeneid* see p. 3.

[88] Compare Valerius Flaccus' return to Apollonius for inspiration.

[89] See Heslin 2005: 158–60. For the oblique presence of this prophecy in the *Iliad* see Chapter 1. Mendelsohn 1990: 297 n. 9 sees in the proem an allusion to Verg. *Ecl.* 4.7, a poem that analogises to divine birth the coming of a mortal saviour. By alluding both to mythological theomachy and (via Vergil) to dependence on an elevated human being, the opening of the *Achilleid* suggests the combined influence of epic heroism and imperial cult.

[90] On the *Achilleid*'s playfulness see, e.g., Hinds 2000: 236–44, Heslin 2005, Feeney 2004b. Barchiesi 1996 gives due weight to the theomachic energy of the poem.

7

The War of the Worlds
HANNIBAL AS THEOMACH IN SILIUS ITALICUS' *PUNICA*

> No, just the bare bones of a name, all rock and ice and storm and abyss. It makes no attempt to sound human. It is atoms and stars. It has the nakedness of the world before the first man—or of the cindered planet after the last.
>
> —FOSCO MARAINI

> As I said this, I suddenly beheld the figure of a man, at some distance, advancing towards me with superhuman speed. He bounded over the crevices in the ice, among which I had walked with caution; his stature also, as he approached, seemed to exceed that of man.
>
> —MARY SHELLEY

> This was the foulest and most lamentable crime to befall the Roman state since the foundation of the city. At a time when Rome had no foreign enemy, and when, if our customs had so allowed, the gods were favourably inclined, the temple of Jupiter Optimus Maximus, which had been founded with due auspices by our ancestors as a token of our empire, which neither Porsenna nor the Gauls could violate when the city was surrendered to the one and captured by the others, now was burned by the madness of the emperors.
>
> —TACITUS

> Rise, unknown avenger, from my bones.
>
> —VERGIL

Silius depicts Hannibal's theomachic qualities early in Book 1 of the *Punica* and in increasingly emphatic terms thereafter, culminating in the confrontation between the Carthaginian leader and Jupiter in Book 12. The poet thus combines a stereotypical portrait of Hannibal's impiety in the existing historiographical tradition with the literary figure of the theomach that had become especially prominent in imperial epic.[1] Critics have shown some of the many links between Hannibal and other theomachs, such as the Giants, Lucan's Caesar, or Statius' Capaneus, but from the point of view of a literary history of theomachy what is perhaps more striking is Hannibal's falling short of the paradigm.[2] His selective reverence for the gods, such as Juno and Hercules, means that he offers no real intellectual threat to the divine, as, for instance, Ovid's theomachs do. And his withdrawal from Rome in the face of Jupiter's opposition cuts short the theomachic encounter to which so much of the poem builds up. As we saw in the previous chapter, the most fully realised theomachy in Silius' poem is in fact performed by a Roman—the confrontation of the consul Scipio with the river Trebia in *Punica* 4. The theomachs of other epics, even if they ultimately fail in their ambitions, at least exert some kind of pressure on the gods through their antagonism; Hannibal, by contrast, for all his impiety, offers little by way of systematic opposition to the gods. Furthermore, Silius uses the hero's potentially most theomachic moments—his crossing of the Alps and assault on the Capitol—to underline the power and supremacy of Jupiter in the world of the *Punica*.

In adopting Hannibal as a means to devastate Rome, Juno at once elevates and limits the hero. For when Silius says that 'she dares to match him alone against the fates' (*hunc audet solum componere fatis*, *Pun.* 1.39), Hannibal, for all his extraordinary powers, appears as an instrument of the goddess's will. Juno's favour, however, doesn't prevent Silius from following historiographical tradition in describing Hannibal's disregard for the gods: *armato nullus diuum pudor* ('when armed he had no shame of gods', *Pun.* 1.58). Indeed, Hannibal himself confirms the characterisation through the oath his father, Hamilcar, has him swear as a young boy (*Pun.* 1.116–19):

> non superi mihi, non Martem cohibentia pacta,
> non celsae obstiterint Alpes Tarpeiaque saxa.
> hanc mentem iuro nostri per numina Martis,
> per manes, regina, tuos.
>
> The gods will not obstruct me, nor the treaty that
> constricts Mars, nor the lofty Alps and Tarpeian rocks.

---

[1] Livy 21.4.9: *nihil sancti, nullus deum metus, nullum ius iurandum, nulla religio* ('no regard for the sacred, no fear of the gods, no respect for oaths, no religious scruples'). On Livy's handling of the tradition see Levene 1993: 44–7, Moore 2010: 163–5.

[2] See, e.g., Fucecchi 1990b, Marks 2005: 168–9, Muecke 2007, R. J. Littlewood 2013: 206–11 (Giants); Ahl, Davis, and Pomeroy 1986: 2511–19, Marks 2005: 275 n. 106, Tipping 2010a: 89–92 (Caesar). The similarities between Hannibal and Capaneus require little elaboration and have already been well discussed by Ripoll 1998: 340–8; my separate treatment of the two characters in Chapters 7 and 8 illustrates key points of contrast. These differences derive not just from the two heroes' individual characterisation but also, more importantly, from the theologically dissimilar epics in which they appear (a larger distinction the two chapters also make clear).

> I vow this intent by the godhead of our own Mars,
> and by your shade, my Queen.

Despite Hannibal's dismissal of divine opposition, however, it's important to note the piety of sorts displayed in his sacred oath to a god and to a ghost.[3] Not only is Hannibal an instrument of Juno, then, his religiosity, however limited, also makes him a far less radical specimen of the theomach than some of his Ovidian and Lucanian predecessors and his Statian counterparts. When the Carthaginian priestess foresees the eventual confrontation of Hannibal and Jupiter, her language suggests a suitably elemental and sublime battle (*Pun.* 1.134–7):

> heu quaenam subitis horrescit turbida nimbis
> tempestas, ruptoque polo micat igneus aether!
> magna parant superi. tonat alti regia caeli,
> bellantemque Iouem cerno.

> Oh, what wild storm shudders with sudden
> clouds, and the fiery air flashes in the broken sky!
> The gods prepare great things. The palace of the high heaven thunders,
> and I see Jupiter going to war.

The passage builds expectation for the pivotal conflict during the siege of Rome in *Punica* 12, but we already know that for Hannibal, at least, this contest can be no more than a purely martial one, since he lacks the conceptual ambition of those theomachs who deny conventional theology. The lines immediately following the end of the prophecy only emphasise the absence of any intellectual threat from Hannibal's impiety (*Pun.* 1.137–9):

> uenientia fata
> scire ultra uetuit Iuno, fibraeque repente
> conticuere. latent casus longique labores.

> Juno forbade [the prophetess]
> to know further the coming fates, and the victims suddenly
> fell silent. Misfortunes and long labours lie hidden.

In this epic, the gods control access to knowledge, and theomachy symbolises no alternative model—at least, no seriously entertained one—of understanding the nature and operation of the world. The theological scrutiny traditionally applied by the theomach has become a strangely passive acceptance on the part of Hannibal.

Hannibal's two most clearly theomachic acts are the scaling of the Alps and the siege of Rome, two goals which are twinned in the hero's dreams (*Pun.* 1.64–5) and form part of a system of imagery linking the literal walls of Rome

---

[3] On the provocation of appropriating Mars, an especially Roman deity, see Feeney 1982 ad 1.118.

to the figurative wall represented by the Alps (*Pun.* 3.509–10).[4] In each episode Silius uses the notion of theomachy both to aggrandise Hannibal and to demonstrate the seemingly unbridgeable gulf between mortality and divinity. The majority of the chapter will be devoted to illustrating this simultaneous process of elevation and undercutting, but we shall also identify two complicating factors. First, Silius invests Hannibal with considerable metapoetic significance, a role which the hero can play easily given the suggestive concepts of loftiness and audacity that attach to his march across the Alps and attempt to ascend the Capitol. These two scenes—the points of highest drama in the work—thus put Silius' conventional, ethical condemnation of impiety in tension with theomachy's aesthetic importance for the *Punica*. The concluding section of this chapter, in particular, will show how the increasingly hollow theomachic rhetoric of Hannibal in Book 17 nevertheless culminates in the idea that fame may ultimately be the most successful form of theomachy, a fame that Silius appropriates and magnifies through the *Punica*.

A second problem arises from the contemporary significance of Hannibal's intention to burn the Capitol. As the epigraph from Tacitus' *Histories* (Tac. *Hist.* 3.72) well illustrates, the historical burning of the Capitol during the civil wars of AD 69 could be seen as a moment hugely revealing of the condition of Rome.[5] What Hannibal—and other theomachic figures, like the Gauls—had failed to do aspirants to the principate, themselves Romans, had now done. And in doing so, these men had become the desecrators of Jupiter's temple and thus the truest theomachs of all. Lying behind Silius' ostensible contrasts between Hannibal and the pious Romans, then, is a context in which Hannibal appears not as the Carthaginian other but as an image of what the empire had become.

Entering the Abodes of the Gods: Philosophy, Metapoetry, and Panegyric on the Alps

In order to convey both a sense of Hannibal's achievement in crossing the Alps and the scale of the task, Silius draws on the language of the sublime. Mountains in general, and the Alps in particular, have offered theorists and poets of the sublime a central example of the kind of phenomenon that generates a sublime attitude in the viewer or reader.[6] Silius evokes the sublime especially clearly in his initial description of the mountains (*Pun.* 3.483–6):[7]

> quantum Tartareus regni pallentis hiatus
> ad manes imos atque atrae stagna paludis

---

[4] On the theme of walls in the *Punica* see von Albrecht 1964: 24–46.
[5] See Joseph 2012: 98–106.
[6] Day 2013: 4–5 and index s.v. 'Mountains'.
[7] Cf. Schrijvers 2006: 104–6; for other sublime aspects of the Alps episode see Hardie 2009b: 132, 2013: 132–5.

> a supera tellure patet, tam longa per auras
> erigitur tellus et caelum intercipit umbra.

> As far as the Tartarean chasm of the pale kingdom
> stretches down to the dead below and to the pools of the black swamp
> from the earth above, so high does the earth rise
> through the air and block the sky with its shadow.

The simile shares its evocation of vertical, cosmological distance with a reference in a lacunose passage of Longinus' *Peri Hypsous*: ... τὸ ἐπ' οὐρανὸν ἀπὸ γῆς διάστημα· καὶ τοῦτ' ἂν εἴποι τις οὐ μᾶλλον τῆς Ἔριδος ἢ Ὁμήρου μέτρον ('... the distance from earth to heaven; and someone might well call this the measure of Eris or of Homer', Longin. 9.5).[8] Besides its connection to literary critical discourse, however, the simile also has a direct source in the epic tradition, the Sibyl's description of Tartarus to Aeneas (*Aen.* 6.577–9):

> tum Tartarus ipse
> bis patet in praeceps tantum tenditque sub umbras
> quantus ad aetherium caeli suspectus Olympum.

> Then Tartarus itself
> opens into the deep and reaches towards the shades
> twice as far as one gazes up towards airy Olympus.

Silius thus takes a description of cosmological expanses beyond the earth and applies it to a feature of the known world. Moreover, Vergil's Aeneas never descends to Tartarus, which is why the Sibyl must describe it to him as they proceed to Elysium, whereas Hannibal will himself reach the summit of the Alps. One particular point of contrast between the Vergilian and Silian passages is suggestive in this context. Silius claims that the Alps rise as high as Tartarus falls below the earth, but according to the Sibyl, Olympus is only half as high above the earth as Tartarus' depth. Based on these premises, Silius hints at the Alps towering even above Olympus (and above Homer's Strife, too). That the Alps are indeed higher than Mount Olympus is a geographical fact, of course, but the implication of the comparison is more important. For the Alps start to become a locus of Gigantomachic energy as their sublimity places them in tension with the home of the gods.[9] It's striking, in this regard, to see how the Vergilian passage from which Silius draws his description of the Alps continues straight after the account of Tartarus' depths (*Aen.* 6.580–4):

---

[8] Longinus' mention of distance indicates that the missing quotation comes from the passage in which Strife grows until her head strikes heaven (*Il.* 4.440–3).

[9] In making the Alps the home of winds and storms (*Pun.* 3.491–2), Silius also relocates and appropriates the Gigantomachic energy of Aeolus' cave in the *Aeneid*. On Vergil's cave of the winds see Hardie 1986: 90–7. At the beginning of *Punica* 4, Fama represents the Alps as 'rocks threatening heaven' (*saxa minantia caelo*, *Pun.* 4.2).

hic genus antiquum Terrae, Titania pubes,
fulmine deiecti fundo uoluuntur in imo.
hic et Aloidas geminos immania uidi
corpora, qui manibus magnum rescindere caelum
adgressi superisque Iouem detrudere regnis.

Here the ancient race of the Earth, her Titanic offspring,
hurled down by the lightning bolt, struggle in the depths.
Here too I saw the twin Aloidae with their immense
bodies, who threatened to tear down the great heaven
with their hands and dislodge Jupiter from his high kingdom.

Of the most egregious sinners punished in hell, the very first to be mentioned by the Sibyl are the Giants and their theomachic brethren. The Giant-like Aloidae who strive to pile Pelion on Ossa in particular exemplify the Longinan sublime (Longin. 8.2, referring to *Od*. 11.315–17). Silius amplifies the sense of a Gigantomachic sublime as theorised by Longinus, and evident also in Vergil's Tartarus, by imitating the Aloidae's piling of mountains in order to convey the height of the Alps: *mixtus Athos Tauro Rhodopeque adiuncta Mimanti / Ossaque cum Pelio cumque Haemo cesserit Othrys* ('Athos mixed with Taurus and Rhodope joined to Mimas, and Pelion piled on Ossa and Othrys on Haemus—all cede to the Alps', *Pun*. 3.494–5).[10] Silius accumulates not only the conventional pairing of Pelion and Ossa but also a whole host of other mountains, many of which, like Rhodope and Mimas, are themselves associated with theomachy.[11] Just as Longinus sees the sublimity of Strife as applicable to Homer himself, so too the sublimity of the Alps acts as a catalyst for Silius' own sublimity, which consists in the surpassing of Vergil's Tartarus by the reality of the Alps, and the surpassing of Vergil's Aeneas and Aloidae by the historical feat of Hannibal.

The relation between sublimity and originality is evident in the very act of crossing the Alps (*Pun*. 3.496–9):

primus inexpertas adiit Tirynthius arces.
scindentem nubes frangentemque ardua montis
spectarunt superi longisque ab origine saeclis
intemerata gradu magna ui saxa domantem.

The first to enter the unexplored citadels was the Tirynthian.
The gods watched him as he was cutting through the clouds and breaking

[10] Cf. Fucecchi 1990b: 40. Silius' echo of the list of mountains set ablaze by Phaethon (Ov. *Met*. 2.217–26), noted by Schrijvers 2006: 105 n. 27, evokes both the sublime and the theomachic elements of Ovid's episode.

[11] Cf. Luc. 7.450 and my discussion at p. 175 n. 38. Venus, always prone to exaggerate the scale of human theomachy (cf. p. 19 above), will later speak of Hannibal's crossing of the Alps in terms greater than the feat of the Aloidae: *Alpibus imposuit Libyam* ('he has placed Libya on the Alps', *Pun*. 3.563). Hannibal piles not just mountains but an entire country on top of an entire mountain range, an image of continental and tectonic proportions.

the heights of the mountain, and mastering the rocks with great force, rocks that were undefiled by any step in the long ages since their creation.

Hercules here plays his familiar role of pioneer and civiliser of the natural world.[12] The collocation *primus inexpertas*, in particular, suggests the role of the culture hero or innovator as described in two poems by Tibullus: Osiris is said to be the one who 'first entrusted seeds to the untried earth' (*primus inexpertae conmisit semina terrae*, Tib. 1.7.31), and an unnamed farmer the one who 'first led dances from unskilled art' (*primus inexperta duxit ab arte choros*, Tib. 2.1.56). It is Hercules' exceptional quality, however, that leads him to initiate no familiar and easily replicable feature of human life, such as agriculture or art, but rather something that defies imitation and stands as a paradigm of uniqueness.

The Alps are, however, inhabited, as the Carthaginians will find out when attacked by mountain tribes (*Pun.* 3.540–6), and as Livy's Hannibal points out to his men 'unacquainted' (*inexpertis*, Livy 21.29.7) with the Alps (Livy 21.30.6–7):

> quid Alpes aliud esse credentes quam montium altitudines? fingerent altiores Pyrenaei iugis: nullas profecto terras caelum contingere nec inexsuperabiles humano generi esse. Alpes quidem habitari, coli, gignere atque alere animantes

> What else do you believe these Alps to be other than the heights of mountains? Let's say they are higher than the peaks of the Pyrenees: surely, there can be no lands that touch the sky, or are insurmountable by the human race? The Alps are indeed inhabited, cultivated, living things are born and bred there.

And yet in one important detail, as we have seen, Silius' account of the Alps differs from that of Livy's Hannibal—the mountains do indeed seem to touch, even overtop, the heavens. Moreover, in ascending them, the Carthaginian troops believe that 'they are fighting against the gods' (*diuisque repugnent*, *Pun.* 3.502). Set against the more theomachic mise en scène, Silius attempts to elevate the correspondingly theomachic Hannibal above his historiographical predecessor, and concomitantly to elevate the *Punica* over its historiographical source.

In order to achieve this combined heroic and literary success, Hannibal must lay a new claim to originality. Whereas the Livian Hannibal emphasises that the mountains are inhabited by tribes and hence have already yielded to

---

[12] Hercules' immense reach is conveyed not only in the feat itself but also in the very syntax of the passage: two participles represent him cutting through the clouds and subduing the heights, but we must wait almost two lines until we see him taming the rocks, with *domantem* placed as the very last word of the sentence. On this passage see also Santini 1991: 95–6.

men, Silius' hero is concerned rather with the opposite—the possibility of treading an entirely new path (*Pun.* 3.512-17):[13]

> nec mora commotum promissis ditibus agmen
> erigit in collem et uestigia linquere nota
> Herculis edicit magni crudisque locorum
> ferre pedem ac proprio turmas euadere calle.
> rumpit inaccessos aditus atque ardua primus
> exsuperat summaque uocat de rupe cohortes.

> And without delay he led the column, moved by his rich promises,
> up the hill, and told the troops to leave behind the famous traces
> of great Hercules, to set their feet on new places
> and proceed with a path all their own.
> He broke the inaccessible approaches and was the first
> to master the heights and summon his soldiers from the highest crag.

Just as in the case of Scipio outdoing Achilles at the Trebia in Book 4, so here too Silius shows a historical figure pushing beyond Hercules, the greatest hero of all.[14]

Ironically, the notion of treading new ground is itself a clichéd trope for the composition of original poetry. Silius' *inaccessos*, in particular, recalls Manilius' claim to originality at the beginning of Book 3 of the *Astronomica* (Man. 3.1-3):[15]

> in noua surgentem maioraque uiribus ausum
> nec per inaccessos metuentem uadere saltus
> ducite, Pierides.

> As I rise to new heights and dare deeds greater than my strength,
> not fearing to go through inaccessible passes,
> lead me, Muses.

Manilius' proclaimed novelty and the absence of fear point to a wider, philosophical context for the ascent of Hannibal, whom Silius describes as 'undisturbed by the Alps or any horror of the place' (*non Alpibus ille nec ullo / turbatus terrore loci, Pun.* 3.503-4). That fearlessness, combined with his claim to be the first to enter new heights, also recalls Lucretius' Epicurus, thanks to whose teachings 'the terrors of the mind flee, the walls of the world part asunder' (*diffugiunt animi terrores, moenia mundi / discedunt*, Lucr. 3.16-17). For Hannibal, however, the walls in question are those of Rome (*moenia Romae, Pun.* 3.509),

---

[13] On the contrast between the Livian Hannibal's rationalising approach to the Alps and Livy's own riposte to Polybian rationalism at 21.32.7, see Feldherr 2009: 313-18, Levene 2010: 149-55.

[14] On Hercules as a model for Hannibal see Asso 2010: 179-89.

[15] Note also the claim of Seneca's Hercules to have seen places 'inaccessible to all' (*inaccessa omnibus*, HF 606), i.e., the underworld. For Hercules as a metapoetic figure see Chapter 4.

which will not, of course, fall.[16] Nor is this the only contrast. Lucretius, earlier in the same passage in *De Rerum Natura* 3, envisages his relationship with his predecessor, Epicurus, far differently from Hannibal's relationship to any of his models (Lucr. 3.3–6):[17]

> te sequor, o Graiae gentis decus, inque tuis nunc
> ficta pedum pono pressis uestigia signis,
> non ita certandi cupidus quam propter amorem
> quod te imitari aueo.

> I follow you, O glory of the Greek race, and now in your
> imprinted marks I plant the tracks of my feet,
> desiring not to compete with you so much as, because of my love,
> I wish to imitate you.

Lucretius emphasises his close and deferential following of Epicurus, even if in other places he describes the novelty of putting Epicurean doctrine in Latin verse, whereas Hannibal gives far greater importance to his own originality as he departs from Hercules' *uestigia*.[18] Finally, after describing the *moenia mundi* falling away, Lucretius goes on to imagine the homes of the gods in terms diametrically opposed to the weather conditions found at the top of mountains (Lucr. 3.18–22):

> apparet diuum numen sedesque quietae
> quas neque concutiunt uenti nec nubila nimbis
> aspergunt neque nix acri concreta pruina
> cana cadens uiolat semperque innubilus aether
> integit, et large diffuso lumine ridet.

> The gods and their peaceful abodes appear,
> which no winds shake nor clouds spray
> with rain, nor does white snow, hardened with harsh frost,
> violate them by falling there, but the air which is always without clouds
> protects them, and smiles broadly with dappled light.

Hannibal's ascent neither reveals the gods to him nor secures the tranquillity that philosophy seeks as its goal. Instead, his rise, for all its spectacular sublimity,

---

[16] After his victory at Cannae, Hannibal imagines burning the Capitol in terms reminiscent of Epicurus' philosophical ascent: *ac iam claustra manu, iam moenia flamma / occupat* ('and now he lays hands on the barricade, now he attacks the walls with flame', *Pun.* 10.335–6); cf. *claustra* (Lucr. 1.71), *flammantia moenia* (Lucr. 1.73). Hannibal's subsequent disturbance by a dream sent by Juno emblematises the gap between Epicurus and himself.

[17] Compare also Epicurus, described as *primus* (Lucr. 3.2), with Silius' Hercules (*Pun.* 3.496) and Hannibal (*Pun.* 3.516); Cf. Hardie 2013: 134.

[18] Lucretius' originality: Lucr. 1.136–9. Konstan 1988 discusses the metapoetics of the opening of *De Rerum Natura* 3 and the claims to originality underlying the deference to Epicurus.

must lead to a fall—both literally, in the descent to Italy, and metaphorically, in the eventual victory of Rome.

The extended intertextual connection between Hannibal and Lucretius/Epicurus has more than one precedent. Andrew Feldherr has recently argued that Livy's Hannibal also shows signs of Lucretian influence for many of the same reasons seen in Silius' account.[19] For Feldherr, awareness of the Epicurean intertext generates two largely conflicting responses in the audience: on the one hand, we gain a sense of detachment as we contrast the struggles of the Carthaginians with the beatific experience of a philosophical ascent; on the other hand, Hannibal's attempt to banish his troops' fear by puncturing rumours about the Alps makes him into another Epicurus crusading against the *fama deum*. That ambiguity changes in Silius, for his Hannibal is less concerned to deflate *fama* than to follow, and even surpass, the mythological example of Hercules.[20] If the Lucretian intertext provides any reason for viewing Hannibal's ascent positively, it lies in the hero's bold claim to originality that carries with it the merits of Silius' own poetic project.[21]

Besides Hercules and the Livian Hannibal, however, Lucan's Caesar also performs the same feat: *iam gelidas Caesar cursu superauerat Alpes* ('now Caesar had swiftly surmounted the icy Alps', Luc. 1.183).[22] This one-line account alludes to Hannibal's example, but in its brevity it reaffirms the exceptional speed and irresistible force of Caesar.[23] When Silius says that Hannibal 'first surmounts the heights' (*ardua primus / exsuperat*, Pun. 3.516–17), he thus alludes not only to Livy (*nec inexsuperabiles*, Livy 21.30.7) but also to Lucan's Caesar (*superauerat*). Both heroes, moreover, share a close connection with the thunderbolt, which in Hannibal's case derives from his family name, Barca (meaning 'thunderbolt' in Punic), and which Lucan makes into an important recurring motif of Caesar's power.[24] Finally, later in Silius' account, the language used to describe Hannibal's men cutting down a forest will closely echo Lucan's language in the episode of the Massilian grove: *iamque ubi nudarunt silua densissima montis* ('and now where they stripped the mountain of its

---

[19] Feldherr 2009: 318–29; Cf. Hardie 2009b: 129–31, 2013: 132–5.

[20] For the role of the personified (and theomachic) *Fama* in advertising Hannibal's competition with Hercules, see *Pun.* 4.1–9.

[21] Cf. Tipping 2010a: 69–70, 98–106 on the metapoetics of Hannibal's excess.

[22] Not once but twice: *super euolat Alpem* ('he flies over the Alps', Luc. 3.299).

[23] On Lucan's broader assimilation of Hannibal's and Caesar's invasions of Italy see Ahl 1976: 107–12. For other similarities between the two heroes see von Albrecht 1964: 54–5, Brouwers 1982: 82–4, and the references at p. 232 n. 2 above. In Petronius' *Satyrica*, the character Eumolpus recites a poem on the civil war (often separately designated the *Bellum Ciuile*) in which he describes Caesar crossing the Alps in similarly allusive style (*Sat.* 122.1–123.1 = *BC* 144–208). On the grouping of Caesar, Hercules, and Hannibal in Eumolpus' narration, and on the Gigantomachic and metapoetic aspects, see Connors 1998: 121–34.

[24] On the symbolic relation between the thunderbolt and Caesar see Chapter 5. Lucan's Caesar may partly have inherited this symbolism from his association with Hannibal. The Scipios, too, were connected to *fulmina* through poetic and etymological traditions (see *Pun.* 7.106–7 with the commentary of R. J. Littlewood 2011: 74–5).

thickest wood', *Pun.* 3.640); cf. *inter nudatos stabat densissima montis* ('it stood, very dense, among the mountains stripped bare', Luc. 3.428).[25] The Alps may be the home of storm winds (*Pun.* 3.491–2), but Hannibal—like Caesar at Massilia—has a good claim to being an even more potent symbol of violence and sublimity.

And yet there is one fundamental difference between the worlds that Caesar and Hannibal inhabit. For whereas Caesar's sublime power fills a vacuum left by the absent Olympian gods, Hannibal operates in a world filled with plotting and intervening deities. Nowhere is this divine presence more apparent than in the crossing of the Alps. For between the Carthaginians' arrival at the peak of the mountain range (*uertice*, *Pun.* 3.555) and their descent (*delatus*, *Pun.* 3.631), Silius portrays an exchange between an anxious Venus and Jupiter, in which the latter reassures the former by prophesying the eventual Roman victory and the (much later) glory of the Flavian dynasty. In other words, at the true summit of the poem, unseen by Hannibal camped atop the Alps, the gods contemplate reaches of time utterly beyond the human hero's ken.

The theological point is reinforced at the end of the book, when Bostar returns to the army to report the ambiguous prophecy of Jupiter Ammon. The oracle claims that no one will penetrate into Italy deeper than Hannibal so long as his victories are feared (*Pun.* 3.708–10). Whereas the Carthaginians understand the prophecy to imply Hannibal's success, the audience knows that it signifies the enduring invincibility of Rome: Hannibal's failure will represent the high-water mark for Rome's enemies. In addition to the audience's hindsight, however, Jupiter's earlier speech had explicitly revealed the outcome of the war and Rome's later history, thereby pre-empting the need to interpret the oracle. Silius' epic mode, rich in divine action and speech, gives the audience direct access to the gods and the knowledge that comes from them. Through the divine conversation, then, and through the co-ordination between Jupiter's speech and the oracle, Silius reaffirms conventional epic theology and religion. He does so, moreover, in the face of a Hannibal who leaves much to be desired compared to his theomachic and Epicurean models.

It's important to consider, however, the significance of the part of Jupiter's speech that does not appear in the oracle—the panegyric of the Flavians.[26] Venus' initial complaint incorporates elements of two speeches by the Vergilian Venus in *Aeneid* 1 (229–53) and 10 (18–62), both of which bemoan the perilous state of the Trojans despite the promises of Fate and Jupiter.[27] Jupiter's

---

[25] Day 2013: 116–20, 132–3 builds on Feldherr's reading of Livy to suggest that the same complex of Lucretian sublimity and mountain ascent also applies to Lucan's Caesar, whose attitude to superstition has points of contact with Lucretius' philosophical rationalism. Cf. Chapter 5 on the Massilia episode, though note the qualifications about Caesar's powerful remystifications.

[26] On Jupiter's speech, especially the possible connections between Scipio and Domitian, see the detailed reading at Marks 2005: 209–22, with further scattered comments at 222–44. Cf. Schubert 1984: 55–70, Ripoll 1998: 509–15, Hartmann 2004: 98–122, Fucecchi 2012, Penwill 2013: 46–50.

[27] Spaltenstein 1986: 246–7.

speech, likewise, takes it cues from the Vergilian Jupiter's reply to Venus in *Aeneid* 1 (257–96), in which the god prophesies the glory of Aeneas' descendants. Vergil has Jupiter twice mention the deification of mortals across this long span of time—first Aeneas (*Aen.* 1.259–60), then Caesar (*Aen.* 1.289–90). Silius' Jupiter, however, shows signs of a much changed religious context. That transformation is well illustrated by the shift from the praise of the Roman heroes of the Punic war as 'not unworthy of our heaven' (*nostro / non indigna polo*, *Pun.* 3.585–6) to the 'heavenly valour' that carries Vespasian 'to the stars' (*uirtus caelestis ad astra*, *Pun.* 3.594): with the jarring transition from mid-republic to high empire, litotes gives way to the most literal and hyperbolic forms of expression. The sanctified status of the Julio-Claudians is recognised in passing (*sacris Iulis*, *Pun.* 3.595), but Jupiter returns to Vespasian's divinity once again in emphatic terms: *sed superum sedem nostrosque tenebit honores* ('but he will hold the seat of the gods and our honours', *Pun.* 3.602). The address to Domitian is even more direct and elevating: *nam te longa manent nostri consortia mundi* ('for a long-enduring share of our heaven awaits you', *Pun.* 3.611). All of these individual claims lead up to Domitian's restoration of the Capitoline temple of Jupiter and the vision of the collectively deified Flavian family (*Pun.* 3.622–9):

> ille etiam, qua prisca, uides, stat regia nobis,
> aurea Tarpeia ponet Capitolia rupe
> et iunget nostro templorum culmina caelo.
> tunc, o nate deum diuosque dature, beatas
> imperio terras patrio rege. tarda senectam
> hospitia excipient caeli, solioque Quirinus
> concedet, mediumque parens fraterque locabunt;
> siderei iuxta radiabunt tempora nati.

> But he, you see, will place a golden Capitol on the Tarpeian
> rock, where now our ancient palace stands,
> and will join the tops of the temples with our sky.
> Then, O child of gods and creator of divinities, rule the happy
> lands with a father's sway. The heavens will welcome
> your old age at last, and Quirinus will cede to you
> his throne, and your father and brother will place you between them;
> nearby the brows of your deified son will shine forth.

The contrast could not be clearer between Hannibal, desirous of scaling the Capitol (*Iouis culmen*, *Pun.* 3.510), and Domitian, who survived its burning during the civil war (*Tarpei culminis ignes*, *Pun.* 3.609) and has now, following another fire in AD 80, rebuilt it more splendidly than ever.[28] Whereas Hannibal

---

[28] For the rebuilding of the temple see Stat. *Silv.* 4.3.16–17, Suet. *Dom.* 5, Mart. 9.3.7 with the commentary of Henriksén 2012: 29–30, and in general Darwall-Smith 1996: 96–7, 105–10.

must descend from the summit of the Alps, a Gigantomachic mountain range that threatens the sky, the meeting of the roof of the new temple of Jupiter with the heavens merely foreshadows the eventual ascent of the emperor.

And yet, despite the seemingly felicitous conjoining of imperial panegyric and epic theology, and the superficial assimilation of the high points of republic and empire, the ultimate fulfilment of Hannibal's theomachic goal during the civil war should give us pause.[29] For if, as the oracle of Jupiter Ammon suggests, Hannibal exposes the limits of Roman vulnerability, then the burning of the Capitol in AD 69, alluded to at *Pun.* 3.609–10, implies that something has gone seriously awry.

More troubling still is the implication of the allusions to Lucan's Caesar both before and after the exchange between Venus and Jupiter. In having Hannibal re-echo Caesar, and thereby reaffirming a connection between the two heroes already present in the *Bellum Civile*, Silius blurs the line between foreign and civil war.[30] As a result, Hannibal emerges as a precursor to Caesar and hence to the very emperors that Jupiter praises, both *sacris Iulis* and their Flavian successors. Furthermore, at the topographical summit of the poem, in its most panegyrical passage, the surrounding allusions to Caesar recall Lucan's quite different conception of the relationship between the emperors and the Olympian gods. On that view, a cynical reader might well conclude that Domitian's sky-reaching temple does in fact resemble the Alps, and that Dido's *ultor* may not be Hannibal after all, but rather Caesar and his self-destructive and theomachic heirs.[31]

Theology and Politics at the Capitol

After the Carthaginians grow enervated by the luxuries of Capua in Book 11, they begin the new campaign in Book 12 with a series of failed attempts to take various Greek cities in southern Italy. The mounting frustration prompts Hannibal to make exhortatory speeches to his troops, which recur to theomachic rhetoric: first, at Naples, Hannibal reminds his men of Mago's promise that they would soon feast in the temple of Capitoline Jupiter (*Pun.* 12.48, referring to *Pun.* 10.375–6); second, at Cumae, Hannibal draws the by now familiar analogy

---

[29] Compare Hannibal's dreams in Book 1 (*nocturno penetrat Capitolia uisu*, 'in his nocturnal visions he penetrates the Capitol', *Pun.* 1.64) with Jupiter Ammon's prophecy that no one will be able 'to penetrate more deeply into the bowels of the Ausonian race' (*altius Ausoniae penetrare in uiscera gentis, Pun.* 3.709). In the end, Hannibal will only penetrate Rome figuratively as he surveys the city: *penetraret in omnes / spectando partes* ('he would have penetrated into all its parts with his gaze', *Pun.* 12.569–70). Cf. Muecke 2007: 86. On Hannibal's gaze see Lovatt 2013b: index s.v. 'Hannibal', esp. 94–8.

[30] For other intimations of civil war in the *Punica* see Ahl, Davis, and Pomeroy 1986: 2518; Marks 2010b; Tipping 2010a: 35–44. On the projection of the Roman self onto the foreign or mythological other in Flavian epic, especially in the *Punica*, see Augoustakis 2010b.

[31] On Domitian's similarly lofty palace see Mart. 8.36, Stat. *Silv.* 4.2.18–31, and pp. 318–19.

between the scaling of the Alps and Rome's walls, describing the mountains as 'beating the heavens' (*caelum / pulsantes, Pun.* 12.71–2). Thus, even these early detours set the tone and the theomachic theme that will dominate Book 12.

The account of the temple of Phoebus at Cumae, seemingly a digressive allusion to the *Aeneid*, shares the same theomachic concerns. Vergil's treatment of the same temple focuses on an ecphrasis of the images on its doors and on Daedalus' grief for the death of Icarus (*Aen.* 6.14–33). Silius' speaker, by contrast, speaks of Daedalus' audacity, which consists not only in flight itself but also in its wider implications for human power: *aetherias aliena tollere in auras / ausus se penna atque homini monstrare uolatus* ('daring to raise himself to the upper air on wings not his own and to show humankind the art of flight', *Pun.* 12.92–3).[32] The consequent alarm of the gods (*superosque nouus conterruit ales*, 'and the novel winged creature terrified the gods', *Pun.* 12.95) thus follows as much from a concern about the potentially enlarged capacities of all humankind as from the strange and unsettling sight of Daedalus himself.[33] As at Lucan's Massilia and Silius' Trebia, human industry and technology pose the greatest threat to the divine.[34] Moreover, Silius' sustained trope of verticality, inspired partly by Hannibal's Alpine crossing, continues here in the symbolism of the rise and descent of Daedalus and Icarus for Hannibal's own fortunes.

As if the example of the overreaching Daedalus were not lesson enough for Hannibal, the Carthaginian leader is given a guided tour of the area around the Bay of Naples, a prominent feature of which is the site of Hercules' defeat of the Giants (*Pun.* 12.133–51). Frances Muecke has argued that this geographical excursus offers Hannibal an ecphrastic vision of his own place in the *Punica*'s mythological symbolism.[35] Although he worships Hercules (*Pun.* 3.14–16), this site offers the strongest hint yet that Hannibal should be more closely associated with the Giants, an association that the poem has made abundantly clear to the reader on numerous occasions thus far, and which will be sealed later in Book 12 when Hannibal confronts Jupiter. One can push Muecke's point further, however, by linking the details of the excursus with

---

[32] Vergil also calls Daedalus *ausus*, but the inventor is described only as 'daring to trust himself to the heavens' (*ausus se credere caelo, Aen.* 6.15), rather than daring 'to raise himself' there, as in Silius' version. Silius further emphasises the audacity at the end of Virrius' speech: *audaces alas* ('daring wings', *Pun.* 12.103). Contrast the more positive images of Rome raising her gaze to the sky (*tollebat ad aethera uultus, Pun.* 12.319), and Ennius' poetry raising Roman commanders to the heavens (*attolletque duces caelo, Pun.* 12.411).

[33] The locus classicus for the idea of human flight as a threat to the gods is Aristophanes' *Birds*, on which see Romer 1994, Versnel 2011: 480–4.

[34] Cf. pp. 160 and 207–8. Note also Silius' references only a few lines later to Hercules' making of a road across the Lucrine Lake, and the transformation of Lake Avernus into a spa (*Pun.* 12.116–21). Leigh 2010: 221–3 refers to the latter in particular in his discussion of Caesar's rationalism in the grove-cutting episode of the *BC*. As my treatment of the Trebia and Daedalus illustrates, however, the felling of trees is only one facet of a much larger concept of technology as theomachy. In this regard, note also Hannibal's transportation of his fleet across land at *Pun.* 12.434–48.

[35] See Muecke 2007, which also takes account of various intertextual connections between *Punica* 12 and the *Aeneid*.

Silius' broader characterisation of Hannibal as theomach. Despite the violent motions of the Giants and Titans trapped beneath the mountains, and the consequent seismic activity that causes even 'the heavens to pale with fear' (*expallescere caelum*, *Pun.* 12.146), Silius emphasises the Giants' impotence. Although the fiery Iapetus, for instance, might wish to continue fighting the gods, it is in another's hands—implicitly Jupiter's—whether the Titan can ever climb out of his prison: *si quando euadere detur, / bella Ioui rursus superisque iterare uolentem* ('if he is ever allowed to escape, wishing once again to renew the war against Jupiter and the gods', *Pun.* 12.150–1). The ultimate power of Jupiter is apparent from much earlier in the poem, for instance in the god's prophecy to Venus in Book 3, but it is a fact of Silius' world to which Hannibal remains stubbornly resistant. In the literary history of theomachy, Hannibal's is a particularly unthreatening resistance, since the hero opposes Jupiter, and not the gods in general, and for no other reason than the close identification between Jupiter and Rome. This is theomachy reduced to mere nationalism.

When Hannibal subsequently attacks Rome, Silius paints a vivid picture of Jupiter's intervention, ordering the other gods to defend the city, summoning an epic storm of northerly and southerly winds, and casting his thunderbolt directly at Hannibal (*Pun.* 12.605–26). Just as against the Trebia Scipio had 'held up the rushing river with his shield' (*clipeoque ruentem sustulit amnem*, *Pun.* 4.652), Hannibal, his shield struck by lightning, remains 'determined not to yield' (*non cedere certi*, *Pun.* 12.624). Here, however, lies the difference: Scipio could threaten to curb the river with a feat of Roman engineering, but in this case it is the god who combines divine force and the power of metallurgy: *et fluxit ceu correptus fornacibus ensis* ('and his sword liquefied as if thrust in a furnace', *Pun.* 12.626).[36] Hannibal bravely offers a Lucretian riposte: *caecum e nubibus ignem / murmuraque a uentis misceri uana docebat* ('he informed them that the fire from the clouds was blind and the rumblings stirred up by the winds were empty', *Pun.* 12.628–9). The notion that the natural phenomena of lightning and thunder are frequently confused for divine signs is an Epicurean one, and the verb *doceo*, moreover, has strong Lucretian resonances.[37] Moreover, Hannibal's language, as Marco Fucecchi notes, alludes to that of Vergil's Iarbas (*Aen.* 4.208–10), whose Epicurean-influenced rhetoric was discussed in Chapter 2.[38] Yet Hannibal's rare moment of philosophical

---

[36] The word *fornacibus* equivocates between technology and mythology: its immediate context is the human activity of forging, but in the larger context of Jupiter's lightning it evokes the furnaces of the Cyclopes in which the god's thunderbolts are forged. Silius' *liquefacta* (*Pun.* 12.625) suggests that he may have been thinking of Vergil's description of Etna at *G.* 1.471–3. Spaltenstein 1990: 197 and von Albrecht 1964: 35 n. 37 see an allusion to Luc. 7.159, which strengthens the civil war subtext underlying the attack on the Capitol. Fucecchi 1990b: 32 n. 21 notes in addition Sen. *QNat.* 2.31.1, which describes the melting of a sword struck by a thunderbolt.

[37] For Lucretius' views on lightning see Chapter 2. For Lucretius' use of *doceo* see, e.g., Lucr. 1.265 and 1.931, besides many other instances.

[38] Fucecchi 1990b: 32–3; cf. Lovatt 2013b: 96–7. On Iarbas see Chapter 2.

iconoclasm is undermined in two important ways: first, it follows from such a graphic vision of Jupiter's action that it can only seem like empty rhetoric, and second, it sits entirely out of place with Hannibal's own acceptance of epic theology throughout the poem.[39] Carefully balanced against Hannibal's recourse to natural meteorology, moreover, are the Romans' pious prayers to Capitoline Jupiter (*Pun.* 12.639–45). These prayers recall the pious sacrifices earlier in the book after the Romans hear the Delphic oracle's unusually straightforward pronouncement that the worst of the war is over, that the Romans should sacrifice to the gods, and that they will see Jupiter himself fighting on their behalf (*Pun.* 12.320–41). The contrast between Hannibal's erroneous impiety and the Romans' explicitly corroborated piety could not be more emphatic.

If Silius' account of the first storm were insufficiently sublime, the second combines references to mountains, the underworld, and Typhoeus in a concentration of sublime imagery (*Pun.* 12.657–60):

> intonat ipse,
> quod tremat et Rhodope Taurusque et Pindus et Atlas.
> audiuere lacus Erebi, mersusque profundis
> agnouit tenebris caelestia bella Typhoeus.

> [Jupiter] himself thundered,
> and Rhodope and Taurus and Pindus and Atlas shook.
> The lakes of Erebus heard, and sunk in the deepest
> shadows Typhoeus recognised war in heaven.

Silius brings into view both the summits and depths of the world, a sublimity that is thoroughly anti-Lucretian and anti-Lucanian in its dependence on the power of Jupiter. Hannibal retreats but once again tries to reduce the clear signs of divinity to mere weather: *uentis hiemique fugaces / terga damus?* ('do we flee, routed by winds and storms?', *Pun.* 12.677–8). Compared with the true sublimity of Jupiter, however, it's Hannibal himself who is reduced to appearing as a Salmoneus-like simulacrum of the god's awesome majesty: *rursus in arma uocat trepidos clipeoque tremendum / increpat atque armis imitatur murmura caeli* ('again he calls his frightened men to arms, and he clashes on his shield with a terrible din, and with his armour he imitates the roar of heaven', *Pun.* 12.684–5).[40] It is this particular excess that finally prompts Jupiter to demand that Juno curb Hannibal's overreaching (*Pun.* 12.697–700):

---

[39] Lovatt 2013b: 98 rightly points to the tension between Hannibal's rationalist 'historical-scientific gaze' and Silius' epic theology, but it's important to recognise, as I have argued, that Hannibal is hardly a rationalist tout court. Indeed, it is characteristic of almost all theomachs, with the telling exception of Lucretius' Epicurus, that despite their radical rhetoric they buy into elements of the very theological system for which they typically show contempt.

[40] Salmoneus was a mythological king who was killed by Jupiter's lightning for playing the role of the god and simulating his thunder. On this passage see von Albrecht 1964: 37, Fucecchi 1990b: 33; for other appearances of Salmoneus in Roman epic see *Aen.* 6.585–94, Man. 5.91–6, Val. Fl. 1.662–5. A similar

>   etiamne parabit
> nostras ille domos, nostras perrumpere in arces?
> siste uirum. namque, ut cernis, iam flagitat ignes
> et parat accensis imitari fulmina flammis.

>   And will he prepare also
> to break into our homes and our citadels?
> Stop that man! For, as you see, already he demands fires
> and prepares to imitate my thunderbolts with his kindled flames.

In this passage, perhaps more explicit than any other in the epic tradition, Silius makes clear the fundamental inextricability of theomachy and the aspiration to divinity, but he does so in a way that highlights the categorical separation of the human and divine, and thus the inevitable failure of Hannibal.[41]

It's important to take stock at this point and to notice the consequence of making this moment so pivotal to the epic and of framing Hannibal's overreaching in this particular way. Livy only briefly relates that two storms prevented Hannibal from taking Rome (Livy 26.11.2–3), and although the episode significantly occurs at the beginning of the second half of the decade when the fortunes of the two sides start to shift, it nevertheless offers a striking contrast to Silius' epic account. The scene in *Punica* 12 not only massively amplifies the storms, it also includes a third storm culminating in the direct confrontation of Hannibal and Jupiter.[42] All these adaptations are the standard accoutrements of epic and tragedy in the wake of Ovid and Seneca, especially the focus on the theomachic sublime. But in choosing to place such emphasis on Hannibal's theomachy, Silius makes the fulcrum of the Punic War something other than a struggle between two nations, or even a contest between two men: history is fashioned not just as mythology but as itself a continuation of an eternal, cosmological conflict.[43] Nor is this conflict

---

story is told of an Alban king (called Remulus or Romulus Silvius, among other names): see Diod. Sic. 7.5.11, Dion. Hal. *Ant. Rom.* 1.71.3, Livy 1.3.9, Ov. *Met.* 14.617–18; cf. Frier 1999: 54–5. At *Pun.* 12.684 the MSS' garbled *uenus* (obelised by Delz) has often been emended to *armis* (from the very earliest editions), though Bauer's *minis* has much to recommend it: it avoids the repetition of *arma* in the previous line, develops rather than recapitulates the action of Hannibal striking his shield, and enhances the sound effects created by *imitatur murmura*.

[41] For Hannibal's presumption, cf. his description of himself as *Hannibal aequatus superis* ('Hannibal equalled to the gods', *Pun.* 4.810). Tipping 2010a: 68 n. 47 lists other passages where Hannibal is treated as a god. Through its divine voices, however, the poem repeatedly emphasises the limits placed on Hannibal: Jupiter pronounces as much in Book 6 (*Pun.* 6.600–5), and after the heights of Hannibal's achievements at Cannae Juno shows herself to be perfectly aware that Jupiter will not allow the Carthaginian leader to enter Rome (*Pun.* 10.350). Juno then sends a dream to Hannibal clearly foreshadowing the events of Book 12 (*Pun.* 10.357–68).

[42] Cf. Ripoll 1998: 343 n. 154, Pomeroy 2000: 166 n. 48.

[43] The idea of attacking a wall is canonically associated with theomachy from the *aristeia* of Patroclus in *Iliad* 16, on which see Chapter 1. Patroclus' conflict with Apollo, however, is significantly less direct than Hannibal's with Jupiter.

an allegory or higher-order counterpart of human action, as in the *Aeneid*, but instead it is fought with mortals and within the ambit of human history.

Against that context it's worth reiterating that Silius' Jupiter is alarmed not so much by the physical contest as by Hannibal's pretension to his power. Like the consternation caused by Daedalus' flight mentioned earlier in Book 12, the allusion to Salmoneus reveals what really troubles the gods.[44] This is where the centring of the battle, and indeed the focus of the *Punica* as a whole, on the Capitol takes on greater significance. The burning of the Capitol in AD 69—the fulfilment of what Hannibal fails to do—and the rebuilding of it first by Vespasian and again later by Domitian, whom in Book 3 Silius had cast, respectively, as a god and a god-in-waiting, represent the stakes of civil war: one side will be remembered as Giants while the other will go on to become regents and partners of the Olympian gods.[45] By presuming to take the Capitol by force, and by imitating and promising to displace Jupiter, Hannibal threatens to undermine the categories of piety and impiety that distinguish the pretenders from the true authorities, the rebels from the emperors. There is, then, some irony in Juno's attempt to dissuade Hannibal from persisting in his attack: *quo ruis, o uecors, maioraque bella capessis / mortali quam ferre datum?* ('where do you rush, madman? Do you undertake greater wars than mortals are allowed?', *Pun.* 12.703–4).[46] These greater wars will be fought after the fall of Nero in Silius' own lifetime.

Despite the problematic historical subtext, through Juno's speech Silius seems largely to reaffirm the conventional theological and political hierarchies that structure his epic. In an allusion to *Aeneid* 2, where Venus had shown to Aeneas the gods destroying Troy (*Aen.* 2.601–23), Juno now reveals to Hannibal the gods protecting Rome (*Pun.* 12.704–25), a reversal which both assimilates and distinguishes the protagonists of the two epics.[47] Juno's pointing out of her fellow Olympians culminates in the image of Jupiter Tonans, wrathful and surrounded by storms and fire. When she describes him wielding his aegis (*aegida*, *Pun.* 12.720), she recalls precisely the word used by the Pythia earlier in the book (*aegida*, *Pun.* 12.336), thereby confirming the accuracy of the Delphic prophecy.[48] Arthur Pomeroy has noted that *aegida* also alludes to a passage in the *Aeneid* (*Aen.* 8.352–4):[49]

---

[44] Cf. Santini 1991: 79.

[45] Cf. Fucecchi 1990b: 35–6. For the related notion, voiced by Hannibal, that Jupiter will depart the Capitol as a result of the Carthaginians' attack see *Pun.* 12.517: *demigrantem Tarpeia sede Tonantem*; cf. the more violent *deiectum* (*Pun.* 6.713) and *detraxi* (*Pun.* 17.227). Hannibal imagines burning the Capitol immediately after his success at Cannae: *Tarpeia incendia* (*Pun.* 10.336).

[46] Cf. Lovatt 2013b: 98 with n. 47.

[47] Ahl, Davis, and Pomeroy 1986: 2500–1; Pomeroy 2000: 159–60; Lovatt 2013b: 95–6.

[48] Nor is the Delphic oracle the only prophetic power to be corroborated, for as early as Book 1 the priestess of Dido's cult, too, foresaw 'Jupiter waging war' (*bellantemque Iouem*, *Pun.* 1.137).

[49] Pomeroy 2000: 167 n. 49.

> Arcades ipsum
> credunt se uidisse Iouem, cum saepe nigrantem
> aegida concuteret dextra nimbosque cieret.

> The Arcadians
> believe that they have seen Jupiter himself, when often
> he shakes his darkening aegis and stirs the clouds with his right hand.

Whereas the speaker, Evander, distances himself from the folk belief in Jupiter's presence, Silius brings that same aegis-wielding Jupiter right into the action of the *Punica*.

More striking than Silius' affirmation of traditional epic theology, however, is the sophistication seen in his treatment of the aegis, and the subtle nuances that go into creating this multivalent image. Juno describes the aegis as 'pouring out flames' (*flammasque uomentem*, *Pun.* 12.720). The intra- and intertextual significance of this phrase runs wide and deep, encompassing many of the theological issues raised by imperial poetry's representation of theomachy.[50] Pomeroy takes the phrase as an allusion to Vergil's Cacus, whom we see 'spewing out fire' (*uomens ignis*, *Aen.* 8.199) in his confrontation with Hercules. Pomeroy reads the overlap of monstrous thief and supreme deity as 'particularly alarming' and concludes that 'Hannibal is no Hercules and wisely avoids the challenge'.[51] The point about the problematic nature of the intertext is well taken, but Pomeroy's interpretation, restricted to a footnote, requires elaboration. As is well known, Vergil himself complicates any simple understanding of this image of Cacus not only through Hercules' own monstrous violence in the episode but also by the use of a very similar phrase to describe the divinely forged helmet of Aeneas (*galeam flammasque uomentem*, *Aen.* 8.620).[52] It is the latter phrase, indeed, on which Silius' description of Jupiter is more closely, indeed exactly, modelled. It will not do, then, simply to see Jupiter's appearance as alarming because of its overlap with Cacus, for it primarily recalls Aeneas' divine power. The complexity of the Vergilian image is further compounded shortly after the description of Aeneas' helm, when on the shield of the hero Vulcan portrays Augustus, 'whose happy brows pour out twin flames' (*geminas cui tempora flammas / laeta uomunt*, *Aen.* 8.680-1).[53] Thus, Silius' initial association of Hannibal and Aeneas is balanced against the subsequent association of Jupiter and Aeneas, while the character of Jupiter's power is coloured by its proximity both to Cacus and to Augustus.

Vergil's diction had already contained more than just political or ethical significance; it participated in a philosophical dialogue too. For Lucretius had

---

[50] Several, but not all, of the intra- and intertexts are noted at Spaltenstein 1990: 40, 202, 470.
[51] Pomeroy 2000: 167 n. 50.
[52] On assimilations of Hercules, Cacus, Augustus, and Aeneas see Lyne 1987: 27-35, Morgan 1998.
[53] On the connection between Augustus and Romulus implied by the similarity of this line to *Aen.* 6.779, see D. West 1993: 15.

described the volcano of Etna spewing forth fire (*uomat ignis*, Lucr. 1.724, with *flammarum* at 723). Monica Gale has well discussed Lucretius' technique of demythologisation, where the poet exploits mythological imagery and language to emphasise, by contrast, the truth of natural scientific accounts of phenomena. Gale sees precisely this technique in operation in the description of Etna, with the diction suggestive of the violence of Enceladus or Typhoeus trapped beneath the mountain, even as the context of the passage praises the rationalism of Empedocles and other early philosophers.[54] Vergil harnesses the volcanic power of Etna for Aeneas' arms forged by Vulcan, whose furnace is located within Etna (*Aen.* 8.416–53); Silius takes this appropriation a step further in making the aegis of Jupiter himself take on the qualities of Etna/Typhoeus.[55] The rejoinder to Lucretius' demythologisation of the volcano, and his Epicurean view of the gods, is emphatic as a wrathful Jupiter intervenes directly in human affairs.[56]

Nor do the significance of the image and the resulting polarisations end there. For Silius had described fire pouring from the helmet of Hannibal in Book 1 (*Pun.* 1.460–3):

> letiferum nutant fulgentes uertice cristae,
> crine ut flammifero terret fera regna cometes
> sanguineum spargens ignem; uomit atra rubentes
> fax caelo radios.

> The plumes sway, flashing balefully from his crest,
> as when a comet terrifies fierce kings with its flaming tail,
> scattering bloody fire; the black flame spews ruddy
> rays in the sky.

Besides this intratextual connection between Books 1 and 12, Silius also alludes intertextually to Vergil once again, for Aeneas is described in much the same terms (*Aen.* 10.270–3):

> ardet apex capiti cristisque a uertice flamma
> funditur et uastos umbo uomit aureus ignis:
> non secus ac liquida si quando nocte cometae
> sanguinei lugubre rubent.

> His helmet flashes and a flame pours out from the top of his crest
> and his golden boss spews vast fires:
> just as when comets on a clear night
> glow blood red and ominous.

---

[54] Gale 1994: 187 n. 98, 2000: 120–3. For the early association of Etna and Typhoeus see Ps.-Aesch. *PV* 363–72.

[55] Similar language appears repeatedly in Ovid's treatments of Etna/Typhoeus: see Ov. *Met.* 5.353, *Pont.* 2.10.23–4, *Ib.* 597–8; cf. Sen. *Phoen.* 314–16. Ov. *Fast.* 1.569–74 uses the phrase in explicitly associating Cacus with Typhoeus.

[56] *quantis pascat ferus ignibus iras* ('with what great fires he fiercely feeds his anger', *Pun.* 12.721).

Already in *Punica* 1, then, Hannibal is aligned with the awesome, and at one point even Giant-like, Aeneas of Vergil's tenth book.[57] But the two heroes' similarity becomes enmeshed in a series of further assimilations and contrasts woven into Book 12 in particular, especially in the complex polysemy of the fiery aegis of Jupiter, which brings both Cacus and Augustus into Silius' intricate tapestry, as well as Etna and Typhoeus. As in Silius' other theomachic moments, Homer, too, has a role to play: for the model lying behind the image of the fiery brow and its connection to the aegis is taken from *Iliad* 18, when Athena places her aegis on Achilles and he appears with his head blazing to terrify the Trojans and mark a turning point in the battle (*Il.* 18.203–31). The context of Achilles at his most godlike inspires both Vergil and Silius to reflect on the divine qualities of their heroes, but the Roman poets, of course, live in a world where the flame can signify an individual, like Aeneas or Augustus, who will become a god in his own right.

The care the poet has taken to work out his theme is evident from his use of the same image in the final book of the *Punica*, thus forming a neat symmetry with its appearance in Book 1 and emphasising the pivotal, even if not mathematically central, nature of Book 12. As Hannibal and Scipio line up for battle at Zama, Silius describes the Roman consul thus: *flammam ingentem frons alta uomebat* ('his lofty brow pours forth a huge flame', *Pun.* 17.398). For each reader who sees Scipio as taking on the mantle of Silius' Jupiter and Vergil's Augustus and Aeneas, along with Homer's Achilles, another will see Scipio aligned with Silius' Hannibal and Vergil's Cacus, along with Etna and Typhoeus.[58] Silius' allusions both to his own poem and to others', principally the *Aeneid*, thus possess a density of significance and reveal a mastery of poetic craft not normally associated with the *Punica*. And yet the multiple layers of imagery and allusion bring together god, hero, emperor, and villain in ways that provoke deep reflection on the implications of Hannibal's theomachy and its location before the Capitol. Mortals and gods are aligned and opposed, their respective natures assimilated and distinguished: this is the one of the key principles of theomachy, and it lies at the heart of Flavian epic.

Failure, Fame, and the Refraction of Theomachy

After their fortunes wane following the failed assault on Rome, the Carthaginians attempt to reprise the theomachic feats that marked their, and the epic's, apogee. With the Romans in the ascendancy, however, these attempts can only appear anticlimactic. Hasdrubal's crossing of the Alps, for instance, earns him the title of a second Hannibal (*Pun.* 15.516) and prompts a personification of

---

[57] On *Aeneid* 10 see Chapter 2 and, for its reception in Statius' *Thebaid*, pp. 274–7.
[58] On Livy's assimilation of Scipio to Hannibal in the later part of the third decade see Rossi 2004.

Italy to claim that for Hannibal only war with the gods remains (*Pun.* 15.527–8). But her intervention leads to the Carthaginian disaster at the Metaurus and the snuffing out of the vaguest possibility of another attack on the gods.[59] So too, when Hannibal departs for Libya, he regrets his failure to drag Jupiter from his throne (*Pun.* 17.225–7) and orders his fleet to return to Italy. But Neptune rouses a storm of epic proportions, just as Aeolus had done near the beginning of the *Aeneid*, and Hannibal, nearly shipwrecked, wishes that he had been struck by Jupiter's thunderbolt at Rome (*Pun.* 17.266–7). In other words, he asks to have played the part of Capaneus, a striking contrast to Aeneas, who in the same position wishes to have fallen at the hands of Diomedes.[60] Hannibal's self-elevating urge sets him apart from Aeneas: he deems Jupiter, not a mere mortal theomach like Diomedes, to be his proper opponent.[61] The emotion of regret that pervades not just Hannibal's speech but his appearances throughout Book 17, however, indelibly colours his characteristically impious rhetoric: the theomachic moment has passed, and no attempt to recreate it will succeed.[62] Where an epic storm of this nature should inspire the theomach, like Caesar or Capaneus, to reach ever greater heights and to take the poem along with him, Hannibal, despite his grandiloquent speech, falls into the self-doubt of an Aeneas at the beginning of his epic, a heroic trajectory marked by reversal and uncertainty.[63]

At Zama, Hannibal persists in attempting to raise the spectre of theomachy (*Pun.* 17.317–19):

> horrescamne ipsos, ueniant si ad proelia diuos,
> cum stetis, turmae, uidi contermina caelo
> quas iuga calcantes summas uolitare per Alpes?

> Should I fear the gods themselves, if they come to battle,
> when you stand with me, my men, whom I saw trampling peaks
> level with the sky and flying across the top of the Alps?

Silius' audience is by now well trained to intuit the rhetorical move that Hannibal makes to his troops—climbing the Alps was a successful theomachy that

---

[59] Hasdrubal's last words before being killed are to wish that Hannibal should burn the Capitol and mix his ashes with those of the shrine of Jupiter (*Pun.* 15.800–5). At this point, however, when the Carthaginians' fortunes have ebbed, the continuity of such rhetoric from Hannibal's earlier speeches only emphasises the ever-receding possibility of theomachy.

[60] Cf. p. 74.

[61] Compare the prayers of the Romans in Book 12, who believed that Hannibal could fall to no one but Jupiter (*Pun.* 12.643–5). Cf. Themis speaking about Capaneus at Ov. *Met.* 9.404–5.

[62] Hannibal's regret is a leitmotif of Book 17; later on, when faced with the defeat at Zama, he wishes that he had died at sea (*Pun.* 17.559–60). On the decline of Hannibal in the second half of the *Punica*, and the hero's stubborn refusal to accept reality, see Fucecchi 1990a.

[63] On Caesar and the storm see Day 2013: 143–56; on Capaneus see pp. 290–1 below. Hannibal will suffer a literal loss of direction at the end of Zama as he turns from a figure embodying epic teleology to one emblematic of the wandering, repetition, and error characteristic of romance (*Pun.* 17.522–617); on the relation between these two narrative structures see Quint 1993.

makes anything possible, even the overcoming of the gods in battle. But we already know this claim to be false from the confrontation with Jupiter in Book 12, an episode of which Hannibal reminds his men at *Pun.* 17.324–7. Furthermore, the only god to appear at Zama is Juno, who comes with the purpose of rescuing her favourite. There is, then, a clear irony in the simile describing Hannibal's *aristeia* at Zama (*Pun.* 17.474–8):

> ut, cum fulminibus permixta tonitrua mundum
> terrificant summique labat domus alta parentis,
> omne hominum terris trepidat genus, ipsaque ob ora
> lux atrox micat, et praesens adstare uiritim
> creditur intento perculsis Iuppiter igne.

> As when thunder mixed with lighting terrifies the world
> and the lofty abode of the highest father totters,
> the whole race of men on earth is frightened, and a dreadful light
> flashes over their very faces, and to a man they believe that
> Jupiter stands present and that they are struck by his fire.

Silius draws once again on the sublime language expressive of divine power to aggrandise Hannibal's *aristeia* and by extension the battle itself: the result of Zama may be a given, but the mode of its telling is of central importance to the success of the epic. The image of Jupiter striking mortals with his thunderbolt, however, recalls the scene of Hannibal's own failure at Rome.[64] Far from elevating Hannibal, the simile re-emphasises the gap between human and divine that the epic has maintained from the outset.

After being tricked by Juno into following a phantom of Scipio, Hannibal continues to speak in theomachic terms that appear increasingly out of place given his current predicament (*Pun.* 17.548–50):

> fulmineus ductor 'quisnam se numine caeco
> composuit nobis' inquit 'deus? aut latet idem
> cur monstro? tantumne obstat mea gloria diuis?'

> The thunderous general said, 'What god, concealing his divinity,
> pits himself against me? Why does he hide behind
> this portent? Is my glory such an impediment to the gods?'

Hannibal's misunderstanding of the situation is especially piquant: he perceives a contest with the divine—even literal theomachy, if one hears in *composuit* the verb's application to the pairing of gladiatorial combatants—when in fact Juno is attempting to save him from death at the hands of a mortal

---

[64] On the connections between the attack on the Capitol in Book 12 and the battle of Zama in Book 17 see Marks 2005: 194–200.

opponent.[65] The transformation in his circumstances has resulted in his rhetoric appearing empty if not downright bathetic.

Hannibal's final speech, too, returns to the idea of his glory in competition with the gods (*Pun.* 17.606–10):[66]

> caelum licet omne soluta
> in caput hoc compage ruat terraeque dehiscant,
> non ullo Cannas abolebis, Iuppiter, aeuo,
> decedesque prius regnis, quam nomina gentes
> aut facta Hannibalis sileant.

> Even if the whole of heaven with its frame
> disturbed were to rush down on my head and the earth gape open,
> you will never wipe out the memory of Cannae, Jupiter,
> but you will vacate your kingdom before the nations
> will be silent about the name and deeds of Hannibal.

Unlike all the hollow threats and boasts earlier in the book, Hannibal here finally touches on a way in which his theomachic ambitions might come to some fruition. Hannibal recasts the Punic War not as a clash of nations but as a medium for his own individual fame, placing that fame in tension with the power of Jupiter. It's instructive to compare the terms in which Hannibal imagines his own death with its likely source in the *Aeneid*. Loyal to her husband's shade, Dido wishes for death before she might break her marriage vows: *sed mihi uel tellus optem prius ima dehiscat / uel pater omnipotens adigat me fulmine ad umbras* ('but I would wish that the deep earth gape open for me first, or that the omnipotent father strike me to the shades with his thunderbolt', *Aen.* 4.24–5). Hannibal, by contrast, pictures a universal catastrophe akin to Stoic ecpyrosis, one that involves not just the opening of the earth but also the collapse of the heavens. For his fame to outlast not only such a disaster but also the end of Jupiter's reign would seem impossible, of course—for who would be left to report it?—but it is precisely the paradox that emphasises the power of fame to endure and to overcome all impediments.

The link between theomachy and fame reconnects Hannibal with his memorable crossing of the Alps, but it also evokes the topos of the *mache parapotamios* discussed in the previous chapter, in which Scipio and the Trebia struggled over the memory and existence of the river in sharp counterpoint to Scamander's threat to obliterate any trace of Achilles. Hannibal is thus well attuned to the dynamics of epic fame and its theomachic element. From this metapoetic point of view it's striking that his speech, which goes on to describe his continued threat to the Romans, should include the suggestive word *uiuam*, and not once but twice (*Pun.* 17.612, 615). In such a self-reflexive and self-authorising context, the verb clearly recalls Ovid's claim at the end of the

---

[65] *OLD* s.v. *compono* 3. Cf. *Pun.* 1.39 with Feeney 1982 ad loc.
[66] Cf. Bessone 2013a: 93–6.

Metamorphoses to achieve immortality through his art even in defiance of Jupiter (esp. *uiuam*, *Met.* 15.879).[67] Whereas Ovid had made his fame contingent on the spatial and temporal bounds of Roman power, however, Hannibal defies even the end of the world to blot out his name.

Silius acknowledges Scipio's fame too: *mansuri compos decoris per saecula rector* ('the leader possessed glory that would remain through the ages', *Pun.* 17.625). But the claim is qualified by an adjectival phrase in apposition with Scipio: *securus sceptri* ('secure in power', *Pun.* 17.627).[68] Power, as the *Punica* clearly illustrates, is no guarantee of permanence.[69] It is still Hannibal, represented in art, who draws the attention of all at Scipio's triumph: *sed non ulla magis mentesque oculosque tenebat, / quam uisa Hannibalis campis fugientis imago* ('but nothing held the minds and eyes of people more than the sight of a picture of Hannibal fleeing the field', *Pun.* 17.643–4).[70] Through comparisons with Bacchus, Hercules, and Quirinus—figures emblematic of the divinisation of mortals—Silius ends his poem with the image of the victorious Scipio as a truer figure of the divine than Hannibal ever was (*Pun.* 17.645–54).[71] But it is Hannibal who had voiced in his final speech the radical and theomachic thought that fame—the measure not only of his own heroism but also of Silius' epic—might transcend the Roman and imperial gods.

---

[67] Compare also Ovid's *abolere* (*Met.* 15.872) with Hannibal's *abolebis* (*Pun.* 17.608). Silius thereby suggests that Cannae is Hannibal's artistic achievement and legacy. On the Ovid passage see pp. 114–15. On the significance of Hannibal alluding to Ovid (and Horace) cf. Tipping 2010a: 70 with further bibliography at n. 51.

[68] On the meaning of this phrase see McGuire 1997: 101–2, Marks 2005: 113–14.

[69] The Roman audience would have known all too well that Scipio, too, would fall from grace. Cf. Livy 38.53.9–11 with Briscoe 2008: 170–9.

[70] Cf. Tipping 2010a: 104.

[71] On the imperial aspects of Bacchus and Hercules see Marks 2005: 224–7. On Hercules as a model for Scipio and as a paradigm of human divinity see Asso 2010: 189–92. On the legend of Scipio's divinity see pp. 227–8 with n. 82. Domitian's building of a temple to Hercules on the Via Appia in AD 94, which contained a statue of the hero with the features of the emperor, marked the beginning of a closer association with Hercules reflected in the poetry of Martial and Statius (see esp. *Ep.* 9.64 with the commentary of Henriksén 2012: 271–3). Domitian could even surpass Hercules: Mart. *Ep.* 9.101.23.

8

Theomachy and the Limits of Epic
CAPANEUS IN STATIUS' *THEBAID*

> Who is that great one who seems as if he minds not
> the fire and lies scornful and scowling,
> so that the rain seems not to ripen him?
> —DANTE ALIGHIERI

> At that time, then, I felt a strong disgust with reality. I did not approve, I did not accept the universe as it was. My attitude was scornful and proud like that of a Capaneus stuck in a terrestrial hell. And I tried to deny reality, to deny copies of reality, to despise the rules of real life, and to remake, in my own way, a different and more perfect reality.
> —GIOVANNI PAPINI

> If I were free I'd like to write a book with my philosophy in it. But for now, all I can do is tell it to you two wretches. If you can use it, fine. If not, and you get out of here alive and I don't, which would be rather strange, you can spread it about and maybe it will be of use to somebody. Who knows? Not that it matters much to me, though. I don't have the makings of a philanthropist.
> —PRIMO LEVI

Capaneus' defiance of the gods, familiar from the mythological tradition, marks him out as an especially strong instance of the theomach. His challenge to Jupiter to confront him in Book 10 of Statius' *Thebaid*—*nunc age, nunc totis in me conitere flammis, / Iuppiter!* ('now come, now strive against me with all your flames, Jupiter!' *Theb.* 10.904–5)—amplifies the typically impious characterisation visible, for example, in Aeschylus' *Septem* (*Sept.* 427–9):

> θεοῦ τε γὰρ θέλοντος ἐκπέρσειν πόλιν
> καὶ μὴ θέλοντός φησιν, οὐδὲ τὴν Διὸς
> Ἔριν πέδοι σκήψασαν ἐμποδὼν σχεθεῖν.

> For he says he will utterly destroy the city whether god is willing
> or unwilling, and that not even strife with Zeus,
> though it fall before him in the plain, will stand in his way.

The particular point of interest created by Statius is that his Capaneus explicitly addresses certain theological issues. This is a character who, at various points in the *Thebaid*, casts doubt on the validity of divination and sacrifice (*Theb.* 3.616–8, 10.847), sounds oddly like an Epicurean (*Theb.* 3.659–60), declares the gods to be a human fiction (*Theb.* 3.661), deifies his valour and arms (*Theb.* 3.615–6, 9.548–50), and calls himself a 'despiser of the gods' (*Theb.* 9.550), all of which bombastic rhetoric culminates in the theomachic challenge itself.

There is, of course, a glaring inconsistency in Capaneus both claiming that the gods do not exist and challenging Jupiter to combat, and it's precisely such paradoxes that have led critics to see his attitude to the gods as intellectually shallow.[1] That verdict on Statius' Capaneus as a dubious and foolish figure is in line with the conventional characterisation familiar from Aeschylus. For many readers it was no doubt the obvious and intuitive response, as it was for Dante in the *Inferno*. In this chapter, however, I attempt to expose the limitations of such a response in light of a close reading of the hero's appearances and other related episodes in the *Thebaid*.[2] The dismissal of Capaneus will be seen to depend on an overly literal reading of his rhetoric, which assumes a unified consistency as a prerequisite for intellectual heft and integrity.[3]

More interpretive avenues open up, however, if one accepts that through his hero Statius does not seek to offer a coherent and systematic theology, but rather to interrogate conventional beliefs in the divine. On that view, it becomes easier to understand the logic of the hero's challenge. The provocation of divine wrath subjects the gods to a kind of empirical test: their inaction will support the claim that they do not exist, or that they are impotent or unmoved, while their reaction, to Capaneus' detriment, will establish both their existence and their interventionism. And yet, any recuperation of Capaneus' radical views faces several more serious problems—his death by the thunderbolt of Jupiter, the fulfilment of various prophecies and auguries in the poem, and the large swathes of the epic given over to vivid descriptions of the gods' interaction and participation in events. Casting doubt on the existence of the divine

---

[1] Cf., e.g., Vessey 1973: 158: 'Capaneus' brief excursion into philosophy is glib and banal, consisting merely of insult and a threadbare *sententia*'. Ahl 1986: 2899 follows suit: 'Capaneus' wisdom is no more extensive than a few Epicurean clichés which provide a pretext for his assault on heaven'.

[2] Recent scholarship on the *Thebaid* has offered more nuanced readings of Capaneus, though none takes his rhetoric, let alone his 'philosophy', especially seriously (contrast the reactions of Papini and Levi to Dante's Capaneus in the epigraphs to this chapter). See, e.g., Klinnert 1970; Delarue 2000: 31, 83–5, and 396; Lovatt 2001; Lovatt 2005: 128–39; Leigh 2006. My approach differs from these in its focus on Statius' epic theology. This chapter significantly expands on Chaudhuri (forthcoming b).

[3] On the problematic effect that assumptions of coherence and consistency can have on our understanding of a narrative see Levene 2010: 317–92 on Livy.

in Lucan's *Pharsalia*, an epic devoid of typical divine action, would be one thing, but to do so in Statius' *Thebaid* is another matter entirely.

Some features of the poem, however, should give us pause before dismissing Capaneus as yet another foolish theomach, albeit one who has learned a few philosophical slogans. In the final book of the epic, for instance, responsibility for the burial of the Argive dead falls entirely to Athens and its king, Theseus, whose intervention is secured by the appeals of the widows of the deceased heroes: the gods are conspicuous only by their almost total absence. The end of the poem, therefore, in contrast to so many of the *Thebaid*'s models—the *Iliad*, *Aeneid*, and *Metamorphoses*—consists of an emphatically human resolution of a plot that had been partly initiated and fuelled by divine action.[4] By virtue of his appearance as a substitute deus ex machina Theseus reactivates and instantiates the theological debate set in motion by Capaneus' rhetoric: when, for once, humans take near total charge of bringing events to a conclusion, it is natural to revisit earlier questions of whether the gods are powerful, present, or even real. Throughout the poem, uncertainty and inconsistency abound in the treatment of the morality of the gods, mantic practices, and the utility of belief in the divine, and in the multiple explanations of the causes of events. Moreover, fluctuations in the narrator's tone—at one moment self-assured, at another tentative—are more marked than in the case of earlier epics and invite the reader's scrutiny. In Statius' tangled and disordered world, knowing the divine is especially fraught with difficulty and mistrust. Set against such a view of the *Thebaid*, and from the perspective of its conclusion, Capaneus' rhetoric sounds less like mindless bravado and more like the poem's illustration of one way to approach the philosophical and theological problems it poses.

That epic poets built such open-ended dialogues into their works is now well-established thanks to the scholarship of the last two decades, but Statius' place in that tradition, especially with regard to the central role of the theomach, remains understudied.[5] One of the principal ways in which Statius brings the theological and philosophical elements of the generic tradition into his poem is through allusions in Capaneus' characterisation. The hero's interrogative function emerges not only from his own speech and behaviour but also from the intertexts that shape him, principally from Vergil, Ovid, and Lucretius. The primary method of this chapter, therefore, is to examine the implications of Statius' complex intertextuality, especially the effect of combining

---

[4] Death or burial also dominates the end of all three earlier epics—Hector's, Turnus', and Julius Caesar's—but in each case there is a strong divine presence instrumental in leading up to the close: Zeus and Hermes enable the *Iliad*'s denouement, as do Jupiter, Juno, and Iuturna for the *Aeneid* and Jupiter and Venus for the *Metamorphoses*.

[5] On competing theological discourses in the Latin epic tradition see, e.g., Hardie 1986, Farrell 1991, Myers 1994, O'Hara 2007, Feldherr 2010. Feeney 1991, which does treat the *Thebaid*, remains the best treatment of the poem's theology to date.

several—often conflicting—source texts. These readings present the *Thebaid* as a radically decentring work of art that exploits the symbolic potential of the theomach to suggest—but never resolve—multiple views of the nature of the world and humankind's place within it.

The chapter focuses on the two main appearances of Capaneus in the epic— first on his agon with the prophet Amphiaraus, and then on the theomachy itself. Although the agon's immediate focus is the significance of the augury performed by the prophet Amphiaraus, the arguments of the two heroes quickly reveal a more radical disagreement about the validity of divinatory knowledge and even the status of the gods themselves. Whereas Amphiaraus represents the world of the *Thebaid* in accordance with the mainstream tradition of classical epic, as we see the gods in the works of Homer, Vergil, and Ovid, Capaneus' view resembles the more unconventional perspectives of Lucretius and Lucan. The agon thus functions as a synecdoche for two ways of understanding the epic world—either as populated by, and subject to, vigorously participatory gods or as distant from, or entirely devoid of, such gods. Since critics have had little to say about Capaneus' speeches in the agon—and that too has been largely dismissive—I offer a new reading of the episode, which highlights the rhetorical and intellectual force of his words, especially in light of their allusive background.

Nevertheless, Statius' repeated and extensive descriptions of divine action suggest that of the two views Amphiaraus' is prima facie the correct one. That conclusion is complicated, however, in a number of different ways, of which I focus on two. First, confidence in Amphiaraus is undermined at various points in the poem both through his assimilation to his antagonist Capaneus and through questions concerning the morality and effectiveness of the prophet's knowledge of the divine. Second, in the account of Capaneus' theomachy, Statius builds on the hero's earlier Epicurean and atheist rhetoric to turn the act from a simple and traditional impiety into a more powerful challenge against the enabling fictions of the *Thebaid* and the entire epic world. In the course of the argument I suggest that Capaneus represents Statius' philosophical poetics: through the character of the theomach the author figures his own testing of one of the main generic conventions of epic—the nature and operation of divine power.

I finally turn to the last phase of the epic as exemplifying Statius' response to the prior discourse on the divine. I argue, in particular, that the diminished presence of the divine, while not corroborating Capaneus' view precisely, nevertheless moves the epic world much closer to it. In light of this conclusion, it becomes clear that by altering the parameters of epic theology the theomach has an instrumental role in opening the way to Statius' novel resolution, and that such a negotiation between opposed points of view is essential to Statius' poetics. In the end, the *Thebaid* differs from both the mainstream epic tradition and its idiosyncratic counterparts, such as Lucretius' and Lucan's poems, not only by incorporating various, and often conflicting, epic theologies but also by illustrating its own process of compromise among them. The figure of Capaneus is fundamental to the working out of that process.

Capaneus and his Predecessors

Midway through Book 3 Amphiaraus and his fellow seer Melampus perform an augury through which they foresee the defeat of the Argive expedition.[6] Although the army clamours for war, they wait on the approval that Amphiaraus refuses to give. At this crucial juncture, with the progress of the epic potentially derailed, Capaneus enters the scene to argue against the prophet's opposition to the war. Statius departs from the tradition evident in Aeschylus' *Septem*, in which Tydeus, not Capaneus, is Amphiaraus' antagonist (*Sept.* 570-5). Whether following another version or innovating, Statius deliberately casts Capaneus in this more prominent and fully characterised role, and he positions the theomach as a more systematic opponent of Amphiaraus' pious world view.

Statius describes Capaneus with a richly intertextual epithet, *superum contemptor* (*Theb.* 3.602), which, as many critics have noted, recalls Vergil's description of the Etruscan tyrant Mezentius (*contemptor diuum*, *Aen.* 7.648, *contemptor deum*, *Aen.* 8.7).[7] In commenting on the Vergilian epithet, Servius makes the aptness of Statius' allusion clear: CONTEMPTORQUE DEUM MEZENTIUS *quis enim iustius quam sacrilegus contra pios et praepararet bellum et gereret?* ('MEZENTIUS DESPISER OF THE GODS For who could be more appropriate than a sacrilegious person to prepare and wage war against the pious?' Serv. ad *Aen.* 8.7).[8] Although the two characters will be connected by a number of verbal and thematic echoes throughout the *Thebaid*, Servius' comment also indicates a key point of contrast: where Mezentius merely opposes the 'pious', that is, the Trojans, Capaneus will attempt to fight the gods themselves. The epithet also alludes to a number of impious figures in Ovid's *Metamorphoses*—Pentheus, Polyphemus, and the race of humans born from the blood of the Giants.[9] Through this single phrase Statius signals both the tradition of impiety in which Capaneus follows and the antagonistic attitude to the divine that the hero brings to the upcoming agon.[10] At the same time, Capaneus

---

[6] On this scene see Manolaraki 2013 and Tuttle 2013. On the Roman historical practice of augury see, e.g., Linderski 1986, Vaahtera 2001, and Santangelo 2013 (who focuses on the late republic extending into the Augustan period); on divination in general under the empire see Vigourt 2001. For the Augustan poets' negotiation of the significance of augury cf. Green 2009.

[7] See Leigh 2006: 226 with nn. 36-7.

[8] On Mezentius see Chapter 2.

[9] Pentheus (*contemptor superum*, *Met.* 3.514), Polyphemus (*contemptor Olympi*, *Met.* 13.761), race born from Giants (*propago / contemptrix superum*, *Met.* 1.160-1)—on all of whom see Chapter 3 passim.

[10] Cf. p. 307 n. 26 and n. 000 for the similar contempt of Caligula and the Claudii.

possesses the truly theomachic qualities missing from Vergil's impious hero, and indeed Statius amplifies them far beyond anything seen in common models like Polyphemus.

The first of Capaneus' two speeches begins by inciting the gathered horde and dismissing the power of prophecy (*Theb.* 3.607-18):

> 'quae tanta ignauia' clamat,
> 'Inachidae uosque o socio de sanguine Achiui?
> unius (heu pudeat!) plebeia[11] ad limina ciuis
> tot ferro accinctae gentes animisque paratae
> pendemus? non si ipse cauo sub uertice Cirrhae
> (quisquis is est, timidis famaeque ita uisus) Apollo
> mugiat insano penitus seclusus in antro,
> expectare queam dum pallida uirgo tremendas
> nuntiet ambages. uirtus mihi numen et ensis
> quem teneo! iamque hic timida cum fraude sacerdos
> exeat, aut hodie, uolucrum quae tanta potestas,
> experiar.'

> 'What great cowardice is this,' he shouts,
> 'you sons of Inachus, and you, Achaeans of allied blood?
> Do we hang on the plebeian threshold—for shame!—of but one citizen,
> so many nations girded with iron and ready in spirit?
> Not if he himself from beneath the cavernous height of Cirrha
> —not if Apollo (whoever he is, seeming thus to cowards and rumour)
> were to bellow in the deep seclusion of his mad cave,
> could I wait for the pale virgin to announce
> her dread riddles. Valour is my god and the sword
> that I hold! Now let this priest come out with his fearful deceit,
> or today I shall test what is this supposedly great power of birds.'

Capaneus' caricature of the Delphic oracle alludes to Vergil's description of the Cumaean Sibyl, just after she has foretold the new Trojan War that awaits Aeneas in Latium (*Aen.* 6.98-101):[12]

> talibus ex adyto dictis Cumaea Sibylla
> <u>horrendas</u> canit <u>ambages antroque remugit</u>,

---

[11] On *plebeia*, sometimes emended to *Phoebeia*, see Snijder 1968: 239-40. The tone of aristocratic contempt suits Capaneus' characterisation (see previous note).

[12] Cf. Lactantius ad *Theb.* 3.613. The commentator had earlier noted that the phrase *quae tanta ignauia* (*Theb.* 3.607) alludes to Tarchon's speech at *Aen.* 11.733, though the two passages are more closely connected (cf. *Theb.* 3.614-15 with *Aen.* 11.738-40). Statius turns Tarchon's slight against Bacchic revels into Capaneus' more thoroughgoing dismissal of religion. In *Thebaid* 10, Menoeceus, a contrasting doublet for Capaneus, will echo the impious hero's words when lying to his father about his intention to fulfil a prophecy (*Theb.* 10.723-6). On Menoeceus see Fantham 1995, Franchet d'Espèrey 1999: 374-82, Heinrich 1999, and Ganiban 2007: 136-48.

> obscuris uera inuoluens: ea frena furenti
> concutit et stimulos sub pectore uertit <u>Apollo</u>.
>
> In such words the Cumaean Sibyl chants from her shrine
> dread riddles and bellows from her cave,
> wrapping truth in darkness: as she rages
> Apollo shakes the reins and applies the goads beneath her breast.

The Vergilian intertext presents two interpretive options. On the one hand, Capaneus' unconscious echo of the *Aeneid* seems to highlight the hero's ignorance of the oft-verified power of prophecy: just as the Sibyl's prediction about the war in Latium came true, so too will Amphiaraus' pessimistic forecast about the Theban war. The rhetorical effect of Capaneus' sarcasm, however, works quite differently and points not to his ignorance but rather to the radical implications of his disbelief. By having Capaneus (albeit unknowingly) turn the Sibyl's words against her Vergilian image of divine and oracular authority, Statius casts his hero as rejecting the conventional assumptions both of epic poetry and of Greco-Roman religion.[13] It isn't sloppiness that leads Capaneus to lump together Greek oracles and Roman auguries: his dismissal of the Roman ritual practice of taking the auspices before going to war is part of a comprehensive attack on the gods that encompasses both Greek and Roman worlds, both literary and historical conceptions of the divine.

Into the resulting theological vacuum steps the hero himself (*Theb.* 3.615–16): *uirtus mihi numen et ensis / quem teneo!* ('valour is my god and the sword that I hold!'), invoking in the process the words of Vergil's Mezentius: *dextra mihi deus et telum, quod missile libro, / nunc adsint!* ('now let my right hand, my god, and the weapon I poise to hurl be favourable!' *Aen.* 10.773–4).[14] Despite their long-standing association, however, it's important to distinguish between the two heroes. Mezentius' impiety extends only as far as a lack of concern for the divine: *nec diuum parcimus ulli* ('nor do we show regard for any of the gods,' *Aen.* 10.880).[15] But even this sentiment comes after he has seen Aeneas kill his son, so it expresses, rather more than impiety, the extent of his desire for vengeance. Unlike Mezentius, however, who accepts both the existence and the ultimate power of the divine (*ast de me diuum pater atque hominum rex / uiderit*, 'but about me the father of the gods and king of men will see,' *Aen.* 10.743–4), Capaneus, by contrast, is much more thoroughgoing in his impiety, especially since he is provoked by nothing more than his own impatience and bellicosity.[16]

---

[13] Capaneus' position likewise encourages a rereading of the Vergilian passage, undermining the authority prophecy grants to the foundation of Rome.
[14] Cf. Lactantius ad *Theb.* 3.615. On Capaneus' autonomy see Klinnert 1970: 62–3, 70–1, 75–8, 133–42.
[15] See Chapter 2.
[16] Cf. *Theb.* 3.598–603. See also Ripoll 1998: 341.

Capaneus' boast about his sword alludes to a number of other impious heroes in the epic and tragic tradition, principally Apollonius' Idas (Ap. Rhod. 1.466–71):[17]

ἴστω νῦν δόρυ θοῦρον, ὅτῳ περιώσιον ἄλλων
κῦδος ἐνὶ πτολέμοισιν ἀείρομαι, οὐδέ μ' ὀφέλλει
Ζεὺς τόσον ὁσσάτιόν περ ἐμὸν δόρυ, μή νύ τι πῆμα
λοίγιον ἔσσεσθαι μηδ' ἀκράαντον ἄεθλον
Ἴδεω γ' ἑσπομένοιο, καὶ εἰ θεὸς ἀντιόωτο·
τοῖόν μ' Ἀρήνηθεν ἀοσσητῆρα κομίζεις.

Let my rushing spear be witness now, with which beyond all others
I carry off glory in wars—nor does Zeus aid me
so much as my spear—that no grief
shall be deadly nor any challenge unfulfilled
while Idas follows, even if a god should encounter us;
such an aid am I whom you bring from Arene.

Even Idas, however, though he claims the superiority of his spear over the strength of Zeus, gives no indication that the gods might not exist. Statius, in fact, makes Capaneus' traditional boast about his arms into a significantly more provocative claim by having the hero explicitly cast doubt on the status of Apollo (*quisquis is est, timidis famaeque ita uisus*, *Theb*. 3.612). This intellectual position has received relatively little attention in the scholarship, which by and large still focuses on moral evaluation. Tim Stover, for instance, argues that 'by using Apollonius' Idas as a model for his Capaneus, Statius underscores and reinforces Capaneus' utterly criminal nature'.[18] Stover is right to observe the accumulation of negative *exempla* in the figure of Capaneus, but the subtle differences between character and model, and between the world of the *Thebaid* and its predecessors, suggest that Statius had greater purpose in his elaborate intertextual games than merely to reaffirm the conventional view of impiety.

The final words of Capaneus' speech contain a further allusion that develops the sceptical characterisation of the hero: 'let this priest come out, or today I shall test what great power there is in birds' (*sacerdos / exeat, aut hodie, uolucrum quae tanta potestas, / experiar*, *Theb*. 3.616–18). The verb *experiar* alludes to Lycaon's test of Jupiter's identity, discussed in Chapter 3 (*Met*. 1.222–3):

---

[17] Stover 2009, esp. 440–3, has convincingly argued for Statius' knowledge and use of the episode in the *Argonautica* (on which see J. J. Clauss 1993: 79–80). Idas' speech recalls the boasts of Parthenopaeus and Capaneus in Aeschylus' *Septem* (see pp. 44–6 and 218–19). Wißmann 2000: 453–4 argues that Apollonius' agon alludes to the confrontation of Tydeus and Amphiaraus in the *Septem*. Statius demonstrates an awareness of the interconnectedness of the tradition through his allusions to different versions of the same topos. For the relationship between the Statian agon and the near contemporary scene in Silius' *Punica* depicting a similar agon between Flaminius and the seer Corvinus, see Chapter 6.

[18] Stover 2009: 440.

experiar deus hic discrimine aperto / an sit mortalis, nec erit dubitabile uerum ('I shall test with clear distinction whether this one is god or mortal: nor will the truth be open to doubt').[19] As we saw in the reading of the Lycaon episode, *experiar* strongly suggests the acquisition of knowledge by empirical testing, which Ovid had contrasted with the response of the Arcadian people (*Met.* 1.220–1): *signa dedi uenisse deum, uulgusque precari / coeperat; inridet primo pia uota Lycaon* ('I gave signs that a god had come, and the people began to pray: Lycaon first mocked their pious prayers'). Statius draws on this Ovidian conflict between the pious acknowledgement of supernatural signs and the impious valorisation of the purely physical world to structure the agon in the *Thebaid*, in which Capaneus can threaten to 'test' the power of augury by the measure of his own might. In the context of augury, the verb *experiar* bears a further Ovidian irony. In the *Fasti*, Romulus thinks to determine the foundation of the city by augury: *magna fides auium est: experiamur aues* ('there is great faith in birds: let us test the birds', *Fast.* 4.814). Picking up on the Ovidian intratextuality between the *Fasti* and the *Metamorphoses*, Capaneus applies Lycaon's scepticism to the activity in which Romulus has such confidence. Just as Capaneus casts doubt on Apollo in terms that parody the prophetic power of Vergil's Sibyl, so too he casts doubt on augury in terms that parody the foundation of Rome—he thus threatens on more than one front the numinous authority that poetry and civic mythology lent to Roman identity.

The Agon: Two World Views

In response to Capaneus' speech 'the Achaean mob roars with joy and fulfils his frenzy with its approval' (*laetum fremit adsensuque furentem / implet Achaea manus*, *Theb.* 3.618–9). Amphiaraus picks up the motif of Capaneus' madness in his reply (*Theb.* 3.620–4):

> alio curarum agitante tumultu
> non equidem effreno iuuenis clamore profani
> dictorumque metu, licet hic insana minetur,
> elicior tenebris; alio mihi debita fato
> summa dies, uetitumque dari mortalibus armis.

---

[19] As the representative example of Ovid's *propago / contemptrix superum* (*Met.* 1.160–1), Lycaon already bears an affinity to Capaneus, the *superum contemptor*. For Capaneus' second allusion to Lycaon's *experiar* see below. Contrast Silius' use of *experiar* at *Pun.* 4.608: Silius turns the theomachic empiricist attitude to a good purpose, namely, the testing not of the gods but of the limits of Roman power, here represented by the vulnerability of an elephant to a Roman spear. This small example of redirecting theomachic characteristics to a more legitimate goal occurs within a larger example of the same phenomenon—Scipio's *mache parapotamios*. For the river battle is an attempt to appropriate the sublimity of the theomachic Achilles for the aggrandisement of Scipio, with Achilles' impiety carefully moderated throughout. See Chapter 6.

> By a different, troubling welter of cares—
> not by the unbridled clamour of this sacrilegious youth,
> nor by fear of his words, though his threats be insane—
> am I drawn from the darkness; by another fate is my last day
> owed to me, forbidden to be given to mortal arms.

Amphiaraus' accusations of madness (*insana*; cf. also *uesane*, *Theb.* 3.627) respond to Capaneus' own labelling of the Delphic cave—and by extension the whole matter of prophecy—as *insano* (*Theb.* 3.613).[20] Capaneus later responds by redirecting Amphiaraus' charge of madness: *tuus o furor auguret uni / ista tibi* ('let that frenzy of yours augur those things for you alone', *Theb.* 3.648-9). He takes advantage of the well-established idea of prophetic frenzy, using it as a basis to judge Amphiaraus mad in a more general sense.[21] Moreover, just as the seer attempts to isolate Capaneus (*unique tacet tibi noster Apollo*, 'to you alone is our Apollo silent', *Theb.* 3.628), so too that same language will now be turned against him (*uni... tibi*). But this is no simple exchange of mutual insults; for each side labels as mad a way of thinking that is fundamentally antithetical to the speaker's own view, whether Capaneus' scepticism about the gods or Amphiaraus' confidence in omens. Framing such a clash of fundamentally irreconcilable world views in terms of madness is nothing new in literature; Tiresias makes much the same accusation against Pentheus in the *Bacchae* (*Bacch.* 325-6): κοὐ θεομαχήσω σῶν λόγων πεισθεὶς ὕπο. / μαίνῃ γὰρ ὡς ἄλγιστα ('and I shall not fight the god persuaded by your words. For you are most grievously mad'). Statius' innovation is to give Capaneus' 'madness' at least the semblance of a more intellectually coherent position—a deliberate attempt to demolish the entire edifice underlying Amphiaraus' authority, rather than overweening pride for its own sake.

Amphiaraus' announcement that he will disclose the future to the waiting crowd, with the pointed exception of Capaneus, suggests that the revelation might persuade the rest of the Argives not to pursue the war (*Theb.* 3.626-8). He then asks a series of rhetorical questions forcing the men to attend to the absurdity of wishing to go to war (*Theb.* 3.629-35):

> quo, miseri, fatis superisque obstantibus arma,
> quo rapitis? quae uos Furiarum uerbera caecos
> exagitant? adeone animarum taedet? et Argos
> exosi? nil dulce domi? nulla omina curae?

---

[20] Nau 2005: 158-73 offers a good summary of the scene and the basic themes, especially the rhetoric of madness; on other rhetorical features of the agon see Frings 1991: 10-16. For the fullest treatment of madness in the *Thebaid* see Hershkowitz 1998: 247-301; cf. Lovatt 2001, who discusses the agon on p. 118, for important qualifications, including the additional complications presented by madness' metapoetic aspect (113-17).

[21] For *furor* used of a diviner's inspiration see Cic. *Div.* 1.66. For the similar association between μάντις ('seer') and μαίνομαι ('to be mad') in Greek, see, e.g., Pl. *Ti.* 71e-72a (where the relationship is implicit but clear); cf. Pl. *Phdr.* 244c, Cic. *Div.* 1.1.

quid me Persei secreta ad culmina montis
ire gradu trepido superumque inrumpere coetus
egistis?

Where, wretched ones, when the fates and the gods obstruct your arms,
where are you rushing? What lash of the Furies drives you on
blindly? Are you so weary of life? And is Argos
hateful? Is there no sweetness at home? Have you no care for the omens?
Why did you force me to go to the secret peaks of the Persean mountain
with trembling step and to burst in on the gatherings of the gods?

The standard supernatural apparatus of epic—fates, councils of the gods, Furies, and omens—appears among the many competing influences mentioned by Amphiaraus, as the prophet reasserts a vision of the world that had been attacked or dismissed by Capaneus. He goes on to justify his opposition to the war through the unique authority granted to his mantic powers: 'I have seen the portents of great ruin' (*uidi ingentis portenta ruinae*, *Theb*. 3.640). And yet despite his sense of conviction, the speech is filled with a sense of futility. Far from being able to profit from his special insight, Amphiaraus appears bound to his fate. The use of the verb *ago* both in and immediately before his speech describes and echoes his subjection to external powers: *tandem prorumpere adactus / Oeclides* ('at last the son of Oecleus is impelled to burst forth', *Theb*. 3.619–20); *sed me uester amor nimiusque arcana profari / Phoebus agit* ('but my love for you and too mighty Phoebus drive me to foretell hidden matters', *Theb*. 3.625–6); *quid me... egistis* ('why did you force me...?' *Theb*. 3.633–5). The speech culminates in an explicit submission: *sed quid uana cano, quid fixos arceo casus? / ibimus* ('but why do I prophesy empty things, why do I ward off fixed fate? We will go', *Theb*. 3.646–7). What began as a bold riposte to Capaneus, and as an attempt to convince the Argives of their folly, over the course of the speech has become Amphiaraus' realisation of his own impotence. This resignation is the logical consequence of his belief in the veridicality of divination. Unlike Roman augury, which merely gauged the gods' approval or disapproval and formed the basis of subsequent decision-making, Amphiaraus has seen an image of the very future itself, and the specificity of that knowledge leaves no room for manoeuvre.[22] There is, then, something scrupulously consistent about Amphiaraus' world view just as there is about Capaneus'—each believes in an extreme conception of the human will, either in its maximal independence from the gods or in its maximal subjection to them.

---

[22] As Cicero, himself an augur, says of the Romans in *De Divinatione*: *non enim sumus ii nos augures, qui auium reliquorumue signorum obseruatione futura dicamus* ('for we augurs are not the sort who declare the future by observation of birds or other signs', *Div*. 2.70). Snijder 1968: 188 notes that the haruspicy and augury are, nonetheless, depicted with a number of Roman touches.

There is one point, however, on which Amphiaraus appears very much mistaken. Twice the seer claims that the gods stand in the way of the war: *fatis superisque obstantibus arma* ('when the fates and the gods obstruct your arms', *Theb.* 3.629); *proicite arma manu: deus ecce furentibus obstat, / ecce deus!* ('cast your weapons from your hands: look—a god stands in the way of your frenzy, a god!', *Theb.* 3.643-4). This sentiment not only appears at odds with Amphiaraus' own yielding to fate but contrasts strikingly with the efforts of Jupiter and Mars to set the war in motion, in particular earlier in Book 3 itself.[23] It's true that Jupiter intends the destruction of Argos as well as Thebes, and in that sense the gods will thwart the expedition, but Amphiaraus is entirely oblivious to the irony that the verb *obsto* poorly conveys what the gods have actually been doing.[24] This question of knowing, or failing to know, the divine is one to which the agon will return, but Amphiaraus' misinterpretation already cedes important ground to Capaneus' aggressive scepticism about divination.

Indeed, Capaneus' response to Amphiaraus focuses on the presumption divination makes on the gods' actual interest or involvement in human affairs, a presumption which assumes not only the possibility of knowledge, but also active and interested (or, in other words, epic) gods (*Theb.* 3.657-61):

> tua prorsus inani
> uerba polo causas abstrusaque nomina[25] rerum

---

[23] Cf. *Theb.* 3.234-5, 575-8. Lactantius ad *Theb.* 3.643 identifies the *deus* as Apollo, suggesting that the augury is designed to counter the desire for war. This interpretation, however, faces several problems: first, as the god of prophecy Apollo may be Amphiaraus' patron, but the augury itself is closely associated with Jupiter (cf. *Theb.* 3.471-82); second, whatever the identity of the *deus* at *Theb.* 3.643-4, there is no uncertainty about the comprehensiveness of *fatis superisque* at *Theb.* 3.629; third, even if Amphiaraus correctly suggests that Apollo discourages the war, he seems to have no awareness of the destructive role of Jupiter.

[24] Lactantius ad *Theb.* 3.641 notes that Venus and Juno are opposed to the war, but Amphiaraus is clearly not suggesting that only *some* gods are against the war. Under the same lemma, however, Lactantius also raises the possibility that *diuumque metus* might refer to a fear shared by all the gods because Capaneus will attack the heavens. If this is so, the gods nevertheless persist in encouraging a war that ultimately fulfils the hero's theomachic tendencies.

[25] The reading of P, *nomina*, is much contested, with other MSS having *semina*, and some commentators emending to *omina* (cf. *Theb.* 2.263); the transmitted text of Lactantius supports *semina*, pace Sweeney, who (via Schindel) accepts Baehrens' highly implausible *momina*. Whatever the true reading, Capaneus' rhetorical question effectively denies that augury can provide information about the world. What kind of information that is, however, depends partly on the word in question. If *omina* (following D. E. Hill 1983, as I do elsewhere), then Capaneus rejects augury on its own terms—it does not reveal the truth of omens, if such things even exist. The manuscript variants, *nomina* or *semina*, on the other hand, along with *causas* earlier in the line, suggest natural, and specifically materialist, philosophy. In either case, Capaneus rejects augury for the different reason that it does not provide scientific—i.e., true—knowledge. The phrase *causas rerum* alludes to Epicureanism via Vergil: *felix qui potuit rerum cognoscere causas* ('happy is he who knows the causes of things', *G.* 2.490). For natural philosophy as the way to know the *causas rerum* see Sen. *QNat.* 2.53.3 (though Seneca views Etruscan divination by lightning as a product of such philosophy; cf. Hine 1981: 420); cf. Ov. *Met.* 15.68. Luc. 1.67 uses such philosophical language for the purpose of knowing about civil war (which is itself cast in cosmological terms throughout the poem). For *nomina rerum* cf. *Silv.* 2.6.8, Lucr. 5.72, 1029. Especially Lucretian is *semina rerum* (12 times in Lucr., e.g., 1.59), but see also Ov. *Met.* 1.9, 419, Sen. *Ben.* 3.29.4, Luc. 10.208. Lovatt 2013a: 62

> eliciunt? miseret superum, si carmina curae
> humanaeque preces. quid inertia pectora terres?
> primus in orbe deos fecit timor!

> Can your words really coax
> from the empty sky the causes and hidden names of things?
> Pitiable are the gods if they take heed of humans' hymns
> or prayers. Why do you terrify sluggish hearts?
> Fear first made gods in the world!

Capaneus here alludes to the provocations of Iarbas at *Aen.* 4.206–18, discussed in Chapter 2, though he speaks with greater conviction than his Vergilian predecessor.[26] Just as Servius notes the Epicurean flavour of Iarbas' speech, so too Lactantius remarks that Statius is here following Epicurus (ad *Theb.* 3.659): *totum hoc secundum Epicurum dicit poeta.*[27] To substantiate his point the commentator quotes a passage from Lucretius' *De Rerum Natura* that describes the impassivity of the gods:

> omnis enim diuum per se natura necessest
> immortali aeuo summa cum pace fruatur
> semota a nostris rebus seiunctaque longe
> nec bene promeritis capitur, nec tangitur ira.[28]

> For the whole nature of the gods in itself necessarily
> enjoys immortal age in the deepest peace,

reads Capaneus as making 'a sarcastic suggestion that Amphiaraus is a Lucretian figure, who could use his words to influence the world'. When talking to Dis in the underworld, Amphiaraus asserts his knowledge of 'causes and beginnings' (*causas elementaque*, *Theb.* 8.92), on which see Masterson 2005: 303, Seo 2013: 180. In general, on the role of physical explanation in ancient ethics see Inwood 2007.

[26] Cf. esp. Statius' *inani* and *terres* with Vergil's *terrificant*, *inania*, and *inanem*. Whereas Iarbas hopes his challenge will spur his father into action, Capaneus' scepticism is more than rhetorical.

[27] Cf. Taisne 1999: 170; Delarue 2000: 31, 83–5, 396; Leigh 2006: 231–2. Neri 1986: 2016–17 sees an Epicurean-Stoic conflict behind the rhetoric of Capaneus and Amphiaraus. The sarcasm in Capaneus' words certainly stands in pointed contrast to the philosophical, and even divinatory, character of Sen. *QNat.* 1.1.4: *uidebimus an rerum omnium certus ordo ducatur et alia aliis ita implexa sint, ut quod antecedit aut causa sit sequentium aut signum; uidebimus an diis humana curae sint, an series ipsa, quid factura sit, certis rerum notis nuntiet* ('We shall then see whether a fixed order is observed in all events, and whether one event is so entwined with another that what precedes is either cause or at least token of what follows. We shall then see, too, whether mortal affairs concern the gods, and whether the very series of events announces by sure signs what it will bring about'). Neri cites this passage from the *QNat.* in the same article, but in a separate discussion of Seneca's attitude to fate and divination (Neri 1986: 2046–51).

[28] The quotation given by Lactantius corresponds to the manuscript and modern readings of Lucr. 2.646–48 and 651. In addition to minor differences in word order, the commentator's version skips lines 649–50, which describe the self-sufficiency of the gods, free from pain and danger; the gist of both versions is, however, the same. The full passage also appears twice in our text of Lucr. (1.44–49 and 2.646–51). Although the repetition may cause textual critics some consternation (see, e.g., Bailey 1947: 601–3), it has no bearing on the fact that Lactantius closely identified Capaneus' thought at *Theb.* 3.659–60 with Lucretius' thought on the detachment and impassivity of the gods. For a Stoic response to this Epicurean view see, e.g., Sen. *Ben.* 4.3–8.

> far removed and separated from our affairs,
> and it is neither taken with good services, nor touched by anger.

Lactantius could equally well have chosen other passages from the *De Rerum Natura* on the tranquillity and distance of the gods (Lucr. 2.1093–4, 5.146–55), or on the futility of divination and augury (Lucr. 4.1239, 6.381–6), or on the bad religious practices that follow from superstitious and mistaken beliefs about the gods (Lucr. 5.73–5, 6.43–79), all of which express the sentiment that the gods are far removed from natural and human affairs and that therefore our appeals to them are rendered useless. And while Capaneus' language here mimics, but does not copy, that of Lucretius, Lactantius is nevertheless right to observe the rejection of religious superstition Capaneus shares with the Epicurean Lucretius.[29]

Consistent with their dismissal of divine intervention in human affairs, Capaneus and Lucretius also share a disdain for oracles. Lucretius, for instance, ironically appropriates oracular language to emphasise the supremacy of his scientific epistemological methods over traditional forms that are both unreasoned and false (*sanctius... quam / Pythia*, Lucr. 5.111–12).[30] But whereas Lucretius asserts that his philosophy is not only more reasoned than oracular methods but also more holy (*sanctius*, Lucr. 5.111), thus offering an alternative form of piety, Capaneus has neither interest nor use for piety of any kind, whether in a traditional or alternative form.[31] The extremity of Capaneus' attitude emerges clearly from the contrast between his and Lucretius' claims about the role of fear in religion. The philosopher explains, for instance, how fear of the gods led to the veneration of holy places (Lucr. 5.73–75):

> et quibus ille modis diuom metus insinuarit
> pectora, terrarum qui in orbi sancta tuetur
> fana lacus lucos aras simulacraque diuom.
>
> ...and in what ways that fear of the gods insinuated its way
> into our hearts, which in our world keeps holy
> the shrines, pools, groves, altars, and images of the gods.

Capaneus, on the other hand, deems even Apollo to be a figment of fear and rumour (*Theb.* 3.612), and now extends his hypothesis to all the gods: *primus in*

---

[29] Lactantius follows his quotation of Lucretius with one from Vergil, in which Dido casts doubt on Aeneas' claim to have been instructed to leave Carthage by the gods (*Aen.* 4.379–80): *scilicet is superis labor est, ea cura quietos / sollicitat* ('truly, this is work for gods, this care troubles their peace'). In contrast to Lucretius, of course, Vergil, like Statius, presents his gods as very much involved in human affairs. Statius, however, makes Capaneus' speech more ostentatiously philosophical than Dido's. For another Epicurean statement of this sort in Roman epic, cf. Luc. 7.454–5: *mortalia nulli / sunt curata deo* ('mortal affairs concern no god'), discussed in Chapter 5.

[30] Cf. Lucr. 1.734–41 where Lucretius claims that even the wrong-headed ideas of well-intentioned philosophers should be considered superior to oracles.

[31] Summers 1995 argues that Lucretius attacks not just the superstitious aspect of religion but all Roman religious practices; this radical attitude to traditional piety is thus distinguished from the more accommodating position of Epicurus.

orbe deos fecit timor! (*Theb.* 3.661).[32] The sentiment, which explains the existence of religion as a fiction that brings order and civilisation to society, including the notion of gods, is known from as early as a famous fragment of the *Sisyphus*, a satyr drama or tragedy attributed usually to Critias but by some to Euripides: πυκνός τις καὶ σοφὸς γνώμην ἀνήρ / <θεῶν> δέος θνητοῖσιν ἐξευρεῖν ('some shrewd man of clever judgement invented fear of gods for mortals', *TrGF* 43 fr. 19.12–13 Snell).[33] This kind of anthropological conspiracy theory clearly goes beyond, and is in fact contradictory to, anything in the writings of Epicurus or Lucretius, both of whom describe the gods as passive, but very much in existence. The opponents of Epicureanism, on the other hand, sometimes suggested that the philosophy dresses an otherwise impious atheism in the guise of a more acceptable and elaborate system of belief.[34] One way to interpret Capaneus' atheism, then, is as an exposé of true Epicurean sentiments—the hero merely gives voice to, and thereby confirms, the slippage from disinterested to non-existent gods. If intended as a caricature of Epicureanism, however, Capaneus has entered so far into parody that Statius' point has become rather lost. For the bellicose, raging warrior—even if we set his atheist claims to one side— would seem to be not just an exaggeration but quite the opposite of an Epicurean.[35] If by pressing for an allegorical reading we arrive at a dead end, a better alternative is to examine the rhetorical effect of Capaneus' claims and the interpretive directions opened by the Lucretian intertext.[36]

---

[32] The *fama* of Apollo, which Capaneus scorns, should perhaps be associated with the *fama deum* by which Lucretius' Epicurus is similarly undaunted (Lucr. 1.68). Capaneus' words at 3.661 also appear in a fragmentary poem attributed to Petronius (fr. 28 Mueller).

[33] On the fragment see Sutton 1981, Kahn 1997, Collard 2007: 56–68, O'Sullivan 2012.

[34] Cf., e.g., Cotta's argument, following Posidonius, at Cic. *Nat. D.* 1.115–24. Epicureans naturally defended themselves against the charge, as attested by Philodemus' treatise *De Pietate* (on which see Obbink 1996).

[35] While Lucretius does not explicitly claim that Epicureans disapprove of war per se, the opening allegory of the work in which Venus subdues Mars is a clear indication of the Epicurean preference for peace. Lucretius also criticises war both as the result of avarice (Lucr. 5.1423–35) and as false security against the fear of death (Lucr. 2.37–54), since only philosophy can truly and permanently release the mind from its irrational anxieties. On the Epicurean attitude to peace, see the passage from Diogenes of Oenoanda quoted in Fowler 1989: 149, and cf. 145: 'What matters for the Epicurean is the chance to lead a quiet life'. Fowler 1997 argues for such a thing as Epicurean anger, but even this enlarged conception can't accommodate Capaneus' frenzy and war lust. Capaneus' *furor* may offer one point of resemblance, however, with Lucretius. In the *genethliacon* for Lucan, Statius lists several canonical Latin poets, including Lucretius, who yield to the superiority of the poet of the *Pharsalia*: *et docti furor arduus Lucreti* ('and the high frenzy of the learned Lucretius', *Silv.* 2.7.76; cf. p. 290 n. 97). Statius may here be referring to the legend of Lucretius' madness, brought on by a love philtre, as related by Jerome and immortalised by Tennyson. Since the date and origin of that story remain a mystery, however, it may be more plausible to assume that Statius is simply characterising the Epicurean poet's radical views as mad or inspired. Statius' own view of Lucretius is unknown, but his *Silvae* certainly reveal a strongly Epicurean flavour; see Newlands 2002: 137–42, 170–5; Newlands 2011: index s.v. 'Epicureanism'; and cf. André 1996, Zeiner 2005: 178–90.

[36] Capaneus' inconsistencies have their own Lucretian resonance. The topic of 'l'anti-Lucrèce chez Lucrèce', i.e., whether Lucretius was deliberately or unintentionally inconsistent, has long preoccupied scholars (see O'Hara 2007: 55–76, with further bibliography).

A precedent for using a character to bring an Epicurean perspective into an epic is provided by none other than Vergil's Mezentius. As we saw in Chapter 2, Leah Kronenberg has argued that Mezentius can be read as an allegorical Epicurean, drawing on the evidence of several intertextual connections between Mezentius' attitude to death and Lucretius' *De Rerum Natura*.[37] She finds that the effect of incorporating Epicurean associations within Mezentius is not only to unsettle preconceptions about the individual character but also to deepen the larger dialogue on how philosophical considerations interact with literary interpretation:

> Even an Epicurean Mezentius, however, invites a critical examination of Epicurean doctrine and probes the limits of its claims to provide a secure means to *voluptas*. More than anything, then, Mezentius' character, like Dido's, provokes debate and presents competing perspectives on the values he represents.... Virgil's allegories are not perfect and pure representations of a particular philosophy, and his characters seamlessly intertwine philosophic allusions with other sorts of literary models and codes. Thus, it is ultimately up to Virgil's readers to decide which philosophic voices to recognize and also which to commend.[38]

Strikingly, the reception of Mezentius in Capaneus, not noted by Kronenberg, suggests that Statius was already aware of an Epicurean reading of Mezentius, which he substantially developed in the representation of Capaneus. Through the agon between Capaneus and Amphiaraus, moreover, Statius places philosophical 'debate' and 'competing perspectives' at the centre of his audience's attention far more directly than Vergil had. Nor do the two characters argue in terms that merely allude to philosophical differences—they explicitly spell out those differences and act according to those beliefs. If an Epicurean reading of Mezentius 'has the potential to reconfigure the moral universe of the text', Statius goes one step further in making it impossible for the reader to miss that potential: whatever one thinks of the attitudes of Capaneus and Amphiaraus, their outlooks suggest utterly different ways of understanding the world of the *Thebaid* and engaging with the remainder of the poem.[39]

What Madness Is This?: The Ambivalence of Amphiaraus

The rhetorical crescendo of Capaneus' speech returns to *furor*, one of the key points of contention between the two heroes (*Theb.* 3.661–9):

> et tibi tuto
> nunc eat iste furor; sed prima ad classica cum iam
> hostilem Ismenon galeis Dircenque bibemus,

---

[37] Kronenberg 2005.
[38] Kronenberg 2005: 427–8.
[39] Kronenberg 2005: 427.

> ne mihi tunc, moneo, lituos atque arma uolenti
> obuius ire pares uenisque aut alite uisa
> bellorum proferre diem: procul haec tibi mollis
> infula terrificique aberit dementia Phoebi:
> illic augur ego et mecum quicumque parati
> insanire manu.
>
>   So now while safe
> let that frenzy come to you; but at the first trumpet blast, as
> we drink from our helms the hostile waters of Ismenus and Dirce,
> do not try to get in my way, I warn you, when I desire
> the clarion call and arms, nor by entrails and the sighting of birds
> seek to put off the day of battle: far away will be that soft
> ribbon of yours and the madness of dread Phoebus:
> there I shall be augur and all who are prepared with me
> to be frenzied in fight.

If up to this point the two heroes have tried to attach the negative connotations of madness to the other's thought and behaviour, in this passage Capaneus embraces madness (*insanire*) as a virtue in war, distinguishing it from the prophetic frenzy (*furor, dementia*) he attributes to Amphiaraus.[40] Helen Lovatt takes issue with what she sees as a rhetorical sleight of hand:

> This is doubly ironic because Amphiaraus in his role as prophet is specifically excluded from prophetic madness. He does not go into trances or commune with the dead: his area of expertise is augury from birds, a quasi-scientific exercise in observation.[41]

Such a distinction between artful divination, which proceeds by observation, and inspired frenzy is certainly a Roman one, as attested, for example, by Quintus in Book 1 of Cicero's *De Divinatione*.[42] As far as Capaneus is concerned, however, the distinction has no relevance, since augury is nothing but

---

[40] Cf. Lovatt 2001: 118: '[Capaneus] sets up a deliberate opposition between the madness of prophecy and the madness of war, in which the madness of war is privileged as the good and right madness'. When Capaneus claims to be augur, the irony (though not the words) may recall Lucretius' own claim to make oracular pronouncements. Lucretius in turn seems to inherit this claim from a (possibly less ironic) tradition that saw Epicurus as a kind of oracle. See Smith 1982: 60 n. b for references. Later in the poem, Capaneus uses a similar rhetorical ploy of appropriating the language of prophecy: *sunt et mihi prouida dextrae / omina* ('prescient too are the omens of my right hand', *Theb.* 10.485–6). As Lactantius ad *Theb.* 10.485 suggests, the rhetoric is directed in particular against Thiodamas, prophetic successor to Amphiaraus and leader of the night raid in Book 10 (cf. Capaneus' refusal to join the raid at *Theb.* 10.257–9, both because it involves trickery and because the idea came from an oracle).

[41] Lovatt 2001: 118.

[42] See, e.g., Cic. *Div.* 1.34. Quintus' distinction also reveals Roman chauvinism against a Greek practice. Neri 1986: 2016 suggests a link between the arguments of the *De Div.* and Statius' agon; Manolaraki 2013: 103–7 draws a similar connection to the preceding augury. On the scientific character of Amphiaraus' augury cf. Lact. ad *Theb.* 7.701: EXPERIENTIA CAELI *doctrina et scientia auguriorum* (KNOWLEDGE OF HEAVEN: knowledge and skill of auguries').

irrational superstition, a view that had likewise received a lengthy airing in Book 2 of the *De Divinatione*, wherein Marcus criticises Quintus' defence of divination.[43] For the force of Capaneus' point doesn't depend on whether Amphiaraus enters into a divinatory frenzy or not, but rather on what he perceives as the wrongheadedness of the seer's beliefs, which for rhetorical purposes chimes well with the notion of prophetic madness. For Capaneus, just as for Marcus, the specific type of divination does not matter at all—the entire system is nonsensical. Moreover, it's important to recognise just how radically Capaneus poses that question: whereas the Marcus of the *De Divinatione* can attack false superstition while wishing to preserve religious institutions and believing in the existence of the divine, Statius draws on a host of interconnected poetic and philosophical traditions—from the *Sisyphus* fragment to Lucretius, from Vergil's Mezentius to Ovid's Lycaon—in order to make Capaneus' rejection of the divine as comprehensive and richly developed as possible.[44]

Capaneus' ironic claim to be an augur foreshadows his ultimate assimilation with Amphiaraus through the prophet's frenzied *aristeia* in Book 7. Immediately prior to the *aristeia*, the poet describes Capaneus' brief confrontation with the priest Eunaeus, a scene which recalls the issues fought over in the agon. Statius dwells on this otherwise inconsequential episode in part to emphasise Capaneus' impiety, but also to prepare for Amphiaraus' abandonment of his pious and prescient credentials in favour of the momentary and heedless experience of war.

As the fighting begins, Eunaeus, a Theban priest of Bacchus, comes out to the front lines to dissuade the troops from joining battle. As in the agon, the poet draws attention to the relationship between religious inspiration and madness, and asks what persuades Eunaeus to change his 'accustomed frenzy' (*adsuetum furorem*, *Theb.* 7.651); as the priest intervenes in the melee, he is described as maddened by the god (*lymphante deo*, *Theb.* 7.662).[45] Eunaeus is thus both changed and unchanged; his madness remains, but he has exported it to a different context, from the grove to the battlefield. Eunaeus then attempts

---

[43] Cic. *Div.* 2.70–83. Marcus' scepticism may not represent Cicero's own opinion, of course, but the fact that Cicero could present such a substantial attack suggests that at least some philosophically inclined Romans could take a very negative view of divination (*non necesse est fateri partim horum errore susceptum esse, partim superstitione, multa fallendo?* 'isn't it necessary to admit that these [divinatory] practices are taken up partly out of error, partly out of superstition, and often through deceit?', Cic. *Div.* 2.83). On the complexities involved in interpreting the *De Div.* see the works cited at p. 9 n. 27, along with Guillaumont 1984 and 2006, and the introduction to Wardle 2006.

[44] For Marcus' defence of religious institutions and belief see Cic. *Div.* 2.148. Cicero is more accepting of divination at *Leg.* 2.32, though there too he emphasises the fundamental premise of the existence of the gods.

[45] Lactantius notes this 'change' in his gloss on *mutare furorem* (*Theb.* 7.651): *ut sacra Liberi in furorem bellorum insania commutares*. By also glossing *lymphante deo* (*Theb.* 7.662), he makes sure that this new madness is not missed: *hoc est furiis incitante*.

to persuade the men to desist from fighting, but the poem offers little evidence to support his particular argument (*Theb.* 7.663–8):

> prohibete manus, haec omine dextro
> moenia Cirrhaea monstrauit Apollo iuuenca;
> parcite, in haec ultro scopuli uenere uolentes.
> gens sacrata sumus: gener huic est Iuppiter urbi
> Gradiuusque socer; Bacchum haud mentimur alumnum
> et magnum Alciden.

> Stay your hands! Apollo revealed these walls
> with the favourable omen of Cirrha's heifer.
> Forbear! Rocks came willingly of their own accord to form them.
> We are a sacred people: this city's son-in-law is Jupiter,
> Mars its father-in-law; we do not lie that Bacchus
> and great Hercules are its children.

Eunaeus justifies the city's and its people's sacred status first by adducing the omens and supernatural phenomena surrounding the foundation of Thebes, and secondly by listing the gods connected to the city. Whatever the truth of the foundation tales—which Capaneus will scorn in Book 10—and despite any favour Bacchus or Hercules may have for Thebes, the first two gods mentioned in Eunaeus' speech are Jupiter and Mars, the very gods conspiring to destroy Thebes as well as Argos.[46] The invocation of these gods as a reason not to fight could not be more ironic given their essential and enthusiastic role in the war.

It's appropriate that this priest, whose spiritual frenzy has been displaced onto the battlefield, must then confront the god despiser Capaneus, who claimed that he would take up an augur's madness in battle. The inadequacy of prophetic inspiration and religious service in this new martial context is amply illustrated by the ease with which Capaneus dispatches his opponent: *sic tum congressu Capaneus gauisus iniquo* ('so then did Capaneus rejoice in the unequal combat', *Theb.* 7.675). The line alludes to Vergil's description of the encounter between Mezentius and Aeneas, in which the latter fights at a disadvantage against his mounted opponent (*urgetur pugna congressus iniqua*, *Aen.* 10.889).[47] The result of Vergil's 'unequal fight' is, however, reversed, for whereas the wounded Mezentius, though on horseback, is no match for Aeneas, Capaneus makes short work of Eunaeus.[48] The effect of the change is to associate

---

[46] For Jupiter's destructive impulse and his collusion with Mars see *Theb.* 1.214–47, 3.218–52, and 7.1–89. For Bacchus' affection for Thebes see *Theb.* 7.145–92. Hercules' allegiance is hesitant since he is connected to both cities (*Theb.* 10.890–1). Eunaeus' misreading of the gods' will echoes that of Amphiaraus, who claims that the gods stand in the way of the Argive expedition.

[47] Cf. Lact. ad *Theb.* 7.675. The phrase *congressus iniquus* also alludes to Val. Fl. 6.322, where it's used of Gesander's fight with Canthus. For Gesander as another Mezentius, noticed by Statius, see Wijsman 2000: passim, esp. 67–8.

[48] Cf. p. 71.

Capaneus with the victor, Aeneas, as well as his primary model of Mezentius.[49] The unexpected triangulation of heroes will make greater sense as Statius develops a complex pattern of identifications and reversals over the remainder of Book 7.

At the beginning of Amphiaraus' *aristeia*, Statius elevates the hero and glances forward to the remarkable form of his death—the swallowing of his chariot by the earth: *eminet ante alios iam formidantibus arua / Amphiaraus equis* ('Amphiaraus shines forth beyond the others, though his horses already fear the ground', *Theb.* 7.690–1).[50] Saddened by the imminent death of his devotee, Apollo 'adds a vain lustre' to Amphiaraus' final moments (*decus addit inane, Theb.* 7.692), while Mars renders him invincible against mortal weapons (*ne quid mortalia bello / laedere tela queant, Theb.* 7.696–7).[51] The hero, conscious of his impending doom, becomes the stronger for this awareness (*uires fiducia leti / suggerit, Theb.* 7.699–700). Whether due to the gods' influence or his own final burst of energy, Amphiaraus is said to reach new heights of prophetic and martial power (*Theb.* 7.700–11):

> inde uiro maioraque membra diesque
> laetior et numquam tanta experientia caeli,
> si uacet: auertit morti contermina Virtus.
> ardet inexpleto saeui Mauortis amore
> et fruitur dextra atque anima flagrante superbit.
> hicne hominum casus lenire et demere Fatis
> iura frequens? quantum subito diuersus ab illo
> qui tripodas laurusque sequi, qui doctus in omni
> nube salutato uolucrem cognoscere Phoebo!
> innumeram ferro plebem, ceu letifer annus
> aut iubar aduersi graue sideris, immolat umbris
> ipse suis.
>
> Then the hero's limbs grew greater, and the day brighter
> and never did he possess such great knowledge of the heavens,
> if he had the leisure: valour, neighbour of death, turns him.

---

[49] Capaneus' wish that Eunaeus were not just a priest of Bacchus but even the god himself (*Theb.* 7.678–9) makes him also into another Erysichthon, who explicitly rejects the gods (*qui numina diuum sperneret, Met.* 8.739–40) and wishes that the sacred tree he is about to cut down were not merely loved by the goddess, but rather the goddess herself: *non dilecta deae solum, sed et ipsa licebit / sit dea, iam tanget frondente cacumine terram* (*Met.* 8.755–6). Capaneus voices another variant on this sentiment when he wishes that the Nemean serpent he is about to strike were indeed a favourite of the gods (*Theb.* 5.568).

[50] On the *aristeia* see Seo 2013: 161–3.

[51] Most commentators rightly choose *addit inane* over the alternative manuscript readings (see Smolenaars 1994: 324–5). Of these variants, *abdidit omne* ('took away all glory'), while clearly mistaken, is striking—perhaps a case of the scribe refusing to countenance Apollo's conferring any glory on the raging Amphiaraus?

> He burns with insatiable love of savage War,
> and revels in the might of his hand and exults in his blazing spirit.
> Is this he who so often alleviated the fortunes of men and took the laws
> from the Fates? How suddenly changed from him
> who knew how to follow the tripods and the laurels,
> to greet Phoebus and understand the bird in every cloud!
> Like some plague year or grievous ray of baleful star,
> with his sword he sacrifices a countless host
> to his own shade.

Despite this prodigious excellence, the prophetic and martial abilities of Amphiaraus appear mutually exclusive: led by valour, he turns away from the 'great knowledge of the heavens'. Instead of resembling his Theban counterpart Eunaeus, Amphiaraus' behaviour, as Lovatt has observed, looks a good deal more like that of Capaneus.[52] Beyond mere resemblance, however, what really clinches the assimilation of the two characters is the seer's newfound love of war (*Mauortis amore*, *Theb.* 7.703), which precisely echoes that of Capaneus, even in its metrical *sedes* (*Mauortis amore*, *Theb.* 3.598). In this light, Capaneus' earlier claim to be augur in battle takes on a new significance: the heroic *aristeia* becomes a state more powerful than any inspiration. Capaneus' ironic image of 'augury' may distance him from the Amphiaraus of peacetime, but it also foreshadows the prophet as we see him now—enraged, impassioned, and destructive.

By describing Amphiaraus as 'sacrificing' opponents, Statius recalls the actions of Achilles and Aeneas, both of whom take captives to sacrifice to the shades of Patroclus and Pallas, respectively.[53] Although Amphiaraus doesn't take captives as such—the idea of sacrifice appears more figurative—Lovatt reads the seer's sacrifice of 'countless' numbers to his 'own' shade as an augmentation of his epic predecessors.[54] She notes that the phrase *immolat umbris* (*Theb.* 7.710) picks up on Vergil, who uses *immolet umbris* to describe what Aeneas intends to do with his captives (*Aen.* 10.519).[55] The connection between Amphiaraus and Aeneas, as Mark Masterson has observed, goes even further.[56] Soon after the mention of Aeneas' intended human sacrifice, the Trojan hero kills Haemonides, a priest of Apollo (*Aen.* 10.537–42). Within that very passage the same words of sacrifice appear in slightly modified form: *lapsumque superstans / immolat ingentique umbra tegit* ('standing over him as he fell, he sacrificed him and covered him with his huge shadow', *Aen.*

---

[52] Lovatt 2001: 107: 'he becomes increasingly dominated by the madness of battle, until he seems to have become so berserk as to be indistinguishable from his anti-type, Capaneus'. Juhnke 1972: 120–3 argues that Amphiaraus' *aristeia* alludes to that of Diomedes in *Iliad* 5, which even gives it a theomachic quality.
[53] *Il.* 21.26–32; *Aen.* 10.517–20.
[54] Lovatt 2001: 107–8.
[55] Lovatt 2001: 107 n. 14.
[56] Masterson 2005: 294–8.

10.540–1).⁵⁷ The meaning of *umbra* may have shifted from 'shade' to 'shadow', but Vergil's use of the same vocabulary at *Aen.* 10.519 and 10.541 strongly foregrounds the image of Aeneas as sacrificer. The *umbra* at *Aen.* 10.541 not only describes Aeneas' literal shadow, then, but also glances both backwards at the shade of Pallas and forwards at the shade that Haemonides will become. The fact that Aeneas' victim is a priest of Apollo, Masterson concludes, has a bearing on the reading of Amphiaraus, who thus becomes both sacrificer and shade while recalling both Aeneas and his priestly victim.⁵⁸

It's now possible to see how the earlier intertextual association between Capaneus and Aeneas, as well as Mezentius, foreshadows the various unexpected identifications and reversals involved in the assimilation of Capaneus and Amphiaraus. Moreover, it's no coincidence that the Aeneas of Vergil's tenth book should be a model for Statius' impious or frenzied heroes, since it's in that book of the *Aeneid* that the hero is at his most destructive and even merits the famous simile comparing him to the Giant Aegaeon (*Aen.* 10.565–8).⁵⁹ Statius has taken a phase of profound instability and devastation in Vergil's text and used it to undermine identities and polarities in the *Thebaid* about which the reader might have felt more certain beforehand.

Prophecy, Science, and the Powers of Explanation

The ambivalence of Amphiaraus emerges even before his *aristeia*, however, through Statius' questioning of the morality and utility of prophecy. Following Amphiaraus' augury, for instance, Statius condemns both the desire for and the methods of knowing the future (*Theb.* 3.551–65):

> unde iste per orbem
> primus uenturi miseris animantibus aeger
> creuit amor? diuumne feras hoc munus, an ipsi,
> gens auida et parto non umquam stare quieti,
> eruimus quae prima dies, ubi terminus aeui,
> quid bonus ille deum genitor, quid ferrea Clotho
> cogitet? hinc fibrae et uolucrum per nubila sermo

---

⁵⁷ In part of his comment ad *Theb.* 7.710–11, Lactantius notes how *immolat* can refer piquantly to a priest's death and adduces Aeneas' killing of Haemonides as an example. Sweeney 1997: 494 questions the authenticity of the entire comment because some lines on the irony of *immolat* seem to copy a remark of Servius on the *Aeneid* passage. There is no reason, however, to doubt Lactantius' spotting of the connection between Amphiaraus and Haemonides, which does not appear in Servius.

⁵⁸ Masterson 2005: 296–7. Putnam 2011: 32 observes a further irony within the *Aeneid*: Haemonides closely recalls the Sibyl, since the same phrase is used to describe both (*Phoebi Triuiaeque sacerdos*, 'a priest of Phoebus and Trivia', *Aen.* 6.35, 10.537). Aeneas' killing of Haemonides thus suggests a reversal of the piety he showed to the Sibyl, a reversal that Statius takes up and expands in Amphiaraus' *aristeia*.

⁵⁹ On the Aegaeon simile see pp. 78–80. On Aeneas and Mezentius see Quint 2001: esp. 55–9.

astrorumque uices numerataque semita lunae
Thessalicumque nefas. at non prior aureus ille
sanguis auum scopulisque satae uel robore gentes
mentibus his usae; siluas amor unus humumque
edomuisse manu; quid crastina uolueret aetas
scire nefas homini. nos, prauum et flebile uulgus,
scrutati penitus superos: hinc pallor et irae,
hinc scelus insidiaeque et nulla modestia uoti.

> From where did that sick passion
> for the future first arise for wretched mortals through the world?
> Would you say that this is a gift of the gods, or do we ourselves—
> a greedy race never content to rest with what has been gained—
> search out what is the first day or when the end of life,
> what the good father of the gods or iron Clotho thinks?
> From this follow entrails and the speech of birds through the clouds
> and the positions of the stars and the calculated paths of the moon
> and Thessalian abomination. But that earlier golden
> race of our ancestors and the people born from rocks or oak
> were not of that mind; their only love was to tame the woods and the soil
> by hand; it was forbidden for humans to know
> what tomorrow's time would bring. We, a depraved and lamentable crowd
> probe deep the gods: from this follow fear and anger,
> from this, crime and treachery and immoderate prayer.

Despite their different connotations, augury, haruspicy, astrology, and witchcraft belong to the same spectrum of practice, certainly inasmuch as they frequently deal with the interpretation of omens.[60] Moreover, the poet clearly does not intend to contrast acceptable public and state-sanctioned practices with illegitimate or disreputable forms, since here he lumps augury, an official element of Roman public religion, together with witchcraft, a distinctly murkier activity: the passage thus unequivocally condemns all forms of enquiry into the future.[61] Even if the poet declares the desire to know the future morally wrong, however, he doesn't dispute the fundamentally veridical quality of the various methods—mantic arts can and do tell the truth, as suggested by

---

[60] See MacBain 1982, Potter 1994. After examining the entrails (*fibris*, *Theb*. 3.456), Amphiaraus and Melampus seek omens (*omina*, *Theb*. 3.459) in the sky, which turn out to be a bird augury.

[61] The phrase *scire nefas* (*Theb*. 3.563) will be recalled in Tiresias' *scire nefastum* (*Theb*. 4.516), where the Theban seer calls on an obscure (possibly Orphic) power greater than the gods (see Lactantius ad loc.; the witch Erichtho threatens to invoke a similarly unnamed and omnipotent deity at Luc. 6.744–9). The phrase *scire nefas* famously refers to prophetic arts at Hor. *Carm*. 1.11.1. It also describes magic that can draw Jupiter from heaven at Ov. *Fast*. 3.325. The conjunction of prophecy, magic, and witchcraft under the rubric of forbidden knowledge makes it all the more difficult to isolate Amphiaraus from negative associations. For Lucan, knowledge of whether Caesar or Pompey had more just cause for war is *scire nefas* (Luc. 1.126–7): to enquire about such dire matters is akin to practising the dark arts.

Amphiaraus' foreknowledge of the expedition's failure. But apparent veridicality can't settle the dispute on the status or moral value of prophecy in the epic. There is, for example, a significant difference between Amphiaraus as the judicious and scrupulous reader of supernatural signs and Amphiaraus as the practiser of mantic activities that colour him as greedy, depraved, lamentable, and a harbinger of immorality in the company of Thessalian witches, a disjunction whose ramifications are all the more striking given the contrast drawn in the agon between the pious seer and the impious Capaneus.

The poet's condemnation of the origin and practice of mantic activities, however, sits uneasily with a passage from Book 6 decrying wasted omens. In the last act of the funeral games, Adrastus attempts to shoot an arrow into a marked tree at the other end of the circus, and although he hits the target, the arrow mysteriously returns to the king. Immediately before the king shoots, the poet remarks on humans' ignorance of omens (*Theb.* 6.934–7):

> quis fluere occultis rerum neget omina causis?
> fata patent homini, piget inseruare, peritque
> uenturi praemissa fides: sic omina casum
> fecimus, et uires hausit Fortuna nocendi.

> Who would deny that omens flow from hidden causes of things?
> The fates lie open for humans, yet they resist observing them, and
> the advance pledge of the future is wasted: thus we have made omens
> into chance, and Fortune has derived its power to harm.

Whereas in Book 3 the poet spoke of humans' 'sick passion for the future' (*uenturi aeger amor*, *Theb.* 3.552–3), here he rues the missed opportunity to know the future.[62] The change in attitude is directed against the Argive leaders, who offer physical or natural explanations for the sign (*Theb.* 6.942–6):

> multa duces errore serunt: hi nubila et altos
> occurrisse Notos, aduersi roboris ictu
> tela repulsa alii. penitus latet exitus ingens
> monstratumque nefas: uni remeabile bellum,
> et tristes domino spondebat harundo recursus.

> The leaders discuss many things in error: some say the clouds and high
> winds met, and others that by the opposing force of the wood
> the arrow ricocheted back. Deep hidden lies the prodigious event
> and the signified abomination: to its master alone
> did the arrow promise a return from war and a sad retreat.

---

[62] Legras 1905: 173 finds the passages inconsistent, but Snijder 1968: 220–1 disagrees. Lovatt's sense that the poet deploys the inconsistency to comment on the problem of interpretation is more compelling than Vessey's explanation that Statius was more concerned with literary impact than philosophical coherence (Lovatt 2005: 285 and n. 14 citing Vessey 1970: 440). On inconsistency as a feature of Roman epic see O'Hara 2007 (building on O'Hara 1994).

One should not neglect the evident humour here as the Seven against Thebes—almost proverbially impious and bellicose, and fresh from the blood and sweat of athletic competition—suddenly engage in a spot of amateur donnishness. Indeed, the humour only sharpens the apparent message that to focus on physical or natural explanations alone is a pretension that leads to false and dangerous reductionism, while other forms of understanding—prophecy, augury, and the like—might hit on the truth and ward off disaster.[63]

While the poet himself assumes the inherent truth of omens and prophecies, however, the unfolding of the plot casts doubt on the utility of an epistemological method that provides only partial knowledge and leads to perverse outcomes. Subject to the whim of the gods, even the special connection of prophets to the truth seems to drop out of service at the most crucial moments.[64] Further, information derived from supernatural sources also turns out to be unhelpful in determining the particular course of action one should take, since, despite the accuracy of signs, their fulfilment doesn't accord with the expectations of the characters. Oracles and signs are repeatedly seen to define the way people behave, encouraging Adrastus' welcome of Tydeus and Polynices in Book 1 (*Theb.* 1.395-7, 482-510) and discouraging Lycurgus from joining the war in Book 5 (*Theb.* 5.643-9); yet these characters' consequent actions, far from helping them avoid disaster, even facilitate it.

Thus, the poet's claim in Book 6 that omens are wasted through inattention to hidden causes is belied by the poem, in which prophets, despite their apparent foreknowledge, are as vulnerable to misfortune as sceptics—Amphiaraus enjoys no better fate than Capaneus. As the seer says at the end of the agon: *sed quid uana cano, quid fixos arceo casus? / ibimus* ('but why do I prophesy empty things, why do I ward off fixed fate? We will go', *Theb.* 3.646-7). If the ignorant Capaneus and sapient Amphiaraus are bound by the same fate, we might reasonably wonder if the poem offers any clear sense of the utility of augury, prophecy, and the like.[65] The poet's notion of a wasted omen thus seems to make little sense: humans are not harmed by ignorance or misreading signs, as the poet alleges, but rather by fate, and no amount of knowledge—of any kind—can obviate that fate. Measured by utility, prophetic knowledge is no better than mistaken explanations of a physical or natural kind; to interpret Adrastus' arrow's flight as an omen, the poem suggests, could no more have helped the king avoid disaster than any of the speculative natural philosophy floated by the Argive leaders.

---

[63] Vergil suggests that disaster, whether political or meteorological, can be avoided if we attend to signs and omens (*G.* 1.424-97). Meliboeus regrets not paying heed to omens at *Ecl.* 1.16-17.

[64] Amphiaraus falls foul of just such caprice in Book 1 when he cannot foresee the risks of admitting Polynices and Tydeus into the Argive royal family because his own patron god does not allow it: *non docte futuri / Amphiarae uides, etenim uetat auctor Apollo* ('nor do you see it, Amphiaraus knowledgeable of the future, for the authority of Apollo forbids it', *Theb.* 1.398-9).

[65] On the inefficacy of prophecy and powerlessness of prophets see Dominik 1994: 112-14, 121-2, 198; Tuttle 2013.

Despite his scepticism about the merits of rationalising explanations, Statius frequently accommodates just such explanations throughout the poem. The earthquake that swallows Amphiaraus, for instance, is attributed to various causes, including blasts of air, erosion by water, or the actions of Neptune or personified Earth (*Theb.* 7.809–16).[66] The uncertainty articulated in such passages' *siue... seu...* structure alludes to the philosophical, especially Epicurean, practice known as the *pleonachos tropos*, according to which a writer offers multiple plausible explanations for phenomena while remaining agnostic about the correct one.[67] As the example of the earthquake shows, however, Statius goes beyond—indeed, undermines—any materialist philosophical model by incorporating divine causation within his broad epistemological range.[68] Denis Feeney has suggested that the different kinds of explanation reflect the pervasive conflict in the *Thebaid* among its various realms—primarily heaven, hell, and earth.[69] To this I would add, however, that the mannerism's rhetorical force is to set the terms according to which the epic world is to be understood. Statius' uncertainty in this regard, as much as it accommodates a full and varied range of causes, leaves open the possibility that one class of explanation—whether supernatural or physical—is simply mistaken.

The attraction of natural philosophical explanations is even felt on Olympus. Just prior to the chariot race in Book 6, the poet switches our view to Olympus, where the god Apollo sings to the Muses (*Theb.* 6.358–65):[70]

> orsa deum, nam saepe Iouem Phlegramque suique
> anguis opus fratrumque pius cantarat honores.
> tunc aperit quis fulmen agat, quis sidera ducat
> spiritus, unde animi fluuiis, quae pabula uentis,
> quo fonte inmensum uiuat mare, quae uia solis
> praecipitet noctem, quae porrigat, imane tellus
> an media et rursus mundo succincta latenti.
> finis erat, differt auidas audire sorores.

---

[66] See Smolenaars 1994: 386–7, Taisne 1999: 170, Franchet d'Espèrey 2001: 25–6.

[67] See, e.g., Epicurus, *Ep. Pyth.* 87.2, Lucr. 5.526–33. The mannerism is discussed by Asmis 1984: 321–30, Bénatouïl 2003. Statius' reception of the *pleonachos tropos* was already mediated by the work of earlier poets, such as Ovid and Lucan. In the *Metamorphoses*, for instance, Ovid can use the trope to accommodate divine explanations (e.g., the account of human origins at *Met.* 1.78–81 or the enquiry of Myrrha's nurse at *Met.* 10.397–9) or in terms more reminiscent of natural philosophy (e.g., Pythagoras' account of Etna at *Met.* 15.342–50). Cf. Luc. 2.7–15 on fate versus chance. On the reception of the trope in Latin epic see Myers 1994: 54–5, 140, 153–4; O'Hara 2007: 123–8; Schiesaro 2002: 66 (Ovid); Bartsch 1997: 189 n. 23 (Lucan); Franchet d'Espèrey 2001; Seo 2013: 168–78 (Statius); Hardie 2009b: 231–63 (across the epic tradition).

[68] Whereas Franchet d'Espèrey 2001: 25–6 sees the passage, especially the last of the *siue* clauses, as affirming the gods and fate as the source of human suffering, my reading places greater emphasis on the uncertainty underlying the existence of multiple types of explanatory discourse (in this respect my analysis has more in common with Delarue 2000: 276–80).

[69] Feeney 1991: 345, 349–50.

[70] For the lacuna in the passage see the apparatus of D. E. Hill 1983: 145.

He began with the deeds of the gods, for often of Jupiter and of Phlegra and
    of his own
feat of the serpent and the honours of his brothers did he devotedly sing.
Then he reveals what spirit drives the thunderbolt, or leads
the stars, from where comes the violence of rivers, what feeds the winds,
from which source the immense sea draws life, which path of the sun
hastens the night, which lengthens it, whether the earth be lowest
or in the middle and girded in turn by a hidden world.
That was the end, and he puts off the sisters eager to hear more.

Apollo devotedly (*pius*, *Theb.* 6.359) sings the tale of the Gigantomachy, amongst other stories of divine feats, but he then goes on to sing of various subjects of natural science (*Theb.* 6.360–4)—accounts of the thunderbolt, stars, rivers, winds, and cosmology—topics which the poet lists at greater length than the preceding stories of divine achievements, and without any explicit motivation from duty or piety.[71] Apollo's sudden turn from Jupiter at Phlegra to explanations of natural phenomena in the style of didactic poetry or philosophy is jarring, not least because he devotes considerably more space to those topics than he did to the mythical narratives. With its surprising scientific accents, the god's song is even said to leave its audience of Muses wanting more (*Theb.* 6.365), as if conventional tales of Phlegra seem worn by comparison.

The epic tradition on which Statius draws might provide a partial answer for Apollo's choice of repertoire. Lactantius associated at least some of the questions with Epicurean enquiry of a particularly Lucretian flavour (ad *Theb.* 6.363–4):

> thesis philosophica: terra elementorum omnium ima sit an suspensa, ut Lucretius? ergo utrum uoluatur caelum, quod accidit si media est terra, <an>, quod si in imo desinit, caelum esse dicat<ur> immobile? sed cum disputantium discordat opinio, uerum non dicit, <ni>si qui rite cognouit originum causas. unde Vergilius: 'felix qui potuit rerum cognoscere causas'.[72]

> A philosophical thesis: whether the earth is the lowest of all elements or suspended, as Lucretius says. Then whether the sky turns, which happens if the earth is in the middle, or whether, if it stops at the bottom, the sky is said to be immovable. But when the opinion of those disputing the

---

[71] Contrast Apollo's relatively straightforward singing of Phlegra, without any didactic subversion, at Val. Fl. 5.692–3. Cf. Stat. *Silv.* 4.2.52–6.

[72] As the apparatus of Sweeney's text of Lactantius indicates, there are several problems with the manuscript readings here, not least the fact that the comment is paired with the wrong lemma (*Theb.* 6.362–3) when its content clearly relates to 363–4. The textual issues, however, do not affect the basic fact—relevant to my argument—that at least one ancient reader was prompted to think of philosophical comparanda, in particular Lucretius.

question is at variance, he does not speak the truth, except who has rightly discovered the causes of origins. Whence Vergil: 'happy is he who has been able to discover the causes of things'.

In his edition of Lactantius' commentary, Sweeney even identifies two passages from the *De Rerum Natura* that might have prompted Lactantius' remark, both of which come from adjacent discussions in Book 5 about the formation of the world and the movement of heavenly bodies: the first describes 'bodies of the earth' taking up 'the lowest places' (*terrai corpora... imas capiebant omnia sedes*, Lucr. 5.449–51); the second offers two theories of celestial motion—whether 'the great circle of heaven turns round' (*magnus caeli si uortitur orbis*, Lucr. 5.510) or 'the whole of heaven remains at rest' (*caelum omne manere / in statione*, Lucr. 5.517–8).[73] Whether or not Lactantius is right to see a specific reference to Lucretius here matters less than the recognisably philosophical style of the questions addressed by Apollo: whatever Statius' precise source, he clearly invokes the language and imagery of natural philosophy, for which Lucretius was an obvious point of reference.[74] Further uncertainties remain— whether Apollo's song parodies Capaneus' Epicurean reading habits, for instance, or whether, as Frederick Ahl has suggested, the irony stems from the deflation of myth, perhaps even of the gods themselves, being placed in the mouth of a god.[75] In either case, it's striking that Apollo, patron god of Amphiaraus, should adopt an idiom congenial to the philosophy associated with Capaneus, which in the agon had been used against the prophet. By attributing such unexpected philosophical concerns to a god, Statius draws further attention to the competing discourses over which Amphiaraus and Capaneus had argued, and which structure one's response to the *Thebaid*. In a world where explanatory discourses multiply, and warriors sound like philosophers, even the language of the gods cannot remain unchanged.

Capaneus' Theomachy: Philosophical Poetics

Statius offers several possible reasons for Capaneus' theomachy, including infernal inspiration (*Theb.* 10.831–6):

---

[73] Sweeney 1997: 411. For the common, though not wholly accepted, identification of Vergil's *felix* (G. 2.490) with Lucretius, and for wider discussion of the *Georgics*' debt to the *De Rerum Natura*, see Farrell 1991: 275–324.

[74] Cf., for instance, a very similar list of topics associated with Ovid's Pythagoras (Ov. *Met.* 15.66– 72), a passage that alludes simultaneously to Lucretius and Empedocles (see Hardie 1995), and the scientific song of Vergil's Iopas (*Aen.* 1.742–6), which also alludes to Lucretius (P. Gordon 2012: 62–5).

[75] Ahl 1986: 2901: 'Statius' Olympian narrator is quite possibly conceding that the gods themselves are simply naive explanations of phenomena that exist in endless inter-relationships and thus that he himself is but a fiction, a form that has emerged in an attempt to give definition to the indefinable'. On the poem's 'constantly changing perspectives and frames of reference' see Ahl 1986: 2898.

>   siue ille profunda
> missus nocte furor, Capaneaque signa secutae
> arma Iouem contra Stygiae rapuere sorores,
> seu uirtus egressa modum, seu gloria praeceps,
> seu magnae data fama neci, seu laeta malorum
> principia et blandae superum mortalibus irae.

> Whether that frenzy
> sent by deep night, and the Stygian sisters following
> Capaneus' standards took his arms against Jupiter,
> or valour beyond limits, or headlong glory,
> or the fame given to a great death, or the prosperous beginnings
> of evils and the divine anger that flatters mortals.

Notable once again are the different categories of explanation, ranging from supernatural compulsion to the tendencies of Capaneus' character.[76] Statius makes no attempt to clarify how any of these factors relate, whether they are more or less plausible, complementary or competing. It's impossible to discern, therefore, whether Tisiphone—instructed by Dis in Book 8 to set Capaneus' theomachy in motion—wholly brings about the hero's crazed actions or merely lends an encouraging hand to an already unhinged individual.[77] Moreover, as Feeney has argued, Statius' complex combination of active mythological gods, allegorical personifications, and extreme human passions makes it all the more difficult to disentangle clear conceptions of divine influence and human agency.[78] The different explanations of Capaneus' action, and by extension the *pleonachos tropos* more generally, point to the central issue in the theomachy—how we are to understand the nature of the world—and this is precisely the ground over which Capaneus and the gods contend.

As he scales the walls of the city, Capaneus claims to test the truth of divine power (*Theb.* 10.845–7):

> 'hac' ait 'in Thebas, hac me iubet ardua uirtus
> ire, Menoeceo qua lubrica sanguine turris.
> experiar quid sacra iuuent, an falsus Apollo.'

---

[76] Cf. Hutchinson 1993: 219: '[Statius] calls forth a complex and ambivalent response towards what might look an impressively simple impiety. He sets out in profusion possible causes of what Capaneus did ('whether it was that…', *sive…seu*, etc.), and hence possible evaluations.' See also Franchet d'Espèrey 2001: 28–9.

[77] Dis' instruction responds to what he sees as Jupiter's autocratic and imperialistic disregard for his brother's kingdom: *quaere deis qui bella ferat, qui fulminis ignes / infestumque Iouem clipeo fumante repellat* ('seek one to carry war to the gods, to repel with smoking shield the fires of the thunderbolt and hostile Jupiter', *Theb.* 8.76–7). For the strongest assertion of the view that the humans of the poem are mere pawns and unwitting casualties of supernatural powers see Dominik 1994: 1–75, and esp. 111–29, condensed and updated in Dominik 2012.

[78] Feeney 1991: 364–91.

> 'This way into Thebes', he says, 'this way my high valour bids me
> go, where the tower is slippery with Menoeceus' blood.
> I shall test what sacrifice avails, or whether Apollo is false'.

The verb *experiar* repeats a similar usage by Capaneus in the agon—*uolucrum quae tanta potestas, / experiar* ('I shall test what is this supposedly great power of birds', *Theb.* 3.617–18)—and therefore emphasises the original allusion to Ovid's Lycaon. While the allusion has been noted, critics have yet to offer any account of its effect or any reason for the attention drawn to it by the repetition.[79] Just as in the agon, here too, I suggest, the empiricism of Lycaon is of primary relevance. Lycaon seeks to test the identity of a god using physical means—attempted murder and the feeding of human flesh. For Capaneus, the empiricism implied by *experiar*, by analogy, takes the form of a martial test: if his efforts in battle are successful they will disprove the efficacy of augury and sacrifice.[80] Moreover, the theomachy, too, functions as a test of his earlier claims that the gods do not intervene in human affairs or do not exist, for surely such impiety ought to provoke a divine response, as indeed it does.[81]

The allusion to Lycaon should be read as part of a larger network of associations in the theomachy scene, including the subsequent comparison to the Aloidae—one of many Gigantomachic motifs applied to Capaneus throughout the poem (*Theb.* 10.848–52):[82]

> dicit, et alterno captiua in moenia gressu
> surgit ouans: quales mediis in nubibus aether
> uidit Aloidas, cum cresceret impia tellus
> despectura deos nec adhuc inmane ueniret
> Pelion et trepidum iam tangeret Ossa Tonantem.

> Thus he speaks, and with alternating step against the captive walls
> he rises triumphant: even as the sky in the middle of the clouds
> saw the Aloidae, when impious earth rose
> to look down on the gods, and vast Pelion was yet to come
> and Ossa already touched the anxious Thunderer.

---

[79] Leigh 2006: 225 n. 32 notes the similarity. Ripoll 2006: 243 identifies the Ovidian council of the gods before the Lycaon episode with the Statian scene of the gods arguing during Capaneus' assault; cf. Fucecchi 2013: 115.

[80] Cf. Lact. ad *Theb.* 10.847: QUID SACRA IVVENT *quid prosit Thebanis mors Menoecei sacris inuenta* ('WHAT SACRIFICE AVAILS What the death of Menoeceus, devised as a sacrifice, avails the Thebans'). On the futility of Menoeceus' self-sacrifice see Heinrich 1999, Dominik 1994: 106.

[81] For Dante's reception of the combined ideas of empiricist enquiry and physical testing see p. 86 n. 14.

[82] The comparison with the Aloidae, used to describe Capaneus at *Theb.* 10.849–52, also occurs at *Theb.* 6.719–21, where it's used of Hippomedon's prodigious discus throw. Lovatt suggests that the lines from Book 6 are probably spurious, perhaps the comment of a scholiast or scribe (Lovatt 2005: 111–12). Taisne 1994: 121–6 highlights the presence of Gigantomachic imagery in Capaneus' assault and in Statius' poetry more generally; cf. S. J. Harrison 1992.

Matthew Leigh has suggested that this simile forms part of a systematic attempt on the part of the poet to figure the sublimity of the hero. In particular, Leigh lists several Lucretian images as contexts for Statius' own depiction of Capaneus.[83] Among these, Leigh notes the passage in Book 5 of the *De Rerum Natura*, discussed in Chapter 2, where Lucretius allegorises his refutation of the immortality of the world as a kind of Gigantomachy (Lucr. 5.113–21). In light of the philosophical associations of Capaneus seen thus far, the relevance of Lucretius to Capaneus' theomachy goes well beyond Leigh's primary concern with aesthetic sublimity. Rather, Epicureanism's materialist perspective and its consequent revaluation of the meaning of piety and impiety share a great deal in common with Statius' representation of his hero, from his irreverence towards oracles and holy places (cf. Lucr. 1.734–41, 5.73–5) to his suggestion that gods do not care for human prayers, a passage that Lactantius had long ago identified with Epicurean thought.

Besides Lucretius' Gigantomachic allegory, Leigh also cites the mention of the Aloidae at the beginning of the pseudo-Aristotelian *De Mundo* as evidence for the analogy between philosophy's successful aspiring to the heavens and the Giants' more literal, and failed, assault.[84] As we saw in Chapter 2, the trope goes back to Plato's *Sophist*, in which the character of the Eleatic Stranger casts materialist philosophers as Giants who 'drag everything down to earth from heaven and the unseen, simply grasping rocks and oaks with their hands' (Pl. *Soph.* 246a). The legacy of this image lives on not only in Lucretius' didactic poem but also in Statius' epic, in which the materialist Capaneus imitates the Giants, rends the stone walls of Thebes (*Theb.* 10.877–82), and grasps a firebrand of oak (*Theb.* 10.843).[85] One need not go so far as to take Statius to be alluding to Plato; rather, the evidence of the trope, the fullest example of which is to be found in the *Sophist*, provides a context against which to understand the curiously materialist attributes that Statius gives to Capaneus.[86]

In view of the philosophical associations at work, the Lycaon allusion and the Gigantomachic trope have more in common than merely the mythological detail that Lycaon was born from the blood of the Giants (*Met.* 1.151–67). For the salient feature of Lycaon's challenge to Jupiter, as we saw in Chapter 3, is its empiricism: rather than accepting the *signa* of the god—whatever they might be—Lycaon seeks observable criteria of divinity in the belief that knowledge is acquired through experience. That empiricism, however poetically and imprecisely represented, is a hallmark of a philosophical manner of thinking

---

[83] Leigh 2006: 231–2; cf. Taisne 1999: 170–3, Lovatt 2013b: 108–11.
[84] Leigh 2006: 232 n. 65 citing Ps.-Arist. *Mund.* 1.1.
[85] Cf. the description of Capaneus' shield at Eur. *Phoen.* 1130–3, which bears an image of a Giant carrying a city torn from its foundations.
[86] Cf. Ware 2012: 128–34 on the cosmological significance of Claudian's Giants, esp. *Rapt.* 1.42–3, where the Giants are closely identified with the elements themselves.

associated especially with Epicureanism and Stoicism but visible earlier too.[87] Lycaon and Capaneus thus resemble not only the impious Giants of mythology but also the allegorical Giants of Plato or Lucretius, who give privileged importance to the evidence of the physical senses.[88] There is no need to press the allegory very far or to parse out whether the theomachs' attitudes are emblematic of a particular school of empiricism or of a generally rationalistic approach to theology. Ovid and Statius could exploit poetic licence and disregard philosophical niceties in appropriating their inherited traditions for their own purposes. Statius gives to the empiricism of Lycaon, redeployed in Capaneus, a new energy that draws more closely on philosophical imagery and idiom. Capaneus' testing of the gods thus becomes an even more explicit and radical interrogation of the beliefs and practices that underlie religion.

Capaneus' elevation works in intratextually—as well as intertextually—suggestive ways, too. His trajectory—first upwards as he scales Thebes, then downwards after being struck by the thunderbolt—pointedly reverses that of Menoeceus earlier in Book 10, who falls to his death before his spirit demands from Jupiter a place in the firmament. Capaneus' motion and spatial position also connect him to Amphiaraus once again, through imagery that continues to build on the pattern of cosmic symbolism. The description of Capaneus 'hanging in empty air' *(uacuoque sub aere pendens, Theb.* 10.681) recalls Amphiaraus' own account of being swallowed up by the earth: *pendens et in aere uoluor operto* ('hanging and whirled along in covered air', *Theb.* 8.110). The intratextuality brings the two heroes together when, in spatial terms, they could not be further apart. Yet some distance remains: while Amphiaraus describes his penetration of the earth in terms of passivity and helplessness, Capaneus seems to have attained, or even exceeded, the limit of human powers. The image of suspension occurs again later in Book 8, when Thiodamas' prayer to *Tellus* represents the earth as 'hanging in empty air': *aere pendentem uacuo* (*Theb.* 8.311).[89] Capaneus' elevation thus assimilates the hero to the earth itself, the fabled mother of the Giants. The image of Capaneus, almost a Giant in his own

---

[87] On Epicurean empiricism see Kleve 1977, De Lacy and De Lacy 1978: 165–82, Taylor 1980, Everson 1990, Allen 2001: 194–241, Asmis 2009, Giovacchini 2012. On the relation of empiricism to Stoic theology see Inwood 2005 on Seneca's *QNat.*, and Graver 1999 and Algra 2009 for the broader philosophical background. Cf. also Sext. Emp. *Math.* 8.56-8.

[88] In lumping together materialism and empiricism—i.e., ontology and epistemology—I do not mean to suggest that the nuances of each are insignificant. Rather, what matters to the poets—irrespective of the philosophers—is a broader distinction between two ways of viewing the world, one emphasising matter and perceptual experience, the other emphasising the intangible and the unseen.

[89] Cf. *Theb.* 6.363–4 with Lact. ad loc. (on which see above on Apollo's natural philosophical song on the position of the earth within the universe). The image of the hanging earth is fairly common; see, e.g., Lucr. 2.602–3, Ov. *Met.* 1.12–13, Man. 1.173, Luc. 5.94. An intertextuality of a different kind brings the image of 'hanging in air' from the realm of physics to the realm of aesthetics. In a poem in praise of the Colosseum, Martial describes the tomb of Mausolus in exactly these terms (*Spect.* 1.5–6): *aere nec uacuo pendentia Mausolea / laudibus inmodicis Cares in astra ferant.* It is tempting to think of Capaneus' elevation as representing this typically Flavian concern with wonder, immensity, and impossibility (on which see Newmyer 1984). See further Chapter 9.

right, hanging in mid-air, about to threaten the heavens, a hero that represents within the epic an idiosyncratic and confrontational philosophy—this idea becomes freighted with cosmic symbolism. Taken together with Amphiaraus' penetration of the underworld, the human heroes appear not so much pawns of the supernatural powers as agents of terrestrial imperialism.[90]

Statius emphasises the rationalist motive underlying Capaneus' acts of destruction when the hero mocks the walls of Thebes and the legend of their construction (*Theb.* 10.873–7):[91]

>   humilesne Amphionis arces,
> pro pudor, hi faciles, carmenque imbelle secuti,
> hi, mentita diu Thebarum fabula, muri?
> et quid tam egregium prosternere moenia molli
> structa lyra?
>
>   Are these Amphion's lowly towers—
> for shame!—are these the compliant walls that followed
> an unwarlike song, that ancient lying tale of Thebes?
> And what is so extraordinary about laying low walls built
> by a soft lyre?

Lovatt interprets the hero's attack on *carmen* and *fabula* as undermining poetry itself and its creative power: either it doesn't create at all—it is a lie—or what it does create is feeble. She goes on to read Capaneus as rending not only the Theban landscape but also the fabric of the poem:[92]

> Here he turns his hostility against poetry itself, denying poetry its effectiveness as a creator. It is as if he is striving to reach outside his own poetic world and claim a glory free from association with potentially false and intrinsically unwarlike poetry. In attacking the gods and insulting the walls of Amphion, he is striving to attain a greater reality, to leave the screen and come down into the real world.

---

[90] The list of possible explanations for the earthquake in Book 7 includes the idea of antagonism between earth, on the one hand, and Jupiter and Dis, on the other: *seu uati datus ille fragor, seu terra minata est / fratribus* ('whether that rupture was bestowed upon the seer, or earth threatened the brothers', *Theb.* 7.815–16). In Thiodamas' prayer, his elevation of the spirit of Amphiaraus above Phoebus sounds a competitive, if not theomachic, note: *tibi sacra feram praesaga, tuique /numinis interpres te Phoebo absente uocabo. / ille mihi Delo Cirrhaque potentior omni, / quo ruis, ille adytis melior locus* ('I shall carry on your foreknowing rites, and as mediator of your godhead I shall call on you in Phoebus' absence. That place is more powerful for me than Delos and all Cirrha, that place where you hasten is better than any shrine', *Theb.* 8.335–8). On the Thiodamas passage and ideas of succession see Hardie 1993: 111–13.

[91] Leigh 2006: 226: 'His assault on Thebes is not just an expression of his heroic etiquette, it is also a vehicle for his militant rationalism'. In the following quotation, there is some uncertainty about the text, especially *humilesne*, and about how the passage should be punctuated (see Hill's apparatus). For my purposes, however, the basic sense is secure enough.

[92] Lovatt 2001: 114. See also Lovatt 2005: 133.

Lovatt is right on the mark to see Capaneus attempting to move beyond his poetic world. In specifying that Amphion's song was 'unwarlike' and the lyre 'soft', however, Capaneus may not be generalising about poetry in toto. Instead, he leaves open the possibility of a different kind of poetry, one that sings of war rather than creation, one that is symbolised not by a feeble city wall but rather by the might of the hero who destroys such fragile constructions. That poetry is, of course, epic, a genre which began with, and was fundamentally defined by, the attempt to sack a city.[93] But it is a view of epic both narrow and extreme, harking back to the genre's Iliadic roots but at the same time dismissing the long-standing ktistic and religious elements on which Vergil in particular had placed such a premium. In Capaneus' resolutely physical and rational view of the world, which eliminates the legends and gods fundamental to both mythological and historical epic, the hyperepic hero threatens to deconstruct epic as traditionally conceived. What is left, in theory, is a strange hybrid—a poetry neither mythological nor historical, which celebrates the limitlessness of human power—a philosophical epic.

Philosophical doesn't mean didactic or doctrinaire, however, in the manner of Lucretius or Manilius. As we have seen, Statius uses the hero's appearances not only to give voice to a materialist position but also to participate in a dialogue about the existence and power of a realm beyond the physical. Thus, Capaneus' perspective on the world is always situated within a rich context that can support or undermine his view. Nowhere is this more evident than in Statius' scene change from Capaneus' dismantling of the city walls to Olympus, where the gods argue before Jupiter about the fate of the Thebans and Argives (*Theb.* 10.883–96).[94] The vivid description of exactly the kind of divine action in which Capaneus does not believe places the traditional epic world in direct confrontation with the materialist world.[95] The picture of Bacchus beseeching Jupiter to use the thunderbolt (*Theb.* 10.886–9) and of Hercules hesitating with his drawn bow (*Theb.* 10.890–1) anticipates Capaneus' provocation of those very gods (*Theb.* 10.899–906):

> 'nullane pro trepidis,' clamabat, 'numina Thebis
> statis? ubi infandae segnes telluris alumni,
> Bacchus et Alcides? piget instigare minores:
> tu potius uenias (quis enim concurrere nobis
> dignior?); en cineres Semelaeaque busta tenentur!

---

[93] See, especially, Patroclus' theomachic assault on the Trojan wall in *Iliad* 16, discussed in Chapter 1.

[94] See Ripoll 2006 on the epic tradition of fractious divine councils, esp. 255 on the twinning of divine and human theomachy in this passage of the *Thebaid*.

[95] On Statius as 'anti-Lucrèce' see Taisne 1999: 167–9. There may be a further irony at *Theb.* 10.897: *non tamen haec turbant pacem Iouis* ('yet this does not trouble Jupiter's calm'). Jupiter's imperturbability assimilates him to an Epicurean god even as he faces a distinctly un-Epicurean divine quarrel and just as he is about to hurl his thunderbolt in equally un-Epicurean fashion. It's Statius' habit to press such conflicting characterisations to the limit and even beyond.

> nunc age, nunc totis in me conitere flammis,
> Iuppiter! an pauidas tonitru turbare puellas
> fortior et soceri turres excindere Cadmi?'

> 'Does none of you gods,' he shouted, 'stand for fearful
> Thebes? Where are the sluggish nurslings of this abominable land,
> Bacchus and Alcides? It shames me to provoke lesser beings:
> Rather come you—for who is worthier
> to confront me?—look, the ashes and tomb of Semele are in my power!
> Now come, now strive against me with all your flames,
> Jupiter! Or are you braver at frightening trembling girls
> with thunder and razing the towers of your father-in-law Cadmus?'

Capaneus had already answered these rhetorical questions for himself in the agon—either the gods are not interested enough in human affairs to respond to his provocations or they simply do not exist. For such egregious blasphemy to go unpunished would constitute serious evidence in favour of Capaneus' attitude to the gods. What Capaneus doesn't see, of course, is the view of heaven to which the reader has been granted privileged access.

Jupiter regards Capaneus' challenge as another Gigantomachy and as an example of a lesson that has gone unheeded: *quaenam spes hominum tumidae post proelia Phlegrae! / tune etiam feriendus?* ('what hope is there for men after the battles of arrogant Phlegra! Must you too be struck?' *Theb.* 10.909–10).[96] For the gods—understandably—there is no philosophical subtext to Capaneus' theomachy, since their own participation in the scene decisively pre-empts any question of their existence and power. And yet Statius wittily attributes to the gods a tinge of doubt concerning Jupiter's thunderbolt (*dubio pro fulmine pallent, Theb.* 10.920), while Capaneus' ascent recalls in imagery and characterisation, if not in diction, Lucretius' heroic portrayal of Epicurus, discussed in Chapter 2.[97] Like Epicurus (Lucr. 1.68–71), Capaneus is disbelieving of stories about the gods, undaunted by superstitious warnings and thunderbolts, and his looking up at the walls (*Theb.* 10.840) and elevation in mid-air (*Theb.* 10.861, 918) suggest Epicurus' movement from looking up at the sky to passing beyond the bounds of the world (Lucr. 1.66–7, 72–3).[98]

---

[96] On the relative merits of P's *quae non* against the variant reading *quaenam* see T. Gärtner 2001 and 2003.

[97] On Capaneus and Epicurus see Taisne 1999: 173, Leigh 2006: 231–2, Lovatt 2013b: 108–11. In the catalogue of epic poets in the *genethliacon* to Lucan, Statius writes of the 'high frenzy' of Lucretius (*et docti furor arduus Lucreti, Silv.* 2.7.76)—*furor* and *arduus*, two apt words for Statius' mad and sublime hero (*furor*, 10.832; *ardua uirtus*, 10.845).

[98] The river simile describing Capaneus' destruction of Thebes (*Theb.* 10.864–9) echoes a Lucretian simile illustrating the force of natural elements and analogical argument (Lucr. 1.280–9). Cf. Hardie 2009b: 206, 209–10. Statius' allusion reinforces the combined destructiveness of the elements and materialist philosophy. Statius is also looking back to the river simile used of Diomedes before his theomachy (*Il.* 5.87–92), on which see Taisne 1999: 171–2 with nn. 37–8, and Chapter 1.

Statius' subsequent description of the storm gathered by Jupiter represents a decisive riposte to the materialist or sceptical point of view (*Theb.* 10.913–17):

ipsa dato nondum caelestis regia signo
sponte tonat, coeunt ipsae sine flamine nubes
accurruntque imbres: Stygias rupisse catenas
Iapetum aut uictam supera ad conuexa leuari
Inarimen Aetnamue putes.

The heavenly palace itself, with no sign yet given,
thunders of its own accord, the clouds themselves gather without any wind
and rainstorms hasten: you would think that Iapetus
had broken his Stygian chains or that subdued Inarime or Etna
was raised to the vault above.

The detail of the absence of the winds marks the storm's cause as unequivocally supernatural, especially as it follows the thundering of Jupiter's palace.[99] When Statius explicitly describes Capaneus struck by a thunderbolt 'driven by the full force of Jupiter' (*toto Ioue fulmen adactum, Theb.* 10.927), we see in a single action the god demonstrate his power and refute the hero's claims. Moreover, at the moment of Capaneus' death, Statius separates the hero's body and soul in one final rejection of the materialist view: *sed membra uirum terrena relinquunt, / exuiturque animus* (but his earthly body deserts the hero, and his spirit is stripped away, *Theb.* 10.937–8). Despite all the hero's provocations, and despite all of the philosophical allusions, Statius' Jupiter asserts his authority within the world of the *Thebaid*. However radical Capaneus' threat, this epic is not, after all, to be an adventure in a post-divine world.

The Twilight of the Gods

If at the close of Book 10 the epic's theology would seem to have been settled, the remaining two books not only reopen earlier questions, they do so far more radically than before. After an abundance of speech and action by both Jupiter and Tisiphone at the beginning of Book 11, the unparalleled impiety of

---

[99] On the application of Gigantomachic imagery to both Capaneus and Jupiter see Lovatt 2005: 133–9. Such assimilations and confusions make theomachy appear ethically more ambiguous. This is especially true in the case of the intratextual allusion in Capaneus' death (*Theb.* 10.935–9), which points back to Asopus' war on Jupiter fought in revenge for the rape of his daughter Aegina (*Theb.* 7.320–7). Statius constructs the allusion not only through the repeated image of a theomach scarcely yielding in the face of Jupiter's thunderbolt but also through the shared diction of the two passages (e.g., *stetit / stat, igne / ignibus, cessit / cessissent, anhelit / anhelat, fulmineum / fulmen, in caelum / in sidera*). Jupiter's simple narrative of human and Gigantic impiety thus occludes his own Gigantism and the possible justifications for theomachy resulting from his tyrannical behaviour.

the fraternal duel drives off from the scene first the gods and then the Furies. As a consequence, the twelfth and final book describes very little divine action, and even that only as a backdrop to the various human attempts to resolve the plot of the poem.[100] Critics have long noted this extraordinary diminishing of the gods' presence in the final phase of the *Thebaid*. In particular, Feeney's masterful account of Statius' handling of the divine demonstrates the series of transitions from fully characterised Olympian deities through personified abstractions to the almost entirely allegorical figure of *Clementia* described in Book 12.[101] This movement has two main functions: first, to explore the human attempts at resolution in the absence of divine influence, and second, to offer a commentary on the ways in which divine action in poetry ought to be understood. Where Feeney's interests in Statius' generic innovations intersect with my own is in his observation that Statius 'ends up in Lucan's camp, by eventually removing the gods from the scene altogether'.[102] As the comparison to the godless and revolutionary *Pharsalia* suggests, the end of the *Thebaid* looks curiously like Capaneus' vision of a world where the gods are distant or non-existent and matters are settled by the force of human might and will.[103]

Three passages, in particular, continue and develop Capaneus' testing of the mythological and theological conventions of epic. First, the hero's wife, Evadne, revisits the question of the Argives' monstrous nature, so frequently alluded to in the preceding books. Second, a comparison between Theseus and Jupiter suggests a new way of understanding the relationship between men and gods in the epic. And third, an allusion to Capaneus in Theseus' triumph over Creon picks up a discourse on divine action initiated in the scene of the fight over Hippomedon's body in Book 9 and suggests a novel way of resolving the questions raised by the earlier episode.

Many critics continue to debate the question of whether or not Theseus is a true source of moral authority at the end of the poem, a question as intractable

---

[100] Despite the withdrawal of several gods in the face of the duel, others—including Hecate, Ceres, Juno, and Iris—appear early on in Book 12, either participating in the Argive women's mourning or assisting them in their expedition (*Theb.* 12.129–40). Juno, in particular, intervenes directly in affairs, securing the favour of Athens' patron deity, Pallas, towards the Argive widows (*Theb.* 12.291–4, 464–7), and appealing in direct speech to the moon to illuminate Argia's search for her husband's body (*Theb.* 12.295–311). Only female gods, then, play any sort of prominent role in the final book of the epic. Although an analogue can clearly be seen with the human protagonists of the book, the Argive widows, this gendering of divine action means that there is no active, male heavenly counterpart to Theseus. Indeed the closest thing to any such pairing is the brief mention of Pallas beating her shield before the Athenians march to Thebes (*Theb.* 12.606–10).

[101] Feeney 1991: 355–91; cf. Schetter 1960: 26–9, Bessone 2011: 55-8. On *Clementia* see Burgess 1972, Braund 1996: 9–12, Ganiban 2007: 214–19, McNelis 2007: 163–5.

[102] Feeney 1991: 358.

[103] Ornytus prepares for this view when, near the beginning of the book, he encourages the train of mourning Argive women to call on Theseus' aid: *bello cogendus et armis / in mores hominemque Creon* ('by war and arms must Creon be forced into human conduct', 12.165-6). See Pollmann 2004: 129, Rieks 1967: 222.

as that of Aeneas' moral authority at the close of Vergil's epic.[104] More amenable to analysis is the fact that Theseus has sole authority at the close of the *Thebaid*. Whether a model of justice or a deeply ambivalent figure, Theseus is the one individual able to end Creon's tyranny, to grant the Argives funeral rites, and to bring the epic to some kind of resolution. In the process of accomplishing these feats we see little to no divine intervention either for or against him.[105] Indeed, as we shall see, rather than operating under the influence of, or in conjunction with, the gods, Theseus comes to resemble them.

Book 12 forces the reader to re-evaluate not only the operation of Statius' epic world but also the Argive heroes and their characteristic impiety. The latter question comes to the fore when Evadne, wife of Capaneus, appeals to Theseus to ensure the burial of the Argive princes against the edict of Creon (*Theb.* 12.552-8):[106]

> nec querimur caesos: haec bellica iura uicesque
> armorum; sed non Siculis exorta sub antris
> monstra nec Ossaei bello cecidere bimembres.
> mitto genus clarosque patres: hominum, inclute Theseu,
> sanguis erant, homines, eademque in sidera, eosdem
> sortitus animarum alimentaque uestra creati,
> quos uetat igne Creon.

> We do not complain that they were killed: these are the laws of war and
> the vicissitudes of arms; but they were not monsters born from Sicilian
> caves, nor double-bodied creatures of Ossa who died in the war.
> I omit their family and famed fathers: they were of the blood of men,
> renowned Theseus, men born to the same stars,
> to the same human lot, the same nourishment as you,
> whom Creon keeps from the fire.

In direct contrast to many descriptions of the heroes, Evadne denies that the champions are to be identified with monsters and asserts their human nature, emphasised by the repetition *hominum...homines*.[107] In speaking of monsters

---

[104] For the more positive view of Theseus see, e.g., Hardie 1993: 44-8, Braund 1996, Ripoll 1998: 446-51, Franchet d'Espèrey 1999: 294-6, Delarue 2000: 368-74. Most recently, McNelis 2007: 160-77 sees Theseus as a source of resolution for the narrative. For the more critical view of Theseus see, e.g., Dominik 1994: 92-8, Davis 1994: 471, and Hershkowitz 1998: 296-301; Burgess 1978: 346-63 and Ahl 1986: 2894-8 view Theseus as a complex and ambivalent character offering a relatively simple solution to the problem posed by Creon's tyranny. Most recently, Ganiban 2007: 212-32 sees Theseus as the best example of a flawed model of autocracy.

[105] Cf. Hardie 1993: 48: 'Here at last, perhaps, is a self-sufficient epic "man"'; also Bessone 2013b: 159-61.

[106] On Theseus' apparent lack of engagement with Evadne or the other lamenting women see Markus 2004: 116.

[107] Hippomedon is likened to Polyphemus (*Theb.* 6.716-18), and to a Centaur twice, once with his own horse (*Theb.* 4.139-44), and then with Tydeus' horse (*Theb.* 9.220-4). In the presence of Adrastus, Tydeus claims (*Theb.* 1.457-60) that Polynices' refusal to share the shelter during the storm compares

she alludes in particular to Cyclopes and Centaurs, but Capaneus had earlier been compared to precisely those creatures: *unus ut e siluis Pholoes habitator opacae / inter et Aetnaeos aequus consurgere fratres* ('as one who lives in the woods of dark Pholoe, or who stands equal among Aetnaean brethren', *Theb.* 3.604–5).[108] Given the imagery applied to Evadne's husband in particular, Feeney wryly points out that 'Evadne is on thin ice in her claim that the Argives were not gigantesque monsters'.[109] And yet Evadne's measured argument—she has no quarrel about the heroes' death in battle but seeks only the right of burial—militates against her natural bias and already suggests that there may be more to her speech than the irony observed by Feeney. The cogency of Evadne's point is lost, however, if one assumes that her irony is unintentional and that she doesn't understand the implications of her own rhetoric. Moreover, the stark contrast she draws between monsters and men attests not so much to her erroneous judgement as to the distorting effect of the hyperbolic comparisons pervasive in the *Thebaid* and in the wider epic tradition: if poetry, especially Statius' poetry, thrives on magnifying its characters to mythical proportions, Evadne's distinction, however problematic, acts as a sobering corrective.[110] Taking Capaneus to be a Giant, for instance, risks conflating similes and allusions with more radical identity claims. By contrast, Evadne suggests that considerable interpretive care needs to be taken before determining the scope and implications of such resemblances.[111] In this regard, like her husband, she undermines the poetic exaggerations on which epic relies for its power; further, she does so all the more persuasively for the lack of his typical grandiloquence. And yet, by the end of her speech, she too falls prey to the same rhetorical impulse when she wishes that Hercules not envy Theseus'

unfavourably with the mutual tolerance of Centaurs, Cyclopes, and other monsters (though Tydeus may be guilty of some hypocrisy since the narrator does not indicate that either party was willing to share, *Theb.* 1.408–13). When Tydeus refers to his birthplace as *monstriferae Calydonis* (*Theb.* 1.453), he alludes to the Calydonian boar; however, the frequent association of Tydeus and the animal (e.g., *Theb.* 1.488–90) adds the ironic sense that he too is a monster born from Calydon. Finally, Tydeus' cannibalism suggests that these men were not in fact born to 'the same nourishment' as Theseus.

[108] Cyclopes traditionally inhabited Sicily, especially the area near Etna, while Centaurs traditionally inhabited Mount Pelion (and by association Mount Ossa) and Mount Pholoe (cf. *OCD* s.v. 'Cyclopes', 'Centaurs'). The phrase *Ossaei bimembres*, though certainly referring to Centaurs, may also allude to the Giants; the mountain of Ossa readily evokes the Gigantomachy (e.g., *Theb.* 8.79, 10.852). The word *bimembres*, too, could allude to the double bodies of Giants, which according to legend walked on snakes instead of legs (Capaneus refers to this mythical physiognomy at *Theb.* 5.569–70); cf. Naev. fr. 19.2 Morel = 45 Warmington *bicorpores Gigantes*. On Centaurs and Cyclopes as symbols of brute force in the *Thebaid* see Franchet d'Espèrey 1999: 193–7. On Statius' allusions to Vergilian and Ovidian treatments of the Centauromachy to figure civil war see Parkes 2009: 488–92.

[109] Feeney 1991: 361 n. 156. Cf. *Theb.* 2.595–601, where Tydeus is compared to the Hundred-Hander Briareus.

[110] Cf. Bessone 2013b: 160–1.

[111] Evadne's denial that the heroes were monsters may suggest to an Epicurean reader—or perhaps a reader such as her husband—the Lucretian arguments that creatures such as Centaurs do not exist (Lucr. 4.732–43, 5.878–81). On the Lucretian passages see Gigandet 1998: 134–55, Campbell 2007: 46–52, Nelis 2009: 258–9. On *bimembres*, Centaurs, and poetic credibility cf. Ov. *Met.* 15.281–4.

Theomachy and the Limits of Epic

similar feats (*nec sacer inuideat paribus Tirynthius actis*, *Theb.* 12.584). This inconsistency, too, recalls her husband, in particular the way in which his provocations of the gods sat uneasily with his materialist or atheist slogans.

Undeterred by Evadne's earlier assertion of the common humanity of the Argive champions and Theseus, Statius instead picks up her closing elevation of the Athenian king to the level of a divinity. Immediately following her speech the poet refers to Theseus as *Neptunius heros* (*Theb.* 12.588), thereby emphasising his divine parentage. As well as a subsequent comparison to Mars, Statius also likens Theseus to Jupiter himself (*Theb.* 12.650-5):[112]

> qualis Hyperboreos ubi nubilus institit axes
> Iuppiter et prima tremefecit sidera bruma,
> rumpitur Aeolia et longam indignata quietem
> tollit hiems animos uentosaque sibilat Arctos;
> tunc montes undaeque fremunt, tunc proelia caecis
> nubibus et tonitrus insanaque fulmina gaudent.

> As when cloudy Jupiter steps on the Hyperborean pole
> and makes the stars tremble at the beginning of winter,
> Aeolia is broken and the storm indignant at its long rest
> lifts its spirits and the windy North whistles;
> then mountains and waves roar, then the blind clouds do battle
> and thunder and crazed lightning rejoice.

The description of winter storms evokes the image of Jupiter as god of lightning, the same Jupiter who raised a storm above Thebes before destroying Capaneus with the thunderbolt. And yet the storm's impatience—*longam indignata quietem*—recalls Capaneus' 'heart long since scornful of peace' (*longam pridem indignantia pacem / corda*, *Theb.* 3.599-600). And the epithet used of the lightning—*insana*—makes Jupiter's weaponry appear to belong more appropriately to the mad Capaneus.[113] The simile thus raises moral questions relevant to critics' ethical readings, but also questions of the identity and power of Theseus, who blurs the distinction between Jupiter and Capaneus through the dangerous extent of his might. In embodying both god and theomach, however, Theseus offers a new solution to the problem of the divine apparatus: at one stroke he turns it from reality to metaphor, thus fulfilling Capaneus' vision while assuming the power traditionally invested in Jupiter.

Theseus will again recall Capaneus with his final speech over the body of Creon (*Theb.* 12.778-81):[114]

---

[112] Theseus is compared to Mars at *Theb.* 12.733-5.

[113] For *insanus* associated with Capaneus see *Theb.* 3.669; 10.32, 919.

[114] For comparison with the end of the *Aeneid*, to which Statius alludes, see Ganiban 2007: 226-8; cf. Bernstein 2013: 244-7. Note the striking contrast between the descriptions of the deaths of Turnus and Creon. Vergil depicts the flight of Turnus' spirit to the underworld—the fate of his body and soul—in unmistakably dualist terms: *ast illi soluuntur frigore membra / uitaque cum gemitu fugit indignata sub*

adsistit Theseus grauis armaque tollens,
'iamne dare extinctis iustos' ait 'hostibus ignes,
iam uictos operire placet? uade atra dature
supplicia, extremique tamen secure sepulcri'.

Theseus stands grimly above him, and taking his arms
he says, 'Now does it please you to give just fires to your deceased
enemy, now to bury the defeated? Go to receive your dark
punishments, yet sure of your final burial'.

As Lucia Caiani has noted, the passage echoes Capaneus' speech over the corpse of Hippomedon in Book 9: *interea iustos dum reddimus ignes, / hoc ultor Capaneus operit tua membra sepulcro* ('meanwhile, until we bestow just fires, Capaneus, your avenger, covers your body in this tomb', *Theb.* 9.564–5).[115] The tomb in question is a makeshift construction built from the arms of Hypseus, who had despoiled Hippomedon and was in turn slain by Capaneus. In order to understand the significance of Capaneus' reference to fires and a tomb, we need to look back to the beginning of the scene when Juno beseeches Jupiter to allow Hippomedon burial on land (*Theb.* 9.514–21):

'en meus Hippomedon, cui gentis origo Mycenae
Argolicique lares numenque ante omnia Iuno
(sic ego fida meis?), pelagi crudelibus ibit
praeda feris? certe tumulos supremaque uictis
busta dabas: ubi Cecropiae post proelia flammae,
Theseos ignis ubi est?' non spernit coniugis aequas
ille preces, leuiterque oculos ad moenia Cadmi
rettulit, et uiso sederunt flumina nutu.

'See, my Hippomedon, whose descent is from Mycenae
and whose home is Argos, for whom Juno comes before all gods
(am I thus faithful to my own?), will he go to feed the cruel
beasts of the sea? Assuredly you granted tombs and the final
pyres to the vanquished: where are the Cecropian flames after the battle,

---

umbras ('and his limbs were loosened by the chill of death, and his life, indignant, fled with a groan to the shades', *Aen.* 12.951–2). In the *Thebaid*, Theseus prepares the audience for a similar glimpse into Creon's fate: *Argolici, quibus haec datur hostia, manes, / pandite Tartareum chaos ultricesque parate / Eumenidas, uenit ecce Creon!* ('Argive spirits, to whom this sacrifice is given, open Tartarean chaos and prepare the avenging Eumenides—behold, Creon comes!' *Theb.* 12.771–3). Absent from the following description of Creon's death, however, is any hint of the eschatology suggested either a few lines earlier in the *Thebaid* or at the equivalent point of the *Aeneid*: *ille oculis extremo errore solutis / labitur* ('with his gaze wandering loosened at the last, he falls', *Theb.* 12.777–8). Far from the punishment promised by Theseus, far from the realms of heaven and hell that have structured and motivated so much of the action of the epic, Statius tellingly offers only the physical details of death.

[115] Caiani 1990: 272. Cf. also *tremens* (*Theb.* 12.774) / *tremibunda* (*Theb.* 9.552), *labitur* (*Theb.* 12.778) / *labitur* (*Theb.* 9.556), and *adsistit* (*Theb.* 12.778) / *adsistens* (*Theb.* 9.557). Caiani's article offers excellent discussion of the many inter- and intratextual allusions running through this episode.

> where is the fire of Theseus?' He did not spurn the just prayers
> of his consort, and he lightly drew his gaze to the walls
> of Cadmus, and seeing his nod the rivers settled.

Juno's use of the verb *dabas*—whether referring to a specific promise on Jupiter's part or to a general ethical norm guaranteed by the god—implies that the Argives' burial and Theseus' future intervention depend on Jupiter.[116] Jupiter appears to confirm her understanding of events by calming the waters, thereby enabling Hippomedon to leave the river, shortly after which the beleaguered hero dies. The subsequent fight over Hippomedon's arms and Capaneus' temporary measure of burial invite the audience to wonder whether Juno's plea on behalf of Hippomedon is better answered by Jupiter's calming of the river or by Capaneus' godless heroism.[117] And yet the true significance of the scene from Book 9 is not realised until Theseus, standing over the body of Creon at the denouement of the epic, alludes to Capaneus' speech. For in the relatively godless context of Book 12, and given Theseus' allusion to the godless Capaneus of all people, it appears that Jupiter has little to no role in granting just fires and tombs to the dead; rather, Theseus, a successor to Capaneus and mortal analogue to Jupiter, represents the human agent of an equally human piety.[118]

For a human to discharge a role traditionally dependent on the gods of epic thus continues the poem's running theological debate, in which Capaneus is perhaps the most vocal and explicit participant. Capaneus' position, or variety of positions, promotes the ideas that distant or non-existent gods do not influence mortal affairs, and that human will can be effected by one's agency and might. Those ideas, however subtly corroborated in places throughout the poem, are repeatedly set against a world of rich, and seemingly potent, divine action. In the final book of the *Thebaid*, however, the epic world has changed— not to fit Capaneus' vision of it, to be sure, but certainly closer to his valorisation of human agency and the physical, visible realm than seemed the case for the majority of the poem. The gods may remain, even if we see a somewhat different cast of deities from before, but they play distinctly secondary roles to the human protagonists, both Theseus and the widows of the fallen. That the end of the poem should experiment with a different kind of relationship between gods and mortals only continues, and to some extent cashes out, the earlier provocations repeatedly voiced and embodied by the theomach Capaneus.

---

[116] Cf. Dewar 1991: 157.

[117] For Capaneus' self-conscious impiety in this scene see esp. *Theb.* 9.548–50 with Dewar 1991: 162.

[118] Cf. Caiani 1990: 272–5.

9

The Politics of Theomachy

> The King shall be enthroned in a position of revered worship and shall not be violated. No person shall expose the King to any sort of accusation or action.
> —2007 CONSTITUTION OF THAILAND, CHAPTER 2, SECTION 8

> Every tyrant deep down is only an anarchist who has seized the crown and who brings everyone to heel. There is though, another idea in the anarchy of Heliogabalus. Believing himself god, identifying himself with his god, he never makes the mistake of inventing a human law, an absurd and preposterous human law through which he as god would speak.
> —ANTONIN ARTAUD

> The gods too, if it is right to say, are made by poetry and such great majesty needs the voice of a singer.
> —OVID

> He who fashions sacred visages from gold or marble, that man does not make gods: the one who asks makes them.
> —MARTIAL

In Domitian's new Forum Transitorium, one of the scenes from the frieze, still visible today, represents Minerva's punishment of Arachne after the mortal girl challenges the goddess to a contest of weaving. In light of Domitian's adoption of Minerva as patron goddess, the scene puts the mythological story to clear political use: overreaching against gods and emperors, the frieze warns, is much the same thing and will end in much the same way.[1] Admonitory

---

[1] On Domitian and Minerva see Girard 1981, D'Ambra 1993: 3–18.

mythological images were nothing new: on the doors of the Temple of Palatine Apollo, Augustus' patron deity, was depicted the figure of Niobe, who boasted of her superiority over the goddess Latona.[2] This kind of context, coupled with the far more ambivalent handling of these myths in Ovid's *Metamorphoses*, invites a similarly political reading of the theomachies treated in this book.

Critics have offered political interpretations of the theomach before: William Dominik has argued that Capaneus represents an opponent of the emperor, for instance, while John Fitch has read the maddened Hercules as alluding to the stereotype of the tyrannical emperor, such as Caligula, as we saw in Chapter 4.[3] This approach has not been without its problems. Dominik's reading of the *Thebaid* as a subversive critique of Domitian, for example, received considerable criticism for relying on highly tendentious sources and for taking an overly allegorical approach to the poem.[4] Although the search for hidden criticism of the emperor has fallen out of favour in recent years, Dominik's willingness to tackle the politics of the epic head-on nevertheless remains a signal virtue.[5] Much recent work on the *Thebaid*, by contrast, while offering brilliant literary analyses, has not taken up imperial politics as a substantial theme.[6] Helen Lovatt, for instance, has commented incisively on the consequences of Statius' assimilation of Jupiter and Capaneus and the confusing application of Gigantomachic imagery to both god and hero:[7]

---

[2] See Kellum 1985, P. Zanker 1988.

[3] Dominik 1994: 166: '[Jupiter's] treatment of Capaneus recalls Domitian's wonted treatment of direct critics of his regime'. For Hercules as Caligula see Fitch 1987: 368.

[4] For criticism of Dominik's working assumptions see Hardie 1996. In Dominik's defence, he clearly states in his preface that he intends to offer a reading of how the *Thebaid* may have been understood in particular historical circumstances, that is, if interpreting the poem from a senatorial, anti-Domitianic point of view. See Dominik 1994: xiii–xiv, where he cites Hirsch's concept of a work's 'significance' (as opposed to the author's intended 'meaning') as a theoretical justification for his approach.

[5] Cf. Cowan 2009: '*Herrscherkritik* is a path oft-trodden and not always with the most careful of steps. However, it is surely possible to discuss Flavian politics and their relationship (and difference) from Augustan politics without simply looking for coded attacks on the *princeps*'. For the possibility of political criticism under tyranny see Ahl 1984a, 1984b, Bartsch 1994, Rutledge 2009.

[6] Three recent English monographs on the *Thebaid*, for example, have primarily focused on poetics to very good effect, but while they all acknowledge the relevance of contemporary politics, they generally avoid specific claims about links between the poem and imperial rule. See Lovatt 2005: 109, Ganiban 2007: 231–2, and McNelis 2007: 2–8. In a recent review of Ganiban's book, for instance, Cowan 2009 notes the avoidance of 'the politics of Domitianic Rome, or indeed politics more generally'. Continental scholarship has generally been more receptive, esp. Bessone 2011; Ripoll 1998 touches on political themes across Flavian epic, while Hartmann 2004 analyses the most explicitly political passages, esp. the panegyrics, in Statius and Silius. Politics more broadly conceived, however—the politics of imperial family relations or socio-economic exchange—receives extensive treatment in Bernstein 2008, Augoustakis 2010b, and Coffee 2009. Silius is far better situated in his Domitianic context than Statius thanks to the detailed and substantial reading of Marks 2005, though the *Punica* too would benefit from being viewed through a wider historicist lens. M. Wilson 2013 warns against rooting the *Punica* too deeply within a Flavian context given that Silius, who was born under Tiberius, lived through a significantly greater proportion of the first century AD.

[7] Lovatt 2005: 137–8.

Politically, this makes the distinction between legitimised and illegitimate authority extremely difficult to maintain. Is Capaneus a freedom fighter or a terrorist? Is Jupiter a monstrous tyrant or an efficient ruler?

Lovatt's rhetorical questions are on the mark, but a consideration of contemporary Roman political and religious practice enables us to press much further and to see why a contemporary reader might have felt the same uncertainty about the representation of legitimacy and tyranny in the *Thebaid*.

The possibility of a fresh approach to the politics of Latin literature has been opened up by recent studies that move interpretation away from allegory and subversive criticism to the domain of interdiscursivity.[8] Critics have increasingly abandoned the project of treating a text as a roman-à-clef to be deciphered in favour of locating a work's themes and forms of expression within a cultural context, and identifying the ways—sometimes similar, sometimes diverse—in which the rhetoric of various literary and cultural discourses functions. In this chapter, then, I focus not on theomachy per se but rather on the imperial contexts against which attacks on the gods or attempts to usurp the gods might have been understood. The emperors' divine aspect generated a discourse that developed over the course of the first century AD in response to the ideology of individual emperors and criticism of their rule.[9] As I have argued at several points in this book, it's highly plausible that theomachy emerged as a central topos of Silver Latin literature as a result of this developing discourse, since epic and tragedy provided a ready-made vehicle through which to think about the possibility of mortals being elevated to divinity and the attendant risks and implications. The particularly bold and grandiose character of Silver Latin theomachy—compared with Greek and even Augustan versions—can be explained not only by the familiar recourse to a period style and the desire to exceed previous authors but also by a political context that made divinity and its discontents a more pressing issue for contemporary Romans.

This chapter, divided into three parts, offers a series of readings of different political engagements with impiety—including, in part 1 ('Undermining the Emperor'), Ovid's exile poetry and a Tacitean account of a treason trial; in part 2 ('The Theomachic Revolution'), Lucan's response to imperial deification and Suetonius' representation of Caligula; and, in part 3 ('Domitian, Augustus, and Dynastic Competition'), Statius' exploration of imperial ideology. In each case I examine the implications of the relevant cultural and political discourses for a reading of theomachy. I argue that these discursive contexts figure the theomach sometimes as an opponent of the emperor and sometimes as a tyrant, with the two extremes united by a common revolutionary zeal to push the

---

[8] On the term see Riggsby 2006: 5, and cf. pp. 4–5 above. Other studies in this vein include Roller 2001 and Feldherr 2010; Habinek 1998 is formative.

[9] For bibliography on the imperial cult see p. 11 n. 35.

limits of their world.[10] Viewed through the lens of Roman politics, then, theomachy points to the ambitions and failures shared by rebels and tyrants alike. In the final section, which focuses on Statius' *Silvae* as well as his *Thebaid*, I suggest that the pushing of limits represented by theomachy captures not only an aspect of Rome's politico-religious tradition but also a characteristically Flavian meta-discourse about the very conception of limits, especially in relation to the achievements of earlier ages.

Undermining the Emperor

The figuring of Capaneus as an opponent of the emperor appears as early as Ovid's exile poetry. In several poems Ovid describes his punishment by Augustus through the image of Capaneus' destruction by Jupiter. Because these passages, however, offer little by way of detail concerning Ovid's wrongdoing, they have received less comment than, for example, the famous invocation of the myth of Actaeon to represent the poet's error and disproportionate penalty (*Tr.* 2.103-8).[11] Nevertheless, the choice to assimilate himself to the impious Capaneus appears an odd one for a poet seeking to minimise the seriousness of his transgression and to reassure the emperor of his unwavering devotion, despite the epic grandeur the mythical comparison provides.

Given the alleged aim of securing a recall from exile, Ovid puts the myth of Capaneus to surprisingly self-aggrandising use: *illo nec leuius cecidi, quem magna locutum / reppulit a Thebis Iuppiter igne suo* ('nor did I fall more lightly than the boaster whom Jupiter cast back from Thebes with his own fire', *Tr.* 5.3.29-30). It's difficult to determine whether the poet is more self-conscious or self-incriminating here, as his claim to have suffered the same fate as Capaneus repeats the very fault—boasting—for which the hero had been punished. The issue of self-promotion and fame is subsequently made even more explicit: *notior est factus Capaneus a fulminis ictu, / notus humo mersis Amphiaraus equis* ('Capaneus was made more famous by the lightning stroke, Amphiaraus famed because his horses sank beneath the earth', *Pont.* 3.1.51-2). It might have been a shrewd, and perfectly comprehensible, move for Ovid to concede publicly that his punishment had turned him into a negative exemplum, like Capaneus, but, strikingly, this isn't what he does. Instead, he mitigates Capaneus' impious arrogance by pairing him with Amphiaraus, the sole member of the Seven to be famous for his piety. Moreover, together with other, sympathetic perspectives on Capaneus' fall (*Tr.* 3.5.5-8, 4.3.61-4), these claims to renown

---

[10] In this respect, the readings bear a close resemblance to the philosophical interpretation of Capaneus' role in Chapter 8.

[11] On the Actaeon image see Ingleheart 2006, McGowan 2009: 195-7; on the possible reasons for Ovid's exile see Syme 1978: 215-29.

suggest a distinct lack of contrition on the poet's part. Far from distinguishing his own error from Capaneus' challenge to Jupiter, as one might reasonably have expected him to do, Ovid goes so far as to humanise the hero and even glorify himself by association with the hero's death.

Even when Ovid acknowledges partial responsibility for his fate, allusion to Capaneus problematises his pose of deference to Augustus. At the end of *Tristia* 4.8, Ovid uses the familiar image of the thunderbolt to concede the emperor's maximal power (*Tr.* 4.8.45–52):[12]

> nil adeo ualidum est, adamas licet alliget illud,
>   ut maneat rapido firmius igne Iouis;
> nil ita sublime est supraque pericula tendit
>   non sit ut inferius suppositumque deo.
> nam quamquam uitio pars est contracta malorum,
>   plus tamen exitii numinis ira dedit.
> at uos admoniti nostris quoque casibus este,
>   aequantem superos emeruisse uirum.

> Nothing is so strong, though adamant binds it,
>   as to remain too firm for the rapid fire of Jupiter;
> nothing is so sublime or reaches so far above dangers
>   that it is not below and subject to the god.
> For although a part of my ills was brought about by my fault,
>   the anger of the god has given still greater ruin.
> But you be warned by my fate also,
>   to deserve well of a man equal to the gods.

The reference to punishment by Jupiter's fire recalls the repeated use of Capaneus in the other exile poems, but the decision to allude to the hero in this poem in particular is especially perplexing, since the ostensibly awestruck tone of the passage sits uneasily with Ovid's implied identification with a figure notorious for his dismissal of the gods. Moreover, although this passage would seem to acknowledge Augustus' divine power—*numinis ira*—it ends on a less certain note, asserting that the emperor equals the gods (*aequantem superos*),

---

[12] In the exile poetry, Ovid frequently refers to Jupiter's *fulmen* and related vocabulary as a metaphor for Augustus' power. See, e.g., *Tr.* 1.1.81–2, 1.3.11–12, 2.33, 2.144, 2.179, 4.8.45–52, 5.2.53; *Pont.* 1.7.46. At *Pont.* 3.6.27–8, Ovid contrasts Augustus' reasoned and merciful justice with the haphazard thunderbolts of Jupiter, but the prolonged association of Jupiter and Augustus throughout the exile poetry threatens to override this single and selective distinction. Moreover, the idea that the thunderbolt strikes indiscriminately forms an important part of the Lucretian argument for natural meteorology over divinely caused lightning (Lucr. 6.387–422); such Lucretian resonances undermine the very divine authority Augustus sought to arrogate. The thunderbolt was also a metaphor for political power under the republic; Livy reports that the Rhodian envoy Astymedes used the image in mitigating his city's offence against Rome: *etiam deos aliqui uerbis ferocioribus increpant, nec ideo quemquam fulmine ictum audimus* ('some even assail the gods with overbold language, but we have not heard that anyone has for that reason been struck by a thunderbolt', Livy 45.23.19).

while emphasising with the poem's final word that he is still a man (*uirum*).[13] Although far less egregious than Capaneus' impiety, Ovid's subtle reduction of Augustus gives some indication of the way in which Capaneus' traditional impiety could take on a new significance in the imperial age.

For someone wishing to make the point that their punishment was too severe for the crime, Ovid makes a rather odd choice, I have suggested, in using the example of Capaneus. Unlike Actaeon, whom Ovid can plausibly absolve of deliberate impiety, Capaneus is so wilful that he literally asks to be punished. But it's precisely the egregiousness of Capaneus' attitude, however sympathetically Ovid treats the character, that explains Ovid's adoption of the myth. By assimilating himself to such an extreme figure, Ovid puts his wrongdoing and consequent punishment in perspective: the absurd disproportion of the comparison points to a similar disproportion in the punishment. Furthermore, the rhetorical purpose of using the example of Capaneus goes beyond mere hyperbole: during this period impiety had acquired a specifically political significance. Opposition to the emperor was frequently couched in terms of the *crimen maiestatis*, often abbreviated simply to *maiestas*, a charge of treason under the republic that, under the principate, had been extended to include diminution of the emperor's majesty, often in its divine aspect.[14] The Greek sources on this period generally refer to the charge as one of 'impiety' (ἀσέβεια), and Tacitus, the main Roman source, even refers to one instance as 'impiety against the emperor' (*impietatis in principem*, Ann. 6.47). Equally explicit is the collocation used to describe the charges against the two Julias: *laesarum religionum ac uiolatae maiestatis* ('harming religion and violating majesty', Tac. Ann. 3.24).[15] Invoked in the unambiguously political context of Ovid's punishment, Capaneus' proverbial impiety suggests precisely the kind

---

[13] Ovid uses similar diction to describe Augustus as a man equalling the gods at *Pont.* 1.2.118. In his comment on this passage, Gaertner 2005: 207 notes the similarity to *Pun.* 4.810, where Silius uses the phrase of Hannibal. It is important to add, however, that as a result of poets applying these terms to figures as wildly different as Augustus and Hannibal (or, at least, ostensibly different), it becomes more difficult to distinguish true elevation from impious overreaching, no matter the intent of the speaker (on the Silian passage cf. p. 247 n. 41). On Ovid's scrutinising of claims to divinity in the *Metamorphoses* see Chapter 3.

[14] There were any number of ways to fall foul of the charge, as attested by the frequent citations in Tacitus; see Bauman 1974: 3 and passim for a full account of the charge, including the attendant legal problems. In AD 95 Domitian executed two senators under the charge of *maiestas*, Acilius Glabrio and Flavius Clemens, for what Dio calls 'atheism' (ἀθεότητος, 67.14.2; cf. Suet. *Dom.* 15.1). We do not know how political this particular charge was; it may be that the two men were associated with Judaism or Christianity or some other rejection of the Roman gods. On these charges see Robinson 1995: 96; Southern 1997: 115–16, with 114–15 on philosophers; and Jones 1992: 115–17. Although this episode postdates—and hence can't have influenced—the composition of the *Thebaid*, it nevertheless emphasises the political significance of impiety in Domitian's reign. For a literary-cultural view of *maiestas*, focused on Ovid's account of the birth of the goddess Maiestas in *Fasti* 5, see N. Mackie 1992, Labate 2010: 210–14. Balsley 2011 reads the Lycaon episode in the *Metamorphoses* (see Chapter 3) as alluding to a *maiestas* trial.

[15] See Bauman 1974: 3, 13.

of undermining of the emperor and even revolution from which Ovid would wish to distance himself as far as possible.

More revealing than the case of Ovid, however, is that of Thrasea Paetus in Tacitus' *Annals*, which offers the most detailed exploration of the link between impiety and revolution.[16] When Cossutianus Capito brings a charge of *maiestas* against Thrasea Paetus, the informer includes the following allegation: *eiusdem animi est Poppaeam diuam non credere, cuius in acta diui Augusti et diui Iuli non iurare. spernit religiones, abrogat leges* ('it is characteristic of the same spirit not to believe in the divinity of Poppaea as not to swear by the acts of the divine Augustus and divine Julius. He rejects religious scruples, he abrogates the laws', *Ann.* 16.22). Tacitus portrays Capito as 'unjust' (*iniquus*, *Ann.* 16.21), but, however morally compromised, the form of the allegation highlights the role of impiety in defining Thrasea's threat to the regime.[17] The danger partly lies in Thrasea's exemplarity, a theme that runs through Capito's speech (*Ann.* 16.22): Thrasea is like Cato to Nero's Caesar; his followers imitate his habits, though not yet his outright opposition; the provinces and armies avidly read the *acta diurna* to know his latest principled stand; he follows in the line of Tubero and Favonius, opponents of the Gracchi and Julius Caesar, respectively; he is even a new Brutus; most dangerous of all, Thrasea's example might set greater political movements into effect: *secessionem iam id et partis et, si idem multi audeant, bellum esse* ('already it is the secession of a party, and, if many dare the same, it is war', *Ann.* 16.22). Once Capito has made Thrasea appear to be at the head of a revolution, the consequences are strictly binary: *aut transeamus ad illa instituta, si potiora sunt, aut noua cupientibus auferatur dux et auctor* ('either let us change to his rules, if they are better, or let the leader and author of the revolutionaries be removed', *Ann.* 16.22). The hypothetical choice is, of course, purely rhetorical, since accepting Thrasea's new rules would necessarily entail the end of imperial authority. This fundamental challenge to the emperor leaves no room for compromise—either incumbent or opponent must be destroyed. But perhaps Capito's finest move is to portray Thrasea as the real tyrant. He 'has followers, or rather henchmen' (*et habet sectatores uel potius satellites*, *Ann.* 16.22), and 'although his sect vaunts liberty in order to overthrow tyranny', in the end 'they will be the ones to attack liberty itself' (*ut imperium euertant libertatem praeferunt: si peruerterint, libertatem ipsam adgredientur*, *Ann.* 16.22). Capito's rhetorical appropriation of terms aside, his formulation works because it builds on an intuitive concern that the intransigence of the radical will merely lead to a new tyranny.

---

[16] The association between impiety and revolution continues to this day, as the epigraphs to this chapter illustrate.

[17] Scepticism about Tacitus' specific presentation of the episode, however legitimate, does not negate its contribution to an understanding of the discursive role of impiety in challenges to imperial authority. Rutledge 2001: 115–18 gives a good account of the rhetorical moves; see also Rudich 1993: 149–60, Wilkinson 2012: 64–77.

Capito's attack on Thrasea for impiety and subversion presents one way of looking at the theomach's threat to the gods: not to punish the theomach would suggest that his vision of the world may be better or more ethical than conventional theology. It is for the sake of the preservation of that theology that the theomach, just as Thrasea, must die.[18] But Capito's rhetoric also suggests that the theomach's vision of the world isn't so different from the divine perspective after all: the violence and self-assertion that drive opposition to the gods threaten merely to supplant divine tyranny with a state of nature dominated by individual strength.

Read against these Ovidian and Tacitean contexts, then, Statius' amplification of Capaneus' impiety acquires a particular piquancy. As I argued in the previous chapter, Capaneus' varied claims—Epicurean, atheist, theomachic—represent a battery of attacks that test the integrity and limits of the epic world. On a politicised reading, however, those same attacks test not only the poetic fiction inhabited by the character but also the theological vision shaped by imperial ideology. Rather than simple blasphemy, Statius' Capaneus offers a series of provocations to reflect on the nature of the divine and its relationship to humankind; at the same time, he is no armchair philosopher but a violent radical willing to take his beliefs (or disbelief) to the furthest extreme.

The Theomachic Revolution

A significant intermediary between the figure of the theomach and the Roman emperor is, as we saw in Chapter 5, Lucan's Caesar. Among other sources, Lucan draws on the heroic model of Senecan tragedy—the impious and seemingly unlimited protagonist, like Atreus—in representing Caesar in the *Bellum Civile*. Lucan's fusion of theomach and autocrat in the person of Caesar means that characters following in this tradition, such as Capaneus and Silius' Hannibal, are at most one step removed from the Lucanian reflection of imperial ideology.[19]

---

[18] Statius' theomach and Tacitus' opponents of the emperor also share a death wish. Capaneus is called 'lavish of his life' (*largusque animae*, *Theb.* 3.603), which Lactantius ad loc. compares with Horace's *animaeque magnae / prodigum Paulum* ('Paulus prodigal of his great life', *Carm.* 1.12.37–8) and Vergil's *est hic, est animus lucis contemptor* ('this here is a spirit that is contemptuous of the light', *Aen.* 9.205). For Tacitus, Thrasea's grandstanding meant only that 'he endangered himself, but did not mark the beginning of freedom for others' (*sibi causam periculi fecit, ceteris libertatis initium non praebuit*, *Ann.* 14.12). By contrast, Tacitus famously praises his father-in-law, Agricola, for his quiet amelioration of Domitian's cruelty over the suicidal exhibitionism of the emperor's more forthright opponents (*Agr.* 42.4–5; cf. the *fama* given as one of the motivations for Capaneus' theomachy, if indeed *fama*, and not *fata*, is the correct reading at *Theb.* 10.835). The theomach well illustrates not only the futility but also the arrogance of openly opposing the emperor.

[19] Fantham 1995 speaks of 'Capaneus' Caesarian self-aggrandizement'. In lexical terms, Capaneus' bellicosity comes closest to an echo of Caesar: cf. *at numquam patiens pacis longaeque quietis / armorum* ('but never suffering peace nor long rest from arms', Luc. 2.650–1) with Statius' *longam indignantia*

What distinguishes Caesar from the consistently theomachic Capaneus, however, is the uncertainty about his precise relationship to the *BC*'s absent gods and the multiplicity of theomachic tensions in the poem. Caesar's impiety and violence naturally suggest the role of the theomach, and yet, after the Battle of Pharsalus, Caesar sees the bloodshed as proof of fortune and divine favour: *fortunam superosque suos in sanguine cernit* ('in the blood he sees his fortune and his gods', Luc. 7.796).[20] From the beginning of the poem, however, the narrator questions the moral weight of such backing: *uictrix causa deis placuit, sed uicta Catoni* ('the victorious cause pleased the gods, but the defeated cause pleased Cato', Luc. 1.128). This opposition has the curious result of placing Cato, rather than Caesar, in the role of the theomach.[21] Finally, in one further reversal, the poet turns the practice of imperial deification itself into a kind of theomachy at the end of his impassioned, and strikingly inconsistent, speech just before the battle of Pharsalus (Luc. 7.445–59).[22] Although uttered in a vastly different tone from Capaneus' attacks on the gods, this embittered speech, with its suggestions of absent, impotent, or non-existent gods, is the closest Lucan comes to prefiguring the combination of atheism, Epicureanism, and sheer antagonism that Statius will attribute to his hero.[23]

Lucan's union of philosophical radicalism with political revolution represents a fundamental intervention in the discourse of theomachy, one that shapes the terms against which Statius' Capaneus must be understood and that suggests quite the opposite interpretation from Ovid's use of Capaneus. Furthermore, set against the context of imperial deification, Capaneus' materialist and atheist rhetoric no longer appears part of a simple binary opposition between the secular and the religious. Rather, Capaneus' aggressive assertion of his world view, and the concomitant belief in his own supremacy, recalls Caesar's embodiment of rationalism, for instance at the Massilian grove, even as that rationalism yields to a powerful remystification as Caesar increasingly displaces the gods. In political terms, then, theomachy—however fuelled by philosophical disenchantment—seems inevitably to lead to yet another form of religion. Capaneus thus ceases to look like the Ovidian or Tacitean opponent of the emperor, but rather resembles the theomachic emperor himself.

---

pacem ('scorning the long peace', *Theb*. 3.599) and *impatiens* four lines below at *Theb*. 3.603. The comparison of Caesar with Bellona (Luc. 7.567–8) may also lie behind the Thebans' identification of Capaneus with the goddess (*Theb*. 10.853–5). Of the nine times the goddess's name comes up in the *Thebaid* (and once in the *Achilleid*) this is the only instance in which she is identified with any particular character. Both Caesar and Capaneus also allude to Ovid's Erysichthon: compare Luc. 3.433–5 with *Met*. 8.741–4; *Theb*. 5.568, 7.678–9 with *Met*. 8.755–6. On Caesar and Hannibal see Chapter 7.

[20] On Caesar as representative, rather than antagonist, of the divine see Fantham 2003.
[21] Cf. Chapter 5.
[22] On this passage see pp. 173–6.
[23] On Capaneus' complex of attitudes to the gods, including a marked strain of Epicureanism, see Chapter 8. For the possibility of a politicised Epicureanism see Momigliano 1941, Fowler 1989.

In Chapter 4, I explored the idea of a slippage between imperial deification and theomachy through the representation of Caligula. I now wish to return briefly to that example to illustrate what theomachy might signify beyond the tyranny and excessive ambition of the emperor. Once again, I treat Caligula not as a straightforwardly historical figure but according to the manner of his portrayal, and I intend the reading not to refer to Caligula specifically but to imperial power broadly conceived in Caligulan terms. I suggest that the characterisation of Caligula as a revolutionary—not just in theological or political matters but in cultural ones as well—fleshes out the deeper significance of theomachy: it represents an attempt to transcend not only the gods or the emperor but also the norms of a society. There is, of course, a trivial sense in which any behaviour considered impious by definition violates social norms— such is the case with the numerous tyrants featuring in mythology and political thought, such as Busiris, who practises human sacrifice, or Xerxes, whose yoking of the Hellespont allegorises his attempt to deprive Greece of her freedom.[24] The case of Caligula, however, reveals a struggle to define Roman imperial values, and in particular aesthetic values. In this way, the earlier political and aesthetic readings of theomachy overlap, as the metapoetic symbolism discussed at many points in this book combines with the emperor's desire to surpass his predecessors.

In Suetonius' biography, our fullest account of Caligula, the emperor resembles a weaker version of Capaneus.[25] On the one hand, like Capaneus the *contemptor superum*, Caligula threatens Jupiter (*Calig.* 22.4), mocks miracles (*Calig.* 51.1), and despises the gods (*deos contemneret, Calig.* 51.1).[26] Jupiter even seems to play a role in the emperor's death: first, Caligula dreams that the god kicks him down to earth (*Calig.* 57.3), and second, according to one account of his assassination, the word 'Jupiter' is the password that Caligula says right before Chaerea strikes him dead (*Calig.* 58.2-3). On the other hand, unlike Capaneus, Caligula believes in the gods and is frightened by thunder and lightning (*Calig.* 51.1).[27] Moreover, he possesses obviously unheroic qualities, such

---

[24] For Busiris' impiety as an allegorisation of the Egyptians' 'extreme disregard for established customs' (τὴν ὑπερβολὴν τῆς ἀνομίας), specifically hospitality towards strangers, see Diod. Sic. 1.67.11. For Xerxes' impiety see Aesch. *Pers.* 745-51, and cf. Mikalson 2003: 44-7 on Herodotus' treatment.

[25] Statius accords with the tyrannical representation of Caligula at *Silv.* 3.3.69-75 (*tyrannum*, 72). In the same passage he also describes the emperor as 'driven by the Furies' (*Furiis agitatus*, 70), a charge that could be levelled at Capaneus (e.g., *Theb.* 10.831-3).

[26] Caligula intensifies the impious and tyrannical instincts of his ancestors, the Claudii of the early republic. See Livy 3.57.2 (*deorum contemptor*), 9.34.22 (*contemptu deorum*), with Wiseman 1979: 55-139, Vasaly 1987: 212-22; cf. Suet. *Tib.* 2.2. For the aristocratic arrogance of the Claudii see, e.g., Suet. *Tib.* 2.4, and cf. Capaneus' disparaging use of *plebeia* at *Theb.* 3.609 (on which see Snijder 1968: 239-40). Legras 1905: 216 suggested that Capaneus' particular combination of bellicosity and aristocracy recalls Coriolanus: 'une sorte de Coriolan qui méprise les plébéiens'.

[27] Caligula's interaction with gods demonstrates his belief in them, even if erratic and prone to violence and transgression: witness his rebuilding of temples (*Calig.* 21), or his prayer that Minerva supervise his daughter Julia Drusilla's upbringing (*Calig.* 25).

as his unspectacular military record (*Calig.* 43-47) and personal cowardice (*Calig.* 51).[28] Thus, to the extent that Capaneus alludes to imperial antagonism against the divine—of which Caligula is the best specimen—he represents the strongest form of that attitude, appropriate both to convey the high style of the epic genre and to enact the most stringent testing of the gods.

Caligula's transgressiveness consists partly in his desire to publish or literalise what ought to remain discreet or symbolic. That desire can seem to take on a positive aspect, for example his lifting of the censorship of earlier historians upon his accession (*Calig.* 16.1):

> Titi Labieni, Cordi Cremuti, Cassi Seueri scripta senatus consultis abolita requiri et esse in manibus lectitarique permisit, quando maxime sua interesset ut facta quaeque posteris tradantur.

> He allowed the writings of Titus Labienus, Cremutius Cordus, and Cassius Severus, which had been suppressed by decrees of the senate, to be sought, circulated, and read, saying that it was very much in his own interest that whatever happened be handed down to posterity.

Caligula's exact motivation for doing so is unclear—here it is only said to be 'in his own interest'—but besides sending a signal of his openness, the action has further resonances in light of his later decline, resonances to which we shall return. The same desire to make matters more public and transparent, however, can be seen in its negative form too. In a discussion about kingship, Suetonius claims that Caligula 'was not far from assuming at once a diadem and changing the appearance of the principate for the form of monarchy' (*nec multum afuit quin statim diadema sumeret speciemque principatus in regni formam conuerteret*, *Calig.* 22.1). The word *speciem* here, whether focalised through Caligula or not, makes abundantly clear that the principate was in actuality no different from a monarchy. The emperor's subsequent over-identification with the divine should be read in a similar way: in taking on all the trappings of divinity—the offerings, statues, temples, and worship—Caligula was merely spelling out what Augustus had handled with delicacy and Tiberius had rejected with apparent modesty. But if the fact of being emperor was to all intents and purposes a kind of divinisation, the rhetorical handling of that fact—however delicate or modest—simply occluded the political reality. When modern historians draw distinctions between degrees of divinisation, they comply rather too willingly with the projections of imperial ideology.[29] There was no right or wrong way to be

---

[28] Caligula's dressing up like the gods replete with their weapons (*Calig.* 52.1), in particular Jupiter, suggests the myth of Salmoneus rather than Capaneus—the weak imposter rather than the martial challenger. Cf. pp. 179-90 on the story of Augustus dressing up as Apollo.

[29] See Gradel 2002 for the argument that divinity in the ancient world was more a matter of degree than of kind. Gradel is too quick, however, to dismiss alternative notions of divinity, which stress the polarity of human and divine, as merely Christianising misperception (see esp. 1-26). Although divine honours for the emperor may represent an elevation in status rather than an absolute separation from

divine, however, only a popular or unpopular way to be emperor. Caligula merely made explicit what Ovid had already understood, as we saw in Chapter 3: whatever the senate, inscriptions, and coins might say to legitimise or qualify a claim to divinity, to be emperor was in one perfectly comprehensible way to be god.[30] On this view, Caligula was not so much mad as intolerably candid about the nature of imperial power.

Viewed from any distance, the line between exploring and exploiting the scope of imperial power may be difficult to make out, but Suetonius nevertheless offers a confident assessment of Caligula's psychology: *nihil tam efficere concupiscebat quam quod posse effici negaretur* ('he desired to do nothing so much as what was said could not be done', *Calig.* 37.2). On that traditional view, Caligula's various feats can be attributed to a gross disregard for proper limits. His riding across the Gulf of Baiae on a bridge of boats, for instance, was regarded by some as a bid to outdo Xerxes' bridging of the Hellespont (*Calig.* 19).[31] Suetonius also reports, however, that Caligula's motivation may have come from elsewhere, from an occasion when an astrologer to the emperor Tiberius had claimed that the young Caligula's chances of becoming emperor were as likely as his riding a horse across the Gulf of Baiae. It follows that by bridging the gulf, thereby accomplishing the astrologer's *adynaton*, Caligula asserted his own claim to the principate. His very concept of accession to power is thus framed as the fulfilment of the impossible, as a defiance of others' doubt, and as a heroic innovation.

Caligula's excess is further manifested in his extravagance and continued defiance of the natural world—incredible luxuries, lavish construction projects, building piers in stormy seas, tunnels through the hardest rock, the raising of plains, and the levelling of mountains (*Calig.* 37).[32] This mannerist distortion of norms extends to the emperor's taste in literature (*Calig.* 34.2):

---

humanity, Romans need only have looked to mythology and literature to see divinity as mutually exclusive with humanity. Examples of such categorical difference abound in Homer and Hesiod, and make their presence very strongly felt in Roman imperial poetry, especially in the first half of Ovid's *Metamorphoses*. Authors problematised such distinctions, of course, but those distinctions must have been conceptually available in the first place in order for them to be problematised. Throughout this book I have argued that the imperial poets negotiate these different conceptions of divinity rather than assuming any particular one to be correct. For a detailed critique of Gradel along these lines see Levene 2012; cf. also Iossif and Lorber 2011: 702–4. See Ando 2008: x–xii, xvi–xvii for a different approach to Roman theology focused on its empiricist outlook.

[30] Immediately after mentioning the funeral of Augustus and the decreeing of a temple and divine rites to him, Tacitus says that 'all prayers were then directed towards Tiberius' (*uersae inde ad Tiberium preces*, *Ann.* 1.11). Of this transition Hardie 2007a: 155 says: 'prayers to a god are replaced by, converted into, prayers to a mortal ruler, a reversal of the *Metamorphoses*' concluding transformation of human ruler into god'. Tacitus' irony here highlights what divinity had become: an emperor was to all intents and purposes a god regardless of theological niceties, and the people show their understanding of the situation when addressing their prayers to Tiberius and not to the deceased Augustus. Note that the senators who later in *Ann.* 1.11 stretch their hands to heaven, to the statue of Augustus, and to Tiberius are hedging their bets because they cannot decipher the intentions of the new emperor.

[31] See also Joseph. *AJ* 19.5–6. On the date of the bridge see Wardle 2007.

[32] For the theomachs' defiance of the natural world cf., e.g., Chapter 6.

cogitauit etiam de Homeri carminibus abolendis, cur enim sibi non licere dicens, quod Platoni licuisset, qui eum e ciuitate quam constituebat eiecerit? sed et Vergili ac Titi Liui scripta et imagines paulum afuit quin ex omnibus bibliothecis amoueret, quorum alterum ut nullius ingenii minimaeque doctrinae, alterum ut uerbosum in historia neglegentemque carpebat.

He thought even of destroying the poetry of Homer, saying why should the same not be allowed to him as had been allowed to Plato, who threw Homer out of the state which he designed? Moreover, he was little short of removing the writings and images of Vergil and Livy from all the libraries, disparaging the former as of little talent and learning and the latter as verbose and careless in his history.

We will never know what Plato would actually have done with Homeric poetry had he ever been given the power to create his ideal republic, but Caligula thought he knew and, moreover, he was in a position to make the hypothetical a reality. Similarly, what for most people would merely be a contrarian stance on the quality of Vergil's and Livy's writings was for Caligula an opportunity to turn literary criticism into a policy.[33] His idiosyncrasy goes well beyond aesthetic judgment; the passage is set in the context of Caligula's assault on the statues of famous men of the past and on the contemporary legal profession (*Calig.* 34.1–2). Suetonius adds that new statues could only be erected with Caligula's permission and that the emperor threatened lawyers if they did not agree with his wishes. This battery of iconoclastic attacks thus maximises the emperor's authority in multiple realms of culture: religious cult, literature, and the law. At this point, it should be easier to understand—no matter how eccentric and unreliable Suetonius' characterisation—why Caligula might have revoked the ban on various historians of the late republic and early empire. Their histories had been censored because they offered a critical view of Julius Caesar and his successors. In making those texts accessible, Caligula was not only signalling his openness, he was implementing part of a larger and more radical ideological program to break with convention and make public and real what had previously been private and theoretical.

This view of Caligula as above all an iconoclast shares important ground with Capaneus beyond their contempt for the gods. As I discussed in Chapter 8, Helen Lovatt and Matthew Leigh have both read Capaneus as a figure for Statius' transgressive poetics: Lovatt sees the hero attempting to break through the fiction into an unattainable reality, while Leigh takes Capaneus to be a more direct allegory for Statius' own Bloomian struggle with Vergil.[34] Building

---

[33] Evidence for adverse opinions of Vergil in Flavian times comes from Maternus in Tacitus' *Dialogus* (12.6): *pluris hodie reperies, qui Ciceronis gloriam quam qui Vergilii detrectent.* Cf. Gossage 1969: 68. Caligula's supposed distaste for Vergil doesn't prevent him from quoting the poet (*Calig.* 45.2).

[34] Lovatt 2001: 114 and 2005: 133, Leigh 2006.

on these and other ideas, I argued that Capaneus represents one voice in a larger debate on the very nature of epic and its theology, and on the possibilities—though ultimately foreclosed—for the genre's development. Statius presents Capaneus as one who seeks to expose fictions and who surpasses the feats of his ancestors and peers, as a character who takes epic to a logical extreme and then attempts to go still further, threatening the very integrity of the genre.[35] By now I hope it's clear that this isn't a purely literary reading of Capaneus, nor is it a reading of Capaneus alone. For Hannibal, Hercules, Caesar, and to some extent their Ovidian predecessors too, all exert some pressure on their genre through their determination to do what cannot be done and to overturn existing authorities. In doing so they reflect not only the desire of their authors to establish their identity and legacy but also the potentialities of imperial power as articulated by perhaps its most honest holder—Caligula—and by his theomachic successors, Nero and Domitian.[36]

Domitian, Augustus, and Dynastic Competition

Despite the Greek mythological subject matter of the *Thebaid*, the preface of the poem points to its engagement with issues of human-divine boundary crossing, specifically imperial ideology. This interest isn't confined to the brief panegyric of Domitian, where it might be expected, but it also emerges through a subsequent invocation to the Muse Clio, which uses an allusion to Horace to link the subject matter of the *Thebaid* to long-standing questions about the relationship between the emperor and the gods.

Statius' programmatic statements in the prologue introduce an apparent distinction between the mythological epic and its historical context. The poet emphasises his choice not to write a historical epic, supposedly because he lacks the inspiration and the daring to sing of Domitian's military achievements (*Theb.* 1.16–31):[37]

---

[35] Most of these elements are discussed in Chapter 8. For Capaneus' surpassing of his ancestors see *Theb.* 3.601–2, of his peers *Theb.* 10.748–51. At *Theb.* 3.602–3 most translators take *aequi / impatiens* to mean that Capaneus is intolerant of 'justice', but the same phrase used by Tacitus of Agrippina the Elder (Tac. *Ann.* 6.25) suggests that Capaneus is 'intolerant of rivalry' or 'impatient of equality'. Cf. *Theb.* 1.189–90.

[36] Suetonius labels Nero a *religionum... contemptor* (*Ner.* 56.1). His biography shows many of the same tyrannical characteristics that we see in Caligula, and indeed Nero is even said to have admired his uncle Caligula (*Ner.* 30.1). Common characteristics include, but are not limited to, jealousy (*Ner.* 24.1, 53.1), extravagance (*Ner.* 27.2–3, 42.2), lavish building projects (*Ner.* 31.1–3), cowardice (*Ner.* 46.1, 49.2–3), and self-regard (*Ner.* 55.1). For a spirited defence of Nero as the most self-consciously theatrical of rulers see Champlin 2003; for an attempt to read his intellectual interests and technological ambitions sympathetically see Hine 2006: 63–7. The standard biography remains M. T. Griffin 1985. For Domitian see below.

[37] On this passage see Hartmann 2004: 70–87, Penwill 2013: 37–43.

> limes mihi carminis esto
> Oedipodae confusa domus, quando Itala nondum
> signa nec Arctoos ausim spirare triumphos
> bisque iugo Rhenum, bis adactum legibus Histrum
> et coniurato deiectos uertice Dacos
> aut defensa prius uix pubescentibus annis
> bella Iouis. tuque, o Latiae decus addite famae
> quem noua maturi subeuntem exorsa parentis
> aeternum sibi Roma cupit (licet artior omnes
> limes agat stellas et te plaga lucida caeli,
> Pliadum Boreaeque et hiulci fulminis expers,
> sollicitet, licet ignipedum frenator equorum
> ipse tuis alte radiantem crinibus arcum
> imprimat aut magni cedat tibi Iuppiter aequa
> parte poli), maneas hominum contentus habenis,
> undarum terraeque potens, et sidera dones.
>
> Let the limit of my song be
> the disordered house of Oedipus, since not yet may I dare to tell
> in inspired fashion of Italian standards and Northern triumphs,
> the Rhine twice yoked, the Danube twice brought under laws
> and the Dacians cast down from their conspiring peak
> or earlier still the wars fought in adolescent years
> in defence of Jupiter.
> And you, o glory added to the renown of Latium,
> succeeding to the new endeavours of your father's mature years,
> whom Rome desires to be her own forever (though a narrower path
> leads all the stars, and the bright region of the sky
> unfamiliar with the Pleiades or Boreas or the cleaving thunderbolt
> tempts you, though the tamer of the fiery-footed steeds
> himself sets upon your locks the far-shining diadem
> or Jupiter yields to you an equal part
> of the great sky), may you remain contented with rule over men,
> master of sea and earth, and may you give stars to the sky.

The panegyric, similar in tone if not in diction to Lucan's praise of Nero in the *Bellum Civile* (Luc. 1.33–66), focuses on Domitian's entitlement to a place in heaven and the poet's hope that that occasion, which necessarily signifies the emperor's death as a prerequisite of deification, is located far off in the future. As so often in panegyric, the honoree collapses the normal distinction between human and divine: Domitian will receive the crown of Apollo or rule jointly with Jupiter. With that conventional crescendo, Statius would seem to have discharged the burden of a poet's obligation to his emperor, at least for now (*Theb.* 1.32–4):

> tempus erit, cum Pierio tua fortior oestro
> facta canam: nunc tendo chelyn; satis arma referre
> Aonia.

> There will be a time when emboldened by Pierian frenzy
> I shall sing your deeds: now I string my lyre; it is enough to tell of
> Aonian arms.

In committing to compose an imperial epic at some unspecified point in the future, and thus temporarily deflecting the obligation to write one now, Statius participates in the familiar topos of the *recusatio*, which works by treating the poem at hand—the *Thebaid*—as a lesser poem than the putative epic for the emperor.[38] Behind the false modesty and literary posturing lies an apparently concrete opposition between contemporary reality and mythology. The remainder of the preface, however, whets the reader's appetite for the actual (supposedly inferior) poem to follow. Statius therefore offers a selective summary of the *Thebaid*—a contents page, as it were—listing the alternate rule of Thebes, madness, strife, the brothers' funeral pyre, Creon's savage edict, the sheer quantity of slaughter, and the heroes' *aristeiai* (*Theb.* 1.33–45). Having left Domitian far behind, we are now firmly located in the epic's mythological plot, and indeed immediately upon concluding his contents page, the poet transports us to Oedipus' cave and the father's curse that may (or may not) drive the fraternal conflict and the plot of the poem. The transition from contemporary Rome to ancient Thebes thus appears sharp and definite, as the poet emphatically moves away from a future obligation to focus on the topic at hand.[39] In the last part of the preface, however, just as he switches to the catalogue of *aristeiai*, Statius subtly undermines the clear dichotomy he has set up (*Theb.* 1.41–5):

> quem prius heroum, Clio, dabis? inmodicum irae
> Tydea? laurigeri subitos an uatis hiatus?
> urguet et hostilem propellens caedibus amnem
> turbidus Hippomedon, plorandaque bella proterui
> Arcados atque alio Capaneus horrore canendus.

> Which of the heroes will you give me first, Clio? Tydeus, limitless
> in his rage? Or the sudden swallowing of the laurel-wreathed seer?
> Swirling Hippomedon too drives me, repelling his river-foe
> with slaughter, and the wars of the brave Arcadian
> must be lamented, and Capaneus must be sung with another thrill.

---

[38] Rosati 2002a argues that Statius' deployment of the Muses comments on the relationship—indeed constitutes the negotiation—between poetic inspiration and political pressure. See also Markus 2003, Gibson 2006, Galli 2013: 60–5. By far the best new treatment of *recusatio* as both a political as well as a poetic gesture is Freudenburg (forthcoming), the Augustan focus of which can profitably be applied, mutatis mutandis, to the Domitianic context.

[39] For Thebes as Rome's 'other' see Hardie 1990; in the context of the *Thebaid* see Braund 2006. On the tradition of Thebes as a foil for Athens in Attic tragedy cf. Zeitlin 1986.

The choice to appeal to Clio, the Muse associated with history (and by extension with imperial panegyric), is striking.[40] One might rather expect to see an address to Calliope, the Muse more commonly associated with epic, whom Statius calls on elsewhere, or even to an unnamed Muse or Muses, a typical epic invocation before a daunting list.[41] The specificity of the invocation, along with the syntactical arrangement *quem... Clio dabis*, forms a well-known allusion to Horace's *Odes* (*Carm.* 1.12.1–3):[42]

> quem uirum aut heroa lyra uel acri
> tibia sumis celebrare, Clio?
> quem deum?
>
> Which man or hero do you take up to celebrate
> with lyre or keen flute, Clio?
> Which god?

Horace's poem, which goes on to list gods, heroes of mythology, and great men of Roman history—Romulus, Camillus, Regulus, and the like—before settling on its intended honoree, Augustus, opens up a number of relevant issues.[43] Most pointedly, the allusion effectively reintroduces into Statius' mythological catalogue the very issue he claimed to have concluded: imperial panegyric. That this reintroduction is deliberate is clear, since Statius also alludes to the same lines of *Odes* 1.12 in *Silvae* 4.2, a poem exalting Domitian and his palace, in which Statius gives thanks for an invitation to dine with the emperor: *qua celebrem mea uota lyra* ('with what lyre am I to celebrate my wishes?' *Silv.* 4.2.7). Unlike the *Thebaid*, the panegyrical content of *Silvae* 4.2 closely echoes

---

[40] On Clio as the Muse of history see Nisbet and Hubbard 1970: 146. Statius will invoke Clio again in Book 10 to find out the cause of Menoeceus' death wish, a passage which emphasises the Muse's historical remit: *memor incipe Clio, / saecula te quoniam penes et digesta uetustas* ('begin mindful Clio, since the generations are in your power and the order of the past', *Theb.* 10.630–1). Valerius Flaccus also appeals to Clio's 'knowledge of the minds of gods and ways of things' (*superum... facultas / nosse animos rerumque uias*, Val. Fl. 3.15–16), but she notably lacks the explicit associations with time and history which she has in the *Thebaid* (note, however, that the context of Valerius' invocation is the mistaken 'civil' war at Cyzicus, a context prominently shared by Flavian history and Statius' Theban mythology). Statius' reference to *Clio mea* at *Silv.* 1.5.14 suggests that she might even be regarded as the distinctive Muse of the *Thebaid*. See Newlands 2002: 209, 217–19.

[41] Besides the invocation by Valerius Flaccus (previous note) this is Clio's only other appearance in Latin epic, in contrast to Calliope, who appears in the *Aeneid* (*Aen.* 9.525), the *Metamorphoses* (*Met.* 5.339), the *Punica* (*Pun.* 3.222, 12.390), and even in the *De Rerum Natura* (Lucr. 6.94). Statius invokes Calliope twice in the *Thebaid*, on both occasions in typical epic contexts: first, before the catalogue of Argive troops (*Theb.* 4.35), and second, in order to sing of battle (*Theb.* 8.374). Statius calls on all the Muses collectively to help him determine the scope of his work (*Theb.* 1.3–4) and to sing of Hippomedon's (*Theb.* 9.315–18) and Capaneus' (*Theb.* 10.831–6) theomachies.

[42] See most recently Georgacopoulou 1996: 173–5 (also illuminating on the other intertexts), Steiniger 1998: 227 (also offers an excellent comparison with the use of the Muses by Valerius Flaccus and Silius Italicus). Statius' *prius* (*Theb.* 1.41) also picks up on Horace's language from later in the same ode (*quid prius dicam*, *Carm.* 1.12.13).

[43] On this ode see Nisbet and Hubbard 1970: 142–69; for its negotiation of Augustus' divinity see Feeney 1998: 56, 111–13; Cole 2001.

the original, Horatian context of *Odes* 1.12: like the Augustan poet, Statius too compares the *princeps* to Jupiter (*Silv.* 4.2.11), Pollux (48), Bacchus (49), and Hercules (50), amongst others.[44]

Horace's contemplation of such a range of comparanda highlights a live problem in early Augustan Rome—the status of this new figure of power, the *princeps*: is he a republican hero, a demigod, or something even greater? In contrast with Horace's list, Statius' heroes in the *Thebaid* are hardly exemplary or auspicious—if the reader did not already know from mythology that they are better known for anger, death, frenzy, lamentation, and horror, Statius' invocation explicitly looks ahead to these characteristics. In light of *Odes* 1.12, then, Statius' text appears deeply ironic, a 'pseudo-célébration', as Sophia Georgacopoulou has called it.[45] But there is more to the intertextuality between *Thebaid* and *Ode* than simply the inversion of fame into infamy, order into disorder. Horace's poem raises the problem of how one conceives of and addresses Augustus' elevated status, and it finds its solution in the harmonious rule of Jupiter and Augustus (*Carm.* 1.12.49–57):

> gentis humanae pater atque custos,
> orte Saturno, tibi cura magni
> Caesaris fatis data: tu secundo
>   Caesare regnes.
>
> ille seu Parthos Latio imminentis
> egerit iusto domitos triumpho
> siue subiectos Orientis orae
>   Seras et Indos,
>
> te minor latum reget aequos orbem.

> Father and guardian of the human race,
> offspring of Saturn, care of great Caesar
> has been given to you by the fates: with Caesar as your second,
>   may you rule.
>
> Whether the Parthians threatening Latium
> he leads, subdued, in just triumph,
> or lying near the Eastern shore,
>   the Seres and the Indians,
>
> under you, he will rule the wide world with justice.

Statius has gone to some lengths to contrast his mythological poem with a putative historical epic on the deeds of Domitian, but the passage in which he

---

[44] The same comparanda appear in *Odes*. 1.12: Bacchus (22), Hercules (25), and the Dioscuri (25). Cf. *Silv.* 4.3.155, and Sil. *Pun.* 3.614–15 with Marks 2005: 222–7 and Tipping 2010a: 16–18, 46, 188.

[45] Georgacopoulou 1996: 174.

does so is nevertheless suffused with the panegyrical language of military triumph, the alignment of Jupiter and Domitian, and ultimately imperial apotheosis. The allusion to Horace in the invocation to Clio thus underscores the continued relevance of contemporary ideological concerns, despite Statius' earlier avowals to the contrary.[46]

Indeed, in this light, the Horatian appeal to Clio in the *Thebaid* prompts us to wonder why the impious heroes of Greek mythology are substituting for the familiar and ennobling comparanda of imperial panegyric—not Bacchus but 'swirling' Hippomedon, not Hercules but Tydeus 'limitless in his rage'.[47] Coming so soon after the panegyric to Domitian, which reflects on the emperor's past and future relationship with the gods, the invocation, with its strong allusion to Horace, leaves us with a conundrum: what is the nature of the relationship between a human being at the peak of his powers and the gods? Rather than the largely harmonious relationship described in the Horatian and Statian panegyrics, in the *Thebaid* at least it would often seem to be the antagonistic relationship represented most emphatically in theomachy. Whereas Horace had offered a subtle protreptic to Augustus to remain subordinate to Jupiter (*secundo*, *Carm.* 1.12.51; *minor*, *Carm.* 1.12.57), Statius will depict Hippomedon and Capaneus vying against the very gods.[48] It's difficult to resist the implication that Statius is passing informed commentary on Horace's pious hope: the history of the principate after Augustus had frequently shown not only emperors transgressing the boundary between human and divine but also 'revolutionaries' cast as opposing the divinity of the ruler.[49]

---

[46] Georgacopoulou 1996: 176 n. 29 privileges hymn over panegyric or history in the symbolism of Clio, but the distinction is hardly a clear one, and to ignore the historical signposting here misses the political significance of Statius' allusion to Horace. Steiniger 1998: 227–8 argues that the invocation to Clio suggests history, but she doesn't explore the possible implications.

[47] Moreover, and again quite unlike Horace's list, these heroes appear to make their own demands of the poet, each one competing for attention through the outlandishness or emotional intensity surrounding his *aristeia*. Lactantius' gloss on *urguet* reads: *compellit ad scribendum*. This compulsion is emphasised by the gerundival force of *ploranda* (*Theb.* 1.44) and *canendus* (*Theb.* 1.45). The heroes' effect on the poet resembles Bacchus' influence on one of his followers: *en urgues (alium tibi, Bacche, furorem / iuraui)*... ('you drive me (I swore a different frenzy to you, Bacchus)...', *Theb.* 4.396–7). Describing divine influence in this way imputes a similar power to the heroes and suggests that the poet suffers a kind of possession. Cf. *Silv.* 5.3.234: *Thebais urguebat*, though with a somewhat different sense.

[48] On the relationship between protreptic and patronage in imperial poetry see Braund 1998.

[49] It is perhaps partly as a response to this historical phenomenon that Capaneus acquires his importance in the poem and at the end of the preface. The extant evidence of the myth, whether from epic, tragedy, or mythography, neither gives the hero particular prominence nor indicates that his death was the last before the fraternal duel (Apollod. *Bibl.* 3.73, for instance, places Capaneus' death in the early stages of the war). It is probable, therefore, that Statius deliberately chose to give Capaneus greater weight. Lactantius suggests that the diction used of Capaneus at 1.45 also signals special emphasis: *bene 'alio horrore', maiore impetu dictionis. ut ipse alibi de Capaneo: 'grauioraque tela mereri'* ('rightly "with another thrill", with greater force of diction. As he himself says elsewhere of Capaneus: "to deserve heavier weaponry"', Lact. *ad Theb.* 1.45). Sweeney 1997: 8 emends *grauioraque tela mereri*

Evidence from outside the *Thebaid* makes Domitian's relationship with the gods a matter of particular interest. Especially beguiling is Pliny's comment in the *Panegyricus* on Domitian's delusion of divinity (*Pan.* 33.4):[50]

demens ille uerique honoris ignarus, qui crimina maiestatis in harena colligebat, ac se despici et contemni, nisi etiam gladiatores eius ueneraremur, sibi male dici in illis, suam diuinitatem suum numen uiolari interpretabatur, cumque se idem quod deos, idem gladiatores quod se putabat.

That man was mad and ignorant of true honour, who gathered charges of *maiestas* in the arena, and thought he was being looked down upon and despised unless we worshipped even his gladiators, and interpreted insults against them as violations of his divinity and godhead, thinking himself the same as the gods, and his gladiators the same as him.

Even leaving aside Pliny's undoubted bias, however, there is evidence to suggest that Domitian raised the association of god and emperor to a new level.[51] He took an active role in the deification of his family through consecration of the temple to the Flavian *gens* and the representation of his brother's apotheosis on the soffit of the Arch of Titus.[52] He erected an obelisk which celebrates in hieroglyphs the divinity of the Flavian dynasty, and also, according to

---

(*Theb.* 5.585), recorded in all the manuscripts, to *non mihi iam solito uatum de more canendum* ('departing from the customary manner of bards', *Theb.* 10.829), thus identifying the prologue's *alio horrore* with the higher register required to sing of the theomachy. However, the reading of the manuscripts is certainly interpretable and could be retained (cf. D. E. Hill 2000: 58). Lactantius' connection of *alio horrore* to Jupiter's *grauiora tela* not only offers an example of more forceful diction, it also draws an analogy between the thrill of the poetic voice and the heavier weaponry itself. Ovid furnishes evidence for *grauiora* as an aesthetic term when Orpheus appeals for inspiration to sing of lighter themes than Gigantomachy: *Iouis est mihi saepe potestas / dicta prius; cecini plectro grauiore Gigantas / sparsaque Phlegraeis uictricia fulmina campis. / nunc opus est leuiore lyra* ('the power of Jupiter has often been recounted by me before; with a heavier lyre have I sung the Giants and the victorious thunderbolts cast on the Phlegraean plains. Now there is need for a lighter lyre', *Met.* 10.149–52). In the context of Capaneus' Gigantomachic associations, Statius' *grauiora tela* thus picks up the Ovidian term for grand poetry, which Lactantius sees flagged from the first mention of Capaneus at *Theb.* 1.45. Cf. *Silv.* 1.5.1, where Statius uses the simple positive *graui plectro* to describe his mode of composing the *Thebaid*. Lovatt 2005: 134 n. 61 suggests another potential allusion to the *Metamorphoses*.

[50] On the unreliability of the sources concerning Domitian see, e.g., Waters 1964, 1969; Jones 1973, 1979, 1992; Syme 1983; Saller 1990; Southern 1997; Flower 2006: 234–75. Dominik 1994: 135–6 admits the senatorial bias but generally downplays factors such as the imposition of Trajanic ideology. On the problem of establishing Statius' attitude to Domitian in the *Silvae* see Geyssen 1996: esp. 1–16, Nauta 2002: 412–29. On the same problem in the interpretation of the *Punica* see Marks 2005: 211–12, 245–52, 283–8.

[51] See Charlesworth 1935, Hannestad 1986: 140–1, Friesen 1993: 119; *contra* Gering 2012: 117–39. Fears 1977: 222–6 argues against the view that Domitian sought to identify himself with Jupiter, but nevertheless accepts that 'Domitian went beyond conservative Roman tastes in the readiness with which he accepted adulation as a divinity' (224). Cf. Fears 1981: 74–80. Carter 2001: 20–34 and Marks 2005: 222–35 conveniently gather much of the evidence for Domitian's relationship with the divine along with copious bibliography. I offer a more condensed account here.

[52] See P. J. E. Davies 2000: 142–58.

Jean-Claude Grénier, the emperor's own divinity.[53] Some of Domitian's coinage, moreover, represented the emperor with the thunderbolt, a symbol of Jupiter's power.[54] And Domitian was even addressed as *dominus et deus*, though the exact usage and implications of this honorific have been the subject of much debate.[55] Reflecting that context, the panegyrical poems within Statius' *Silvae* abound with comparisons of the emperor to the gods.[56] Such hyperbolic rhetoric can even overlook potential tensions in the name of maximal praise. To return to *Silvae* 4.2, its celebration of Domitian's new palace puts the emperor in seemingly unthreatening competition with Jupiter (*Silv.* 4.2.20–2):[57]

> stupet hoc uicina Tonantis
> regia, teque pari laetantur sede locatum
> numina.
>
> The nearby palace of the Thunderer
> is amazed, and the gods delight that you are placed
> in an equal abode.

In the panegyric in the *Thebaid*, too, Statius can contemplate the possibility upon Domitian's death of Jupiter yielding to the emperor an equal part of the heavenly sky (*magni cedat tibi Iuppiter aequa / parte poli*, *Theb.* 1.29–30).

Statius' tone and projection of Domitianic ideology is further consistent with the poetry of his contemporary Martial, who assimilates Domitian to Jupiter by calling him 'ruler of the world and parent of the earth' (*mundi rector et parens orbis*, Mart. 7.7.5) and 'Thunderer' (*Tonantem*, Mart. 7.99.1).[58] Indeed, when Martial takes his turn to describe the height of Domitian's palace, the language of praise goes beyond divine associations and even exploits the imagery of theomachy: *Thessalicum breuior Pelion Ossa tulit* ('Ossa bore Thessalian Pelion less high', Mart. 8.36.6). The scale of Gigantomachy pales in comparison

---

[53] See Grénier 1987, 1996; Lembke 1994 expresses scepticism about Grénier's interpretation. Newlands 2002: 8–17 discusses the obelisk in her concise summary of Domitian's relationship with divinity. The obelisk currently stands in the Piazza Navona, but its original location was probably in the Isis temple complex in the Campus Martius.

[54] E.g., *BMC* 2: lxxxv. See Jones 1992: 108 with 220 nn. 53–4. Cf., e.g., *Silv.* 3.3.158–60, which continues the trope of the thunderbolt of imperial punishment that we saw in Ovid's exile poetry, as well as Plin. *Ep.* 3.11.3.

[55] See, e.g., Suet. *Dom.* 13.2, Dio 67.4.7; however, the title doesn't appear in the existing epigraphic record. For full treatment of sources and scholarship, see Jones 1992: 108–9, who expresses scepticism that Domitian ordered others to use the title, preferring to see it as a flattering address that the emperor chose not to reject; Dominik 1994: 158–60 views the title as part of a de facto apotheosis. See also Gradel 2002: 160.

[56] Statius compares or identifies Domitian with Jupiter at *Silv.* 1.6.27 (*nostri Iouis*), 3.4.18 (*Iuppiter Ausonius*), 4.2.11 (*cum Ioue*), and likens him to a god at 1.1.62 (*dei*), 4.3.128 (*deus*), 5.1.37–8 (*deus...propior Ioue*), 5.2.170 (*proximus ille deus*). Cf. Seager 2010: 342–9.

[57] On the potential anxieties underlying the poem see Newlands 2002: 260–83.

[58] On the representation of Domitian's relationship with the divine in Martial's *Epigrams* see Sullivan 1991: 137–45, Pitcher 1998: 65–72, Leberl 2004: 291–321, Henriksén 2012: xxiv–xxxi.

with the lofty palace, yet another testament to the nature-defying feats of Flavian engineering.[59] But we can look higher still: *haec, Auguste, tamen, quae uertice sidera pulsat, / par domus est caelo sed minor est domino* ('yet this house, Augustus, which strikes the stars with its top, is equal to the heavens but less than its master', Mart. 8.36.11–12). The frequency of the image of striking the stars in imperial poetry makes it more difficult to disentangle positive from negative connotations. For balanced against Horace's *sublimi feriam sidera uertice* ('I shall strike the stars with my lofty head', *Carm.* 1.1.36), for instance, is Vergil's description of the gigantic and theomachic Cyclops, Polyphemus: *altaque pulsat / sidera* ('and he strikes the lofty stars', *Aen.* 3.619–20).[60] In conjunction with the prior mention of Pelion and Ossa, far from emptying his imagery of problematic significance, Martial embraces it: Domitian is an emperor so transcendent as to surpass the celestial ambitions of any poet or theomach. In this poem, and in this age, theomachy can even offer a hyperbolic model—not just a cautionary tale—against which imperial power and achievement are to be understood.

The divine associations in contemporary panegyric are thus an intensification of the associations to be found in the material evidence: the temple of the Flavian *gens*, the Arch of Titus, and the Pamphili obelisk.[61] Together, the texts and monuments suggest a coherent ideology that lent itself to exaggeration or distortion in the wake of Domitian's downfall. Since we lack a similar breadth of evidence for many earlier emperors—no equivalent of Martial or Statius survives from the age of Caligula, for instance—it's difficult to say with any certainty how far Domitian's ideological ambitions exceeded those of his predecessors.[62] Given that the practices of imperial cult and apotheosis existed in one form or another from Caesar onwards, Statius' concern with the elevation of mortals in the prologue of the *Thebaid*, and in the narrative itself, engages with a system or tradition of imperial practice as well as with the literature concerning Domitian's particular ideology. But the coincidence of concern with the emperor as god across all our forms of evidence—the occasional poetry of Martial and Statius, the building program, and the (albeit exaggerated) claims of the hostile sources—strongly suggests that Domitian's relationship with the divine (or, at least, that relationship as representative of a more systemic phenomenon) provided a special impetus for Statius' thinking in the *Thebaid*.

---

[59] For another example of engineering as theomachy see pp. 206–8. Lines 7–8 of the epigram invoke the sublimity of mountains, another site of theomachic power (see Chapter 7). On the Flavian fascination with height see Vout 2012: 95–102; but not only Flavian: cf. Petron. *Sat.* 120.1.87.

[60] For an extensive list of parallels see Schöffel 2002: 336 n. 4.

[61] On allusions to Domitian's architectural and decorative practice in the *Thebaid* see Keith 2007.

[62] Nero, for example, had even appeared radiate on certain coins, a mark linked to divinity that had previously only been conferred on deceased emperors. See Champlin 2003: 116–17 with 300 n. 8 (and 112–44 for Nero's close association with Sol); Fears 1977: 325–8 argues that Nero's coinage need not be taken as a claim to divinity. Levy 1988 suggests that Caligula may have appeared radiate even earlier, though with the implication of divine sanction for his rule rather than divine status.

Finally, it should be borne in mind that Statius, and indeed anyone living around the time of Domitian, would have had one further way of thinking about theomachic competitiveness—not as the confrontation between subject and ruler, nor even ruler and god, nor yet between rival emperors, but rather the confrontation of dynasties. Domitian, the third in his line, held sway over a vast empire, and was presiding over the greatest urban transformation in Rome since the time of Augustus.[63] That is the context that best explains a poem like *Silvae* 1.1, for instance, in which Statius imagines that the equestrian statue of Alexander, now bearing the head of Julius Caesar, cedes to the newer and greater equestrian statue of Domitian (*Silv.* 1.1.84–90).[64] The emperor's statue even competes with famous monuments of the gods (*Silv.* 1.1.99–104). His sword is earlier compared to that of Orion, a comparison that suggests immense size but also recalls the mythological hero's theomachic qualities (*Silv.* 1.1.43–45).[65] *Silvae* 1.1 thus suggests the elevation of Domitian to near divine status, a move supported by the favourable comparisons with Alexander and Caesar.[66] Those comparisons, however, raise Domitian above not only individuals but also dynasties—the Hellenistic rulers and, especially, the Julio-Claudians, whom the Flavians replaced after a protracted civil war. When Romans vie with gods, those gods are as likely to come from the Palatine as Olympus—indeed, as imperial literature suggests, the two are hardly extricable.[67]

The opening poem of the *Silvae* exemplifies a tendency towards maximisation which typifies Roman art of the middle to late first century and saturates the *Thebaid* in particular.[68] The theme of excess and outlandishness may have been a topos of Roman literature, but the witnesses of the established Flavian dynasty were in a quite different position from a Horace or a Seneca or a Lucan

---

[63] See D'Ambra 1993: 33–46; cf. Marks 2010a: 36–7. Referring to large-scale architectural and ceremonial developments relating to the imperial palace, Paul Zanker concludes that 'Domitian's new public and residential style set the standard down to the time of Maxentius' (P. Zanker 2002: 107).

[64] See Newlands 2002: 51–73, Dewar 2008, Marks 2010a: 29. On the triangulation of Alexander, Domitian, and Scipio in the *Punica* see Marks 2005: 227–9 (cf. 142–7). On *Silv.* 1.1 in general see Leberl 2004: 143–67.

[65] On Orion's theomachic aspect cf. Sen. *HF* 12.

[66] Alexander and Caesar are key figures in the history of divinised monarchy. Alexander's association with Zeus, and even with Bacchus through his conquering of the east, sets a pattern for Hellenistic kings (see Badian 1981; on Alexander's reception in Rome see Spencer 2002). As the Roman republic came into closer contact with Hellenistic kingdoms, this practice became more familiar to Roman culture, leading to Greek divine honours for generals serving in the east (e.g., Pompey); see most recently Cole 2014. Although Caesar's death technically antedates the principate, Octavian made him the first in the line of deified Roman leaders (as did Suetonius in the *Vitae Caesarum*). Both Alexander and Caesar may have enjoyed some worship while alive, even if full apotheosis had to wait until their deaths. See Weinstock 1971; Gradel 2002: 54–72, 261–5.

[67] Martial compares Domitian favourably to his predecessors, e.g., Mart. 5.19.1–6, 8.11.7–8.

[68] For Flavian art as the culmination of this aesthetic see Newmyer 1984; cf. Rieks 1967: 212–13. Newlands 2002: 23 argues that in the *Silvae* Statius goes to the limits of panegyric in order to describe and accommodate the emperor's near limitless power.

in seeing those excesses as part of a large-scale, intergenerational power play that could elevate not only individuals but also entire families to the heavens. From that perspective the *Thebaid*'s concern with theomachy responds not just to political struggles narrowly conceived—as involving either the emperor or his opposition—but to a larger notion of revolution in which the rebels and tyrants of this chapter all participated, and which Flavian culture helped shape. It is owed to Domitian as much as to the anxiety of literary influence that Statius shows such extraordinary self-consciousness about the pressure to reinvent and supersede—pressures that animate theomachy and the poetry of hyperbole alike.[69] Thus, the elevation and competition with the divine typical of the epic tradition—the theomachies of Diomedes and Achilles in the *Iliad*, for instance—overlap with the contemporary concerns of first-century AD Rome. The conjunction of these two different streams of influence—one literary, the other sociopolitical—explains why the *Thebaid* is so interested in these questions of being like, and vying with, the gods. It is, I suggest, the ideological positioning of Domitian that shaped Statius' particular exploration of the shared project of epic and empire—a testing of the limits of human power.[70]

---

[69] Cf. Ripoll 1998: 531 n. 297.

[70] As one who had composed epic poetry himself, Domitian would have been well placed to understand the connection. Cf. Quintilian's praise of the emperor's suitability for the genre: *quis enim caneret bella melius quam qui sic gerit?* ('For who could sing of wars better than one who wages them so [well]?', *Inst.* 10.1.91). For evaluation of the evidence for Domitian's writing of epic see Coleman 1986: 3088–91. Marks 2010c: 198–9 sees Domitian's combining of poet and warrior roles as contributing to the obsolescence of historical epic.

Epilogue

And Zeus blasted Asclepius with lightning... as Stesichorus said in his *Eriphyle*, because he revived Capaneus and Lycurgus.

—PHILODEMUS

Then you leave us nothing, but we are gods in vain, neither contributing any providence to affairs nor worthy of sacrifice, truly just like drills or axes? Indeed, you think you despise me with good reason, because though I'm clutching the thunderbolt, as you see, I suffer you expounding all these things before us.

—LUCIAN

That I might move the turning spheres of heaven:
For earth and all this airy region
Cannot contain the state of Tamburlaine.

—CHRISTOPHER MARLOWE

If there is any god in heaven, of which I'm not sure,
his concern is on high, and not down here:
there is no man who has witnessed him for certain,
but the cowardly people believe from fear.

—MATTEO MARIA BOIARDO

A learned woman is thought to be a comet, that bodes mischief, whenever it appears. To offer to the world the liberal education of women is to deface the image of God in man, it will make women so high, and men so low, like fire in the house-top, it will set the whole world in a flame.

—BATHSUA MAKIN

Epilogue

The ease with which Jupiter dispatches Capaneus—with just the one thunderbolt—has left most critics feeling that the hero poses no real threat to the existing order.[1] In this book, by contrast, I have argued that the threat of the theomach—not only Capaneus, but also Hercules, Achilles, and others—resides in the potential to undermine the enabling fictions of the world he or she inhabits. For a brief moment, Patroclus can sack Troy, Niobe can nullify Latona, Hannibal can overcome history, and Capaneus can eliminate the gods altogether. These imagined scenarios threaten to take the works in which they appear in a radically different direction from that allowed by plot or genre, and the gods soon reassert their authority to enforce traditional limits. But not in every case. Lucan's *Bellum Civile* offers one perspective on what the consequences are for the genre and the world when the gods do not police these boundaries—an epic without hope or end, and a vision of tyranny and unlimited desire as the common condition of human nature. And yet, beyond this pessimism, Lucan's proliferation of theomachs in Caesar, Pompey, and Cato illustrates the larger symbolic function of theomachy and the hermeneutic challenge it poses the reader. For the poets, especially the ones writing in early imperial Rome, suggest a variety of ways in which the theomach's view might be realised—if not by theomachy proper then by poetic, philosophical, or political means. Fame, the *Iliad* suggests, can breach the divide between mortal and immortal, as, according to the Roman models, can equanimity, scepticism, and poetic and imperial apotheosis. Rather than offering a simple didactic moralism, the theomach is instrumental in generating a dialogue on the broader symbolism of fighting the gods, its stakes and implications.

The Neronian and Flavian theomach, who grew out of a unique convergence of cultural influences and historical pressures, offers a distinctive contribution to the legacy of Roman epic and tragedy. To describe that afterlife in any detail would require a book of its own, but the remaining pages nevertheless attempt to provide at least a glimpse of some important moments in the later literary tradition. The examples focus on the poetry of the European Renaissance, when writers and readers were well attuned to the nuances of their classical heritage, and when the problems raised by classical theomachy appeared of particularly direct relevance.[2] Many of the literary, intellectual, religious, and political developments taking place across Europe from the fifteenth to the seventeenth century—changing conceptions of the epic genre, materialist philosophies, claims of apostasy, and a growing centralisation of

---

[1] For the inequality of the contest see, e.g., Dominik 1994: 30, 166; McNelis 2007: 144. Leigh, who views Capaneus as a figure for Statius' poetic struggle against Vergil, acknowledges the difficulty of challenging the canon (2006: 239 n. 103), judging the assault 'futile but not ignoble' (241). Lovatt does see the hero as posing a threat, but only inasmuch as he provokes 'a response which in its extremity is gigantic and destructive' (2005: 136).

[2] Hardie 1993: xii remarks on the affinity between imperial and Renaissance epic. For a broader consideration of the early modern reception of Latin literature see Brockliss et al. 2012.

state power—share clear resemblances with the ancient contexts discussed in earlier chapters. Those similarities, set against important historical differences, make the theomach a source of especially potent creative energy during the period.

By the time of the Renaissance, of course, the representation of the theomach would have to adapt to Christian theology, since a monotheistic religion with an eternal and truly omnipotent God allowed no possibility of change in the divine order nor even the kinds of direct confrontation that we have seen in this book.[3] Even when theomachy does occur, as in the scene of the War in Heaven in Book 6 of Milton's *Paradise Lost* (*PL*), God himself does not participate, but sends his Son to bring the conflict to an end.[4] And when in the Great Council of Book 2 the devils debate how they might respond to their fall, they ignore the speech of the martial theomach, Moloch, which encourages a familiar and doomed assault on heaven (*PL* 2.51–105). Instead, they favour Satan's novel conception, voiced by Beelzebub, of guerrilla tactics targeting God's creation, humankind (*PL* 2.310–78). It's hard not to see in these two scenes a rejection not only of the martial epic tradition, as Miltonists have argued, but also of classical theomachy in particular. Indeed, some early modern critics considered it both implausible and indecorous to depict Satan raging and striving against God in high epic style, let alone embarking on theomachy proper.[5] Milton's tone in the account of the War in Heaven has generated particular controversy, with generations of critics disputing whether the scene is ultimately bathetic, a parody of epic tropes rather than a true instantiation of classical theomachy within *Paradise Lost*.[6] The scholarly debate itself, however, and especially the real discomfort provoked by theomachy, testify to the continued relevance of the theomach, and to the development of the role in post-classical literature. Furthermore, the analysis offered in this book suggests that, however important the distinctions between epic and parody or between bellicosity and guile, the concept of classical theomachy is sufficiently broad to encompass extremes from the crafty Lycaon to the bombastic Capaneus. A departure from martial epic, therefore, isn't necessarily a departure from theomachy tout court, however closely the two categories might otherwise be intertwined. But even more important than the range of theomachic attitudes and of the tones in which they're described is the sublimity of the theomachic moment itself, when it is precisely a sense of risk and uncertainty that defines the scene's power. The struggle between mortal and

---

[3] At *Paradise Lost* 3.315–43 God speaks of giving the Son power and of a final, universal sharing in God's nature after the Last Judgement, but this orchestrated transition is entirely different from the revolutionary cycles of classical myth. For the effect on the epic genre of the transition from polytheistic to monotheistic religion see T. Gregory 2006.

[4] On the Son as epic hero see Bond 2011: 169–84.

[5] E.g., Boileau, *L'Art poétique* 3.205–8.

[6] See Stein 1953: 17–37, Revard 1980, T. Gregory 2006: 43 n. 9.

god, often literally raised to the heights, enables starkly contrasting visions of the world—some radical, others conservative—and challenges the reader to wonder how seriously any of these fictions should be taken. It is that moment of rupture and provocation, channelled not only through questions of artistic tone or aesthetics but also through questions of philosophy and politics, that draws its strongest inspiration from imperial Rome and leaves its mark on the subsequent tradition.[7]

The maddened Hercules, too, deeply influences the early modern conception of heroism. Stretching across the Renaissance from the eponymous paladin of Ariosto's *Orlando Furioso* to the biblical protagonist of Milton's *Samson Agonistes*, the delusional and self-destructive Hercules casts a dark shadow over the zealous violence of these Christian heroes.[8] Christopher Marlowe had also duly noted the rhetorical possibilities opened up by the grandiose hero of Senecan drama.[9] In the epigraph above (*2 Tamburlaine* 4.2.118–20), Tamburlaine alludes to the theomachic Hercules' false sense of ascent at *Hercules Furens* 958–61, but Marlowe takes Seneca's epicisation of the tragic hero to its logical extreme. His Tamburlaine disregards the conventional trajectory imposed by the genre to triumph at the end of the play, thus requiring a sequel to reach the eventual limit of his capacities.[10] Indeed, Tamburlaine is a hero who can get away with saying 'were Egypt Jove's own land, / Yet would I with my sword make Jove to stoop' (*1 Tamburlaine* 4.4.79–80) since Jupiter is no more than a figment of classical antiquity. However rhetorical his theomachy, Tamburlaine appears to be the rare exception who defies the gods with impunity, at least until he eventually succumbs to human mortality at the end of the sequel.[11] Marlowe has done something quite striking with his Senecan inheritance: whereas madness fully brought out Hercules' theomachic instincts, for Tamburlaine theomachy is rather the condition of his existence, the defining feature of his imperialist desires, and one of the animating forces underlying the rhetorical manner that would be so influential for Elizabethan drama. Nor is Hercules the only theomach underlying this intricate character. Patrick Cheney has recently

---

[7] See, e.g., Quint 2004 on Phaethontic imagery and Epicurean beliefs in Satan's voyage to Earth; cf. the epigraph to the introduction from *Paradise Lost* (*PL* 6.99–102).

[8] On the importance of the *Hercules Furens* for the *Orlando Furioso* see Ascoli 1987; for *Samson Agonistes* see Wittreich 2002: 32–8.

[9] On the larger debt of European tragedy to Senecan rhetoric see Braden 1985.

[10] Among our Roman texts, generic cross-fertilisation shapes Seneca's *HF* and Statius' *Thebaid* in particular, but the early modern period sees an even more radical breakdown of distinctions between epic and tragedy. In the first part of *Tamburlaine*, for instance, it's hard not to imagine the audience privileging the epic rise of the eponymous hero over the fall of the Turkish king, Bajazeth. Similarly, Milton's *Paradise Lost* owes some of the complexity of its dynamic to its original conception as a tragedy (and to its debt to earlier tragedies, such as Grotius' *Adamus Exul*).

[11] Marlowe leaves unclear how exactly the audience is to understand the cause and implications of Tamburlaine's death. Although Tamburlaine is already an old man, his sudden illness follows shortly upon his burning a copy of the Qur'an, suggesting the punishment of the Muslim hero by his own god. On Tamburlaine and religion see Shell 2010: 44–7.

argued for the importance of Lucan's Caesar, too, and the Lucanian mode of the sublime in representing Tamburlaine's imperial ambitions.[12] The intertext is one of which Tamburlaine himself is aware as he compares his army favourably to that of Lucan's Caesar (*1 Tamburlaine* 3.3.152–5, especially 'Nor in Pharsalia was there such hot war', 154). For Cheney, Caesar's consistently tyrannical characterisation highlights by contrast Tamburlaine's slide from freedom fighter to tyrant. That slippage, however, shows what we now know to be the duality characteristic of the Roman theomach, not only Caesar's own conjoining of rationalistic and mythologising aspects but also the civilising and Titanic facets of Hercules and the divine and tyrannical stereotypes of the Roman emperor.

It is Capaneus, however, who presents an especially intriguing case, as emerges from his reception in the Italian tradition. The most famous appearance of Capaneus in Italian literature is Dante's use of the hero to represent the sin of blasphemy in the seventh circle of the *Inferno*.[13] But more in line with Statius' ambivalent treatment are the three main chivalric epics of the fifteenth and sixteenth century, each of which includes a knightly pagan character modelled on Capaneus. Superficially, at least, the early modern epicists Boiardo, Ariosto, and Tasso follow Dante in replacing Capaneus' error about the power of Jupiter with the analogous failure to acknowledge the Christian God. Where they differ from the medieval perspective is in the further significance of the blasphemous pagan knight, who brings into the poems a strain of humanist thought that challenges the dominant Christian ideology and reflects contemporary intellectual currents with which the authors engaged.[14]

What reception study of the theomach might look like can be illustrated by a slightly closer look at one aspect of Capaneus' reception in Tasso's *Gerusalemme Liberata* (*GL*). First published in full in 1581, Tasso's fictionalised treatment of the First Crusade combines its historical subject matter with the strong influence of the earlier chivalric tradition. Indeed, Tasso incorporates Capaneus' pre-existing reception in Boiardo and Ariosto into the figure of Argante, one of the three principal opponents of the crusaders.[15] Yet the Statian pedigree of Tasso's Argante isn't the most striking use of Capaneus in the *Liberata*; for Tasso, unlike Boiardo and Ariosto, actually mentions Capaneus by name. Intriguingly, however, the name is not used in conjunction with a pagan hero, such as Argante, whose blasphemy might intuitively be associated with the impiety of Capaneus. Rather, it is a Christian figure, the Swiss knight Alcasto,

---

[12] Cheney 2009: 104–5.

[13] See the epigraphs to Chapter 8.

[14] The epigraph from Boiardo (*Orlando Innamorato* 2.3.22) reveals a glimpse of Capaneus' intellectual legacy, on which see further Chaudhuri (forthcoming c).

[15] See Foltran 1992–93, who nevertheless privileges Vergilian intertexts. Tasso may have been influenced by a contemporary translation of Statius' epic composed by his acquaintance Erasmo di Valvasone. A study of Statius' reception in Valvasone's *Angeleida* (1590)—a source for Milton's *Paradise Lost*—is a desideratum; for preliminaries see the indices of Borsetto 2005 s.v. 'Theb (Stazio)' and 'Papinio Stazio, Publio'.

who enjoys this dubious privilege: *Alcasto il terzo vien, qual presso a Tebe / già Capaneo, con minaccioso volto* ('Alcasto comes third with threatening visage, like Capaneus long before against Thebes', *GL* 1.63). The reason for the comparison can be better understood when one considers the contemporary significance of the Swiss in Tasso's day. By the late sixteenth century the Swiss Confederacy had long been one of the primary centres of Reformation theology, where such famous and controversial figures as Zwingli, Bullinger, and Calvin had developed and disseminated their ideas; by the time of the *Liberata*'s publication many of the cantons were already strongholds of Protestantism. From the perspective of Counter-Reformation Italy, then, the impiety of Capaneus supplies an apt analogue for the contemporary heresy of the Swiss, which is foreshadowed by and embodied in the figure of Alcasto. Although Alcasto can hardly lay claim to Capaneus' martial prowess in his appearances through the poem, his heretical symbolism has chilling resonances with the contemporary Christian history at which the *Liberata* anxiously glances. In the light of his later reception, Statius' impious hero comes alive as part of a long-standing tradition of negotiating questions of religious belief and political authority—a legacy that should encourage us to re-evaluate the place of the theomach, and of Neronian-Flavian literature more generally, in the epic tradition and in the cultural identity of early modern Europe.[16]

Critics may locate the end of the heyday of European epic and tragedy soon after the European Renaissance, but the story of theomachy continues through the Romantic poetry of Shelley and the dawning atheism of much twentieth-century philosophy. Even today theomachy sits at the centre of Philip Pullman's bestselling trilogy, *His Dark Materials*, which draws its inspiration from the rebellion of Milton's Satan. Current debates about the place of religion in Western society are also described in familiar antagonistic terms: for example, a news article from 2006 could be titled 'Dawkins v God—Stop the Fight'.[17] As the Renaissance Christian and modern atheist examples make clear, then, theomachy is more than just a scene of literary or mythological heroism—it is a mode of contemplating and representing views of the divine. The boxing metaphor of the newspaper headline operates at one extreme of the spectrum of complexity, its sensationalism appropriate to the journalistic genre; while we may doubt that the editor was fully cognisant of the literary history of theomachy, however, the choice of combative metaphor nevertheless continues a long-standing tradition of pairing violent martial imagery with no less violent philosophical or pseudo-philosophical rhetoric.

What emerges from the earlier chapters of this book, and from this brief and selective glance at post-classical literature, is that the significance of

---

[16] I hope to expand on this point elsewhere, focusing especially on Tasso's main Christian hero, Rinaldo, who combines—surprisingly—elements of Lucan's Caesar (cf. Burrow 1993: 97–9) and Statius' Capaneus (cf. Maier 1963: 620–3).

[17] Kamm 2006.

theomachy extends beyond the immediate and obvious concern with gods or God. For as the ancient examples make amply clear, theomachy chafes at the limits of the world—limits that are theological, to be sure, but also more broadly metaphysical, epistemological, and political.[18] When, in the epigraph above, the seventeenth-century intellectual and feminist Bathsua Makin sarcastically imagines an educated woman as a Phaethon-like theomach, her argument is much less concerned with piety than with the limits placed on women and the limited conceptions of men. Theomachy is not, then, a concept merely useful to an age that believes in conventional notions of divinity, but rather a figure for something much larger—a test of whatever limits human societies feel at the borders of our experience, limits that define who we are and what we can be. In dramatising such a wide range of conflicts, which touch on all members of society in one way or another, theomachy becomes more than a litmus test of religious, sacrilegious, or non-religious attitudes—it is a place where religion, philosophy, politics, and poetry meet, where art and history combine to show humanity at its extreme limit, and where the encounter of god and mortal illustrates the spirit of enquiry and uncertainty common to us all. If classical theomachy teaches us one thing, it is to shift attention from the result of the battle to the fight itself, for it is in the moment of collision, and in the welter of beliefs that come together, that we learn how the world is defined—a literary experiment on a sublime scale in search of its very own God particle.[19]

Yet fundamentally—underlying physics and theology, politics and poetry—theomachy is an experiment in ethics. Through the rise and fall of the theomach, authority (divine or human) impresses on the audience both its own validity and recognition of the hierarchies of power. A closer examination of theomachy thus enables a closer scrutiny of authority: as the theomach probes potential weaknesses in authority and instabilities in the hierarchies of power, so with that knowledge comes the opportunity for authority to evolve or change altogether. Simply to diminish or to lionise the theomach, then, as so many critics have done, is to misread the hero's function both in the poetry that gave the figure its richest form and in the subsequent literary tradition. The war against god is no parable of folly, nor a covert celebration of atheism, but rather the means of understanding the premises upon which worlds are built and the uncomfortable allegiances to which our moral choices commit us.

---

[18] Cf. Porter 2012: 68 on the historical emergence of the sublime as 'an effort to conceive entities that lay at the limits of thought (whether this was in confrontation with the materiality of sensation or the essence of divinity)'. The theomachic sublime, as we have seen on many occasions throughout this book, arises from precisely the confrontation between the material and the immaterial, the desire to touch and to see, on the one hand, versus the intangible and the invisible on the other.

[19] I thank Ben Sadock for identifying the metaphor of the particle collider latent in an earlier draft. That many physicists dislike the term 'God particle' by which the media often refer to the Higgs boson only strengthens the force of the analogy—a continuing struggle over the intellectual frameworks and metaphors that construct and define our universe.

BIBLIOGRAPHY

Acosta-Hughes, B., and S. A. Stephens. 2012. *Callimachus in Context: From Plato to the Augustan Poets*. Cambridge: Cambridge University Press.
Adler, E. 2003. *Vergil's Empire: Political Thought in the Aeneid*. Lanham: Rowman & Littlefield.
Ahl, F. M. 1976. *Lucan: An Introduction*. Ithaca: Cornell University Press.
Ahl, F. M. 1984a. 'The Art of Safe Criticism in Greece and Rome'. *AJP* 105: 174–208.
Ahl, F. M. 1984b. 'The Rider and the Horse: Politics and Power in Roman Poetry from Horace to Statius'. *ANRW* 2.32.1: 78–110.
Ahl, F. M. 1986. 'Statius' *Thebaid*: A Reconsideration'. *ANRW* 2.32.5: 2803–2912.
Ahl, F. M. 2008. *Two Faces of Oedipus: Sophocles' Oedipus Tyrannus and Seneca's Oedipus*. Ithaca: Cornell University Press.
Ahl, F. M., M. A. Davis, and A. Pomeroy. 1986. 'Silius Italicus'. *ANRW* 2.32.4: 2492–2561.
Albrecht, M. von. 1964. *Silius Italicus: Freiheit und Gebundenheit römischer Epik*. Amsterdam: P. Schippers.
Algra, K. 2009. 'Stoic Philosophical Theology and Graeco-Roman Religion'. R. Salles (ed.). *God and Cosmos in Stoicism*. Oxford: Oxford University Press: 224–51.
Allen, J. 2001. *Inference from Signs: Ancient Debates about the Nature of Evidence*. Oxford: Oxford University Press.
Alvar, J. 1985. 'Materiaux pour l'étude de la formule *sive deus, sive dea*'. *Numen* 32: 236–73.
Anderson, R. (ed.). Forthcoming. *Belief and Its Alternatives in Greek and Roman Religion*. Cambridge: Cambridge University Press.
Anderson, W. S. 1972. *Ovid's Metamorphoses: Books 6–10*. Norman: University of Oklahoma Press.
Anderson, W. S. 1997. *Ovid's Metamorphoses: Books 1–5*. Norman: University of Oklahoma Press.
Ando, C. 2008. *The Matter of the Gods: Religion and the Roman Empire*. Berkeley: University of California Press.
Ando, C. 2010a. 'The Ontology of Religious Institutions'. *History of Religions* 50: 54–79.
Ando, C. 2010b. '*Praesentia Numinis*. Part 1: The Visibility of Roman Gods'. *Asdiwal* 5: 45–73.
André, J.-M. 1996. 'Stace témoin de l'épicurisme campanien'. G. Giannantoni and M. Gigante (eds.). *Epicureismo greco e romano*. 3 vols. Naples: Bibliopolis: 909–28.
Ariemma, E. M. 2010. '*Fons cuncti Varro mali*: The Demagogue Varro in *Punica* 8–10'. Augoustakis 2010a: 241–76.
Armstrong, D., J. Fish, P. A. Johnston, and M. B. Skinner (eds.). 2004. *Vergil, Philodemus, and the Augustans*. Austin: University of Texas Press.
Ascoli, A. R. 1987. *Ariosto's Bitter Harmony: Crisis and Evasion in the Italian Renaissance*. Princeton: Princeton University Press.
Asmis, E. 1984. *Epicurus' Scientific Method*. Ithaca: Cornell University Press.

Asmis, E. 2009. 'Epicurean Empiricism'. J. Warren (ed.). *The Cambridge Companion to Epicureanism*. Cambridge: Cambridge University Press: 84–104.
Asso, P. 2010. 'Hercules as a Paradigm of Roman Heroism'. Augoustakis 2010a: 179–92.
Asso, P. (ed.). 2011. *Brill's Companion to Lucan*. Leiden: Brill.
Attridge, H. W. 1978. 'The Philosophical Critique of Religion under the Early Empire'. *ANRW* 2.16.1: 45–78.
Augoustakis, A. (ed.). 2010a. *Brill's Companion to Silius Italicus*. Leiden: Brill.
Augoustakis, A. 2010b. *Motherhood and the Other: Fashioning Female Power in Flavian Epic.* Oxford: Oxford University Press.
Augoustakis, A. (ed.). 2013. *Ritual and Religion in Flavian Epic*. Oxford: Oxford University Press.
Auvray, C.-E. 1989. *Folie et douleur dans Hercule furieux et Hercule sur l'Oeta. Recherches sur l'expression esthétique de l'ascèse stoïcienne chez Sénèque*. Bern: P. Lang.
Axelsson, K. 2007. *The Sublime: Precursors and British Eighteenth-Century Conceptions.* Bern: P. Lang.
Badian, E. 1981. 'The Deification of Alexander the Great'. H. J. Dell (ed.). *Macedonian Studies in Honor of Charles F. Edson*. Thessaloniki: Institute for Balkan Studies: 27–71.
Badian, E. 1996. 'Alexander the Great between Two Thrones and Heaven: Variations on an Old Theme'. Small 1996: 11–26.
Baier, T. (ed.). 2012. *Götter und menschliche Willensfreiheit: von Lucan bis Silius Italicus.* Munich: Beck.
Bailey, C. 1947. *Titi Lucreti Cari De Rerum Natura Libri Sex*. 3 vols. Oxford: Oxford University Press.
Bakker, E. J. 2013. *The Meaning of Meat and the Structure of the Odyssey*. Cambridge: Cambridge University Press.
Balsley, K. 2011. 'Truthseeking and Truthmaking in Ovid's *Metamorphoses* 1.163–245'. *Law and Literature* 23: 48–70.
Baraz, Y., and C. S. van den Berg (eds.). 2013. *AJP. Special Issue: Intertextuality*. Baltimore: Johns Hopkins University Press.
Barchiesi, A. 1996. 'La guerra di Troia non avrà luogo'. *AION* 18: 45–62.
Barchiesi, A. 1999. 'Venus' Masterplot: Ovid and the *Homeric Hymns*'. P. R. Hardie, A. Barchiesi, and S. Hinds (eds.). *Ovidian Transformations: Essays on the Metamorphoses and Its Reception*. Cambridge: Cambridge Philological Society: 112–26.
Barchiesi, A. 2001. 'Genealogie letterarie nell'epica imperiale: fondamentalismo e ironia'. E. A. Schimdt (ed.). *L'histoire littéraire immanente dans la poésie latine*. Geneva: Fondation Hardt: 315–54.
Barchiesi, A. 2002. Review of D. Nelis, *Vergil's Aeneid and the Argonautica of Apollonius Rhodius. CJ* 98: 89–91.
Barchiesi, A. 2005. *Ovidio: Metamorfosi*. Vol. 1: *Libri I–II*. Milan: A. Mondadori.
Barchiesi, A. 2008a. 'Le cirque du soleil'. J. Nelis-Clément and J.-M. Roddaz (eds.). *Le cirque romain et son image*. Bordeaux: Ausonius: 521–37.
Barchiesi, A. 2008b. '*Senatus consultum de Lycaone*: concili degli dèi e immaginazione politica nelle *Metamorfosi* di Ovidio'. *MD* 61: 116–45.
Barchiesi, A. 2009. 'Phaethon and the Monsters'. Hardie 2009c: 163–88.
Barchiesi, A. 2011. 'Roman Callimachus'. B. Acosta-Hughes, L. Lehnus, and S. Stephens (eds.). *Brill's Companion to Callimachus*. Leiden: Brill: 511–33.

Barchiesi, A., and G. Rosati. 2007. *Ovidio: Metamorfosi*. Vol. 2: *Libri III–IV*. Milan: A. Mondadori.
Barchiesi, A., J. Rüpke, and S. Stephens (eds.). 2004. *Rituals in Ink: A Conference on Religion and Literary Production in Ancient Rome*. Stuttgart: Steiner.
Barkan, L. 1986. *The Gods Made Flesh: Metamorphosis and the Pursuit of Paganism*. New Haven: Yale University Press.
Barker, E., and J. Christensen. 2011. 'On Not Remembering Tydeus: Diomedes and the Contest for Thebes'. *MD* 66: 9–44.
Barrett, A. A. 1990. *Caligula: The Corruption of Power*. New Haven: Yale University Press.
Bartsch, S. 1994. *Actors in the Audience: Theatricality and Doublespeak from Nero to Hadrian*. Cambridge, Mass.: Harvard University Press.
Bartsch, S. 1997. *Ideology in Cold Blood: A Reading of Lucan's Civil War*. Cambridge, Mass.: Harvard University Press.
Bartsch, S. 2012. 'Ethical Judgment and Narratorial Apostrophe in Lucan's *Bellum Civile*'. T. Baier (ed.): 87–98.
Bartsch, S., and D. Wray (eds.). 2009. *Seneca and the Self*. Cambridge: Cambridge University Press.
Bassett, E. L. 1963. 'Scipio and the Ghost of Appius'. *CP* 58: 73–92.
Bauman, R. A. 1967. *The Crimen Maiestatis in the Roman Republic and Augustan Principate*. Johannesburg: Witwatersrand University Press.
Bauman, R. A. 1974. *Impietas in Principem: A Study of Treason against the Roman Emperor with Special Reference to the First Century A.D.* Munich: Beck.
Beagon, M. 2009. 'Ordering Wonderland: Ovid's Pythagoras and the Augustan Vision'. Hardie 2009c: 288–309.
Beard, M. 1986. 'Cicero and Divination: The Formation of a Latin Discourse'. *JRS* 76: 33–46.
Beard, M. 1987. 'A Complex of Times: No More Sheep on Romulus' Birthday'. *PCPS* 33: 1–15.
Beard, M. 2007. *The Roman Triumph*. Cambridge, Mass.: Belknap Press of Harvard University Press.
Beard, M., and J. Henderson. 1998. 'The Emperor's New Body: Ascension from Rome'. M. Wyke (ed.). *Parchments of Gender: Deciphering the Bodies of Antiquity*. Oxford: Oxford University Press: 191–219.
Beard, M., J. North, and S. Price. 1998. *Religions of Rome*. 2 vols. Cambridge: Cambridge University Press.
Bénatouïl, T. 2003. 'La méthode épicurienne des explications multiples'. T. Bénatouïl, V. Laurand, and A. Macé (eds.). *L'épicurisme antique*. Strasbourg: Université Marc Bloch: 15–47.
Bernstein, N. W. 2008. *In the Image of the Ancestors: Narratives of Kinship in Flavian Epic*. Toronto: University of Toronto Press.
Bernstein, N. W. 2013. 'Ritual Murder and Suicide in the *Thebaid*'. Augoustakis 2013: 233–48.
Bessone, F. 2011. *La Tebaide di Stazio. Epica e potere*. Pisa: F. Serra.
Bessone, F. 2013a. 'Critical Interactions: Constructing Heroic Models and Imperial Ideology in Flavian Epic'. Manuwald and Voigt 2013: 87–105.
Bessone, F. 2013b. 'Religion and Power in the *Thebaid*'. Augoustakis 2013: 145–61.

Billerbeck, M. 1999. *Seneca: Hercules Furens*. Leiden: Brill.
Billerbeck, M., and S. Guex. 2002. *Sénèque. Hercule furieux*. Bern: P. Lang.
Bishop, J. D. 1966. 'Seneca's *Hercules Furens*: Tragedy from *modus vitae*'. *C&M* 27: 216–24.
Blomart, A. 1997. 'Die *evocatio* und der Transfer fremder Götter von der Peripherie nach Rom'. H. Cancik and J. Rüpke (eds.). *Römische Reichsreligion und Provinzialreligion*. Tübingen: Mohr Siebeck: 99–111.
Bloom, H. 1982. *Agon: Towards a Theory of Revisionism*. Oxford: Oxford University Press.
Bloom, H. 1997. *The Anxiety of Influence: A Theory of Poetry*. 2nd ed. Oxford: Oxford University Press.
Bloom, H. 2003. *A Map of Misreading*. 2nd ed. Oxford: Oxford University Press.
Bloom, H. 2011. *The Anatomy of Influence: Literature as a Way of Life*. New Haven: Yale University Press.
Bond, C. 2011. *Spenser, Milton, and the Redemption of the Epic Hero*. Newark: University of Delaware Press.
Borsetto, L. 2005. *Erasmo di Valvasone. Angeleida*. Alessandria: Edizioni dell'Orso.
Boyd, B. W. (ed.). 2002. *Brill's Companion to Ovid*. Leiden: Brill.
Boyd, T. W. 1995. 'A Poet on the Achaean Wall'. *Oral Tradition* 10: 181–206.
Boyle, A. J. (ed.). 1983. *Seneca Tragicus: Ramus Essays on Senecan Drama*. Berwick: Aureal Publications.
Boyle, A. J. 1997. *Tragic Seneca: An Essay in the Theatrical Tradition*. London: Routledge.
Boyle, A. J. 2008. *Octavia (Attributed to Seneca)*. Oxford: Oxford University Press.
Boys-Stones, G. R. 2010. 'Hesiod and Plato's History of Philosophy'. G. R. Boys-Stones and J. H. Haubold (eds.). *Plato and Hesiod*. Oxford: Oxford University Press: 31–51.
Braden, G. 1970. 'The Rhetoric and Psychology of Power in the Dramas of Seneca'. *Arion* 9: 5–41.
Braden, G. 1985. *Renaissance Tragedy and the Senecan Tradition: Anger's Privilege*. New Haven: Yale University Press.
Braden, G. 1993. 'Herakles and Hercules: Survival in Greek and Roman Tragedy (With a Coda on *King Lear*)'. R. Scodel (ed.). *Theater and Society in the Classical World*. Ann Arbor: University of Michigan Press: 245–64.
Braund, S. M. 1996. 'Ending Epic: Statius, Theseus and a Merciful Release'. *PCPS* 42: 1–23.
Braund, S. M. 1998. 'Praise and Protreptic in Early Imperial Panegyric: Cicero, Seneca, Pliny'. M. Whitby (ed.). *The Propaganda of Power: The Role of Panegyric in Late Antiquity*. Leiden: Brill: 53–76.
Braund, S. M. 2006. 'A Tale of Two Cities: Statius, Thebes, and Rome'. *Phoenix* 60: 259–73.
Braund, S. M. 2009. *Seneca: De Clementia*. Oxford: Oxford University Press.
Braund, S. M., and G. Gilbert. 2003. 'An ABC of Epic *ira*: Anger, Beasts, and Cannibalism'. Braund and Most 2003: 250–85.
Braund, S. M., and G. W. Most (eds.). 2003. *Ancient Anger: Perspectives from Homer to Galen*. Cambridge: Cambridge University Press.
Bremmer, J. N. 2007. 'Atheism in Antiquity'. M. Martin (ed.). *The Cambridge Companion to Atheism*. Cambridge: Cambridge University Press: 11–26.
Briscoe, J. 2008. *A Commentary on Livy, Books 38–40*. Oxford: Oxford University Press.
Brockliss, W., P. Chaudhuri, A. Haimson Lushkov, and K. Wasdin. 2012. 'Introduction'. W. Brockliss, P. Chaudhuri, A. Haimson Lushkov, and K. Wasdin (eds.). *Reception and the Classics: An Interdisciplinary Approach to the Classical Tradition*. Cambridge: Cambridge University Press: 1–16.

Brouwers, J. H. 1982. 'Zur Lucan-Imitation bei Silius Italicus'. J. den Boeft and A. H. M. Kessels (eds.). *Actus: Studies in Honour of H. L. W. Nelson*. Utrecht: Instituut voor Klassieke Talen: 73–87.

Brown, L. 1998. 'Innovation and Continuity: The Battle of Gods and Giants, *Sophist* 245–249'. J. Gentzler (ed.). *Method in Ancient Philosophy*. Oxford: Oxford University Press: 181–207.

Brunt, P. A. 1989. 'Philosophy and Religion in the Late Republic'. Griffin and Barnes 1989: 174–98.

Buchan, M. 2004. *The Limits of Heroism: Homer and the Ethics of Reading*. Ann Arbor: University of Michigan Press.

Burgess, J. F. 1972. 'Statius' Altar of Mercy'. *CQ* 22: 339–49.

Burgess, J. F. 1978. 'Man and the Supernatural in Statius' *Thebaid*: A Study in Consistency of Theme and Mood'. Ph.D. Thesis, University of Reading.

Burkert, W. 1985. *Greek Religion*. J. Raffan (trans.). Cambridge, Mass.: Harvard University Press.

Burnyeat, M. F. 1982. 'Gods and Heaps'. M. Schofield and M. C. Nussbaum (eds.). *Language and Logos: Studies in Ancient Greek Philosophy Presented to G. E. L. Owen*. Cambridge: Cambridge University Press: 315–38.

Burrow, C. 1993. *Epic Romance: Homer to Milton*. Oxford: Oxford University Press.

Busch, A. 2009. 'Dissolution of the Self in the Senecan Corpus'. Bartsch and Wray 2009: 255–82.

Caiani, L. 1990. 'La pietas nella *Tebaide* di Stazio: Mezenzio modello di Ippomedonte e Capaneo'. *Orpheus* 11: 260–76.

Cairns, D. L. 2003. 'Ethics, Ethology, Terminology: Iliadic Anger and the Cross-Cultural Study of Emotion'. Braund and Most 2003: 11–49.

Campbell, G. 2007. 'Bicycles, Centaurs and Man-Faced Ox-Creatures: Ontological Instability in Lucretius'. Heyworth et al. 2007: 39–62.

Canter, H. V. 1937. 'Ill Will of the Gods in Greek and Latin Poetry'. *CP* 32: 131–43.

Carter, W. 2001. *Matthew and Empire: Initial Explorations*. Harrisburg: Trinity Press International.

Carvounis, A. 2007. 'Final Scenes in Quintus of Smyrna, *Posthomerica* 14'. M. Baumbach and S. Bär (eds.). *Quintus Smyrnaeus: Transforming Homer in Second Sophistic Epic*. Berlin: Walter de Guyter: 241–58.

Cavell, S. 1999. *The Claim of Reason: Wittgenstein, Skepticism, Morality, and Tragedy*. Rev. ed. Oxford: Oxford University Press.

Champlin, E. 2003. *Nero*. Cambridge, Mass.: Belknap Press of Harvard University Press.

Charlesworth, M. P. 1935. 'Some Observations on Ruler-Cult Especially in Rome'. *HThR* 28: 5–44.

Chaudhuri, P. N. 2013. 'Flaminius' Failure? Intertextual Characterization in Silius Italicus and Statius'. Manuwald and Voigt 2013: 379–97.

Chaudhuri, P. N. Forthcoming a. 'Classical Quotation in *Titus Andronicus*'. *ELH: English Literary History* 81.

Chaudhuri, P. N. Forthcoming b. 'Testing the Gods: Belief in Roman Imperial Epic'. R. Anderson (forthcoming).

Chaudhuri, P. N. Forthcoming c. 'The *Thebaid* in Italian Renaissance Epic: The Case of Capaneus'. C. E. Newlands and W. J. Dominik (eds.). *Brill's Companion to Statius*. Leiden: Brill.

Cheney, P. 2009. *Marlowe's Republican Authorship: Lucan, Liberty, and the Sublime*. Basingstoke: Palgrave Macmillan.

Chignell, A., and M. C. Halteman. 2012. 'Religion and the Sublime'. Costelloe 2012: 183–202.

Chinn, C. 2010. '*Nec discolor amnis*: Intertext and Aesthetics in Statius' Shield of Crenaeus (*Theb.* 9.332–338)'. *Phoenix* 64: 148–69.

Clauss, J. J. 1989. 'The Episode of the Lycian Farmers in Ovid's *Metamorphoses*'. *HSCP* 92: 297–314.

Clauss, J. J. 1993. *The Best of the Argonauts: The Redefinition of the Epic Hero in Book 1 of Apollonius's Argonautica*. Berkeley: University of California Press.

Clauss, M. 1999. *Kaiser und Gott: Herrscherkult im römischen Reich*. Stuttgart: B. G. Teubner.

Clay, D. 1998. *Paradosis and Survival: Three Chapters in the History of Epicurean Philosophy*. Ann Arbor: University of Michigan Press.

Clay, J. S. 1983. *The Wrath of Athena: Gods and Men in the Odyssey*. Princeton: Princeton University Press.

Coffee, N. 2009. *The Commerce of War: Exchange and Social Order in Latin Epic*. Chicago: University of Chicago Press.

Cohen, D. 1991. *Law, Sexuality, and Society: The Enforcement of Morals in Classical Athens*. Cambridge: Cambridge University Press.

Cole, S. 2001. 'The Dynamics of Deification in Horace's *Odes* 1–3'. S. R. Asirvatham, C. O. Pache, and J. Watrous (eds.). *Between Magic and Religion: Interdisciplinary Studies in Ancient Mediterranean Religion and Society*. Lanham: Rowman & Littlefield: 67–91.

Cole, S. 2006. 'Elite Scepticism in the *Apocolocyntosis*: Further Questions'. Volk and Williams 2006: 175–82.

Cole, S. 2014. *Cicero and the Rise of Deification at Rome*. Cambridge: Cambridge University Press.

Coleman, K. M. 1986. 'The Emperor Domitian and Literature'. *ANRW* 2.32.5: 3087–3115.

Coleman, K. M. 1988. *Statius: Silvae IV*. Oxford: Oxford University Press.

Collard, C. 2007. *Tragedy, Euripides and Euripideans: Selected Papers*. Exeter: Bristol Phoenix Press.

Collins, D. 1998. *Immortal Armor: The Concept of Alkē in Archaic Greek Poetry*. Lanham: Rowman & Littlefield.

Collins, D. 2004. *Master of the Game: Competition and Performance in Greek Poetry*. Cambridge, Mass.: Harvard University Press.

Connors, C. 1998. *Petronius the Poet: Verse and Literary Tradition in the Satyricon*. Cambridge: Cambridge University Press.

Conte, G. B. 1994. *Genres and Readers: Lucretius, Love Elegy, Pliny's Encyclopedia*. G. W. Most (trans.). Baltimore: Johns Hopkins University Press.

Conte, G. B. 2007. *The Poetry of Pathos: Studies in Virgilian Epic*. S. J. Harrison (ed.). Oxford: Oxford University Press.

Costelloe, T. M. (ed.). 2012. *The Sublime: From Antiquity to the Present*. Cambridge: Cambridge University Press.

Cowan, R. 2009. Review of R. T. Ganiban, *Statius and Virgil: The Thebaid and the Reinterpretation of the Aeneid*. *BMCR*. June 31. <http://www.bmcr.brynmawr.edu/2009/2009-06-31.html>.

Cowan, R. Forthcoming. *After Virgil: The Poetry, Politics and Perversion of Roman Epic*. Exeter: Bristol Phoenix Press.

Crane, G. 1990. 'Ajax, the Unexpected and the Deception Speech'. *CP* 85: 89–101.
D'Ambra, E. 1993. *Private Lives, Imperial Virtues: The Frieze of the Forum Transitorium in Rome*. Princeton: Princeton University Press.
Darwall-Smith, R. H. 1996. *Emperors and Architecture: A Study of Flavian Rome*. Brussels: Latomus.
Dauge, Y. A. 1981. *Le barbare. Recherches sur la conception romaine de la barbarie et de la civilisation*. Brussels: Latomus.
Davies, J. P. 2004. *Rome's Religious History: Livy, Tacitus and Ammianus on Their Gods*. Cambridge: Cambridge University Press.
Davies, P. J. E. 2000. *Death and the Emperor: Roman Imperial Funerary Monuments, from Augustus to Marcus Aurelius*. Cambridge: Cambridge University Press.
Davis, P. J. 1994. 'The Fabric of History in Statius' *Thebaid*'. C. Deroux (ed.). *Studies in Latin Literature and Roman History*. Vol. 7. Brussels: Latomus: 464–83.
Day, H. J. M. 2013. *Lucan and the Sublime: Power, Representation and Aesthetic Experience*. Cambridge: Cambridge University Press.
Degl'Innocenti Pierini, R. 2005. 'Gli *sparsa miracula* di Ovidio (*Met.* 2.193) e Seneca (*Epist.* 90.43)'. *Prometheus* 31: 59–64.
De Lacy, P. H., and E. A. De Lacy. 1978. *Philodemus: On Methods of Inference*. Rev. ed. Naples: Bibliopolis.
Delarue, F. 2000. *Stace, poète épique. Originalité et cohérence*. Leuven: Peeters.
Delz, J. 1987. *Sili Italici Punica*. Stuttgart: B. G. Teubner.
Detienne, M. 1981. 'Between Beasts and Gods'. R. L. Gordon (ed.). *Myth, Religion and Society: Structuralist Essays*. Cambridge: Cambridge University Press: 215–28.
Dewar, M. J. 1991. *Statius: Thebaid IX*. Oxford: Oxford University Press.
Dewar, M. J. 1994. 'Laying It On with a Trowel: The Proem to Lucan and Related Texts'. *CQ* 44: 199–211.
Dewar, M. J. 2008. 'The Equine Cuckoo: Statius' *Ecus Maximus Domitiani Imperatoris* and the Flavian Forum'. J. J. L. Smolenaars, H.-J. van Dam, and R. R. Nauta (eds.). *The Poetry of Statius*. Leiden: Brill: 65–84.
Dominik, W. J. 1994. *The Mythic Voice of Statius: Power and Politics in the Thebaid*. Leiden: Brill.
Dominik, W. J. 2012. 'Critiquing the Critics: Jupiter, the Gods and Free Will in Statius' *Thebaid*'. Baier 2012: 187–98.
Due, O. S. 1962. 'An Essay on Lucan'. *C&M* 23: 68–132.
Due, O. S. 1974. *Changing Forms: Studies in the Metamorphoses of Ovid*. Copenhagen: Gyldendal.
Duff, J. D. 1928. *Lucan: The Civil War*. Cambridge, Mass.: Harvard University Press.
Du Quesnay, I. M. Le M. 1995. 'Horace, *Odes* 4.5: *pro reditu Imperatoris Caesaris Divi filii Augusti*'. S. J. Harrison (ed.). *Homage to Horace: A Bimillenary Celebration*. Oxford: Oxford University Press: 128–87.
Duret, L. 1988. 'Néron-Phaéthon ou la témérité sublime'. *REL* 66: 139–55.
Dynneson, T. L. 2008. *City-State Civism in Ancient Athens: Its Real and Ideal Expressions*. Bern: P. Lang.
Dyson, J. T. 1996. 'Dido the Epicurean'. *CA* 15: 203–21.
Dyson, S. L. 1970. 'Caepio, Tacitus and Lucan's Sacred Grove'. *CP* 65: 36–8.
Easterling, P. E. 2006. 'Notes on Notes: The Ancient Scholia on Sophocles'. S. Eklund (ed.). *Syncharmata: Studies in Honour of Jan Fredrik Kindstrand*. Uppsala: Uppsala Universitet: 21–36.

Eden, P. T. 1984. *Seneca: Apocolocyntosis*. Cambridge: Cambridge University Press.
Edmunds, L. 2001. *Intertextuality and the Reading of Roman Poetry*. Baltimore: Johns Hopkins University Press.
Elliott, J. 2013. *Ennius and the Architecture of the Annales*. Cambridge: Cambridge University Press.
Esposito, P. 2012. 'Su alcuni miti tragici in Lucano e nell'epica flavia'. Baier 2012: 99–126.
Essler, H. 2011. *Glückselig und unsterblich: Epikureische Theologie bei Cicero und Philodem (mit einer Edition von Pherc. 152/157, Kol. 8–10)*. Basel: Schwabe Verlag.
Everson, S. (ed.). 1990. *Epistemology*. Cambridge: Cambridge University Press.
Fabre-Serris, J. 2009. 'Constructing a Narrative of *mira deum*: The Story of Philemon and Baucis (Ovid, *Metamorphoses* 8)'. Hardie 2009c: 231–47.
Fairclough, N. 2003. *Analysing Discourse: Textual Analysis for Social Research*. London: Routledge.
Fantham, E. 1995. 'The Ambiguity of *Virtus* in Lucan's *Civil War* and Statius' *Thebaid*'. *Arachnion* 3. <http://www.cisi.unito.it/arachne/num3/fantham.html>.
Fantham, E. 1996. '*Religio…dira loci*: Two Passages in Lucan *De Bello Civili* 3 and Their Relation to Virgil's Rome and Latium'. *MD* 37: 137–53.
Fantham, E. 2003. 'The Angry Poet and the Angry Gods: Problems of Theodicy in Lucan's Epic of Defeat'. Braund and Most 2003: 229–49.
Fantham, E. 2006. 'The Perils of Prophecy: Statius' Amphiaraus and His Literary Antecedents'. Nauta et al. 2006: 147–62.
Fantham, E. 2011. 'A Controversial Life'. Asso 2011: 3–20.
Farrell, J. 1991. *Vergil's Georgics and the Traditions of Ancient Epic: The Art of Allusion in Literary History*. Oxford: Oxford University Press.
Farrell, J. 2007. 'Horace's Body, Horace's Books'. Heyworth et al. 2007: 174–93.
Fears, J. R. 1977. *Princeps a Diis Electus: The Divine Election of the Emperor as a Political Concept at Rome*. Rome: American Academy in Rome.
Fears, J. R. 1981. 'The Cult of Jupiter and Roman Imperial Ideology'. *ANRW* 2.17.1: 3–141.
Feeney, D. C. 1982. 'A Commentary on Silius Italicus Book 1'. Ph.D. Thesis, Oxford University.
Feeney, D. C. 1991. *The Gods in Epic: Poets and Critics of the Classical Tradition*. Oxford: Oxford University Press.
Feeney, D. C. 1993. 'Towards an Account of the Ancient World's Concepts of Fictive Belief'. C. Gill and T. P. Wiseman (eds.). *Lies and Fiction in the Ancient World*. Exeter: University of Exeter Press: 230–44.
Feeney, D. C. 1998. *Literature and Religion at Rome: Cultures, Contexts, and Beliefs*. Cambridge: Cambridge University Press.
Feeney, D. C. 2004a. 'Interpreting Sacrificial Ritual in Roman Poetry: Disciplines and Their Models'. Barchiesi et al. 2004: 1–21.
Feeney, D. C. 2004b. '*Tenui…latens discrimine*: Spotting the Differences in Statius' *Achilleid*'. *MD* 52: 85–105.
Feeney, D. C. 2007. 'The History of Roman Religion in Roman Historiography and Epic'. J. Rüpke (ed.). *A Companion to Roman Religion*. Malden: Blackwell: 129–142.
Feldherr, A. 2002. 'Metamorphosis in the *Metamorphoses*'. Hardie 2002a: 163–79.
Feldherr, A. 2009. 'Delusions of Grandeur: Lucretian "Passages" in Livy'. Hardie 2009c: 310–29.

Feldherr, A. 2010. *Playing Gods: Ovid's Metamorphoses and the Politics of Fiction*. Princeton: Princeton University Press.
Fenik, B. 1968. *Typical Battle Scenes in the Iliad: Studies in the Narrative Techniques of Homeric Battle Description*. Wiesbaden: Steiner.
Fenno, J. B. 2005. '"A Great Wave against the Stream": Water Imagery in Iliadic Battle Scenes'. *AJP* 126: 475–504.
Ferri, R. 2003. *Octavia: A Play Attributed to Seneca*. Cambridge: Cambridge University Press.
Finglass, P. J. 2011. *Sophocles: Ajax*. Cambridge: Cambridge University Press.
Fish, J., and K. R. Sanders (eds.). 2011. *Epicurus and the Epicurean Tradition*. Cambridge: Cambridge University Press.
Fishwick, D. 1987–2005. *The Imperial Cult in the Latin West: Studies in the Ruler Cult of the Western Provinces of the Roman Empire*. 3 vols. Leiden: Brill.
Fitch, J. G. 1979. '*Pectus o nimium ferum*: Act V of Seneca's *Hercules Furens*'. *Hermes* 107: 240–8.
Fitch, J. G. 1981. 'Sense-Pauses and Relative Dating in Seneca, Sophocles and Shakespeare'. *AJP* 102: 289–307.
Fitch, J. G. 1987. *Seneca's Hercules Furens*. Ithaca: Cornell University Press.
Fitch, J. G. 2002. *Seneca: Tragedies*. Vol. 1. Cambridge, Mass.: Harvard University Press.
Fitch, J. G., and S. McElduff. 2002. 'Construction of the Self in Senecan Drama'. *Mnemosyne* 55: 18–40.
Fletcher, K. F. B. 2006. 'Vergil's Italian Diomedes'. *AJP* 127: 219–59.
Flower, H. I. 2006. *The Art of Forgetting: Disgrace and Oblivion in Roman Political Culture*. Chapel Hill: University of North Carolina Press.
Foltran, D. 1992–93. 'Dalla "Liberata" alla "Conquistata": intertestualità virgiliana e omerica nel personaggio di Argante'. *Studi Tassiani* 40–41: 89–134.
Forbes Irving, P. M. C. 1990. *Metamorphosis in Greek Myths*. Oxford: Oxford University Press.
Ford, A. L. 1992. *Homer: The Poetry of the Past*. Ithaca: Cornell University Press.
Fowler, D. P. 1989. 'Lucretius and Politics'. Griffin and Barnes 1989: 120–50.
Fowler, D. P. 1997. 'Epicurean Anger'. S. M. Braund and C. Gill (eds.). *The Passions in Roman Thought and Literature*. Cambridge: Cambridge University Press: 16–35.
Fowler, D. P. 2007. 'Laocoon's Point of View: Walking the Roman Way'. Heyworth et al. 2007: 1–17.
Franchet d'Espèrey, S. 1999. *Conflit, violence et non-violence dans la Thébaïde de Stace*. Paris: Les Belles lettres.
Franchet d'Espèrey, S. 2001. 'Le problème des motivations multiples (*sive... sive*) dans la *Thébaïde* de Stace'. A. Billault (ed.). *Opōra: la belle saison de l'hellénisme. Études de littérature antique offertes au recteur Jacques Bompaire*. Paris: Presses de l'Université de Paris-Sorbonne: 23–31.
Frede, D., and A. Laks (ed.). 2002. *Traditions of Theology: Studies in Hellenistic Theology, Its Background and Aftermath*. Leiden: Brill.
Frederiksen, M. 1984. *Campania*. N. Purcell (ed.). London: British School at Rome.
Freudenburg, K. Forthcoming. '*Recusatio* as Political Theater: Horace's Letter to Augustus'. *JRS* 104.
Frier, B. W. 1999. *Libri Annales Pontificum Maximorum: The Origins of the Annalistic Tradition*. Ann Arbor: University of Michigan Press.

Friesen, S. J. 1993. *Twice Neokoros: Ephesus, Asia, and the Cult of the Flavian Imperial Family.* Leiden: Brill.

Frings, I. 1991. *Gespräch und Handlung in der Thebais des Statius.* Stuttgart: B. G. Teubner.

Frings, I. 1992. *Odia fraterna als manieristisches Motiv: Betrachtungen zu Senecas Thyest und Statius' Thebais.* Stuttgart: Steiner.

Fucecchi, M. 1990a. 'Il declino di Annibale nei *Punica*'. *Maia* 42: 151–66.

Fucecchi, M. 1990b. 'Empietà e titanismo nella rappresentazione siliana di Annibale'. *Orpheus* 11: 21–42.

Fucecchi, M. 2012. 'Epica, filosofia della storia e legittimazione del potere imperiale: la profezia di Giove nel libro III dei *Punica* (e un'indicazione di percorso per l'epos storico)'. Baier 2012: 235–54.

Fucecchi, M. 2013. 'Looking for the Giants: Mythological Imagery and Discourse on Power in Flavian Epic'. Manuwald and Voigt 2013: 107–22.

Gaertner, J. F. 2005. *Ovid: Epistulae Ex Ponto, Book I.* Oxford: Oxford University Press.

Gale, M. R. 1994. *Myth and Poetry in Lucretius.* Cambridge: Cambridge University Press.

Gale, M. R. 2000. *Virgil on the Nature of Things: The Georgics, Lucretius, and the Didactic Tradition.* Cambridge: Cambridge University Press.

Galinsky, G. K. 1972. *The Herakles Theme: The Adaptations of the Hero in Literature from Homer to the Twentieth Century.* Oxford: Blackwell.

Galinsky, G. K. 1975. *Ovid's Metamorphoses: An Introduction to the Basic Aspects.* Berkeley: University of California Press.

Galinsky, G. K. 1996. *Augustan Culture: An Interpretive Introduction.* Princeton: Princeton University Press.

Galli, D. 2013. 'Recusatio in Flavian Epic Poetry: Valerius Flaccus' *Argonautica* (1.7–21) and Statius' *Thebaid* (1.17–33)'. Manuwald and Voigt 2013: 55–65.

Ganiban, R. T. 2007. *Statius and Virgil: The Thebaid and the Reinterpretation of the Aeneid.* Cambridge: Cambridge University Press.

Gärtner, T. 2001. 'Statius *Theb.* 10,909f. im Lichte spätantiker Imitationen'. *MH* 58: 123–8.

Gärtner, T. 2003. 'Nochmals zu Statius, *Theb.* 10,909f.'. *MH* 60: 210.

Gärtner, U. 2005. *Quintus Smyrnaeus und die Aeneis: zur Nachwirkung Vergils in der griechischen Literatur der Kaiserzeit.* Munich: Beck.

Georgacopoulou, S. A. 1996. 'Clio dans la *Thébaïde* de Stace: à la recherche du *kléos* perdu'. *MD* 37: 167–91.

Gering, J. 2012. *Domitian, dominus et deus? Herrschafts- und Machtstrukturen im Römischen Reich zur Zeit des letzten Flaviers.* Rahden: Verlag Marie Leidorf.

Geyssen, J. W. 1996. *Imperial Panegyric in Statius: A Literary Commentary on Silvae 1.1.* Bern: P. Lang.

Gibson, B. J. 2006. 'The *Silvae* and Epic'. Nauta et al. 2006: 163–84.

Gigandet, A. 1998. *Fama Deum. Lucrèce et les raisons du mythe.* Paris: J. Vrin.

Gildenhard, I. 2011. *Creative Eloquence: The Construction of Reality in Cicero's Speeches.* Oxford: Oxford University Press.

Gildenhard, I., and A. Zissos. 2000. 'Ovid's Narcissus (*Met.* 3.339–510): Echoes of Oedipus'. *AJP* 121: 129–47.

Gildenhard, I., and A. Zissos. 2004. 'Ovid's *Hecale*: Deconstructing Athens in the *Metamorphoses*'. *JRS* 94: 47–72.

Gillespie, S., and P. R. Hardie (eds.). 2007. *The Cambridge Companion to Lucretius*. Cambridge: Cambridge University Press.

Giovacchini, J. 2012. *L'empirisme d'Epicure*. Paris: Classiques Garnier.

Girard, J.-L. 1981. 'Domitien et Minerve: une prédilection impériale'. *ANRW* 2.17.1: 233–45.

Gladhill, C. W. 2012. 'Gods, Caesars and Fate in *Aeneid* 1 and *Metamorphoses* 15'. *Dictynna* 9. <http://dictynna.revues.org/820>.

Glauthier, P. 2011. 'Science and Poetry in Imperial Rome: Manilius, Lucan, and the *Aetna*'. Ph.D. Thesis, Columbia University.

Glenn, J. M. 1971. 'Mezentius and Polyphemus'. *AJP* 92: 129–55.

Goldberg, S. M. 1995. *Epic in Republican Rome*. Oxford: Oxford University Press.

Goldhill, S. D. 1988. 'Doubling and Recognition in the *Bacchae*'. *Métis* 3: 137–56.

Gordon, P. 1998. 'Phaeacian Dido: Lost Pleasures of an Epicurean Intertext'. *CA* 17: 188–211.

Gordon, P. 2012. *The Invention and Gendering of Epicurus*. Ann Arbor: University of Michigan Press.

Gordon, R. 2001. 'The Roman Imperial Cult and the Question of Power'. L. Golden (ed.). *Raising the Eyebrow: John Onians and World Art Studies: An Album Amicorum in His Honour*. Oxford: Archaeopress: 107–22.

Gossage, A. J. 1969. 'Virgil and the Flavian Epic'. D. R. Dudley (ed.). *Virgil*. London: Routledge & K. Paul: 67–93.

Gotoff, H. C. 1984. 'The Transformation of Mezentius'. *TAPA* 114: 191–218.

Gowing, A. M. 2005. *Empire and Memory: The Representation of the Roman Republic in Imperial Culture*. Cambridge: Cambridge University Press.

Gradel, I. 2002. *Emperor Worship and Roman Religion*. Oxford: Oxford University Press.

Graver, M. R. 1999. 'Commentary on Inwood'. *Proceedings of the Boston Area Colloquium in Ancient Philosophy* 15: 44–54.

Green, S. J. 2003. 'Collapsing Authority and "Arachnean" Gods in Ovid's Baucis and Philemon (*Met.* 8.611–724)'. *Ramus* 32: 39–56.

Green, S. J. 2009. 'Malevolent Gods and Promethean Birds: Contesting Augury in Augustus's Rome'. *TAPA* 139: 147–67.

Green, S. J. 2010. 'Undeifying Tiberius: A Reconsideration of Seneca, *Apocolocyntosis* 1.2'. *CQ* 60: 274–6.

Gregory, J. 1985. 'Some Aspects of Seeing in Euripides' *Bacchae*'. *G&R* 32: 23–31.

Gregory, T. 2006. *From Many Gods to One: Divine Action in Renaissance Epic*. Chicago: University of Chicago Press.

Grénier, J.-C. 1987. 'Les inscriptions hiéroglyphiques de l'obélisque Pamphili'. *MEFRA* 99: 937–61.

Grénier, J.-C. 1996. '*Obeliscus Domitiani*'. E. M. Steinby (ed.). *Lexicon Topographicum Urbis Romae*. Vol. 3. Rome: Quasar: 357–8.

Griffin, A. H. F. 1991. 'Philemon and Baucis in Ovid's *Metamorphoses*'. *G&R* 38: 62–74.

Griffin, J. 1980. *Homer on Life and Death*. Oxford: Oxford University Press.

Griffin, J. 1985. *Latin Poets and Roman Life*. London: Duckworth.

Griffin, M. T. 1985. *Nero: The End of a Dynasty*. New Haven: Yale University Press.

Griffin, M. T. 1992. *Seneca: A Philosopher in Politics*. Oxford: Oxford University Press.

Griffin, M. T., and J. Barnes (eds.). 1989. *Philosophia Togata: Essays on Philosophy and Roman Society*. Oxford: Oxford University Press.

Grillo, L. 2012. *The Art of Caesar's Bellum Civile: Literature, Ideology, and Community*. Cambridge: Cambridge University Press.

Grimal, P. 2010. 'Is the Eulogy of Nero at the Beginning of the *Pharsalia* Ironic?'. Tesoriero et al. 2010: 59–68.

Guillaumont, F. 1984. *Philosophe et augure. Recherches sur la théorie cicéronienne de la divination*. Brussels: Latomus.

Guillaumont, F. 2006. *Le De divinatione de Cicéron et les théories antiques de la divination*. Brussels: Latomus.

Gustafsson, G. 2000. *Evocatio Deorum: Historical and Mythical Interpretations of Ritualised Conquests in the Expansion of Ancient Rome* Uppsala: Uppsala University.

Habinek, T. N. 1998. *The Politics of Latin Literature: Writing, Identity, and Empire in Ancient Rome*. Princeton: Princeton University Press.

Habinek, T. N. 2002. 'Ovid and Empire'. Hardie 2002a: 46–61.

Halliwell, F. S. 1990. 'Human Limits and the Religion of Greek Tragedy'. *Literature and Theology* 4: 169–80.

Halliwell, F. S. 2012. *Between Ecstasy and Truth: Interpretations of Greek Poetics from Homer to Longinus*. Oxford: Oxford University Press.

Hammer, D. 2002. *The Iliad as Politics: The Performance of Political Thought*. Norman: University of Oklahoma Press.

Hannestad, N. 1986. *Roman Art and Imperial Policy*. Aarhus: Aarhus University Press.

Hardie, P. R. 1986. *Virgil's Aeneid: Cosmos and Imperium*. Oxford: Oxford University Press.

Hardie, P. R. 1988. 'Lucretius and the Delusions on Narcissus'. *MD* 20–21: 71–89.

Hardie, P. R. 1990. 'Ovid's Theban History: The First "Anti-*Aeneid*"?'. *CQ* 40: 224–35.

Hardie, P. R. 1993. *The Epic Successors of Virgil: A Study in the Dynamics of a Tradition*. Cambridge: Cambridge University Press.

Hardie, P. R. 1994. *Virgil, Aeneid: Book IX*. Cambridge: Cambridge University Press.

Hardie, P. R. 1995. 'The Speech of Pythagoras in Ovid *Metamorphoses* 15: Empedoclean *Epos*'. *CQ* 45: 204–14.

Hardie, P. R. 1996. 'The Case for the Prosecution'. Review of W. J. Dominik, *The Mythic Voice of Statius: Power and Politics in the Thebaid*. *CR* 46: 27–8.

Hardie, P. R. 1997a. 'Closure in Latin Epic'. D. H. Roberts, F. M. Dunn, and D. P. Fowler (eds.). *Classical Closure: Reading the End in Greek and Latin Literature*. Princeton: Princeton University Press: 139–62.

Hardie, P. R. 1997b. 'Questions of Authority: The Invention of Tradition in Ovid *Metamorphoses* 15'. T. N. Habinek, A. Schiesaro (eds.). *The Roman Cultural Revolution*. Cambridge: Cambridge Philological Society: 182–98.

Hardie, P. R. 1997c. 'Virgil and Tragedy'. Martindale 1997: 312–26.

Hardie, P. R. 1999. 'Metamorphosis, Metaphor, and Allegory in Latin Epic'. M. Beissinger, J. Tylus, and S. L. Wofford (eds.). *Epic Traditions in the Contemporary World: The Poetics of Community*. Berkeley: University of California Press: 89–107.

Hardie, P. R. (ed.). 2002a. *The Cambridge Companion to Ovid*. Cambridge: Cambridge University Press.

Hardie, P. R. 2002b. *Ovid's Poetics of Illusion*. Cambridge: Cambridge University Press.

Hardie, P. R. 2007a. 'Contrasts'. Heyworth et al. 2007: 141–73.

Hardie, P. R. 2007b. 'Lucretius and Later Latin Literature in Antiquity'. Gillespie and Hardie 2007: 111–28.

Hardie, P. R. 2009a. 'Introduction: Paradox and the Marvellous in Augustan Literature and Culture'. Hardie 2009c: 1–18.
Hardie, P. R. 2009b. *Lucretian Receptions: History, The Sublime, Knowledge*. Cambridge: Cambridge University Press.
Hardie, P. R. (ed.). 2009c. *Paradox and the Marvellous in Augustan Literature and Culture*. Oxford: Oxford University Press.
Hardie, P. R. 2012. *Rumour and Renown: Representations of Fama in Western Literature*. Cambridge: Cambridge University Press.
Hardie, P. R. 2013. 'Flavian Epic and the Sublime'. Manuwald and Voigt 2013: 125–38.
Harries, B. 1990. 'The Spinner and the Poet: Arachne in Ovid's *Metamorphoses*'. *PCPS* 36: 64–82.
Harrison, G. W. M. (ed.). 2000. *Seneca in Performance*. London: Duckworth.
Harrison, S. J. 1991. *Vergil: Aeneid 10*. Oxford: Oxford University Press.
Harrison, S. J. 1992. 'The Arms of Capaneus: Statius, *Thebaid* 4.165–77'. *CQ* 42: 247–52.
Harrison, T. 2000. *Divinity and History: The Religion of Herodotus*. Oxford: Oxford University Press.
Harrison, T. Forthcoming. *Greek Religion: Belief and Experience*. London: Bloomsbury Publishing.
Hartmann, J. M. 2004. *Flavische Epik im Spannungsfeld von generischer Tradition und zeitgenössischer Gesellschaft*. Bern: P. Lang.
Heiden, B. 1987. '*Laudes Herculeae*: Suppressed Savagery in the Hymn to Hercules (Verg. A. 8.285–305)'. *AJP* 108: 661–71.
Heinrich, A. J. 1999. '*Longa retro series*: Sacrifice and Repetition in Statius' Menoeceus Episode'. *Arethusa* 32: 165–95.
Henderson, J. 2000. 'The Camillus Factory: *per astra ad Ardeam*'. *Ramus* 29: 1–26.
Henderson, J. 2010. 'Lucan/The Word at War'. Tesoriero et al. 2010: 433–91.
Henriksén, C. 2012. *A Commentary on Martial, Epigrams Book 9*. Oxford: Oxford University Press.
Henry, D., and B. Walker. 1965. 'The Futility of Action: A Study of Seneca's *Hercules Furens*'. *CP* 60: 11–22.
Herington, C. J. 1966. 'Senecan Tragedy'. *Arion* 5: 422–71.
Hershkowitz, D. 1998. *The Madness of Epic: Reading Insanity from Homer to Statius*. Oxford: Oxford University Press.
Hesk, J. P. 2003. *Sophocles: Ajax*. London: Duckworth.
Hesk, J. P. 2006. 'Homeric Flyting and How to Read It: Performance and Intratext in *Iliad* 20.83–109 and 20.178–258'. *Ramus* 35: 4–28.
Heslin, P. J. 2005. *The Transvestite Achilles: Gender and Genre in Statius' Achilleid*. Cambridge: Cambridge University Press.
Heyworth, S. J., P. G. Fowler, and S. J. Harrison (eds.). 2007. *Classical Constructions: Papers in Memory of Don Fowler, Classicist and Epicurean*. Oxford: Oxford University Press.
Hickson, F. V. 1993. *Roman Prayer Language: Livy and the Aeneid of Vergil*. Stuttgart: B. G. Teubner.
Hill, D. E. 1983. *P. Papini Stati Thebaidos Libri XII*. Leiden: Brill.
Hill, D. E. 2000. 'Lactantius on Statius'. Review of R. D. Sweeney, *Lactantii Placidi in Statii Thebaida Commentum*. *CR* 50: 57–9.
Hill, T. D. 2004. *Ambitiosa Mors: Suicide and the Self in Roman Thought and Literature*. London: Routledge.

Hinds, S. 1985. 'Booking the Return Trip: Ovid and *Tristia* 1'. *PCPS* 31: 13–32.
Hinds, S. 1987a. 'Generalising about Ovid'. *Ramus* 16: 4–31.
Hinds, S. 1987b. *The Metamorphosis of Persephone: Ovid and the Self-Conscious Muse*. Cambridge: Cambridge University Press.
Hinds, S. 1998. *Allusion and Intertext: Dynamics of Appropriation in Roman Poetry*. Cambridge: Cambridge University Press.
Hinds, S. 2000. 'Essential Epic: Genre and Gender from Macer to Statius'. M. Depew and D. D. Obbink (eds.). *Matrices of Genre: Authors, Canons, and Society*. Cambridge, Mass.: Harvard University Press: 221–44.
Hine, H. M. 1981. *Seneca: Natural questions, Book Two*. New York: Arno Press.
Hine, H. M. 2004. '*Interpretatio Stoica* of Senecan Tragedy'. M. Billerbeck and E. A. Schmidt (eds.). *Sénèque le tragique*. Geneva: Fondation Hardt: 173–209.
Hine, H. M. 2006. 'Rome, the Cosmos, and the Emperor in Seneca's *Natural Questions*'. *JRS* 96: 42–72.
Hogan, J. C., and D. J. Schenker. 2002. 'Challenging Otherness: A Reassessment of Early Greek Attitudes toward the Divine'. A. Mahoney and R. Scaife (eds.). *Ancient Journeys: A Festschrift in Honor of Eugene Numa Lane*. The Stoa: A Consortium for Electronic Publication in the Humanities. <http://www.stoa.org/hopper/text.jsp?doc=Stoa:text:2001.01.0001>.
Holmes, B. 2010. *The Symptom and the Subject: The Emergence of the Physical Body in Ancient Greece*. Princeton: Princeton University Press.
Holmes, N. 1999. 'Nero and Caesar: Lucan 1.33–66'. *CP* 94: 75–81.
Housman, A. E. 1926. *M. Annaei Lucani Belli Civilis Libri Decem*. Oxford: Blackwell.
Hunink, V. 1992. *M. Annaeus Lucanus: Bellum Civile, Book III*. Amsterdam: J. C. Gieben.
Hunter, R. L. 2006. *The Shadow of Callimachus: Studies in the Reception of Hellenistic Poetry at Rome*. Cambridge: Cambridge University Press.
Hutchinson, G. O. 1993. *Latin Literature from Seneca to Juvenal: A Critical Study*. Oxford: Oxford University Press.
Ingleheart, J. 2006. 'What the Poet Saw: Ovid, the Error and the Theme of Sight in *Tristia* 2'. *MD* 56: 64–86.
Innes, D. C. 1979. 'Gigantomachy and Natural Philosophy'. *CQ* 29: 165–71.
Inwood, B. 2005. *Reading Seneca: Stoic Philosophy at Rome*. Oxford: Oxford University Press.
Inwood, B. 2007. 'Moral Causes: The Role of Physical Explanation in Ancient Ethics'. P. K. Machamer, and G. Wolters (eds.). *Thinking about Causes: From Greek Philosophy to Modern Physics*. Pittsburgh: University of Pittsburgh Press: 14–36.
Iossif, P. P., and C. C. Lorber. 2011. 'More than Men, Less than Gods: Concluding Thoughts and New Perspectives'. P. P. Iossif, A. S. Chankowski, and C. C. Lorber (eds.). *More than Men, Less than Gods: Studies on Royal Cult and Imperial Worship*. Leuven: Peeters: 691–710.
Jacobs, J. 2010. 'From Sallust to Silius Italicus: *Metus hostilis* and the Fall of Rome in the *Punica*'. J. F. Miller and A. J. Woodman (eds.). *Latin Historiography and Poetry in the Early Empire: Generic Interactions*. Leiden: Brill: 123–39.
Jaillard, D. 2011. 'The Seventh Homeric Hymn to Dionysus: An Epiphanic Sketch'. A. Faulkner (ed.). *The Homeric Hymns: Interpretative Essays*. Oxford: Oxford University Press: 133–50.

James, A. 2007. *Quintus of Smyrna: The Trojan Epic—Posthomerica.* Baltimore: Johns Hopkins University Press.
Janan, M. W. 2009. *Reflections in a Serpent's Eye: Thebes in Ovid's Metamorphoses.* Oxford: Oxford University Press.
Jenkinson, J. R. 1974. 'Sarcasm in Lucan i. 33–66'. *CR* 24: 8–9.
Johnson, P. J. 2008. *Ovid before Exile: Art and Punishment in the Metamorphoses.* Madison: University of Wisconsin Press.
Johnson, P. J., and M. Malamud. 1988. 'Ovid's *Musomachia*'. *Pacific Coast Philology* 23: 30–8.
Johnson, W. R. 1987. *Momentary Monsters: Lucan and His Heroes.* Ithaca: Cornell University Press.
Jones, B. W. 1973. 'Some Thoughts on Domitian's Perpetual Censorship'. *CJ* 68: 276–7.
Jones, B. W. 1979. *Domitian and the Senatorial Order: A Prosopographical Study of Domitian's Relationship with the Senate, A.D. 81–96.* Philadelphia: American Philosophical Society.
Jones, B. W. 1992. *The Emperor Domitian.* London: Routledge.
Joseph, T. A. 2012. *Tacitus the Epic Successor: Virgil, Lucan, and the Narrative of Civil War in the Histories.* Leiden: Brill.
Juhnke, H. 1972. *Homerisches in römischer Epik flavischer Zeit: Untersuchungen zu Szenennachbildungen und Strukturentsprechungen in Statius' Thebais und Achilleis und in Silius' Punica.* Munich: Beck.
Kahn, C. H. 1997. 'Greek Religion and Philosophy in the *Sisyphus* Fragment'. *Phronesis* 42: 247–62.
Kamerbeek, J. C. 1948. 'On the Concept of θεομάχος in Relation with Greek Tragedy'. *Mnemosyne* 4: 271–83.
Kamerbeek, J. C. 1953. *The Plays of Sophocles: Commentaries.* Vol. 1: *The Ajax.* Leiden: Brill.
Kamm, O. 2006. 'Dawkins v God—Stop the Fight'. *The Times Online.* November 2. <http://www.thetimes.co.uk/tto/law/columnists/article2048822.ece>.
Keith, A. M. 2002. 'Sources and Genres in Ovid's *Metamorphoses* 1–5'. B. W. Boyd 2002: 235–70.
Keith, A. M. 2007. 'Imperial Building Projects and Architectural Ecphrases in Ovid's *Metamorphoses* and Statius' *Thebaid*'. *Mouseion* 7: 1–26.
Keith, A. M. 2010. 'Dionysiac Theme and Dramatic Allusion in Ovid's *Metamorphoses* 4'. I. Gildenhard and M. Revermann (eds.). *Beyond the Fifth Century: Interactions with Greek Tragedy from the Fourth Century BCE to the Middle Ages.* Berlin: Walter de Gruyter: 187–217.
Kellum, B. A. 1985. 'Sculptural Programs and Propaganda in Augustan Rome: The Temple of Apollo on the Palatine'. R. Winkes (ed.). *The Age of Augustus.* Providence: Center for Old World Archaeology and Art, Brown University: 169–76.
Ker, J. 2006. 'Seneca, Man of Many Genres'. Volk and Williams 2006: 19–41.
Ker, J. 2009. *The Deaths of Seneca.* Oxford: Oxford University Press.
King, K. C. 1987. *Achilles: Paradigms of the War Hero from Homer to the Middle Ages.* Berkeley: University of California Press.
Kiso, A. 1984. *The Lost Sophocles.* New York: Vantage Press.
Klein, F. 2009. '*Prodigiosa mendacia uatum*: Responses to the Marvellous in Ovid's Narrative of Perseus (*Metamorphoses* 4–5)'. Hardie 2009c: 189–212.

Kleve, K. 1977. 'Empiricism and Theology in Epicureanism'. *Symbolae Osloenses* 52: 39–51.
Klinnert, T. C. 1970. 'Capaneus-Hippomedon: Interpretationen zur Heldendarstellung in der Thebais des P. Papinius Statius'. Ph.D. Thesis, University of Heidelberg.
Knox, B. M. W. 1961. 'The *Ajax* of Sophocles'. *HSCP* 65: 1–37.
Kohn, T. D. 2013. *The Dramaturgy of Senecan Tragedy*. Ann Arbor: University of Michigan Press.
Konstan, D. 1988. 'Lucretius on Poetry: III.1–13'. *Colby Quarterly* 24: 65–70.
Krischer, T. 1971. *Formale Konventionen der homerischen Epik*. Munich: Beck.
Kronenberg, L. J. 2005. 'Mezentius the Epicurean'. *TAPA* 135: 403–31.
Krostenko, B. A. 2000. 'Beyond (Dis)belief: Rhetorical Form and Religious Symbol in Cicero's *De Divinatione*'. *TAPA* 130: 353–91.
Kyriakou, P. 2001. 'Warrior Vaunts in the *Iliad*'. *RhM* 144: 250–77.
Labate, M. 2010. *Passato remoto. Età mitiche e identità augustea in Ovidio*. Pisa: F. Serra.
Lane Fox, R. 2009. *Travelling Heroes: In the Epic Age of Homer*. New York: Alfred A. Knopf.
La Penna, A. 1999. 'Mezentius: A Tragedy of Tyranny and of Ancient Titanism'. P. R. Hardie (ed.). *Virgil: Critical Assessments of Classical Authors*. Vol. 4. London: Routledge: 345–75.
Laudizi, G. 1989. *Silio Italico. Il passato tra mito e restaurazione etica*. Galatina: Congedo.
Lawall, G. 1983. '*Virtus* and *pietas* in Seneca's *Hercules Furens*'. Boyle 1983: 6–26.
Lawrence, S. E. 1998. 'The God That Is Truly God and the Universe of Euripides' *Heracles*'. *Mnemosyne* 51: 129–46.
Leach, E. W. 1974. 'Ekphrasis and the Theme of Artistic Failure in Ovid's *Metamorphoses*'. *Ramus* 3: 102–42.
Lee, A. G. 1984. *Ovid: Metamorphoses Book I*. London: Bristol Classical Press.
Leberl, J. 2004. *Domitian und die Dichter: Poesie als Medium der Herrschaftsdarstellung*. Göttingen: Vandenhoeck & Ruprecht.
Lefkowitz, M. R. 1989. '"Impiety" and "Atheism" in Euripides' Dramas'. *CQ* 39: 70–82.
Legras, L. 1905. *Étude sur la Thébaïde de Stace*. Paris: Société Nouvelle de Librairie et d'Édition.
Leigh, M. 1997. *Lucan: Spectacle and Engagement*. Oxford: Oxford University Press.
Leigh, M. 2006. 'Statius and the Sublimity of Capaneus'. M. J. Clarke, B. G. F. Currie, and R. O. A. M. Lyne (eds.). *Epic Interactions: Perspectives on Homer, Virgil, and the Epic Tradition: Presented to Jasper Griffin by Former Pupils*. Oxford: Oxford University Press: 217–41.
Leigh, M. 2010. 'Lucan's Caesar and the Sacred Grove: Deforestation and Enlightment in Antiquity'. Tesoriero et al. 2010: 201–38.
Lembke, K. 1994. *Das Iseum Campense in Rom: Studie über den Isiskult unter Domitian*. Heidelberg: Verlag Archäologie und Geschichte.
Levene, D. S. 1993. *Religion in Livy*. Leiden: Brill.
Levene, D. S. 2010. *Livy on the Hannibalic War*. Oxford: Oxford University Press.
Levene, D. S. 2012. 'Defining the Divine in Rome'. *TAPA* 142: 41–81.
Levy, B. E. 1988. 'Caligula's Radiate Crown'. *GNS* 38: 101–7.
Lieberg, G. 1973. 'Die *theologia tripartita* in Forschung und Bezeugung.' *ANRW* 1.4: 63–115.
Liebeschuetz, J. H. W. G. 1979. *Continuity and Change in Roman Religion*. Oxford: Oxford University Press.
Linderski, J. 1982. 'Cicero and Roman Divination'. *PP* 37: 12–38.

Linderski, J. 1986. 'The Augural Law'. *ANRW* 2.16.3: 2146–2312.

Lipka, M. 2009. *Roman Gods: A Conceptual Approach*. Leiden: Brill.

Littlewood, C. A. J. 2004. *Self-Representation and Illusion in Senecan Tragedy*. Oxford: Oxford University Press.

Littlewood, R. J. 2011. *A Commentary on Silius Italicus' Punica 7*. Oxford: Oxford University Press.

Littlewood, R. J. 2013. 'Patterns of Darkness: Chthonic Illusion, Gigantomachy, and Sacrificial Ritual in the *Punica*'. Augoustakis 2013: 199–216.

Liveley, G. 2011. *Ovid's Metamorphoses: A Reader's Guide*. London: Continuum.

Louden, B. 1993. 'Pivotal Contrafactuals in Homeric Epic'. *CA* 12: 181–98.

Lovatt, H. 2001. 'Mad about Winning: Epic, War and Madness in the Games of Statius' *Thebaid*'. *MD* 46: 103–20.

Lovatt, H. 2005. *Statius and Epic Games: Sport, Politics, and Poetics in the Thebaid*. Cambridge: Cambridge University Press.

Lovatt, H. 2010. 'Interplay: Silius and Statius in the Games of *Punica* 16'. Augoustakis 2010a: 155–78.

Lovatt, H. 2013a. 'Competing Visions: Prophecy, Spectacle, and Theatricality in Flavian Epic'. Augoustakis 2013: 53–70.

Lovatt, H. 2013b. *The Epic Gaze: Vision, Gender and Narrative in Ancient Epic*. Cambridge: Cambridge University Press.

Lowrie, M. 2009. *Writing, Performance, and Authority in Augustan Rome*. Oxford: Oxford University Press.

Lucarini, C. M. 2004. 'Le fonti storiche di Silio Italico'. *Athenaeum* 92: 103–26.

Lyne, R. O. A. M. 1987. *Further Voices in Vergil's Aeneid*. Oxford: Oxford University Press.

Lyons, D. 1997. *Gender and Immortality: Heroines in Ancient Greek Myth and Cult*. Princeton: Princeton University Press.

MacBain, B. 1982. *Prodigy and Expiation: A Study in Religion and Politics in Republican Rome*. Brussels: Latomus.

Maciver, C. A. 2012. *Quintus Smyrnaeus' Posthomerica: Engaging Homer in Late Antiquity*. Leiden: Brill.

Mackie, C. J. 1998. 'Achilles in Fire'. *CQ* 48: 329–38.

Mackie, C. J. 1999. 'Scamander and the Rivers of Hades in Homer'. *AJP* 120: 485–501.

Mackie, C. J. 2008. *Rivers of Fire: Mythic Themes in Homer's Iliad*. Washington, D. C.: New Academia Publishing.

Mackie, H. S. 1996. *Talking Trojan: Speech and Community in the Iliad*. Lanham: Rowman & Littlefield.

Mackie, N. 1992. 'Ovid and the Birth of Maiestas'. A. Powell (ed.). *Roman Poetry and Propaganda in the Age of Augustus*. London: Bristol Classical Press: 83–97.

Maier, B. 1963. *Torquato Tasso. Opere*. Vol. 3: *Gerusalemme liberata*. Milan: Rizzoli.

Manolaraki, E. 2013. '"Consider in the Image of Thebes": Celestial and Poetic Auspicy in the *Thebaid*'. Augoustakis 2013: 89–108.

Mansfeld, J. 1999. 'Theology'. K. Algra, J. Barnes, J. Mansfeld, and M. Schofield (eds.). *The Cambridge History of Hellenistic Philosophy*. Cambridge: Cambridge University Press: 452–78.

Manuwald, G., and A. Voigt (eds.). 2013. *Flavian Epic Interactions*. Berlin: Walter de Gruyter.

Marincola, J. 1997. *Authority and Tradition in Ancient Historiography*. Cambridge: Cambridge University Press.
Marks, R. D. 2005. *From Republic to Empire: Scipio Africanus in the Punica of Silius Italicus*. Bern: P. Lang.
Marks, R. D. 2010a. 'Julius Caesar in Domitianic Poetry'. N. Kramer and C. Reitz (eds.). *Tradition und Erneuerung: mediale Strategien in der Zeit der Flavier*. Berlin: Walter de Gruyter: 13–40.
Marks, R. D. 2010b. 'Silius and Lucan'. Augoustakis 2010a: 127–53.
Marks, R. D. 2010c. 'The Song and the Sword: Silius's *Punica* and the Crisis of Early Imperial Epic'. K. A. Raaflaub and D. Konstan (eds.). *Epic and History*. Malden: Wiley-Blackwell: 185–211.
Markus, D. D. 2003. 'The Politics of Epic Performance in Statius'. A. J. Boyle and W. J. Dominik (eds.). *Flavian Rome: Culture, Image, Text*. Leiden: Brill: 431–67.
Markus, D. D. 2004. 'Grim Pleasures: Statius' Poetic *consolationes*'. *Arethusa* 37: 105–35.
Marti, B. M. 1952. 'Seneca's *Apocolocyntosis* and *Octavia*: A Diptych'. *AJP* 73: 24–36.
Martin, R. P. 1989. *The Language of Heroes: Speech and Performance in the Iliad*. Ithaca: Cornell University Press.
Martindale, C. 1997. *The Cambridge Companion to Virgil*. Cambridge: Cambridge University Press.
Masters, J. 1992. *Poetry and Civil War in Lucan's Bellum Civile*. Cambridge: Cambridge University Press.
Masterson, M. 2005. 'Statius' *Thebaid* and the Realization of Roman Manhood'. *Phoenix* 59: 288–315.
Mastronarde, D. J. 1978. 'Are Euripides *Phoinissai* 1104–1140 interpolated?'. *Phoenix* 32: 105–28.
Mastronarde, D. J. 1986. 'The Optimistic Rationalist in Euripides: Theseus, Jocasta, Teiresias'. M. Cropp, E. Fantham, and S. E. Scully (eds.). *Greek Tragedy and Its Legacy: Essays Presented to D. J. Conacher*. Calgary: University of Calgary Press: 201–11.
Matthews, M. 2008. *Caesar and the Storm: A Commentary on Lucan, De Bello Civili, Book 5, lines 476–721*. Bern: P. Lang.
Mayer, R. G. 1981. *Lucan: Civil War VIII*. Warminster: Aris & Phillips.
Mayer, R. G. 1994. '*Personata Stoa*: Neostoicism and Senecan Tragedy'. *JWI* 57: 151–74.
Mazzoli, G. 1968. 'Due note anneane'. *Athenaeum* 46: 354–68.
Mazzoli, G. 1970. *Seneca e la poesia*. Milan: Ceschina.
McDermott, W. C., and A. E. Orentzel. 1977. 'Silius Italicus and Domitian'. *AJP* 98: 24–34.
McDonnell, M. A. 2006. *Roman Manliness: Virtus and the Roman Republic*. Cambridge: Cambridge University Press
McGowan, M. M. 2009. *Ovid in Exile: Power and Poetic Redress in the Tristia and Epistulae Ex Ponto*. Leiden: Brill.
McGuire, D. T. 1997. *Acts of Silence: Civil War, Tyranny, and Suicide in the Flavian Epics*. Hildesheim: Olms-Weidmann.
McNamara, J. 2010. 'The Frustration of Pentheus: Narrative Momentum in Ovid's *Metamorphoses*, 3.511–731'. *CQ* 60: 173–93.
McNelis, C. 2007. *Statius' Thebaid and the Poetics of Civil War*. Cambridge: Cambridge University Press.
Meijer, P. A. 2007. *Stoic Theology: Proofs for the Existence of the Cosmic God and of the Traditional Gods*. Delft: Eburon.

Mellinghoff-Bourgerie, V. 1990. *Les incertitudes de Virgile. Contributions épicuriennes à la théologie de l'Énéide*. Brussels: Latomus.
Mendelsohn, D. 1990. 'Empty Nest, Abandoned Cave: Maternal Anxiety in *Achilleid* 1'. *CA* 9: 295–308.
Michel, A. 1969. 'Rhétorique, tragédie, philosophie: Sénèque et le sublime'. *GIF* 21: 245–57.
Mikalson, J. D. 1991. *Honor Thy Gods: Popular Religion in Greek Tragedy*. Chapel Hill: University of North Carolina Press.
Mikalson, J. D. 2003. *Herodotus and Religion in the Persian Wars*. Chapel Hill: University of North Carolina Press.
Miller, J. F. 2009. *Apollo, Augustus, and the Poets*. Cambridge: Cambridge University Press.
Momigliano, A. 1941. Review of B. Farrington, *Science and Politics in the Ancient World*. *JRS* 31: 149–57.
Momigliano, A. 1984. 'The Theological Efforts of the Roman Upper Classes in the First Century B. C.' *CP* 79: 199–211.
Moore, T. 2010. 'Livy's Hannibal and the Roman Tradition'. W. Polleichtner (ed.). *Livy and Intertextuality*. Trier: WVT: 135–67.
Morgan, L. 1998. 'Assimilation and Civil War: Hercules and Cacus (*Aen.* 8.185–267)'. H.-P. Stahl (ed.). *Vergil's Aeneid: Augustan Epic and Political Context*. London: Duckworth: 175–98.
Morrison, J. V. 1992. 'Alternatives to the Epic Tradition: Homer's Challenges in the *Iliad*'. *TAPA* 122: 61–71.
Morrison, J. V. 1997. '*Kerostasia*, the Dictates of Fate, and the Will of Zeus in the *Iliad*'. *Arethusa* 30: 276–96.
Most, G. W. 2012. 'The Sublime, Today?'. B. Holmes and W. H. Shearin (eds.). *Dynamic Reading: Studies in the Reception of Epicureanism*. Oxford: Oxford University Press: 239–66.
Motto, A. L., and J. R. Clark. 1981. '*Maxima virtus* in Seneca's *Hercules Furens*'. *CP* 76: 100–17.
Motto, A. L., and J. R. Clark. 1988. *Senecan Tragedy*. Amsterdam: A. M. Hakkert.
Muecke, F. 2007. 'Hannibal at the "Fields of Fire": A "Wasteful Excursion"? (Silius Italicus, *Punica* 12, 113–157)'. *MD* 58: 73–91.
Muellner, L. C. 1996. *The Anger of Achilles: Mēnis in Greek Epic*. Ithaca: Cornell University Press.
Murray, G. 1946. *Greek Studies*. Oxford: Oxford University Press.
Myers, K. S. 1994. *Ovid's Causes: Cosmogony and Aetiology in the Metamorphoses*. Ann Arbor: University of Michigan Press.
Mynors, R. A. B. 1969. *P. Vergili Maronis Opera*. Oxford: Oxford University Press.
Nagler, M. N. 1974. *Spontaneity and Tradition: A Study in the Oral Art of Homer*. Berkeley: University of California Press.
Nagy, G. 1979. *The Best of the Achaeans: Concepts of the Hero in Archaic Greek Poetry*. Baltimore: Johns Hopkins University Press.
Narducci, E. 2002. *Lucano. Un'epica contro l'impero. Interpretazione della Pharsalia*. Rome: GLF Editori Laterza.
Nau, R. 2005. 'Capaneus: Homer to Lydgate'. Ph.D. thesis, McMaster University.
Nauta, R. R. 2002. *Poetry for Patrons: Literary Communication in the Age of Domitian*. Leiden: Brill.

Nauta, R. R., H.-J. van Dam, and J. J. L. Smolenaars (eds.). 2006. *Flavian Poetry*. Leiden: Brill.

Nehrkorn, H. 1971. 'A Homeric Episode in Vergil's *Aeneid*'. *AJP* 92: 566-84.

Nelis, D. 2001. *Vergil's Aeneid and the Argonautica of Apollonius Rhodius*. Leeds: Francis Cairns.

Nelis, D. 2009. 'Ovid, *Metamorphoses* 1.416-51: *noua monstra* and the *foedera naturae*'. Hardie 2009c: 248-67.

Nelis, D. 2011. 'Praising Nero (Lucan, *De Bello Civili*, 1.33-66)'. G. Urso (ed.). *Dicere laudes. Elogio, comunicazione, creazione del consenso*. Pisa: ETS: 253-64.

Neri, V. 1986. 'Dei, Fato e divinazione nella letteratura latina del I sec. d. C'. *ANRW* 2.16.3: 1974-2051.

Nesselrath, H.-G. 1992. *Ungeschehenes Geschehen: 'Beinahe-Episoden' im griechischen und römischen Epos von Homer bis zur Spätantike*. Stuttgart: B. G. Teubner.

Newlands, C. E. 2002. *Statius' Silvae and the Poetics of Empire*. Cambridge: Cambridge University Press.

Newlands, C. E. 2011. *Statius: Silvae, Book II*. Cambridge: Cambridge University Press.

Newmyer, S. T. 1984. 'The Triumph of Art over Nature: Martial and Statius on Flavian Aesthetics'. *Helios* 11: 1-7.

Nisbet, R. G. M., and M. Hubbard. 1970. *A Commentary on Horace: Odes, Book 1*. Oxford: Oxford University Press.

Oakley, S. P. 1997. *A Commentary on Livy, Books VI-X*. Vol. 2. Oxford: Oxford University Press.

Obbink, D. D. 1996. *Philodemus: On Piety, Part 1*. Oxford: Oxford University Press.

O'Hara, J. J. 1990. *Death and the Optimistic Prophecy in Vergil's Aeneid*. Princeton: Princeton University Press.

O'Hara, J. J. 1994. 'They Might Be Giants: Inconsistency and Indeterminacy in Vergil's War in Italy'. *Colby Quarterly* 30: 206-26.

O'Hara, J. J. 2007. *Inconsistency in Roman Epic: Studies in Catullus, Lucretius, Vergil, Ovid and Lucan*. Cambridge: Cambridge University Press.

Olson, S. D. 1995. *Blood and Iron: Stories and Storytelling in Homer's Odyssey*. Leiden: Brill.

Ormand, K. 2010. 'Lucan's *Auctor Vix Fidelis*'. Tesoriero et al. 2010: 324-45.

O'Sullivan, P. 2012. 'Sophistic Ethics, Old Atheism, and "Critias" on Religion'. *CW* 105: 167-85.

Otis, B. 1970. *Ovid as an Epic Poet*. 2nd ed. Cambridge: Cambridge University Press.

Owen, E. T. 1946. *The Story of the Iliad*. Ann Arbor: University of Michigan Press.

Owen, W. S. H. 1968. 'Commonplace and Dramatic Symbol in Seneca's Tragedies'. *TAPA* 99: 291-313.

Owen, W. S. H. 1969. 'Seneca, *Hercules Furens*, Line 12'. *CJ* 64: 225-6.

Padel, R. 1995. *Whom Gods Destroy: Elements of Greek and Tragic Madness*. Princeton: Princeton University Press.

Padilla, M. W. 1998. *The Myths of Herakles in Ancient Greece: Survey and Profile*. Lanham: University Press of America.

Papadopoulou, T. 2004. 'Herakles and Hercules: The Hero's Ambivalence in Euripides and Seneca'. *Mnemosyne* 57: 257-83.

Papadopoulou, T. 2005. *Heracles and Euripidean Tragedy*. Cambridge: Cambridge University Press.

Papaioannou, S. 2005. *Epic succession and Dissension: Ovid, Metamorphoses 13.623–14.582, and the Reinvention of the Aeneid*. Berlin: Walter de Gruyter.
Parkes, R. 2009. 'Hercules and the Centaurs: Reading Statius with Vergil and Ovid'. *CP* 104: 476–94.
Parkes, R. 2012. *Statius, Thebaid 4*. Oxford: Oxford University Press.
Parks, W. 1990. *Verbal Dueling in Heroic Narrative: The Homeric and Old English Traditions*. Princeton: Princeton University Press.
Pelling, C. B. R. 2011. *Plutarch: Caesar*. Oxford: Oxford University Press.
Penwill, J. 2013. 'Imperial Encomia in Flavian Epic'. Manuwald and Voigt 2013: 29–54.
Peppard, M. 2011. *The Son of God in the Roman World: Divine Sonship in Its Social and Political Context*. Oxford: Oxford University Press.
Phillips, O. C. 1968. 'Lucan's Grove'. *CP* 63: 296–300.
Pitcher, R. A. 1998. 'Martial's Debt to Ovid'. F. Grewing (ed.). *Toto notus in orbe: Perspektiven der Martial-Interpretation*. Stuttgart: Steiner: 59–76.
Platt, V. J. 2011. *Facing the Gods: Epiphany and Representation in Graeco-Roman Art, Literature, and Religion*. Cambridge: Cambridge University Press.
Pollmann, K. F. L. 2004. *Statius, Thebaid 12*. Paderborn: F. Schöningh.
Pomeroy, A. J. 2000. 'Silius' Rome: The Rewriting of Vergil's Vision'. *Ramus* 29: 149–68.
Pomeroy, A. J. 2010. 'To Silius through Livy and His Predecessors'. Augoustakis 2010a: 27–45.
Porter, J. I. 2007. 'Lucretius and the Sublime'. Gillespie and Hardie 2007: 167–84.
Porter, J. I. 2010. *The Origins of Aesthetic Thought in Ancient Greece: Matter, Sensation, and Experience*. Cambridge: Cambridge University Press.
Porter, J. I. 2011. 'Making and Unmaking: The Achaean Wall and the Limits of Fictionality in Homeric Criticism'. *TAPA* 141: 1–36.
Porter, J. I. 2012. 'Is the Sublime an Aesthetic Value?'. I. Sluiter and R. M. Rosen (eds.). *Aesthetic Value in Classical Antiquity*. Leiden: Brill: 47–70.
Potter, D. S. 1994. *Prophets and Emperors: Human and Divine Authority from Augustus to Theodosius*. Cambridge, Mass.: Harvard University Press.
Price, S. R. F. 1984. *Rituals and Power: The Roman Imperial Cult in Asia Minor*. Cambridge: Cambridge University Press.
Price, S. R. F. 1987. 'From Noble Funerals to Divine Cult: The Consecration of Roman Emperors'. D. Cannadine and S. R. F. Price (eds.). *Rituals of Royalty: Power and Ceremonial in Traditional Societies*. Cambridge: Cambridge University Press: 56–105.
Purves, A. C. 2006. 'Falling into Time in Homer's *Iliad*'. *CA* 25: 179–209.
Putnam, M. C. J. 1995. *Virgil's Aeneid: Interpretation and Influence*. Chapel Hill: University of North Carolina Press.
Putnam, M. C. J. 2011. *The Humanness of Heroes: Studies in the Conclusion of Virgil's Aeneid*. Amsterdam: Amsterdam University Press.
Quint, D. 1989. 'Repetition and Ideology in the *Aeneid*'. *MD* 23: 9–54.
Quint, D. 1993. *Epic and Empire: Politics and Generic Form from Virgil to Milton*. Princeton: Princeton University Press.
Quint, D. 2001. 'The Brothers of Sarpedon: Patterns of Homeric Imitation in *Aeneid* 10'. *MD* 47: 35–66.
Quint, D. 2004. 'Fear of Falling: Icarus, Phaethon, and Lucretius in *Paradise Lost*'. *Renaissance Quarterly* 57: 847–81.

Rawson, E. 1975. 'Caesar's Heritage: Hellenistic Kings and Their Roman Equals'. *JRS* 65: 148–59.
Redfield, J. M. 1994. *Nature and Culture in the Iliad: The Tragedy of Hector*. Rev. ed. Durham: Duke University Press.
Reiche, H. 1971. 'Myth and Magic in Cosmological Polemics: Plato, Aristotle, Lucretius'. *RhM* 114: 296–329.
Revard, S. P. 1980. *The War in Heaven: Paradise Lost and the Tradition of Satan's Rebellion*. Ithaca: Cornell University Press.
Richardson, N. J. 1993. *The Iliad: A Commentary*. Vol. 6: Books 21–24. Cambridge: Cambridge University Press.
Riedweg, C. 1990. 'The "Atheistic" Fragment from Euripides' *Bellerophontes* (286 N^2)'. *ICS* 15: 39–53.
Rieks, R. 1967. *Homo, humanus, humanitas: zur Humanität in der lateinischen Literatur des ersten nachchristlichen Jahrhunderts*. Munich: Fink.
Riggsby, A. M. 2006. *Caesar in Gaul and Rome: War in Words*. Austin: University of Texas Press.
Riley, K. 2008. *The Reception and Performance of Euripides' Herakles: Reasoning Madness*. Oxford: Oxford University Press.
Ripoll, F. 1998. *La morale héroïque dans les épopées latines d'époque flavienne. Tradition et innovation*. Leuven: Peeters.
Ripoll, F. 2002. 'Les scènes d'ornithomancie dans les épopées latines d'époque flavienne'. *Latomus* 61: 929–60.
Ripoll, F. 2006. 'Adaptations latines d'un thème homérique: la théomachie'. *Phoenix* 60: 236–58.
Ripoll, F. 2009. 'Mythe et tragédie dans la *Pharsale* de Lucain'. J.-P. Aygon, C. Bonnet, and C. Noacco (eds.). *La mythologie de l'Antiquité à la modernité. appropriation—adaptation—détournement*. Rennes: Presses Universitaires de Rennes: 85–98.
Roberts, W. R. 1907. *Longinus: On the Sublime*. Cambridge: Cambridge University Press.
Robinson, O. F. 1995. *The Criminal Law of Ancient Rome*. Baltimore: Johns Hopkins University Press.
Roche, P. A. 2009. *Lucan: De Bello Civili, Book 1*. Oxford: Oxford University Press.
Roller, M. B. 2001. *Constructing Autocracy: Aristocrats and Emperors in Julio-Claudian Rome*. Princeton: Princeton University Press.
Romer, F. E. 1994. 'Atheism, Impiety and the *limos Mēlios* in Aristophanes' *Birds*'. *AJP* 115: 351–65.
Rosati, G. 2002a. 'Muse and Power in the Poetry of Statius'. E. Spentzou and D. P. Fowler (eds.). *Cultivating the Muse: Struggles for Power and Inspiration in Classical Literature*. Oxford: Oxford University Press: 229–51.
Rosati, G. 2002b 'Narrative Techniques and Narrative Structures in the *Metamorphoses*'. B. W. Boyd 2002: 271–304.
Rosati, G. 2009. '*Latrator Anubis*: Alien Divinities in Augustan Rome, and How to Tame Monsters through Aetiology'. Hardie 2009c: 268–87.
Rose, A. 1979–80. 'Seneca's *HF*: A Politico-Didactic Reading'. *CJ* 75: 135–42.
Rosenmeyer, T. G. 1989. *Senecan Drama and Stoic Cosmology*. Berkeley: University of California Press.
Rossi, A. F. 2004. 'Parallel Lives: Hannibal and Scipio in Livy's Third Decade'. *TAPA* 134: 359–81.

Ruck, C. A. P. 1976. 'Duality and the Madness of Herakles'. *Arethusa* 9: 53–75.
Rudich, V. 1993. *Political Dissidence under Nero: The Price of Dissimulation*. London: Routledge.
Rüpke, J. 2005. 'Varro's *tria genera theologiae*: Religious Thinking in the Late Republic'. *Ordia Prima* 4: 107–29.
Russell, D. A. 1964. *'Longinus' on the Sublime*. Oxford: Oxford University Press.
Rutherford, R. B. 1986. 'The Philosophy of the *Odyssey*'. *JHS* 106: 145–62.
Rutledge, S. H. 2001. *Imperial Inquisitions: Prosecutors and Informants from Tiberius to Domitian*. London: Routledge.
Rutledge, S. H. 2009. 'Writing Imperial Politics: The Social and Political Background'. W. J. Dominik, J. Garthwaite, and P. A. Roche (eds.). *Writing Politics in Imperial Rome*. Leiden: Brill: 23–61.
Saller, R. P. 1990. 'Domitian and His Successors: Methodological Traps in Assessing Emperors'. *AJAH* 15: 4–18.
Sammons, B. 2010. *The Art and Rhetoric of the Homeric Catalogue*. Oxford: Oxford University Press.
Santangelo, F. 2013. *Divination, Prediction and the End of the Roman Republic*. Cambridge: Cambridge University Press.
Santini, C. 1991. *Silius Italicus and His View of the Past*. Amsterdam: J. C. Gieben.
Scheid, J. 2005. 'Augustus and Roman Religion: Continuity, Conservatism, and Innovation'. G. K. Galinsky (ed.). *The Cambridge Companion to the Age of Augustus*. Cambridge: Cambridge University Press: 175–93.
Schein, S. L. 1984. *The Mortal Hero: An Introduction to Homer's Iliad*. Berkeley: University of California Press.
Schetter, W. 1960. *Untersuchungen zur epischen Kunst des Statius*. Wiesbaden: O. Harrassowitz.
Schiesaro, A. 2002. 'Ovid and the Professional Discourses of Scholarship, Religion, Rhetoric'. Hardie 2002a: 62–75.
Schiesaro, A. 2003. *The Passions in Play: Thyestes and the Dynamics of Senecan Drama*. Cambridge: Cambridge University Press.
Schiesaro, A. 2009. 'Seneca and the Denial of the Self'. Bartsch and Wray 2009: 221–36.
Schmiel, R. C. 2003. 'Composition and Structure: The Battle at the Hydaspes (Nonnos *Dionysiaca* 21.303–24.178)'. D. Accorinti and P. Chuvin (eds.). *Des Géants à Dionysos. Mélanges de mythologie et de poésie grecques offerts à Francis Vian*. Alessandria: Edizioni dell'Orso: 469–81.
Schmitzer, U. 1990. *Zeitgeschichte in Ovids Metamorphosen: mythologische Dichtung unter politischem Anspruch*. Stuttgart: B. G. Teubner.
Schöffel, C. 2002. *Martial, Buch 8*. Stuttgart: Steiner.
Schofield, M. 1986a. 'Cicero for and against Divination'. *JRS* 76: 47–65.
Schofield, M. 1986b. '*Euboulia* in the *Iliad*'. *CQ* 36: 6–31.
Schotes, H.-A. 1969. *Stoische Physik, Psychologie und Theologie bei Lucan*. Bonn: R. Habelt.
Schrijvers, P. H. 2006. 'Silius Italicus and the Roman Sublime'. Nauta et al. 2006: 97–111.
Schubert, W. 1984. *Jupiter in den Epen der Flavierzeit*. Bern: P. Lang.
Scodel, R. 1982. 'The Achaean Wall and the Myth of Destruction'. *HSCP* 86: 33–53.
Scodel, R. 2004. 'The Modesty of Homer'. C. J. Mackie (ed.). *Oral Performance and Its Context*. Leiden: Brill: 1–19.

Seager, R. 2010. 'Domitianic themes in Statius' *Silvae*'. *Papers of the Langford Latin Seminar* 14: 341–74.
Segal, C. 1983. 'Dissonant Sympathy: Song, Orpheus, and the Golden Age in Seneca's Tragedies'. Boyle 1983: 229–51.
Segal, C. 1997. *Dionysiac Poetics and Euripides' Bacchae*. Rev. ed. Princeton: Princeton University Press.
Seo, J. M. 2013. *Exemplary Traits: Reading Characterization in Roman Poetry*. Oxford: Oxford University Press.
Shaw, P. 2006. *The Sublime*. London: Routledge.
Shay, J. 1994. *Achilles in Vietnam: Combat Trauma and the Undoing of Character*. New York: Atheneum.
Shell, A. 2010. 'Tragedy and Religion'. E. Smith and G. A. Sullivan (eds.). *The Cambridge Companion to English Renaissance Tragedy*. Cambridge: Cambridge University Press: 44–57.
Shelton, J.-A. 1978. *Seneca's Hercules Furens: Theme, Structure and Style*. Göttingen: Vandenhoeck & Ruprecht.
Silk, M. S. 1985. 'Heracles and Greek Tragedy'. *G&R* 32: 1–22.
Simpson, C. J. 1996. 'Caligula's Cult: Immolation, Immortality, Intent'. Small 1996: 63–71.
Sklenář, R. 2003. *The Taste for Nothingness: A Study of Virtus and Related Themes in Lucan's Bellum Civile*. Ann Arbor: University of Michigan Press.
Slatkin, L. M. 1991. *The Power of Thetis: Allusion and Interpretation in the Iliad*. Berkeley: University of California Press.
Small, A. M. (ed.). 1996. *Subject and Ruler: The Cult of the Ruling Power in Classical Antiquity*. Ann Arbor: Journal of Roman Archaeology.
Smith, M. F. 1982. *Lucretius: De Rerum Natura*. W. H. D. Rouse (trans.). 2nd ed. Cambridge, Mass.: Harvard University Press.
Smolenaars, J. J. L. 1994. *Statius: Thebaid VII*. Leiden: Brill.
Snijder, H. 1968. *P. Papinius Statius: Thebaid: A Commentary on Book III*. Amsterdam: A. M. Hakkert.
Southern, P. 1997. *Domitian: Tragic Tyrant*. London: Routledge.
Spaltenstein, F. 1986. *Commentaire des Punica de Silius Italicus*. Vol. 1: *Livres 1 à 8*. Geneva: Droz.
Spaltenstein, F. 1990. *Commentaire des Punica de Silius Italicus*. Vol. 2: *Livres 9 à 17*. Geneva: Droz.
Spencer, D. 2002. *The Roman Alexander: Reading a Cultural Myth*. Exeter: University of Exeter Press.
Stahl, H.-P. 1981. 'Aeneas, an Unheroic Hero?'. *Arethusa* 14: 157–77.
Staley, G. A. 2010. *Seneca and the Idea of Tragedy*. Oxford: Oxford University Press.
Stanford, W. B. 1954. *The Ulysses Theme: A Study in the Adaptability of a Traditional Hero*. Oxford: Blackwell.
Stanley, K. 1993. *The Shield of Homer: Narrative Structure in the Iliad*. Princeton: Princeton University Press.
Star, C. 2012. *The Empire of the Self: Self-Command and Political Speech in Seneca and Petronius*. Baltimore: Johns Hopkins University Press.
Stein, A. S. 1953. *Answerable Style: Essays on Paradise Lost*. Minneapolis: University of Minnesota Press.

Steiniger, J. 1998. 'Saecula te quoniam penes et digesta vetustas: die Musenanrufungen in der Thebais des Statius'. Hermes 126: 221–37.
Stevens, P. T. 1986. 'Ajax in the Trugrede'. CQ 36: 327–36.
Stover, T. 2008. 'Cato and the Intended Scope of Lucan's Bellum Civile'. CQ 58: 571–80.
Stover, T. 2009. 'Apollonius, Valerius Flaccus, and Statius: Argonautic Elements in Thebaid 3.499–647'. AJP 130: 439–55.
Stover, T. 2011. 'Aeneas and Lausus: Killing the Double and Civil War in Aeneid 10'. Phoenix 65: 352–60.
Stover, T. 2012. *Epic and Empire in Vespasianic Rome: A New Reading of Valerius Flaccus' Argonautica*. Oxford: Oxford University Press.
Sullivan, J. P. 1991. *Martial, the Unexpected Classic: A Literary and Historical Study*. Cambridge: Cambridge University Press.
Summers, K. 1995. 'Lucretius and the Epicurean Tradition of Piety'. CP 90: 32–57.
Sutton, D. F. 1981. 'Critias and Atheism'. CQ 31: 33–8.
Sweeney, R. D. 1997. *Lactantii Placidi in Statii Thebaida Commentum*. Stuttgart: B. G. Teubner.
Syed, Y. 2004. 'Ovid's Use of the Hymnic Genre in the Metamorphoses'. Barchiesi et al. 2004: 99–113.
Syme, R. 1978. *History in Ovid*. Oxford: Oxford University Press.
Syme, R. 1983. 'Domitian: The Last Years'. Chiron 13: 121–46.
Taisne, A.-M. 1994. *L'esthétique de Stace. La peinture des correspondances*. Paris: Les Belles Lettres.
Taisne, A.-M. 1999. 'Le De rerum natura et la Thébaïde de Stace'. R. Poignault (ed.). *Présence de Lucrèce*. Tours: Centre de Recherches A. Piganiol: 165–75.
Taplin, O. 1992. *Homeric Soundings: The Shaping of the Iliad*. Oxford: Oxford University Press.
Tarrant, R. J. 1978. 'Senecan Drama and Its Antecedents'. HSCP 82: 213–63.
Tarrant, R. J. 1985. *Seneca's Thyestes*. Atlanta: Scholars Press.
Tarrant, R. J. 1995. 'Greek and Roman in Seneca's Tragedies'. HSCP 97: 215–30.
Tarrant, R. J. 1997. 'Aspects of Virgil's Reception in Antiquity'. Martindale 1997: 56–72.
Tarrant, R. J. 2004. *P. Ovidi Nasonis Metamorphoses*. Oxford: Oxford University Press.
Tarrant, R. J. 2006. 'Seeing Seneca Whole?'. Volk and Williams 2006: 1–17.
Taylor, C. C. W. 1980. '"All Perceptions Are True"'. M. Schofield, M. F. Burnyeat, and J. Barnes (eds.). *Doubt and Dogmatism: Studies in Hellenistic Epistemology*. Oxford: Oxford University Press: 105–24.
Tesoriero, C., F. Muecke, and T. Neal (eds.). 2010. *Oxford Readings in Classical Studies: Lucan*. Oxford: Oxford University Press.
Thomas, R. F. 1988. 'Tree Violation and Ambivalence in Virgil'. TAPA 118: 261–73.
Thome, G. 1979. *Gestalt und Funktion des Mezentius bei Vergil, mit einem Ausblick auf die Schlussszene der Aeneis*. Bern: P. Lang.
Thompson, L. 1964. 'Lucan's Apotheosis of Nero'. CP 59: 147–53.
Thompson, L., and R. T. Bruère. 2010. 'Lucan's Use of Virgilian Reminiscence'. Tesoriero et al. 2010: 107–48.
Thornton, A. 1976. *The Living Universe: Gods and Men in Virgil's Aeneid*. Leiden: Brill.
Tietze Larson, V. S. 1991. 'The Hercules Oetaeus and the Picture of the Sapiens in Senecan Prose'. Phoenix 45: 39–49.

Tipping, B. 2007. '*Haec tum Roma fuit*: Past, Present, and Closure in Silius Italicus' *Punica*'. Heyworth et al. 2007: 221-41.

Tipping, B. 2010a. *Exemplary Epic: Silius Italicus' Punica*. Oxford: Oxford University Press.

Tipping, B. 2010b. 'Virtue and Narrative in Silius Italicus' *Punica*'. Augoustakis 2010a: 193-218.

Tracy, J. 2011. 'Internal Evidence for the Completeness of the *Bellum Civile*'. Asso 2011: 33-53.

Trinacty, C. V. Forthcoming. *Senecan Tragedy and the Reception of Augustan Poetry*. Oxford: Oxford University Press.

Turkeltaub, D. 2010. 'Reading the Epic Past: The *Iliad* on Heroic Epic'. P. Mitsis and C. Tsagalis (eds.). *Allusion, Authority, and Truth: Critical Perspectives on Greek Poetic and Rhetorical Praxis*. Berlin: Walter de Gruyter: 129-52.

Tuttle, A. 2013. 'Argive Augury and Portents in the *Thebaid*'. Augoustakis 2013: 71-88.

Tyler, J. 1974. 'Sophocles' *Ajax* and Sophoclean Plot Construction'. *AJP* 95: 24-42.

Usener, H. 1869. *M. Annaei Lucani Commenta Bernensia*. Stuttgart: B. G. Teubner.

Usher, M. D. 2007. 'Theomachy, Creation, and the Poetics of Quotation in Longinus Chapter 9'. *CP* 102: 292-303.

Vaahtera, J. 2001. *Roman Augural Lore in Greek Historiography: A Study of the Theory and Terminology*. Stuttgart: Steiner.

Vasaly, A. 1987. 'Personality and Power: Livy's Depiction of the Appii Claudii in the First Pentad'. *TAPA* 117: 203-26.

Venini, P. 1971. *Studi staziani*. Pavia: Tipografia del Libro.

Vernant, J.-P., and P. Vidal-Naquet. 1988. *Myth and Tragedy in Ancient Greece*. J. Lloyd (trans.). New York: Zone Books.

Versnel, H. S. 1990. *Inconsistencies in Greek and Roman Religion*. Vol. 1: *Ter Unus: Isis, Dionysos, Hermes*. Leiden: Brill.

Versnel, H. S. 2011. *Coping with the Gods: Wayward Readings in Greek Theology*. Leiden: Brill.

Vessey, D. W. T. C. 1970. 'The Games in *Thebaid* VI'. *Latomus* 29: 426-41.

Vessey, D. W. T. C. 1973. *Statius and the Thebaid*. Cambridge: Cambridge University Press.

Vian, F. 1952. *La guerre des Géants. Le mythe avant l'époque hellénistique*. Paris: Librairie C. Klincksieck.

Vigourt, A. 2001. *Les présages impériaux d'Auguste à Domitien*. Paris: de Boccard.

Volk, K. 2001. 'Pious and Impious Approaches to Cosmology in Manilius'. *MD* 47: 85-117.

Volk, K. 2006. 'Cosmic Disruption in Seneca's *Thyestes*: Two ways of Looking at an Eclipse'. Volk and Williams 2006: 183-200.

Volk, K., and G. D. Williams (eds.). 2006. *Seeing Seneca Whole: Perspectives on Philosophy, Poetry and Politics*. Leiden: Brill.

Von Glinski, M. L. 2012. *Simile and Identity in Ovid's Metamorphoses*. Cambridge: Cambridge University Press.

Vout, C. 2012. *The Hills of Rome: Signature of an Eternal City*. Cambridge: Cambridge University Press.

Walbank, F. W. 1967. 'The Scipionic Legend'. *PCPS* 13: 54-69.

Wald, E. 2012. *The Dozens: A History of Rap's Mama*. Oxford: Oxford University Press.

Wardle, D. 1994. *Suetonius' Life of Caligula*. Brussels: Latomus.

Wardle, D. 2006. *Cicero: On Divination, Book 1*. Oxford: Oxford University Press.

Wardle, D. 2007. 'Caligula's Bridge of Boats—AD 39 or 40?' *Historia* 56: 118-20.

Ware, C. 2012. *Claudian and the Roman Epic Tradition*. Cambridge: Cambridge University Press.
Waters, K. H. 1964. 'The Character of Domitian'. *Phoenix* 18: 49–77.
Waters, K. H. 1969. '*Traianus Domitiani continuator*'. *AJP* 90: 385–405.
Watkins, C. 1977. 'On μῆνις'. *Indo-European Studies* 3: 686–722.
Weinstock, S. 1971. *Divus Julius*. Oxford: Oxford University Press.
West, D. 1993. 'On Serial Narration and on the Julian Star'. *PVS* 21: 1–16.
West, M. L. 1969. 'The Achaean Wall'. *CR* 19: 255–60.
Wheeler, S. M. 1999. *A Discourse of Wonders: Audience and Performance in Ovid's Metamorphoses*. Philadelphia: University of Pennsylvania Press.
White, P. 2002. 'Ovid and the Augustan Milieu'. B. W. Boyd 2002: 1–25.
Whitehorne, J. E. G. 1983. 'The Background to Polyneices' Disinterment and Reburial'. *G&R* 30: 129–42.
Whitman, C. H. 1958. *Homer and the Heroic Tradition*. Cambridge, Mass.: Harvard University Press.
Whitmarsh, T. Forthcoming. *Battling the Gods: The Struggle against Religion in Ancient Greece and Rome*. London: Faber & Faber.
Wickkiser, B. L. 1999. 'Famous Last Words: Putting Ovid's Sphragis Back into the *Metamorphoses*'. *MD* 42: 113–42.
Wijsman, H. J. W. 2000. '*Gesander alter Mezentius* (Valerius Flaccus 6.279–385)'. *Mnemosyne* 53: 58–70.
Wilkinson, S. 2012. *Republicanism during the Early Roman Empire*. London: Continuum.
Williams, G. D. 2012. *The Cosmic Viewpoint: A Study of Seneca's Natural Questions*. Oxford: Oxford University Press.
Willis, I. 2011. *Now and Rome: Lucan and Vergil as Theorists of Politics and Space*. London: Continuum.
Wilson, E. R. 2004. *Mocked with Death: Tragic Overliving from Sophocles to Milton*. Baltimore: Johns Hopkins University Press.
Wilson, M. 2013. 'The Flavian *Punica*?'. Manuwald and Voigt 2013: 13–27.
Winterling, A. 2011. *Caligula: A Biography*. D. L. Schneider, G. W. Most, and P. Psoinos (trans.). Berkeley: University of California Press.
Wiseman, T. P. 1979. *Clio's Cosmetics: Three Studies in Greco-Roman Literature*. Leicester: Leicester University Press.
Wißmann, J. 2000. 'Apollonius Rhodius, *Argonautica* 1, 463ff.: A Marker'. *Mnemosyne* 53: 450–5.
Wistrand, E. K. H. 1956. *Die Chronologie der Punica des Silius Italicus: Beiträge zur Interpretation der flavischen Literatur*. Stockholm: Almqvist & Wiksell.
Wittreich, J. A. 2002. *Shifting Contexts: Reinterpreting Samson Agonistes*. Pittsburgh: Duquesne University Press.
Wöhrle, G. 1999. *Telemachs Reise: Väter und Söhne in Ilias und Odyssee oder ein Beitrag zur Erforschung der Männlichkeitsideologie in der homerischen Welt*. Göttingen: Vandenhoeck & Ruprecht.
Woodruff, P. 2011. *The Ajax Dilemma: Justice, Fairness, and Rewards*. Oxford: Oxford University Press.
Woolf, G. D. 2012. 'Reading and Religion in Rome'. J. Rüpke and W. Spickermann (eds.). *Reflections on Religious Individuality: Greco-Roman and Judaeo-Christian Texts and Practices*. Berlin: Walter de Gruyter: 193–208.

Wray, D. 2009. 'Seneca and Tragedy's Reason'. Bartsch and Wray 2009: 237–54.
Yamagata, N. 1994. *Homeric Morality*. Leiden: Brill.
Yasumura, N. 2011. *Challenges to the Power of Zeus in Early Greek Poetry*. London: Bristol Classical Press.
Young, E. 2013. 'Homer in a Nutshell: Vergilian Miniaturization and the Sublime'. *PMLA* 128: 57–72.
Zanker, G. 1992. 'Sophocles' *Ajax* and the Heroic Values of the *Iliad*'. *CQ* 42: 20–5.
Zanker, G. 1994. *The Heart of Achilles: Characterization and Personal Ethics in the Iliad*. Ann Arbor: University of Michigan Press.
Zanker, P. 1988. *The Power of Images in the Age of Augustus*. A. Shapiro (trans.). Ann Arbor: University of Michigan Press.
Zanker, P. 2002. 'Domitian's Palace on the Palatine and the Imperial Image'. A. K. Bowman, H. M. Cotton, M. Goodman, and S. Price (eds.). *Representations of Empire: Rome and the Mediterranean World*. Oxford: Oxford University Press: 105–30.
Zeiner, N. K. 2005. *Nothing Ordinary Here: Statius as Creator of Distinction in the Silvae*. London: Routledge.
Zeitlin, F. I. 1982. *Under the Sign of the Shield: Semiotics and Aeschylus' Seven Against Thebes*. Rome: Edizioni dell'Ateneo.
Zeitlin, F. I. 1986. 'Thebes: Theater of Self and Society in Athenian Drama'. J. P. Euben (ed.). *Greek Tragedy and Political Theory*. Berkeley: University of California Press: 101–41.
Zintzen, C. 1972. '*Alte virtus animosa cadit*: Gedanken zur Darstellung des Tragischen in Senecas *Hercules Furens*'. E. Lefèvre (ed.). *Senecas Tragödien*. Darmstadt: Wissenschaftliche Buchgesellschaft: 149–209.
Zissos, A. 1999. 'The Rape of Proserpina in Ovid Met. 5.341–661: Internal Audience and Narrative Distortion'. *Phoenix* 53: 97–113.
Zwierlein, O. 1984. *Senecas Hercules im Lichte kaiserzeitlicher und spätantiker Deutung*. Wiesbaden: Steiner.

INDEX OF PASSAGES

Aeschylus
Choephori
2: 47 n. 69
Eumenides
162–3: 178 n. 43
Persae
745–51: 307 n. 24
Septem contra Thebas
266: 47 n. 69
417–31: 33 n. 27
424–31: 45–6
425: 50
427–9: 256–7
427–31: 219 n. 57
432–4: 46 n. 64
440–3: 45
468–9: 44
491–4: 44
529–30: 71 n. 38
529–32: 44, 219 n. 57
570–5: 260
694: 46

Ps.-Aeschylus
Prometheus Vinctus
363–72: 250 n. 54
755–68: 34 n. 31

Apollodorus
Bibliotheca
1.27: 70 n. 36
1.34–8: 224 n. 72
1.41: 186
3.73: 316 n. 49
Epitome
5.24–6.6: 44 n. 60

Apollonius Rhodius
Argonautica
1.466–8: 71 n. 38
1.466–71: 218–19, 263
1.481–4: 219
1.487–91: 219–20
3.1226–7: 206 n. 22

Aratus
Phaenomena
634–46: 70 n. 36

Ps.-Aristotle
De Mundo
1.1: 286 n. 84

Author unknown
Aetna
49: 224 n. 72

Boiardo, Matteo Maria
Orlando Innamorato
2.3.22: 326 n. 14

Callimachus
Epigrammata
28.4: 98
Hymni
2.105–13: 213 n. 40

Cassius Dio
67.4.7: 318 n. 55

Catullus
64: 180

Cicero
De Divinatione
1: 10 n. 33
1.1: 265 n. 21
1.29: 222 n. 65
1.34: 272 n. 42
1.66: 265 n. 21
1.77: 214 n. 46, 215, 221 n. 63, 222 n. 65
1.115–24: 270 n. 33
1.127: 86 n. 11
2.20: 222 n. 65
2.70: 86 n. 12, 266 n. 22
2.70–83: 273 n. 43
2.83: 273 n. 43
2.148: 12 n. 38, 273 n. 44
De Domo Sua
112: 85 n. 8
De Finibus
3.66.1–8: 153 n. 106
De Natura Deorum
2.7–8: 222 n. 65
2.76: 85 n. 8
3.43–52: 107 n. 66
3.55: 90 n. 24

Cicero (*continued*)
　De Senectute
　　5: 7 n. 22
　Pro Caelio
　　58: 86 n. 14
　Pro Fonteio
　　30: 7 n. 22
　In Verrem
　　2.4.75: 137 n. 59
　　2.7.72: 7 n. 22

Claudian
　De Raptu Proserpinae
　　1.42–3: 286 n. 86

Coelius Antipater
　fr. 20P: 214 n. 46, 215, 221
　　n. 63, 222 n. 65

Critias
　Sisyphus fragment
　TrGF 43 fr. 19: 42 n. 56
　TrGF 43 fr. 19.12–13: 270

Dante
　Inferno
　　26.97–9: 86 n. 14
　　31.91–2: 86 n. 14

Diodorus Siculus
　1.67.11: 307 n. 24
　7.5.11: 247 n. 40

Dionysius of Halicarnassus
　Antiquitates Romanae
　　1.71.3: 247 n. 40

Epictetus
　Discourses
　　3.24.24: 41 n. 53,
　　　145 n. 83
　　4.1.101: 41 n. 53,
　　　145 n. 83

Epicurus
　Epistle to Pythocles
　　87.2: 281 n. 67

Euripides
　Bacchae
　　45: 40
　　45–6: 53
　　310: 54 n. 83
　　311–12: 54 n. 83
　　325: 40, 53

325–6: 265
500: 94 n. 35
502: 94 n. 35
616–41: 94 n. 34
635–6: 53
789: 53
1255: 40
1255–6: 53
1348: 43
Herakles
　342: 153 n. 104
　1265: 148 n. 90
　1313–39: 148
　1340–6: 153
Ion
　212–15: 206 n. 22
Iphigenia at Aulis
　1408: 40–1
　1408–9: 41
Phoenissae
　1121–2: 46 n. 64
　1130–3: 286 n. 85
Sisyphus fragment
　TrGF 43 fr. 19: 42 n. 56
　TrGF 43 fr. 19.12–13: 270
Troades
　69–86: 44 n. 60

Heraclitus
　Allegoricae Homericae
　　1.1–2: 38–9 n. 48

Hesiod
　Theogony
　　183–6: 224 n. 72
　　820–68: 59 n. 8
　Works and Days
　　109–201: 29 n. 20
　　160: 37 n. 43

Hippocrates
　Epistulae
　　14.22: 41 n. 53

Homer
　Iliad
　　1: 106 n. 64
　　1.5: 85 n. 9
　　1.266–72: 29 n. 20
　　1.396–406: 34
　　1.404: 34
　　2.155–6: 23 n. 13
　　2.204–5: 135 n. 55
　　2.594–600: 38, 43 n. 58
　　4.119–21: 198 n. 10

Homer (*continued*)
  Iliad (*continued*)
    4.401–10: 33
    4.402: 33
    4.405–10: 43
    4.408: 33 n. 28
    4.411–18: 33
    4.440–1: 90 n. 24
    4.440–3: 235 n. 8
    5: 78, 80
    5.85–92: 17
    5.87–92: 290 n. 98
    5.129–32: 18
    5.177–8: 29 n. 19
    5.297–318: 74 n. 56
    5.302–4: 30 n. 21
    5.330–7: 18–19
    5.362: 19
    5.379–80: 19, 80 n. 71
    5.382–404: 19
    5.383–91: 219
    5.385–404: 43 n. 58
    5.392–404: 116 n. 1
    5.405–9: 19–20
    5.431–53: 74 n. 56
    5.432–42: 21
    5.438: 21 n. 9
    5.439: 26
    5.443: 23 n. 10
    5.457: 19 n. 5
    5.459: 21 n. 9
    5.511: 6 n. 17
    5.770–2: 139
    5.800–13: 34
    5.817–21: 20
    5.818: 23 n. 12
    5.846–64: 28
    5.884: 21 n. 9
    6.128–9: 23 n. 12
    6.130–40: 23 n. 12, 43 n. 58
    6.141: 23 n. 12
    6.183: 33 n. 28
    6.200: 33 n. 28, 136 n. 56
    7.91: 204 n. 17
    7.446–53: 37
    7.458: 37
    8.130–4: 24
    8.143–4: 24
    8.169–71: 24
    8.210–11: 24 n. 14
    8.238–44: 198 n. 10
    8.369: 30 n. 22
    12.13–33: 37
    12.22–3: 37
    12.27–33: 38

12.228–9: 217
12.233–43: 217
12.244–50: 217–18
13.18–19: 139
13.27–9: 139
13.723–53: 218
15.361–6: 37 n. 42
16: 289 n. 93
16.87–96: 22
16.433–58: 24 n. 13
16.698–709: 22
16.705: 21 n. 9
16.706: 26
16.707–9: 23
16.710: 6 n. 17, 23 n. 10
16.784–9: 23
16.786: 21 n. 9
18.203–31: 251
20.4: 6 n. 17
20.30: 25
20.61–5: 140
20.67–74: 27
20.97–102: 43
20.367–8: 202
20.371–2: 197 n. 7
20.441–9: 26
20.447: 21 n. 9
20.448: 26, 35 n. 35
20.490–4: 197 n. 7
20.493: 21 n. 9
21: 6
21.2: 199
21.12–16: 197, 204
21.18: 21 n. 9, 197
21.26–32: 276 n. 53
21.33: 212
21.106–13: 199 n. 12
21.130–2: 197, 212
21.136–8: 198
21.153–60: 199 n. 11
21.177: 27 n. 16
21.182–3: 212
21.184–99: 198–9, 212
21.214–20: 200
21.214–26: 212
21.223: 200
21.227: 21 n. 9, 200 n. 13
21.228–32: 200 n. 13
21.240–2: 201
21.248: 207
21.249: 201
21.256: 201
21.257–64: 201–2, 208
21.281–3: 202
21.302–4: 203

Homer (*continued*)
  Iliad (*continued*)
    21.314–15: 203
    21.316–23: 38
    21.318–23: 188, 203, 210
    21.324–7: 204
    21.357–8: 204
    21.379–80: 204
    21.388: 140
    21.389: 27
    21.396–8: 28
    21.406–8: 28
    21.450–7: 30
    21.470: 6 n. 17
    21.516–17: 25
    21.522–5: 28
    22: 177 n. 42
    22.8–9: 30–1
    22.13: 30–1
    22.20: 31
    22.99–103: 218
    22.107: 218
    22.208: 27 n. 16
    23.724: 133 n. 50
    24.602–17: 43 n. 58
  Scholia to *Iliad*
    1.5: 85 n. 9
    5.407: 20 n. 7
    5.443: 22–3 n. 10
    5.511: 6 n. 17
    16.710: 6 n. 17, 22–3 n. 10
    20.4: 6 n. 17
    21.470: 6 n. 17
  Odyssey
    1.70: 44 n. 59
    4.499–511: 44
    4.504: 44
    9.273–8: 70
    11.305–20: 43 n. 58, 59 n. 8
    11.315–17: 139, 236
    11.317: 44 n. 59
    13.128–83: 44 n. 59
    21.215–9: 34–5
  Scholia to *Odyssey*
    1.70: 44 n. 59
    11.317: 44 n. 59

Horace
  Odes
    1.1.35–6: 115 n. 80
    1.1.36: 142, 319
    1.11.1: 278 n. 61
    1.12: 88, 314–15, 315 n. 44
    1.12.1–3: 314
    1.12.13: 314 n. 42
    1.12.22: 315 n. 44
    1.12.25: 315 n. 44
    1.12.37–8: 305 n. 18
    1.12.49–57: 315
    1.12.51: 316
    1.12.57: 316
    2.20.1–5: 115 n. 80
    3.1.1: 98
    3.4.42–58: 140 n. 69
    3.5.1–2: 174 n. 35
    3.5.2: 78
    3.30: 142
    3.30.1–9: 115 n. 80
    3.30.7–16: 143 n. 78
    4.5: 88 n. 18

Josephus
  Antiquitates Judaicae
    19.4–6: 134 n. 51
    19.5–6: 208 n. 29, 309 n. 31

Lactantius
  Commentary on the *Thebaid*
    1.43: 316 n. 47
    1.45: 316–17 n. 49
    3.603: 305 n. 18
    3.613: 261 n. 12
    3.615: 262 n. 14
    3.641: 267 n. 24
    3.643: 267 n. 23
    3.659: 268–9
    4.516: 278 n. 61
    6.363–4: 282–3
    7.651: 273 n. 45
    7.662: 273 n. 45
    7.710–11: 277 n. 57
    10.485: 272 n. 40

Livy
  1.3.9: 247 n. 40
  1.20.4: 148 n. 89
  3.2.5: 7 n. 22
  3.57.2: 307 n. 26
  7.26.1–5: 226
  7.26.4: 226 n. 78
  9.1.11: 7 n. 22
  9.34.22: 307 n. 26
  21.4.9: 232 n. 1
  21.29.7: 237
  21.30.6–7: 237
  21.30.7: 240
  21.32.7: 238 n. 13
  21.54.9: 207 n. 25
  21.63.6: 7 n. 22, 222
  21.63.13–14: 214 n. 46

Livy (*continued*)
  22.3.4–14: 215 n. 47
  22.3.10: 221 n. 63
  22.3.11–12: 214 n. 46
  22.5.2: 222 n. 67
  26.11.2–3: 247
  26.19.6–7: 227 n. 82
  27.13.8: 86 n. 14
  38.53.9–11: 255 n. 69
  45.23.19: 302 n. 12
  Periochae
    19: 222 n. 65

Longinus
  De Sublimitate / Peri Hypsous
    1.4: 141 n. 73
    7.2: 141 n. 73
    8.2: 236
    8.4: 140
    9.5: 139, 235
    9.6: 140
    9.8: 139
    15.4: 141
    36.1: 154

Lucan
  Bellum Civile
    1.9–23: 184 n. 53
    1.33–8: 171
    1.33–66: 312
    1.47–52: 168
    1.51: 176
    1.67: 267 n. 25
    1.74: 168 n. 25
    1.125: 183 n. 52
    1.126–7: 278 n. 61
    1.128: 191, 192, 306
    1.143–50: 163
    1.151–7: 161, 170–1
    1.158–82: 164
    1.163–4: 164
    1.172: 164–5 n. 18
    1.181: 164
    1.183: 240
    1.204: 213
    1.283–91: 165 n. 18
    1.288: 165 n. 18
    1.540–4: 166 n. 20
    2.7–15: 281 n. 67
    2.241: 193
    2.320–2: 189
    2.384: 191
    2.650–1: 305 n. 19
    3.299: 240 n. 22
    3.312–20: 170
    3.319: 170
    3.320: 174
    3.392: 163, 163 n. 16
    3.395: 163 n. 16
    3.399: 162 n. 15
    3.406: 162 n. 15
    3.408–10: 161
    3.428: 241
    3.433: 162
    3.433–5: 162, 306 n. 19
    3.436–9: 159
    3.446–9: 159
    3.453: 163
    3.454: 164
    4.141–3: 208 n. 29
    4.375–6: 165
    5.94: 287 n. 89
    5.274: 164
    5.356: 164, 191
    5.579–80: 161 n. 12
    6.538–53: 180
    6.744–9: 278 n. 61
    7.1–6: 166
    7.144–50: 169
    7.151–84: 214 n. 46
    7.151–206: 172, 173
    7.159: 245 n. 36
    7.168–71: 173, 177
    7.172–6: 172–3
    7.197: 173, 174
    7.201–2: 173
    7.297–8: 175 n. 39
    7.311: 175 n. 39
    7.348–55: 175 n. 39
    7.445–7: 157, 174
    7.445–8: 11–12
    7.445–9: 12
    7.445–59: 173–4, 306
    7.447: 12
    7.450: 236 n. 11
    7.454–5: 269 n. 29
    7.455–9: 157
    7.457: 12
    7.557: 177
    7.557–81: 176, 191 n. 73
    7.567–8: 306 n. 19
    7.567–71: 176
    7.596: 167 n. 23
    7.777–80: 177
    7.781–3: 167 n. 23
    7.792–4: 179
    7.796: 175 n. 39, 306
    7.797–9: 179
    8.713: 187 n. 64
    8.714: 187 n. 64

Lucan (*continued*)
  Bellum Civile (*continued*)
    8.793: 182
    8.800–2: 182
    8.816: 187 n. 64
    8.831–4: 183
    8.832: 189
    8.835–7: 184
    8.843–50: 185
    8.855–8: 186
    8.858–64: 186
    8.861: 187 n. 64
    8.863: 187 n. 62
    8.865–6: 187
    8.869–72: 187
    8.872: 187 n. 64
    9.1–4: 188
    9.7: 189
    9.8: 189
    9.10–11: 186 n. 58, 189
    9.17–18: 189
    9.18: 190
    9.153–61: 183–4
    9.509: 192
    9.509–10: 191
    9.513–14: 190
    9.564–5: 189–90
    9.574–80: 190
    9.584–6: 190
    9.591–3: 191 n. 74
    9.598–600: 193
    9.601–4: 191
    9.617–18: 191 n. 74
    9.884–9: 191 n. 73
    10.34: 161 n. 13
    10.108–10: 165
    10.155–6: 165
    10.208: 267 n. 25
    10.422–5: 165
    10.439–85: 165
    10.456: 164

Lucretius
  De Rerum Natura
    1.44–9: 268 n. 28
    1.59: 267 n. 25
    1.66–7: 58, 290
    1.67: 59
    1.68: 270 n. 32
    1.68–9: 66 n. 24
    1.68–71: 59, 290
    1.70: 59
    1.71: 239 n. 16
    1.72–3: 290
    1.73: 239 n. 16
    1.75: 59
    1.78–9: 58
    1.79: 60
    1.80–3: 62 n. 14
    1.123: 73 n. 47
    1.136–9: 239 n. 18
    1.265: 245 n. 37
    1.280–9: 290 n. 98
    1.716–41: 151 n. 97
    1.722–5: 100
    1.724: 250
    1.734–41: 269 n. 30, 286
    1.925–47: 100 n. 51
    1.926–30: 100 n. 50
    1.931: 245 n. 37
    1.938: 100 n. 50
    1.945: 100
    1.947: 100 n. 50
    2.37–54: 270 n. 35
    2.602–3: 287 n. 89
    2.646–48: 268 n. 28, 268–9
    2.646–51: 268 n. 28
    2.649–50: 268 n. 28
    2.651: 268 n. 28, 268–9
    2.1093–4: 269
    2.1101–4: 59 n. 7
    3.2: 239 n. 17
    3.3–6: 239
    3.16–17: 238
    3.18–22: 239
    3.319–22: 60 n. 10, 151 n. 96
    3.661: 270 n. 32
    4.592–4: 151 n. 98
    4.732–43: 294 n. 111
    4.1239: 269
    5.72: 267 n. 25
    5.73–5: 269, 286
    5.73–75: 269
    5.82–90: 59 n. 7
    5.111–12: 269
    5.113: 99
    5.113–21: 60, 286
    5.146–55: 269
    5.449–51: 283
    5.510: 283
    5.517–18: 283
    5.526–33: 281 n. 67
    5.878–81: 294 n. 111
    5.1029: 267 n. 25
    5.1183–93: 59 n. 7
    5.1423–35: 270 n. 35
    5.1448–53: 87 n. 15
    6.43–79: 269
    6.50–67: 59 n. 7, 66
    6.54–5: 66 n. 23
    6.94: 314 n. 41
    6.323–9: 161 n. 13

Index of Passages

Lucretius (*continued*)
  De Rerum Natura (*continued*)
    6.340–2: 67–8
    6.379–422: 59 n. 7, 66
    6.381–6: 269
    6.387–422: 302 n. 12
    6.420: 85 n. 8
    6.680–702: 100

Manilius
  Astronomica
    1.173: 287 n. 89
    3.1–3: 238
    5.91–6: 246 n. 40

Marlowe, Christopher
  1 Tamburlaine
    3.3.152–5: 326
    4.4.79–80: 325
  2 Tamburlaine
    4.2.118–20: 325

Martial
  De Spectaculis
    1.5–6: 287 n. 89
  Epigrammata
    5.19.1–6: 320 n. 67
    7.7.5: 318
    7.99.1: 318
    8.11.7–8: 320 n. 67
    8.36: 243 n. 31
    8.36.6: 318
    8.36.11–12: 319
    9.3.7: 242 n. 28
    9.64: 255 n. 71
    9.101.23: 255 n. 71

Menander
  Eunuch
    fr. 162 K-T: 41 n. 53

Milton, John
  Paradise Lost
    2.51–105: 324
    2.310–78: 324
    3.315–43: 324 n. 3
    6.99–102: 325 n. 7

Naevius
  Bellum Punicum
    fr. 19.2 Morel: 294 n. 108

Nonnus
  Dionysiaca
    9.208–42: 92 n. 28
    38.190: 137 n. 59

Ovid
  Epistulae ex Ponto
    1.2.118: 303 n. 13
    1.7.46: 302 n. 12
    2.10.23–4: 250 n. 55
    3.1.51–2: 301
    3.6.27–8: 302 n. 12
  Fasti
    1.569–74: 250 n. 55
    3.325: 278 n. 61
    4.814: 264
    5: 303 n. 14
  Ibis
    597–8: 250 n. 55
  Metamorphoses
    1.9: 267 n. 25
    1.12–13: 287 n. 89
    1.76: 84
    1.78–81: 281 n. 67
    1.149–50: 180
    1.151–67: 286
    1.160–1: 260 n. 9, 264 n. 19
    1.171–6: 84 n. 4
    1.184: 227 n. 80
    1.199–205: 113
    1.201: 84 n. 4
    1.204–5: 84
    1.209–10: 85
    1.211–15: 85
    1.213: 85 n. 8
    1.220: 98
    1.220–1: 264
    1.220–3: 85–6
    1.221: 108
    1.222–3: 263–4
    1.224–6: 87
    1.226–31: 87
    1.419: 267 n. 25
    1.747–2.102: 92 n. 28
    1.753: 137
    2.55–6: 166 n. 21
    2.102: 137
    2.104: 137
    2.124: 167
    2.193–4: 151 n. 98
    2.193–200: 137
    2.217–26: 236 n. 10
    2.298ff.: 168 n. 25
    2.327–8: 138 n. 64
    2.329: 167
    2.329–31: 166 n. 21
    2.381–93: 166–7
    2.384: 167 n. 22
    2.394–400: 166 n. 21
    2.731: 91 n. 25
    3.263–6: 89–90

Ovid (*continued*)
  Metamorphoses (*continued*)
    3.266: 119 n. 8
    3.268–72: 90
    3.275–8: 91
    3.280–6: 91
    3.302–4: 92
    3.513–16: 93
    3.514: 93, 260 n. 9
    3.531: 104 n. 58
    3.557–8: 93
    3.568–9: 95
    3.579–80: 96
    3.609: 96
    3.609–10: 93
    3.611–12: 93
    3.629: 93
    3.629–30: 93
    3.636: 93
    3.656: 93
    3.658–9: 93 n. 31
    3.697–700: 94
    3.732–3: 96
    4.389–98: 95 n. 38
    4.687: 91 n. 25
    4.747–9: 84 n. 6
    5.300: 98
    5.305: 98
    5.307: 98
    5.308–9: 98
    5.319–20: 99
    5.321–31: 99
    5.339: 314 n. 41
    5.346–58: 99
    5.353: 250 n. 55
    5.662–78: 99, 100
    6: 178 n. 44
    6.72–4: 102
    6.83–4: 101
    6.87–9: 175 n. 38
    6.121–2: 102
    6.130–1: 102
    6.157–64: 104
    6.158: 104
    6.162: 104
    6.170–2: 104
    6.172: 104
    6.172–6: 104
    6.172–83: 106
    6.177–8: 104
    6.181: 105
    6.182–3: 105
    6.185: 105
    6.186–91: 105
    6.193–7: 105
    6.197–202: 105
    6.203: 105 n. 63

    6.206–9: 105
    6.212–13: 106
    6.217: 106
    6.293: 106
    6.313–15: 106
    8.434: 91 n. 25
    8.611–16: 108
    8.612–13: 109
    8.614: 110
    8.622: 108
    8.689: 109
    8.721–2: 108
    8.724: 109
    8.725–7: 109
    8.739–40: 109, 275 n. 49
    8.741–4: 162, 306 n. 19
    8.754: 162
    8.755–6: 275 n. 49,
      306 n. 19
    8.762: 162
    8.771–3: 163
    8.827: 164 n. 18
    8.829: 164 n. 18
    8.830: 165 n. 19
    8.830–3: 163
    8.832–3: 164
    8.839: 164 n. 18
    8.879–83: 110
    9.16: 110
    9.17: 110
    9.23–6: 122 n. 12
    9.25–6: 110
    9.203–4: 110–11
    9.404–5: 252 n. 61
    10.149–52: 317 n. 49
    10.397–9: 281 n. 67
    13.761: 260 n. 9
    14.32: 91 n. 25
    14.617–18: 247 n. 40
    15: 175
    15.66–72: 283 n. 74
    15.68: 267 n. 25
    15.281–4: 294 n. 111
    15.342–50: 281 n. 67
    15.356–61: 84 n. 6
    15.745–6: 112, 185 n. 55
    15.750: 112
    15.760–1: 106–7, 112
    15.760–78: 80
    15.773–4: 80, 112
    15.785–6: 166
    15.803–6: 112–13,
      143 n. 79
    15.818–9: 113
    15.832–70: 168
    15.844–6: 143 n. 79
    15.846: 115 n. 79

Ovid (*continued*)
  Metamorphoses (*continued*)
    15.847: 115 n. 79
    15.848: 115 n. 79
    15.849: 115 n. 79
    15.868: 115 n. 79
    15.870: 114 n. 77
    15.871: 114
    15.872: 255 n. 67
    15.873: 115 n. 79
    15.874: 115 n. 79
    15.875: 115 n. 79
    15.875–6: 114–15, 142
    15.876: 115 n. 79
    15.877–8: 115, 143 n. 78
    15.879: 114 n. 77, 255
  Tristia
    1.1.81–2: 302 n. 12
    1.3.11–12: 302 n. 12
    2.33: 302 n. 12
    2.103–8: 301
    2.144: 302 n. 12
    2.179: 302 n. 12
    3.5.5–8: 301
    4.3.61–4: 301
    4.8.45–52: 302, 302 n. 12
    5.2.53: 302 n. 12
    5.3.29–30: 301

Scholia to Persius
  2.36: 174, 187

Petronius
  fr. 28: 270 n. 32
  Satyrica
    122.1–123.1: 240 n. 23

Pindar
  Isthmian
    7.44–7: 136 n. 56
    8.26–47: 34 n. 31
  Olympian
    9.29–46: 109 n. 70

Plato
  Phaedrus
    244c: 265 n. 21
  Republic
    378d5–7: 38 n. 48
    568d7–8: 72 n. 42
    574d4–5: 72 n. 42
    575b7: 72 n. 42
  Sophist
    246a: 286
    246a–c: 60–1
    246b: 61
    246c: 61
  Timaeus
    71e–72a: 265 n. 21

Pliny the Elder
  Historia Naturalis
    5.68: 186 n. 57

Pliny the Younger
  Epistulae
    3.11.3: 318 n. 54
  Panegyricus
    33.4: 317

Plutarch
  Alexander
    2.1: 133 n. 47
    3.1–4: 133 n. 47
    6.8: 133
  Antony
    3.6: 186
  Caesar
    47: 172 n. 33

Polybius
  3.80.3–82.8: 215 n. 47

Quintilian
  Institutio Oratoria
    10.1.91: 321 n. 70

Quintus of Smyrna
  Posthomerica
    3.26–9: 31
    3.45–52: 31–2

Sallust
  Bellum Iugurthinum
    85: 128 n. 31

Scribonius Largus
  Compositiones
    ep. 1: 87

Seneca the Elder
  Suasoriae
    1.5: 133 n. 46

Seneca the Younger
  Ad Helviam
    5.1: 149 n. 94
  Agamemnon
    604–9: 146
  Apocolocyntosis
    1.2: 150 n. 95
    11.4: 131

Seneca the Younger (*continued*)
  De Beneficiis
    1.13.3: 153 n. 106
    3.29.4: 267 n. 25
    4.3–8: 268 n. 28
    6.35.1: 149 n. 94
  De Ira
    1.20.2: 141 n. 72
    1.20.8–9: 134
  De Providentia
    5.10–11: 138 n. 62
  De Tranquillitate
    16.4: 153 n. 106
  De Vita Beata
    9.4: 152 n. 101
  Epistulae Morales
    24.4: 153 n. 104
    41.4: 151
    48: 152
    48.11: 152
    53.11–12: 152
    71.30: 150 n. 94
    71.37: 126 n. 26
    73: 152 n. 102
    73.14–16: 150
    90.43: 151 n. 98
    92.30: 152 n. 99
    98.9: 150
  Hercules Furens
    1–5: 119
    6–18: 119
    12: 70 n. 36, 120, 320 n. 65
    21–6: 120
    23: 120
    24: 120
    27–9: 120
    30–42: 121
    35–6: 122
    37–40: 130
    39–40: 122
    46–56: 122–3
    52–4: 123
    57–9: 123
    60–1: 123
    61–3: 123
    63: 124
    64–74: 124
    75: 148 n. 88
    75–82: 125
    79–82: 126
    80: 126 n. 24
    82: 126 n. 24
    84–5: 125
    89–90: 125
    90–1: 126
    92–4: 126
    94: 126 n. 24
    96–8: 126
    99: 126
    109–12: 126
    110–11: 144 n. 82
    117–18: 126–7
    121–2: 127
    164–6: 130
    172–3: 130
    192–5: 130
    195: 193 n. 78
    265–7: 128
    268–70: 128 n. 31
    276: 128
    337–41: 128
    357: 128
    436–8: 128
    438: 129
    439–47: 129
    444–5: 147
    447–8: 129
    449: 129
    450: 129
    457–8: 129
    463: 129
    582: 143 n. 78
    583: 143 n. 78
    606: 238 n. 15
    609–10: 123 n. 18, 143 n. 78
    806: 143 n. 78
    927: 144 n. 82
    944–52: 137–8
    955: 139
    958: 139
    958–9: 142, 143–4
    958–61: 325
    959: 152
    959–63: 132
    961–2: 152
    963–4: 133
    965–73: 139–40
    982–6: 144 n. 82
    1018–19: 144 n. 82
    1038: 144 n. 82
    1082–99: 145
    1157: 148 n. 88
    1201: 145
    1202–10: 146
    1217: 147
    1218: 145, 154
    1239: 145
    1271–2: 149 n. 94
    1274: 151
    1274–5: 149 n. 94

Seneca the Younger (*continued*)
  Hercules Furens (*continued*)
    1276–7: 150 n. 94
    1287–94: 147
    1297: 145 n. 83
    1302–13: 145
    1315: 148
    1321–41: 149
    1338: 154
    1341–4: 148
  Medea
    41: 148 n. 88
    895: 148 n. 88
    937: 148 n. 88
    976: 148 n. 88
    988: 148 n. 88
    1026–7: 143
  Phaedra
    195–203: 126 n. 25
  Phoenissae
    314–16: 250 n. 55
  Quaestiones Naturales
    1.1.4: 268 n. 27
    2.31.1: 245 n. 36
    2.53.3: 267 n. 25
    6.2.8–9: 147
  Thyestes
    108: 166 n. 21
    120–1: 166 n. 20
    272–8: 178 n. 44
    776–8: 166 n. 20
    784–8: 166 n. 20
    789–884: 166
    793–804: 167 n. 22
    812: 224 n. 72
    885–6: 142 n. 77
    885–8: 141–2, 168
    891–2: 166 n. 20
    893–5: 179
    896–7: 168
    908: 169
    911–12: 142
    1077–92: 144 n. 81

Ps.-Seneca
  Hercules Oetaeus
    147–50: 122 n. 12
    1618–41: 193
    1683–4: 193
    1693: 193
    1994–6: 194
  Octavia
    476: 130
    527–32: 130

Servius
  Commentary on the *Aeneid*
    1.44: 69 n. 34
    4.34: 64
    4.210: 66
    4.379: 64 n. 21
    8.7: 69–70, 260
    10.567: 79

Sextus Empiricus
  Adversus Mathematicos
    8.56–8: 287 n. 87
    9.182–90: 107 n. 66

Silius Italicus
  Punica
    1.39: 232, 254 n. 65
    1.42: 80 n. 72
    1.58: 232
    1.64: 243 n. 29
    1.64–5: 233
    1.116–19: 232–3
    1.134–7: 233
    1.137: 248 n. 48
    1.137–9: 233
    1.460–3: 250
    1.611: 152 n. 99
    2.33–5: 228 n. 84
    3.14–16: 244
    3.222: 314 n. 41
    3.442–65: 208 n. 29
    3.483–6: 234–5
    3.491–2: 235 n. 9, 241
    3.494–5: 236
    3.496–9: 236–7, 239 n. 17
    3.502: 237
    3.503–4: 238
    3.509: 238
    3.509–10: 234
    3.510: 242
    3.512–17: 238
    3.516: 239 n. 17
    3.516–17: 240
    3.540–6: 237
    3.555: 241
    3.563: 236 n. 11
    3.585–6: 242
    3.594: 242
    3.595: 242
    3.599: 208
    3.602: 242
    3.609: 242
    3.609–10: 243
    3.611: 242
    3.614–15: 315 n. 44

Silius Italicus (*continued*)
  Punica (*continued*)
    3.622–9: 242
    3.631: 241
    3.640: 240–1
    3.708–10: 241
    3.709: 243 n. 29
    4.1–9: 240 n. 20
    4.2: 235 n. 9
    4.63–5: 214 n. 46
    4.101–42: 220 n. 60
    4.180: 303 n. 13
    4.243–7: 205
    4.253: 205
    4.275–6: 205–6, 224 n. 72
    4.294: 206
    4.298–9: 206 n. 21
    4.520–4: 206
    4.522: 206 n. 24
    4.525: 206
    4.573–4: 207
    4.574: 209
    4.600–1: 206 n. 24
    4.608: 264 n. 19
    4.622–4: 207
    4.625–6: 207
    4.639: 207
    4.640: 207
    4.642: 207
    4.643–8: 207–8
    4.651–2: 209
    4.652: 245
    4.659–66: 209
    4.670–5: 210, 213
    4.675–95: 210
    4.696–7: 210
    4.709–10: 222 n. 64
    4.810: 247 n. 41
    5.16: 222 n. 66
    5.59–62: 222 n. 65
    5.66–9: 214
    5.70–4: 214
    5.75–8: 215
    5.76: 222 n. 66
    5.78–80: 226
    5.80: 226
    5.87–8: 227
    5.96–100: 220
    5.103–4: 222 n. 64
    5.104: 222
    5.110–13: 224
    5.117: 222 n. 67
    5.117–20: 221
    5.121: 220 n. 62
    5.121–9: 221

    5.125–7: 221
    5.126: 222 n. 67
    5.130–9: 224–5, 225 n. 74
    5.131: 225
    5.139: 225
    5.140–1: 225 n. 74
    5.162–3: 221
    5.167–8: 222
    5.179–81: 223
    5.384–91: 228
    5.635–6: 228 n. 84
    5.652–5: 225
    6.600–5: 247 n. 41
    6.713: 248 n. 45
    7.106–7: 240 n. 24
    10.336: 248 n. 45
    10.350: 247 n. 41
    10.357–68: 247 n. 41
    10.375–6: 243
    11.385–409: 223 n. 69
    12.48: 243
    12.71–2: 244
    12.92–3: 244
    12.95: 244
    12.103: 244 n. 32
    12.116–21: 244 n. 34
    12.133–51: 244
    12.146: 245
    12.150–1: 245
    12.319: 244 n. 32
    12-320–41: 246
    12.336: 248
    12.390: 314 n. 41
    12.411: 244 n. 32
    12.434–48: 244 n. 34
    12.517: 248 n. 45
    12.569–70: 243 n. 29
    12.605–26: 245
    12.624: 245
    12.625: 245 n. 36
    12.626: 245
    12.628–9: 245
    12.639–45: 246
    12.643–5: 252 n. 61
    12.657–60: 246
    12.677–8: 246
    12.684–5: 246, 247 n. 40
    12.697–700: 246–7
    12.703–4: 248
    12.704–25: 248
    12.720: 248, 249
    12.721: 250 n. 56
    12.725: 227
    12.728: 31
    13.615–47: 227

Index of Passages

Silius Italicus (*continued*)
  Punica (*continued*)
    13.781–91: 195 n. 1
    15.516: 251
    15.527–8: 252
    15.800–5: 252 n. 59
    16.696–7: 229 n. 86
    17.225–7: 252
    17.227: 248 n. 45
    17.266–7: 252
    17.317–19: 252
    17.324–7: 253
    17.398: 251
    17.474–8: 253
    17.522–617: 252 n. 63
    17.548–50: 253
    17.559–60: 252 n. 62
    17.567–80: 223 n. 69
    17.606–10: 254
    17.608: 255 n. 67
    17.612: 254
    17.615: 254
    17.625: 255
    17.627: 255
    17.643–4: 255
    17.645–54: 255
    17.649–54: 228

Sophocles
  Ajax
    116: 47 n. 69
    117: 47, 50
    118: 48
    127–8: 47
    132–3: 47
    666–8: 51
    758–79: 48–9
    761: 50
    768–9: 50
    777: 50
    779: 50
    1069–72: 50
    1073: 50 n. 75
    1082: 50 n. 75
    1099–1114: 50
    1343–4: 51
  Scholia to *Ajax*
    118: 20 n. 7, 48
    666: 51–2
  Antigone
    127–40: 45 n. 61
    834: 104 n. 59
  Electra
    150: 104 n. 59

Statius
  Achilleid
    1.3–7: 34 n. 33
    1.151–2: 133 n. 49
  Silvae
    1.1.43–5: 320
    1.1.62: 318 n. 56
    1.1.84–90: 320
    1.1.99–104: 320
    1.5.1: 317 n. 49
    1.5.14: 314 n. 40
    1.6.27: 318 n. 56
    2.6.8: 267 n. 25
    2.7.76: 270 n. 35
    2.776: 290 n. 97
    3.3.69–75: 307 n. 25
    3.3.70: 307 n. 25
    3.3.72: 307 n. 25
    3.3.158–60: 318 n. 54
    3.4.18: 318 n. 56
    4.2: 314–15
    4.2.7: 314
    4.2.11: 315, 318 n. 56
    4.2.18–31: 243 n. 31
    4.2.20–2: 318
    4.2.48: 315
    4.2.49: 315
    4.2.50: 315
    4.2.52–6: 282 n. 71
    4.3: 208
    4.3.16–17: 242 n. 28
    4.3.72–94: 208 n. 28
    4.3.155: 315 n. 44
    5.1.37–8: 318 n. 56
    5.2.170: 318 n. 56
    5.3.234: 316 n. 47
  Thebaid
    1.3–4: 314 n. 41
    1.16–31: 311–312
    1.29–30: 318
    1.32–4: 312–13
    1.33–45: 313
    1.41: 314 n. 42
    1.41–5: 313–314
    1.44: 316 n. 47
    1.45: 316 n. 47, 316 n. 49, 317 n. 49
    1.189–90: 311 n. 35
    1.214–47: 274 n. 46
    1.395–7: 280
    1.398–9: 280 n. 64
    1.408–13: 294 n. 107
    1.453: 294 n. 107
    1.457–60: 293 n. 107
    1.482–510: 280
    1.488–90: 294 n. 107

Statius (*continued*)
  Thebaid (*continued*)
    2.263: 267 n. 25
    2.595–601: 294 n. 109
    3.218–52: 274 n. 46
    3.234–5: 267 n. 23
    3.456: 278 n. 60
    3.459: 278 n. 61
    3.460–551: 220 n. 60
    3.471–82: 267 n. 23
    3.551–65: 277–8
    3.552–3: 279
    3.575–8: 267 n. 23
    3.595–6: 205 n. 20
    3.598: 276
    3.598–603: 262 n. 16
    3.599: 306 n. 19
    3.599–600: 295
    3.601–2: 33 n. 27, 311 n. 35
    3.602: 260
    3.602–3: 311 n. 35
    3.603: 305 n. 18, 306 n. 19
    3.604–5: 294
    3.607–18: 261, 261 n. 12
    3.609: 307 n. 26
    3.612: 263, 269
    3.613: 261 n. 12, 265
    3.614–15: 261 n. 12
    3.615: 262 n. 14
    3.615–16: 221, 257, 262
    3.616–18: 257, 263
    3.617–18: 285
    3.619–20: 266
    3.620–4: 264–5
    3.625–6: 266
    3.627: 265
    3.628: 265
    3.629: 267, 267 n. 23
    3.629–35: 265–6
    3.633–5: 266
    3.640: 266
    3.641: 267 n. 24
    3.643–4: 267, 267 n. 23
    3.646–7: 266, 280
    3.648–9: 265
    3.648–51: 221
    3.652: 220 n. 62
    3.653–5: 221
    3.657–61: 267–8
    3.659: 268
    3.659–60: 257, 268 n. 28
    3.660: 220 n. 62
    3.661: 222, 257, 269–70
    3.661–9: 271–2
    3.662: 220 n. 62
    3.665–6: 220

3.668: 221
3.669: 295 n. 113
4.35: 314 n. 41
4.139–44: 293 n. 107
4.165–74: 225 n. 74
4.175–6: 226 n. 75
4.182–6: 44 n. 58
4.396–7: 316 n. 47
4.516: 278 n. 61
5.565–70: 227
5.568: 275 n. 49, 306 n. 19
5.569–70: 294 n. 108
5.585: 316 n. 49
5.643–9: 280
6.84–5: 159 n. 4
6.358–65: 281–2
6.359: 282
6.360–64: 282
6.362–3: 282 n. 72
6.363–4: 282 n. 72, 282–3, 287 n. 89
6.365: 282
6.716–18: 293 n. 107
6.719–21: 285 n. 82
6.934–7: 279
6.942–6: 279
7.1–89: 274 n. 46
7.145–92: 274 n. 46
7.320–7: 228 n. 85, 291 n. 99
7.651: 273, 273 n. 45
7.662: 273, 273 n. 45
7.663–8: 274
7.675: 274, 274 n. 47
7.678–9: 275 n. 49, 306 n. 19
7.690–1: 275
7.692: 275
7.696–7: 275
7.699–700: 275
7.700–11: 275–6
7.701: 272 n. 42
7.703: 276
7.710: 276
7.710–11: 277 n. 57
7.730–5: 228 n. 85
7.809–16: 281
7.815–16: 288 n. 90
8.76: 7
8.76–7: 284 n. 77
8.79: 294 n. 108
8.92: 268 n. 25
8.110: 286 n. 86
8.311: 286 n. 86
8.335–8: 186 n. 56, 288 n. 90
8.374: 314 n. 41
9.220–4: 293 n. 107
9.315: 213
9.315–18: 210–11, 314 n. 41

Statius (*continued*)
　Thebaid (*continued*)
　　9.342–3: 211
　　9.343–4: 211
　　9.344–5: 213 n. 38
　　9.393–4: 211
　　9.442–3: 211
　　9.445: 212
　　9.446–539: 228 n. 85
　　9.469–72: 212
　　9.476–80: 213
　　9.481–510: 213
　　9.506–10: 212
　　9.514–21: 296–7
　　9.540–6: 228 n. 85
　　9.546–59: 228 n. 85
　　9.548–50: 257, 297 n. 117
　　9.550: 257
　　9.552: 296 n. 115
　　9.556: 296 n. 115
　　9.557: 296 n. 115
　　9.564–5: 296
　　10.32: 295 n. 113
　　10.257–9: 272 n. 40
　　10.485–6: 221, 272 n. 40
　　10.630–1: 314 n. 40
　　10.723–6: 261 n. 12
　　10.748–51: 311 n. 35
　　10.827–31: 1–2
　　10.829: 317 n. 49
　　10.831–3: 307 n. 25
　　10.831–6: 283–4, 314 n. 41
　　10.832: 290 n. 97
　　10.835: 305 n. 18
　　10.840: 290
　　10.843: 286
　　10.845: 290 n. 97
　　10.845–7: 284–5
　　10.847: 257, 285 n. 80
　　10.848–52: 285
　　10.849–52: 226 n. 75, 285 n. 82
　　10.852: 294 n. 108
　　10.853–5: 306 n. 19
　　10.861: 287, 290
　　10.864–9: 290 n. 98
　　10.873–7: 288
　　10.877–82: 286
　　10.883–96: 289
　　10.886–9: 289
　　10.890–1: 274 n. 46, 289
　　10.897: 289 n. 95
　　10.899–906: 289–90
　　10.904–5: 256
　　10.909–10: 290
　　10.913–17: 291
　　10.918: 290
　　10.919: 295 n. 113
　　10.920: 290
　　10.927: 291
　　10.935–9: 291 n. 99
　　10.937–8: 291
　　11.119–35: 166 n. 20
　　12.129–40: 292 n. 100
　　12.165–6: 292 n. 103
　　12.291–4: 292 n. 100
　　12.295–311: 292 n. 100
　　12.464–7: 292 n. 100
　　12.552–8: 293
　　12.584: 295
　　12.588: 295
　　12.606–10: 292 n. 100
　　12.650–5: 295
　　12.733–5: 295 n. 112
　　12.771–3: 296 n. 114
　　12.774: 296 n. 115
　　12.777–8: 296 n. 114
　　12.778: 296 n. 115
　　12.778–81: 295–6
　　12.816–817: 3 n. 7

Suetonius
　Augustus
　　70: 179–80
　Caligula
　　16.1: 308
　　19: 208 n. 29, 309
　　21: 307 n. 27
　　22.1: 308
　　22.1–2: 135
　　22.4: 133, 307
　　25: 307 n. 27
　　33.1: 134 n. 53
　　34.1–2: 310
　　34.2: 309–10
　　37: 309
　　37.2: 309
　　43–47: 308
　　45.2: 310 n. 33
　　51: 308
　　51.1: 307
　　52.1: 308 n. 28
　　57.3: 134 n. 53, 307
　　58.2–3: 134 n. 53, 307
　Domitian
　　5: 242 n. 28
　　13.2: 318 n. 55
　　15.1: 303 n. 14
　Galba
　　1.1: 135 n. 53
　Nero: 311 n. 36
　　24.1: 311 n. 36
　　27.2–3: 311 n. 36

Suetonius (*continued*)
   Nero (*continued*)
      30.1: 134–5 n. 53, 311 n. 36
      31.1–3: 311 n. 36
      42.2: 311 n. 36
      46.1: 311 n. 36
      49.2–3: 311 n. 36
      53.1: 311 n. 36
      55.1: 311 n. 36
      56.1: 134 n. 53, 311 n. 36
   Tiberius
      2.2: 222 n. 65, 307 n. 26
      2.4: 307 n. 26

Tacitus
   Agricola
      42.4–5: 305 n. 18
   Annals
      1.11: 309 n. 30
      3.1: 185 n. 54
      3.24: 303
      6.25: 311 n. 35
      6.47: 303
      14.12: 305 n. 18
      15.45: 135 n. 53
      16.21: 304
      16.22: 304
   Dialogus de Oratoribus
      12.6: 310 n. 33
   Histories
      3.72: 234

Tasso, Torquato
   Gerusalemme Liberata
      1.63: 327

Tibullus
   1.7.31: 237
   2.1.56: 237

Valerius Flaccus
   Argonautica
      1.662–5: 246 n. 40
      3.15–16: 314 n. 40
      5.692–3: 282 n. 71
      6.322: 274 n. 47

Varro
   De Re Rustica
      1.18.7–8: 87 n. 15

Vergil
   Aeneid
      1.25–6: 121
      1.33: 113 n. 75

1.36: 121
1.39–45: 44 n. 60
1.46–8: 19 n. 6
1.46–9: 90 n. 23
1.96–8: 74
1.229–53: 241
1.257–96: 242
1.259–60: 143 n. 79, 242
1.289–90: 242
1.742–6: 64 n. 20, 283 n. 74
1.752: 74
2.163–4: 76
2.223–4: 214 n. 46
2.403–15: 44 n. 60
2.601–23: 248
3.570–82: 100
3.619–20: 319
4.24–5: 254
4.173: 66
4.175: 67
4.176–7: 67 n. 27
4.177: 71
4.178–80: 67
4.178–83: 224 n. 72
4.188: 67
4.197: 66
4.206–18: 268
4.208–10: 65, 68, 245
4.210: 66
4.217–18: 66
4.218: 66
4.219–21: 66
4.220–1: 68 n. 32
4.376–80: 64–5
4.379: 64 n. 21
4.379–80: 269 n. 29
4.434: 64
4.469: 93 n. 31
5.647: 86 n. 11
6.14–33: 244
6.15: 244 n. 32
6.35: 277 n. 58
6.98–101: 261–2
6.577–9: 235
6.580–4: 235–6
6.585–94: 69 n. 34, 246 n. 40
6.779: 249 n. 53
7.405: 177
7.406: 177
7.420: 72 n. 41
7.435: 72 n. 41
7.446: 72 n. 41
7.456: 72 n. 41
7.473: 72 n. 41
7.479: 177

Index of Passages

Vergil (*continued*)
  Aeneid (*continued*)
    7.648: 69, 260
    7.653–4: 72
    8.7: 69–70, 260
    8.55: 72
    8.199: 249
    8.285–305: 116 n. 1
    8.352–4: 248–9
    8.416–53: 250
    8.472–4: 72
    8.483–4: 72
    8.485–8: 72
    8.560–71: 71 n. 41
    8.620: 249
    8.680–1: 249
    8.698: 184
    8.703: 176
    9.16: 72 n. 41
    9.184–5: 126 n. 25
    9.205: 305 n. 18
    9.525: 314 n. 41
    9.641: 152
    9.642: 133
    9.644: 133
    9.654–6: 72 n. 41
    9.710–16: 206 n. 21
    9.806: 72 n. 41
    10.18–62: 241
    10.28–30: 76 n. 60
    10.270–3: 250
    10.517–20: 73, 276 n. 53
    10.519: 276, 277
    10.537–42: 80, 276, 277 n. 58
    10.540–1: 276–7
    10.541: 277
    10.565–8: 277
    10.565–70: 78–9
    10.567: 79
    10.623: 72 n. 41
    10.686: 72 n. 41
    10.743–4: 71, 262
    10.762–8: 70
    10.763: 70
    10.765: 70
    10.767: 71
    10.773: 220 n. 62
    10.773–4: 71, 262
    10.822: 73 n. 47
    10.838: 71
    10.844: 71
    10.861–2: 71
    10.880: 71, 262
    10.889: 71, 274
    11.123: 72 n. 41
    11.173–5: 71 n. 41
    11.275–8: 76
    11.282–7: 75
    11.291–2: 76
    11.530: 72 n. 41
    11.733: 261 n. 12
    11.738–40: 261 n. 12
    11.897: 72 n. 41
    12.19: 72 n. 41
    12.149: 72 n. 41
    12.598: 72 n. 41
    12.793–7: 76–7
    12.922–3: 77
    12.951–2: 296 n. 114
  Eclogues
    1.6: 78
    1.16–17: 280 n. 63
    4.7: 230 n. 89
    5.51–2: 115 n. 80
    5.56–7: 115 n. 80
  Georgics
    1.424–97: 280 n. 63
    1.466–8: 166
    1.471–3: 100, 245 n. 36
    1.477: 73 n. 47
    1.497: 166 n. 20
    1.498–501: 168
    2.490: 267 n. 25, 283 n. 73
    3.8–9: 115 n. 80

Xenophon
  Memorabilia
    2.1.24–34: 153 n. 105
  Oeconomicus
    16.3: 41 n. 53

GENERAL INDEX

Achilles
  and Aeneas, 27, 43
  and Apollo, 25–6, 30–2, 41
  and Athena, 203, 251
  and Capaneus, 32
  and generational competition, 30–2, 34, 38
  and Hector, 26, 202
  and Hephaestus, 27, 197, 201 n. 15, 204
  and Hippomedon, 210–14
  between mortal and god, 26–31, 41
  in *Posthomerica*, 31–2
  and Scamander, 19, 25, 27, 38–9, 188, 197–205
  and Scipio, Publius (father of Africanus), 205–10
  and Scipio Africanus, 251
  theomachy of, 16, 19, 21–2, 25–32, 34, 38–9, 41, 43, 188, 197–205
  and Zeus, 25, 27, 34, 199
Aegaeon, 34, 57–8, 78–9, 153 n. 107, 227, 230, 277. *See also* Briareus
Aeneas
  and Achilles, 27, 43
  and Aegaeon, 57, 78–9
  and Amphiaraus, 276–7
  and Apollo, 43, 276–7
  and Capaneus, 274–5
  and Diomedes, 21, 74–7
  and Hannibal, 249–52
  and Mezentius, 71–3
  piety *vs.* impiety of, 73, 80
  and theomachy, 57–8, 76–81, 276–7
Aeneid (Vergil)
  Anna (sister of Dido) in, 63–6
  Atlas in, 124–5
  and *Bellum Civile*, 176–7, 184
  Cacus in, 116 n. 1, 249–51
  Epicurean theology in, 63–9, 72–4, 271
  Fama in, 64, 66–9, 71
  fulmen in, 65–8, 77, 79
  Gigantomachy and Giants in, 5, 57–8, 64, 67, 68–9, 236, 319
  heroism in, 27
  Iarbas in, 63–9, 268
  influence on Flavian epic, 1–3, 36, 230
  influence on Senecan tragedy, 3 n. 7
  Iulus in, 133, 152, 177

  origins of Roman theomachy in, 56–8, 63–81
  piety *vs.* impiety in, 57–8, 73, 76–81, 260–1
  psychoanalytic model applied to, 2–3
  and *Punica*, 235–6, 241–2, 244–5, 248–52, 254
  Sibyl in, 235–6, 261–2
  terminology of theomachy in, 7
  and *Thebaid*, 260–2, 268, 271, 274–7
  theomach manqué in, 57–8, 69–77
Aeschylus. *See also in Index of Passages*
  Eumenides, 178
  Prometheus Bound (Ps.-Aeschylus), 6
  Septem contra Thebas (*Seven Against Thebes*), 39, 41, 43–7, 219, 256–7, 260
agon, 214–30, 259–60, 264–83
Ahl, Frederick, 283
Ajax (Sophocles), 47–52
Ajax (the Greater), son of Telamon
  and Athena, 44, 47, 50–1
  and Atreidae (Agamemnon and Menelaus), 47, 50–2
  independence of, 44
  madness of, 42, 47–9, 52
  theomachy of, 42, 44, 47–52
Ajax (the Lesser), son of Oileus, 43–4, 47 n. 68, 49–50, 69 n. 34
Alcasto, 326–7
Alexander the Great, 133, 320
allegory, 5, 7 n. 22, 14, 38–9 n. 48, 68, 72, 84, 88, 101, 109, 126, 153, 164, 170–1, 173–4, 193, 248, 270–1, 286–7, 292, 299–300, 307, 310
Aloidae, 19, 30, 219, 236, 285–6
Amphiaraus
  and Aeneas, 276–7
  ambivalence of, 271–7
  and Capaneus, 220, 227, 259–83, 287–8, 301–2
  and *Thebaid*'s explanatory discourse, 277–83
  world view of, 264–71
Ando, Clifford, 10
Aphrodite, 18–20, 40, 57, 75. *See also* Venus
Apollo
  and Achilles, 25–6, 30–2, 41
  and Aeneas, 43, 276–7
  as Augustus' patron deity, 299
  and Diomedes, 21
  and Flaminius, 226–7
  and Iulus, 133

Apollo (*continued*)
   and Laomedon, 30
   Latona as mother of, 105–6
   monumentality and fame of, 37
   and Niobe, 105–6, 299
   and Patroclus, 19, 22–3, 26
   and Phaethon, 92, 166–8
Apollonius, *Argonautica*, 5, 71 n. 38, 215, 218–21, 227, 230 n. 88, 263
   Idas in, 218–20, 263
   Idmon in, 218–20, 227
apotheosis. *See* deification
Ares, 19, 28, 34, 44. *See also* Mars
Argante, 326
Argonautica. *See* Apollonius; Valerius Flaccus
Ariosto, Ludovico, *Orlando Furioso*, 325–6
aristeia, 6 n. 17, 16–17, 20–1, 23 n. 11, 25, 27–9, 34, 43, 78–9, 197, 204–5, 207, 209–11, 214, 247 n. 43, 253, 273, 275–7, 313, 316 n. 47
Aristophanes, *Birds*, 6, 244
atheism, 10, 14, 54 n. 82, 85 n. 8, 107 n. 66, 180, 259, 270, 295, 303 n. 14, 305–6, 327–8
Athena. *See also* Pallas
   and Achilles, 203, 251
   and Ajax (the Greater), 47, 50–1
   and Ajax (the Lesser), 44
   and Ares, 28
   and Diomedes, 18–20, 34, 40, 43
augury. *See* divination
Augustan literature, 4–5, 8, 12, 20 n. 8, 57–8, 78, 88, 102, 111, 113, 115, 121, 142–3, 154, 160, 167, 169, 188, 313 n. 38, 315
Augustus
   Actium, 57, 176, 184
   Apollo as patron deity of, 299
   banquet of the gods, 179–80
   biography of, 179–80
   deification of, 77–8, 84, 88, 103, 106–7, 111–15, 131–3, 135, 168, 308, 315
   in Horatian panegyric, 314–16
   in Ovid's exile poetry, 301–5
   and religion, 58, 77–8, 114, 299 (*see also* deification *subentry*)
authority, 2, 10, 11 n. 35, 13–14, 19, 22–3 n. 10, 33, 35, 38, 43, 46–7, 50–5, 68–70, 81, 84 n. 5, 92, 96–9, 102–3, 119, 131 n. 43, 143 nn. 78–9, 148, 181, 200, 208, 210 n. 32, 219, 222 n. 67, 228, 262, 264–6, 291–3, 300, 302 n. 12, 304, 310, 323, 327–8

Bacchae (Euripides)
   Pentheus in, 42–3, 265
   personal confrontation of human and god in, 53–5
   sight and knowledge in, 92

   theomachy in, 39–43, 52–5, 92, 265
Bacchus
   and Acoetes, 93–7
   and Hercules, 124, 129
   and Pentheus, 83, 89, 92–7, 103
Barker, Elton, 35–6
belief. *See* empiricism; epistemology; fiction; religious belief
Bellerophon, 33 n. 28, 39 n. 49, 45 n. 62, 136
Bellum Civile (Lucan)
   and *Aeneid*, 176–7, 184
   Anubis in, 183, 189
   Battle of Pharsalus in, 158, 166–81
   Caesar as god in, 176–81
   Caesar in, 18, 29, 39, 159–92, 213, 240–1, 243, 252, 305–6, 323, 326
   Cato in, 156–7, 181–2, 189–93, 306, 323
   disenchantment with religion and politics in, 11–12, 29, 156–94, 305–11, 323
   Erichtho in, 177, 180
   feasting and hunger in, 158, 162–5, 178–80, 191
   fulmen in, 161, 170–1, 174, 240
   Gigantomachy in, 169–73
   and *Hercules Oetaeus*, 192–4
   as historical epic without gods, 36, 156–94, 258
   madness in, 177–8
   Massilian grove episode in, 158–65, 240–1, 306
   natural world/elemental images in, 18, 158–71, 181, 240–1, 306
   Osiris in, 183–4
   politics in, 157–8, 164–5, 168, 171–2, 175–6, 180–1, 184–5, 305–12
   Pompey, Gnaeus, in, 183–4
   Pompey the Great in, 156–7, 181–92, 323
   post-classical literature influenced by, 326
   power of the gods in, 172–6
   remystification in, 158, 160, 166–81, 306
   Set in, 183–4, 186
   sublimity in, 158, 181–92, 241, 326
Bloom, Harold, 2, 36
Boiardo, Matteo Maria, 326
Briareus, 34, 116, 294. *See also* Aegaeon
building and engineering, 37–9, 87, 96, 203, 206 n. 21, 207–8, 210 n. 32, 244–5, 309

Caesar (character in *Bellum Civile*)
   and Cato, 191
   and Erysichthon, 158, 160–5, 191
   feasting and hunger of, 158, 162–5, 178–80, 191
   godlike attributes of, 176–81
   and Hannibal, 240–1, 243, 252
   and Lycurgus, 160
   madness of, 177–8

General Index

Caesar (character in *Bellum Civile*) (*continued*)
  in Massilian grove episode, 158–65, 240–1, 306
  monumentality and fame of, 39
  natural world/elemental images describing, 18, 161, 170–1
  and Orestes, 178
  political allusions through, 164–5, 168, 171–2, 175–6, 180–1, 184–5, 305–6
  post-classical literature influenced by, 326
  Rubicon crossing by, 213
  sublimity associated with, 181–2
  theomachy of, 156–65, 323
Caesar, Julius
  deification of, 11, 111–14, 131, 133, 168, 320
  religious symbolism used by, 9
Caiani, Lucia, 296
Caligula
  biography of, 127, 133–5, 307–10
  and Capaneus, 307, 310–11
  divine aspirations of, 135, 308–9
  and Hercules, 127, 131, 133–6, 299
  and Jupiter, 133–5, 307
  madness of, 134–6
  non-deification of, 131, 307
  radicalism of, 307–11
Callimachus, 98, 213
Capaneus
  and Achilles, 32
  and Aeneas, 274–5
  and Amphiaraus, 220, 259–83, 287–8, 301–2
  and Caligula, 307, 310–11
  death of, 24, 291, 302
  and Dis, 20, 284
  epic conventions and limits scrutinised through, 14, 256–97
  and Erysichthon, 275 n. 49
  and Flaminius, 216, 220–3, 225 n. 74, 227, 229
  generational comparisons to, 31–3, 36
  as Giant, 45–7, 226–7, 285–8, 294, 299–300
  Greek theomachy, in relation to, 20, 24–6, 31–3, 45–6
  and Hypseus, 228, 296
  and Idas, 218–20, 263
  impiety of, 260–4, 286, 303–5
  independence of, 45–7
  and Jupiter, 1–3, 7, 25–6, 257, 289–91, 302, 323
  and Lycaon, 263–4, 285–7
  madness of, 264–5, 272, 274, 284
  and Mezentius, 260, 262, 271, 274–5
  natural world/elemental images describing, 18
  overreaching and the limits of theomachy of, 24–6
  philosophy influencing actions of, 9, 47, 283–91
  political allusions through, 299–307, 310–11, 316
  post-classical literature influenced by, 326–7
  predecessors of, 260–4
  religious belief explored through, 10, 256–97
  sublimity associated with, 286
  terminology of theomachy applied to, 7
  theomachy of, 256–97
  world view of, 264–71
  and Zeus, 45–6
Cato (in *Bellum Civile*)
  alluded to in *Hercules Oetaeus*, 193
  sublimity associated with, 181–2, 189–92
  theomachy of, 156–7, 306, 323
Centaurs, 139–40, 293–4
Ceres, 109, 162, 164
Cheney, Patrick, 325–6
Christensen, Joel, 35–6
Christianity, 7, 82, 86 n. 14, 303 n. 14, 308 n. 29, 324–7
Cicero
  De Divinatione, 9, 89, 272–3
  De Natura Deorum, 89
  on Flaminius, 215
  philosophical influences on, 9, 10
  terminology of theomachy in, 7
Claudius (emperor), 131–3, 135
contemptor deorum, 7, 69–70, 76, 93, 109, 134 n. 53, 146, 260, 264 n. 19, 305 n. 18, 307, 311 n. 36
Cyclops, 70, 294, 319

Dante, *Inferno*, 86 n. 14, 257, 326
Day, Henry, 158, 161, 182, 186–7
deification, 11–12, 29, 43, 77–8, 83–4, 88, 103, 106–8, 110–15, 117, 120, 124, 127–36, 145, 150, 152–3, 157, 168, 175, 181–2, 184–5, 188, 192–3, 306–21, 317–21, 323
De Rerum Natura (Lucretius)
  and *Aeneid*, 63–9, 72–4, 271
  Epicurean theology in, 57, 269, 290
  fulmen in, 59, 66, 68
  Gigantomachy in, 58–62, 68, 286
  materialism in, 60–2
  originality in, 238–9
  origins of Roman theomachy in, 56–63, 66, 68
  philosophical influences on, 9, 60–2
  sublimity in, 62–3
  superstition attacked in, 58–62, 160, 269
  and *Thebaid*, 259, 268–70, 282–3, 286, 290
Diana (Artemis), 70, 80, 105–6, 120 n. 9
Dido, 63–6, 68, 74–5, 254
Diomedes
  and Aeneas, 21, 74–7
  and Aphrodite, 18–20, 57, 75

Diomedes (*continued*)
  and Apollo, 21
  and Ares, 34
  and Athena, 18–20, 34, 40, 43
  and legitimisation of theomachy, 16,
    17–20, 40
  theomachy of, 6, 16–21, 24–5, 33–4, 40, 43, 57,
    74–8, 80
  and Venus, 80
  and Zeus, 17–18, 24
Dionysus, 39–43, 53–4, 196 n. 6. *See also*
    Bacchus
Dis, 20, 117, 123, 284. *See also* Hades
divination, 9, 12 n. 38, 88, 220, 257, 259–60,
    264, 266–9, 272–3, 276–8, 280, 285
Dominik, William, 299
Domitian
  Arch of Titus dedicated by, 317, 319
  deification of/of family of, 312–13, 317–19
  and dynastic conflict, 320–1
  and Flavian epic, 196, 242, 248, 299, 311–21
  Forum Transitorium of, 298–9
  Pamphili obelisk set up by, 317, 319
  Volturnus pacified by, 208

earthquakes/seismic activity, 100, 147, 245, 281,
    288 n. 90
elemental images. *See* natural world/elemental
    images
emperors. *See also specific emperors*
  dynasties of, 320–1
  excesses of, 180, 320–1
  imperial cult or deification of, 11–12, 29,
    77–8, 83–4, 88, 103, 106–7, 111–15, 127, 131–6,
    157, 168, 175, 181, 184–5, 306–21
  politics involving (*see* politics)
  undermining of, 301–5
empire, Roman
  emperors of (*see* emperors)
  excesses of, 164–5, 180, 320–1
  politics of (*see* politics)
  reading theomachy in, 8–14
  terminology of theomachy applied to
    enemies of, 7 (*see also* Roman theomachy)
empiricism, 10–11, 83, 85–9, 101, 124–5, 257,
    264, 285–7
engineering. *See* building and engineering
epic. *See also specific poets and titles*
  Capaneus as symbol of, 2–3
  compendious, 36
  different kinds of, 36
  Flavian (*see* Flavian epic)
  Greek, 15–39
  heroism in (*see* heroism)
  historical, with gods, 36, 195

  historical, without gods, 11–12, 36, 156–94, 258
  imperial cult or deification of emperors in,
    11–12 (*see also under* emperors)
  limits of, in *Thebaid*, 256–97
  mythological, 36, 195, 313
  philosophical, 289
  theomachy in (*see* theomachy)
  and tragedy overlap, 6 n. 14, 13, 40
Epicureanism. *See also De Rerum Natura*
  and *Aeneid*, 63–9, 72–4, 271
  and *De Rerum Natura*, 57–63, 269, 290
  and *Hercules Furens*, 119
  and *Metamorphoses*, 100–1
  and *Thebaid*, 259, 268–71, 282–3,
    286, 290
Epicurus. *See also* Epicureanism
  originality of, 238–9
  theomachy of, 25, 57–63, 160
epiphany, 85 n. 8, 91–6, 101, 105 n. 61
epistemology, 6, 9–11, 25, 54, 75, 85–7, 89–97,
    109, 148, 203, 215, 233, 241, 259, 264, 266–8,
    275–6, 278 n. 61, 280, 286–7, 314 n. 40, 328
Erysichthon
  and Caesar, 158–65, 191
  and Capaneus, 275 n. 49
  story of, responding to Pirithous, 109–10
  terminology of theomachy applied to, 7
ethics, theomachy as experiment in, 328
Etna. *See* volcanoes
Euripides. *See also in Index of Passages*
  Bacchae, 39–43, 52–5, 92, 264–5
  Bellerophon, 39 n. 49, 45 n. 62, 136
  Herakles, 52, 117
  Iphigenia at Aulis, 41, 53

fame, 37–9, 68 n. 32, 69, 76, 115, 130, 144, 187–8,
    203–4, 214, 234, 254–5, 301, 315, 323
Feeney, Denis, 4, 281, 284, 292, 294
Feldherr, Andrew, 95–6, 240
fiction, 63–9, 311
Fishwick, Duncan, 131
Fitch, John, 133–4, 137, 299
Flaminius
  and Apollo, 226–7
  and Capaneus, 216, 220–3, 225 n. 74, 227, 229
  and Corvinus, 214–15, 220–2, 226–8
  and Gigantomachy, 223–8
  and Idas, 218–20
  impiety of, 222–3
  and Jupiter, 227
Flavian epic. *See also specific epics*
  agon over omens in, 214–30, 259–60, 264–83
  and *Iliad*, 20, 31, 36, 195–218, 230, 251
  impiety and independence in, 44, 46–7, 222–3,
    260–4, 286, 303–5

General Index

Flavian epic (*continued*)
  intertextuality in/with, 216–23, 225 n. 74, 226, 229, 240, 248–51, 258–64, 268–70, 277, 282–3, 315–16
  paradigms of theomachy in, 195–230
  river battles in, 196–7, 205–14, 245, 254
  Vergil's influence on, 230
Fucecchi, Marco, 245
fulmen (thunderbolt / lightning)
  in *Aeneid*, 39, 65–8, 77, 79
  in *Bellum Civile*, 18, 161, 170–1, 174, 186, 240
  in *De Rerum Natura*, 59, 66, 68
  lightning in Greek theomachy, 24, 45–6, 199
  in *Metamorphoses*, 92, 167
  political power symbolised by, 301, 302 n. 12, 318
  in *Punica*, 214–15, 227, 233, 236, 240, 245–7, 252–3
  in *Thebaid*, 3, 257, 289–91, 295, 323
Furies, 7, 144 n. 82, 177–8, 266, 284, 292

Gale, Monica, 59, 250
Gauls, 7, 205–6, 224–8, 231, 234
gender, 8 n. 23, 292 n. 100, 328
generational competition, 29–36, 38, 43, 142 n. 75
genre, 2, 5–6, 8, 11, 13, 36, 39–40, 56, 78, 84, 89, 95 n. 40, 109, 155, 158, 175 n. 39, 214, 289, 308, 311, 321 n. 70, 323–5, 327
Georgacopoulou, Sophia, 315
Giants. *See also* Gigantomachy *and* Titans
  and Achilles, 32
  and Aloidae, 219, 236, 285–6
  and Capaneus, 45–7, 226–7, 285–7, 294, 299–300
  and Fama, 64, 67–9
  and Hercules, 119–20, 125–6, 139–40, 147
  impiety and independence of, 45–6
Gigantomachy
  in *Aeneid*, 5, 57–8, 64, 67–9, 236, 319
  in *Bellum Civile*, 169–73
  in *De Rerum Natura*, 58–62, 68, 286
  in *Hercules Furens*, 119–20, 125–6, 139–40, 147
  politics symbolised through, 46, 318–19
  in *Punica*, 205–6, 223–8, 235–6, 244–5
  in *Thebaid*, 226–7, 285–8, 291 n. 99, 293–4, 299–300
  theomachy vs., 5
  and Typhonomachy, 99–100
gods. *See also* deification; religion; theology; *specific gods by name*
  absence of, in historical epic, 11–12, 36, 156–94, 258
  imitators of, 6, 92
Gradel, Ittai, 131
Greek epic and tragedy. *See also specific poets and titles*

  death of theomach in, 23–4, 44, 50–1, 54
  didacticism and politics in, 39–55
  distinction between mortal and divine in, 16, 26–31, 41
  generational competition in, 29–36, 38, 43
  independence in, 43–52
  legitimacy of theomachy in, 16–20, 40
  madness of theomachs in, 42, 47–9, 52
  metapoetic treatment of, 16–17, 35–6
  monumentality and fame in, 37–9
  natural world or elemental images in, 17–18, 24, 27, 196–214 (*see also under* rivers)
  overreaching and the limits of theomachy in, 16, 21–6, 57, 80
  personal confrontation of human and god in, 53–5
  piety and impiety in, 40, 43–52
  theomachy in, 6, 15–55, 57, 74–5, 78, 80, 92, 188, 196–214, 251, 264–5
Grénier, Jean-Claude, 318

Hades, 19, 116. *See also* Dis
Halliwell, Stephen, 13–14
Hannibal
  and Aeneas, 249–52
  and Caesar, 240–1, 243, 252
  and earlier theomachs, 31
  failure of, 251–5
  fame of, 254–5
  and Hercules, 232, 237–8, 244, 249
  and Juno, 31, 232–3, 248, 253
  and Jupiter, 25–6, 31, 231–3, 244–55
  originality of, 236–40
  overreaching and the limits of theomachy of, 25, 26, 227, 231–4, 244–55
  scaling of the Alps by, 233–43
  siege of Rome by, 233
  theomachy of, 13, 25, 26, 31, 227, 231–55
  tragedy and epic overlap in, 13
Hardie, Philip
  on Fama, 64, 67, 71
  on Gigantomachy, 5, 58
  on metapoetics, 36
  on Pentheus and Bacchus, 95, 111
  on sublimity, 13 n. 39, 64
Hera, 19, 27, 116, 204. *See also* Juno
Herakles. *See also* Hercules
  generational comparisons to, 30, 38
  and Hades, 19
  and Hera, 19
  madness of, 52, 117
  theomachy of, 17, 19–20, 30, 38, 52, 117
Hercules. *See also* Herakles
  and Achelous, 83, 107–11
  and Cacus, 249

Hercules. *See also* Herakles (*continued*)
    and Caesar, 193
    and Cato, 193
    deification of, 110–11, 116–55, 192–4
    generational comparisons involving, 36
    and Hades, 116
    and Hannibal, 232, 237–8, 244, 249
    and Hera, 116
    Hercules Furens on, 25, 40, 116–55, 325
    Hercules Oetaeus on, 192–4
    originality of, 237
    philosophical example of, 153
    and Scipio Africanus, 227–8
    semi-divine nature of, 5, 6 n. 15, 14, 107–8, 110–11, 116, 122
Hercules Furens (Seneca)
    Amphitryon in, 127–9, 145, 148
    ascent inverted in, 25, 117, 126
    Atlas in, 124–5
    Bacchus in, 124, 129
    and Caligula, 127, 131, 133–6, 299
    cosmic disorder in, 120, 126
    deification and tyranny in, 127–36
    Dis in, 117, 123
    Gigantomachy in, 119–20, 125–6, 139–40, 147
    Greek influences on, 117
    Juno in, 117, 119–27, 132, 144, 149
    madness in, 52, 117, 126–7, 132, 134–44, 154, 299, 325
    and Medea, 143–4
    metapoetic treatment of, 141–3
    natural world/elemental images in, 147–8
    and *Octavia*, 129–30
    and Phaethon, 136–8, 141
    philosophical influences on, 12, 118–19, 138–9, 145, 151–5
    politics in, 12, 127, 129–36, 138, 299
    post-classical literature influenced by, 325
    sublimity in, 138–44, 152, 154
    suicide in, 145–8, 154
    theomachy and deification in, 116–55
    Theseus in, 145, 148, 154
    tragic theomachy in, 40
    wisdom achieved in, 149–53
Hercules Oetaeus (Ps.-Seneca), 192–4
heroism
    Ajax on, 47–50
    epic focus on, 13, 16, 27, 30, 210
    of Hercules, 145, 325
    Iliad on, 17–18, 36, 201, 204
    limits of, 13, 36
    Punica on, 207, 216, 223, 227, 229, 255
    Thebaid on, 210
Hippomedon
    and Ismenus, 210–14
    natural world/elemental images for, 27
    theomachy of, 44, 210–14, 316

tomb of, 296–7
and Typhon, 44
Homer. *See Iliad*; *Odyssey*; *Index of Passages*
Horace, *Odes*, 78, 88, 98, 142, 314–16, 319
hunger
    Caesar's, as metaphor for excess, 158, 162–5, 180, 191
    Erysichthon's, 109, 158, 162–4, 191

Iliad (Homer)
    Achilles in, 16, 19, 21–2, 25–32, 34, 38–9, 41–3, 188, 197–205, 251
    agon over omens in, 216–18
    Diomedes in, 6, 16, 17–20, 21, 24–5, 33–4, 40, 43, 57, 74–5, 78, 80
    Dione in, 19–20, 30, 57, 75
    distinction between mortal and divine in, 16, 26–31, 41
    generational competition in, 29–36, 38, 43
    Hector in, 24–6, 202, 216–20
    Hephaestus in, 27, 197, 201 n. 15, 204
    independence of theomachs omitted in, 43
    Laomedon in, 30–1, 38
    legitimisation of theomachy in, 16, 17–20, 40
    Longinus' allusions to, 139–41
    monumentality and fame in, 37–9
    natural world/elemental images in, 17–18, 27, 196–205
    overreaching and the limits of theomachy in, 16, 21–6, 57, 80
    Patroclus in, 6, 16, 19, 21–6
    Polydamas in, 216–20
    and *Punica*, 20, 31, 36, 195–210, 216–18, 230, 251
    river battle in, 19, 25, 27, 38, 39, 188, 196–214
    Sthenelus in, 24, 33, 43
    sublimity in, 139
    and *Thebaid*, 36, 195–205, 210–14, 230
    theomachy in, 6, 16–43, 57, 74–5, 78, 80, 188, 196–214, 251
imperial cult. *See* emperors
imperialism, 184, 284 n. 77, 288, 325
impiety *vs.* piety
    in *Aeneid*, 57–8, 73, 76–81, 260–1
    Giants', 45–6
    Greek theomachy, 40, 43–52
    in politics, 303–6, 316
    in *Punica*, 47, 222–3
    in *Thebaid*, 44, 46–7, 222–3, 260–4, 286, 303–5
interdiscursivity, 4, 300
intertextuality, 3, 8, 195–6, 216, 221–3, 229–30, 258. *See also specific poets and titles*
Ixion, 69 n. 34, 108–9

Juhnke, Herbert, 195
Julio-Claudian dynasty, 14, 20 n. 8, 131, 135 n. 53, 158, 172, 176, 242, 320

General Index 381

Juno. *See also* Hera
  in *Aeneid*, 65, 76–7, 80, 120–1
  and Hannibal, 31, 232–3, 248, 253
  and Hercules, 117, 119–27, 132, 144, 149
  and Semele, 89–92
  in *Thebaid*, 296–7
Jupiter
  and Aeneas, 76–80
  Ammon, 189–90, 192, 241, 243
  and Augustus, 77–8, 315
  and Baucis and Philemon, 109–10
  in *Bellum Civile*, 170–1, 173–4, 183, 185–91
  and Caligula, 133–5, 307
  and Capaneus, 1–3, 7, 25–6, 257, 289–91, 302, 323
  and Domitian, 316, 318
  and Flaminius, 227
  and Hannibal, 25–6, 31, 231–3, 244–55
  and Hercules, 110–11, 116–17, 122–3, 129, 132, 148–9
  and Iarbas, 65–8
  and Juno, 76–7, 89–92
  and Lycaon, 83–9, 94, 98–104, 106, 263–4
  and Niobe, 104–5, 107
  and Ovid, 112, 114–15
  in *Punica*, 214, 222, 227, 231–3, 241–55
  and Semele, 89–92
  in *Thebaid*, 221, 257, 267, 274, 289–92, 295–7, 299–300, 316, 318, 323
  and Venus, 241–2

King, Katherine, 32
knowledge. *See* epistemology
Kronenberg, Leah, 72–3, 271
Krostenko, Brian, 9

Lactantius, 268–9, 282–3, 286
La Penna, Antonio, 73–4, 152
Latona (Leto), 40, 103–7, 299
Leigh, Matthew
  on *Bellum Civile* (Lucan), 158, 160–2, 193
  on Capaneus, 2–3, 286, 310
  on sublimity, 13
lightning. *See fulmen*
Livy
  Flaminius in, 214–15, 222
  Hannibal in, 237, 240, 247
  terminology of theomachy in, 7
Longinus, *De Sublimitate* / *Peri Hypsous*, 13–14, 62, 118, 138–41, 154, 235–6
Lovatt, Helen, 272, 276, 288–300, 310
Lucan. *See Bellum Civile*; *Index of Passages*
Lucretius. *See De Rerum Natura*; *Index of Passages*

Lycaon
  and Capaneus, 263–4, 285–7
  and Jupiter, 9–10, 83–9, 98–101, 103, 263–4
madness
  of Ajax (son of Telamon), 47–9, 52
  of Arachne, 101
  of Caesar, 177–8
  of Caligula, 134, 136
  of Capaneus, 264–5, 272, 274, 284
  of Diomedes, 76
  of Hercules/Herakles, 52, 117, 126–7, 132, 134–44, 154, 299, 325
  of Niobe, 104
  of Pentheus, 42, 265
maiestas, 84 n. 5, 300, 303–4, 317
Makin, Bathsua, 328
Manilius, *Astronomica*, 8, 238, 289
Marlowe, Christopher, *Tamburlaine the Great, Parts 1 and 2*, 325–6
Mars, 149, 267, 274–5, 295. *See also* Ares
Martial, 318–19
Martin, Richard, 35
Masters, Jamie, 213
Masterson, Mark, 276–7
materialism, 60–2, 68, 83, 99, 103–7, 267 n. 25, 281, 286, 289–91, 295, 306, 323
McNelis, Charles, 213
Medea, 13, 52, 143–4
memory and theomachy, 38, 182, 187–8, 204, 210 n. 32, 254. *See also* fame
Mercury, 65, 67, 109
Metamorphoses (Ovid)
  Achelous in, 83, 107–11, 116–17, 122 n. 12, 161
  Acoetes in, 93–7
  and *Aeneid*, 80
  Arachne in, 97, 101–3, 298
  art in, 97–103
  Baucis and Philemon in, 108–9
  censorship of, 114–15
  compendious epic of, 36
  empiricism in, 83, 85–9, 101, 285–7
  Epicurean allusions in, 99–101
  Erysichthon in, 161–5
  Flavian epics influenced by, 195, 260, 263–4, 275 n. 49, 285–7
  fulmen in, 92
  and Greek theomachy, 54
  Hercules in, 83, 107–11
  Lelex in, 108–10
  Lycaon in, 10, 83–9, 98–101, 103, 263–4, 285–7
  materialism in, 83, 99, 103–7
  metapoetics in, 98–9, 101, 142
  morality in, 96–103, 109

Metamorphoses (Ovid) (*continued*)
   natural world/elemental images in, 92, 109, 110, 161–8
   Niobe in, 10, 83, 103–7
   Pentheus in, 7, 54, 83, 89, 92–7, 103
   Phaethon in, 92, 136–7, 166–8
   Pierides in, 97–101
   Pirithous in, 7, 108–11
   politics in, 83, 88, 96, 103, 106–7, 111–15
   religious belief tested by theomachy in, 10, 82–115, 263–4
   Semele in, 89–92
   sight and knowledge in, 89–97, 104
   terminology of theomachy in, 7
   and *Thebaid*, 260, 263–4, 275 n. 49, 285–7
   tragedy's influence on, 6 n. 14, 40
metapoetics
   Bloom's psychoanalytic model of, 2, 36
   in Greek epic and tragedy, 16–17, 35–6
   in Roman theomachy, 36, 98–9, 101, 141–3, 213
Mezentius
   and Capaneus, 260, 262, 271, 274–5
   terminology of theomachy applied to, 7
   theomachy of, 57, 69–74, 76, 78
Mikalson, Jon, 40, 42
Milton, John
   Paradise Lost, 5, 8 n. 23, 324–7
   Samson Agonistes, 115 n. 110, 325
Minerva. *See* Athena; Pallas
Momigliano, Arnaldo, 8
morality. *See* religion
mountains, 126, 140, 173, 175 n. 38, 186 n. 57, 206, 233–44, 246, 319 n. 59. *See also* volcanoes
Muecke, Frances, 244
Muses
   Calliope, 98–100, 314
   Clio, 311, 313–14, 316
   and Pierides, 97–101
   and Thamyris, 38–9, 40
   in *Thebaid*, 210–11, 213, 281–2, 311, 313–14, 316

Nagy, Gregory, 35, 37
natural world/elemental images
   agricultural taming of, 202–3, 208
   earthquakes/seismic activity, 100, 147, 245, 281, 288 n. 90
   engineering as taming of, 208, 245
   in Greek theomachy, 17–18, 24, 27, 196–205
   lightning/thunderbolts in, 18 (*see also fulmen*)
   in Massilian grove episode, 158–65, 240–1, 306
   mountains, 126, 140, 173, 175 n. 38, 186 n. 57, 206, 233–44, 246, 319 n. 59 (*see also* volcanoes)
   rivers (*see* rivers)
   in Roman theomachy, 17–18, 27, 84, 92, 99–100, 109–10, 126, 140, 147–8, 151 n. 97, 158–71, 173, 175, 181, 186 n. 57, 196–7, 202–3, 205–14, 233–47, 250–1, 281–3, 288 n. 90, 294 n. 108, 319 n. 59
   sublimity expressed through, 181
   sun/solar images, 166–9, 175
   volcanoes, 99, 100, 126, 151 n. 97, 250–1, 294 n. 108
Neptune, 101. *See also* Poseidon
Nero
   and *Bellum Civile*, 157–8, 168–9, 171–2, 176
   biography of, 311 n. 36
   deification of, 168
   in *Octavia*, 130
Niobe, 10, 40, 83, 103–7, 299

Odysseus, 47–8, 50–1
Odyssey (Homer), 5, 34–5, 44, 70, 139, 195
Oedipus, 89, 313
Orion, 70–1, 74, 120
Ovid. *See Metamorphoses*; Index of Passages

Padel, Ruth, 42
Pallas, 97, 101–3, 298. *See also* Athena
Parthenopaeus, 44–5
patricide, 34 n. 33
Patroclus
   and Apollo, 19, 22–3, 26
   overreaching and the limits of theomachy, 21–6
   and Sarpedon, 22
   theomachy of, 6, 16, 19, 21–6
Pentheus
   and Bacchus, 83, 89, 92–7, 103
   death of, 54, 95–6
   and Dionysus, 39–43, 53–4
   madness of, 42, 265
   terminology of theomachy applied to, 7
   theomachy of, 39–43, 52–4, 83, 89–97, 99, 103, 265
   and Tiresias, 53, 93, 265
Phaethon, 92, 136–8, 141, 166–8
philosophy and theomachy, 8–14, 42 n. 56, 47, 62, 99–100, 118–19, 138–9, 145, 151–5, 283–91. *See also* empiricism; epistemology; Epicureanism; materialism; Stoicism; theology
Phoebus. *See* Apollo
piety. *See* impiety *vs.* piety
Plato
   Sophist, 60–2, 286
   terminology of theomachy in, 6
Pliny the Younger, *Panegyricus*, 317
politics
   in *Bellum Civile*, 157–8, 164–5, 168, 171–2, 175–6, 180–1, 184–5, 305–12
   disenchantment with, 157–8, 164–5, 168, 171–2, 175–6, 180–1, 184–5, 305–11
   dynastic, 320–1

politics (*continued*)
　emperors in (*see* emperors)
　fulmen as symbol of political power, 302 n. 12, 318
　Gigantomachy as political symbol, 46, 318–19
　Greek tragedy on, 42 n. 56, 46–7, 50–2, 54
　in *Hercules Furens*, 127–36, 138
　imperial context for understanding, 300–21
　imperial cult or deification of emperors in, 11–12, 29, 77–8, 83–4, 88, 103, 106–7, 111–15, 127, 131–6, 157, 168, 175, 181, 184–5, 306–9, 315–21
　and impiety as revolution, 303–6, 316
　and the origins of Roman theomachy, 77–81
　in Ovid, 83, 88, 96, 103, 106–7, 111–15, 301–5
　in *Punica*, 240–51
　religious belief influenced by, 83–4, 88, 96, 103, 106–7, 111–15, 127, 131–6, 305–21 (*see also* imperial cult *subentry*)
　in Statius, 299–307, 310–21
　in Tacitus, 303–5, 309 n. 30
　in *Thebaid*, 299–307, 310–21
　theomachy's relationship to, 8–14, 29, 42 n. 56, 46–7, 50–2, 54, 77–81, 83–4, 88, 96, 103, 106–7, 111–15, 127, 129–36, 138, 157–8, 164–5, 168, 171–2, 175–6, 180–1, 184–5, 240–51, 298–321
　and the undermining of emperors, 301–5
Polyphemus, 7, 70–1, 74, 319
Pomeroy, Arthur, 248–9
Pompey the Great, 156–7, 181–92, 323
Poseidon. *See also* Neptune
　and Ajax (son of Olieus), 44
　and Laomedon, 30
Price, Simon, 131
Prometheus, 6, 46 n. 64
psychoanalytic model of literature, 2–3, 36
Pullman, Philip, *His Dark Materials*, 8 n. 23, 327
Punica (Silius Italicus)
　and *Aeneid*, 235–6, 241–2, 244, 248–51, 254
　agon over omens in, 214–30
　Corvinus in, 214–15, 220–2, 226–8
　fame of theomach in, 39, 254–5
　Flaminius in, 214–30
　fulmen in, 214–15, 233, 240, 245–7, 252–3
　Gigantomachy in, 205–6, 223–8, 235–6, 244–5
　Hannibal in, 13, 25, 26, 31, 227, 231–55
　as historical epic, 36, 195
　and *Iliad*, 20, 31, 36, 195–210, 216–18, 230, 251
　impiety and independence in, 47, 222–3
　irony, reversal and foreshadowing in, 223–30
　natural world/elemental images in, 18, 27, 196–7, 205–10, 233–47, 250–1
　originality of theomach in, 236–40
　overreaching and the limits of theomachy in, 25–6, 227, 231–4, 244–55
　panegyric in, 241–2
　politics in, 240–51
　river battles in, 205–10, 245, 254
　Scipio, Publius (father of Africanus) in, 18, 27, 39, 205–10, 245, 254
　Scipio Africanus in, 227–9, 255
　sublimity in, 234–7, 241, 246, 264 n. 19

Quintus of Smyrna, *Posthomerica*, 31–2

reception, 16, 56, 118, 271, 281 n. 67, 326–7
religion
　and belief (*see* religious belief)
　defined by art and morality, 96–103
　gods in (*see* gods)
　and imperial cult or deification (*see* deification)
　and impiety/piety (*see* impiety *vs.* piety)
　and politics, 83–4, 88, 96, 103, 106–7, 111–15, 127, 131–6, 305–21 (*see also* imperial cult *subentry*)
　theological understanding of (*see* theology)
religious belief
　and atheism (*see* atheism)
　Christian, 7, 82, 86 n. 14, 303 n. 14, 308 n. 29, 324–7
　disenchantment with traditional, 11–12, 156–94, 305–11, 323
　post-classical, 324–8
　remystification of, 158, 160, 166–81, 306
　science *vs.*, 277–83
　sight and knowledge influencing, 89–97, 104
　and superstition, 58–62, 160, 269, 273
　in *Thebaid*, 10, 256–97
　theomachy testing and shaping, 9–12, 82–115, 263–4
Renaissance literature, 155 n. 110, 323–7
republic, Roman, 157, 161, 170, 181–2, 185, 191, 242–3, 302 n. 12, 303, 307 n. 26, 310, 315, 320 n. 66
revolution, 14, 123, 134, 175, 300–1, 303–11, 316, 321, 324 n. 3
rivers
　Achelous, 83, 107–11, 116–17, 122 n. 12, 161, 199
　in Flavian epic, 196–7, 205–14, 245, 254
　flooding of, 84, 201–2, 207, 209
　in Greek theomachy, 17–19, 25, 27, 38–9, 188, 196–205
　Ismenus, 210–14
　Rhine pacified by Vespasian, 208
　in Roman theomachy, 18, 27, 83–4, 107–11, 196–7, 205–14, 245, 254
　Rubicon crossed by Caesar, 213
　Scamander, 19, 25, 27, 38–9, 188, 197–214
　Trebia, 205–10, 245, 254
　Volturnus pacified by Domitian, 208

Salmoneus, 6, 69 n. 34, 246, 248, 308 n. 28
Scamander
    and Achilles, 19, 25, 27, 38–9, 188, 197–205
    and Ismenus, 210–14
    and Trebia, 205–10
scepticism, 9–10, 64–5, 67, 83, 86, 93, 98–9,
        104–5, 107–11, 114, 122 n. 12, 129, 144, 157,
        159–61, 172, 174, 181, 188 n. 68, 190–1, 215,
        218, 220, 222, 263–5, 267–8, 273 n. 43, 280–1,
        291, 304 n. 17, 323
science, 59, 62, 64 n. 20, 68, 87, 100–1, 151, 246
        n. 39, 250, 267 n. 25, 269, 272, 277–83
Scipio Africanus
    dualism of, 229
    fame of, 255
    and Hercules, 227–8
Scipio, Publius (father of Africanus), 18, 27, 39,
        205–10, 245, 254
seismic activity. *See* earthquakes/seismic activity
Seneca the Younger. *See also* Hercules Furens;
        Index of Passages
    Apocolocyntosis, 127, 131–3, 135
    Atreus, 13, 141–2, 168–9, 175, 178–9
    Epistles, 150–2
    Medea, 13, 52, 143–4
    Thyestes, 52, 131, 141–2, 166, 168–9, 175, 179
    tragedy and epic overlap in, 13, 40
    and Vergil, 3 n. 7
Servius, 63, 66, 260, 268
Shelley, Percy Bysshe, 327
sight, 54, 61, 73 n. 47, 89–97, 104, 123, 139–41, 144
        n. 82, 147 n. 87, 154–5, 173–4, 204 n. 17, 244,
        246, 255, 266, 292, 295, 297, 305
Silius Italicus. *See also Punica; Index of Passages*
    Statius as contemporary of, 196, 216
Silver Latin literature, 3–4, 36, 300
Sisyphus (Critias or Euripides), 270
Sklenář, Robert, 189, 192
Slatkin, Laura, 34
Sophocles. *See also in Index of Passages*
    Ajax, 47–52
    Thamyris, 38–40
Statius. *See also Thebaid; Index of Passages*
    Achilleid, 34 n. 33, 230
    Silvae, 208, 301, 314–15, 318, 320
Stoicism
    and *Aeneid*, 73–4, 152
    and *Bellum Civile*, 189, 192
    and *Hercules Furens*, 118–19, 126, 149–53
storms, 13, 17–18, 66, 74, 161 n. 12, 181, 205, 228,
        233, 235 n. 9, 241, 245–8, 252, 291, 293–4
        n. 107, 295. *See also fulmen*
Stover, Tim, 263
sublimity
    in *Bellum Civile*, 158, 181–92, 241, 326

    in *De Rerum Natura*, 62–3
    in *Hercules Furens*, 138–44, 152, 154
    in *Punica*, 234–7, 241, 246, 264 n. 19
    in *Thebaid*, 286, 290 n. 97
    theomachic sublime, 13–14, 62–3, 324, 328
Suetonius
    Augustus, 179–80
    Caligula, 127, 133–5, 307–10
    Nero, 311 n. 36
superstition, 58–62, 160, 269, 273

Tacitus
    Annals, 303–5, 309 n. 30
    Cossutianus Capito, 304–5
    Histories, 234
    Thrasea Paetus, 304–5
Tasso, Torquato, *Gerusalemme Liberata*, 326–7
technology. *See* building and engineering
Thebaid (Statius)
    Adrastus in, 279–80
    and *Aeneid*, 260–2, 268, 271, 274–7
    agon over omens in, 220–3, 259–60, 264–83
    ambivalence of Amphiaraus in, 271–7
    Capaneus in (*see* Capaneus)
    and comparison with Greek heroes, 31,
        34 n. 33
    contemporary with *Punica*, 196, 216
    and *De Rerum Natura*, 259, 268–70, 282–3,
        286, 290
    Eunaeus in, 273–6
    Evadne in, 292–5
    fulmen in, 3, 257, 289–91, 295, 323
    Gigantomachy in, 226–7, 285–8, 291 n. 99,
        293–4, 299–300
    Hippomedon in, 27, 44, 210–14, 296–7, 316
    Hypseus in, 228, 296
    and *Iliad*, 36, 195, 210–14, 220, 230
    impiety and independence in, 44, 46–7, 222–3,
        260–4, 286, 303–5
    limits of epic depicted through, 256–97
    materialism in, 267 n. 25, 281, 286,
        289–91, 295
    madness in, 264–5, 272–4, 284
    Menoeceus in, 261 n. 12, 285, 287, 314 n. 40
    and *Metamorphoses*, 260, 263–4, 275 n. 49,
        285–7
    metapoetic treatment of, 36, 213
    as mythological epic, 36, 195, 313
    natural world/elemental images in, 196–7,
        210–14, 281–3, 288 n. 90
    philosophical influences on, 9, 47, 282–91
    politics in, 299–307, 310–21
    post-classical literature influenced by, 326–7
    religious belief explored in, 10, 256–97
    river battle in, 210–14

Thebaid (Statius) (*continued*)
  science and explanations for omens in, 277–83
  Statius' Vergil reflected in, 1–2, 3 n. 7, 36
  sublimity in, 286, 290 n. 97
  terminology of theomachy applied to, 7
  Tisiphone in, 7, 284
  twilight of the gods in, 291–7
Thebes, 17, 24–5, 31, 33–4, 36, 43–7, 52–3, 89, 92–3, 95–7, 103–5, 127–8, 195, 262, 267, 273–4, 278 n. 61, 285–90, 292 n. 100, 295, 301, 306 n. 19, 313
theology, 9 nn. 27–8, 10, 12, 14, 29, 39, 54, 57, 100, 172, 175, 180, 191, 195, 233, 241, 243, 246, 249, 257–9, 287, 291, 305, 311, 324, 327–8. *See also* religion
theomachy. *See also specific poets and titles*
  art as a theme of, 97–103
  disenchantment with religion and politics in, 11–12, 156–94, 305–11, 323
  distinction between mortal and divine in, 27, 29
  and empiricism, 10–11, 83, 85–9, 101, 124–5, 257, 264, 285–7
  Flavian (*see* Flavian epic)
  generational competition in, 31, 34 n. 33, 36
  Gigantomachy *vs.*, 5 (*see also* Gigantomachy)
  in Greek epic and tragedy (*see* Greek epic and tragedy)
  heroism in (*see* heroism)
  in historical epic with gods, 36, 195
  in historical epic without gods, 11–12, 36, 156–94, 258
  and impiety (*see* impiety *vs.* piety)
  madness of (*see* madness)
  and memory, 38, 182, 187–8, 204, 210 n. 32, 254 (*see also* fame)
  metapoetic treatment of, 36, 98–9, 101, 141–3, 213
  and monumentality and fame, 39, 254–5 (*see also* fame)
  and morality, 96–103, 109, 117
  and natural world or elemental images (*see* natural world/elemental images)
  origins of Roman, 56–81
  overreaching and the limits of, 25–6, 227, 231–4, 244–55
  personal confrontation of human and god in, 54
  and philosophy, 8–14, 42 n. 56, 47, 62, 99–100, 118–19, 138–9, 145, 151–5, 283–91 (*see also* empiricism; epistemology; Epicureanism; materialism; Stoicism; theology)
  and politics (*see* politics)
  post-classical literature influenced by Roman, 323–8

  in early imperial contexts, 8–14
  religious belief tested and shaped through, 9–12, 82–115, 263–4 (*see also* religious belief)
  sight and knowledge as themes in, 89–97, 104 (*see also* sight; epistemology)
  study of, 1–6
  and sublimity, 13–14, 62–3, 138–44, 152, 154, 158, 181–92, 234–7, 241, 246, 286
  superstition attacked through, 58–62, 160, 269, 273
  symbolic function of, 323–8
  terminology of, 6–8, 41 n. 53
  theomach manqué and limitation of, 57–8, 69–77, 160
Theseus
  in *Hercules Furens*, 145, 148, 154
  in *Metamorphoses*, 109
  in *Thebaid*, 258, 292–3, 295–7
thunderbolts. *See fulmen*
Tiberius, 131, 308–9
Tiresias, 53, 93, 265
Titans. *See also* Giants
  Achilles in *Posthomerica* compared to, 32
  in *Hercules Furens*, 125, 143, 147
  and Prometheus, 6
Tower of Babel, 37–9
tragedy. *See also specific poets and titles*
  and epic overlap, 6 n. 14, 13, 40
  Greek, 39–55
  Renaissance, 155 n. 110, 325–6
  Roman, 40, 52
  Senecan, 3 n. 7, 52, 121, 144, 146, 155 n. 110, 192, 305
treason. *See maiestas*
Turkeltaub, Daniel, 24
Tydeus, 33–4, 36, 260, 280
Typhoeus (Typhon)
  in *Bellum Civile*, 186
  and Juno, 125
  in *Metamorphoses*, 92, 99–100
  in *Punica*, 246, 250–1
  in *Septem*, 44
Typhonomachy, 99–100
tyranny, 7, 14, 52, 59–60, 66 n. 23, 72–3, 96, 103, 125, 127–36, 142, 176, 184–5, 192, 260, 291 n. 99, 293, 299–301, 304–5, 307, 311 n. 36, 321, 323, 326

Uranus, 34

Valerius Flaccus, *Argonautica*, 5, 230 n. 88, 274 n. 47, 282 n. 71, 314 n. 40
Varro, 8–9, 87

Venus. *See also* Aphrodite
   in *Aeneid*, 241–2
   and Diomedes, 80
   Greek *vs.* Roman treatment of, 20 n. 8
   on killing of Caesar and fighting the divine, 112–13
   in *Punica*, 241–2
Vergil. *See Aeneid*; *Index of Passages*
Vespasian, 208, 242, 248
Virgil. *See* Vergil
vision. *See* sight
volcanoes, 99–100, 126, 151 n. 97, 250–1, 294 n. 108
Volk, Katharina, 131

women. *See also specific characters*
   bacchants, 54
   limitations placed on, theomachy as symbol of, 328
   Theban women, 96, 104–5
   as theomachs, 8 n. 23

Xanthus. *See* Scamander
Xerxes, 307, 309

Zeitlin, Froma, 46
Zeus. *See also* Jupiter
   and Achilles, 25, 27, 34, 199
   and Capaneus, 45–6
   and Cyclops, 70
   and Diomedes, 17–18, 24
   generational competition involving, 34
   on monumentality and fame, 37
   and Prometheus, 6